MINOR LEAGUE
2012 BASEBALL ANALYST

BY ROB GORDON AND JEREMY DELONEY

7th Edition

TRIUMPH
BOOKS

Triumph Books and colophon are registered trademarks of Random House, Inc.

This book is available in quantity at special discounts for your group or organization. For further information, contact:

Triumph Books
542 South Dearborn Street
Suite 750
Chicago, Illinois 60605
(312) 939-3330
Fax (312) 663-3557

Printed in U.S.A.
ISBN: 978-1-60078-588-7

Cover design by Veronica Corzo-Duchardt <veronica@winterbureau.com>
Front cover photograph by Cliff Welch/Icon Sports Media, Inc.

Acknowledgments

Rob Gordon:

Producing this book continues to be a labor of love, but would not have been possible without the support of family, friends, and the wonderful folks at BaseballHQ.com.

In 2003 Ron Shandler gave me the opportunity to do something I'd wanted to do all of my life—write about baseball. Ron is one of the smartest baseball people I've ever had the pleasure of meeting. But beyond that Ron has been very supportive, friendly, and loyal—and I owe him a huge thank you for giving Jeremy and I the chance to write and publish this book.

Deric McKamey took me under his wing, showed me the ropes, and spent countless hours explaining what scouts look for and how to break down a player's strengths and weaknesses. Deric's total recall of the most obscure minor league players still amazes me. Deric has moved on to bigger and better things in professional baseball, but his imprint on the structure and content of this book lives.

Jeremy Deloney and I are now in our third edition of the MLBA and each year I'm more and more impressed with his comprehensive and astute knowledge of the minor leagues. Jeremy sees tons of games in the Midwest League and elsewhere and is able to quickly and concisely analyze a player's potential. Jeremy continues to be one of the best and most insightful baseball writers working today. This book would not be possible without the countless hours and sleepless nights he puts into it.

I would also like to thank Brent Hershey. Brent served as my editor at BaseballHQ.com throughout the year and throughout this book. Without his sage advice and careful attention to detail, the writing and analysis here would not be as clear, accurate, or as concise as it is. Brent also knows a great deal about minor leaguers and probably sees as many games as I do. Brent's work is largely behind the scenes, but it has been an invaluable addition.

Many other baseball people provided invaluable support and encouragement over the years. They include Jeff Barton, Jim Callis, John Sickels, Ray Murphy, Rick Wilton, Patrick Davitt (who does a great job with BaseballHQ Radio), Todd Zola, Greg Ambrosius, Jason Grey, Joe Sheehan, Jeff Erickson, Lawr Michaels, Jason Griffin of the Toledo Mudhens, Mark Murray of the St. Louis Cardinals, Steve Moyer, Nate Ravitz, Phil Hertz (Go Blue!), Jock Thompson, and Doug Dennis, who continues to be one of the funniest baseball writers working today.

Some day someone will write a story about Baseball Unlimited. Until then I'll just have to thank in the league—Michael Hartman, Steve Hartman, Michael Cooney, Bob Hathaway, Doug Hathaway, Raj Patel, Derald Cook, Todd Hooper, Dave Dannemiller, Ted Maizes, Nick Gleckman, Greg Murrey, Randy Jones, and John Mundelius. You guys rock and may BU live forever!

The kids from Dearborn Baseball have been a blast to coach. Watching them go from T-ball to kids pitch to travel ball over the past seven years has been incredible. There is no bigger reward than teaching kids about baseball and good sportsmanship.

My colleagues at the University of Michigan, Wayne State University, and Siena Heights University are too numerous to mention by name but you have all been very supportive, particularly David Smith, John Stratman, Joe Turrini, and Mark Guevara

who have been my companions at numerous opening day games in Detroit and listened to me drone on endlessly about the next "can't miss prospect" and the importance of a quality change-up. Also a big thank you to Andy Wible, Susan Gass, Ching-Yune Sylvester, Chris Bass, Craig Regester, Liz Faue, Tim Dodd, Allison Friendly, and Bill Blackerby.

I would especially like to thank my family. My two boys—Bobby and Jimmy—make the sky bluer, the sun brighter, and the crack of the bat all the more sweet. My mother Sandra Bovenkerk Gordon took me on an annual birthday trip to Chicago to see the Cubs play and drove me to countless baseball practices and little league games and my father Robert W. Gordon III took me to Chicago to see the great Roberto Clemente play in his last season and has shared my passion for the game of baseball. My sister Susan Arntson helped raised me and tried to keep me out of trouble. Thank you! She has an amazing family. Her husband Jeff and her kids Rachael, Josh, Marrisa, and Jake seem like more than just regular family.

Finally—a huge thank you to my amazing and beautiful wife Paula Jean Walker-Gordon. Not only has she has been incredibly supportive and tolerant throughout this process, but she is a complete wiz at MS Excel and helped me compile all of the data that appears in this book. This may sound like a cliché, but I really would not have been able to do this without her in my life.

Jeremy Deloney:

I'm known to spend most nights and weekends watching sports of all sorts. Whether it be March Madness, the NHL playoffs, the college football season (despite its "playoff" inadequacies), or various tennis tournaments, I can be found sitting in the front of my TV with chips, an adult beverage or two, and most importantly, my remote control. Put simply, I love sports.

But baseball has an altogether different feel for me. From spring training to the final out of the World Series in November, the game brings about a completely distinctive emotion and appreciation. There isn't much better than studying box scores first thing in the morning. Times have changed with newspapers no longer playing a major role in sports media, but the box score remains my favorite thing to peruse. Add to that the beauty and grace of the game itself and you've got yourself a game that transcends all sports.

This is my third edition of the MLBA and though it may be long and sometimes tedious work, I have great satisfaction with its contents. The concept of "good enough" is not in the core of my beliefs, whether it be in my parenting, daily worklife, or writing a prospect book. With that said, I would like to give special thanks to the following people:

My wife, Amy, who continues to be the highlight of my life. This was a challenging year for our family as we moved from Ohio to Michigan (don't worry, I'm still a Buckeye) after I took a new job. Not only did Amy lead the efforts in the moving process, but she got our new house ready for Christmas on a short schedule. She is the most amazing wife, mother, and friend that anybody could have. She makes me laugh, smile, and appreciate how lucky

I am. I can't picture my life without her. Writing a book while packing/unpacking is difficult and Amy provided me with the flexibility and patience necessary to complete such an endeavor. It may be cliché, but I wouldn't be where I'm at today without her support and love.

My three children, Owen, Ethan, and Madeline, who continue to put smiles on my face and warmth in my heart. Each of my children is very unique. They aren't big into baseball, but I believe they understand my passion. They have the potential to do anything they want to do in life and I will continue to support anything they decide to do.

My parents, Bill and Nancy Deloney, for their support and encouragement. They were instrumental in my family's move to Michigan as they allowed us to live at their house during our transition period. Without that support, the move would've been exponentially more difficult and stressful. I am very blessed to have parents who instilled a sound work ethic in me. I learned a great deal from them throughout my life and I'm sure they have a few more lessons to share as I progress into middle age.

My brothers, BJ and Andy, who I respect a great deal. While we are similar in a lot of ways, we have differences. They both are University of Michigan fans—I don't understand that at all. Outside of that, we all are family-oriented with a respect and passion for sports.

Rob Gordon, who has co-written this book with me for three years and a respected colleague at BHQ. We each bring different strengths to the table, but I'm proud to work with him. He has a broad knowledge of prospects and someone I look to for another opinion.

The leadership at BHQ, Ron Shandler and Ray Murphy, for their continued support and allowing me the opportunity to write for their outstanding organization.

TABLE OF CONTENTS

Introduction. 1

Insights 3

Organization Ratings/Rankings 19

Batters 20

Pitchers 69

Major League Equivalents. 114

Mega-Lists 123

Glossary 135

Team Affiliations. 138

by Jeremy Deloney

Welcome to the *2012 Minor League Baseball Analyst*, the seventh edition of the annual prospect book. Rob Gordon and I are back and excited to share our prospect assessments with you. As the years go by, it seems that minor league analysis gets a little trickier as more and more websites are devoted to following prospects. While many sites claim to be experts, few can match the background of the crew at BaseballHQ.com. From the beginning with Deric McKamey—now a scout with the Cardinals—to the current cast, the quality remains the same. We hope you enjoy the contents.

The format of the book has remained the same over the years and we've taken your suggestions and comments very seriously. After all, you are our clients and we want to satisfy your thirst for prospect analysis. You will continue to get broad-based analysis on over 1,000 players and plenty of lists to peruse. As in previous editions, I covered the American League; Rob covered the National League. We don't expect you to agree with everything Rob and I bring to you, but we want to give you our perspectives and assessments.

I've mentioned in previous editions that selecting the players for the book is the most difficult task of all. Other than writing the prospect profiles, I spend more time on deciding who makes the cut versus who sits it out. In many ways, I'm like the NCAA Tournament committee, without the stench of backroom deals and shady goings-on. There are probably some players that would rank in a Top 1,000 list that you won't see in the book. Rob and I try to balance higher ceiling prospects with the close-to-the-majors players, some who are given 6 or 7 ratings. This is done purposely as we believe there are players who will reach the majors this year for whom we want to provide analysis. There is plenty of time for a 17-year-old international signee to make the cut in future editions.

BaseballHQ.com's **Prospect Rating System** has garnered several questions and comments since it was introduced in 2007. The Potential Ratings is a two-part system in which a player is assigned a number rating based on his upside potential (1-10) and a letter rating based on the probability of reaching that potential (A-E). A "10" implies a Hall of Fame potential whereas a "1" is a minor league roster filler. Certainly you will not find a player less than 6 in the 2012 MLBA. The MLBA is filled with prospects of varying probability ratings, however.

The rating system is not a "be all, end all" system, in that an 8A player may actually be a 9D player. We rate players first by the upside potential. If a position player offers five tools or the potential for five tools, that player will receive a high number. If that same player has a history of poor performance or is in the lower depths of the minors, he may be assigned a low letter rating. Our goal isn't to squelch debate; rather it is to shed light on a player's ultimate potential. What is the difference between an 8A and a 9D? Good question—one that is difficult to answer. This depends on such factors including, but not limited to his athleticism, tools, ability to improve, and historical performance. Ratings can and will change, depending on the aforementioned factors. Our goal is to give you a snapshot of a player's ultimate upside and likelihood of success.

I often hear that the book is mostly about statistical analysis and, while mostly true, there are poignant **essays** that provide a little more color to the black and white numbers you see in the book's meaty middle. This year, we revisit a few topics from previous editions while keeping consistent with the AFL recaps and draft analysis for each major league organization. Guest columnist Brent Hershey dives into players who were selected in the '10 draft and didn't perform up to expectations in the '11 campaign. He provides insight on whether those players can turn it around. Take your time with the essays and use the batter and pitcher boxes in the middle of the book to make your own assessment. We'd love to hear your opinions.

The **Organization Ratings/Rankings** began in the '09 edition of the MLBA and we're delighted to bring them back once again. Ratings/grades/rankings are always difficult on a macro-scale with organizations. Given the vast amount of player movement —whether it is trades, Rule 5 drafts, waiver claims, or player graduations—the ratings are very fluid. When I first started to outline the various organizations, Oakland jumped out as a system that lacked balance. It was tough to come up with a list of prospects that truly belonged in a Top 15 list. After they made trades with Arizona, Boston, and Washington, they not only added upside, but they enhanced their depth. Though they still don't have the highest grade, they showed considerable improvement. Or look at Kansas City. They graduated several prospects from last year's book—Mike Moustakas, Eric Hosmer, Salvador Perez, Aaron Crow, for instance—but they still have a well-rounded and strong organization that ranks as one of the best in baseball.

The meat and potatoes of the book continues to be the **hitter and pitcher profiles**. We bring you expanded stats, tool assessments, expected arrival dates, draft info, potential roles, and their ultimate rating. While a player's skills may improve or regress from year to year, our goal is to quantify and measure a player at one certain point in time. Equally important as the statistical tables is the tool analysis. Over-analysis of statistics in the minor leagues can be a dangerous proposition. Not only are there severe hitters/pitchers environments, but these are mostly still young players who are developing their bodies and their games. Don't get too caught up in a hitter's BA or a pitcher's ERA —look deeper at their skills and how their tools project. That's where Rob and I come into play. It's one thing to look at an OBP and draw conclusions. It's another thing to provide reasons why the OBP is at a certain level and why it may get better or get worse.

Evaluating a hitter is based on several factors, including but not limited to bat speed, pitch recognition, plate discipline, power, and the ability to use the entire field. These factors can be evident in a player's stats, but some cannot. How does a player make adjustments? Does he have a loose swing with projection? Is he solely a fastball hitter who struggles with breaking stuff? There can be a lot of noise in statistical evaluation of a hitter. Park factors, age vs. level, hidden injuries, and a player's makeup can be such distractions. The job of a scout is to filter out the noise and gauge a player's future worth. Of course, we expect some disagreement from time to time. But isn't that part of the fun?

Pitching assessment also has its challenges. Certain statistics paint a colorful picture. ERA, Dom, Ctl, HR per game, and Cmd are very valuable. But how does an ERA in the hitter-friendly California League compare to an ERA in the spacious ballparks of the Florida State League? The pitcher profiles in the MLBA attempt to paint a picture beyond what the stats may say. Take a look at the types of pitches and their velocities that are provided in the book. Evaluating pitching can be much more difficult than hitters. Often times, a pitcher's command simply clicks and the prospect sees his status rise considerably. Sometimes, a pitcher loses his pitchability and can't throw strikes. We attempt to determine if those skills can return.

The **Major League Equivalents** are a staple of the MLBA and is discussed in great detail later in the book. This is always a "bookmark-able" section because it is fascinating to see how a prospect's body of work may translate to the big leagues. Please keep in mind that the actual MLEs are not projections. They represent how a player's previous performance might look at the major league level. However, the MLE stat line can be used in forecasting future performance in just the same way as a major league stat line would.

The **Mega-Lists** section is the generally the most discussed portion of the MLBA. Everybody loves lists and enjoys debating the merits of everybody's lists. The lists include: Top 100 prospects for 2012 (one from Rob, one from me, and one cumulative list with help from other contributors to BHQ), top 15 prospects by organization, top prospects by position, top 100 fantasy prospects for 2012, and top "category" prospects.

While much discussion is centered on rankings, we encourage you to focus on the player rating system. The #10 prospect in the Royals organization may be a Top 3 prospect in the Brewers organization. Prospect lists can change quickly and I could even make a few changes tomorrow morning. Every prospect evaluator has certain biases—that is human nature, after all. However, Rob and I look at the total body of work and eventually have to put our rankings on paper. I don't get too caught up in rankings. Is there really that much difference between a prospect ranked #25 versus one who is ranked #85? Just because I have some player ranked lower than Rob doesn't mean I don't like that player. There are an inordinate number of factors at play that ultimately dictate the rankings.

Take a look at the **Top 100 Archive** at the back of the book. You'll see a number of hits and misses. I have sometimes read critiques of prospect sites from readers who think the evaluator is nuts because "they didn't like Player X". We all make mistakes. I'll admit that I was way off on Andy Marte. He was one of the best pure prospects I've ever seen. I was convinced that he was going to evolve into a sure-fire superstar based upon his athleticism, power potential, pure hitting ability, and solid-average glove work. But I wasn't alone. Most other prospect evaluators made the same mistake. That's just the nature of the business. I'd like to think we're more accurate than the local weatherman, but that may be up for debate. Again, I encourage you to look past the rankings and focus on the skills assessments and player ratings.

We hope you enjoy the seventh edition of the MLBA. We'll continue to provide you valuable analysis whether you play fantasy sports or just love watching the game. We hope you find the assessments to be worthwhile and encourage you to provide feedback. We strive to improve each and every year and to provide you with the analysis that you find most valuable. Enjoy!

Who Can Become a Part of the Next Generation of 20/20 Stars?

by Jeremy Deloney

Compared to the major leagues, there has been a dearth of players compiling 20 HR/20 SB (20/20) in the minors. Shorter seasons and developing tools are just a few of the reasons for this discrepancy. Prospecting in the minor leagues is mostly about projection—how a player's physical abilities evolve as they add strength, become more efficient, and learn their strengths and weaknesses. A 20/20 season is certainly one sign of a positive all-around skillset and this essay will focus on some of the names associated with this well-rounded feat.

There were only four players who achieved the 20/20 mark in the minors in 2011—**Kalian Sams** (OF, SEA), **Kole Calhoun** (OF, LAA), **Brett Jackson** (OF, CHC) and **Tim Wheeler** (OF, COL). Of the four, only Jackson and Wheeler project to be everyday players in the big leagues.

The 25-year-old Sams was signed by the Mariners out of the Netherlands in 2006. Between Low-A and High-A, the right-handed batter hit .231/.291/.483 with 24 HR and 26 SB. Though he set a career-high in HR, his power output is nothing out of the ordinary—he smashed 20 HR in '10. The 26 SB, on the other hand, was a pleasant surprise—his previous career-high was 10, in '07. While he has plenty of pop in his bat, his secondary skills are subpar. Sams is a career .210 hitter with a .289 OBP. Further, he strikes out in abundance and has poor defensive abilities.

The Angels selected the 24-year-old Calhoun in the 8th round of the '10 draft and he paid immediate dividends in High-A batting .324/.410/.547 with 22 HR and 20 SB. He took advantage of a hitter-friendly environment that combined with his mature plate approach to produce his solid offensive season. He's short and strong, but his power doesn't project well because of limited bat speed. Because of his shrewd instincts, Calhoun is able to steal bases despite fringe-average speed. He has the potential to reach the majors, but likely as a reserve because he lacks a standout tool. Defensively, he also is limited to an outfield corner where his power may not be sufficient.

Wheeler, 23, has the potential to be a solid regular for the Rockies, perhaps as early as 2013. After hitting only 12 HR in High-A in '10, the left-handed hitter exploded with 33 HR and 21 SB while hitting .287/.365/.535 in Double-A. He may not hit for much of a BA in the majors due to his inability to make consistent contact and current struggles against left-handed pitching, but he offers wiry strength and plenty of athleticism in his 6'4" 205-pound frame. As he fills out and ages, he likely will slow down, but he knows how to run the bases. He was a former first round pick in '09.

The left-handed hitting Jackson is one of the top prospects in all of baseball. The 23-year-old hit .274/.379/.490 with 20 HR and 21 SB while splitting time between Double-A and Triple-A. He draws plenty of walks which allows him to get on base and use his speed effectively. He has improved his power production without sacrificing other attributes of his game. Jackson is also a standout defender in CF with a strong, accurate arm. Put simply, he has no apparent weakness and all tools grade as above average. He is one of the most likely candidates to continue his 20/20 ways in the majors.

Some notable prospects who came close include: Bryce Harper (OF, WAS), Denny Almonte (OF, SEA), Blake Tekotte (OF, SD), Brandon Jacobs (OF, BOS), and Vince Catricala (3B, SEA).

While the minor leagues featured only four 20/20 players in '11, this has been the norm. Over the last four seasons, the highest output of 20/20 players in the minors has been five, in '09. There were only four such prospects in '08 and three in '10. Some familiar names have accomplished this feat in the minors over that time frame: Brandon Belt (1B/OF, SF), Danny Espinosa (INF, WAS), Chris Heisey (OF, CIN) and Nelson Cruz (OF, TEX). Others include a prospect-turned-priest, Grant Desme (OF, OAK), and the recently deceased Greg Halman (OF, SEA). Nick Franklin (SS, SEA) also put together a 20/20 season in '10 and remains one of the better infield prospects in baseball.

A 20/20 occurrence in the major leagues is far from rare. In fact, there have been 41 20/20 seasons in the majors since '08 (compared to 16 in the minors). Eight players accomplished the feat in '08, 14 in '09, 7 in '10, and 12 in '11. The 41 occurrences have been accomplished by 27 different players. Of those 27 major leaguers, only five of them have gone 20/20 in the minors—Matt Kemp (OF, LA), Ryan Braun (OF, MIL), Ian Kinsler (2B, TEX), Chris Young (OF, ARI), and Nelson Cruz (OF, MIL). Therefore, 22 players who achieved the 20/20 status in the big leagues never reached that level in the minors.

The quest to find the prospects most likely to reach the 20/20 pinnacle in the majors can be a difficult task. Reaching the majors, in and of itself, isn't easy and then earning the playing time to amass stats is doubly arduous. Add in the need/desire to develop the other half of the game—glovework—and this may be an exercise in futility. Nevertheless, here are some minor leaguers with the skill set to potentially become 20/20 artists in the big leagues.

The Twins have long believed in the power-speed combination of 23-year-old **Joe Benson** (OF, MIN). He wasn't as solid as '10, but still showed progress in his plate discipline and instincts. In Double-A, he batted .285/.388/.495 with 16 HR and 13 SB. He was invited to the big leagues as a September callup and struggled. Regardless, with a little fine-tuning, Benson could evolve into a HR/SB dynamo. He hit 27 HR in '10 while stealing 19 bases and his SB could increase as he uses his plus speed more effectively on base.

There is little doubt about **Gary Brown**'s (OF, SF) speed or baserunning acumen for him to achieve 20+ SB in the big leagues. He stole 53 bases in '11 while hitting .336/.407/.519 with 34 doubles and 14 HR in High-A. He makes easy contact and can get on base with his disciplined eye. He doesn't look like a power hitter and projects as a leadoff batter, but he has excellent bat speed and has the strength to hit balls out to the entire ballpark. His game is more about speed and defense, but Brown certainly has the capacity to produce 20+ HR and SB.

The Blue Jays acquired **Anthony Gose** (OF, TOR) in '10 and he's shown marked improvement in key parts of his game. Sure, he strikes out a lot (154 times in '11), but he easily set a career high in HR and walks while drastically reducing the number of times he was caught stealing. For the '11 campaign, the 21-year-old hit .253/.349/.415 with 16 HR and 70 SB. Gose is a terrific CF with a strong arm and plus range. Though he doesn't project well in BA due to the whiffs, he has sufficient bat speed and strength for average pop. This may eventually result in 20 HR.

He led the minors in walks in '11 (104), but there is more to **Robbie Grossman's** (OF, PIT) game than his on-base skills. The 22-year-old switch-hitter has average power and good speed, though none of those tools are considered plus. What separates him from others are his smarts and ability to make adjustments. He has the swing path and strength to eventually hit 20 HR while maintaining his 20+ SB totals. Grossman repeated High-A and batted .294/.418/.451 with 34 doubles, 13 HR, and 24 SB.

Bryce Harper (OF, WAS) not only was 3 HR from achieving the 20/20 mark, but he had a stellar all-around season in his first year as an outfielder. He batted .297/.392/.501 with 17 HR and 26 SB between Low-A and Double-A as an 18-year-old. His pedigree stands on its own merit. Though he could use a little polish, he does everything well and should become a middle-of-the-order run producer and perennial All-Star in the near term. There is no question of his ability to hit 20+ HR in the big leagues. Whether he can steal 20+ is the key. Harper has above average speed at present, though he will likely slow down as he gets older.

The Red Sox drafted 21-year-old **Brandon Jacobs** (OF, BOS) in the 10th round of the '09 draft as a raw talent who appeared to have a brighter future in football. He has vastly exceeded expectations thus far and hit a solid .303/.376/.505 with 17 HR and 30 SB in Low-A, his first year in full-season ball. He projects well in both the power and speed departments mostly due to his athleticism and plus strength. Jacobs has a large frame that may eventually hinder his speed, but he has improved his baserunning and instincts and should continue to steal 20+ bases on a regular basis.

Few prospects can match the five tools of **Rymer Liriano** (OF, SD). En route to winning the Low-A Midwest League MVP, he batted .319/.383/.499 with 30 doubles, 12 HR, and 65 SB. The 20-year-old has very high upside based upon his plentiful underlying skills. Though 12 HR is his career high, he has plus bat speed and excellent strength that should easily get him to the 20 HR mark on an annual basis. Liriano has also shown an improved approach that should continue to get him on base and utilize his plus speed.

Jake Marisnick (OF, TOR) had a breakout campaign in Low-A by hitting .320/.392/.496 with 14 HR and 37 SB while playing above average defense in CF. He's long and strong at 6'4" 200 pounds and has exciting upside. While he only hit 14 HR, the Midwest League is known for curtailing long balls and he should eclipse 20+ HR as soon as next season. He has a clean, quick swing from the right side. Speed-wise, Marisnick is able to use his plus speed effectively and has a patient approach to increase the number of times he gets on base.

One prospect who we can dream on is 23-year-old **Starling Marte** (OF, PIT). The right-handed hitter is a solid all-around talent whose power hasn't developed as quickly as expected. He did hit a career-high 12 HR in '11, but he focuses on putting the ball in play and using his plus speed to his advantage. Marte batted .332/.370/.500 with 38 doubles, 12 HR, and 24 SB. He is an outstanding defender in CF with plus range and a strong, accurate arm. There is hope that more power will come as he learns to turn on pitches and increase the leverage in his swing.

Despite exemplary batting skills, **Christian Yelich** (OF, FLA) has flown under the radar. The 20-year-old batted .312/.388/.484 with 15 HR and 32 SB in Low-A. The sweet lefty swinger has a long, lean frame that needs more strength and he should routinely hit 20+ HR once he physically matures. Yelich has good speed, though not plus, and he is an instinctive baserunner who reads pitchers well. He doesn't fit the classic power-hitter or fleet-footed outfielder roles, but he can do anything on the baseball field well.

2011 Arizona Fall League Wrap-up

by Rob Gordon and Jeremy Deloney

With the 2011 Arizona Fall League finished, we take a look back at the 10 Best and 10 Worst AFL performances. In most cases, one shouldn't read too much into how a player performs in the AFL. Historically, the league has been stocked with top-flight position prospects but quality pitching in the AFL is rare as a thunderstorm in Phoenix. Thus, stats have always favored the hitters, and this year was no exception. Still, every year a handful of players have seasons, either good or bad, that impact their prospect status. Here's a shot at weeding out the contenders from the pretenders in the Valley of the Sun.

10 Best Performances

Nolan Arenado, 3B, COL
2011 stats: .298/.349/.487 with 32 2b, 20 HR, and 47 BB/53 K in 517 AB at High-A
AFL stats: .388/.423/.636 with 12 2b, 6 HR, and 8 BB/14 K in 121 AB
Why it matters/Why it doesn't: Arenado won the 2011 AFL MVP and hit safely in 26 of 29 contests. Defensively he looked solid and showed a great two-strike approach and a willingness to go the other way. The latest word out of Denver is that Arenado, despite playing all of 2011 at High-A, will be given a chance to make the Rockies opening day roster next spring. Cooler heads may prevail, but Arenado did more to improve his status than any other player in the AFL.

Wil Myers, OF, KC
2011 stats: .254/.353/.393 with 23 2b, 8 HR, 52 BB/87 K in 354 AB at Double-A
AFL stats: .360/.481/.674 with 5 2b, 4 HR, 20 BB/18 K in 86 AB
Why it matters/Why it doesn't: The 20-year-old suffered through a knee injury in 2011 and used the AFL to redeem himself. Myers led the AFL in walks and triples and finished 2nd in OBP and 3rd in Slg. The right-handed hitter was a standout with the bat and showed improvement with the glove in the outfield, his first full season since converting from catcher. He has all the ingredients to be an All-Star in the big leagues, though he may need another full season in the minors to tap into his above average power potential and glovework in RF.

Adam Eaton, OF, ARI
2011 stats: .318/.434/.463 with 22 2b, 10 HR, 72 BB/76 K, and 34 SB in 456 AB in High-A and Double-A
AFL stats: .344/.410/.475 with 8 2b, 2 HR, 14 BB/29 K, and 8 SB in 122 AB
Why it matters/Why it doesn't: While Arenado was the most interesting player to watch in the AFL (Non-Bryce Harper Division) Eaton was the most fun to watch. List at 5'9", Eaton was frequently confused with the bat boy prior to the game, but once the game started he had everyone's attention. He hustled everything out, put the ball into play, hit the ball hard at times, played good defense, and was on base all the time. If you are looking for the next Jose Altuve, look no further.

Kevin Mattison, OF, MIA
2011 stats: .260/.353/.406 with 17 2b, 8 HR, 58 BB/127 K, and 38 SB in 503 AB at Double-A
AFL stats: .349/.433/.624 with 2 2b, 6 HR, 15 BB/30 K, and 9 SB in 109 AB
Why it matters/Why it doesn't: It matters because now we know who Kevin Mattison is. Prior to the AFL, Mattison was a 26-year-old career minor leaguer who had a good season at Double-A and a career OPS of .699. The Marlins did add him to their 40-man roster and so he is exempt from the Rule 5 draft—but unfortunately he is still a 26-year-old at Double-A.

Michael Choice, OF, OAK
2011 stats: .285/.376/.542 with 8 2b, 30 HR, 61 BB/124 K in 467 AB at High-A
AFL stats: .318/.423/.667 with 5 2b, 6 HR, 9 BB/12 K in 66 AB
Why it matters/Why it doesn't: Choice put up terrific numbers in his pro debut after being selected in the first round of the 2010 draft. This offensive production continued into the AFL where he worked on shortening his swing. Not only did he make good contact, but he continued his power-hitting ways. He likely won't be a .300 hitter in the majors with his vicious stroke, but he at least has shown the ability to make adjustments against good pitching.

Aaron Hicks, OF, MIN
2011 stats: .242/.354/.368 with 31 2b, 5 HR, 78 BB/110 K in 443 AB at High-A
AFL stats: .294/.400/.559 with 8 2b, 3 HR, 18 BB/21 K in 102 AB
Why it matters/Why it doesn't: The 22-year-old has an abundance of tools, but hasn't yet lived up to expectations. Everybody talks about his plate discipline, but the power hasn't developed. Hicks tapped into his power in the AFL and appears to finally "get it," hitting with authority and swinging at drivable pitches. Now that he's becoming a more complete player, he just might emerge and give the Twins a power-hitting athlete with above average defense.

Bryce Harper, OF, WAS
2011 stats: .297/.392/.501 with 24 2b, 17 HR, 59 BB/87 K, and 26 SB in 387 AB in Low-A and Double-A
AFL stats: .333/.400/.634 with 6 2b, 6 HR, and 11 BB/22 K in 93 AB.
Why it matters/Why it doesn't: It matters because we got another chance to see just how good Harper is going to be; he was once again the youngest player in the AFL. After starting 1-for-18, Harper blitzed through the rest of the season and though he wasn't awe-inspiring in every AB and certainly has some work to do, he did something to make you sit up and take notice almost every night. His stint in the AFL probably doesn't change any plans the Nationals have, but Harper looks like he could play in the majors right now and hold his own.

Jedd Gyorko, 3B, SD
2011 stats: .333/.400/.552 with 47 2b, 25 HR, 64 BB/114 K in 576 AB in High-A and Double-A
AFL stats: .437/.500/.704 with 4 2b, 5 HR, and 10 BB/15 K in 71 AB
Why it matters/Why it doesn't: Gyorko had a fantastic full-season debut marked by solid plate discipline. The 2nd rounder out of West Virginia is a professional hitter with a stocky body and a nice swing. His performance in the AFL helps solidify his prospect

status and with the move of James Darnell to the OF creates a path to full-time AB at 3B, possibly as soon as mid-2012.

Robbie Grossman, OF, PIT

2011 stats: .294/.418/.451 with 34 2b, 13 HR, 104 BB/111 K, 24 SB in 490 AB at High-A

AFL stats: .375/.472/.625 with 7 HR, 20 BB/18 K, and 6 SB in 104 AB

Why it matters/Why it doesn't: Grossman had a solid season at High-A, showing nice speed and good plate discipline, but his power explosion in the AFL raised his visibility to a different level. Even though the AFL is a hitter's haven, putting up that Slg to go along with his 24 regular-season stolen bases makes Grossman an interesting player to watch in 2012.

Miguel De Los Santos, LHP, TEX

2011 stats: 7-6 with a 5.04 ERA, 46 BB/142 K, and a .219 BAA in 94.2 IP in High-A and Double-A

AFL stats: 5-0 with a 3.26 ERA, 15 BB/40 K, and a .178 BAA in 30.1 IP

Why it matters/Why it doesn't: De Los Santos has flown under the radar despite being one of the top strikeout artists in the minors. He's proven difficult to hit and was at his best in the AFL. Not only did he continue to register Ks with his plus-plus change-up, but he sequenced his pitches better and kept hitters guessing as to what was coming next. He still needs to clean up his walks, but it was encouraging to see him dominate very good hitters.

Danny Hultzen, LHP, SEA

2011 stats: Did not pitch professionally (signed late)

AFL stats: 1-0 with a 1.40 ERA, 5 BB/18 K, and a .225 BAA in 19.1 IP

Why it matters/Why it doesn't: The 21-year-old made his pro debut in the AFL and he could reach the majors in 2012. Hultzen may not be a power pitcher, but his plus command and ability to locate his fastball are already among the tops in the Mariners system. He pitched aggressively with his 90-94 mph fastball and mixed in a solid slider. He'll need to enhance the look of his change-up, but he has the makeup and moxie to become a legitimate challenger for a rotation slot in spring training.

10 Worst Performances

Mike Trout, OF, LAA

2011 stats: .326/.414/.544 with 18 2b, 11 HR, 45 BB/76 K, and 33 SB in 353 AB in Double-A and .220/.281/.390 in 123 AB in the majors

AFL stats: .245/.279/.321 with 5 2b, 1 HR, 5 BB/33 K, and 3 SB in 106 AB

Why it matters/Why it doesn't: After slaughtering minor league pitching in 2011, Trout disappointed in the AFL. He may have been tired—physically and emotionally—after a long season, but he didn't impress by becoming more aggressive at the plate and abandoning the professional approach that vaulted him into the top-prospect conversation. Trout is still a gem and should become a perennial All-Star, particularly with his speed and instincts for the game.

Matt Adams, 1B, STL

2011 stats: .300/.357/.566 with 32 HR, 40 BB/90 K in 463 AB at AA

AFL stats: .250/.258/.475 with 4 HR, 3 BB/28 K in 80 AB

Why it matters/Why it doesn't: With Albert Pujols signing in LAA, the AFL was a chance for Adams to showcase his bat as a possible replacement. Adams is a proven minor league hitter with a career line of .316/.365/.552. Unfortunately, he fell flat on his face in the AFL, with a terrible 0.11 batting eye. Adams is still a good prospect, but his fall league performance did not help.

Anthony Gose, OF, TOR

2011 stats: .253/.349/.415 with 20 2b, 16 HR, 62 BB/154 K, and 70 SB in 509 AB in Double-A

AFL stats: .250/.348/.433 with 5 2b, 3 HR, 13 BB/41 K, and 7 SB in 120 AB

Why it matters/Why it doesn't: The 21-year-old has a long and lean frame that oozes potential, but he didn't show much improvement in his brief stint in the AFL. Gose is trying to find offensive consistency with his raw approach and his mechanical swing. He does a nice job of getting on base and using his speed, but he could make much better contact and legging out infield grounders. The Blue Jays won't put much pressure on him because he's so raw, but they still expect bigger things.

Tyson Gillies, OF, PHI

2011 stats: .154/.154/.308 with 2 2b, 0 HR, 0 BB/1 K, and 0 SB in 13 AB at High-A

AFL stats: .178/.302/.233 with 2 2b, 1 HR, 14 BB/24 K, and 4 SB in 90 AB

Why it matters/Why it doesn't: Gillies frequently showcased his good speed and plus throwing arm from right field. At the plate, however, Gillies looked overmatched. Gillies has just 120 AB over the past two seasons due to injuries and an off-field drug charge, so it was not surprising that he struggled. But at some point he will have to make up for lost time and the AFL showed he is still very raw.

Matt Dominguez, 3B, MIA

2011 stats: .249/.309/.405 with 18 2b, 12 HR, 28 BB/55 K in 358 AB in Triple-A and .244/.292/.333 in 45 AB in the majors

AFL stats: .226/.305/.393 with 2 2b, 4 HR, 8 BB/19 K in 84 AB

Why it matters/Why it doesn't: It matters because Dominguez continued to prove he can't hit. After five minor league seasons, Dominguez owns a stat line of .255/.325/.418. It doesn't really matter how good he is defensively, being Brandon Inge without the power or the ability to work behind the plate just isn't going to cut it.

Tim Beckham, SS, TAM

2011 stats: .271/.328/.408 with 28 2b, 12 HR, 42 BB/120 K, and 17 SB in 524 AB in Double-A and Triple-A

AFL stats: .244/.364/.489 with 6 2b, 4 HR, 15 BB/25 K, and 3 SB in 90 AB

Why it matters/Why it doesn't: The former number one overall selection in the draft had a nice year with the bat, but there are many concerns about his glovework. Beckham impressed with his power, but he still struggles with breaking balls and he can be too passive at the plate. He committed several errors in the AFL, and may have to move away from SS and possibly to the outfield. He's a terrific athlete with some potential, however, he needs to produce and find consistency.

Jason Stoffel, RHP, HOU

2011 stats: 2-3 with a 4.53 ERA, 25 BB/50 K, and a .272 BAA in 47.2 IP at Double-A

AFL stats: 0-1 with a 6.87 ERA, 21 BB/21 K, and a .271 BAA in 18.1 IP

Why it matters/Why it doesn't: Stoffel was part of the trade for Jeff Keppinger. Stoffel struggled after coming to Houston (5.63 ERA after the trade compared to 3.98 ERA pre-trade) and the AFL was a chance to impress the Astros and maybe create an opening to compete for a spot in the Astros pen come spring 2012. Instead, Stoffel's struggles with command left him behind in the count against some very good minor league hitters, who often either walked or teed off. Stoffel still has very good stuff, but will need to dramatically improve his command before he will get a shot at the majors.

Andy Oliver, LHP, DET

2011 stats: 8-12 with a 4.71 ERA, 80 BB/143 K, and a .272 BAA in 147 IP in Triple-A and 0-1 with a 6.52 ERA in 9.2 IP in the majors

AFL stats: 0-1 with a 5.82 ERA, 16 BB/15 K, and a .288 BAA in 17 IP

Why it matters/Why it doesn't: The jury is out on what caused Oliver's downfall during the second half of the season and into the AFL. Not only couldn't he throw strikes, but he was carved up by right-handed hitters. Oliver is still very tough on lefties and has the velocity and breaking ball to become a potent #2 starter. He has a tendency to overthrow which causes his mechanics and release point to get out of whack. Don't count him out, but it may take awhile to recover.

Steven Hensley, RHP, SEA

2011 stats: 4-8 wih a 4.65 ERA, 40 BB/68 K, and a .295 BAA in 100.2 IP in Double-A

AFL stats: 1-1 with an 11.30 ERA, 16 BB/15 K, and a .354 BAA in 14.1 IP

Why it matters/Why it doesn't: Much more was expected of Hensley. The Mariners have used him as a starter, but he will likely be best served in the bullpen because of his two average to above-average pitches. In the AFL, he didn't throw strikes and often overthrew. His arm is strong, he just needs to harness his arm action to find value as a reliever.

Ryan Wheeler, 3B, ARI

2011 stats: .294/.358/.465 with 30 2b, 16 HR, 45 BB/102 K, and 3 SB in 480 AB at Double-A

AFL stats: .292/.330/.377 with 9 2b, 0 HR, 7 BB/24 K, and 0 SB in 106 AB

Why it matters/Why it doesn't: Wheeler had a breakout season in 2011, showing some nice pop and hitting for average and doing it at Double-A. The AFL provided an opportunity to show that the progress he made this year was legit. Unfortunately, Wheeler looked sluggish both at the plate and in the field. Offensively his bat lacked quickness and his body simply isn't very athletic. Defensively Wheeler has no business playing 3B and looked at least a step or two slow compared to Arenado, Mike Olt, and Jefry Marte—not to mention Dominguez.

Poor Performers from the 2010 Draft

by Brent Hershey

A myriad of factors can go into a top draft pick playing far below expectations. Youth, maturity level, physical challenges, top-flight competition—all can play a part in a player's failure to adjust to his first professional experience. But as the minor leagues and its prospects continue to gain prominence and publicity, expectations grow to unrealistic heights. Development from a raw high-schooler or even a seasoned college player into a usable big-leaguer normally takes time. As usual, some members of the first-round class of the 2010 draft struggled to produce. Here's a quick look at some of the disappointing performances of first-round 2010 picks, and the player's chances of regaining their prospect sheen.

The selection of **Delino DeShields** (2B, HOU) at #8 overall was a bit of risk, given that many observers didn't feel he had the upside of a Top 10 pick. He signed early, though, and had brief success in 76 rookie-ball AB (.289/.337/.395) in 2010. But he scuffled in his full-season debut in 2011, hitting just .220 in the SAL. He showed off his excellent speed, though, with 30 SB, and did hit 9 HR. His nemesis was the strikeout—188 Ks in 119 games, something that he'll need to work on to reach his power/speed ceiling. He draws plenty of walks (10% bb%) and has a short stroke at the plate. Houston seems committed to him as a second baseman (played there all of 2011), though he could end up in CF in time. He seems unlikely to return Top-10 value, though multiple skills, good bloodlines, and his age (just 19) will give him plenty of chances to improve.

Even moreso than the Astros, the Cubs took criticism for their selection of **Hayden Simpson** (RHP, CHC) as the 16th overall pick in 2010. It's very early, but score one for the critics: Simpson was horrible in the MWL with a 5.72 ERA in 16 starts, and then got worse after he was demoted to rookie league (8.15 ERA in 17 IP). The Cubs talked about his four-pitch mix with plus control and command on draft day, but with a combined 4.3 Ctl and 102 hits given up in just 79 IP in his first professional exposure, Simpson was not fooling anyone. There were reports all year of decreased fastball velocity. Two additional items hamper his quest for a rebound. First, at 6'0" and 170 lbs, he does not possess an ideal frame for a first round pick, let alone a power pitcher. Second, he was a college junior when selected and will play most of 2012 at 23 years old, so he's not young by any standards. He's a long way from the majors at this point.

Josh Sale (OF, TAM) was taken the pick after Simpson at #17 and was widely viewed as one of the best high-school hitters in the draft. A strong hitter with great hand-eye coordination and excellent bat speed, Sale regularly put on batting practice shows but had trouble translating that success to game action. He hit just .210 with 4 HR in 214 AB at rookie-level Princeton in 2011. But he maintained an excellent approach for a 20-year-old (10% walk rate; 81% contact rate) and his notable work ethic and excellent makeup suggest that he'll attempt to make adjustments. Though he has only average footspeed, the power potential might be worth waiting for.

Mike Foltynewicz (RHP, HOU) has a classic power-pitcher's build at 6'4" 200 lbs., but the results from his first full season at Low-A Lexington (4.97 ERA) weren't much to get excited about. Despite having one of the top fastballs in the system, he only managed a 5.9 Dom, confirming whispers that he tends to rely too heavily on his low-90s heater. The team did leave the 19-year-old out there for 26 starts and 134 innings, and inconsistency more than just ineptitude characterized his season. Additional development of breaking stuff is his next task, but many see a mid-rotation innings eater—rather than a frontline starter—as his ceiling.

Kellin Deglan (C, TEX) has had a rough professional career with the bat since being selected 22nd overall in 2010 out of a British Columbia high school. He got 110 AB that summer, hitting .191/.256/.255. In 2011, he was assigned to full-season Hickory in the SAL, and again struggled, hitting just .227 with a .668 OPS in 291 AB. A left-handed hitter with power potential (did hit 6 HR in 2011), his inability to make consistent contact (69% ct%) is a current roadblock. He's fine defensively, but his hitting will need to improve to avoid being a one-way catcher as he ascends the organizational ladder.

Chevez Clarke (OF, LAA) was selected 30th overall as a high-schooler from Georgia. Clarke is a switch-hitting CF with incredible bat speed and five-tool potential. Chevez stayed in extended spring training in 2011 with hopes of improving on his dismal Arizona Rookie League performance from 2010 (.216 BA, .667 OPS, 66% contact rate). His second time through the circuit in 2011 was amazingly similar: .226 BA, .684 OPS, 66% contact rate. He remains just a raw tools guy—very good defense with HR and SB potential, but as of yet, no results to show for it. At just 20 years old, there's still time, but his lack of improvement as he repeated entry level should have the Angels at least a bit concerned.

Justin O'Conner (C, TAM) is another first-round catcher whose defense is ahead of his bat. Signed away from a college commitment to Arkansas, O'Conner showed plus-plus power in high school and has occasionally flashed it as a pro (12 HR in 339 career AB). His incredible bat speed often goes to waste, however, as his swing gets long and contact has become increasingly infrequent—78 strikeouts in just 48 games (178 AB) in 2011. He hit just .157 at short-season Princeton. It's too early to give up on his power, but he looks overmatched at the plate.

Aaron Sanchez (RHP, TOR) fell to the sandwich round because of signability concerns, and the Blue Jays snatched him up. He signed quickly, and got in 10 starts in 2010 with fabulous results: a combined 2.16 ERA with 37 strikeouts in 25 IP. The Jays continued to take it slow in 2011, limiting Sanchez to just 54 IP, where his ERA ballooned to 5.30. His peripherals, though, remained strong, with a 9.3 Dom and 2.2 Cmd between short-season Bluefield and Vancouver. Sanchez is tall and thin, and his mid-90s fastball should gain velocity as his frame fills out. In addition, he has a plus curveball. He'll need to refine his Ctl (4.3 in 2011), but he's on track to take a huge step up in 2012. Sanchez is likely to start at full-season Lansing (MWL).

Ryan Bolden (OF, LAA) possesses exciting raw power and speed, but a lot like organization mate Clarke, strikeouts have hindered him from making an impact. Poor pitch recognition and problems with breaking balls contributed to his .168/.252/.228 slash-line from 2011's Arizona Rookie League. He fanned in 48 of his 101 AB, though did steal eight bases in nine attempts. He'll play the 2012 season at just 20 years old, and already profiles as a corner outfielder. Scouts agree that he'll always struggle with BA, and he'll need to cut down on the swings and misses to survive at higher levels.

The Rangers signed **Luke Jackson** (RHP, TEX) away from a commitment to Miami for $1.545 million. He features a low- to mid-90s fastball, with a curve and changeup that are still developing. Aggressively assigned to Hickory (SAL) for his professional debut, Jackson's stats showcase his struggle: 5.64 ERA in 19 starts (75 IP). He gave up too many home runs (9) and walked a bunch (5.8 Ctl), but was a whiff machine (9.4 Dom), something worth nothing for a 19-year-old in a full-season league. Jackson is still learning on the job, and his inconsistent mechanics have led to the control problems. But as he fills out his 6'2" 178 lb. frame and repeats his delivery, his upside remains substantial.

After an accomplished career at Arizona State, **Seth Blair** (RHP, STL) seemed like he might not need much minor-league seasoning when the Cardinals took him at #46 overall in 2010. But he went through a rough season at low-A Quad Cities (MWL) where he couldn't throw strikes (6.8 Ctl). He did have good Dom (7.7), but overall, his ERA was a hefty 5.29. Blair has a good four-pitch mix led by a low-90s fastball, but some mechanical refinements (repeating his arm slot) would make him more efficient. He has the stuff and experience to rebound and jump back on the fast track.

Like Luke Jackson, **Peter Tago** (RHP, COL) got dropped into the full-season SAL without any prior pro experience just one year out of high school. And like Jackson, he failed to live up to his lofty promise. Tago got 19 starts, pitched 90 innings, and came away with a 7.07 ERA. He has a projectable frame and a clean, repeatable delivery. His fastball sits in the low-90s with lots of movement from a low three-quarters arm angle, though his secondary stuff needs improvement. After being touted as a strike-thrower pre-draft, Tago encountered control problems at Asheville (7.2 Ctl). Still just 19, there's plenty of time.

Deep Sleepers Outside the Top 100

by Jeremy Deloney

A study of Top 100 prospect lists will usually yield at least 50 prospects that are generally included on most, if not all, of the lists. From recent first round picks to multi-tooled players, the lists are adorned with household names, at least with the onset of multiple prospect sites online. The remaining players on the list are still fairly common names, but are generally considered solid prospects nonetheless. This essay will feature 10 minor leaguers who, for whatever reason, are unlikely residents on most Top 100 lists entering the 2012 campaign. Some are recent international signees while others simply haven't performed as well as their tools project them to play.

Often lost in the shuffle in a deep farm system, **Jason Adam** (RHP, KC) gives the Royals plenty of reasons to be optimistic about his future within the organization. He was selected in the fifth round of the '10 draft and pitched most of the '11 season in Low-A as a 19-year-old. Now 20, the 6'4" 225 pound right-hander was 6-9 with a 4.23 ERA, 2.2 Ctl, and 6.6 Dom while posting a .235 oppBA. Those numbers may not be eye-popping, but he showed improvement throughout the season.

Adam has a big, durable frame that could eventually lead him to the middle of the big league rotation. His best current pitch is a big fastball in the 91-96 mph range that he spots impeccably to both sides of the plate. He has the velocity to pitch up, though he can overthrow which hinders pitch movement. His curveball can be a knockout pitch, thrown with excellent arm speed and featuring big-breaking action. Lagging behind is his change-up which is below average. With his arm strength, age, and potential for three average to above average offerings, Adam offers upside and could advance quickly through the minors with more polish.

Blessed with size, athleticism, and a ton of projection, 20-year-old **Aaron Altherr** (OF, PHI) is as aesthetically-pleasing as any prospect in the lower minors. While his performance hasn't matched the above average raw tools, he offers scintillating upside. The 6'5" 190 pound right-handed hitter began the '11 campaign in Low-A where he struggled mightily and was sent back to short-season ball where he still didn't perform as expected. Altherr batted .243/.291/.339 with 18 doubles, 6 HR, and 37 SB between the two levels. Further, he showed little grasp of the strike zone by whiffing 99 times while drawing only 24 walks.

Because of his crude abilities, it is important to look past the statistical outputs. Altherr has above average bat speed and covers the plate well thanks to his long, strong arms. He projects to hit for a moderately-high BA as a result. Once he adds more leverage to his swing, uses his lower half more, and learns to turn on pitches better, he could tap into his power potential and become an offensive force. Altherr runs very well and can play either LF or CF.

The Phillies are known for drafting and signing raw athletes and **Maikel Franco** (3B, PHI) has a chance to shine if given ample development time. The 19-year-old hasn't yet achieved success outside of short-season ball, but he oozes tools. He began the '11 campaign in short-season and was later promoted to Low-A. However, he was demoted back after he struggled against advanced pitching. For the season, the right-handed hitter batted .247/.318/.360 with 19 doubles and 3 HR.

Signed out of the Dominican Republic in '10, Franco is already a solid defender at 3B. He exhibits above average range to go along with a strong, accurate arm. He should stick at that position, though some scouts see an eventual move to an outfield corner. Regardless of his future position, Franco has the potential to become a middle-of-the-order run producer. He isn't particularly big, but he has explosive bat speed which gives him plus raw power to all fields. He brings a mature approach to the plate and makes excellent contact for a young hitter. Franco will attempt to master Low-A to begin '12 and he could move quickly if everything clicks.

Long and lean at 6'7" 180 pounds, **Joan Gregorio** (RHP, SF) tantalizes with loads of projection and quality arm speed and athleticism. The '11 season was his first campaign in the U.S. and he pitched very well. In 12 starts in Rookie ball, he went 3-0 with a 2.32 ERA in 50.1 innings. He posted a 2.8 Ctl and 7.7 Dom while holding the opposition to a .235 BA. Gregorio is only 19 years old and showed nice poise and moxie despite his lack of experience in professional ball.

The future looks bright for Gregorio as he combines a low three-quarters delivery and quick arm to produce an 86-94 mph fastball at present. Because of his long limbs and loose arm action, the velocity should increase a bit as he matures. Additionally, he already exhibits above average command of his fastball. If he can keep that while adding a few ticks, it could become one of the top fastballs in the minors. His secondary pitches need work, but that isn't much different than other young hurlers. Gregorio shows the potential for a solid-average curveball, though his change-up is inconsistent. He'll need the change-of-pace pitch to battle left-handed hitters. He'll likely return to short-season ball in '12, but he has a very high ceiling.

Tall shortstops are often moved off of the position and that very well may be the case for **Rosell Herrera** (SS, COL), but his bat has the potential to play anywhere on the diamond. The switch-hitting 19-year-old was signed in '09 from the Dominican Republic and played in the U.S. for the first time in '11. The 6'3" Herrera spent all season in Rookie ball and hit .284/.361/.449 with 6 doubles, 8 triples, and 6 HR while stealing 5 bases. Due to the presence of the highly-touted Trevor Story (SS, COL), the Rockies moved Herrera to 3B on occasion.

Herrera possesses a clean, line drive stroke, but he could tap into his very projectable power with a little more loft in his swing. He has a solid understanding of the strike zone, though he has a tendency to expand it when attempting to crush a ball. When he makes contact, he hits the ball square and hard and can drive it to all fields, particularly from the left side of the plate. With more at bats, he should eventually hit for both BA and power. Herrera runs well and could steal 15+ bases in the future. As a defender, he has solid arm strength and sufficient range to stick at SS, though a move to 3B or RF is likely.

Nick Kingham (RHP, PIT) is often overlooked when perusing the Pirates stable of arms in the minors. The 20-year-old isn't as highly rated as RHPs Gerrit Cole, Jameson Taillon, Luis Heredia, or Stetson Allie, but he has been successful since his selection in the fourth round of the '10 draft out of high school. The tall and lean righty finished third in the short-season New York-Penn League in ERA while starting 15 games. Kingham went 6-2 with a 2.15 ERA, 1.9 Ctl, and 6.0 Dom while holding the opposition to a .238 BA.

Kingham already throws a heavy ball at 90-95 mph and does an effective job of keeping it on the ground. Velocity and ample pitch movement give his fastball the potential to become a legitimate plus pitch at the major league level. He throws with clean arm action and he uses his 6'5" height well to deliver the ball on a downward plane. While his slider is quite inconsistent, it features excellent late break on occasion and can get swings and misses from time to time. He possesses good feel for a change-up which gives him leverage against left-handed hitters. With his moxie and pitchability, there is no reason why Kingham won't find success at Low-A in '12. His upside doesn't match that of his organization mates, but he could become a dependable and durable #3 starter.

The Angels were pleased to select **Nick Maronde** (LHP, LAA) in the third round of the '11 draft, but they were more than ecstatic when he dominated short-season ball in his pro debut. The 22-year-old was a reliever at the University of Florida in '11 and was converted to a starter upon signing. Not only did he find pro ball to his liking, but he should be able to stick in the starting rotation going forward. In 11 starts, he went 5-0 with a 2.14 ERA, 2.9 Ctl, and 9.7 Dom. He also held hitters to a .217 BA.

With a very fast arm, Maronde aggressively peppers the strike zone with 89-95 mph heat and it features solid, late action down in the strike zone. Though he can be guilty of using his fastball too much, he has shown the capacity to use his secondary pitches to retire hitters. Maronde has a hard slider that has been effective against left-handed hitters and his change-up is a work in progress. However, once he learns to sequence his pitches and repeat his delivery more consistently, he could become a high strikeout lefty in the majors. At worst, he could move back to the bullpen where he could play a pivotal role in the late innings as either a setup man or a closer.

The Athletics signed **Renato Nunez** (3B, OAK) to a $2.2 million bonus in '10 and they plan to bring him to the U.S. in '12 to unleash him in short-season ball. He'll be 18 when the season starts and he has arguably the most upside of any position player in the organization. Nunez played in the Dominican Summer League in '11 and hit .268/.301/.407 with 12 doubles and 5 HR in 194 at bats. The right-handed hitter stands 6'1" 185 pounds and features several average to well above average tools.

Nunez has all the requisite tools to be an offensive machine in the middle of a lineup. He has incredible strength for someone his age and he has a sound swing from the right side. While he has a very aggressive approach, he can punish balls to all parts of the ballpark. Because of his bat speed, plate coverage, and simple stroke, he has the potential to hit for both BA and well above average power. Nunez is also a good athlete who runs relatively well. He won't be a big base stealer, but he can leg out extra base hits. He should stick at 3B due to his soft hands and strong arm. He'll need to improve his footwork and throwing accuracy, but he has plenty of time to enhance his skills. Nunez will likely simmer in the minors for a while, but the payoff could be huge.

It isn't often to see a pitcher post an 8.60 ERA and 8.6 Ctl in short-season ball and be considered a deep sleeper prospect. However, **David Perez** (RHP, TEX) offers huge upside and exhibits the traits desired in a top of the rotation starter. The 6'5" 200 pounder struggled with his command in his first season in the U.S. Signed out of the Dominican Republic in '09, he went 1-4 with a 12.8 Dom in 9 starts covering 30.1 innings in his pro debut. He also held hitters to a .223 BA.

If Perez can harness his arm strength and throw consistent strikes, then he could become a #1-2 starter in the big leagues. He has lots of moving parts in his delivery and he repeats it well, but it hasn't yielded much success. He has outstanding velocity now, sitting between 90-94 mph and often touching 97. With a few mechanical tweaks and adjustments, he could add a few more ticks down the line. He is currently, and projects to be, a strikeout artist with his plus fastball and ability to spin a curveball. His long, lanky frame gives him some deception, but he'll need to refine his change-up in order to avoid being hit hard by left-handed hitters. Perez could become scary good if everything clicks for him.

Signed to a $1.2 million bonus from the Dominican Republic in '10, **Danry Vasquez** (OF, DET) is a pivotal player in the Tigers future. As a 17-year-old in Rookie ball, he batted .272/.306/.350 with 8 doubles, 2 HR, and 3 SB in 206 at bats. He didn't show much patience at the plate, striking out 34 times while drawing only 7 walks. The left-handed hitter spent his time in RF and was among the most dynamic players in the Gulf Coast League.

The 6'3" 170 pounder is a natural hitter who hits hard line drives to the entire field. He possesses a sweet lefty swing with few exploitable holes. While he didn't exhibit much pop in his pro debut, his bat speed and loose stroke should yield plus power down the line. He's long and lean and should become quite a physical specimen when he fully matures. Vasquez is a good athlete with quick movements, though he doesn't project to steal many bases. As a defender, he features a strong, accurate arm and enough range to be effective in a corner. He needs to refine his jumps and routes, but he should become a capable defender in due time.

2011 First-Year Player Draft Recap

by Rob Gordon and Jeremy Deloney

AMERICAN LEAGUE

BALTIMORE ORIOLES

The Orioles may not have had the deepest draft and may not churn out the most quantity of big leaguers, but the success of this draft is solely predicated on the development of RHP Dylan Bundy, the fourth overall pick. He could advance quickly with a mature arsenal of pitches and moxie well beyond his years. The rest of the draft focused on signable college players, led by 3B Jason Esposito (2nd). He brings outstanding glovework to the table and should have enough bat to reach the majors. RHPs Mike Wright (3rd) and Kyle Simon (4th) could make it as either back-end starters or late relievers, but both have generally lower ceilings. The Orioles often draft very conservatively and this one was really no different. However, Bundy and 3B Nick Delmonico (6th) could become stars if both develop the way the Orioles hope.

Sleeper: RHP Mark Blackmar (16th) is very athletic and has the potential for three average offerings. He also provides projection and could throw harder in the near-term.

Grade: B-

BOSTON RED SOX

Few organizations can match the recent quantity and quality of picks of the Red Sox. Their ability to stockpile draft picks and their willingness to spend lavishly are basic tenets of building a terrific draft class. They had four picks in the first and supplemental first rounds and selected players with high upsides. RHP Matt Barnes (1st) could reach the majors quickly while C Blake Swihart (1st) was the top prep catcher available. LHP Henry Owens (supplemental 1st) gives them a solid lefty with potential and OF Jackie Bradley (supplemental 1st) dropped in the draft due to an injury-plagued college season. Overall, the Red Sox gave six-figure bonuses to 14 draftees and seven-figure bonuses to 4 of them.

Sleeper: 3B Nick Moore (30th) was given a six-figure bonus despite his late round selection. He provides excellent athleticism and power potential.

Grade: A

CHICAGO WHITE SOX

Their farm system ranks among the worst in baseball and this draft didn't help. They selected mostly college players, many of whom project as spare parts. Nevertheless, a few stand out. OF Keenyn Walker (supplemental 1st) is as fast as any player drafted and could develop power down the line. RHP Erik Johnson (2nd) is big and strong with an excellent fastball. One player who could find his way to the majors quickly is C Kevan Smith (7th) who showed surprising offensive skills in his pro debut. However, he was also a senior sign from the University of Pittsburgh and offers a low ceiling. Drafts are difficult to grade in such a short period of time, but the selections this year were surprising, given the amount of talent that fell due to signability concerns.

Sleeper: LHP Blair Walters (11th) could be a quick-mover with an average fastball and plus slider.

Grade: D

CLEVELAND INDIANS

The Indians needed an influx of talent from this draft and got it. SS Francisco Lindor (1st) immediately becomes their top prospect with a terrific bat/glove combination unmatched in this draft. RHP Dillon Howard (2nd) also becomes their top pitching prospect with a big fastball that rarely comes out of his hand straight. Both players have exciting upside and give hope to a system that has seen young players elevated to the big leagues or traded to other organizations. C Jake Lowery (4th) and RHP Jake Sisco (3rd) are valuable prospects who project well. The Indians did a nice job of mixing high school and college players along with high ceiling vs. low upside players. The draft will ultimately ride on the success of Lindor and Howard.

Sleeper: RHP Cody Anderson (14th), who increased his velocity in junior college, only needs to improve his secondary offerings to rise up prospect charts.

Grade: B

DETROIT TIGERS

In recent years, the Tigers have been known for pouncing on players who have fallen in the draft due to high price tags. While those players were available this year, the Tigers went into a different route. They didn't have a first round pick, but settled on C James McCann (2nd) with their first selection. He has a good glove and should reach the majors independent of his offensive potential. Detroit loves the power stroke of 1B Aaron Westlake (3rd) and he also has a chance to hit for power. The Tigers preferred college players and they infused a lot of position players into a weak farm system. The best pitcher selected was LHP Brian Flynn (7th) who has a large, durable frame and a fastball to match.

Sleeper: OF Tyler Gibson (15th) could be the best athlete in the Tigers draft and has plus power potential.

Grade: C-

KANSAS CITY ROYALS

The Royals loaded up on high school players early in the draft, before focusing on college players, then turning back to prep stars. OF Bubba Starling (1st) was given a $7.5 million bonus for signing and has as much upside as any in the organization. He was a tough sign due to his scholarship to play quarterback at Nebraska, but there was little doubt the Royals would get him into the fold. RHP Bryan Brickhouse (3rd) was also given a seven-figure bonus and offers projection and an already plus fastball. While the focus on high school players early may mean it will be awhile before the Royals take advantage of their talents, the payoff could be huge. Two late picks, RHPs Jake Junis (29th) and Mark Binford (30th) were early round talents from the high school ranks who fell due to high price tags. The Royals gave them significant signing bonuses and both figure into their future plans.

Sleeper: SS Jack Lopez (16th) has an outstanding glove and could become a top prospect in the organization if his bat develops.

Grade: B

LOS ANGELES ANGELS

The highlight of the draft clearly was 1B C.J. Cron (1st), but the remainder of the selections were rather non-descript. The Angels didn't have a second round pick, but found success with LHP Nick Maronde (3rd) from the University of Florida who dominated short-season ball upon signing. They drafted other players with intriguing tools, but few have all-around star capabilities. The Angels like developing bullpen options and they took a few players that project well for late inning roles. Maronde could also be a quick-moving reliever, but he will likely be developed as a starter.

Sleeper: RHP Daniel Vargas-Vila (28th) who had a stellar debut despite a less-than-stellar pedigree. He deceives hitters with a quality three pitch arsenal.

Grade: C-

MINNESOTA TWINS

In previous drafts, the Twins have generally chosen college pitchers in the early round. Due to a need for middle infield help, they opted for SS Levi Michael (1st) from the University of North Carolina. He is a relatively polished player who may eventually have to move to 2B. Supplemental first round picks 3B Travis Harrison and RHP Hudson Boyd give the Twins two young, heavily scouted high schoolers they can develop. As history suggests, the organization likes to pick college relievers and their selections in rounds 2 through 4 could become dependable big league bullpen mates—RHP Madison Boer, LHP Corey Williams, and RHP Matt Summers. Much of the draft selections appear to be organizational role players.

Sleeper: RHP Josh Burris (17th) is a converted catcher who has exemplary arm strength and a feel for a power curveball, but below average command at present.

Grade: B

NEW YORK YANKEES

The Yankees clearly went the prep route in this draft—their first six signees were all from the high school ranks. They did select LHP Sam Stafford in the 2nd round out of Texas, but they failed to ink him to a contract. 3B Dante Bichette Jr (supplemental 1st) immediately becomes one of their better prospects and offers plus power potential, similar to his father. He was named the Gulf Coast League MVP after hitting .342/.446/.505. Selections from cold weather states, RHP Jordan Cote (3rd) and Matt Duran (4th), likely will need several years of seasoning before they reach the majors, though RHP Branden Pinder (16th) could be wearing pinstripes in just a few seasons. C Greg Bird (5th) was given the highest bonus ($1.1 million) of any Yankees signee. Few draftees are considered "can't miss" and it may take at least 3-5 years to adequately grade this draft.

Sleeper: RHP Mark Montgomery (11th) could advance rapidly as a hard-throwing reliever with a dynamite slider.

Grade: C-

OAKLAND ATHLETICS

Similar to the Angels, Oakland didn't draft a class with eye-popping upside, but they chose safer picks who could eventually develop into something useful. The gem of the class is RHP Sonny Gray (1st) who throws hard despite his size. His curveball is already a plus pitch and he will be given a shot to move up the ladder quickly. 3B B.A. Vollmuth (3rd) has a power bat, but is quite crude with the other parts of his game. OF Bobby Crocker (4th) fits the Athletics mold and has potential to be a solid, everyday player. The Athletics have a dearth of pitching in their system and this draft didn't solve those issues, though Gray could be a steal.

Sleeper: RHP Nathan Kilcrease (30th) may only stand 5'6", but he knows how to pitch and has a solid-average cuveball.

Grade: C

SEATTLE MARINERS

The Mariners went heavy for college players and they should enjoy their first two picks for several years to come. LHP Danny Hultzen (1st) debuted in the Arizona Fall League and has few weaknesses in his arsenal. He throws hard and has good secondary offerings, including a terrific change-up. SS Brad Miller (2nd) does everything well and should be a solid-average middle infielder. He is a good defender with the potential to become a top-of-the-order hitter due to his contact-making ability and disciplined approach. There were intriguing selections such as RHP Carter Capps (supplemental 3rd) who has a very high upside and the number of catchers drafted (5 in the first 19 rounds).

Sleeper: LHP Cameron Hobson (11th) had a stellar debut and has good command of a three pitch mix.

Grade: B

TAMPA BAY RAYS

With 10 of the first 60 picks in the draft, the Rays took advantage and signed an equal assortment of prep stars and college players. They weren't shy with spending either—18 signees with six-figure bonuses—as many of their draftees have very high ceilings and have become some of their better prospects. Few can match the upside of RHP Taylor Guerrieri (1st) with his hard, crisp pitch mix. They also selected quite a few high school infielders, led by SS Jake Hager (1st) and the late-blooming SS Brandon Martin (supplemental 1st). Peppered into the selections were lower-ceiling prospects such as LHP Grayson Garvin (supplemental 1st) and RHP Lenny Linsky (2nd) who could reach the majors quickly as a deceptive reliever. This draft has the potential to bear delicious fruit, but the player development system must cultivate the talent.

Sleeper: 1B John Alexander (8th) has a rare combination of plus athleticism and raw power. He's tall and strong and just needs time to develop.

Grade: A

TEXAS RANGERS

They had a relatively quiet draft and surprised many with their early round selections. Still, they were able to snag a few players in the mid-rounds who should eventually find their way to the majors. The Rangers opted for LHP Kevin Matthews (1st) early and he offers nice velocity despite his light frame. Supplemental first round pick OF Zach Cone has all the tools necessary to be a solid everyday player, but he didn't produce in his junior year at Georga and slid in the draft. Two pitchers who could move quickly include LHP Will Lamb (2nd) and RHP Kyle Hendricks (8th). They both have strong arms that project well in pro ball.

Sleeper: RHP Connor Sadzeck (11th) throws hard and has the potential to develop a plus slider, but he needs to refine his command.

Grade: D

TORONTO BLUE JAYS

They may not have signed their first round selection (RHP Tyler Beede), but the Blue Jays signed four supplemental first rounders and loaded up on high-ceiling high school players, particularly pitchers. OFs Jacob Anderson (supplemental 1st) and Dwight Smith Jr (supplemental 1st) highlight the position players selected. The Blue Jays already had plentiful pitching depth in the minors and only enhanced it with this draft. LHP Daniel Norris (2nd) was given the largest bonus in the draft class and brings a plus fastball and knockout curveball to the table. RHPs Joe Musgrove (supplemental 1st) and Kevin Comer (supplemental 1st) may spend the next several seasons simmering in the minors, but they have great potential as well.

Sleeper: 3B Matt Dean (13th) who slid in the draft due to signability questions was given a large signing bonus as a prep infielder. He has exciting power potential and plus instincts for the game.

Grade: A-

NATIONAL LEAGUE

ARIZONA DIAMONDBACKS

In a year when there was a deep pool of pitching talent, the Diamondbacks jumped in aggressively. The Diamondbacks had two of the first seven picks in the draft, getting the 7th overall pick for failing to sign Barret Loux in the 6th spot in 2010. The club selected Trevor Bauer (RHP) with the 3rd pick and flame-throwing prepster Archie Bradley (RHP). Recognizing that the strength of the organization was the depth they had in position players, GM Kevin Towers and Scouting Director Ray Montgomery followed up by grabbing two college hurlers, lefty Andrew Chaffin from Kent State and righty Anthony Meo from Coastal Carolina. In all, the Diamondbacks spent $11.9 million on the draft and picked up more quality pitching than any other team in baseball.

Sleeper: Kyle Winkler (RHP) from TCU would have been a second or third round pick in previous years, but slipped due to depth of quality arms. Winkler features a 90-94 mph fastball, a mid-80 slider, and a decent change-up. At 5'11" he is a bit undersized, but has good stuff and at worst should reach the majors as a reliever.

Grade: A

ATLANTA BRAVES

Because of their recent success and the large number of compensation picks in the '11 draft, the Braves had only two of first 100 players taken. Not surprisingly they dipped into the large pool of collegiate hurlers, taking Florida State lefty Sean Gilmartin with the 28th pick. Overall the Braves spent a modest $3.7 million in the draft and their first four picks were all college players signed to modest bonuses. The Braves stayed conservative in later rounds and their largest bonus outside of rounds 1-5 was a $400,000 bonus to 14th rounder Navery Moore. The Braves did get a big arm in Santa Clara righty J.R. Graham. Graham has a mid-to-upper-90s fastball, but he only has two legitimate offerings and is just 6'0" 175 pounds. Gilmartin is a solid pick, but in total this group is devoid of any star talent.

Sleeper: Tommy La Stella (2B) is a short, athletic infielder out of Costal Carolina who was taken in the 8th round. La Stella has some nice offensive upside and had an impressive professional debut, hitting .328/.401/.543 with 13 doubles, 9 home runs, and 26 BB/28 K in 232 AB in the SAL. His defense might be a bit light, but the bat looks very good.

Grade: C+

CHICAGO CUBS

In the Cubs second draft under the ownership of Tom Ricketts, the club invested heavily in the draft, spending a club record $12 million. Not only did the Cubs hand out a $5 million bonus to the toolsy and projectable Javier Baez (SS), but they went over slot on a handful of other players as well, landing power hitting Dan Vogelbach (1B) in the 2nd round and two advanced collegiate players, Zeke DeVoss (OF) and Louisville closer Tony Zych (RHP), in rounds 3-4. The Cubs also signed the hard-throwing Dylan Maples (RHP) away from a scholarship to North Carolina by giving the 14th round pick a $2.5 million bonus. Under the direction of Scouting Director Tim Wilken, the Cubs have tended towards college players, so the picks of Baez and Vogelbach represent a bit of a departure and will determine the success of this draft class for the Cubs.

Sleeper: Neftali Rosario (C) is an interesting catching prospect and looks like a steal in the 6th round. Rosario is already a solid defender and had a nice pro debut in the Arizona Rookie League, hitting .294/.351/.490 in 102 AB. He lacks plate discipline but is a strong defender with a good arm.

Grade: B+

CINCINNATI REDS

Despite not having any additional 1st or 2nd round picks, the Reds did a nice job of adding to their talent pool. First round pick Robert Stephenson is a hard-throwing high school right-hander whose fastball tops out at 97 mph. After Stephenson, the Reds grabbed toolsy Gabriel Rosa (2nd), a high school OF from Puerto Rico and Tony Cingrani (3rd), a talented lefty from Rice. One of their better picks was in 5th round when they took Louisville 2B Ryan Wright. Wright has an advanced bat and had a solid pro debut. If Cingrani and Stephenson develop as expected, this is a nice haul for a modest $6.4 million.

Sleeper: Amir Garrett (LHP) is strong high school lefty with a 92-95 mph fastball and a 6'6" frame. He also has the makings of a decent change and curveball, but is very raw on the mound. The Reds gave him $1 million to steal him away from St. Johns.

Grade: B

COLORADO ROCKIES

The Rockies have earned a reputation for scouting, drafting, and developing home grown talent, yet their drafts in the past 3-4 years have yielded sparse results. In particular, the Rockies have struggled in drafting and developing pitching prospects. Most of their best young arms were signed as international free agents, while domestic picks such as Greg Reynolds, Christian Friedrich, Casey Weathers, Peter Tago, and Tyler Matzek (all 1st round picks) have yet to contribute in the majors. In 2011, the Rockies hope to reverse that trend with 20th overall pick Tyler Anderson. Anderson is a college lefty from Oregon and has a good 89-93 mph fastball. With their supplemental 1st round pick, the Rockies snagged toolsy and athletic Trevor Story, a high school kid from Texas who had a solid professional debut, hitting for power and average. The Rockies were not big spenders in 2011, doling out just $4 million in bonuses. If Story and Anderson pan out, they will get solid talent for a minimal investment.

Sleeper: Chris Jensen (RHP, COL) has a good 90-94 mph fastball with a nice slider. If he can develop a 3rd offering, he could emerge as a solid back-of-the-rotation starter. If not, the fastball/slider combination is good enough to be a solid reliever. Jensen had a good debut, going 2-1 with a 2.65 ERA, 10 BB/28 K, and a .206 oppBA in 37.1 IP.

Grade: B

HOUSTON ASTROS

Because of the lack of progress from '10 and '09 1st rounders Delino DeShields Jr. and Jio Mier, the Astros system remains relatively thin, leaving the organization a lot of work to do. Recent trades have partially filled the void, but club still needs more talent. The good news is that the Astros finally departed from their tendency towards taking projectable high school players with their first round picks, nabbing Connecticut OF George Springer 11th overall. Unfortunately there are few impact players in the group. The Astros did grab two power right-handers, Adrian Houser and Jack Armstrong, in rounds 2-3 but both have some work to do. In a year when the draft was very deep, the Astros needed to make more of an impact.

Sleeper: Kyle Hallock (LHP) is a short lefty from Kent State. He doesn't overpower, but does have four solid offerings including a good curve and a plus change-up. Hallock doesn't have a lot of upside, but had a solid pro debut—2.63 ERA, 17 BB/61 K and a .241 oppBAA in 61.2 IP.

Grade: C

LOS ANGELES DODGERS

Given the state of the Dodgers this past summer, it was not surprising to see them be very frugal in the draft. The club spent only $3.5 million and landed a very thin crop of prospects. First rounder Chris Reed (16th overall) was a closer at Stanford, but the Dodgers will attempt to move him into a starting role. Reed features a 91-94 mph fastball with good movement, a plus 82-84 mph slider, and decent change-up, but he started just one game in college and has to be considered a project at this point. The Dodgers did nab some useful players in high school 3B Alex Santana (2nd) and North Carolina State backstop Pratt Maynard (3rd), but did not spend more than $150,000 on any pick after the 3rd round. There wasn't much the Dodgers could do here, but they missed a great opportunity.

Sleeper: O'Koyea Dickson (1B) was a 12th rounder, but had an impressive debut, hitting .333/.402/.603 with 13 home runs in 189 AB in rookie ball. Dickson drives the ball well with good bat speed. At 5'10" 220 lbs. he is physically mature, but a bit short for 1B. If he can handle the position defensively, he has some potential.

Grade: D

MIAMI MARLINS

The Marlins stuck with their tried and true strategy of taking high upside high school players early in the draft. In '09 they picked high school lefty Chad James and in '10 they went with 1B Christian Yelich. Both of those picks have worked out nicely, so the Marlins stayed the course by selecting Jose Fernandez, a high school right-hander from Tampa, FL with the 14th overall pick. Fernandez has plus stuff, is fairly polished for his age, and projects as a solid front-end starter. They followed that up with college lefty Adam Conley, who worked as a starter and a closer at Washington State. The Marlins failed to sign their 3rd and 4th round picks, but did manage to sign high upside prepster Mason Hope (RHP) in the 5th round. Despite missing out on some important picks, the Marlins still did a solid job of acquiring some decent pitching.

Sleeper: Charlie Lowell (LHP) is a strong, durable 6'4" lefty from Wichita State. He has a good 90-94 mph fastball, slider, and a decent change-up. He doesn't have any projection left, but could turn into a decent mid-rotation lefty.

Grade: B

MILWAUKEE BREWERS

The Brewers failed to sign their first round pick in 2010 (Dylan Covey) and so had two of the first 15 picks. To their credit, they didn't waste those picks, selecting and signing two of the best arms in the draft. In particular, the Brewers decision to pick Georgia Tech lefty Jed Bradley was a gutsy move. The compensation pick for not signing Covey was only good for this year, so the Brewers had to sign Bradley or lose the pick. As a college junior, Bradley could have gone back to college and so he had some negotiating leverage, but the Brewers got a deal done. They also took Texas starter Taylor Jungmann with the 12th overall pick. Jungmann was one of the more consistent Division I starters in the country in '11 and features a mid-90s fastball. The Brewers didn't stop there and six of their first eight picks were pitchers and include Jorge Lopez (2nd), Drew Gagnon (3rd), and David Goforth (7th). If Jungmann and Bradley live up to expectations, this draft will look very good in 2-3 years.

Sleeper: Nick Ramirez (1B) was the Brewers 4th round pick out of Cal State Fullerton. Ramirez was a two way player in college and served as the teams closer. He has solid power potential and had a nice pro debut, hitting .271/.305/.496 with 21 doubles and 11 home runs.

Grade: A-

NEW YORK METS

In 2011 the Mets were a bit riskier than they had been in previous drafts. Instead of opting for signable college players, Mets Scouting Director Chad McDonald opted for one of the least known, but most projectable players in the draft, Brandon Nimmo (13th overall). Nimmo is from Wyoming and did not have a high school baseball team, instead playing American Legion Ball and touring widely on the showcase circuits. After taking Nimmo, the Mets went after high school righty Michael Fulmer (1-S) and North Carolina State righty Cory Mazonni (2nd). Given the organization's needs and the depth of the draft, it was not surprising that five of the Mets first six picks were pitchers. If Nimmo and the arms develop, the Mets will have gone a long way towards filling significant needs.

Sleeper: Danny Muno (SS) was an 8th round pick out of Fresno State who had an impressive professional debut, hitting .355/.466/.514 in the NYPL. He is a professional hitter with a quick bat who sprays the ball to all fields. His plus plate discipline gives him a chance to hit for average as he moves up. He played SS in college but was moved to 2B when drafted and profiles well there.

Grade: B-

PHILADELPHIA PHILLLIES

The Phillies stuck with their standard player acquisition mode, drafting toolsy, high-upside, but raw players. The club has enough top end talent in the majors, that they seem content with the diamond in the rough approach. The Phillies first pick was supplemental 1st rounder OF Larry Greene (39th overall). Greene has plus raw power and at 6'2" 235 pounds, he is already physically mature. Whether or not Greene can hit as a pro remains to be seen. The Phillies followed up by taking speedster SS Roman Quinn in round two and then safe college picks 3B Harold Martinez (2nd) and then LHP Adam Morgan (3rd). SS Mitch Walding has size and speed, but will likely have to move off SS due to a below-average arm. There are some interesting projects in this group, but no sure things.

Sleeper: Tyler Greene (SS) was taken in the 11th round and has nice athleticism. He has a good bat and moderate power. Mostly likely he moves off SS, but has enough speed to play OF or 2B where his plus arm strength would play well. Greene had a decent pro debut, hitting .276/.386/.379 in the GCL.

Grade: C

PITTSBURGH PIRATES

The Pirates have been committed to building through the draft since current GM Neal Huntington took over in 2007. Their 2011 was an even more aggressive and earned the club a stern warning

from Commissioner Bud Selig. The Pirates spent an MLB record $17 million in bonuses. The Pirates had the first overall pick in the draft and selected UCLA righty Gerrit Cole and promptly gave him an $8 million bonus. The club wasn't done and picked 5-tool OF Josh Bell in round two, luring him away from a football scholarship to Texas with a $5 million bonus. Cole has top-of-the-rotation stuff, including a 93-98 mph fastball that tops out at 100 mph. If Cole and Bell live up to their potential, this draft provides the club with two elite players.

Sleeper: Clay Holmes (RHP, PIT) was a 9th round pick with 2nd round talent. He got lost in deep pool of high school power arms and the Pirates scooped him up and agreed to a $1.2 million bonus. Holmes has a nice 90-93 mph fastball and at 6'5" 230 pounds he has a nice power-pitching frame.

Grade: A

SAN DIEGO PADRES

Padres GM Jed Hoyer and Scouting Director Jason McLeod built the deepest farm system in baseball before moving into similar roles for the Chicago Cubs. The 2011 draft was one of their last acts for the Padres and it was a good one. The Padres had two first round picks and three supplemental 1st round picks and the club managed to sign 4 of the 5 picks, landing two high upside hurlers in RHP Joe Ross (25th overall) and Michael Kelly (48th overall), 2B Corey Spangenberg (10th overall), SS Jace Peterson (58th overall), and C Austin Hedges (82nd overall). The Padres failed to sign high school backstop Brett Austin, but still netted a quality group of pitchers and position players. Spangenberg got off to a quick start as a pro, hitting .316/.419/.418 at two different levels. While Hoyer and McLeod have moved on, they definitely didn't leave the cupboard bare.

Sleeper: Kevin Quackenbush (RHP) was an 8th round pick after serving as the closer for South Florida. He uses a 90-93 mph fastball with great effect. He hides the ball well and has some nice deception. He also throws a slider and a change-up and had an impressive debut striking out 71 in 42 IP and limiting opposing hitters to a .172 oppBA.

Grade: A

SAN FRANCISCO GIANTS

For the second year in a row the Giants under the direction of GM Brian Sabean and Amateur Scouting Director John Barr went college heavy in the draft. Six of the Giants first seven picks were college players, highlighted by first rounder 2B Joe Panik (29th overall) and 2nd rounder C Andrew Susac from Oregon State. Sandwiched between Panik and Susac, is high school right-hander Kyle Crick. Crick has some work to do, but has some nice upside. The Giants landed a solid group of college position players and strong-armed pitchers, but little in the way of impact talent.

Sleeper: Joe Osich (LHP) is a 6th round pick out of Oregon State. Osich had Tommy John surgery in '10 and lingering concerns about his arm emerged again this past spring. He has a good 92-95 mph fastball, a slider, and an inconsistent change-up. He has good stuff and could develop into an impact reliever. Can spot fastball effectively and should move up quickly, though it will likely be in relief.

Grade: B

ST. LOUIS CARDINALS

The Cardinals under the direction of recently departed Scouting Director Jeff Luhnow continued to draft a mix of polished college players and projectable high schoolers. 1st round pick Kolten Wong (22nd overall) looks to be a professional hitter and had one of the best pro debuts of any pick in the draft, hitting .335/.401/.510 with 15 doubles, 5 home runs, 9 SB, and 21 BB/24 K in the MWL. 2nd round pick Charlie Tilson and 3rd rounder C.J. McElroy are true CF with plus speed. The Cardinals didn't break the bank on this draft, spending just $4.6 million, but Wong looks like a sure thing and if Tilson or McElroy click they will get good bang for their buck.

Sleeper: Danny Miranda (RHP) was an 8th round pick out of the University of Miami where he served as their closer. At 5'11", he isn't going to blow hitters away and his fastball rarely breaks 90 mph, but he has good stuff and gets hitters out. Miranda had a solid debut, 2.64 ERA, 7 BB/27 K, and 15 saves in 30.2 IP.

Grade: B

WASHINGTON NATIONALS

The Nationals continue to break the bank as they stockpile premium young talent. In 2009, the Nationals landed Stephen Strasburg and spent $11.5 million in 2009. In 2010, they drafted Bryce Harper and spent $11.9 million. This year, the National drafted 3B Anthony Rendon (6th overall), widely considered the best position player in the draft and spent a whopping $15 million. In to Rendon, the Nationals went over slot to land RHP Alex Meyer ($2 million), projectable OF Brian Goodwin ($3 million) and TCU lefty Matt Purke ($2.75 million). Even if the Nationals bat .500 with these picks, it would be a coup and the club will likely lament the changes implemented in the new CBA.

Sleeper: Matt Skole (3B) was a 5th round pick out of Georgia Tech. He has good raw power from the left-hand side. He also has good plate discipline and an improved approach at the plate. Defensively he is below average with stiff hands and limited range and will likely have to move to a new position with Zimmerman and Rendon blocking him at 3B.

Grade: A+

2011-2012 Top 20 International Prospects

by Rob Gordon

Each year there is a bevy of talented international players who emerge on the professional baseball scene. Despite the creation of the World Baseball Classic and the brief appearance of baseball as an Olympic sport, these international players do not get a lot of exposure until they sign professional contracts and come to the U.S. In order to shed some light on these players, this article will take a look at the top 20 international prospects for 2011-2012. Since the focus of the MLBA is on prospects, this list will not include international players over the age of 30, but does include international Non-Drafted Free Agents (NDFA) who have signed or remain unsigned at the time of the publication of this book (January 2012). For each player we have provided a scouting report, an ETA to the majors, a player rating, and a brief summary of their contractual status.

1. Yu Darvish, RHP, Hokkaido Nippon Ham Fighters

Darvish is the top international player available and has been for the past several years. The 25-year-old Darvish has an impressive array of offerings. His fastball sits in the 92-95 mph range and tops out at 99 mph. It has good late life and runs in right-handed batters. Darvish also has a plus, late breaking slider that is a true swing-and-miss offering, a plus 12-6 curveball, and a good change-up. At 6'5" 215 pounds he is lean and athletic, but so far has been very durable. He has nice simple mechanics, a repeatable delivery, and generates easy velocity. In 2011 Darvish was 18-6 with a 1.44 ERA and 276 K in 232 IP. The Texas Rangers won the rights to negotiate with Darvish.
MLB Debut: 2012
Potential Rating: 9C

2. Yoenis Cespedes, CF, Cuba

The 26-year-old Cespedes defected from Cuba in July and instantly became the most coveted international position player. At 5'11" 215, Cespedes is physically strong and athletic. At the plate he generates good power for his size. He has plus bat speed and can crush elevated fastballs. He is quick through the ball and makes consistent, hard contact. His swing can get long at times and he can be overly aggressive. Defensively he moves well and has a plus throwing arm. He has above-average speed and should be able to stick in CF once he signs. He projects as a .280-.300 hitter with 20-25 home run, 15 SB potential, above-average defensive CF.
MLB Debut: 2012
Potential Rating: 9D

3. Norichika Aoki, OF, Yakult Swallows

Aoki is widely considered to be the best pure hitter on the international scene. The 29-year-old hits from the left side, makes consistent contact, has plus plate discipline, and above-average speed. Aoki barrels the ball well and has good hand-eye coordination. He uses his speed well, but is not a burner with tons of SB potential. Defensively he covers ground and is a good defender in either CF or LF. At 5'10" 170 pounds, he doesn't have much power, but he has been a consistent .300 with a .400 OBA. The Milwaukee

Brewers won the rights to negotiate with Aoki and he profiles better in the NL, either as a #2 hitter or a solid 4th OF.
MLB Debut: 2012
Potential Rating: 7B

4. Elier Hernandez, OF, KC

The 16-year-old Hernandez was considered one of the best Latin American prospects available in 2011 and was signed by the Royals to a $3.05 million deal. Hernandez has a very nice line-drive stroke. It is a simple approach and he uses his lower half well to generate plus bat speed without sacrificing contact ability. He projects to have above-average power down the road. He is athletic but has only average speed and may slow down as he matures. That likely makes him a corner OF once he reaches the majors, but he should have enough power and ability to hit to be a full-time regular. He has some exciting potential.
MLB Debut: 2016
Potential Rating: 9E

5. Ronald Guzman, OF, TEX

Guzman is a tall, projectable OF from the Dominican Republic. The Rangers signed the 16-year-old for a team record $3.5 million. At 6'4" 195 lbs. Guzman is a long, lean, projectable left-handed OF. Guzman has a good approach at the plate and currently makes consistent contact and is willing to use the whole field. He doesn't have plus bat speed and his swing can get a bit long so it isn't clear if he will hit for both average and power. He isn't as physical or athletic as your typical Dominican teenager, but looks like he should be able to hit. Defensively he is a below-average runner with a below-average arm that will likely limit him to LF or 1B as a professional. He could take some time to develop.
MLB Debut: 2016
Potential Rating: 9E

6. Nomar Mazara, OF, TEX

The Texas Rangers signed the 16-year-old Mazara to a $5 million bonus. The 6'3" 185 lbs. Mazara has plus raw power from the left-hand side. He has good bat speed, and a tall, strong frame that suggests future power. His exaggerated leg-kick when he swings will likely have to be corrected if he is to hit for average and power and there are definite concerns about his ability to make consistent contact in game action. He moves well defensively and has a solid throwing arm. If he can hit, he has the potential to develop into an above-average corner OF.
MLB Debut: 2016
Potential Rating: 9E

7. Tsuyoshi Wada, LHP, BAL

The Orioles signed the 31-year-old Wada to a two-year, $8.15 million deal. The 5'11" Wada does not overpower hitters. His fastball sits in the 85-88 mph range and rarely breaks 90 mph. He also throws a slow curve and a decent change-up and is a consistent strike-thrower. In 2011, Wada was 16-5 with a 1.51 ERA and 40 BB/168 K in 182 IP. Wada is your prototypical finesse lefty, but he knows how to pitch and should be able to slot into the back end of the Orioles rotation.
MLB Debut: 2012
Potential Rating: 7C

8. Victor Sanchez, RHP, SEA

Sanchez was widely considered the top prospect in Venezuela in 2011 and signed for a bonus in the range of $2 million. The 16-year-old Sanchez is only 6'0", but has a nice 88-92 mph fastball, a good slider, a nice change-up, and a seldom used curveball. Sanchez hits his spots well and is fairly polished for such a young hurler, but he doesn't have much projection or upside from here. Still Sanchez is mature and will likely move more quickly than other international pitchers.
MLB Debut: 2016
Potential Rating: 8D

9. Roberto Osuna, RHP, TOR

Osuna is a 16-year-old right-handed pitcher from Mexico. He has a quick arm and generates nice velocity, despite his 6'0" 185-pound frame. His fastball sits in the 88-92 range and tops out at 94 mph. He also has a good curveball and a change-up that has potential. Reports are that he has a good feel for pitching and he signed with the Blue Jays.
MLB Debut: 2016
Potential Rating: 8D

10. Wilmer Becerra, SS, TOR

The Blue Jays also signed 16-year-old SS Wilmer Becerra. Becerra is 6'3" 175 lbs. and has some lean athleticism to his frame. He has good size, speed, and nice range. Defensively he could play either SS or the OF, but his arm is below-average so a corner OF slot might be the best fit. At the plate, there are questions about his hit tool as he can be overly aggressive and struggles with pitch recognition. He does have good bat speed and is projectable, but is also very raw and has work to do.
MLB Debut: 2016
Potential Rating: 8E

11. Hisashi Iwakuma, RHP, Tohoku Golden Eagles

The 30-year-old right-hander is widely considered to be the 2nd best pitching prospect in Japan behind Yu Darvish. Iwakuma has yet to sign with a major league club, but will do so this off-season. Iwakuma features a 90-93 mph 4-seam fastball, a splitter, a 78-82 mph slider, and a 70-73 mph curveball. He missed time with shoulder fatigue and isn't overpowering. Still has he good control and could be a solid #4 or #5 starter in the majors.
MLB Debut: 2012
Potential Rating: 7C

12. Hiroyuki Nakajima, SS, Seibu Lions

The New York Yankees won the rights to negotiate with Nakajima when he was posted in December but were unable to sign him to a contract. The 29-year-old Japanese SS has a bit of power, but is more of a line-drive hitter. Nakajima has solid plate discipline and hit .302/.360/.448 with 16 home runs and 20 SB. While his overall numbers have been off the past several seasons, he still has some nice upside.
MLB Debut: 2016
Potential Rating: 6B

13. Adalberto Mondesi, SS, KC

The 16-year-old Mondesi is the son of former major leaguer Raul Mondesi. The younger Mondesi is tall and wiry, but should add strength as he fills out. The Royals signed Mondesi for a $2 million bonus. The switch-hitting Mondesi has a nice line-drive approach, good bat speed, and should develop more as he matures. He has above-average speed and a decent throwing arm and has good enough actions to be an everyday regular at short.

MLB Debut: 2016
Potential Rating: 8D

14. Enrique Acosta, SS, CHC

The Cubs signed the 16-year-old Acosta to a $1.1 million bonus. At 6'1" 180 lbs., he was one of the more polished hitters on the international market in '11. Acosta has a nice swing, bat speed, and good approach at the plate. He should develop at least moderate to above-average power once he matures. Defensively he is below average and will need to work hard to stay at the position. Most likely a move to 3B or the OF will be in the future.

MLB Debut: 2016
Potential Rating: 8D

15. Manual Marcos, OF, BOS

The Red Sox signed the 16-year Marcos for $800,000. At 6'0"175 lbs., Marcos is not a physically imposing youngster, but he does run well and has a solid bat. Marcos has plus to plus-plus speed and profiles as a speedy, CF with a bit of pop, but more likely a guy with solid gap power. He is a good defender with a strong throwing arm. He might not have as much upside as others on this list, but because of his speed and defense, is more likely to reach his potential.

MLB Debut: 2016
Potential Rating: 8E

16. Jose Ruiz, C, SD

There weren't many quality backstops on the international market in '11 and Ruiz was the best available. At 6'2" 180 lbs., Ruiz has good size and is stronger than many of his contemporaries. Offensively, Ruiz has questions about his ability to hit. He does have good raw power and if his hit tool comes along he could be a solid big leaguer. He moves well behind the plate, has a decent arm, and should be able stick behind the plate.

MLB Debut: 2016
Potential Rating: 8D

17. Wei-Ying Chen, LHP, Chunichi Dragons

Chen is a 26-year-old lefty from Japan who negotiated to become a free agent ahead of schedule and so did not need to be posted. Chen features an 88-91 mph fastball, a splitter, curveball, and a change-up, but none of the offerings are considered to be plus. Chen does command all of his offerings well and works both sides of the plate. When he does sign, he could compete for a 4th or 5th starter spot for a team looking for a finesse lefty.

MLB Debut: 2016
Potential Rating: 6C

18. Mark Malave, C, CHC

The Cubs were active on the international market in '11. In addition to Acosta, the Cubs signed the 16-year-old Malave. The 6'1"200 pounder is a switch-hitting catcher has good raw power, but does not have plus bat speed and might struggle to hit. He has a strong throwing arm, but he isn't very agile and will need to work hard to stick behind the plate.

MLB Debut: 2016
Potential Rating: 8D

19. Dawel Lugo, SS, TOR

The Blue Jays were the most active club on the international market in 2011. The Jays signed Osuna, Becerra, and 16-year-old SS Dawel Lugo from the Dominican Republic for a $1.3 million bonus. Lugo has a solid bat with good bat speed and makes hard contact. He can be a bit aggressive at the plate and doesn't use his lower half very well and will need to develop better plate discipline. At 6'0" 175 he has good size and could develop moderate power as he develops. Lugo is only an average runner with questionable range and an average arm. His actions at SS are a bit long and he needs to improve his footwork. He does have good athleticism and might be able to stick at SS, but could also be moved to 3B or the OF.

MLB Debut: 2016
Potential Rating: 8E

20. Helsin Martinez, OF, Dominican Republic

The 16-year-old Martinez has as much raw power as any Latin American prospect on the free agent market. At 6'5" 190 lbs., he has a tall, muscular frame and could add power and strength as he matures. As with many tall hitters, Martinez' swing can get long. Martinez needs to retool his approach to hitting and scouts question whether or not he will be able to hit as a professional. Because of his size he is fairly raw defensively as he is still growing into his body. He runs reasonably well, but projects to be average to a tick below as he fills out. Martinez is even further away than many others on this list, but because of his size and strength is a player to keep an eye on. As of now, Martinez has yet to land with an MLB team, but will likely do so soon.

MLB Debut: 2016
Potential Rating: 8E

ORGANIZATION RATINGS/RANKINGS

Each organization is graded on a standard A-F scale in four separate categories, and then after weighing the categories and adding some subjectivity, a final grade and ranking are determined. The four categories are the following:

Hitting: The quality and quantity of hitting prospects, the balance between athleticism, power, speed, and defense, and the quality of player development.

Pitching: The quality and quantity of pitching prospects and the quality of player development.

Top-end Talent: The quality of the top players within the organization. Successful teams are ones that have the most star-quality players. These are the players who are a teams' above average regulars, front-end starters, and closers.

Depth: The depth of both hitting and pitching prospects within the organization.

Overall Grade: The four categories are weighted, with top-end talent being the most important and depth being the least.

TEAM	Hitting	Pitching	Top-End Talent	Depth	Overall
San Diego Padres	A-	A	A	A+	A
Tampa Bay Rays	B	A-	A-	A-	A-
Washington Nationals	A	B	A	B	A-
Colorado Rockies	A-	B	B+	A-	A-
Kansas City Royals	B-	A-	A-	B+	B+
Boston Red Sox	A-	B-	B	B+	B+
Toronto Blue Jays	B	B+	A-	B+	B+
Arizona Diamondbacks	B-	B+	B	B+	B+
Pittsburgh Pirates	C+	A	A-	B	B+
Los Angeles Angels	B+	C	B	B	B
Atlanta Braves	B-	A	B+	B	B
Seattle Mariners	B	B	B	B+	B
Texas Rangers	B-	B	A-	B	B
Los Angeles Dodgers	C-	A-	B	B	B
St. Louis Cardinals	B	A-	B+	B	B
Cincinnati Reds	C+	B-	C+	B-	B-
New York Mets	C	A-	B	B-	B-
Cleveland Indians	C+	B	B	B-	B-
Oakland A's	C+	B-	C+	C+	C+
Minnesota Twins	B	C+	B	C	C+
Miami Marlins	C+	C+	C	C+	C+
New York Yankees	B	C-	B+	C	C+
San Francisco Giants	B	C-	B-	B	C+
Chicago Cubs	B-	C	C+	B-	C
Philadelphia Phillies	C-	B-	C	B	C
Houston Astros	B-	C	B-	C-	C
Detroit Tigers	D	C+	B-	D-	C-
Baltimore Orioles	C	D	B+	D-	C-
Milwaukee Brewers	D	B+	B-	D	C-
Chicago White Sox	D	C-	D	D	D

BATTERS

POSITIONS: Up to four positions are listed for each batter and represent those for which he appeared (in order) the most games at in 2011. Positions are shown with their numeric designation (2=CA, 3=1B, 7=LF, 0=DH, etc.)

BATS: Shows which side of the plate he bats from—right (R), left (L) or switch-hitter (S).

AGE: Player's age, as of April 1, 2012.

DRAFTED: The year, round, and school that the player performed at as an amateur if drafted, or where the player was signed from, if a free agent.

EXP MLB DEBUT: The year a player is expected to debut in the Major Leagues.

PROJ ROLE: The role that the batter is expected to have for the majority of his Major League career, not necessarily his greatest upside.

SKILLS: Each skill a player possesses is graded and designated with a "+", indicating the quality of the skills, taking into context the batter's age and level played. An average skill will receive three "+" marks.

- **PWR:** Measures the player's ability to drive the ball and hit for power.
- **BAVG:** Measures the player's ability to hit for batting average and judge the strike zone.
- **SPD:** Measures the player's raw speed and base-running ability.
- **DEF:** Measures the player's overall defense, which includes arm strength, arm accuracy, range, agility, hands, and defensive instincts.

PLAYER STAT LINES: Player statistics for the last five teams that he played for (if applicable), including college and the Major Leagues.

TEAM DESIGNATIONS: Each team that the player performed for during a given year is included.

LEVEL DESIGNATIONS: The level for each team a player performed is included. "AAA" means Triple-A, "AA" means Double-A, "A+" means high Class-A, "A-" means low Class-A, and "Rk" means rookie level.

SABERMETRIC CATEGORIES: Descriptions of all the sabermetric categories appear in the glossary.

CAPSULE COMMENTARIES: For each player, a brief analysis of their skills/statistics, and their future potential is provided.

ELIGIBILITY: Eligibility for inclusion is the standard for which Major League Baseball adheres to; 130 at-bats or 45 days on the 25-man roster, not including the month of September.

POTENTIAL RATINGS: The Potential Ratings are a two-part system in which a player is assigned a number rating based on his upside potential (1-10) and a letter rating based on the probability of reaching that potential (A-E).

Potential

10:	Hall of Famer	5:	MLB reserve
9:	Elite player	4:	Top minor leaguer
8:	Solid regular	3:	Average minor leaguer
7:	Average regular	2:	Minor league reserve
6:	Platoon player	1:	Minor league roster filler

Probability Rating

A: 90% probability of reaching potential
B: 70% probability of reaching potential
C: 50% probability of reaching potential
D: 30% probability of reaching potential
E: 10% probability of reaching potential

SKILLS: Scouts usually grade a player's skills on the 20-80 scale, and while most of the grades are subjective, there are grades that can be given to represent a certain hitting statistic or running speed. These are indicated on this chart:

Scout Grade	HR	BA	Speed (L)	Speed (R)
80	39+	.320+	3.9	4.0
70	32-38	.300-.319	4.0	4.1
60	25-31	.286-.299	4.1	4.2
50 (avg)	17-24	.270-.285	4.2	4.3
40	11-16	.250-.269	4.3	4.4
30	6-10	.220-.249	4.4	4.5
20	0-5	.219-	4.5	4.6

CATCHER POP TIMES: Catchers are timed (in seconds) from the moment the pitch reaches the catcher's mitt until the time that the middle infielder receives the baseball at second base. This number assists both teams in assessing whether a base-runner should steal second base or not.

1.85	+
1.95	MLB average
2.05	-

Adams, David — 4 — New York (A)

Bats R Age 25 · 2008 (3) Virginia · EXP MLB DEBUT: 2012 · POTENTIAL: Starting 2B · 7B

Pwr +++ · BAvg +++ · Spd ++ · Def +++

Year	Lev	Team	AB	R	H	HR	RBI	Avg	OB	Slg	OPS	bb%	ct%	Eye	SB	CS	x/h%	Iso	RC/G
2009	A	Charleston (SC)	259	32	75	0	34	290	374	394	768	12	81	0.71	8	4	33	104	5.38
2009	A+	Tampa	231	37	65	7	41	281	354	498	852	10	83	0.67	3	4	46	216	6.20
2010	AA	Trenton	152	31	47	3	32	309	382	507	889	11	80	0.58	5	2	45	197	6.80
2011	Rk	GCL Yankees	56	13	24	1	11	429	475	643	1118	8	82	0.50	2	1	42	214	9.41
2011	A+	Tampa	52	6	16	0	4	308	357	365	723	7	85	0.50	0	2	19	58	4.48

Fundamentally-sound infielder who saw limited action while recovering from foot surgery. When healthy, hits to all fields by using quick hands and level swing plane. Brings selective eye to plate and drives ball for doubles. Secondary skills not as strong as speed and range is a little short. Has taken awhile to recover, but has talent.

Adams, Matt — 3 — St. Louis

Bats L Age 23 · 2009 (23) Slippery Rock St · EXP MLB DEBUT: 2012 · POTENTIAL: Starting 1B · 8D

Pwr ++++ · BAvg ++++ · Spd + · Def ++

Year	Lev	Team	AB	R	H	HR	RBI	Avg	OB	Slg	OPS	bb%	ct%	Eye	SB	CS	x/h%	Iso	RC/G
2009	Rk	Johnson City	115	15	42	6	25	365	411	574	985	7	83	0.45	0	0	29	209	7.40
2009	A-	Batavia	130	16	45	4	27	346	397	523	920	8	84	0.52	0	0	33	177	6.78
2010	A	Quad Cities	464	71	144	22	88	310	356	541	897	7	83	0.42	5	1	44	231	6.38
2011	AA	Springfield	463	80	139	32	101	300	356	566	922	8	81	0.44	0	1	41	266	6.68

Adams is a strong, muscular hitter with plus power. He has solid bat speed and good plate discipline that gives him the tools to hit for average and power. Career minor league line of .316/.365/.552 shows the offensive potential. His body is thick and he is a below average defender. 1B is the only option, but will likely get a chance with Pujols leaving town.

Adams, Ryan — 4 — Baltimore

Bats R Age 25 · 2006 (2) HS (LA) · EXP MLB DEBUT: 2011 · POTENTIAL: Starting 2B · 7B

Pwr +++ · BAvg ++ · Spd ++ · Def ++

Year	Lev	Team	AB	R	H	HR	RBI	Avg	OB	Slg	OPS	bb%	ct%	Eye	SB	CS	x/h%	Iso	RC/G
2008	A	Delmarva	448	68	138	11	57	308	360	462	822	7	76	0.33	12	5	30	154	5.71
2009	A+	Frederick	215	27	62	2	25	288	346	381	728	8	81	0.46	2	4	26	93	4.55
2010	AA	Bowie	530	81	158	15	68	298	355	464	819	8	77	0.39	2	3	37	166	5.68
2011	AAA	Norfolk	377	46	107	10	37	284	337	454	790	7	73	0.29	5	2	38	170	5.39
2011	MLB	Baltimore	89	9	25	0	7	281	326	326	652	6	72	0.24	0	0	16	45	3.49

Consistent producer who reached BAL, owns compact swing that produces moderate BA with gap power. Has the skill set to be offensive 2B with lots of doubles and potential for double-digit HR. Recognizes pitches, but RHP have been difficult to master. Speed and defense are both below average, though glovework has improved despite poor range.

Adrianza, Ehire — 6 — San Francisco

Bats B Age 22 · 2006 NDFA D.R. · EXP MLB DEBUT: 2013 · POTENTIAL: Starting SS · 8C

Pwr + · BAvg ++ · Spd +++ · Def ++++

Year	Lev	Team	AB	R	H	HR	RBI	Avg	OB	Slg	OPS	bb%	ct%	Eye	SB	CS	x/h%	Iso	RC/G
2008	AAA	Fresno	6	2	3	0	0	500	625	667	1292	25	83	2.00	0	0	33	167	12.98
2009	A	Augusta	388	54	100	2	46	258	330	327	658	10	83	0.64	7	1	20	70	3.82
2010	A+	San Jose	445	70	114	3	35	256	327	348	676	10	80	0.54	33	15	26	92	4.01
2011	A	Augusta	143	18	33	3	17	231	317	378	694	11	78	0.56	3	2	42	147	4.26
2011	A+	San Jose	230	34	69	3	27	300	364	470	833	9	80	0.50	5	1	43	170	6.02

Athletic SS with plus defense, good speed, and a strong arm - can make all the plays and is best defender in the organization. Switch-hitter has a good understanding of the strike zone and showed some signs of life once he reached the CAL. Hit tool is still an open question. Short, compact stroke could lead to moderate power.

Aguilar, Jesus — 3 — Cleveland

Bats R Age 21 · 2007 FA (Venezuela) · EXP MLB DEBUT: 2013 · POTENTIAL: Starting 1B · 8E

Pwr ++++ · BAvg +++ · Spd + · Def ++

Year	Lev	Team	AB	R	H	HR	RBI	Avg	OB	Slg	OPS	bb%	ct%	Eye	SB	CS	x/h%	Iso	RC/G
2010	Rk	AZL Indians	112	15	29	7	22	259	291	482	773	4	71	0.15	1	1	34	223	4.81
2010	A-	Mahoning Vall	123	8	30	2	17	244	306	366	672	8	77	0.39	2	0	37	122	3.82
2011	A	Lake County	349	58	102	19	69	292	357	544	901	9	72	0.36	1	0	47	252	6.91
2011	A+	Kinston	113	12	29	4	13	257	323	389	712	9	75	0.39	1	0	24	133	4.21

Big and strong infielder who had breakout campaign and impressed in AFL. Established easy career high in HR once he added loft and leverage to crude swing. Has power to all fields, but length in swing can be exploited. Reads pitches well and hits LHP and RHP. Secondary skills aren't up to snuff, though plays passable defense.

Ahmed, Nick — 6 — Atlanta

Bats R Age 22 · 2011 (2) Connecticut · EXP MLB DEBUT: 2014 · POTENTIAL: Backup SS · 7C

Pwr ++ · BAvg ++ · Spd +++ · Def +++

Year	Lev	Team	AB	R	H	HR	RBI	Avg	OB	Slg	OPS	bb%	ct%	Eye	SB	CS	x/h%	Iso	RC/G
2009	NCAA	Connecticut	191	34	55	2	20	288	346	366	713	8	86	0.65	11	3	18	79	4.41
2010	NCAA	Connecticut	267	57	80	4	43	300	368	375	743	10	88	0.94	34	8	15	75	4.86
2011	NCAA	Connecticut	183	51	61	2	35	333	416	448	864	12	90	1.44	23	6	25	115	6.54
2011	Rk	Danville	248	46	65	4	24	262	342	379	721	11	81	0.65	18	6	29	117	4.60

Athletic three year starter at Connecticut had solid pro debut, hitting .262 with 13 doubles, 4 home runs, and 18 SB. Solid across the board tools, but none stand out. Has solid plate discipline, but might not have enough offense to be a regular.

Akins, Jordan — 89 — Texas

Bats R Age 20 · 2010 (3) HS (GA) · EXP MLB DEBUT: 2014 · POTENTIAL: Starting OF · 8D

Pwr +++ · BAvg +++ · Spd +++ · Def +++

Year	Lev	Team	AB	R	H	HR	RBI	Avg	OB	Slg	OPS	bb%	ct%	Eye	SB	CS	x/h%	Iso	RC/G
2010	Rk	AZL Rangers	107	14	20	0	8	187	223	252	476	4	67	0.14	5	1	25	65	0.99
2011	Rk	AZL Rangers	180	37	51	2	31	283	306	428	734	3	77	0.14	13	2	35	144	4.45

Tall, lean, and athletic outfielder with chance to be standout due to power and speed combo. Possesses raw abilities that project well and has instincts to move rapidly. Produces above average bat speed and should see power improve with additional leverage in swing. Gets good jumps in OF and could stick in CF as arm speed grades above average.

Alcantara, Yoan — 9 — San Diego

Bats R Age 19 · 2009 NDFA D.R. · EXP MLB DEBUT: 2015 · POTENTIAL: Starting CF · 8D

Pwr +++ · BAvg +++ · Spd +++ · Def +++

Year	Lev	Team	AB	R	H	HR	RBI	Avg	OB	Slg	OPS	bb%	ct%	Eye	SB	CS	x/h%	Iso	RC/G
2011	Rk	AZL Padres	210	50	73	7	46	348	360	586	946	2	88	0.16	8	2	38	238	6.66

Strong, toolsy OF was the most dynamic player in the AZL. He hit for average with power and speed. Defensively he covers ground well and has a strong throwing arm. Can be overly aggressive at the plate, but plate discipline improved as the season progressed. Hit 6 of his 8 home runs in August. If plate discipline can improve, he has the tools to star.

Alfaro, Jorge — 2 — Texas

Bats R Age 19 · 2010 FA (Columbia) · EXP MLB DEBUT: 2015 · POTENTIAL: Starting C · 9D

Pwr ++++ · BAvg ++ · Spd ++ · Def +++

Year	Lev	Team	AB	R	H	HR	RBI	Avg	OB	Slg	OPS	bb%	ct%	Eye	SB	CS	x/h%	Iso	RC/G
2011	A-	Spokane	160	18	48	6	23	300	317	481	798	2	66	0.07	1	0	33	181	5.48

Tall, raw, and athletic backstop has chance to be standout with both glove and bat. Swings hard and doesn't walk much, though bat speed is well above average. Exhibits raw power to all fields and natural hitting acumen that allows him to hit for BA. Strong arm and agility are both stellar, but footwork and release need improvement.

Almonte, Abraham — 78 — New York (A)

Bats B Age 23 · 2005 FA (DR) · EXP MLB DEBUT: 2013 · POTENTIAL: Starting OF · 8E

Pwr +++ · BAvg ++ · Spd ++++ · Def +++

Year	Lev	Team	AB	R	H	HR	RBI	Avg	OB	Slg	OPS	bb%	ct%	Eye	SB	CS	x/h%	Iso	RC/G
2007	Rk	GCL Yankees	160	29	46	3	16	288	370	406	776	12	79	0.62	8	9	22	119	5.32
2008	A	Charleston (SC)	443	61	101	8	46	228	302	359	661	10	77	0.47	29	10	35	131	3.75
2009	A	Charleston (SC)	440	63	123	5	56	280	333	391	724	7	82	0.43	36	5	24	111	4.47
2010	A+	Tampa	57	9	15	0	3	263	333	351	684	10	72	0.38	5	3	27	88	4.17
2011	A+	Tampa	537	92	144	4	52	268	333	382	715	9	81	0.52	30	11	29	114	4.49

Short and stout outfielder with equally compact and swing. Returned with aplomb after shoulder surgery wiped out most of '10 campaign. Brings patient approach to plate and has strength to hit hard line drives. Inconsistent swing mechanics, including hitch in stroke, mute BA potential, but runs well and can play any outfield position.

Almonte, Denny — 789 — Seattle

Bats B Age 23 · 2007 (2) HS (FL) · EXP MLB DEBUT: 2013 · POTENTIAL: Starting OF · 8E

Pwr ++++ · BAvg ++ · Spd +++ · Def ++++

Year	Lev	Team	AB	R	H	HR	RBI	Avg	OB	Slg	OPS	bb%	ct%	Eye	SB	CS	x/h%	Iso	RC/G
2007	A-	Everett	20	0	2	0	1	100	143	100	243	5	45	0.09	1	0			
2008	A	Wisconsin	374	38	93	10	51	249	303	420	723	7	60	0.19	14	10	40	171	5.02
2009	A	Clinton	409	58	95	13	58	232	276	408	685	6	64	0.17	14	6	43	176	4.11
2010	A+	High Desert	494	71	126	22	76	255	291	457	748	5	61	0.13	13	6	40	202	5.16
2011	A+	High Desert	504	75	135	24	97	268	298	490	789	4	68	0.14	18	12	43	222	5.30

Strong and athletic outfielder who repeated High-A and was slightly better, though was 3rd in CAL in Ks. Actually reduced K rate, but is a free swinger with poor pitch recognition. Set career high in Ks and has bat speed and strength to produce plus pop to all fields. Runs well for size and has good instincts on base. Solid defender at any spot.

Almonte, Zoilo — 79 — New York (A)

EXP MLB DEBUT: 2013 | POTENTIAL: Starting OF | 8E

Bats B Age 23
2005 FA (DR)
Pwr +++
BAvg +++
Spd +++
Def +++

Year	Lev	Team	AB	R	H	HR	RBI	Avg	OB	Slg	OPS	bb%	ct%	Eye	SB	CS	x/h%	Iso	RC/G
2009	A-	Staten Island	259	43	71	7	39	274	352	440	792	11	78	0.53	15	7	39	166	5.47
2010	A	Charleston (SC)	227	33	63	10	35	278	339	485	823	8	71	0.32	7	6	40	207	5.84
2010	A+	Tampa	238	26	62	3	26	261	326	366	691	9	73	0.35	8	1	26	105	4.13
2011	A+	Tampa	259	38	76	12	54	293	369	514	882	11	77	0.52	14	4	39	220	6.57
2011	AA	Trenton	175	23	44	3	23	251	307	377	684	7	74	0.31	4	1	34	126	3.94

Short and strong hitter who is starting to realize power potential. Set career highs in HR, SB, and BA. Improved strength and leverage in swing are credited with power output while he is good runner and can steal bases. Can be jammed inside and will strike out due to approach. Relegated to corner OF where arm is solid, but range is limited.

Alonso, Yonder — 3 — San Diego

EXP MLB DEBUT: 2010 | POTENTIAL: Starting 1B | 9C

Bats L Age 25
2008 (1) Miami-FL
Pwr ++++
BAvg ++++
4.50 Spd ++
Def ++

Year	Lev	Team	AB	R	H	HR	RBI	Avg	OB	Slg	OPS	bb%	ct%	Eye	SB	CS	x/h%	Iso	RC/G
2010	AA	Carolina	101	19	27	3	13	267	383	406	789	16	84	1.19	4	2	30	139	5.68
2010	AAA	Louisville	406	50	120	12	56	296	354	470	825	8	81	0.49	9	1	38	175	5.71
2010	MLB	Cincinnati	29	2	6	0	3	207	207	276	483	0	66	0.00	0	0	33	69	0.95
2011	AAA	Louisville	358	46	106	12	56	296	376	486	862	11	83	0.77	6	5	38	190	6.33
2011	MLB	Cincinnati	88	9	29	5	15	330	398	545	943	10	76	0.48	0	0	31	216	7.25

Pure hitter with good bat speed, contact ability, and plate discipline. Short, compact stroke, OB ability, and willingness to use the whole park hints at future potential. Finally got a chance in the majors and all he did was hit .330 in 88 AB. Thick lower half leaves him with below average speed. Trade to San Diego gives him a chance to finally play 1B, but will need to beat out Rizzo.

Altherr, Aaron — 8 — Philadelphia

EXP MLB DEBUT: 2014 | POTENTIAL: Starting CF | 8D

Bats R Age 21
2009 (9) HS, (AZ)
Pwr +++
BAvg +++
Spd ++++
Def ++++

Year	Lev	Team	AB	R	H	HR	RBI	Avg	OB	Slg	OPS	bb%	ct%	Eye	SB	CS	x/h%	Iso	RC/G
2009	Rk	GCL Phillies	84	10	18	1	11	214	283	286	568	9	82	0.53	6	1	22	71	2.61
2010	Rk	GCL Phillies	115	12	35	1	15	304	322	400	722	3	81	0.14	10	3	23	96	4.14
2010	A-	Williamsport	94	11	27	0	10	287	343	426	769	8	86	0.62	2	3	37	138	5.22
2011	A-	Williamsport	269	41	70	5	31	260	294	375	670	5	81	0.25	25	4	27	115	3.59
2011	A	Lakewood	147	20	31	1	15	211	266	272	538	7	68	0.23	12	0	23	61	1.89

Raw, toolsy CF prospect struggled in the SAL and was sent to the NYP where he rebounded some. He has a nice blend of speed and power potential. Struggles with off-speed and breaking balls, but shows a willingness to drive the ball the other way. He covers ground well and has a strong throwing arm. Has plus speed and good tools, but will need to hit for average.

Amarista, Alexi — 4 — Los Angeles (A)

EXP MLB DEBUT: 2011 | POTENTIAL: Utility player | 6B

Bats B Age 23
2007 FA (Venezuela)
Pwr +
BAvg +++
Spd ++++
Def +++

Year	Lev	Team	AB	R	H	HR	RBI	Avg	OB	Slg	OPS	bb%	ct%	Eye	SB	CS	x/h%	Iso	RC/G
2010	A+	Rancho Cucam	297	39	90	4	39	303	345	448	793	6	86	0.45	17	10	32	145	5.26
2010	AA	Arkansas	191	25	55	1	20	288	333	325	658	6	92	0.87	4	1	7	37	3.81
2010	AAA	Salt Lake	65	13	26	0	9	400	409	585	994	2	94	0.25	4	2	35	185	7.26
2011	AAA	Salt Lake	363	49	106	4	50	292	332	419	751	6	85	0.39	15	8	31	127	4.75
2011	MLB	LA Angels	52	2	8	0	5	154	185	250	435	4	85	0.25	0	0	50	96	1.04

Small and athletic infielder who struggled in majors, but has skill set of utility player. Can be tough out by making easy contact and has excellent speed and baserunning instincts. Should hit for good BA by using quick bat and use of entire field. Lacks power and pitch selectivity. Defense is OK and can play middle infield and OF corners.

Amaya, Gioskar — 5 — Chicago (N)

EXP MLB DEBUT: 2014 | POTENTIAL: Starting 3B/2B | 8D

Bats R Age 19
2009 NDFA Venz.
Pwr +++
BAvg ++++
Spd ++
Def ++

Year	Lev	Team	AB	R	H	HR	RBI	Avg	OB	Slg	OPS	bb%	ct%	Eye	SB	CS	x/h%	Iso	RC/G
2011	Rk	AZL Cubs	204	37	77	0	36	377	415	510	925	6	81	0.33	13	8	25	132	6.96

Short, strong infield prospect had an impressive debut. Amaya has a quick bat and ability to make consistent, line-drive contact. Power is more of the gap variety right now. Amaya has good range, soft hands, and positions himself well. Range and arm are a bit short for SS, but works just fine at 3B, but power might not be enough for the hot corner.

Anderson, Bryan — 2 — St. Louis

EXP MLB DEBUT: 2009 | POTENTIAL: Backup C | 6B

Bats L Age 25
2005 (4) HS (CA)
Pwr ++
BAvg ++++
Spd +
Def ++

Year	Lev	Team	AB	R	H	HR	RBI	Avg	OB	Slg	OPS	bb%	ct%	Eye	SB	CS	x/h%	Iso	RC/G
2009	Rk	GCL Cardinals	16	3	5	1	2	313	450	500	950	20	75	1.00	1	0	20	188	7.83
2009	AAA	Memphis	163	22	40	4	11	245	289	399	688	6	74	0.24	1	0	35	153	3.90
2010	AAA	Memphis	270	39	73	12	42	270	337	448	785	9	80	0.50	0	0	33	178	5.13
2010	MLB	St. Louis	32	1	9	0	4	281	303	344	647	3	78	0.14	0	0	22	63	3.26
2011	AAA	Memphis	335	39	94	8	37	281	350	409	759	10	77	0.47	1	1	29	128	4.97

Athletic catcher with good bat speed and plate discipline, giving him doubles power and the ability to hit for average. Decent plate discipline and contact ability hint at upside, but lack of power tempers potential impact. Below average defense with an average arm makes him a backup at best. His stock is well down from three years ago.

Anderson, Jacob — 9 — Toronto

EXP MLB DEBUT: 2015 | POTENTIAL: Starting OF | 9E

Bats R Age 19
2011 (1-S) HS (CA)
Pwr +++
BAvg ++
Spd +++
Def ++

Year	Lev	Team	AB	R	H	HR	RBI	Avg	OB	Slg	OPS	bb%	ct%	Eye	SB	CS	x/h%	Iso	RC/G
2011	Rk	GCL Blue Jays	37	9	15	2	7	405	463	622	1085	10	78	0.50	2	0	27	216	8.98

Tall and athletic physical specimen with massive upside. Has potential to produce mammoth power due to long arms, quick bat, and leverage in swing. Could hit for BA, but needs to reach pitches better and learn to lay off breaking balls out of zone. Solid-average speed and average arm strength are sufficient to become quality RF, but needs more innings.

Anderson, Lars — 3 — Boston

EXP MLB DEBUT: 2010 | POTENTIAL: Starting 1B | 8C

Bats L Age 24
2006 (18) HS (CA)
Pwr +++
BAvg +++
Spd ++
Def +++

Year	Lev	Team	AB	R	H	HR	RBI	Avg	OB	Slg	OPS	bb%	ct%	Eye	SB	CS	x/h%	Iso	RC/G
2010	AA	Portland	62	13	22	5	16	355	420	677	1098	10	74	0.44	1	1	45	323	9.37
2010	AAA	Pawtucket	409	49	107	10	53	262	333	428	761	10	73	0.40	2	2	42	166	5.11
2010	MLB	Boston	35	4	7	0	4	200	333	229	562	17	77	0.88	0	0	14	29	2.78
2011	AAA	Pawtucket	491	65	130	14	78	265	368	422	789	14	76	0.67	5	0	36	157	5.61
2011	MLB	Boston	5	2	0	0	0	0	0	0	0	0	40	0.00	0	0			

Tall and lean infielder who repeated Triple-A and remains stuck in minors despite solid talent on both sides of ball. Uses a patient, and sometimes passive, approach to get on base consistently and generally hits line drives to the gaps. Has the strength and bat speed for plus power, but hasn't realized it yet and struggles with LHP. Good hands and feet at 1B.

Antonio, Mike — 6 — Kansas City

EXP MLB DEBUT: 2014 | POTENTIAL: Starting SS | 8E

Bats R Age 20
2010 (3) HS (NY)
Pwr +++
BAvg +++
Spd +++
Def +++

Year	Lev	Team	AB	R	H	HR	RBI	Avg	OB	Slg	OPS	bb%	ct%	Eye	SB	CS	x/h%	Iso	RC/G
2010	Rk	AZL Royals	163	19	43	1	12	264	298	429	728	5	81	0.26	7	4	47	166	4.51
2011	Rk	Idaho Falls	33	6	10	1	5	303	324	515	839	3	82	0.17	1	0	40	212	5.59
2011	Rk	Burlington	206	30	54	10	37	262	318	461	780	8	88	0.68	10	5	39	199	5.03

Tall and strong infielder who has raw, yet tangible skills. May eventually outgrow SS and move to 3B, but has the arm strength and hands to be asset. Has ample range at present and enough quickness. Best offensive tool is solid, raw power, though he can be pull-conscious. Owns moderate BA potential as swing can get long. Needs to be more consistent.

Arce, Eric — 7 — Toronto

EXP MLB DEBUT: 2015 | POTENTIAL: Starting OF | 8E

Bats L Age 20
2011 (25) Florida State
Pwr ++++
BAvg ++
Spd ++
Def ++

Year	Lev	Team	AB	R	H	HR	RBI	Avg	OB	Slg	OPS	bb%	ct%	Eye	SB	CS	x/h%	Iso	RC/G
2011	NCAA	Florida State	10	3	1	0	1	100	308	100	408	23	90	3.00	0	1	0	0	1.83
2011	Rk	GCL Blue Jays	153	34	41	14	40	268	414	621	1035	20	69	0.79	1	1	56	353	9.29
2011	Rk	Bluefield	19	1	5	0	1	263	333	316	649	10	79	0.50	0	0	20	53	3.65

Stout outfielder who set record for most HR in GCL. Generates plus-plus power to all fields with vicious, uppercut strokes. Uses legs to enhance power, but swing and hitting instincts leave BA potential low. Works counts and draws walks, but strikes out in abundance. Below average speed and range limit him to LF.

Arcia, Orlando — 6 — Milwaukee

EXP MLB DEBUT: 2015 | POTENTIAL: Starting SS | 7D

Bats R Age 17
2011 NDFA D.R.
Pwr +++
BAvg +++
Spd +++
Def +++

Year	Lev	Team	AB	R	H	HR	RBI	Avg	OB	Slg	OPS	bb%	ct%	Eye	SB	CS	x/h%	Iso	RC/G
2011		Did not play																	

Not an off-the charts prospect, but he has nice athleticism and does everything a bit above average. Arcia is only 17, but already has some nice gap power and could develop at least average power. Has good plate discipline and above-average speed. He is the younger brother of Twins prospect Oswaldo Arcia.

Arcia, Oswaldo

9 | **Minnesota** | EXP MLB DEBUT: 2014 | POTENTIAL: Starting OF | **9D**

Bats L Age 21
2007 FA (Venezuela)
Pwr ++++
BAvg +++
Spd ++
Def +++

Year	Lev	Team	AB	R	H	HR	RBI	Avg	OB	Slg	OPS	bb%	ct%	Eye	SB	CS	x/h%	Iso	RC/G
2009	Rk	GCL Twins	167	20	46	5	24	275	335	455	790	8	89	0.83	8	0	39	180	5.34
2010	Rk	Elizabethton	259	47	97	14	51	375	417	672	1089	7	74	0.28	4	4	43	297	9.27
2011	Rk	GCL Twins	8	1	4	0	1	500	500	875	1375	0	88	0.00	0	0	50	375	11.77
2011	A	Beloit	71	18	25	5	18	352	425	704	1129	11	77	0.56	2	2	56	352	9.78
2011	A+	Fort Myers	213	27	56	8	32	263	293	460	753	4	75	0.17	1	1	43	197	4.61

Pure hitting outfielder who missed time with elbow injury but showcased plus power to all fields when healthy. Slugged way thru season with strength and plus bat speed. Covers plate well and puts bat to ball when behind in count. Hits LHP and RHP alike, though will fan frequently. Lacks foot speed for SB and OF range, but is passable defender with average arm strength.

Arenado, Nolan

5 | **Colorado** | EXP MLB DEBUT: 2012 | POTENTIAL: Starting 3B | **9C**

Bats R Age 21
2009 (2) HS (CA)
Pwr ++++
BAvg +++
Spd ++
Def +++

Year	Lev	Team	AB	R	H	HR	RBI	Avg	OB	Slg	OPS	bb%	ct%	Eye	SB	CS	x/h%	Iso	RC/G
2009	Rk	Casper	203	28	61	2	22	300	352	404	756	7	91	0.89	5	2	28	103	4.97
2010	A	Asheville	373	45	115	12	65	308	342	520	862	5	86	0.37	1	3	47	212	5.93
2011	A+	Modesto	517	82	154	20	122	298	356	487	844	8	90	0.89	2	1	36	190	5.89

Strong and well-proportioned, he's quickly developing into one of the better 3B in the minors. Power continues to emerge with 32 doubles along with his 20 HR. Nice inside-out swing and solid two-strike approach; quick and balanced swing should allow him to hit for average and power. Continues to improve defensively and his stock is on the rise.

Arias, Junior

6 | **Cincinnati** | EXP MLB DEBUT: 2014 | POTENTIAL: Starting SS | **9E**

Bats R Age 20
2009 NDFA D.R.
Pwr +++
BAvg +++
Spd +++
Def ++

Year	Lev	Team	AB	R	H	HR	RBI	Avg	OB	Slg	OPS	bb%	ct%	Eye	SB	CS	x/h%	Iso	RC/G
2010	Rk	AZL Reds	195	44	56	6	25	287	329	482	811	6	70	0.21	4	3	38	195	5.70
2011	Rk	Billings	219	47	55	8	30	251	311	452	763	8	66	0.26	7	5	45	201	5.25

Tall, lean, athletic SS is one of the more projectable prospects in the NL. Tools are still raw, but has a live bat, plus bat speed, runs well and has tons of potential. His hit tool projects to be above average, but can be overly aggressive at the plate and will need to be more selective (19 BB/74 K).

Arteaga, Humberto

6 | **Kansas City** | EXP MLB DEBUT: 2015 | POTENTIAL: Starting SS | **8D**

Bats R Age 18
2010 FA (Venezuela)
Pwr +
BAvg +++
Spd +++
Def ++++

Year	Lev	Team	AB	R	H	HR	RBI	Avg	OB	Slg	OPS	bb%	ct%	Eye	SB	CS	x/h%	Iso	RC/G
2011	Rk	AZL Royals	213	30	54	0	28	254	284	324	608	4	82	0.23	8	2	24	70	2.91

Tall and smooth infielder who has upside as defender in middle infield. Has ideal instincts and hands for value with glove. Ranges well to both sides and possesses average, accurate arm. Offensive game lags behind defense. Is adept at bunting and situational hitting, but strength and power aren't up to snuff. Even with more muscle, still projects to below average pop.

Austin, Jay

8 | **Houston** | EXP MLB DEBUT: 2013 | POTENTIAL: Starting CF | **7C**

Bats L Age 21
2008 (2) HS (GA)
Pwr +++
BAvg +++
Spd ++++
Def +++

Year	Lev	Team	AB	R	H	HR	RBI	Avg	OB	Slg	OPS	bb%	ct%	Eye	SB	CS	x/h%	Iso	RC/G
2008	Rk	Greeneville	212	31	42	0	14	198	264	236	500	8	67	0.28	14	6	14	38	1.39
2009	A	Lexington	397	49	106	1	33	267	320	360	680	7	80	0.40	23	13	27	93	3.98
2010	A+	Lancaster	532	83	139	10	59	261	312	414	725	7	76	0.31	54	20	35	152	4.48
2011	A	Lexington	123	9	25	0	16	203	279	260	540	10	74	0.41	6	2	28	57	2.15
2011	A+	Lancaster	315	47	81	3	37	257	320	365	685	8	77	0.40	17	11	30	108	4.04

Plus raw athlete with above average speed and offensive potential. Compact swing and good bat speed are plusses, but he struggled to hit in the CAL. His below-average plate discipline undermines his ability. He needs to improve his approach and be more selective. Arm strength is outstanding and has the range to be an above average defender in CF.

Austin, Tyler

35 | **New York (A)** | EXP MLB DEBUT: 2014 | POTENTIAL: Starting 3B | **8D**

Bats R Age 20
2010 (13) HS (GA)
Pwr +++
BAvg ++++
Spd +++
Def ++

Year	Lev	Team	AB	R	H	HR	RBI	Avg	OB	Slg	OPS	bb%	ct%	Eye	SB	CS	x/h%	Iso	RC/G
2010	Rk	GCL Yankees	2	0	0	0	0	0	0	0	0	0	50	0.00	0	0			
2011	Rk	GCL Yankees	82	13	32	3	22	390	425	622	1047	6	80	0.31	11	0	38	232	8.30
2011	A-	Staten Island	96	16	31	3	14	323	387	542	928	9	76	0.43	7	0	45	219	7.27

Tall and instinctual infielder with impressive raw tools. Has potential to be significant asset with bat. Has above average, professional approach and excellent eye to differentiate between balls and strikes. Exhibits moderate power to all fields and should develop more pop with improved strength. Drafted as C and has strong arm, but still raw with glove.

Avery, Xavier

8 | **Baltimore** | EXP MLB DEBUT: 2012 | POTENTIAL: Starting OF | **8D**

Bats L Age 22
2008 (2) HS (GA)
Pwr ++
BAvg ++
Spd +++++
Def +++

Year	Lev	Team	AB	R	H	HR	RBI	Avg	OB	Slg	OPS	bb%	ct%	Eye	SB	CS	x/h%	Iso	RC/G
2008	Rk	GCL Orioles	175	27	49	0	7	280	319	337	656	5	71	0.20	13	3	18	57	3.53
2009	A	Delmarva	473	55	124	2	36	262	302	340	642	5	77	0.24	30	10	20	78	3.33
2010	A+	Frederick	447	73	125	4	48	280	342	389	731	9	79	0.44	28	14	28	110	4.65
2010	AA	Bowie	107	10	25	3	18	234	281	374	655	6	68	0.21	10	0	36	140	3.48
2011	AA	Bowie	557	72	144	4	26	259	318	343	661	8	72	0.31	36	14	26	84	3.71

Athletic and very fast outfielder who has struggled to live up to potential. Will draw walks from leadoff spot and use speed effectively on base. Strikes out a bunch in an attempt for more pop. Possesses smooth swing, but expands strike zone frequently. Should focus on small ball and speed game. Jumps and routes are fringy, but arm and range are fine for CF.

Baez, Javier

6 | **Chicago (N)** | EXP MLB DEBUT: 2015 | POTENTIAL: Starting 3B/SS | **8D**

Bats R Age 19
2011 (1) HS (FL)
Pwr ++++
BAvg +++
Spd ++
Def ++

Year	Lev	Team	AB	R	H	HR	RBI	Avg	OB	Slg	OPS	bb%	ct%	Eye	SB	CS	x/h%	Iso	RC/G
2011	Rk	AZL Cubs	12	2	4	0	0	333	333	500	833	0	83	0.00	2	0	50	167	5.48
2011	A-	Boise	6	0	1	0	1	167	167	167	333	0	67	0.00	0	0	0	0	

Had the best power of any middle infielder in '11 draft. At 6'0" 180, is strong and physically mature with good bat speed and above-average power. Moves well defensively and has a strong arm, but might lack the speed to play SS in the majors. With size and power, he profiles better at 3B, but does have a strong arm and solid hands. Will make full-season debut in '12.

Bailey, Luke

2 | **Tampa Bay** | EXP MLB DEBUT: 2014 | POTENTIAL: Reserve C | **7D**

Bats R Age 21
2009 (4) HS (GA)
Pwr +++
BAvg ++
Spd ++
Def +++

Year	Lev	Team	AB	R	H	HR	RBI	Avg	OB	Slg	OPS	bb%	ct%	Eye	SB	CS	x/h%	Iso	RC/G
2010	Rk	GCL Rays	137	18	25	5	14	182	273	350	623	11	66	0.36	0	0	52	168	3.17
2011	A	Bowling Green	247	26	55	7	35	223	275	385	660	7	64	0.20	5	1	45	162	3.76

Athletic and agile backstop with more advanced glove than bat at present. Can run into FB with aggressive, long swing and produce good power, but likely to be low BA hitter as he doesn't control strike zone and is very pull conscious. TJ surgery in '09, but arm strength is back. Receives and blocks well while showing leadership behind dish.

Baker, Aaron

3 | **Baltimore** | EXP MLB DEBUT: 2013 | POTENTIAL: Reserve 1B | **7C**

Bats L Age 24
2009 (11) Oklahoma
Pwr ++++
BAvg ++
Spd ++
Def +++

Year	Lev	Team	AB	R	H	HR	RBI	Avg	OB	Slg	OPS	bb%	ct%	Eye	SB	CS	x/h%	Iso	RC/G
2009	A-	State College	227	38	56	3	32	247	340	414	754	12	76	0.59	2	0	45	167	5.21
2010	A	West Virginia	459	64	116	18	79	253	329	453	782	10	75	0.45	3	6	47	200	5.30
2011	A+	Bradenton	386	53	109	15	73	282	356	469	825	10	76	0.48	1	2	36	187	5.82
2011	A+	Frederick	44	8	17	2	9	386	460	591	1051	12	80	0.67	0	0	29	205	8.71
2011	AA	Bowie	46	2	9	0	3	196	196	239	435	0	59	0.00	0	0	22	43	0.22

Big and strong infielder who draws walks and offers plus, raw power, particularly against RHP. Owns a professional approach that allows him to work deep into counts, but struggles with breaking balls are evident. Will always produce loads of Ks and offers few secondary skills. Maintains solid arm strength and is passable defender, but is big and slow with poor agility.

Baldwin, James

8 | **Los Angeles (N)** | EXP MLB DEBUT: 2014 | POTENTIAL: Starting CF | **8D**

Bats L Age 20
2010 (4) HS (NC)
Pwr +++
BAvg ++
Spd +++
Def +++

Year	Lev	Team	AB	R	H	HR	RBI	Avg	OB	Slg	OPS	bb%	ct%	Eye	SB	CS	x/h%	Iso	RC/G
2010	Rk	AZL Dodgers	179	25	49	2	22	274	309	363	672	5	66	0.15	17	3	20	89	3.79
2011	Rk	Ogden	196	47	49	10	39	250	313	480	793	8	62	0.24	22	5	45	230	5.87

Tall, slender, athletic OF is the son of former major league pitcher with the same name. He was a three-sport star in HS so is a bit unpolished. Has plus speed, but struggles with breaking balls and making consistent contact. Not likely to hit for much power, but covers ground well in CF, and has a strong throwing arm. Future leadoff hitter.

Barfield, Jeremy

9 | **Oakland** | EXP MLB DEBUT: 2013 | POTENTIAL: Starting OF | **7D**

Bats R Age 23
2008 (8) San Jacinto JC
Pwr ++++
BAvg ++
Spd ++
Def ++

Year	Lev	Team	AB	R	H	HR	RBI	Avg	OB	Slg	OPS	bb%	ct%	Eye	SB	CS	x/h%	Iso	RC/G
2008	A-	Vancouver	251	28	68	3	41	271	339	375	714	9	83	0.62	5	3	29	104	4.48
2009	A	Kane County	404	48	106	8	52	262	341	389	729	11	76	0.49	1	5	31	126	4.67
2010	A+	Stockton	508	72	138	17	92	272	339	417	757	9	82	0.56	1	1	28	146	4.85
2011	AA	Midland	495	56	127	11	72	257	315	384	699	8	82	0.47	1	1	30	127	4.13

Large-framed outfielder who owns impressive tools, but has been plagued by inconsistency. Blessed with plus raw power, but hasn't translated to production. Aggressive approach leads to many swings and misses while long swing detracts from BA. Arm is ideal for RF, though range and instincts are subpar. Some potential, but staus is dimming.

Baron, Steve

2 | **Seattle** | EXP MLB DEBUT: 2014 | POTENTIAL: Backup C | **6B**

Bats R Age 21
2009 (1-S) HS (FL)
Pwr ++
BAvg ++
Spd ++
Def ++++

Year	Lev	Team	AB	R	H	HR	RBI	Avg	OB	Slg	OPS	bb%	ct%	Eye	SB	CS	x/h%	Iso	RC/G
2009	Rk	Pulaski	106	12	19	2	13	179	230	292	523	6	64	0.18	0	0	42	113	1.63
2010	A-	Everett	198	18	50	3	22	253	275	379	653	3	70	0.10	1	0	34	126	3.40
2010	A	Clinton	154	10	28	1	14	182	232	221	452	6	69	0.21	1	1	14	39	0.61
2011	A	Clinton	198	17	39	4	20	197	260	323	584	8	75	0.35	6	3	44	126	2.62
2011	A+	High Desert	16	3	3	0	1	188	235	250	485	6	63	0.17	0	0	33	63	1.15

Defense-first receiver who projects well defensively with solidly-built frame and nice agility. Combines excellent arm strength with quick release to limit SB. Development of bat has been disappointing, especially in power department. Holes in swing can be exploited and aggressive approach has led to miserable BA/OBP.

Beckham, Tim

6 | **Tampa Bay** | EXP MLB DEBUT: 2012 | POTENTIAL: Starting SS | **8D**

Bats R Age 22
2008 (1) HS (GA)
Pwr +++
BAvg +++
Spd +++
Def +++

Year	Lev	Team	AB	R	H	HR	RBI	Avg	OB	Slg	OPS	bb%	ct%	Eye	SB	CS	x/h%	Iso	RC/G
2008	A-	Hudson Valley	6	5	2	0	0	333	500	500	1000	25	83	2.00	1	0	50	167	9.18
2009	A	Bowling Green	491	58	135	5	63	275	322	389	711	6	76	0.29	13	10	31	114	4.28
2010	A+	Charlotte	465	68	119	5	57	256	343	359	703	12	74	0.52	22	14	28	103	4.42
2011	AA	Montgomery	418	82	115	7	57	275	337	395	732	9	78	0.43	15	4	30	120	4.60
2011	AAA	Durham	106	12	27	5	13	255	275	462	737	3	73	0.10	2	1	37	208	4.32

Fluid and athletic infielder with bevy of tools, but diminishing prospect status. Hit career high in HR and continues to showcase impressive bat speed and strength in hands and wrists. Can be too passive at plate and hasn't made consistent contact. Exhibits quickness and strong arm at SS, but makes lots of throwing errors and takes plays off.

Bell, Josh

9 | **Pittsburgh** | EXP MLB DEBUT: 2015 | POTENTIAL: Starting LF | **9D**

Bats B Age 19
2011 (2) HS (TX)
Pwr ++++
BAvg +++
Spd ++
Def ++

Year	Lev	Team	AB	R	H	HR	RBI	Avg	OB	Slg	OPS	bb%	ct%	Eye	SB	CS	x/h%	Iso	RC/G
2011		Did not play																	

Switch-hitting OF prospect and has plus raw power. At 6'3 205, Bell is strong, has plus bat speed and can hit home runs from both sides. Defensive he is raw, has only average speed, and a fringy arm. Isn't as polished as other high schoolers, but the bat speed and power give him significant upside. Bell will make his pro debut in '12 and has the tools to be a star.

Beltre, Engel

8 | **Texas** | EXP MLB DEBUT: 2012 | POTENTIAL: Starting OF | **8D**

Bats L Age 22
2006 FA (DR)
Pwr +++
BAvg ++
Spd ++++
Def ++++

Year	Lev	Team	AB	R	H	HR	RBI	Avg	OB	Slg	OPS	bb%	ct%	Eye	SB	CS	x/h%	Iso	RC/G
2009	A+	Bakersfield	357	44	81	3	23	227	262	317	579	5	78	0.22	17	7	26	90	2.49
2009	AA	Frisco	14	1	1	0	1	71	71	143	214	0	86	0.00	1	0	100	71	
2010	A+	Bakersfield	263	38	87	5	35	331	358	460	818	4	87	0.32	10	7	23	129	5.33
2010	AA	Frisco	181	14	46	1	14	254	293	337	630	5	87	0.42	8	2	20	83	3.34
2011	AA	Frisco	437	64	101	1	28	231	277	300	577	6	76	0.27	16	6	22	69	2.52

Athletic and projectable prospect who regressed in worst year as pro. Power declined dramatically and was suspended for on-field incident. More tools than production at this point, but has scintillating bat speed and above average power potential. Has blazing speed, but can't use if not on base. Profiles as CF with strong arm and plus range.

Benson, Joe

8 | **Minnesota** | EXP MLB DEBUT: 2011 | POTENTIAL: Starting OF | **8B**

Bats R Age 24
2006 (2) HS (IL)
Pwr ++++
BAvg ++
Spd ++++
Def +++

Year	Lev	Team	AB	R	H	HR	RBI	Avg	OB	Slg	OPS	bb%	ct%	Eye	SB	CS	x/h%	Iso	RC/G
2010	A+	Fort Myers	85	16	25	4	13	294	355	588	943	9	75	0.38	5	0	64	294	7.44
2010	AA	New Britain	374	65	94	23	49	251	322	527	849	9	69	0.34	14	9	53	275	6.29
2011	Rk	GCL Twins	9	2	2	0	0	222	364	333	697	18	78	1.00	1	1	50	111	4.78
2011	AA	New Britain	400	69	114	16	67	285	373	495	868	12	73	0.51	13	9	42	210	6.64
2011	MLB	Minnesota	71	3	17	0	2	239	270	352	622	4	70	0.14	2	2	41	113	3.15

Plus athlete repeated Double-A before ending season in MIN. May struggle to hit for BA as he expands strike zone and swing can get stiff. Ks will likely always be part of equation, but has raw power and above average bat speed. Power-speed combo unmatched in org. Handles CF well with strong arm and above average range, though needs better jumps and routes to stick there.

Bernadina, Roderick

89 | **Baltimore** | EXP MLB DEBUT: 2015 | POTENTIAL: Starting OF | **8C**

Bats R Age 19
2009 FA (Curacao)
Pwr +++
BAvg +++
Spd +++
Def +++

Year	Lev	Team	AB	R	H	HR	RBI	Avg	OB	Slg	OPS	bb%	ct%	Eye	SB	CS	x/h%	Iso	RC/G
2011	Rk	GCL Orioles	184	30	44	4	28	239	320	413	733	11	86	0.85	6	2	48	174	4.85

Young and toolsy prospect who performed well in first season in US. Swings with authority and covers plate well. Uses the entire field and works counts to his advantage. Possesses moderate power potential from quick bat, but struggles with breaking balls at present. Needs to add strength to lean physique and defensive package should improve with more time in OF.

Bethancourt, Christian

2 | **Atlanta** | EXP MLB DEBUT: 2013 | POTENTIAL: Starting C | **8D**

Bats R Age 20
2009 NDFA Panama
Pwr +++
BAvg +++
Spd ++
Def ++

Year	Lev	Team	AB	R	H	HR	RBI	Avg	OB	Slg	OPS	bb%	ct%	Eye	SB	CS	x/h%	Iso	RC/G
2009	Rk	GCL Braves	116	22	33	2	19	284	346	431	777	9	81	0.50	7	0	36	147	5.22
2009	Rk	Danville	50	10	13	2	8	260	339	480	819	11	68	0.38	1	1	54	220	6.10
2010	A	Rome	399	31	100	3	34	251	276	331	607	3	84	0.23	11	3	24	80	2.87
2011	A	Rome	221	25	67	4	33	303	328	430	757	3	88	0.30	6	3	25	127	4.63
2011	A+	Lynchburg	166	11	45	1	20	271	284	325	609	2	79	0.09	3	2	16	54	2.66

Strong, athletic backstop with good defensive actions and the potential to improve. Features a quick release and strong throwing arm that nailed over 35% of baserunners. Uses a short stroke to drive the ball well to all fields and should add power. Plate discipline and contact rate continue to be issues. Shows good actions and soft hands, but still needs some refinement.

Betts, Mookie

46 | **Boston** | EXP MLB DEBUT: 2015 | POTENTIAL: Starting 2B/SS | **8D**

Bats R Age 19
2011 (5) HS (TN)
Pwr ++
BAvg +++
Spd ++++
Def +++

Year	Lev	Team	AB	R	H	HR	RBI	Avg	OB	Slg	OPS	bb%	ct%	Eye	SB	CS	x/h%	Iso	RC/G
2011	Rk	GCL Red Sox	4	0	2	0	2	500	500	500	1000	0	100		1	0	0	0	6.83

Short and athletic infielder who could become catalyst at top of order. Makes splendid contact with compact, level swing and should hit for BA as a result. Bat plane ideal for line drives to gaps and above average speed should allow for infield hits. Power not part of equation, however. Forthcoming move to 2B likely where solid average arm and quickness play best.

Bichette, Dante

5 | **New York (A)** | EXP MLB DEBUT: 2014 | POTENTIAL: Starting 3B | **8C**

Bats R Age 19
2011 (2) HS (FL)
Pwr ++++
BAvg +++
Spd +++
Def +++

Year	Lev	Team	AB	R	H	HR	RBI	Avg	OB	Slg	OPS	bb%	ct%	Eye	SB	CS	x/h%	Iso	RC/G
2011	Rk	GCL Yankees	196	33	67	3	47	342	429	505	934	13	79	0.73	3	3	34	163	7.54
2011	A-	Staten Island	7	1	1	1	1	143	250	571	821	13	71	0.50	0	1	100	429	5.34

Pure-hitting infielder with polished all-around game. Set short-season ball ablaze and was MVP of GCL. Exhibits above-average athleticism in all aspects of game and has bat speed and exciting power potential. Works counts to find pitches to drives and should hit for BA. Owns arm strength and first-step quickness, but will need to improve footwork.

Blackmon, Charles

9 | **Colorado** | EXP MLB DEBUT: 2011 | POTENTIAL: Starting RF/CF | **8D**

Bats L Age 25
2008 (2) Georgia Tech
Pwr +++
BAvg +++
4.20 Spd +++
Def +++

Year	Lev	Team	AB	R	H	HR	RBI	Avg	OB	Slg	OPS	bb%	ct%	Eye	SB	CS	x/h%	Iso	RC/G
2008	A-	Tri-City	290	42	98	2	33	338	373	466	838	5	87	0.43	13	7	29	128	5.75
2009	A+	Modesto	550	87	169	7	69	307	353	433	786	7	85	0.47	30	13	28	125	5.19
2010	AA	Tulsa	337	53	100	11	55	297	358	484	841	9	87	0.74	19	7	37	187	5.91
2011	AAA	Colorado Spgs	243	49	82	10	49	337	385	572	958	7	86	0.56	12	5	40	235	7.15
2011	MLB	Colorado	98	9	25	1	8	255	277	296	573	3	92	0.38	5	1	8	41	2.63

Tall, athletic, speedy OF had a solid season at Triple-A, but struggled when promoted to the majors then broke his foot. Prior to the injury he was an exciting, athletic player. Improved defensively and can play all three OF positions. Makes consistent contact with a quick, compact stroke. Solid plate discipline and ability to put the ball into play lets his speed play up.

Blanke, Michael — 2 — Chicago (A)

EXP MLB DEBUT: 2013 | POTENTIAL: Backup C | 7C

Bats R | Age 23 | 2010 (14) Tampa

- Pwr +++
- BAvg ++
- Spd +
- Def +++

Year	Lev	Team	AB	R	H	HR	RBI	Avg	OB	Slg	OPS	bb%	ct%	Eye	SB	CS	x/h%	Iso	RC/G
2010	Rk	Great Falls	240	35	79	7	43	329	388	508	896	9	86	0.70	0	0	35	179	6.56
2011	A	Kannapolis	170	22	44	2	18	259	304	382	686	6	84	0.39	0	0	36	124	3.99
2011	A+	Winston-Salem	237	25	56	7	25	236	301	363	664	8	82	0.51	0	0	29	127	3.68

Tall and aggressive hitter who has enough talent to be backup at worst. Excels by making consistent, hard contact to entire field and offering average bat speed and power. Long arms provide plate coverage, but holes in swing doesn't project to BA. Strong arm is best defensive trait and is sufficient receiver and blocker.

Blash, Jabari — 789 — Seattle

EXP MLB DEBUT: 2013 | POTENTIAL: Starting OF | 8C

Bats R | Age 22 | 2010 (8) Miami Dade CC

- Pwr ++++
- BAvg ++
- Spd +++
- Def +++

Year	Lev	Team	AB	R	H	HR	RBI	Avg	OB	Slg	OPS	bb%	ct%	Eye	SB	CS	x/h%	Iso	RC/G
2010	Rk	Pulaski	109	21	29	5	20	266	344	477	821	11	60	0.30	1	1	41	211	6.64
2011	A-	Everett	195	26	57	11	43	292	381	574	956	13	67	0.43	10	3	53	282	8.24
2011	A	Clinton	124	13	27	3	13	218	401	347	748	23	65	0.88	5	2	33	129	5.51

Tall and muscular outfielder was standout performer in low minors. Despite patient approach, can be too passive and long swing can be exploited. BA doesn't project well, though has significant power potential with plus strength and leverage. Swing mechanics need improvement. Owns strong arm and good instincts at all outfield positions.

Bogaerts, Xander — 6 — Boston

EXP MLB DEBUT: 2014 | POTENTIAL: Starting 3B | 9D

Bats R | Age 19 | 2009 FA (Aruba)

- Pwr ++++
- BAvg +++
- Spd +++
- Def ++

Year	Lev	Team	AB	R	H	HR	RBI	Avg	OB	Slg	OPS	bb%	ct%	Eye	SB	CS	x/h%	Iso	RC/G
2011	A	Greenville	265	38	69	16	45	260	324	509	834	9	73	0.35	1	3	46	249	5.83

Young but advanced infielder who was relative unknown entering season. Displayed mature game with solid pitch recognition and ability to make hard contact. Aggressive approach muted OBP, but knows the strike zone and can hit for above average pop to all fields. Runs well at present, but likely to outgrow SS and move to 3B. Strong, accurate arm is asset at any spot.

Bolden, Ryan — 789 — Los Angeles (A)

EXP MLB DEBUT: 2014 | POTENTIAL: Starting OF | 8D

Bats R | Age 20 | 2010 (1-S) HS (MS)

- Pwr +++
- BAvg ++
- Spd +++
- Def +++

Year	Lev	Team	AB	R	H	HR	RBI	Avg	OB	Slg	OPS	bb%	ct%	Eye	SB	CS	x/h%	Iso	RC/G
2010	Rk	AZL Angels	150	17	28	0	16	187	256	260	516	9	55	0.21	11	7	21	73	1.91
2011	Rk	AZL Angels	101	12	17	0	13	168	236	228	464	8	52	0.19	8	1	29	59	1.00

Raw and athletic oufielder who suffered thru miserable season in rookie ball. Swings hard with plus bat speed, but doesn't recognize pitches and flails at breaking balls. Should be able to hit for power down the line, but ability to hit for BA is in question. Possesses good secondary skills with good speed and corner OF skills.

Bonifacio, Jorge — 89 — Kansas City

EXP MLB DEBUT: 2015 | POTENTIAL: Starting OF | 9D

Bats R | Age 19 | 2009 FA (DR)

- Pwr +++
- BAvg ++++
- Spd +++
- Def +++

Year	Lev	Team	AB	R	H	HR	RBI	Avg	OB	Slg	OPS	bb%	ct%	Eye	SB	CS	x/h%	Iso	RC/G
2010	Rk	AZL Royals	76	9	16	0	6	211	268	342	610	7	59	0.19	1	2	31	132	3.47
2011	Rk	Burlington	236	26	67	7	30	284	329	492	821	6	75	0.28	5	6	46	208	5.71

Athletic and strong outfielder who showed much promise with all-around game. Plus bat speed generated by smooth, level swing and acute barrel awareness may lead to consistent .300 BA. Offers pop potential, though needs loft and leverage in swing. Runs well, but strong arm is best asset in field. Approach to game is raw and needs to be better running bases.

Borchering, Bobby — 5 — Arizona

EXP MLB DEBUT: 2013 | POTENTIAL: Backup 3B | 7C

Bats B | Age 21 | 2009 (1) HS (FL)

- Pwr ++++
- BAvg ++
- Spd +
- Def ++

Year	Lev	Team	AB	R	H	HR	RBI	Avg	OB	Slg	OPS	bb%	ct%	Eye	SB	CS	x/h%	Iso	RC/G
2009	Rk	Missoula	87	10	21	2	11	241	283	425	708	5	69	0.19	0	0	52	184	4.35
2010	A	South Bend	523	74	141	15	74	270	338	423	761	9	76	0.42	1	1	34	153	4.98
2011	A+	Visalia	531	80	142	24	92	267	329	469	798	8	69	0.30	4	1	39	202	5.54

Strong, powerful switch-hitting 3B continues to hit for power, but not much else. Has plus bat speed and is still young so some offensive potential remains, but has yet to hit above .270 as professional. Lack of range, a below average arm, and inconsistent mechanics make a move off 3B very likely. Made 20 errors in '10 and 27 in '11. Stock is down.

Bradley, Jackie — 8 — Boston

EXP MLB DEBUT: 2014 | POTENTIAL: Starting CF | 8D

Bats L | Age 22 | 2011 (1-S) South Carolina

- Pwr ++
- BAvg +++
- Spd +++
- Def ++++

Year	Lev	Team	AB	R	H	HR	RBI	Avg	OB	Slg	OPS	bb%	ct%	Eye	SB	CS	x/h%	Iso	RC/G
2009	NCAA	South Carolina	255	69	89	11	46	349	426	537	963	12	88	1.10	8	2	27	188	7.43
2010	NCAA	South Carolina	242	56	89	13	60	368	459	587	1046	14	85	1.11	7	3	29	219	8.60
2011	NCAA	South Carolina	162	32	40	6	27	247	337	432	769	12	77	0.58	2	1	43	185	5.19
2011	A-	Lowell	21	5	4	0	0	190	320	190	510	16	76	0.80	0	2	0	0	1.98
2011	A	Greenville	15	2	5	1	3	333	333	600	933	0	80	0.00	0	0	40	267	6.34

Outstanding defender who missed majority of college season after breaking wrist. Has above average instincts, arm strength, and range to patrol CF. Only has average speed, but covers lots of ground from shrewd routes. Hitting ability is big question mark. Inconsistent swing mechanics mute BA potential and swing path not ideal for power development.

Brantly, Rob — 2 — Detroit

EXP MLB DEBUT: 2014 | POTENTIAL: Backup C | 7C

Bats L | Age 22 | 2010 (3) UC Riverside

- Pwr ++
- BAvg +++
- Spd ++
- Def +++

Year	Lev	Team	AB	R	H	HR	RBI	Avg	OB	Slg	OPS	bb%	ct%	Eye	SB	CS	x/h%	Iso	RC/G
2009	NCAA	UC-Riverside	152	25	48	4	23	316	346	454	800	4	89	0.41	0	0	27	138	5.13
2010	NCAA	UC-Riverside	209	50	78	7	39	373	435	569	1005	10	89	0.96	0	1	33	196	7.86
2010	A	West Michigan	188	26	48	1	21	255	336	335	672	11	88	1.05	2	2	25	80	4.21
2011	A	West Michigan	284	42	86	7	44	303	357	440	797	8	86	0.62	2	2	28	137	5.33
2011	A+	Lakeland	146	16	32	3	18	219	245	322	567	3	88	0.29	0	0	28	103	2.48

Athletic and strong backstop with limited offensive upside, but has talent to stick as backup. Consistent, contact-oriented hitter with patient approach and ability to shoot gaps. May not have power requisite of everyday player, but can hit long ball on occasion. Dependable receiver with strong, accurate arm and quick release.

Brentz, Bryce — 9 — Boston

EXP MLB DEBUT: 2013 | POTENTIAL: Starting OF | 8B

Bats R | Age 23 | 2010 (1-S) Middle TN State

- Pwr ++++
- BAvg ++
- Spd +++
- Def ++

Year	Lev	Team	AB	R	H	HR	RBI	Avg	OB	Slg	OPS	bb%	ct%	Eye	SB	CS	x/h%	Iso	RC/G
2009	NCAA	Middle Tenn St	230	79	107	28	73	465	529	930	1459	12	86	0.97	7	4	46	465	12.99
2010	NCAA	Middle Tenn St	184	51	64	15	49	348	437	636	1072	14	78	0.71	4	2	36	288	8.96
2010	A-	Lowell	262	28	52	5	39	198	258	340	598	7	71	0.28	5	4	44	141	2.80
2011	A	Greenville	170	43	61	11	36	359	408	647	1055	8	79	0.40	2	2	39	288	8.42
2011	A+	Salem	288	48	79	19	58	274	334	531	866	8	72	0.33	1	1	44	257	6.25

Athletic and strong outfielder who showed vast improvement after lackluster pro debut in 2010. Offers plenty of loft and leverage in strong swing to produce power to all fields. Bat speed sufficient for BA, but has long, vicious swing and routinely expands strike zone. Owns ideal RF arm along with average speed, but has limited range and instincts.

Brett, Ryan — 4 — Tampa Bay

EXP MLB DEBUT: 2015 | POTENTIAL: Starting 2B | 7B

Bats B | Age 20 | 2010 (3) HS (WA)

- Pwr ++
- BAvg ++++
- Spd +++
- Def ++

Year	Lev	Team	AB	R	H	HR	RBI	Avg	OB	Slg	OPS	bb%	ct%	Eye	SB	CS	x/h%	Iso	RC/G
2010	Rk	GCL Rays	89	8	27	0	9	303	361	404	765	8	81	0.47	12	3	26	101	5.12
2011	Rk	Princeton	240	42	72	3	24	300	368	471	839	10	90	1.08	21	3	42	171	6.13

Very short and quick infielder with uncanny ability to put bat to ball. Knows strike zone very well and rarely swings at bad pitches. Owns natural, quick stroke from both sides and has enough speed and instincts to steal bases. Defense needs work as hands and arm strength aren't ideal. Commits high number of errors due to erratic feet.

Brown, Gary — 8 — San Francisco

EXP MLB DEBUT: 2013 | POTENTIAL: Starting CF | 9D

Bats R | Age 23 | 2010 (1) Cal State Fullerton

- Pwr +++
- BAvg +++
- Spd +++++ (3.80)
- Def +++

Year	Lev	Team	AB	R	H	HR	RBI	Avg	OB	Slg	OPS	bb%	ct%	Eye	SB	CS	x/h%	Iso	RC/G
2009	NCAA	Cal St Fullerton	259	64	88	3	40	340	374	494	868	5	87	0.42	23	8	31	154	6.08
2010	NCAA	Cal St Fullerton	210	63	92	6	41	438	461	695	1156	4	94	0.75	32	5	37	257	9.05
2010	Rk	AZL Giants	22	6	4	0	0	182	308	227	535	15	77	0.80	2	0	25	45	2.40
2010	A-	Salem-Keizer	22	2	3	0	2	136	208	227	436	8	68	0.29	0	1	33	91	0.59
2011	A+	San Jose	559	115	188	14	80	336	387	519	906	8	86	0.60	53	19	32	182	6.63

Exciting CF prospect with surprising power had huge breakout in '11 in part due to improved plate discipline and bb% since turning pro. Makes consistent contact and uses plus speed effectively. Above average defense and an ability to put the bat on the ball. Could stand to tone down his aggressiveness, but is a solid CF with good range and ample arm strength.

Broxton, Keon — 8 — Arizona

EXP MLB DEBUT: 2014 | POTENTIAL: Starting CF | 8E

Bats R | Age 22
2009 (3) Santa Fe JC (FL)
Pwr ++
BAvg ++
4.25 Spd ++++
Def +++

Year	Lev	Team	AB	R	H	HR	RBI	Avg	OB	Slg	OPS	bb%	ct%	Eye	SB	CS	x/h%	Iso	RC/G
2009	Rk	Missoula	272	38	67	11	37	246	296	474	770	7	66	0.20	6	1	46	228	5.34
2010	A	South Bend	531	74	121	5	32	228	312	360	672	11	68	0.38	21	13	34	132	4.10
2011	A	South Bend	78	8	18	0	1	231	294	282	576	8	62	0.23	6	4	11	51	2.63
2011	A+	Visalia	406	69	102	7	44	251	350	362	712	13	65	0.44	27	8	25	111	4.74

Raw and athletic OF who has the potential to develop an interesting power/speed mix. Broxton struggled in '11, failing to hit in the CAL and striking out 142 times. Struggles with pitch recognition and strike zone judgment. Covers ground well and takes good routes. Did steal 33 bases, but not much else going on.

Buckley, Sean — 5 — Cincinnati

EXP MLB DEBUT: 2014 | POTENTIAL: Starting 3B | 7C

Bats R | Age 22
2011 (5) St. Petersburg JC, FL
Pwr ++++
BAvg +++
Spd ++
Def ++

Year	Lev	Team	AB	R	H	HR	RBI	Avg	OB	Slg	OPS	bb%	ct%	Eye	SB	CS	x/h%	Iso	RC/G
2011	Rk	Billings	225	38	65	14	41	289	355	551	906	9	68	0.32	6	4	43	262	7.18

At 6'4" 220, he has good size and a strong bat -- knocked 14 home runs in his pro debut in the Northwest League. At 21, he was not young for that level and will need to prove himself in full-season ball in '12. Decent defender with a strong arm. Value takes a hit if he has to move across the diamond -- a right-handed 1B-only player doesn't have much value.

Burgess, Michael — 9 — Chicago (N)

EXP MLB DEBUT: 2013 | POTENTIAL: Backup OF | 6C

Bats L | Age 23
2007 (1-S) HS (FL)
Pwr ++++
BAvg ++
4.35 Spd ++
Def +++

Year	Lev	Team	AB	R	H	HR	RBI	Avg	OB	Slg	OPS	bb%	ct%	Eye	SB	CS	x/h%	Iso	RC/G
2008	A+	Potomac	71	12	16	6	19	225	313	521	834	11	63	0.35	0	2	56	296	6.26
2009	A+	Potomac	480	63	113	19	71	235	313	410	723	10	72	0.40	12	8	39	175	4.49
2010	A+	Potomac	386	57	101	12	70	262	342	430	772	11	77	0.53	5	2	37	168	5.19
2010	AA	Harrisburg	74	11	21	6	15	284	369	649	1018	12	64	0.37	0	0	62	365	9.37
2011	A+	Daytona	426	61	96	20	68	225	321	427	748	12	74	0.54	1	0	47	202	4.88

Short, muscular OF with plus power but with little idea of how to hit. He has decent bat speed and can hit the ball a long way, but struggles with breaking balls and doesn't make enough contact. He has decent speed and a plus throwing arm, so RF is a good fit. 2012 will be an important year for this former 1st rounder, as so far the results are not encouraging.

Cabrera, Yordy — 6 — Oakland

EXP MLB DEBUT: 2013 | POTENTIAL: Starting SS | 8C

Bats R | Age 21
2010 (2) HS (FL)
Pwr ++++
BAvg +++
Spd +++
Def ++

Year	Lev	Team	AB	R	H	HR	RBI	Avg	OB	Slg	OPS	bb%	ct%	Eye	SB	CS	x/h%	Iso	RC/G
2010	Rk	AZL Athletics	16	3	3	0	0	188	350	250	600	20	69	0.80	0	0	33	63	3.27
2011	A	Burlington	359	59	83	6	47	231	292	368	660	8	69	0.28	23	6	39	136	3.72

Strong infielder struggled in Low-A, but possesses desirable tools for middle infielder. Quick wrists, strength, and bat speed give him chance for plus pop and has speed and instincts to steal bases. Tends to be overly aggressive in approach and swings and misses too often. Could see a move to 3B where his arm strength, hands, and range are ideal.

Calhoun, Kole — 79 — Los Angeles (A)

EXP MLB DEBUT: 2013 | POTENTIAL: Reserve OF | 6B

Bats L | Age 24
2010 (8) Arizona State
Pwr ++
BAvg +++
Spd +++
Def ++

Year	Lev	Team	AB	R	H	HR	RBI	Avg	OB	Slg	OPS	bb%	ct%	Eye	SB	CS	x/h%	Iso	RC/G
2009	NCAA	Arizona State	211	54	66	12	53	313	427	583	1010	17	83	1.20	10	5	47	270	8.36
2010	NCAA	Arizona State	224	61	72	17	59	321	472	616	1088	22	82	1.60	7	6	42	295	9.59
2010	Rk	Orem	202	43	59	7	42	292	407	505	912	16	78	0.87	3	1	42	213	7.34
2011	A+	Inland Empire	512	94	166	22	99	324	409	547	955	12	81	0.76	20	10	39	223	7.53

Short and stocky outfielder who maximizes limited tools. Blends mature approach with decent pop to produce offensive numbers. Stole bases despite fringy speed and defense is ordinary at best, especially with limited arm strength and range. Profiles best in corner OF, but will have to continue to hit to land role.

Calixte, Orlando — 6 — Kansas City

EXP MLB DEBUT: 2015 | POTENTIAL: Reserve INF | 7C

Bats R | Age 20
2011 FA (DR)
Pwr ++
BAvg ++
Spd +++
Def +++

Year	Lev	Team	AB	R	H	HR	RBI	Avg	OB	Slg	OPS	bb%	ct%	Eye	SB	CS	x/h%	Iso	RC/G
2011	A	Kane County	239	19	60	3	31	251	309	318	627	8	71	0.29	11	4	15	67	3.13

Short and athletic infielder who has good tools across the board, but hasn't produced with glove or bat. Owns good bat speed, but free-swinging tendencies mute BA and OBP potential. Strikes out a lot for someone with limited power. Ranges well to both sides and has good arm strength. Has some upside, but needs to find better swing mechanics and consistency.

Candelario, Jeimer — 5 — Chicago (N)

EXP MLB DEBUT: 2015 | POTENTIAL: Starting 3B | 8D

Bats B | Age 18
2011 NDFA D.R.
Pwr +++
BAvg +++
Spd +++
Def ++

Year	Lev	Team	AB	R	H	HR	RBI	Avg	OB	Slg	OPS	bb%	ct%	Eye	SB	CS	x/h%	Iso	RC/G
2011		Did not play																	

17-year-old had an impressive debut in the DSL, hitting .337/.443/.478. At 6'1" 180, he has offensive potential to develop moderate power with good plate dsciipline (50 BB/42 K). Has moderate speed, but needs to work on his defense. He made 17 errors and is still raw, but has nice long-term potential.

Cardenas, Adrian — 456 — Oakland

EXP MLB DEBUT: 2012 | POTENTIAL: Utility player | 7C

Bats L | Age 24
2006 (1-S) HS (FL)
Pwr ++
BAvg ++++
Spd +++
Def +++

Year	Lev	Team	AB	R	H	HR	RBI	Avg	OB	Slg	OPS	bb%	ct%	Eye	SB	CS	x/h%	Iso	RC/G
2009	AA	Midland	325	56	106	3	55	326	397	446	843	10	86	0.86	5	4	29	120	6.14
2009	AAA	Sacramento	183	23	46	1	24	251	315	372	687	9	84	0.59	3	2	39	120	4.20
2010	AA	Midland	194	36	67	3	32	345	441	469	910	15	88	1.43	4	6	27	124	7.16
2010	AAA	Sacramento	210	30	56	1	21	267	322	329	650	7	87	0.61	2	2	18	62	3.68
2011	AAA	Sacramento	491	70	154	5	51	314	374	418	791	9	89	0.84	13	6	24	104	5.42

Versatile and athletic prospect who played a variety of positions, including LF for first time in career. Gets on base consistently by working counts and shooting gaps with level swing path. Makes easy contact with short swing and routinely hits for BA. Not a standout at any position, but makes routine plays with average range and arm.

Carpenter, Matt — 5 — St. Louis

EXP MLB DEBUT: 2011 | POTENTIAL: Backup 3B | 7C

Bats L | Age 26
2009 (13) TCU
Pwr ++
BAvg +++
Spd ++
Def ++

Year	Lev	Team	AB	R	H	HR	RBI	Avg	OB	Slg	OPS	bb%	ct%	Eye	SB	CS	x/h%	Iso	RC/G
2009	A+	Palm Beach	114	13	25	2	9	219	282	342	624	8	79	0.42	1	0	36	123	3.22
2010	A+	Palm Beach	99	17	28	1	16	283	432	404	836	21	86	1.86	0	1	29	121	6.72
2010	AA	Springfield	396	76	125	12	53	316	411	487	898	14	78	0.73	11	2	33	172	7.02
2011	AAA	Memphis	434	61	130	12	70	300	413	463	876	16	84	1.24	5	4	34	164	6.82
2011	MLB	St. Louis	15	0	1	0	0	67	263	133	396	21	73	1.00	0	0	100	67	0.45

Carpenter is an offensive-minded 3B who hit over .300 for 2nd straight season. He has decent power, plate discipline, and makes consistent contact. He should be able to provide solid offense. He is below-average defensively, lacks the arm needed for the position, and with David Freese and Zack Cox in the organization, he doesn't have a clear path to regular AB.

Carroll, Sawyer — 9 — San Diego

EXP MLB DEBUT: 2012 | POTENTIAL: Platoon LF/RF | 7D

Bats L | Age 26
2008 (3-S) Kentucky
Pwr +++
BAvg +++
4.30 Spd ++
Def ++

Year	Lev	Team	AB	R	H	HR	RBI	Avg	OB	Slg	OPS	bb%	ct%	Eye	SB	CS	x/h%	Iso	RC/G
2009	A	Fort Wayne	250	43	79	5	40	316	410	464	874	14	77	0.70	14	5	33	148	6.77
2009	A+	Lake Elsinore	147	28	47	2	42	320	408	531	939	13	78	0.67	4	2	47	211	7.73
2009	AA	San Antonio	82	17	26	1	14	317	440	488	928	18	80	1.13	1	1	35	171	7.76
2010	AA	San Antonio	458	50	110	7	55	240	323	345	668	11	73	0.46	1	7	28	105	3.87
2011	AA	San Antonio	460	68	123	18	71	267	353	463	816	12	79	0.63	11	2	39	196	5.76

Tall/athletic player. Steady upswing in power at Double-A while maintaining solid plate discipline. Runs slightly below average, but is aggressive on the bases. Defensively range is average and lacks arm strength, which makes him better suited for LF. Fourth OF at best.

Carter, Chris — 37 — Oakland

EXP MLB DEBUT: 2010 | POTENTIAL: Starting 1B | 8C

Bats R | Age 25
2005 (15) HS (NV)
Pwr ++++
BAvg ++
Spd +
Def +

Year	Lev	Team	AB	R	H	HR	RBI	Avg	OB	Slg	OPS	bb%	ct%	Eye	SB	CS	x/h%	Iso	RC/G
2010	AAA	Sacramento	465	92	120	31	94	258	359	529	888	14	70	0.53	1	1	52	271	6.90
2010	MLB	Oakland	70	8	13	3	7	186	260	329	588	9	70	0.33	1	0	31	143	2.47
2011	A+	Stockton	24	3	8	3	7	333	429	708	1137	14	67	0.50	0	0	38	375	10.47
2011	AAA	Sacramento	296	55	81	18	72	274	364	530	894	12	71	0.49	5	1	47	257	6.94
2011	MLB	Oakland	44	2	6	0	0	136	174	136	310	4	55	0.10	0	0	0	0	-1.99

Large and muscular hitter can't seem to stick in majors despite best bat speed and power in organization. Struggles to make contact with vicious, uppercut swing and lacks secondary skills. Patient approach leads to nice OBP, but will have to live with fringy BA. Lacks athleticism and range to be sufficient defender at 1B or LF.

Carter, Kes — 8 — Tampa Bay

Bats L Age 22
2011 (1-S) Western KY
Pwr +++
BAvg +++
Spd +++
Def +++

EXP MLB DEBUT: 2014 POTENTIAL: Starting CF **7B**

Year	Lev	Team	AB	R	H	HR	RBI	Avg	OB	Slg	OPS	bb%	ct%	Eye	SB	CS	x/h%	Iso	RC/G
2009	NCAA	W. Kentucky	94	26	36	1	20	383	420	500	920	6	77	0.27	4	2	22	117	6.92
2010	NCAA	W. Kentucky	246	40	84	7	53	341	409	484	892	10	85	0.76	14	3	24	142	6.57
2011	NCAA	W. Kentucky	215	46	74	7	40	344	427	549	976	13	85	0.97	8	1	36	205	7.78
2011	A-	Hudson Valley	13	2	3	0	1	231	333	231	564	13	92	2.00	0	0	0	0	3.26

Tall and very athletic outfielder with potential to be five-tool performer. Bat speed isn't explosive, but has strong swing to produce decent power to the pull side. Often uses opposite field too much and could realize power potential by pulling more. Has solid speed on base and in field where range and arm are suitable for CF.

Castellanos, Nick — 5 — Detroit

Bats R Age 20
2010 (1-S) HS (FL)
Pwr ++++
BAvg ++++
Spd +++
Def +++

EXP MLB DEBUT: 2014 POTENTIAL: Starting 3B **9D**

Year	Lev	Team	AB	R	H	HR	RBI	Avg	OB	Slg	OPS	bb%	ct%	Eye	SB	CS	x/h%	Iso	RC/G
2010	Rk	GCL Tigers	24	5	8	0	3	333	429	417	845	14	79	0.80	0	1	25	83	6.48
2011	A	West Michigan	507	65	158	7	76	312	368	436	804	8	74	0.35	3	2	29	124	5.60

Tall and fundamentally-sound infielder with bat to become middle-of-order run producer. Started year slowly, but finished strong with high BA and moderate pop. Possesses loft and leverage in swing to add more power and long arms provide plate coverage. Should improve pitch recognition with more AB. Runs OK and exhibits agility and strong, accurate arm at 3B.

Castillo, Angel — 9 — Los Angeles (A)

Bats R Age 23
2005 FA (Venezuela)
Pwr ++++
BAvg ++
Spd +++
Def +++

EXP MLB DEBUT: 2013 POTENTIAL: Starting RF **8E**

Year	Lev	Team	AB	R	H	HR	RBI	Avg	OB	Slg	OPS	bb%	ct%	Eye	SB	CS	x/h%	Iso	RC/G
2008	A	Cedar Rapids	45	3	6	0	4	133	133	222	356	0	73	0.00	1	1	67	89	
2009	A	Cedar Rapids	393	56	95	12	61	242	294	389	683	7	72	0.26	16	2	35	148	3.84
2010	A+	Rancho Cucamg	467	72	121	21	70	259	319	454	773	8	70	0.29	12	6	38	195	5.13
2011	AA	Arkansas	347	44	75	6	23	216	265	308	573	6	70	0.22	16	5	25	92	2.32
2011	AAA	Salt Lake	18	3	2	0	1	111	200	167	367	10	72	0.40	1	0	50	56	-0.27

Strong and aggressive hitter who failed to match breakout season in '10 by continuing to expand strike zone. Plus raw power is best attribute, particularly against LHP. Breaking balls give him fits and he can be jammed inside. Walk rate declined while Ks were problematic - BA doesn't project well at all. Nice defender with terrific arm strength.

Castillo, Phillips — 789 — Seattle

Bats R Age 18
2010 FA (DR)
Pwr +++
BAvg ++++
Spd ++
Def +++

EXP MLB DEBUT: 2015 POTENTIAL: Starting OF **9D**

Year	Lev	Team	AB	R	H	HR	RBI	Avg	OB	Slg	OPS	bb%	ct%	Eye	SB	CS	x/h%	Iso	RC/G
2011	Rk	AZL Mariners	170	36	51	1	27	300	357	482	839	8	64	0.25	8	5	47	182	6.87

Projectable and strong outfielder who dazzled in rookie ball by showcasing plus raw power and surprising aptitude for hitting. Should hit for BA due to bat speed and pitch recognition, though swings hard at everything. Very projectable skills, including arm strength. Plays game aggressively and likely to end up in LF due to average speed and range.

Castillo, Welington — 2 — Chicago (N)

Bats R Age 25
2004 NDFA D.R.
Pwr ++
BAvg ++
Spd ++
Def ++++

EXP MLB DEBUT: 2010 POTENTIAL: Backup C **7C**

Year	Lev	Team	AB	R	H	HR	RBI	Avg	OB	Slg	OPS	bb%	ct%	Eye	SB	CS	x/h%	Iso	RC/G
2010	MLB	Chicago Cubs	20	3	6	1	5	300	333	650	983	5	65	0.14	0	0	83	350	8.72
2011	Rk	AZL Cubs	6	2	4	0	0	667	778	1166	1944	33	100		0	0	75	500	20.62
2011	A+	Daytona	42	6	10	1	7	238	333	381	714	13	79	0.67	0	0	40	143	4.56
2011	AAA	Iowa	227	38	65	15	35	286	344	524	868	8	75	0.35	0	0	37	238	6.14
2011	MLB	Chicago Cubs	13	0	2	0	0	154	154	154	308	0	69	0.00	0	0	0	0	

Defensive-oriented catcher with the arm strength and quick release (1.9) needed to halt running game. Castillo receives the ball well and improved his agility. His batting average fluctuates due to marginal plate discipline, but he does have good power to the pull field. Bat continues to lag behind his defense though he does have moderate power.

Castillo, Wilkin — 2 — Colorado

Bats R Age 28
2003 NDFA D.R.
Pwr ++
BAvg ++
4.25 Spd +++
Def +++

EXP MLB DEBUT: 2008 POTENTIAL: Reserve CA/3B **6B**

Year	Lev	Team	AB	R	H	HR	RBI	Avg	OB	Slg	OPS	bb%	ct%	Eye	SB	CS	x/h%	Iso	RC/G
2008	MLB	Cincinnati	32	6	9	0	1	281	303	313	616	3	84	0.20	0	0	11	31	2.92
2009	AAA	Louisville	122	12	27	2	7	221	228	328	556	1	84	0.05	3	1	30	107	2.09
2009	MLB	Cincinnati	3	0	2	0	1	667	667	667	1333	0	100		0	0	0	0	9.99
2010	AAA	Louisville	317	45	81	9	35	256	283	410	693	4	84	0.24	11	3	35	155	3.83
2011	AAA	Gwinnett	279	19	73	5	37	262	282	366	648	3	83	0.17	5	3	25	104	3.24

Athletic backstop has a chance to play at the next level due to plus defense. Behind the dish, he receives the ball well and has average arm strength. Struggles offensively and lacks any type of secondary skill necessary to start. Below average power and weak plate discipline limit his offensive value.

Catricala, Vince — 357 — Seattle

Bats R Age 23
2009 (10) Hawaii
Pwr ++++
BAvg ++++
Spd +
Def +

EXP MLB DEBUT: 2012 POTENTIAL: Starting 1B/3B **8C**

Year	Lev	Team	AB	R	H	HR	RBI	Avg	OB	Slg	OPS	bb%	ct%	Eye	SB	CS	x/h%	Iso	RC/G
2009	NCAA	Hawaii	218	51	76	13	44	349	441	596	1037	14	80	0.84	3	4	36	248	8.58
2009	Rk	Pulaski	219	33	66	8	40	301	354	493	848	8	84	0.53	6	1	36	192	5.88
2010	A	Clinton	496	90	150	17	79	302	373	488	861	10	77	0.50	7	3	39	185	6.30
2011	A+	High Desert	282	56	99	14	61	351	419	574	994	10	84	0.73	8	3	34	223	7.74
2011	AA	Jackson	239	45	83	11	45	347	407	632	1039	9	80	0.51	9	1	52	285	8.45

Tall and strong hitter who broke out in big way with bat. Smashes doubles and HR to all fields and mature eye and hitting acumen project to high BA. Possesses level swing and plus bat speed that make him middle-of-order threat. Very little talent outside of bat. Runs poorly and lacks a defined position. Overall defense is below average, but has average arm strength.

Cavazos-Galvez, Brian — 7 — Los Angeles (N)

Bats R Age 25
2009 (12) U. of New Mexico
Pwr +++
BAvg +++
Spd ++++
Def +++

EXP MLB DEBUT: 2014 POTENTIAL: Starting CF **8D**

Year	Lev	Team	AB	R	H	HR	RBI	Avg	OB	Slg	OPS	bb%	ct%	Eye	SB	CS	x/h%	Iso	RC/G
2009	NCAA	New Mexico	217	64	85	15	63	392	429	737	1166	6	93	0.93	17	3	45	346	9.17
2009	NCAA	Coppin State	90	12	22	0	9	244	364	311	676	16	78	0.85	2	1	27	67	4.33
2009	Rk	Ogden	301	59	97	18	63	322	344	618	962	3	86	0.23	17	8	52	296	6.87
2010	A	Great Lakes	490	76	156	16	77	318	335	520	855	2	88	0.20	43	13	40	202	5.65
2011	AA	Chattanooga	411	60	114	14	61	277	298	470	767	3	85	0.19	13	11	40	192	4.67

Lean, athletic OF prospect can do a bit of everything, but has no standout tool. Can look great in on AB and awful in the next. Punishes mistakes, but can be beat by better pitching. Has solid power potential, runs well, can play all three OF positions. If the plate discipline improves he could be a solid big-league contributor.

Cecchini, Garin — 5 — Boston

Bats L Age 21
2010 (4) HS (LA)
Pwr ++++
BAvg +++
Spd ++
Def +++

EXP MLB DEBUT: 2014 POTENTIAL: Starting 3B **9D**

Year	Lev	Team	AB	R	H	HR	RBI	Avg	OB	Slg	OPS	bb%	ct%	Eye	SB	CS	x/h%	Iso	RC/G
2011	A-	Lowell	114	21	34	3	23	298	389	500	889	13	83	0.89	12	2	47	202	6.84

Tall and strong infielder has a keen knowledge of strike zone and controls bat well. Possesses clean, quick swing and pure hitting ability that should result in plus power down the line. Broken wrist is healed and ready for full-season. Isn't the fleetest prospect around, but isn't a baseclogger either. Displays good hands and clean footwork at 3B.

Ceciliani, Darrell — 8 — New York (N)

Bats L Age 22
2009 (4) Columbia Basin CC
Pwr ++
BAvg +++
6.5/60 Spd +++
Def +++

EXP MLB DEBUT: 2013 POTENTIAL: Starting CF **7C**

Year	Lev	Team	AB	R	H	HR	RBI	Avg	OB	Slg	OPS	bb%	ct%	Eye	SB	CS	x/h%	Iso	RC/G
2009	Rk	Kingsport	158	29	37	2	13	234	292	310	603	8	80	0.42	14	2	22	76	2.92
2010	A-	Brooklyn	271	56	95	2	35	351	403	531	935	8	79	0.43	21	14	35	181	7.31
2011	A	Savannah	421	62	109	4	40	259	340	361	701	11	77	0.54	25	8	28	102	4.38

Solid all-around player without a plus carrying tool. Uses a nice line-drive approach to spray the ball around, but lacks over the fence power. He does have decent plate discipline and a good approach, so should be able to hit for average. Has above-average speed, but isn't a burner. Has a good glove and good instincts, but arm and range might be a bit short for CF.

Chambers, Adron — 7 — St. Louis

Bats L Age 25
2007 (38) Pensacola JC, FL
Pwr ++
BAvg +++
Spd ++++
Def +++

EXP MLB DEBUT: 2011 POTENTIAL: Backup OF **6B**

Year	Lev	Team	AB	R	H	HR	RBI	Avg	OB	Slg	OPS	bb%	ct%	Eye	SB	CS	x/h%	Iso	RC/G
2009	A+	Palm Beach	448	66	127	1	46	283	352	400	751	9	79	0.49	21	12	27	116	5.03
2010	AA	Springfield	252	52	71	5	27	282	360	417	777	11	80	0.62	8	4	27	135	5.30
2010	AAA	Memphis	69	11	20	1	8	290	372	362	734	12	74	0.50	6	1	10	72	4.75
2011	AAA	Memphis	426	73	118	10	44	277	357	415	772	11	79	0.59	22	13	29	138	5.23
2011	MLB	St. Louis	8	2	3	0	4	375	375	625	1000	0	88	0.00	0	0	33	250	7.43

Short, athletic OF prospect with plus speed and a solid approach at the plate. Moderate power likely limits him to a backup role, but speed and range in CF give him value. Chambers is now 25 and looks like a 4th OF at best, but his speed does give him some value.

Chavez, Johermyn — 789 — Seattle

EXP MLB DEBUT: 2012 | POTENTIAL: Starting OF | 8D

Bats R Age 23
2004 FA (Venezuela)
Pwr ++++
BAvg ++
Spd +++
Def +++

Year	Lev	Team	AB	R	H	HR	RBI	Avg	OB	Slg	OPS	bb%	ct%	Eye	SB	CS	x/h%	Iso	RC/G
2007	Rk	GCL Blue Jays	176	29	53	6	21	301	372	494	867	10	72	0.40	7	2	38	193	6.60
2008	A	Lansing	402	40	85	7	39	211	258	323	581	6	68	0.20	9	5	34	112	2.47
2009	A	Lansing	508	87	144	21	89	283	336	474	810	7	73	0.29	10	6	34	191	5.54
2010	A+	High Desert	534	109	168	32	96	315	375	577	952	9	75	0.40	6	9	41	262	7.37
2011	AA	Jackson	439	47	95	13	50	216	295	360	655	10	72	0.40	6	9	35	144	3.58

Tall and muscular hitter who failed to replicate breakout performance. HR and BA fell dramatically and became more aggressive as year passed. Makes hard contact when he connects and has strength for over-the-fence power to all fields. Tendency to chase pitches can be exploited at higher levels. Sufficient range with plus arm in OF.

Chen, Chun-Hsui — 2 — Cleveland

EXP MLB DEBUT: 2013 | POTENTIAL: Starting C | 8D

Bats R Age 23
2007 FA (Taiwan)
Pwr ++++
BAvg ++
Spd +++
Def +++

Year	Lev	Team	AB	R	H	HR	RBI	Avg	OB	Slg	OPS	bb%	ct%	Eye	SB	CS	x/h%	Iso	RC/G
2008	Rk	GCL Indians	115	11	30	3	15	261	336	409	745	10	75	0.45	1	1	30	148	4.83
2009	A-	Mahoning Vall	195	24	42	1	19	215	323	308	631	14	78	0.74	9	2	38	92	3.64
2010	A	Lake County	218	27	68	6	39	312	362	518	880	7	83	0.45	1	1	44	206	6.37
2010	A+	Kinston	172	31	55	6	30	320	443	523	966	18	79	1.06	4	1	42	203	8.12
2011	AA	Akron	412	58	108	16	70	262	332	451	783	9	70	0.35	2	1	40	189	5.38

Strong backstop posted career high in HR, though saw drastic increase in Ks. Tinkered with swing to add loft, but still covers plate well and works counts. Owns quick bat with above average power potential. Not the most mobile catcher and needs to improve blocking and receiving. Plus arm works well, but could use quick release.

Chen, Pin-Chieh — 8 — Chicago (N)

EXP MLB DEBUT: 2014 | POTENTIAL: Starting CF | 7D

Bats L Age 20
2009 NDFA Taiwan
Pwr ++++
BAvg ++
Spd +++
Def +++

Year	Lev	Team	AB	R	H	HR	RBI	Avg	OB	Slg	OPS	bb%	ct%	Eye	SB	CS	x/h%	Iso	RC/G
2010	Rk	AZL Cubs	168	25	49	0	17	292	367	327	694	11	89	1.05	10	7	10	36	4.44
2010	A-	Boise	22	1	7	0	2	318	400	318	718	12	91	1.50	0	1	0	0	4.82
2011	A-	Boise	229	34	69	2	30	301	370	424	794	10	81	0.57	20	6	29	122	5.52

Tall, skinny, athletic OF from Taiwan. Played 2B in his professional debut, but was moved to CF in '11. Controls the bat well with good plate discipline. Should be able to hit for average and has plus speed. Slashing stroke lets his speed play up, but limits power. Is still learning CF, but has good instincts and athleticism.

Chiang, Chih-Hsien — 79 — Seattle

EXP MLB DEBUT: 2012 | POTENTIAL: Starting OF | 8D

Bats L Age 24
2005 FA (Taiwan)
Pwr +++
BAvg +++
Spd ++
Def +++

Year	Lev	Team	AB	R	H	HR	RBI	Avg	OB	Slg	OPS	bb%	ct%	Eye	SB	CS	x/h%	Iso	RC/G
2008	A+	Lancaster	320	47	97	9	59	303	340	459	800	5	84	0.35	2	1	31	156	5.18
2009	A+	Salem	299	37	79	6	38	264	319	415	734	7	84	0.50	2	1	38	151	4.61
2010	AA	Portland	438	54	114	11	65	260	309	420	729	7	85	0.48	2	0	41	160	4.50
2011	AA	Portland	321	68	109	18	76	340	387	648	1035	7	81	0.41	6	2	54	308	8.21
2011	AA	Jackson	130	11	27	0	10	208	243	262	504	4	77	0.20	1	2	26	54	1.52

Lean and athletic outfielder with breakout offensive year. Attacks pitches aggressively and his improved strength leads to greater pull power. Generally shoots gaps with quick swing and possesses ability to hit RHP and LHP. Doesn't steal many bases due to below average wheels. Has potential to be good defender due to arm and average range.

Chirinos, Robinson — 2 — Tampa Bay

EXP MLB DEBUT: 2011 | POTENTIAL: Starting C | 7C

Bats R Age 28
2000 FA (Venezuela)
Pwr +++
BAvg ++
Spd +
Def +++

Year	Lev	Team	AB	R	H	HR	RBI	Avg	OB	Slg	OPS	bb%	ct%	Eye	SB	CS	x/h%	Iso	RC/G
2009	AA	Tennessee	35	4	9	0	5	257	381	343	724	17	89	1.75	0	1	33	86	5.23
2010	AA	Tennessee	264	53	84	15	64	318	412	580	991	14	87	1.20	1	5	46	261	7.89
2010	AAA	Iowa	55	10	20	3	10	364	386	600	986	4	85	0.25	0	0	35	236	7.09
2011	AAA	Durham	282	24	73	6	24	259	328	376	704	9	76	0.42	1	1	27	117	4.24
2011	MLB	Tampa Bay	55	4	12	1	7	218	283	309	592	8	76	0.38	0	0	25	91	2.72

Strong and mobile backstop who converted to catcher full-time in '09. Shows nice defensive skill despite lack of time at position. Best tools still remain with bat as he exhibits sound on-base abilities and good power. Has never been BA hitter, but can shoot gaps with strong swing. Doesn't hit RHP well and could be valuable backup at a few positions.

Choi, Ji-Man — 23 — Seattle

EXP MLB DEBUT: 2014 | POTENTIAL: Platoon C/1B | 7D

Bats L Age 21
2009 FA (South Korea)
Pwr ++
BAvg ++++
Spd ++
Def ++

Year	Lev	Team	AB	R	H	HR	RBI	Avg	OB	Slg	OPS	bb%	ct%	Eye	SB	CS	x/h%	Iso	RC/G
2010	Rk	AZL Mariners	135	23	51	1	23	378	462	541	1002	13	78	0.70	10	1	35	163	8.56
2010	A+	High Desert	43	7	13	1	7	302	388	442	830	12	79	0.67	0	0	23	140	6.02

Patient and polished hitter who missed season due to back and shoulder injuries. Jury is out on future position, though SEA prefers backstop due to potential. Receiving and instincts not where they need to be, but has strong arm when healthy. Knows how to hit and gets on base with professional eye. Prefers lines drives and keeping Ks down.

Choice, Michael — 78 — Oakland

EXP MLB DEBUT: 2013 | POTENTIAL: Starting OF | 9C

Bats R Age 22
2010 (1) UT-Arlington
Pwr ++++
BAvg +++
Spd +++
Def +++

Year	Lev	Team	AB	R	H	HR	RBI	Avg	OB	Slg	OPS	bb%	ct%	Eye	SB	CS	x/h%	Iso	RC/G
2009	NCAA	Texas-Arlington	225	64	93	11	52	413	480	644	1125	11	87	0.97	5	3	29	231	9.31
2010	NCAA	Texas-Arlington	196	67	75	16	59	383	555	704	1259	28	72	1.41	12	4	39	321	12.84
2010	Rk	AZL Athletics	7	1	0	0	0	0	222	0	222	22	71	1.00	0	0			
2010	A-	Vancouver	102	20	29	7	26	284	376	627	1004	13	58	0.35	6	1	66	343	10.05
2011	A+	Stockton	467	79	133	30	82	285	367	542	909	12	71	0.46	9	5	44	257	7.07

Strong outfielder who bypassed Low-A and led CAL in HR. Swings viciously with plus bat speed and owns power to all fields. Works counts and draws walks, but long swing can be exploited. Breaking balls can be problematic, but making strides. Defense plays up due to good routes and jumps, though range and arm are merely average. Can play CF.

Clark, Andrew — 3 — Texas

EXP MLB DEBUT: 2013 | POTENTIAL: Platoon 1B | 7B

Bats L Age 24
2010 (13) Louisville
Pwr +++
BAvg +++
Spd ++
Def +++

Year	Lev	Team	AB	R	H	HR	RBI	Avg	OB	Slg	OPS	bb%	ct%	Eye	SB	CS	x/h%	Iso	RC/G
2009	NCAA	Louisville	254	82	89	9	55	350	466	555	1021	18	89	2.04	1	0	36	205	8.62
2010	NCAA	Louisville	189	52	70	13	61	370	487	667	1154	19	89	2.05	1	1	41	296	10.05
2010	A-	Spokane	217	32	64	1	41	295	398	350	748	15	83	1.03	2	1	16	55	5.20
2011	A	Hickory	355	59	111	12	60	313	415	482	897	15	83	1.00	7	4	32	169	6.94
2011	A+	Myrtle Beach	64	11	19	2	12	297	471	453	924	25	83	1.91	0	0	32	156	7.88

Low-upside infielder with chance to find majors on basis of plate approach and hit tool. Has walked more than fanned in career and knows balls and strikes. Power and bat speed are only moderate, but gets good wood on ball and drives to all fields. Has some value as defensive 1B, but power may not be enough to play everyday.

Clarke, Chevez — 8 — Los Angeles (A)

EXP MLB DEBUT: 2014 | POTENTIAL: Starting CF | 8C

Bats B Age 20
2010 (1) HS (GA)
Pwr +++
BAvg +++
Spd ++++
Def +++

Year	Lev	Team	AB	R	H	HR	RBI	Avg	OB	Slg	OPS	bb%	ct%	Eye	SB	CS	x/h%	Iso	RC/G
2010	Rk	AZL Angels	162	26	35	3	16	216	278	389	667	8	66	0.25	9	2	43	173	3.97
2011	Rk	AZL Angels	195	33	44	3	27	226	284	400	684	8	66	0.24	5	4	41	174	4.25

Short and strong outfielder repeated rookie ball and remains raw in most aspects. Possesses short, quick swing, but aggressive approach mutes BA and OBP. Has potential to hit for plus power as he matures and recognizes pitches better. Strikeouts will likely remain high in near term. Solid CF with ample range and plus arm strength.

Cleary, Delta — 8 — Colorado

EXP MLB DEBUT: 2014 | POTENTIAL: Starting CF | 7D

Bats B Age 22
2008 (32) HS, (AR)
Pwr ++
BAvg ++
Spd ++++
Def +++

Year	Lev	Team	AB	R	H	HR	RBI	Avg	OB	Slg	OPS	bb%	ct%	Eye	SB	CS	x/h%	Iso	RC/G
2008	Rk	Casper	105	22	29	3	9	276	315	400	715	5	82	0.32	4	0	21	124	4.12
2009	A	Asheville	399	53	102	7	45	256	309	376	685	7	78	0.36	32	11	29	120	3.93
2010	A	Asheville	313	54	77	5	35	246	296	348	644	7	76	0.29	18	5	26	102	3.34
2011	A+	Modesto	503	96	118	1	45	235	334	296	630	13	81	0.77	27	16	21	62	3.63

Long, lean, athletic switch-hitting OF prospect bombed in the CAL, hitting just .235/.337/.296. Does have plus speed and managed to swipe 27 bases and drew 75 walks - otherwise, there isn't much going on. Covers ground well in CF and has a strong throwing arm. 2012 might be his last chance to make an impact.

Coleman, Dusty — 6 — Oakland

EXP MLB DEBUT: 2013 | POTENTIAL: Starting SS | 7B

Bats R Age 25
2008 (28) Wichita State
Pwr +++
BAvg ++
Spd +++
Def +++

Year	Lev	Team	AB	R	H	HR	RBI	Avg	OB	Slg	OPS	bb%	ct%	Eye	SB	CS	x/h%	Iso	RC/G
2008	A-	Vancouver	72	13	23	0	6	319	355	458	814	5	64	0.15	1	0	39	139	6.34
2009	A	Kane County	346	56	88	8	42	254	332	410	742	10	67	0.35	18	8	39	156	5.05
2009	A+	Stockton	100	14	22	1	8	220	291	330	621	9	61	0.26	2	2	32	110	3.41
2011	A+	Stockton	462	71	111	15	66	240	309	413	722	9	63	0.27	21	4	41	173	4.82
2011	AAA	Sacramento	36	5	12	0	4	333	351	417	768	3	61	0.07	0	2	25	83	5.61

Lean and athletic infielder who established career highs in 2B, HR, and SB. Struggles to make contact which led to leading CAL in Ks. Aggressive, long swing exploited by good pitching and BA potential is limited. Runs bases with solid-average speed and is good baserunner. Plays with good glove and is blessed with solid-average speed and arm.

Collier, Zach — 7 — Philadelphia

EXP MLB DEBUT: 2014 | POTENTIAL: Starting CF | 8E

Bats L | Age 21
2008 (1-S) HS (CA)
- Pwr ++
- BAvg ++
- 4.10 Spd ++++
- Def ++++

Year	Lev	Team	AB	R	H	HR	RBI	Avg	OB	Slg	OPS	bb%	ct%	Eye	SB	CS	x/h%	Iso	RC/G
2008	Rk	GCL Phillies	129	15	35	0	19	271	356	357	713	12	78	0.61	5	0	29	85	4.63
2009	A-	Williamsport	137	21	31	1	13	226	274	336	610	6	69	0.21	7	0	39	109	2.98
2009	A	Lakewood	298	40	65	0	32	218	274	319	593	7	73	0.29	13	7	35	101	2.84
2011	A	Lakewood	416	50	106	1	36	255	320	349	669	9	76	0.40	35	13	29	94	3.89

Raw, toolsy prospect starting to look like a bust. Made some progress and has plus speed and athleticism, but doesn't really know how to hit. Long swing, marginal pitch recognition, and poor plate discipline keep BA low. Has excellent range in CF, but missed all of '10 with a hamstring injury and will miss the first 50 games of '12 for a drug violation.

Collins, Tyler — 79 — Detroit

EXP MLB DEBUT: 2014 | POTENTIAL: Reserve OF | 6B

Bats L | Age 22
2011 (6) Howard JC
- Pwr +++
- BAvg +++
- Spd +++
- Def +++

Year	Lev	Team	AB	R	H	HR	RBI	Avg	OB	Slg	OPS	bb%	ct%	Eye	SB	CS	x/h%	Iso	RC/G
2011	Rk	GCL Tigers	3	2	1	0	1	333	600	667	1267	40	100		0	0	100	333	13.39
2011	A-	Connecticut	163	28	51	8	31	313	353	534	886	6	90	0.59	6	1	37	221	6.14

Short and stocky outfielder with average tools across board. Offensive package begins with good bat speed and can put charge in ball with short, simple swing. Lacks projectable power, but has line drive stroke for doubles in gaps. Has fringe-average speed with good instincts while on base. Nothing special as corner OF with decent range and enough arm to be useful.

Colon, Christian — 46 — Kansas City

EXP MLB DEBUT: 2013 | POTENTIAL: Starting 2B | 8C

Bats R | Age 23
2010 (1) Cal State Fullerton
- Pwr +++
- BAvg +++
- Spd +++
- Def +++

Year	Lev	Team	AB	R	H	HR	RBI	Avg	OB	Slg	OPS	bb%	ct%	Eye	SB	CS	x/h%	Iso	RC/G
2008	NCAA	Cal St Fullerton	243	59	80	4	39	329	378	444	822	7	90	0.76	13	4	23	115	5.63
2009	NCAA	Cal St Fullerton	255	82	91	8	40	357	412	529	942	9	91	1.00	15	7	29	173	7.02
2010	NCAA	Cal St Fullerton	268	73	96	17	68	358	430	631	1061	11	93	1.89	13	6	39	272	8.41
2010	A+	Wilmington	245	38	68	3	30	278	314	380	694	5	87	0.39	2	4	25	102	4.01
2011	AA	NW Arkansas	491	69	126	8	61	257	320	342	662	9	90	0.90	17	7	19	86	3.91

Smooth and strong infielder brings mature approach to all facets of game. Uses easy, compact swing to make consistent contact and hits to all fields. Situational hitting skills are unmatched and can bunt to get on base. Power ceiling isn't high, but has strength to reach fences. Can play any middle infield slot, though range and average arm may work best at 2B.

Cone, Zach — 8 — Texas

EXP MLB DEBUT: 2013 | POTENTIAL: Starting OF | 8C

Bats R | Age 22
2011 (1-S) Georgia
- Pwr +++
- BAvg +++
- Spd ++++
- Def ++++

Year	Lev	Team	AB	R	H	HR	RBI	Avg	OB	Slg	OPS	bb%	ct%	Eye	SB	CS	x/h%	Iso	RC/G
2009	NCAA	Georgia	93	20	30	4	18	323	370	548	918	7	73	0.28	3	1	37	226	7.03
2010	NCAA	Georgia	212	45	77	10	53	363	403	627	1030	6	84	0.42	13	0	38	264	7.94
2011	NCAA	Georgia	247	39	68	4	34	275	317	385	701	6	81	0.31	13	3	25	109	4.05
2011	A-	Spokane	224	37	45	4	29	201	254	339	593	7	75	0.28	11	2	47	138	2.73

Very athletic outfielder who disappointed in college and short-season ball, but exhibits skills that project well. Present power below average, but should hit for moderate pop with better pitch recognition and selectivity. Has above average speed and plus range while getting good jumps and reads. Defense enhanced by instincts and average, accurate arm.

Cooper, David — 3 — Toronto

EXP MLB DEBUT: 2011 | POTENTIAL: Starting 1B | 8C

Bats L | Age 25
2008 (1) California
- Pwr +++
- BAvg ++++
- Spd +
- Def ++

Year	Lev	Team	AB	R	H	HR	RBI	Avg	OB	Slg	OPS	bb%	ct%	Eye	SB	CS	x/h%	Iso	RC/G
2008	A+	Dunedin	92	10	28	1	13	304	373	435	807	10	83	0.63	0	0	36	130	5.68
2009	AA	New Hampshire	473	62	122	10	66	258	340	389	729	11	81	0.64	0	0	34	131	4.70
2010	AA	New Hampshire	498	59	128	20	78	257	327	442	769	9	85	0.70	0	0	40	185	5.04
2011	AAA	Las Vegas	467	77	170	9	96	364	444	535	979	13	91	1.56	1	3	36	171	7.84
2011	MLB	Toronto	71	9	15	2	12	211	282	394	676	9	80	0.50	0	0	60	183	3.95

Contact-oriented, line-drive hitter was doubles machine and led PCL in BA. Reached TOR, but didn't hit well despite batting pedigree. Draws walks and makes outstanding contact with short, simple stroke. Lacks ideal power for 1B, but can swing for fences on occasion. Does not run well and stiff hands limit effectiveness with glove.

Cowart, Kaleb — 5 — Los Angeles (A)

EXP MLB DEBUT: 2014 | POTENTIAL: Starting 3B | 9C

Bats B | Age 20
2010 (1) HS (GA)
- Pwr ++++
- BAvg ++++
- Spd +++
- Def +++

Year	Lev	Team	AB	R	H	HR	RBI	Avg	OB	Slg	OPS	bb%	ct%	Eye	SB	CS	x/h%	Iso	RC/G
2010	Rk	Orem	5	1	2	1	3	400	500	1000	1500	17	60	0.50	0	0	50	600	17.17
2010	Rk	AZL Angels	21	0	3	0	4	143	143	143	286	0	71	0.00	0	0	0	0	
2011	Rk	Orem	283	49	80	7	40	283	341	420	761	8	71	0.31	11	4	28	138	5.02

Strong and athletic infielder with chance to become solid player with bat and glove. Shortened swing to make better contact, but still has power to all fields. Possesses good pop from both sides and makes proper adjustments for moderate BA despite subpar pitch recognition. Has good quickness and plus arm strength to be solid-average defender.

Cowgill, Collin — 8 — Oakland

EXP MLB DEBUT: 2011 | POTENTIAL: 4th OF | 7C

Bats R | Age 26
2008 (5) Kentucky
- Pwr +++
- BAvg +++
- 4.30 Spd +++
- Def +++

Year	Lev	Team	AB	R	H	HR	RBI	Avg	OB	Slg	OPS	bb%	ct%	Eye	SB	CS	x/h%	Iso	RC/G
2008	A	South Bend	201	31	50	1	17	249	332	358	690	11	70	0.41	1	0	34	109	4.34
2009	A+	Visalia	220	39	61	6	36	277	361	445	807	12	78	0.59	11	4	33	168	5.72
2010	AA	Mobile	502	89	143	16	83	285	358	464	822	10	85	0.78	25	9	38	179	5.77
2011	AAA	Reno	395	95	140	13	70	354	428	554	983	11	84	0.81	30	3	32	200	7.79
2011	MLB	AZ D'backs	92	8	22	1	9	239	300	304	604	8	70	0.29	4	2	18	65	2.84

Short and stocky outfielder with average tools across board. Offensive package begins with good bat speed and can put charge in ball with short, simple swing. Lacks projectable power, but has line drive stroke for doubles in gaps. Has fringe-average speed with good instincts while on base. Nothing special as corner OF with decent range and enough arm to be useful.

Cox, Zack — 5 — St. Louis

EXP MLB DEBUT: 2012 | POTENTIAL: Starting 3B | 8C

Bats L | Age 23
2010 (1) Arkansas
- Pwr +++
- BAvg ++++
- Spd +++
- Def ++

Year	Lev	Team	AB	R	H	HR	RBI	Avg	OB	Slg	OPS	bb%	ct%	Eye	SB	CS	x/h%	Iso	RC/G
2009	NCAA	Arkansas	199	41	53	13	39	266	333	558	891	9	67	0.31	1	2	57	291	7.00
2010	NCAA	Arkansas	238	67	102	9	48	429	500	609	1109	13	84	0.92	11	1	24	181	9.31
2010	Rk	GCL Cardinals	15	0	6	0	1	400	438	467	904	6	80	0.33	0	0	17	67	6.63
2011	A+	Palm Beach	164	22	55	3	20	335	377	439	816	6	82	0.38	2	2	20	104	5.43
2011	AA	Springfield	352	54	103	10	48	293	346	432	778	8	80	0.42	0	1	28	139	5.04

Compact, professional hitter has a short LH stroke and willingness to use the whole field. He has a flat swing that limits present power, but bat speed and plate discipline hint at future growth. He hit .306 in full-season debut and should compete for playing time at some point in '12. He is an instinctual player who runs the bases well. Solid defender at 3B with soft hands.

Coyle, Sean — 4 — Boston

EXP MLB DEBUT: 2014 | POTENTIAL: Starting 2B | 8C

Bats R | Age 20
2010 (3) HS (PA)
- Pwr +++
- BAvg +++
- Spd ++++
- Def +++

Year	Lev	Team	AB	R	H	HR	RBI	Avg	OB	Slg	OPS	bb%	ct%	Eye	SB	CS	x/h%	Iso	RC/G
2010	Rk	GCL Red Sox	10	5	2	0	0	200	273	300	573	9	90	1.00	0	0	50	100	3.13
2011	A	Greenville	384	77	95	14	64	247	349	464	813	14	71	0.55	20	6	51	216	6.01

Short and instinctual prospect who maximizes average tools. Makes consistent, hard contact from simple swing and exemplary hand-eye coordination to hit for BA and surprising, moderate pop. Focuses on hard line drives and knows value of taking pitches. Runs well and can steal bases, but may slow down as he matures. Makes routine plays with average arm.

Cozart, Zack — 6 — Cincinnati

EXP MLB DEBUT: 2011 | POTENTIAL: Reserve SS/2B | 7B

Bats R | Age 26
2007 (2) Mississippi
- Pwr ++++
- BAvg ++
- 4.35 Spd ++
- Def ++++

Year	Lev	Team	AB	R	H	HR	RBI	Avg	OB	Slg	OPS	bb%	ct%	Eye	SB	CS	x/h%	Iso	RC/G
2008	A	Dayton	418	57	117	14	49	280	319	457	776	5	82	0.31	3	3	34	177	4.90
2009	AA	Carolina	462	72	121	10	59	262	350	398	749	12	81	0.72	10	2	34	136	5.00
2010	AAA	Louisville	553	91	141	17	67	255	305	416	721	7	81	0.37	30	4	36	161	4.31
2011	AAA	Louisville	323	57	100	7	32	310	355	467	823	7	84	0.45	9	2	35	158	5.60
2011	MLB	Cincinnati	37	6	12	2	3	324	324	486	811	0	84	0.00	0	0	17	162	4.72

Athletic middle infielder with solid fundamentals. Strong defender with plus arm strength and soft hands, and has decent range despite below average speed. Makes solid contact with modest power and decent plate discipline. Nice MLB debut and should get plenty of AB in a utility role due to solid defense.

Crocker, Bobby — 89 — Oakland

EXP MLB DEBUT: 2014 | POTENTIAL: Starting OF | 8D

Bats R | Age 22
2011 (4) Cal Poly
- Pwr +++
- BAvg +++
- Spd ++++
- Def ++

Year	Lev	Team	AB	R	H	HR	RBI	Avg	OB	Slg	OPS	bb%	ct%	Eye	SB	CS	x/h%	Iso	RC/G
2009	NCAA	Cal Poly	127	31	41	5	24	323	377	488	865	8	71	0.30	10	2	27	165	6.38
2010	NCAA	Cal Poly	67	10	21	1	20	313	352	418	770	6	70	0.20	9	0	24	104	5.09
2011	NCAA	Cal Poly	189	37	64	5	20	339	396	497	893	9	79	0.46	9	2	30	159	6.61
2011	Rk	AZL Athletics	88	14	23	0	4	261	301	375	676	5	75	0.23	2	2	30	114	3.88
2011	A-	Vermont	118	19	38	3	15	322	365	441	806	6	81	0.36	6	1	21	119	5.28

Tall and strong outfielder who is blessed with plus speed and athleticism. Uses whole field with line drive swing, but needs to pull ball to live up to power potential. Knows how to put bat to ball and keeps barrel in hitting zone for long time. Steals bases, but lacks quickness and is destined for LF due to fringy arm strength. Has enough instincts for CF.

Cron, C.J. — 3 — Los Angeles (A)

EXP MLB DEBUT: 2013 | POTENTIAL: Starting 1B | 8B

Bats R Age 22
2011 (1) Utah
Pwr ++++
BAvg +++
Spd +
Def ++

Year	Lev	Team	AB	R	H	HR	RBI	Avg	OB	Slg	OPS	bb%	ct%	Eye	SB	CS	x/h%	Iso	RC/G
2009	NCAA	Utah	246	39	83	11	58	337	373	557	930	5	87	0.45	1	2	37	220	6.63
2010	NCAA	Utah	197	55	85	20	81	431	477	817	1294	8	88	0.74	0	0	42	386	10.68
2011	NCAA	Utah	198	51	86	15	59	434	511	803	1314	14	89	1.48	1	1	49	369	11.52
2011	Rk	Orem	143	30	44	13	41	308	353	629	982	7	76	0.29	0	0	43	322	7.40

Big and strong hitter who served as DH due to torn labrum. Stood out in short season league with mammoth power and natural hitting instincts. Long arms and swing can be exploited, but has ability to put charge into ball when he makes contact. Doesn't run well, but is a passable defender with enough range and arm strength.

Crouse, Michael — 9 — Toronto

EXP MLB DEBUT: 2015 | POTENTIAL: Starting OF | 8E

Bats R Age 21
2008 (16) HS (CAN)
Pwr +++
BAvg ++
Spd ++++
Def +++

Year	Lev	Team	AB	R	H	HR	RBI	Avg	OB	Slg	OPS	bb%	ct%	Eye	SB	CS	x/h%	Iso	RC/G
2008	Rk	GCL Blue Jays	15	2	2	0	0	133	278	267	544	17	53	0.43	1	1	50	133	2.56
2009	Rk	GCL Blue Jays	188	28	41	2	17	218	303	340	644	11	72	0.43	25	5	37	122	3.62
2010	Rk	GCL Blue Jays	96	17	32	4	20	333	390	594	984	9	67	0.28	9	6	44	260	8.61
2010	A	Lansing	88	11	19	2	9	216	324	386	710	14	60	0.40	5	2	47	170	4.99
2011	A	Lansing	364	73	95	14	55	261	341	475	816	11	69	0.39	38	8	47	214	6.01

Tall and extremely athletic outfielder who enjoyed success in first year of full-season ball. Showed off raw but exciting tools by hitting for good power and stealing bases with above average wheels. Overall game is still rough around edges, but additional polish could prove valuable. Plays decent defense in RF with cannon of arm.

Culberson, Charlie — 4 — San Francisco

EXP MLB DEBUT: 2012 | POTENTIAL: Starting 2B | 7C

Bats R Age 23
2007 (1-S) HS, (GA)
Pwr +++
BAvg +++
Spd +++
Def ++

Year	Lev	Team	AB	R	H	HR	RBI	Avg	OB	Slg	OPS	bb%	ct%	Eye	SB	CS	x/h%	Iso	RC/G
2007	Rk	AZL Giants	161	32	46	1	16	286	361	416	777	11	76	0.50	19	1	30	130	5.43
2008	A	Augusta	282	31	66	3	27	234	280	319	599	6	80	0.32	6	6	24	85	2.81
2009	A	Augusta	509	71	125	2	36	246	292	306	598	6	78	0.30	15	4	19	61	2.79
2010	A+	San Jose	503	80	146	16	71	290	334	457	791	6	80	0.33	25	7	33	167	5.14
2011	AA	Richmond	553	69	143	10	56	259	287	382	669	4	77	0.17	14	4	32	123	3.53

Offensive-minded 2B with a nice power and speed mix. Good bat speed, quick hands, and a willingness to use the whole field allow him to drive the ball. Can be overly aggressive at the plate, leading to poor plate discipline. Will need to improve and make more consistent contact. Has decent speed and is a good baserunner. Inconsistent defense will need to be resolved.

Culver, Cito — 6 — New York (A)

EXP MLB DEBUT: 2015 | POTENTIAL: Starting SS | 8C

Bats B Age 19
2010 (1) HS (NY)
Pwr ++
BAvg +++
Spd +++
Def ++++

Year	Lev	Team	AB	R	H	HR	RBI	Avg	OB	Slg	OPS	bb%	ct%	Eye	SB	CS	x/h%	Iso	RC/G
2010	Rk	GCL Yankees	160	21	43	2	18	269	324	363	686	8	74	0.32	6	3	23	94	3.96
2010	A-	Staten Island	43	2	8	0	0	186	314	209	523	16	77	0.80	1	1	13	23	2.20
2011	A-	Staten Island	276	40	69	2	33	250	324	337	660	10	79	0.53	10	0	26	87	3.81

Fundamentally solid infielder who is excellent defender with ideal quickness and smooth actions for SS. Has arm strength to gun down runners from hole and has keen instincts with glove. Not much offensive upside, though exhibits good bat speed despite length in swing. Not much power projection and is nothing more than average runner.

Cunningham, Jarek — 56 — Pittsburgh

EXP MLB DEBUT: 2013 | POTENTIAL: Starting 2B | 7D

Bats R Age 22
2008 (18) HS, (WA)
Pwr +++
BAvg +++
Spd +++
Def +++

Year	Lev	Team	AB	R	H	HR	RBI	Avg	OB	Slg	OPS	bb%	ct%	Eye	SB	CS	x/h%	Iso	RC/G
2008	Rk	GCL Pirates	148	20	47	5	22	318	377	507	883	9	82	0.54	2	1	36	189	6.41
2010	A	West Virginia	488	72	126	12	49	258	301	436	738	6	73	0.23	11	7	44	178	4.63
2011	Rk	GCL Pirates	5	2	2	0	0	400	400	400	800	0	100		0	0	0	0	4.93
2011	A+	Bradenton	310	53	80	15	51	258	297	516	813	5	74	0.21	5	2	55	258	5.52

Athletic 2B prospect has good range, good hands, and solid instincts. Improved power gives him an added tool and makes him a viable starter at 2B. Below average plate discipline and did make 22 errors. Has some work to do, but profiles as a solid offensive 2B.

Cunningham, Todd — 8 — Atlanta

EXP MLB DEBUT: 2013 | POTENTIAL: Backup OF | 7C

Bats B Age 23
2010 (2) Jacksonville State
Pwr ++
BAvg +++
3.90 Spd +++++
Def ++

Year	Lev	Team	AB	R	H	HR	RBI	Avg	OB	Slg	OPS	bb%	ct%	Eye	SB	CS	x/h%	Iso	RC/G
2009	NCAA	Jacksonville St	236	66	80	10	47	339	400	602	1002	9	90	1.00	9	2	41	263	7.79
2010	NCAA	Jacksonville St	237	61	85	11	42	359	449	603	1053	14	86	1.18	21	2	38	245	8.72
2010	A	Rome	231	32	60	1	20	260	302	338	640	6	87	0.47	7	4	22	78	3.49
2011	Rk	GCL Braves	11	2	2	0	4	182	250	364	614	8	55	0.20	1	0	50	182	3.98
2011	A+	Lynchburg	334	59	86	4	20	257	324	353	678	9	86	0.70	14	6	23	96	4.06

He lacks a true standout tool, but should be able to develop into a solid 4th OF. Mature approach and makes consistent contact with a short stroke. Has the strength and bat speed to hit for moderate power, but is more content with putting the ball in play and spraying line drives to the gaps. Runs well, but range is a little short for CF.

Curry, Matt — 3 — Pittsburgh

EXP MLB DEBUT: 2013 | POTENTIAL: Starting 1B | 8D

Bats L Age 23
2010 (16) TCU
Pwr ++++
BAvg +++
Spd +++
Def ++

Year	Lev	Team	AB	R	H	HR	RBI	Avg	OB	Slg	OPS	bb%	ct%	Eye	SB	CS	x/h%	Iso	RC/G
2009	NCAA	Texas Christian	162	30	51	3	31	315	413	444	857	14	75	0.68	2	2	27	130	6.60
2010	NCAA	Texas Christian	248	65	84	18	65	339	462	677	1140	19	80	1.14	12	5	55	339	10.21
2010	A-	State College	197	36	59	7	29	299	415	477	892	17	76	0.83	7	5	36	178	7.08
2011	A	West Virginia	155	39	56	9	34	361	479	671	1150	18	81	1.21	6	2	48	310	10.36
2011	AA	Altoona	302	38	73	6	39	242	316	374	691	10	70	0.37	1	1	34	132	4.17

Strong, athletic power bat with a solid understanding of the strike zone. Doesn't chase pitches he can't handle. Short, compact, powerful stroke and good extension give him good offensive upside. A below average runner but not a base clogger. Solid glove defensively, but the bat will be his ticket as he advances.

Custodio, Claudio — 46 — New York (A)

EXP MLB DEBUT: 2015 | POTENTIAL: Starting SS | 7A

Bats R Age 21
2010 FA (DR)
Pwr +
BAvg ++++
Spd ++++
Def ++++

Year	Lev	Team	AB	R	H	HR	RBI	Avg	OB	Slg	OPS	bb%	ct%	Eye	SB	CS	x/h%	Iso	RC/G
2011	Rk	GCL Yankees	157	46	51	1	19	325	408	414	822	12	75	0.55	26	2	22	89	6.09

Short and quick infielder who led GCL in SB. Possesses level, line drive stroke from right side and has discerning eye at plate which allows for high OBP. Offensive package enhanced by above average wheels. Can beat out infield grounders and tally SB with ease. No evidence of projectable power. Has excellent hands and feet along with average arm strength.

Cuthbert, Cheslor — 5 — Kansas City

EXP MLB DEBUT: 2013 | POTENTIAL: Starting 3B | 9D

Bats R Age 19
2009 FA (Nicaragua)
Pwr ++++
BAvg +++
Spd ++
Def +++

Year	Lev	Team	AB	R	H	HR	RBI	Avg	OB	Slg	OPS	bb%	ct%	Eye	SB	CS	x/h%	Iso	RC/G
2010	Rk	Idaho Falls	60	10	14	2	10	233	270	433	703	5	73	0.19	1	0	50	200	4.08
2010	Rk	AZL Royals	68	14	18	1	5	265	324	412	736	8	72	0.32	1	1	33	147	4.78
2011	A	Kane County	300	33	80	8	51	267	345	397	742	11	78	0.55	2	0	28	130	4.77

Advanced and fundamentally sound infielder who started strong and faded late. Profiles as prototypical 3B with strength, power, and average range. Nabs runners with very strong arm and has soft, quick hands. Swings bat with authority and uses whole field adeptly. Owns above average raw power and should reach potential by learning to read breaking balls better.

Danks, Jordan — 8 — Chicago (A)

EXP MLB DEBUT: 2012 | POTENTIAL: Starting OF | 8D

Bats L Age 25
2008 (7) Texas
Pwr +++
BAvg +++
Spd +++
Def ++++

Year	Lev	Team	AB	R	H	HR	RBI	Avg	OB	Slg	OPS	bb%	ct%	Eye	SB	CS	x/h%	Iso	RC/G
2008	A	Kannapolis	40	10	13	2	7	325	386	625	1011	9	65	0.29	1	0	54	300	9.22
2009	A+	Winston-Salem	118	25	38	3	21	322	412	525	937	13	73	0.56	5	1	42	203	7.78
2009	AA	Birmingham	284	50	69	6	20	243	330	356	686	12	74	0.51	7	3	28	113	4.10
2010	AAA	Charlotte	445	62	109	8	42	245	309	373	682	8	66	0.27	15	6	35	128	4.11
2011	AAA	Charlotte	463	65	119	14	65	257	338	425	764	11	67	0.37	18	4	37	168	5.36

Tall and athletic outfielder who may be putting together complete package. Set career high in HR, SB, and BB, though was 3rd in Ks while repeating IL. Exhibits natural hitting skills with ample plate coverage and average bat speed/power projection. Can be too pull-conscious. Solid defender due to excellent range, strong arm, and instincts.

d'Arnaud, Travis — 2 — Toronto

EXP MLB DEBUT: 2012 | POTENTIAL: Starting C | 8B

Bats R Age 23
2007 (1-S) HS (CA)
Pwr +++
BAvg ++++
Spd ++
Def +++

Year	Lev	Team	AB	R	H	HR	RBI	Avg	OB	Slg	OPS	bb%	ct%	Eye	SB	CS	x/h%	Iso	RC/G
2008	A-	Williamsport	175	21	54	4	25	309	373	463	836	9	83	0.62	1	2	33	154	5.92
2008	A	Lakewood	64	12	19	2	5	297	348	469	817	7	84	0.50	0	0	37	172	5.51
2009	A	Lakewood	482	71	123	13	71	255	314	419	733	8	84	0.55	8	4	42	164	4.59
2010	A+	Dunedin	263	36	68	6	38	259	311	411	722	7	76	0.32	3	1	40	152	4.40
2011	AA	New Hampshire	424	72	132	21	78	311	361	542	904	7	76	0.33	4	2	42	231	6.65

Tall and athletic backstop who underwent thumb surgery after setting career high in HR. EL MVP exhibits quality skills with bat and glove. Hits for nice BA by using hand-eye coordination and short swing. Launches balls to all fields, but drastic increase in Ks was troublesome. Footwork and accuracy need work, but has agility and average arm strength.

Darnell, James — 7 — San Diego

EXP MLB DEBUT: 2011 | POTENTIAL: Starting LF | **8B**

Bats R Age 25
2008 (2) South Carolina
Pwr +++
BAvg +++
4.30 Spd +++
Def +++

Year	Lev	Team	AB	R	H	HR	RBI	Avg	OB	Slg	OPS	bb%	ct%	Eye	SB	CS	x/h%	Iso	RC/G
2010	A	Fort Wayne	25	5	9	1	8	360	467	640	1107	17	84	1.25	0	0	56	280	9.72
2010	AA	San Antonio	373	46	99	10	50	265	343	408	750	11	83	0.69	2	0	32	142	4.91
2011	AA	San Antonio	288	62	96	17	62	333	435	604	1039	15	83	1.08	2	1	45	271	8.63
2011	AAA	Tucson	134	20	35	6	17	261	340	425	765	11	78	0.53	0	0	29	164	4.95
2011	MLB	San Diego	45	2	10	1	7	222	300	333	633	10	84	0.71	1	0	30	111	3.50

Strong 3B/OF prospect put together another impressive season at the plate. Plus plate discipline and solid bat speed allow him to control the strike zone and drive balls to all parts of the field. Struggled once he reached the majors, but should be able to hit for average and moderate to good power. Was moved from 3B to LF, but his bat is his ticket to regular MLB AB.

Davidson, Matt — 35 — Arizona

EXP MLB DEBUT: 2013 | POTENTIAL: Starting 3B | **8D**

Bats R Age 21
2009 (1) HS, (CA)
Pwr ++++
BAvg ++
Spd ++
Def ++

Year	Lev	Team	AB	R	H	HR	RBI	Avg	OB	Slg	OPS	bb%	ct%	Eye	SB	CS	x/h%	Iso	RC/G
2009	A-	Yakima	270	29	65	2	28	241	296	319	614	7	72	0.28	0	2	26	78	3.00
2010	A	South Bend	415	58	120	16	79	289	356	504	860	9	74	0.39	0	2	45	214	6.36
2010	A+	Visalia	71	6	12	2	11	169	289	268	557	14	65	0.48	0	0	25	99	2.18
2011	A+	Visalia	535	93	148	20	106	277	341	465	806	9	73	0.35	0	1	41	189	5.61

Solid follow-up to breakout in '10. Plus raw power and good bat speed, but needs better pitch recognition and to make more consistent contact (147 K). Short, quick stroke and willing to use the whole field. Is now an average defender with good hands, but is a below-average runner. Will need to work hard to stay at 3B.

Davis, Glynn — 8 — Baltimore

EXP MLB DEBUT: 2014 | POTENTIAL: Reserve OF | **7C**

Bats R Age 20
2010 FA (Catonsville CC)
Pwr ++
BAvg +++
Spd ++++
Def +++

Year	Lev	Team	AB	R	H	HR	RBI	Avg	OB	Slg	OPS	bb%	ct%	Eye	SB	CS	x/h%	Iso	RC/G
2011	Rk	GCL Orioles	23	4	10	1	2	435	519	652	1171	15	87	1.33	1	1	30	217	10.14
2011	A-	Aberdeen	255	34	69	1	14	271	336	337	673	9	79	0.47	23	9	22	67	3.91
2011	A+	Frederick	4	0	1	0	0	250	250	250	500	0	75	0.00	0	0	0	0	1.07

Tall and lean outfieler is among fastest prospects in baseball. Solid BA more a result of speed than hitting ability. Needs to hit balls on ground to take advantage of wheels and could improve bunting. Has power potential, but needs to figure out what kind of hitter he wants to be. Possesses plus range in CF with solid arm strength, but raw with routes and reads off bat.

Davis, Kentrail — 8 — Milwaukee

EXP MLB DEBUT: 2013 | POTENTIAL: Starting CF | **8D**

Bats L Age 23
2009 (1-S) Tennessee
Pwr +++
BAvg +++
4.10 Spd +++
Def +++

Year	Lev	Team	AB	R	H	HR	RBI	Avg	OB	Slg	OPS	bb%	ct%	Eye	SB	CS	x/h%	Iso	RC/G
2008	NCAA	Tennessee	206	45	68	13	44	330	400	583	983	10	73	0.43	7	2	34	252	7.96
2009	NCAA	Tennessee	214	58	66	9	30	308	401	528	929	13	78	0.69	4	1	38	220	7.35
2010	A	Wisconsin	245	44	82	3	46	335	409	518	928	11	85	0.86	3	1	41	184	7.27
2010	A+	Brevard County	123	20	30	0	17	244	336	341	677	12	77	0.61	8	2	23	98	4.21
2011	A+	Brevard County	507	76	124	8	46	245	296	361	657	7	81	0.38	33	8	28	116	3.59

Smallish/athletic sparkplug OF struggled in the pitcher-friendly FSL. Runs wells, controls the strike zone, and has a compact stroke and surprising power. Davis has plus speed and is starting to use it better. He can be overly aggressive and strikes out too much. Will need to be more patient to be an effective. Looked better in the AFL and is still a player to watch.

Davis, Khris — 7 — Milwaukee

EXP MLB DEBUT: 2013 | POTENTIAL: Starting LF | **7C**

Bats R Age 24
2009 (7) Cal State Fullerton
Pwr +++
BAvg ++
Spd +++
Def +++

Year	Lev	Team	AB	R	H	HR	RBI	Avg	OB	Slg	OPS	bb%	ct%	Eye	SB	CS	x/h%	Iso	RC/G
2009	Rk	Helena	1	0	0	0	0	0	0	0	0	0	100	#####	0	0	###	0	-2.66
2009	Rk	AZL Brewers	37	7	9	2	8	243	349	514	862	14	70	0.55	4	0	44	270	6.69
2010	A	Wisconsin	457	86	128	22	72	280	384	499	883	14	74	0.64	17	10	41	219	6.84
2011	A+	Brevard County	304	50	94	15	68	309	408	533	941	14	77	0.73	10	5	39	224	7.52
2011	AA	Huntsville	124	10	26	2	16	210	269	331	599	7	81	0.43	0	0	38	121	2.95

Strong, powerful OF prospect had a solid start in the FSL, hitting .309 with 15 home runs, earning a promotion to Double-A -- though struggled once he got there. Swing can get long at times, but he has good power, nice plate discipline, and above-average speed. LF is the most likely destination so power will need to continue to develop. If not, he's a 4th OF.

de la Cruz, Keury — 8 — Boston

EXP MLB DEBUT: 2015 | POTENTIAL: Reserve OF | **7D**

Bats L Age 20
2009 FA (DR)
Pwr ++
BAvg +++
Spd +++
Def +++

Year	Lev	Team	AB	R	H	HR	RBI	Avg	OB	Slg	OPS	bb%	ct%	Eye	SB	CS	x/h%	Iso	RC/G
2010	Rk	GCL Red Sox	198	35	52	6	31	263	321	475	796	8	75	0.34	9	6	44	212	5.48
2011	A-	Lowell	300	31	79	4	24	263	287	390	677	3	81	0.18	15	11	30	127	3.67

Toolsy and talented outfielder who failed to advance past short season ball. Possesses controlled swing with good bat speed and potential for average pop. Profiles more as doubles hitter. Approach and pitch recognition aren't yet up to snuff. Exhibits enough range to be asset in CF and arm strength sufficient for any position.

de la Cruz, Vicmal — 789 — Oakland

EXP MLB DEBUT: 2015 | POTENTIAL: Starting OF | **9E**

Bats L Age 18
2010 FA (DR)
Pwr ++++
BAvg +++
Spd +++
Def +++

Year	Lev	Team	AB	R	H	HR	RBI	Avg	OB	Slg	OPS	bb%	ct%	Eye	SB	CS	x/h%	Iso	RC/G
2011		Did not play																	

Strong and athletic outfielder who has yet to play in US, but exhibited plenty of tools in DSL. Bat speed gives him power potential, but needs experience against breaking balls. Tends to be pull-conscious, but swings with conviction. Isn't afraid to draw walks, but can be too patient. Plays all OF positions with plus speed and range.

Decker, Jaff — 7 — San Diego

EXP MLB DEBUT: 2013 | POTENTIAL: Starting LF | **8D**

Bats L Age 22
2008 (1) HS (AZ)
Pwr +++
BAvg +++
Spd +++
Def +++

Year	Lev	Team	AB	R	H	HR	RBI	Avg	OB	Slg	OPS	bb%	ct%	Eye	SB	CS	x/h%	Iso	RC/G
2008	Rk	AZL Padres	159	51	56	5	34	352	519	541	1060	26	77	1.53	9	1	32	189	9.91
2008	A-	Eugene	10	2	2	0	0	200	333	200	533	17	50	0.40	0	0	0	0	2.21
2009	A	Fort Wayne	358	78	107	16	64	299	433	514	947	19	74	0.92	10	6	40	215	7.99
2010	A+	Lake Elsinore	290	53	76	17	58	262	365	500	865	14	72	0.59	5	4	43	238	6.54
2011	AA	San Antonio	496	90	117	19	92	236	367	417	785	17	71	0.71	15	5	43	181	5.69

Short, compact player with good plate discipline and the ability to hit for average. Struggled as he modified his approach to generate more power. Did hit 19 home runs, but sacrificed too much contact. Plus arm strength, but his lack of athleticism and speed hinder him on defense. Has the potential to hit for average or power, but maybe not both. Did manage to walk 103 times.

Deglan, Kellin — 2 — Texas

EXP MLB DEBUT: 2014 | POTENTIAL: Starting C | **8D**

Bats L Age 20
2010 (1) HS (CAN)
Pwr +++
BAvg ++
Spd ++
Def ++++

Year	Lev	Team	AB	R	H	HR	RBI	Avg	OB	Slg	OPS	bb%	ct%	Eye	SB	CS	x/h%	Iso	RC/G
2010	Rk	AZL Rangers	28	5	8	0	5	286	333	357	690	7	75	0.29	0	0	13	71	4.05
2010	A-	Spokane	82	7	13	1	4	159	225	220	444	8	74	0.33	0	0	23	61	0.70
2011	A	Hickory	291	39	66	6	39	227	308	347	655	10	69	0.37	2	0	33	120	3.67

Tall and athletic catcher whose glove is further along than bat. Possesses agile footwork that combines with quality receiving and blocking. Also owns strong, accurate arm. Swings and misses frequently with a long swing and has difficulty reading breaking balls. Has potential to grow into power, but likely only average hitter at best.

DeJesus, Ivan — 64 — Los Angeles (N)

EXP MLB DEBUT: 2011 | POTENTIAL: Starting SS | **8C**

Bats R Age 25
2005 (2) HS P.R.
Pwr +
BAvg +++
4.35 Spd +++
Def ++++

Year	Lev	Team	AB	R	H	HR	RBI	Avg	OB	Slg	OPS	bb%	ct%	Eye	SB	CS	x/h%	Iso	RC/G
2008	AA	Jacksonville	463	91	150	7	58	324	419	423	843	14	83	0.94	16	2	20	99	6.30
2009	Rk	AZL Dodgers	10	1	2	0	3	200	273	300	573	9	40	0.17	0	0	50	100	4.80
2010	AAA	Albuquerque	533	89	158	7	70	296	336	405	742	6	85	0.40	6	1	27	109	4.58
2011	AAA	Albuquerque	387	61	120	8	59	310	382	432	813	10	82	0.66	4	1	24	121	5.69
2011	MLB	Los Angeles (N)	32	2	6	0	1	188	235	188	423	6	66	0.18	0	0	0	0	0.07

Athletic, sure-handed defender was moved from SS to 2B and made his MLB debut in '11. Quick bat that allows him to shoot line drives to all fields. Will not hit for power, but plays solid defense and uses short, compact stroke to hit for average, though does not walk enough or steal enoug bases to profile as a top of the order hitter.

DeJesus, Jharmidy — 35 — Seattle

EXP MLB DEBUT: 2014 | POTENTIAL: Starting 1B/3B | **8D**

Bats R Age 22
2007 FA (DR)
Pwr ++++
BAvg +++
Spd ++
Def +++

Year	Lev	Team	AB	R	H	HR	RBI	Avg	OB	Slg	OPS	bb%	ct%	Eye	SB	CS	x/h%	Iso	RC/G
2008	Rk	AZL Mariners	127	27	43	6	18	339	404	591	995	10	80	0.56	4	1	44	252	7.89
2008	A-	Everett	90	12	24	4	15	267	313	444	757	6	69	0.21	0	1	33	178	4.83
2009	Rk	Pulaski	169	19	42	4	24	249	306	385	691	8	75	0.33	0	2	31	136	4.00
2011	A-	Everett	201	31	60	4	33	299	356	408	764	8	79	0.43	3	0	22	109	4.94

Tall, lean, and athletic infielder who hasn't developed as much as hoped, but has been victim of injuries. Has never played full-season ball, but has terrific projection when healthy. Owns quick bat with brute, raw power and exhibits natural hitting skills. Decent defender due to strong arm and clean footwork. Just needs to play to show potential.

DeLeon, Kelvin — 9 — New York (A)

Bats L Age 21 | 2007 FA (DR)

EXP MLB DEBUT: 2014 | POTENTIAL: Starting OF | 8E

Pwr ++++ | BAvg ++ | Spd ++ | Def +++

Year	Lev	Team	AB	R	H	HR	RBI	Avg	OB	Slg	OPS	bb%	ct%	Eye	SB	CS	x/h%	Iso	RC/G
2009	Rk	GCL Yankees	201	28	54	7	31	269	323	438	760	7	70	0.26	5	1	37	169	4.99
2010	A-	Staten Island	259	33	61	6	37	236	283	359	642	6	69	0.21	5	1	31	124	3.30
2011	A	Charleston (SC)	453	54	100	14	60	221	272	369	641	7	68	0.22	0	1	38	148	3.30

Lean and athletic outfielder who has yet to capitalize on natural hitting instincts. Uses compact swing to generate plus power to all fields and has enough loft and backspin to hit mammoth shots ... when he makes contact. Continues to be free swinger and offers little to no ability to work counts. Decent defender with strong arm, though below average speed.

Delmonico, Nick — 5 — Baltimore

Bats L Age 19 | 2011 (6) HS (TN)

EXP MLB DEBUT: 2015 | POTENTIAL: Starting 3B | 8C

Pwr ++++ | BAvg +++ | Spd ++ | Def ++

Year	Lev	Team	AB	R	H	HR	RBI	Avg	OB	Slg	OPS	bb%	ct%	Eye	SB	CS	x/h%	Iso	RC/G
2011		Did not play																	

Big and strong hitter whose best tools revolve around offensive game. Takes vicious hacks at pitches, often times when not in strike zone, but balls travels far when he connects. Has plenty of strength in swing for power to all fields. Should hit for BA with a few adjustments. Defense is question mark as he displays poor footwork and stiff hands. Arm is strong for corner position.

Den Dekker, Matt — 8 — New York (N)

Bats L Age 24 | 2010 (5) U. of Florida

EXP MLB DEBUT: 2013 | POTENTIAL: Starting CF | 8C

Pwr +++ | BAvg +++ | 4.10 Spd ++++ | Def ++++

Year	Lev	Team	AB	R	H	HR	RBI	Avg	OB	Slg	OPS	bb%	ct%	Eye	SB	CS	x/h%	Iso	RC/G
2010	NCAA	Florida	247	65	87	13	49	352	422	563	985	11	80	0.61	23	7	26	211	7.72
2010	Rk	GCL Mets	18	2	5	0	5	278	350	389	739	10	72	0.40	0	0	40	111	4.99
2010	A	Savannah	104	21	36	0	15	346	398	471	869	8	73	0.32	3	0	36	125	6.66
2011	A+	St. Lucie	267	54	79	6	36	296	354	494	848	8	76	0.37	12	5	42	199	6.22
2011	AA	Binghamton	272	49	64	11	32	235	304	426	731	9	67	0.30	12	5	42	191	4.73

Speedy CF had a huge breakout season, showing surprising power. Den Dekker runs well and has a short line-drive stroke. Knock on him was that he had below average power, but his extra-base production in 2011 was legit. He frequently sold out for the power and might not be able to hit for average and power. Doesn't get the attention he should.

DeShields, Delino — 4 — Houston

Bats R Age 19 | 2010 (1) HS, (GA)

EXP MLB DEBUT: 2014 | POTENTIAL: Starting 2B | 8D

Pwr +++ | BAvg +++ | 4.3/40 Spd ++++ | Def +++

Year	Lev	Team	AB	R	H	HR	RBI	Avg	OB	Slg	OPS	bb%	ct%	Eye	SB	CS	x/h%	Iso	RC/G
2010	Rk	GCL Astros	9	3	1	0	0	111	200	111	311	10	78	0.50	0	0	0	0	-0.77
2010	Rk	Greeneville	67	11	21	0	8	313	361	433	794	7	73	0.28	5	1	33	119	5.57
2011	A	Lexington	469	73	103	9	48	220	298	322	619	10	75	0.44	30	11	27	102	3.14

8th overall pick in the '10 draft struggled in his full-season debut. He does have good speed. Has good athleticism, a strong throwing arm, covers ground well, and could develop into a solid run producer, but will need to hit. Needs to be more selective and make more contact. Good bat speed and a compact stroke. Still has potential, but will need to show more.

DeVoss, Zeke — 4 — Chicago (N)

Bats B Age 21 | 2011 (3) Miami-FL

EXP MLB DEBUT: 2013 | POTENTIAL: Starting 2B | 7B

Pwr ++ | BAvg ++++ | Spd +++ | Def +++

Year	Lev	Team	AB	R	H	HR	RBI	Avg	OB	Slg	OPS	bb%	ct%	Eye	SB	CS	x/h%	Iso	RC/G
2010	NCAA	Miami	211	49	53	9	33	251	336	450	786	11	76	0.54	24	4	40	199	5.35
2011	NCAA	Miami	215	59	73	2	27	340	478	456	934	21	86	1.90	32	10	25	116	7.94
2011	Rk	AZL Cubs	17	4	5	0	3	294	333	353	686	6	76	0.25	2	0	20	59	3.90
2011	A-	Boise	132	28	41	0	14	311	445	386	831	20	79	1.14	14	4	22	76	6.61

Short but talented 2B prospect has plus offensive tools that include contact ability, speed, and plate discipline. Used advanced understanding of strike zone to hit in pro debut. Doesn't have much power, but did steal 16 bases. Moves well defensively and has a strong arm. Projects as a future lead-off hitter.

Dickerson, Alex — 7 — Pittsburgh

Bats L Age 22 | 2011 (3) Indiana

EXP MLB DEBUT: 2014 | POTENTIAL: Starting LF | 8D

Pwr ++++ | BAvg +++ | Spd ++ | Def ++

Year	Lev	Team	AB	R	H	HR	RBI	Avg	OB	Slg	OPS	bb%	ct%	Eye	SB	CS	x/h%	Iso	RC/G
2009	NCAA	Indiana	238	45	88	14	57	370	414	618	1032	7	80	0.38	2	4	34	248	8.04
2010	NCAA	Indiana	236	62	99	24	75	419	465	805	1270	8	85	0.57	3	2	43	386	10.56
2011	NCAA	Indiana	215	33	79	9	49	367	431	540	970	10	90	1.14	2	1	24	172	7.36
2011	A-	State College	150	25	47	3	19	313	380	493	873	10	81	0.57	0	0	43	180	6.48

Tall, athletic OF had a solid pro debut. Has good power potential and a smooth LH stroke. At times, struggles with quality breaking balls and can be overly pull conscious. Hit righties and lefties equally and made nice adjusments throughout the year. Range and speed are below average so will need to hit to have value.

Dickerson, Corey — 7 — Colorado

Bats L Age 23 | 2010 (8) Meridian CC, MS

EXP MLB DEBUT: 2014 | POTENTIAL: Backup OF | 7D

Pwr +++ | BAvg +++ | Spd ++ | Def ++

Year	Lev	Team	AB	R	H	HR	RBI	Avg	OB	Slg	OPS	bb%	ct%	Eye	SB	CS	x/h%	Iso	RC/G
2010	Rk	Casper	276	54	96	13	61	348	408	634	1042	9	82	0.55	12	6	46	286	8.44
2011	A	Asheville	383	78	108	32	87	282	348	629	978	9	74	0.39	9	6	59	347	7.72

Tall, athletic prospect with impressive power. Hit 27 doubles and 32 home runs, but did not impress in other aspects of his game. Was moved from 3B to CF where he is a an average runner with a below average arm. Home/road split tells an important story. Hit just .193/.280/.363 with 6 home runs on the road.

Dickson, O'Koyea — 3 — Los Angeles (N)

Bats R Age 22 | 2011 (12) Sonoma St

EXP MLB DEBUT: 2013 | POTENTIAL: Backup 1B | 8D

Pwr ++++ | BAvg +++ | Spd ++ | Def ++

Year	Lev	Team	AB	R	H	HR	RBI	Avg	OB	Slg	OPS	bb%	ct%	Eye	SB	CS	x/h%	Iso	RC/G
2011	Rk	Ogden	189	33	63	13	38	333	394	603	997	9	77	0.43	1	1	38	270	7.85

Impressive debut. Drives the ball well with good bat speed. At 5'10", 220 lbs, he is physically mature, but a bit short for 1B. Handles the position well, but will need to rake to have any value.

Dietrich, Derek — 6 — Tampa Bay

Bats L Age 22 | 2010 (2) Georgia Tech

EXP MLB DEBUT: 2013 | POTENTIAL: Starting 3B | 7A

Pwr +++ | BAvg +++ | Spd ++ | Def ++

Year	Lev	Team	AB	R	H	HR	RBI	Avg	OB	Slg	OPS	bb%	ct%	Eye	SB	CS	x/h%	Iso	RC/G
2008	NCAA	Georgia Tech	238	53	79	14	66	332	398	592	990	10	79	0.52	3	1	41	261	7.78
2009	NCAA	Georgia Tech	225	61	70	10	54	311	392	511	903	12	79	0.63	5	0	30	200	6.84
2010	NCAA	Georgia Tech	240	68	84	17	61	350	418	650	1068	10	85	0.76	8	4	42	300	8.54
2010	A-	Hudson Valley	179	33	50	3	20	279	321	419	740	6	77	0.26	2	2	34	140	4.60
2011	A	Bowling Green	480	73	133	22	81	277	330	502	832	7	73	0.30	5	7	45	225	5.85

Strong and steady infielder who finished 3rd in MWL in HR. Showed improved batting eye and ability to use whole field. Generates moderate power, but will likely be doubles hitter at higher levels. Needs better strike zone management and has shown difficulty against LHP. Projects better at 2B or 3B where lack of range and quickness are more suitable.

Dixon, Rashun — 79 — Oakland

Bats R Age 21 | 2008 (10) HS (MS)

EXP MLB DEBUT: 2013 | POTENTIAL: Starting OF | 8E

Pwr +++ | BAvg +++ | Spd ++++ | Def ++

Year	Lev	Team	AB	R	H	HR	RBI	Avg	OB	Slg	OPS	bb%	ct%	Eye	SB	CS	x/h%	Iso	RC/G
2008	Rk	AZL Athletics	179	32	47	8	42	263	330	525	855	9	62	0.26	5	2	45	263	7.06
2009	A-	Vancouver	196	25	42	2	16	214	297	281	577	11	63	0.32	6	4	21	66	2.59
2010	A	Kane County	444	69	122	8	54	275	359	383	741	12	70	0.43	9	7	24	108	4.96
2011	A+	Stockton	456	74	111	11	47	243	314	379	694	9	70	0.35	3	5	32	136	4.15

Ultra athletic prospect with potential for speed and power production. Hit career high in HR and natural power starting to emerge. Advancing moderately while developing swing mechanics. Chases pitches, but can also be tentative at plate. May not hit for BA with long swing and tendency to fan. Raw defender with OK range and routes.

Dominguez, Chris — 5 — San Francisco

Bats R Age 25 | 2009 (3) Louisville

EXP MLB DEBUT: 2013 | POTENTIAL: Starting 1B | 8D

Pwr ++++ | BAvg ++ | Spd ++ | Def ++

Year	Lev	Team	AB	R	H	HR	RBI	Avg	OB	Slg	OPS	bb%	ct%	Eye	SB	CS	x/h%	Iso	RC/G
2009	Rk	AZL Giants	36	8	11	2	8	306	359	528	887	8	75	0.33	1	0	36	222	6.43
2009	A-	Salem-Keizer	181	31	46	9	32	254	289	442	731	5	69	0.16	11	2	33	188	4.39
2010	A	Augusta	559	85	152	21	101	272	315	456	771	6	76	0.26	14	7	38	184	4.89
2011	A+	San Jose	258	40	75	11	40	291	337	465	802	7	72	0.25	8	2	29	174	5.38
2011	AA	Richmond	295	35	72	7	45	244	266	403	670	3	74	0.12	1	5	43	159	3.55

Strong-armed, athletic 3B with plus raw power continues to make progress. Continues to work on shortening his stroke and making more consistent contact, but struggles with pitch recognition and will need to cut down on Ks. Defensively he moves reasonably well and has a strong throwing arm. If contact issues can be resolved, he has enough bat to make an impact.

Dominguez, Matt — 5 — Florida
EXP MLB DEBUT: 2011 | POTENTIAL: Starting 3B | 7B

Bats R Age 22
2007 (1) HS, (CA)
Pwr +++
BAvg +++
4.35 Spd ++
Def +++++

Year	Lev	Team	AB	R	H	HR	RBI	Avg	OB	Slg	OPS	bb%	ct%	Eye	SB	CS	x/h%	Iso	RC/G
2010	AA	Jacksonville	504	61	127	14	81	252	327	411	738	10	81	0.58	0	2	39	159	4.72
2011	A+	Jupiter	18	0	3	0	2	167	211	167	377	5	83	0.33	0	0	0	0	0.19
2011	AA	Jacksonville	15	1	2	0	1	133	278	133	411	17	87	1.50	0	0	0	0	1.34
2011	AAA	New Orleans	325	47	84	12	55	258	309	431	740	7	85	0.48	0	1	37	172	4.55
2011	MLB	Florida	45	2	11	0	2	244	277	333	610	4	82	0.25	0	0	36	89	3.00

A fractured elbow in April cost him 8 weeks and a chance to win the starting 3B job in Florida. When he returned he struggled to hit. Did see action in the majors in September, but fared no better. Possesses plus defense with arm strength, soft hands, and quickness. Has yet to have a breakout season and questions about his ability to hit must be answered.

Domoromo, Luis — 8 — San Diego
EXP MLB DEBUT: 2014 | POTENTIAL: Starting RF | 8D

Bats L Age 20
2008 NDFA Venz.
Pwr +++
BAvg +++
Spd ++++
Def +++

Year	Lev	Team	AB	R	H	HR	RBI	Avg	OB	Slg	OPS	bb%	ct%	Eye	SB	CS	x/h%	Iso	RC/G
2010	A-	Eugene	113	12	31	1	8	274	311	345	656	5	80	0.26	0	0	19	71	3.44
2011	A	Fort Wayne	435	66	123	9	68	283	338	405	742	8	81	0.43	7	7	26	122	4.64

Raw but talented OF prospect had solid full-season debut in the MWL. Good speed and athleticism and plus bat speed hints at long-term power upside. Needs to improve plate discipline and refine overall game, but there is some nice potential here.

Donaldson, Josh — 2 — Oakland
EXP MLB DEBUT: 2010 | POTENTIAL: Platoon C | 7C

Bats R Age 26
2007 (1-S) Auburn
Pwr +++
BAvg ++
Spd ++
Def ++

Year	Lev	Team	AB	R	H	HR	RBI	Avg	OB	Slg	OPS	bb%	ct%	Eye	SB	CS	x/h%	Iso	RC/G
2008	A+	Stockton	188	37	62	9	39	330	385	564	949	8	85	0.59	0	2	39	234	7.09
2009	AA	Midland	455	67	123	9	91	270	379	415	795	15	80	0.87	7	2	38	145	5.77
2010	AAA	Sacramento	294	52	70	18	67	238	339	476	815	13	73	0.57	3	1	47	238	5.77
2010	MLB	Oakland	32	1	5	1	4	156	206	281	487	6	63	0.17	0	0	40	125	0.96
2011	AAA	Sacramento	444	79	116	17	70	261	337	439	777	10	77	0.51	13	4	39	178	5.17

Strong backstop who produces moderate power from average bat speed and strength. Pitch selectivity enhances OBP, but long, loopy swing detracts from BA potential. Possesses average arm, though quick release neutralizes running game. Blocking and receiving may not be good enough to earn starting role, but bat gives him chance.

Dozier, Brian — 46 — Minnesota
EXP MLB DEBUT: 2012 | POTENTIAL: Starting 2B | 7A

Bats R Age 25
2009 (8) Southern Miss
Pwr ++
BAvg ++++
Spd +++
Def +++

Year	Lev	Team	AB	R	H	HR	RBI	Avg	OB	Slg	OPS	bb%	ct%	Eye	SB	CS	x/h%	Iso	RC/G
2009	Rk	Elizabethton	218	38	77	0	14	353	415	431	846	10	88	0.88	3	0	22	78	6.14
2010	A	Beloit	151	24	42	0	17	278	347	338	685	10	89	1.00	6	1	19	60	4.32
2010	A+	Fort Myers	350	44	96	5	42	274	355	354	710	11	88	1.07	10	4	18	80	4.58
2011	A+	Fort Myers	180	32	58	2	22	322	411	472	883	13	89	1.35	13	4	31	150	6.83
2011	AA	New Britain	311	60	99	7	34	318	375	502	876	8	85	0.61	11	7	36	183	6.37

Short and instinctual infielder who makes up for lack of athleticism with mature approach on both sides of the ball. Posted career high in HR, 2B, and SB while featuring good glove at SS. Rarely Ks and will draw walks by being selective at plate. Steals bases more on instincts than speed, but has enough wheels to post double-digit SB. Won't be a star, but should produce.

Drury, Brandon — 5 — Atlanta
EXP MLB DEBUT: 2015 | POTENTIAL: Starting 3B | 8D

Bats R Age 19
2010 (13) HS, (OR)
Pwr +++
BAvg +++
Spd ++
Def ++

Year	Lev	Team	AB	R	H	HR	RBI	Avg	OB	Slg	OPS	bb%	ct%	Eye	SB	CS	x/h%	Iso	RC/G
2010	Rk	GCL Braves	192	20	38	3	17	198	234	292	525	4	74	0.18	2	2	29	94	1.66
2011	Rk	Danville	265	40	92	8	54	347	362	525	886	2	87	0.17	3	0	34	177	5.95

Drury made progress in '11, hitting .347. He has a short, compact stroke allows him to drive the ball into the gaps. Moved to 3B after turning pro; he is a work in progress. Strong throwing arm, but below average speed and range. Will need better plate discipline and pitch recognition to maintain this average, a 2% walk rate isn't going to cut it.

Dugan, Kelly — 379 — Philadelphia
EXP MLB DEBUT: 2014 | POTENTIAL: Starting RF | 7D

Bats B Age 21
2009 (2) HS (CA)
Pwr +++
BAvg ++
Spd ++
Def +++

Year	Lev	Team	AB	R	H	HR	RBI	Avg	OB	Slg	OPS	bb%	ct%	Eye	SB	CS	x/h%	Iso	RC/G
2009	Rk	GCL Phillies	150	18	35	0	8	233	290	300	590	7	80	0.40	9	5	26	67	2.85
2010	Rk	GCL Phillies	33	12	19	1	4	576	622	848	1470	11	88	1.00	2	2	32	273	13.39
2010	A-	Williamsport	60	6	15	0	4	250	308	350	658	8	72	0.29	0	0	40	100	3.75
2011	A-	Williamsport	176	25	50	2	21	284	337	386	723	7	81	0.41	6	0	20	102	4.45

Tall, switch-hitting OF has good raw power, but it doesn't show up in game action. His swing can get long and he still has work to do at the plate. He has good speed and enough arm strength to play a corner OF spot. A back injury limited him to just 47 games in 2011 and he has been injury prone.

Dunston Jr, Shawon — 8 — Chicago (N)
EXP MLB DEBUT: 2015 | POTENTIAL: Starting CF | 8D

Bats L Age 19
2011 (11) HS (CA)
Pwr +++
BAvg +++
Spd +++
Def +++

Year	Lev	Team	AB	R	H	HR	RBI	Avg	OB	Slg	OPS	bb%	ct%	Eye	SB	CS	x/h%	Iso	RC/G
2011		Did not play																	

Tall, projectable CF is the son of former major leaguer by the same name. Dropped to 11th round due to signability concerns. At 6'2" 170, he is still growing into his body and has yet to make his pro debut. Still raw both on offense and defense, but moves well and has nice loose athleticism from the LH side. Will make his pro debut in '12.

Duran, Juan — 8 — Cincinnati
EXP MLB DEBUT: 2014 | POTENTIAL: Starting RF | 8D

Bats R Age 20
2008 NDFA D.R.
Pwr ++++
BAvg ++
Spd ++++
Def ++++

Year	Lev	Team	AB	R	H	HR	RBI	Avg	OB	Slg	OPS	bb%	ct%	Eye	SB	CS	x/h%	Iso	RC/G
2009	Rk	GCL Reds	164	15	29	0	17	177	215	268	483	5	68	0.15	0	0	38	91	1.18
2010	Rk	Billings	201	23	49	6	25	244	309	393	702	9	65	0.27	2	3	35	149	4.38
2011	A	Dayton	367	48	97	16	71	264	327	463	790	8	59	0.22	1	4	40	199	6.16

Tall/athletic outfielder showed some signs of life offensively. Bat speed provides power to all fields, and centers ball well. Decent range with a strong arm, but continued poor plate discipline undercuts potential. He will need to make progress soon to realize his potential. Too much of a free swinger right now.

Dykstra, Allan — 3 — New York (N)
EXP MLB DEBUT: 2013 | POTENTIAL: Starting 1B | 7D

Bats L Age 25
2008 (1) Wake Forest
Pwr ++++
BAvg +++
4.50 Spd +
Def ++

Year	Lev	Team	AB	R	H	HR	RBI	Avg	OB	Slg	OPS	bb%	ct%	Eye	SB	CS	x/h%	Iso	RC/G
2008	NCAA	Wake Forest	186	51	60	16	50	323	492	645	1137	25	76	1.38	7	1	47	323	10.59
2008	A+	Lake Elsinore	24	5	7	1	10	292	452	458	910	23	71	1.00	0	0	29	167	7.70
2009	A	Fort Wayne	411	71	93	11	60	226	383	375	757	20	75	1.01	1	2	39	148	5.44
2010	A+	Lake Elsinore	386	54	93	16	70	241	369	438	806	17	68	0.64	1	4	45	197	6.05
2011	AA	Binghamton	390	57	104	19	77	267	377	474	851	15	66	0.53	1	1	40	208	6.71

Tall, strong 1B prospect generates power from his uppercut swing and draws walks, but is stiff at the plate and can be beat up and in and down and away. Lacks pitch recognition, which cut into his BA ability. Defense is below average, lacking agility and ability to scoop throws in the dirt. Power gives him a chance.

Dykstra, Cutter — 8 — Washington
EXP MLB DEBUT: 2014 | POTENTIAL: Backup CF | 6C

Bats R Age 22
2008 (2) HS (CA)
Pwr ++
BAvg ++++
4.15 Spd ++++
Def +++

Year	Lev	Team	AB	R	H	HR	RBI	Avg	OB	Slg	OPS	bb%	ct%	Eye	SB	CS	x/h%	Iso	RC/G
2008	Rk	AZL Brewers	26	5	7	0	0	269	387	269	656	16	73	0.71	0	1	0	0	3.93
2009	Rk	Helena	209	35	51	5	26	244	331	349	680	11	76	0.54	14	4	22	105	3.98
2009	A	Wisconsin	99	16	21	1	7	212	297	303	600	11	73	0.44	4	2	29	91	2.96
2010	A	Wisconsin	353	66	110	5	39	312	404	411	815	13	80	0.76	27	8	18	99	5.93
2011	A+	Potomac	306	26	65	1	27	212	263	265	528	6	73	0.26	12	4	20	52	1.80

Athletic OF struggled at High-A, hitting just .212 with only 1 home run. Moderate bat speed produces line-drive power. Contact rate and plate discipline eroded badly in '11. He runs the bases aggressively, but has only average speed. Ranges well in CF, but lacks arm strength and proper route-taking. Will need to prove that '11 was a fluke and time is running out.

Eaton, Adam — 9 — Arizona
EXP MLB DEBUT: 2013 | POTENTIAL: Starting CF | 8B

Bats L Age 23
2010 (19) Miami, OH
Pwr +++
BAvg +++
Spd ++++
Def ++++

Year	Lev	Team	AB	R	H	HR	RBI	Avg	OB	Slg	OPS	bb%	ct%	Eye	SB	CS	x/h%	Iso	RC/G
2009	NCAA	Miami	214	67	75	11	48	350	416	617	1033	10	87	0.89	28	1	39	266	8.16
2010	NCAA	Miami	220	64	81	13	55	368	421	709	1130	8	86	0.67	30	4	49	341	9.23
2010	Rk	Missoula	226	48	87	7	37	385	467	575	1043	13	81	0.80	20	8	29	190	8.78
2011	A+	Visalia	244	54	81	6	39	332	430	492	922	15	83	1.02	24	8	30	160	7.31
2011	AA	Mobile	212	31	64	4	28	302	388	429	818	12	83	0.86	10	6	23	127	5.89

Short (5'9"), athletic OF had a breakout season in '11. Isn't going to hit for much power, but he has solid plate discipline, gap power, and plus speed. Because of his size, he doesn't get much attention, but has hit at every stop. Needs to stay back on the ball better, but is a scrappy player who understands the game. Range might be a bit short for CF but he is fun to watch.

Eibner, Brett — 89 — Kansas City

EXP MLB DEBUT: 2013 | POTENTIAL: Starting OF | 8C

Bats R Age 23
2010 (2) Arkansas

- Pwr ++++
- BAvg ++
- Spd +++
- Def +++

Year	Lev	Team	AB	R	H	HR	RBI	Avg	OB	Slg	OPS	bb%	ct%	Eye	SB	CS	x/h%	Iso	RC/G
2008	NCAA	Arkansas	191	36	57	8	48	298	388	497	886	13	76	0.61	3	3	35	199	6.76
2009	NCAA	Arkansas	147	34	34	12	34	231	365	510	875	17	59	0.52	3	5	47	279	7.42
2010	NCAA	Arkansas	216	66	72	22	71	333	435	718	1153	15	75	0.71	3	0	54	384	10.28
2011	A	Kane County	272	46	58	12	31	213	331	408	739	15	67	0.53	2	3	47	195	4.99

Tall and strong outfielder who missed two months with thumb injury and struggled. Exhibits plus power when he makes contact, but swings through pitches with long stroke. Draws walks with patient approach, but inability to make contact hinders BA potential. Arm is ideal for RF and runs well for size. Will need to make progress soon, but has talent to do so.

Eldemire, Gauntlett — 8 — Philadelphia

EXP MLB DEBUT: 2014 | POTENTIAL: Starting CF | 8E

Bats R Age 23
2010 (6) Ohio University

- Pwr +++
- BAvg +++
- Spd +++ (6.3/60)
- Def +++

Year	Lev	Team	AB	R	H	HR	RBI	Avg	OB	Slg	OPS	bb%	ct%	Eye	SB	CS	x/h%	Iso	RC/G
2008	NCAA	Ohio	178	36	47	7	35	264	325	466	791	8	78	0.40	10	1	43	202	5.28
2009	NCAA	Ohio	198	61	62	21	56	313	414	682	1096	15	78	0.79	11	2	47	369	9.18
2010	NCAA	Ohio	201	59	80	16	55	398	478	726	1205	13	77	0.67	16	5	41	328	10.80

Toolsy, athletic OF missed all of '11 with a wrist injury. Prior to the injury he showed good raw power and speed potential. He has plus bat speed, but takes vicious cuts and is likely to strikeout in abundance without a better approach. He runs well and has the potential to be a 20/20, but will need to prove he is healthy in 2012.

Erickson, Gorman — 2 — Los Angeles (N)

EXP MLB DEBUT: 2013 | POTENTIAL: Starting C | 7D

Bats B Age 24
2006 (15) HS, (CA)

- Pwr +++
- BAvg +++
- Spd ++
- Def ++

Year	Lev	Team	AB	R	H	HR	RBI	Avg	OB	Slg	OPS	bb%	ct%	Eye	SB	CS	x/h%	Iso	RC/G
2008	AAA	Las Vegas	5	0	0	0	0	0	0	0	0	0	60	0.00	0	0			
2009	Rk	Ogden	197	40	60	5	36	305	380	482	862	11	82	0.67	0	0	40	178	6.36
2010	A	Great Lakes	261	32	56	2	27	215	305	310	615	12	83	0.76	3	0	32	96	3.43
2011	A+	Rancho Cucamg	226	37	69	6	40	305	412	491	903	15	81	0.98	3	2	38	186	7.15
2011	AA	Chattanooga	142	18	39	7	26	275	327	479	806	7	85	0.50	1	0	38	204	5.27

Tall, strong, switch-htting backstop. Has a solid approach with plus plate discipline, good power, and the ability to hit for average. Erickson is a an average receiver with a decent arm, but his ticket to the majors is his bat. Overall had a solid season of growth offensively and could surprise in '12.

Escobar, Eduardo — 46 — Chicago (A)

EXP MLB DEBUT: 2011 | POTENTIAL: Starting SS | 8C

Bats B Age 23
2006 FA (Venezuela)

- Pwr ++
- BAvg +++
- Spd ++++
- Def ++++

Year	Lev	Team	AB	R	H	HR	RBI	Avg	OB	Slg	OPS	bb%	ct%	Eye	SB	CS	x/h%	Iso	RC/G
2009	A	Kannapolis	464	64	119	3	41	256	300	328	628	6	80	0.32	20	6	17	71	3.18
2010	A+	Winston-Salem	368	57	105	3	39	285	327	402	730	6	79	0.30	8	5	28	117	4.49
2010	AA	Birmingham	202	22	53	3	22	262	294	376	670	4	83	0.26	3	0	26	114	3.63
2011	AAA	Charlotte	489	55	130	4	49	266	304	354	658	5	79	0.26	13	8	24	88	3.51
2011	MLB	Chicago WSox	7	0	2	0	0	286	286	286	571	0	86	0.00	0	0	0	0	2.18

Short and thin infielder with fundamental skills and solid defense. Likely won't have much power in majors, but quick bat and hands produce BA potential. Needs to work counts better in order to get on base and use above average wheels. Plus range at SS with average, accurate arm. Has instincts to be legitimate contributor in number of ways.

Esposito, Jason — 5 — Baltimore

EXP MLB DEBUT: 2014 | POTENTIAL: Starting 3B | 7B

Bats R Age 21
2011 (2) Vanderbilt

- Pwr ++
- BAvg +++
- Spd +++
- Def ++++

Year	Lev	Team	AB	R	H	HR	RBI	Avg	OB	Slg	OPS	bb%	ct%	Eye	SB	CS	x/h%	Iso	RC/G
2009	NCAA	Vanderbilt	237	39	68	4	42	287	332	401	733	6	80	0.33	20	5	26	114	4.47
2010	NCAA	Vanderbilt	262	65	94	12	64	359	432	599	1032	11	87	0.97	31	4	40	240	8.27
2011	NCAA	Vanderbilt	268	55	91	9	59	340	379	530	909	6	83	0.38	15	10	35	190	6.52

Tall and strong infielder with potential to be impact defender. Exhibits quickness and great hands at 3B while possessing strong, accurate arm. Can make routine and difficult plays. A hitch in swing hinders power, but BA potential is average. Can lace line drives to gaps and offer some semblance of over-the-wall power, particularly with fastballs up and in.

Exposito, Luis — 2 — Boston

EXP MLB DEBUT: 2012 | POTENTIAL: Backup C | 7C

Bats R Age 25
2005 (31) St. Petersburg JC

- Pwr +++
- BAvg ++
- Spd +
- Def +++

Year	Lev	Team	AB	R	H	HR	RBI	Avg	OB	Slg	OPS	bb%	ct%	Eye	SB	CS	x/h%	Iso	RC/G
2008	A+	Lancaster	226	31	68	10	37	301	328	509	837	4	79	0.19	0	1	37	208	5.52
2009	A+	Salem	288	28	78	6	45	271	325	424	748	7	83	0.47	3	1	40	153	4.77
2009	AA	Portland	92	14	31	3	12	337	365	489	854	4	71	0.15	1	2	26	152	6.07
2010	AA	Portland	473	65	123	11	94	260	337	416	754	10	81	0.60	1	2	41	156	4.98
2011	AAA	Pawtucket	330	33	80	8	36	242	298	367	664	7	76	0.33	0	2	31	124	3.60

Tall and strong backstop whose production fell off from '10. Became more aggressive and long swing was exploited by good pitching. Has strength and bat speed to produce raw power, but batting eye needs attention. Strong arm enhanced by quick release, but can make inaccurate throws. Should hit enough and defend enough to be backup at worst.

Fairley, Wendell — 8 — San Francisco

EXP MLB DEBUT: 2014 | POTENTIAL: Platoon CF | 6D

Bats L Age 24
2007 (1-S) HS (MS)

- Pwr ++
- BAvg ++
- Spd ++++
- Def +++

Year	Lev	Team	AB	R	H	HR	RBI	Avg	OB	Slg	OPS	bb%	ct%	Eye	SB	CS	x/h%	Iso	RC/G
2008	Rk	AZL Giants	193	39	50	2	17	259	347	337	684	12	81	0.70	7	3	18	78	4.19
2009	A	Augusta	345	47	84	3	42	243	315	333	648	9	70	0.35	2	4	29	90	3.59
2010	A+	San Jose	391	42	114	1	46	292	340	343	683	7	78	0.34	10	6	15	51	3.90
2011	A+	San Jose	208	28	51	2	21	245	311	317	629	9	81	0.51	3	1	20	72	3.34
2011	AA	Richmond	98	11	26	0	7	265	321	337	657	8	72	0.30	2	2	19	71	3.67

Plus athlete with good speed, but struggled in repeat of High-A. Possesses good bat speed and plate discipline, but has not translated that into game action and had just 2 HR and 5 SB on the year. Has good range in CF with average arm strength, but looks like nothing more than a 4th or 5th OF.

Farris, Eric — 4 — Milwaukee

EXP MLB DEBUT: 2012 | POTENTIAL: Backup 2B | 6C

Bats R Age 26
2007 (4) Loyola Marymount

- Pwr ++
- BAvg +++
- Spd +++
- Def +++

Year	Lev	Team	AB	R	H	HR	RBI	Avg	OB	Slg	OPS	bb%	ct%	Eye	SB	CS	x/h%	Iso	RC/G
2009	A+	Brevard County	473	68	141	7	49	298	339	385	723	6	90	0.63	70	6	18	87	4.42
2010	Rk	AZL Brewers	32	5	8	1	9	250	273	500	773	3	91	0.33	1	0	75	250	4.93
2010	AAA	Nashville	230	28	63	2	15	274	301	348	649	4	89	0.36	14	2	19	74	3.47
2011	AAA	Nashville	538	70	146	6	55	271	312	372	684	6	87	0.46	21	7	25	100	3.96
2011	MLB	Milwaukee	1	0	0	0	0	0	0	0	0	0	100		0	0			

Short, athletic speedster held his own in 2nd stint at Triple-A. Missed a big chunk of '10 with a knee injuruy, but was healthy in '11. Singles hitter whose best tools is his speed. Makes all of the plays on defense, but is only average in the field. Could develop into a solid back-up, but lack of power gives him limited potential.

Federowicz, Tim — 2 — Los Angeles (N)

EXP MLB DEBUT: 2011 | POTENTIAL: Starting C | 8D

Bats R Age 24
2008 (7) UNC

- Pwr +++
- BAvg +++
- Spd +++
- Def ++

Year	Lev	Team	AB	R	H	HR	RBI	Avg	OB	Slg	OPS	bb%	ct%	Eye	SB	CS	x/h%	Iso	RC/G
2009	A+	Salem	187	18	48	4	24	257	276	390	666	3	88	0.23	1	0	35	134	3.57
2010	A+	Salem	407	47	103	4	61	253	324	371	695	10	79	0.50	1	1	38	118	4.26
2011	AA	Portland	339	46	94	8	52	277	340	407	747	9	81	0.51	1	0	30	130	4.75
2011	AAA	Albuquerque	83	17	27	6	17	325	429	627	1055	15	76	0.75	0	0	48	301	9.04
2011	MLB	Los Angeles (N)	13	0	2	0	1	154	267	154	421	13	69	0.50	0	0	0	0	0.34

Strong, stocky backstop came over to the Dodgers as part of the Erik Bedard trade. Solid offensive contributor, with a quick bat, moderate power, and decent plate discipline. Defensively has good footwork and a strong throwing arm. Nailed 37% of baserunners in '11 and made his MLB debut. Will compete for the starting job in LA in 2012.

Fields, Daniel — 8 — Detroit

EXP MLB DEBUT: 2014 | POTENTIAL: Starting OF | 8E

Bats R Age 21
2009 (6) HS (MI)

- Pwr +++
- BAvg ++
- Spd ++++
- Def ++

Year	Lev	Team	AB	R	H	HR	RBI	Avg	OB	Slg	OPS	bb%	ct%	Eye	SB	CS	x/h%	Iso	RC/G
2010	A+	Lakeland	375	33	90	8	47	240	337	371	708	13	68	0.46	8	9	30	131	4.56
2011	A+	Lakeland	432	57	95	8	46	220	299	326	626	10	69	0.37	4	4	27	106	3.23

Athletic and toolsy outfielder who repeated High-A and finished 2nd in FSL in Ks. Regressed in most categories, though shows glimpses of upside. Possesses above average speed on base and in CF. Muscular frame should lead to power, particularly as he covers plate well. Struggles against LHP and breaking balls. Arm strength a tad short, but ranges well in CF.

Fleury, Mark — 2 — Cincinnati

EXP MLB DEBUT: 2013 | POTENTIAL: Backup C | 7D

Bats L Age 24
2009 (4) UNC

- Pwr +++
- BAvg ++
- Spd ++
- Def +++

Year	Lev	Team	AB	R	H	HR	RBI	Avg	OB	Slg	OPS	bb%	ct%	Eye	SB	CS	x/h%	Iso	RC/G
2009	Rk	Billings	131	20	26	4	17	198	281	382	663	10	79	0.56	0	1	54	183	3.80
2010	A	Dayton	365	50	93	11	48	255	345	433	777	12	74	0.53	4	1	43	178	5.39
2011	Rk	AZL Reds	7	0	1	0	0	143	400	143	543	30	86	3.00	1	1	0	0	3.46
2011	A+	Bakersfield	169	26	47	3	24	278	387	414	801	15	75	0.71	5	2	30	136	5.90
2011	AA	Carolina	6	1	1	1	2	167	167	667	833	0	50	0.00	0	0	100	500	7.33

Short, compact backstop moves up on the org depth chart with the trade of Grandal. He has a nice LH stroke that generates moderate power. He's shown solid plate discipline and a nice walk rate, but his lack of power likely limits him to a back-up role. Still raw behind the plate, but has a good arm and decent potential.

Flores, Ramon
378 | **New York (A)** | EXP MLB DEBUT: 2014 | POTENTIAL: Starting OF | **8C**

Bats L Age 20 — 2008 FA (VZ)
Pwr +++ | BAvg +++ | Spd +++ | Def +++

Year	Lev	Team	AB	R	H	HR	RBI	Avg	OB	Slg	OPS	bb%	ct%	Eye	SB	CS	x/h%	Iso	RC/G
2009	Rk	GCL Yankees	158	14	31	0	14	196	294	241	535	12	78	0.63	7	5	19	44	2.28
2010	Rk	GCL Yankees	158	33	52	2	22	329	430	481	911	15	86	1.27	4	1	31	152	7.28
2010	A	Charleston (SC)	48	3	12	0	2	250	294	313	607	6	69	0.20	1	0	25	63	2.90
2010	A+	Tampa	28	0	7	0	2	250	250	250	500	0	82	0.00	0	0	0	0	1.26
2011	A	Charleston (SC)	468	59	124	11	59	265	350	400	749	12	80	0.66	13	2	31	135	4.95

Short and lean prospect who established career high in HR and SB. Profiles as top of order hitter with ability to work counts and put bat to ball. Exemplifies ideal plate discipline and balanced swing provides opportunity to hit for BA. Possesses good pop for size, but no more than average. Runs well and has average range in outfield.

Flores, Wilmer
6 | **New York (N)** | EXP MLB DEBUT: 2014 | POTENTIAL: Starting 3B | **8D**

Bats R Age 20 — 2007 NDFA Venz.
Pwr +++ | BAvg ++++ | Spd ++ | Def ++

Year	Lev	Team	AB	R	H	HR	RBI	Avg	OB	Slg	OPS	bb%	ct%	Eye	SB	CS	x/h%	Iso	RC/G
2008	A	Savannah	5	1	2	0	0	400	400	400	800	0	60	0.00	0	0	0	0	5.84
2009	A	Savannah	488	44	129	3	36	264	296	332	628	4	85	0.31	3	3	19	68	3.18
2010	A	Savannah	277	30	77	7	44	278	333	433	767	8	87	0.62	2	1	35	155	5.00
2010	A+	St. Lucie	277	32	83	4	40	300	322	415	737	3	86	0.23	2	4	28	116	4.36
2011	A+	St. Lucie	516	52	139	9	81	269	306	380	686	5	87	0.40	2	2	27	110	3.89

Tall, strong infielder with lots of offensive upside due to his bat speed and potential power, but has yet to have a breakout. Swings aggressively, and does not walk much and is not selective. Lack of speed and range at SS make a move off the position likely. Does have solid arm strength and bat could play at 3B or the OF.

Flowers, Tyler
2 | **Chicago (A)** | EXP MLB DEBUT: 2009 | POTENTIAL: Starting C | **8D**

Bats R Age 26 — 2005 (33) Chipola JC
Pwr ++++ | BAvg ++ | Spd + | Def ++

Year	Lev	Team	AB	R	H	HR	RBI	Avg	OB	Slg	OPS	bb%	ct%	Eye	SB	CS	x/h%	Iso	RC/G
2009	MLB	Chicago WSox	16	3	3	0	0	188	316	250	566	16	50	0.38	0	0	33	63	3.03
2010	AAA	Charlotte	346	43	76	16	53	220	327	434	760	14	65	0.45	2	1	53	214	5.36
2010	MLB	Chicago WSox	11	2	1	0	0	91	333	91	424	27	55	0.80	0	0			
2011	AAA	Charlotte	222	36	58	15	32	261	372	500	872	15	62	0.46	2	0	40	239	7.15
2011	MLB	Chicago WSox	110	13	23	5	16	209	298	409	707	11	65	0.37	0	1	48	200	4.44

Large and strong backstop has struggled in MLB opportunities, but still knocking on door with patient approach and plus power to all fields. Swings hard, but has shortened stroke to make more contact. Possesses decent mobility and agility for size, but receiving still a tad below average. Has enough glove to be more than DH and bat still worthwhile.

Forsythe, Blake
2 | **New York (N)** | EXP MLB DEBUT: 2014 | POTENTIAL: Backup C | **6C**

Bats R Age 22 — 2010 (3) Tennessee
Pwr +++ | BAvg ++ | Spd ++ | Def +++

Year	Lev	Team	AB	R	H	HR	RBI	Avg	OB	Slg	OPS	bb%	ct%	Eye	SB	CS	x/h%	Iso	RC/G
2009	NCAA	Tennessee	196	51	68	15	46	347	458	663	1121	17	73	0.77	5	2	44	316	10.17
2010	NCAA	Tennessee	199	40	57	15	57	286	383	583	966	13	73	0.57	0	1	47	296	7.83
2010	Rk	GCL Mets	10	0	2	0	0	200	273	200	473	9	80	0.50	0	0	0	0	1.36
2010	A-	Brooklyn	101	14	24	3	8	238	313	396	709	10	59	0.27	1	1	38	158	4.83
2011	A	Savannah	370	44	87	9	43	235	336	395	730	13	67	0.46	0	1	43	159	4.97

Strong bodied backstop catcher is the younger brother of Logan Forsythe. Blake has good raw power and decent plate discipline, but the power has not been evident in game action and he has yet to hit for average. Defensively he moves well and has a strong arm and has a chance to stay behind the plate.

Franco, Maikel
5 | **Philadelphia** | EXP MLB DEBUT: 2015 | POTENTIAL: Starting 3B | **8D**

Bats R Age 19 — 2010 NDFA D.R.
Pwr ++++ | BAvg ++ | Spd ++ | Def ++

Year	Lev	Team	AB	R	H	HR	RBI	Avg	OB	Slg	OPS	bb%	ct%	Eye	SB	CS	x/h%	Iso	RC/G
2010	Rk	GCL Phillies	194	23	43	2	29	222	281	330	611	8	76	0.35	0	0	35	108	3.03
2011	A-	Williamsport	202	19	58	2	38	287	366	411	777	11	85	0.83	0	0	34	124	5.40
2011	A	Lakewood	65	6	8	1	6	123	136	200	336	2	77	0.07	0	0	38	77	

Strong, agile 3B prospect from the Dominican Republic made impressive strides in '11. Franco has good bat speed, decent plate discipline, and good hand-eye coordination. At 6'1" 180 lbs., he has good raw power. He is a below average runner, but fields his position well and should stick at 3B. Look for more in '12.

Franklin, Nick
46 | **Seattle** | EXP MLB DEBUT: 2013 | POTENTIAL: Starting SS/2B | **8B**

Bats B Age 21 — 2009 (1) HS (FL)
Pwr +++ | BAvg ++++ | Spd +++ | Def ++++

Year	Lev	Team	AB	R	H	HR	RBI	Avg	OB	Slg	OPS	bb%	ct%	Eye	SB	CS	x/h%	Iso	RC/G
2010	A	Clinton	513	89	144	23	65	281	345	485	830	9	76	0.41	25	10	36	205	5.79
2010	AA	West Tennessee	3	3	2	0	0	667	750	667	1417	25	67	1.00	0	0	0	0	16.56
2011	Rk	AZL Mariners	11	1	1	0	0	91	91	91	182	0	45	0.00	0	0			
2011	A+	High Desert	258	50	71	5	20	275	353	411	764	11	78	0.55	13	1	28	136	5.13
2011	AA	Jackson	83	13	27	2	6	325	371	482	853	7	78	0.33	5	3	26	157	6.02

Athletic and aggressive infielder who didn't match '10 HR output, but has all-around game worthy of top prospect status. Makes consistent contact with strong swing and uses entire field. Power may have been stifled by illness, but projects to average pop. Runs well and plays heady defense, though arm strength may be best suited for 2B.

Frazier, Todd
6357 | **Cincinnati** | EXP MLB DEBUT: 2010 | POTENTIAL: Starting 3B/LF | **7B**

Bats R Age 26 — 2007 (1-S) Rutgers
Pwr ++++ | BAvg ++ | 4.40 Spd ++ | Def +++

Year	Lev	Team	AB	R	H	HR	RBI	Avg	OB	Slg	OPS	bb%	ct%	Eye	SB	CS	x/h%	Iso	RC/G
2009	AA	Carolina	451	59	131	14	68	290	351	481	832	9	85	0.63	7	8	43	191	5.81
2009	AAA	Louisville	63	9	19	2	9	302	362	476	839	9	81	0.50	2	0	37	175	5.88
2010	AAA	Louisville	480	71	124	17	66	258	322	448	770	9	74	0.35	14	4	43	190	5.10
2011	AAA	Louisville	315	47	82	15	46	260	332	467	799	10	74	0.41	17	4	41	206	5.45
2011	MLB	Cincinnati	112	17	26	6	15	232	277	438	715	6	76	0.26	1	0	42	205	4.06

Strong athlete possesses bat speed, nice short stroke, and good power. Improved plate discipline suggests he was unlucky in '11 and should rebound. Makes consistent hard contact and uses the entire field. Features a strong throwing arm, but below average speed. Lack of clarity on position continues to hold him back.

Fuentes, Reymond
8 | **San Diego** | EXP MLB DEBUT: 2014 | POTENTIAL: Starting CF | **8D**

Bats L Age 21 — 2009 (1) HS P.R.
Pwr ++ | BAvg +++ | Spd ++++ | Def +++

Year	Lev	Team	AB	R	H	HR	RBI	Avg	OB	Slg	OPS	bb%	ct%	Eye	SB	CS	x/h%	Iso	RC/G
2009	Rk	GCL Red Sox	145	16	42	1	14	290	322	379	702	5	83	0.29	9	5	21	90	4.05
2010	A	Greenville	374	59	101	5	41	270	316	377	693	6	77	0.29	42	5	25	107	3.99
2011	A+	Lake Elsinore	510	84	140	5	45	275	332	369	701	8	77	0.38	41	14	21	94	4.19

Fast, athletic OF who has the instincts and range to become top-flight CF. Cleaned up swing mechanics and used entire field better. Can hit hard line drives to gaps, but power isn't a strength. Struggles with plate discipline and may not have enough OBP skills to hit leadoff. Takes good routes in OF, though arm strength is a little short.

Galindo, Jesus
8 | **San Francisco** | EXP MLB DEBUT: 2015 | POTENTIAL: Starting CF | **8D**

Bats B Age 21 — 2009 NDFA D.R.
Pwr ++ | BAvg ++ | Spd ++++ | Def ++++

Year	Lev	Team	AB	R	H	HR	RBI	Avg	OB	Slg	OPS	bb%	ct%	Eye	SB	CS	x/h%	Iso	RC/G
2011	A-	Salem-Keizer	239	49	66	2	20	276	345	364	709	9	81	0.54	47	8	21	88	4.40

Proto-typical leadoff prospect. Has plus speed, draws walks, and puts the ball into play. Does not have much power and is still raw in some aspects of his game. He covers ground well in CF and has a strong enough arm keep runners honest. Will need to prove he can hit at higher level, but is an exciting young player.

Gallagher, Austin
53 | **Los Angeles (N)** | EXP MLB DEBUT: 2013 | POTENTIAL: Platoon 1B | **7D**

Bats L Age 23 — 2007 (3) HS, (PA)
Pwr +++ | BAvg +++ | Spd ++ | Def ++

Year	Lev	Team	AB	R	H	HR	RBI	Avg	OB	Slg	OPS	bb%	ct%	Eye	SB	CS	x/h%	Iso	RC/G
2007	Rk	Ogden	197	28	56	4	17	284	347	401	748	9	83	0.58	1	1	27	117	4.80
2008	A+	Inland Empire	307	36	90	5	55	293	354	456	810	9	76	0.40	1	4	43	163	5.72
2009	A	Great Lakes	226	28	58	3	30	257	320	345	665	9	81	0.49	1	1	24	88	3.76
2010	A+	Inland Empire	422	47	123	6	64	291	350	405	755	8	82	0.49	0	2	28	114	4.89
2011	A+	Rancho Cucamg	390	73	114	13	62	292	389	451	841	14	82	0.89	0	1	30	159	6.17

23-year-old 1B with bat speed and plate discipline that should make him an above average hitter. Move from 3B to 1B hurts long-term value, but fared well in repeat of CAL. Swing can get long, but has ability to adjust. Arm strength and soft hands but lacks first-step quickness which will only worsen with maturity so limited to 1B.

Galloway, Isaac
8 | **Florida** | EXP MLB DEBUT: 2012 | POTENTIAL: Starting CF | **8D**

Bats R Age 22 — 2008 (8) HS, (CA)
Pwr +++ | BAvg +++ | 4.00 Spd ++++ | Def ++++

Year	Lev	Team	AB	R	H	HR	RBI	Avg	OB	Slg	OPS	bb%	ct%	Eye	SB	CS	x/h%	Iso	RC/G
2008	Rk	GCL Marlins	199	29	57	1	23	286	300	417	718	2	83	0.12	4	2	33	131	4.17
2009	A	Greensboro	340	44	91	3	30	268	293	382	675	3	74	0.13	15	9	33	115	3.69
2010	A+	Jupiter	100	9	20	0	6	200	238	290	528	5	79	0.24	4	3	30	90	1.97
2011	A	Greensboro	431	56	104	16	54	241	265	418	683	3	72	0.12	17	9	41	176	3.65

Plus athlete with good speed and the ability to impact an offense. Was healthy in '11, but struggled to hit. Drives the ball well to all fields, but will need to improve plate discipline. Possesses above average range and arm strength, but must learn to take better routes. Has power and speed, but also a lot of work to do.

Galvez, Jonathan

6 | San Diego | EXP MLB DEBUT: 2013 | POTENTIAL: Starting 2B | 8C

Bats R Age 21
2007 NDFA D.R.
Pwr +++
BAvg +++
Spd +++
Def ++

Year	Lev	Team	AB	R	H	HR	RBI	Avg	OB	Slg	OPS	bb%	ct%	Eye	SB	CS	x/h%	Iso	RC/G
2009	Rk	AZL Padres	193	45	57	6	27	295	390	503	893	13	77	0.68	14	6	44	207	6.98
2010	A	Fort Wayne	398	64	103	10	49	259	353	397	750	13	70	0.48	18	7	31	138	5.11
2011	A+	Lake Elsinore	488	84	142	13	86	291	346	465	811	8	75	0.33	37	9	38	174	5.64

Wiry, athletic SS had an impressive season in the CAL. Galvez still needs better plate discipline to make more consistent contact, but more than held his own offensively. Stole career high 37 bases in '11. Moves well defensively, but does not have a strong arm as may eventually move over to 2B or the OF.

Galvis, Freddy

6 | Philadelphia | EXP MLB DEBUT: 2012 | POTENTIAL: Starting SS | 8D

Bats B Age 22
2006 NDFA Venz.
Pwr ++
BAvg +++
Spd +++
Def +++

Year	Lev	Team	AB	R	H	HR	RBI	Avg	OB	Slg	OPS	bb%	ct%	Eye	SB	CS	x/h%	Iso	RC/G
2009	A+	Clearwater	251	29	62	1	15	247	276	307	583	4	83	0.23	6	3	18	60	2.57
2009	AA	Reading	61	6	12	1	5	197	222	246	468	3	89	0.29	0	1	8	49	1.33
2010	AA	Reading	502	58	117	5	48	233	276	311	587	6	82	0.34	15	4	21	78	2.70
2011	AA	Reading	422	63	115	8	35	273	318	400	718	6	84	0.41	19	11	30	128	4.32
2011	AAA	Lehigh Valley	121	15	36	0	8	298	315	364	678	2	85	0.17	4	2	19	66	3.67

Slick fielding SS has excellent range, soft hands, a strong arm and true SS actions. He is one of the best defenders in the minors. Offensively has decent bat speed and can square up the ball consistently. He had his best season yet and while his power is below average his speed and defense should play well in the majors.

Garcia, Avisail

9 | Detroit | EXP MLB DEBUT: 2014 | POTENTIAL: Starting OF | 9E

Bats R Age 21
2007 FA (Venezuela)
Pwr +++
BAvg +++
Spd +++
Def +++

Year	Lev	Team	AB	R	H	HR	RBI	Avg	OB	Slg	OPS	bb%	ct%	Eye	SB	CS	x/h%	Iso	RC/G
2009	A	West Michigan	299	36	79	1	31	264	283	324	608	3	77	0.11	8	7	18	60	2.71
2009	A+	Lakeland	8	1	2	0	0	250	250	250	500	0	75	0.00	0	0	0	0	1.07
2010	A	West Michigan	494	58	139	4	63	281	309	356	666	4	77	0.18	20	4	18	75	3.49
2011	A+	Lakeland	488	53	129	11	56	264	291	389	680	4	73	0.14	14	5	26	125	3.65

Strong and aggressive hitter who hasn't yet capitalized on excellent tools. Exhibits bat speed and wrist action for plus power down the line. Doesn't control strike zone at present and flails at breaking balls. Needs to be more patient to hit for BA. Plus arm is best defensive attribute and above average range is enhanced by terrific speed. Likely to repeat High-A.

Garcia, Jonathan

8 | Los Angeles (N) | EXP MLB DEBUT: 2014 | POTENTIAL: Starting CF | 8D

Bats R Age 20
2009 (8) HS, P.R.
Pwr +++
BAvg +++
Spd +++
Def +++

Year	Lev	Team	AB	R	H	HR	RBI	Avg	OB	Slg	OPS	bb%	ct%	Eye	SB	CS	x/h%	Iso	RC/G
2009	Rk	AZL Dodgers	138	22	42	3	21	304	351	500	851	7	73	0.27	4	0	48	196	6.27
2010	Rk	Ogden	239	45	73	10	40	305	357	527	884	7	75	0.32	4	1	42	222	6.50
2011	A	Great Lakes	464	58	106	19	63	228	281	420	701	7	71	0.26	2	1	46	192	4.08

Short, toolsy OF prospect showed improved power, but poor plate discipline led to a .228 BA in the MWL. Has good raw power for his size, runs well, and can drive the ball. Defensively he covers lots of ground and has a strong throwing arm. Still young and will likely get a repeat of the MWL in '12.

Garcia, Leury

6 | Texas | EXP MLB DEBUT: 2013 | POTENTIAL: Starting SS | 7A

Bats B Age 21
2007 FA (DR)
Pwr +
BAvg +++
Spd ++++
Def ++++

Year	Lev	Team	AB	R	H	HR	RBI	Avg	OB	Slg	OPS	bb%	ct%	Eye	SB	CS	x/h%	Iso	RC/G
2008	Rk	AZL Rangers	129	17	27	0	14	209	255	279	535	6	69	0.20	12	3	22	70	1.90
2009	A	Hickory	276	28	64	1	18	232	279	286	565	6	77	0.28	19	6	16	54	2.34
2010	Rk	AZL Rangers	18	5	9	0	2	500	591	611	1202	18	78	1.00	4	2	22	111	11.55
2010	A	Hickory	359	57	94	3	22	262	306	323	629	6	84	0.40	47	9	13	61	3.25
2011	A+	Myrtle Beach	442	65	113	3	38	256	300	342	642	6	77	0.28	30	12	24	86	3.34

Small and wiry infielder who impresses with glove and speed. Runs as well as anybody in system, but must learn to keep ball on ground to take advantage of plus-plus wheels. Hits too many flyballs and lacks plate discipline. Hits from both sides, but not much pop from either. Plus defender who owns quick hands and well above average range.

Garcia, Willy

7 | Pittsburgh | EXP MLB DEBUT: 2015 | POTENTIAL: Starting OF | 8E

Bats R Age 19
2010 NDFA D.R.
Pwr +++
BAvg +++
Spd +++
Def +++

Year	Lev	Team	AB	R	H	HR	RBI	Avg	OB	Slg	OPS	bb%	ct%	Eye	SB	CS	x/h%	Iso	RC/G
2011	Rk	GCL Pirates	177	26	47	5	35	266	309	446	755	6	72	0.22	7	5	38	181	4.85
2011	A-	State College	7	1	2	0	0	286	286	286	571	0	100		0	0	0	0	2.76

Toolsy, international OF from the Dominican Republic. At 6'3" 180 lbs he has room to grow and projects to have above-average power. Has above-average speed, but isn't a burner. Can be overly aggressive at the plate and needs to improve his plate discipline, but will be exciting to watch.

Garfield, Cameron

2 | Milwaukee | EXP MLB DEBUT: 2014 | POTENTIAL: Starting C | 7D

Bats R Age 21
2009 (2) HS, (CA)
Pwr +++
BAvg ++
Spd ++
Def +++

Year	Lev	Team	AB	R	H	HR	RBI	Avg	OB	Slg	OPS	bb%	ct%	Eye	SB	CS	x/h%	Iso	RC/G
2009	Rk	Helena	218	26	54	4	21	248	281	353	634	4	72	0.16	3	4	28	106	3.09
2010	A	Wisconsin	384	41	94	3	46	245	286	318	603	5	81	0.30	2	4	23	73	2.85
2011	Rk	AZL Brewers	36	7	13	2	10	361	395	667	1061	5	75	0.22	0	0	46	306	8.74
2011	A	Wisconsin	17	3	2	0	2	118	167	176	343	6	82	0.33	0	1	50	59	

Strong, powerful defensive-minded backstop can't seem to stay healthy. Dislocated knee resulted in only 53 AB in '11 and he's had only 453 AB since being drafted in 2nd round in '09. Strong arm and receives the ball well. Has some power, but needs to prove he can stay healthy.

Gaynor, Wade

5 | Detroit | EXP MLB DEBUT: 2013 | POTENTIAL: Reserve 3B | 7D

Bats R Age 24
2009 (3) Western Kentucky
Pwr +++
BAvg ++
Spd ++
Def +++

Year	Lev	Team	AB	R	H	HR	RBI	Avg	OB	Slg	OPS	bb%	ct%	Eye	SB	CS	x/h%	Iso	RC/G
2008	NCAA	Western Kentucky	259	56	90	13	48	347	388	598	986	6	88	0.57	11	1	42	251	7.31
2009	NCAA	Western Kentucky	251	83	93	25	78	371	448	781	1228	12	84	0.85	21	4	53	410	10.54
2009	A-	Oneonta	234	37	45	3	23	192	259	282	541	8	78	0.40	8	3	31	90	2.13
2010	A	West Michigan	514	91	147	10	80	286	345	436	780	8	78	0.41	13	5	36	150	5.23
2011	A+	Lakeland	488	58	104	9	56	213	270	338	608	7	72	0.28	2	2	38	125	2.90

Strong infielder who led FSL in Ks. Has been inconsistent with bat production. Can hit LHP hard with gap power and covers plate well due to long arms. Exploited inside due to long swing and fringy bat speed may nullify BA potential. Runs OK for size and has nice arm strength at 3B. Range and footwork may be better off across diamond, but needs to hit.

Gennett, Scooter

4 | Milwaukee | EXP MLB DEBUT: 2014 | POTENTIAL: Starting 2B | 7C

Bats L Age 22
2009 (16) HS, (FL)
Pwr +++
BAvg +++
Spd ++
Def ++

Year	Lev	Team	AB	R	H	HR	RBI	Avg	OB	Slg	OPS	bb%	ct%	Eye	SB	CS	x/h%	Iso	RC/G
2010	A	Wisconsin	482	87	149	9	55	309	351	463	814	6	81	0.34	14	4	35	154	5.49
2011	A+	Brevard County	556	74	167	9	51	300	333	406	739	5	88	0.39	11	10	21	106	4.49

Short, high-energy 2B plays the game with intensity. Gennett has a compact, line-drive approach gives him ability to put the ball into play. Generates a bit of pop, with above-average speed, but average plate discipline will need to be addressed to get on base more. Solid defender with good range, but still learning the position. He has a chance to start in the majors.

Gibbs, Micah

2 | Chicago (N) | EXP MLB DEBUT: 2014 | POTENTIAL: Backup C | 7C

Bats B Age 23
2010 (3) LSU
Pwr ++
BAvg ++
Spd ++
Def ++++

Year	Lev	Team	AB	R	H	HR	RBI	Avg	OB	Slg	OPS	bb%	ct%	Eye	SB	CS	x/h%	Iso	RC/G
2009	NCAA	Louisiana State	238	58	70	6	42	294	402	454	856	15	78	0.83	2	1	34	160	6.56
2010	NCAA	Louisiana State	245	47	95	10	60	388	453	592	1044	11	87	0.94	7	2	28	204	8.33
2010	Rk	AZL Cubs	4	0	0	0	0	0	0	0	0	0	100		0	0			
2010	A-	Boise	148	18	30	0	13	203	267	250	517	8	78	0.39	0	1	23	47	1.87
2011	A	Peoria	306	32	75	2	28	245	349	317	666	14	77	0.71	1	2	23	72	4.04

Switch-hitting backstop possesses solid receiving skills. Good plate discipline, but below average power as a pro. Swing is not smooth and there is concern he will not hit for average. Arm strength is below average, but otherwise he moves well behind the plate and has good actions so should be able to stay at the position. Projects as a backup C.

Gillaspie, Conor

5 | San Francisco | EXP MLB DEBUT: 2008 | POTENTIAL: Starting RF | 7C

Bats L Age 24
2008 (1-S) Wichita St
Pwr +++
BAvg ++++
4.35 Spd ++
Def ++

Year	Lev	Team	AB	R	H	HR	RBI	Avg	OB	Slg	OPS	bb%	ct%	Eye	SB	CS	x/h%	Iso	RC/G
2008	MLB	San Francisco	5	1	1	0	0	200	429	200	629	29	100		0	0	0	0	5.37
2009	A+	San Jose	469	62	134	4	67	286	361	386	747	10	86	0.81	2	3	28	100	4.99
2010	AA	Richmond	491	57	141	8	67	287	337	420	757	7	86	0.55	0	4	29	132	4.88
2011	AAA	Fresno	428	63	127	11	61	297	391	453	844	13	82	0.84	9	9	31	157	6.26
2011	MLB	San Francisco	19	2	5	1	2	263	333	421	754	10	95	2.00	0	0	20	158	4.95

Athletic 3B prospect had another solid season and made his MLB debut. Has good bat speed and extension through the zone to hit for BA and moderate power. Despite a lean/athletic build, he doesn't have much speed or range. Solid plate discpline, but lack of power and sub-par defense could result in a move to a new position.

Gillespie, Cole — 7 — Arizona

EXP MLB DEBUT: 2010 | POTENTIAL: Starting LF/RF | 8C

Bats R Age 28
2006 (3) Oregon St
Pwr + + +
BAvg + + +
4.25 Spd + + +
Def + + +

Year	Lev	Team	AB	R	H	HR	RBI	Avg	OB	Slg	OPS	bb%	ct%	Eye	SB	CS	x/h%	Iso	RC/G
2009	AAA	Nashville	236	29	57	7	27	242	330	424	753	12	76	0.55	6	5	42	182	5.03
2010	AAA	Reno	264	54	76	8	49	288	390	477	867	14	81	0.90	8	5	37	189	6.60
2010	MLB	AZ D'backs	104	11	24	2	12	231	279	365	645	6	72	0.24	1	1	42	135	3.38
2011	AAA	Reno	484	100	145	12	79	300	400	479	879	14	81	0.89	24	5	32	180	6.80
2011	MLB	AZ D'backs	6	2	2	1	4	333	429	833	1262	14	83	1.00	0	0	50	500	10.63

Athletic player with average tools across the board, but does the little things that enhance his value. Produces moderate power and will hit for BA. Hit .300 with 19 doubles, 16, triples, and 12 home runs at Triple-A. Has solid plate discipline. Runs bases intelligently and his average defensive tools play both OF corner positions.

Gillies, Tyson — 7 — Philadelphia

EXP MLB DEBUT: 2012 | POTENTIAL: Starting LF | 7B

Bats L Age 23
2005 (26) Vancouver, BC
Pwr + +
BAvg + + +
Spd + + + + +
Def + + +

Year	Lev	Team	AB	R	H	HR	RBI	Avg	OB	Slg	OPS	bb%	ct%	Eye	SB	CS	x/h%	Iso	RC/G
2008	A+	High Desert	30	4	7	0	1	233	258	300	558	3	80	0.17	1	1	14	67	2.23
2009	A+	High Desert	498	104	170	9	42	341	412	486	898	11	84	0.74	44	19	24	145	6.78
2010	Rk	GCL Phillies	2	3	1	0	1	500	750	500	1250	50	100		0	0	0	0	14.24
2010	AA	Reading	105	15	25	2	6	238	273	333	606	5	77	0.21	2	2	20	95	2.72
2011	A+	Clearwater	13	1	2	0	0	154	154	308	462	0	92	0.00	0	0	100	154	1.60

Strong, athletic, talented OF can't seem to catch a break. On and off field issues have stalled his development. A bad hamstring and an ankle injury limited him to 13 AB. Did see action in the AFL, where he looked healthy. Does have nice pop and good speed with solid plate discipline. Outstanding defender with above average range and strong arm.

Gilmore, Jon — 5 — Chicago (A)

EXP MLB DEBUT: 2013 | POTENTIAL: Reserve INF | 7D

Bats R Age 23
2007 (1-S) HS (IA)
Pwr + +
BAvg + + +
Spd + +
Def + +

Year	Lev	Team	AB	R	H	HR	RBI	Avg	OB	Slg	OPS	bb%	ct%	Eye	SB	CS	x/h%	Iso	RC/G
2008	Rk	Danville	258	27	87	4	31	337	369	473	842	5	84	0.32	0	3	31	136	5.71
2008	A	Rome	102	6	19	0	4	186	202	196	398	2	80	0.10	1	0	5	10	0.13
2009	A	Kannapolis	504	60	138	5	67	274	320	361	681	6	84	0.41	4	3	24	87	3.89
2010	A+	Winston-Salem	568	79	177	5	80	312	350	394	745	6	84	0.38	1	3	19	83	4.60
2011	AA	Birmingham	180	19	51	3	28	283	348	417	765	9	82	0.56	0	0	33	133	5.07

Aggressive and athletic infielder who missed time due to hand injury. Power hasn't developed, but has line drive pop to both gaps. Can go to opposite field too often and needs to pull in order to realize power potential. Hits LHP well and makes contact, but doesn't recognize pitches. Arm is strong, but lacks quickness and sloppy footwork.

Gindl, Caleb — 9 — Milwaukee

EXP MLB DEBUT: 2012 | POTENTIAL: Platoon LF/RF | 7C

Bats L Age 23
2007 (5) HS (FL)
Pwr + + +
BAvg + + +
Spd + + + +
Def + +

Year	Lev	Team	AB	R	H	HR	RBI	Avg	OB	Slg	OPS	bb%	ct%	Eye	SB	CS	x/h%	Iso	RC/G
2007	Rk	Helena	207	40	77	5	42	372	427	580	1007	9	82	0.53	4	4	39	208	8.06
2008	A	West Virginia	508	86	156	13	81	307	384	474	858	11	72	0.44	14	5	35	167	6.55
2009	A+	Brevard County	394	61	109	17	71	277	368	459	827	13	77	0.62	18	4	32	183	5.93
2010	AA	Huntsville	463	61	126	9	60	272	349	406	755	11	83	0.71	10	5	34	134	5.03
2011	AAA	Nashville	472	84	145	15	60	307	389	472	861	12	80	0.68	6	5	30	165	6.34

Short/stocky athlete with a short path to the ball and moderate bat speed. Had nice breakout in '11, due to solid plate discipline that gives him the potential to hit for average. Speed is an asset on the bases, but doesn't translate to range in the OF, but arm strength is above average. Power might be a bit short for a corner slot, but he should be able to play at the next level.

Givens, Mychal — 46 — Baltimore

EXP MLB DEBUT: 2014 | POTENTIAL: Starting 2B | 8E

Bats R Age 22
2009 (2) HS (FL)
Pwr + +
BAvg + + +
Spd + + +
Def + + +

Year	Lev	Team	AB	R	H	HR	RBI	Avg	OB	Slg	OPS	bb%	ct%	Eye	SB	CS	x/h%	Iso	RC/G
2010	A-	Aberdeen	33	8	12	3	5	364	462	727	1189	15	94	3.00	2	1	50	364	10.01
2010	A	Delmarva	18	2	4	0	4	222	391	222	614	22	78	1.25	1	1	0	0	3.68
2010	A+	Frederick	4	2	2	0	1	500	500	500	1000	0	100		0	1	0	0	6.83
2011	A-	Aberdeen	276	30	77	1	30	279	350	337	687	10	86	0.75	14	5	16	58	4.22
2011	A	Delmarva	210	21	41	0	15	195	235	229	464	5	83	0.31	6	6	17	33	1.25

Plus athlete who is blessed with plentiful tools, but is very raw with bat and is prototypical high risk/high reward prospect. Works counts, but borders on passive. Has clean, short swing and makes contact, but needs to tap into natural strength to drive balls. Strong arm is best tool and allows him to make plays. Range and hands are likely best for 2B, but may move to 3B.

Glaesmann, Todd — 89 — Tampa Bay

EXP MLB DEBUT: 2014 | POTENTIAL: Starting OF | 8E

Bats R Age 21
2009 (3) HS (TX)
Pwr + + +
BAvg + +
Spd + + +
Def + + +

Year	Lev	Team	AB	R	H	HR	RBI	Avg	OB	Slg	OPS	bb%	ct%	Eye	SB	CS	x/h%	Iso	RC/G
2009	Rk	GCL Rays	18	1	5	0	2	278	278	333	611	0	83	0.00	1	0	20	56	2.70
2010	Rk	Princeton	236	41	55	4	24	233	273	398	671	5	70	0.19	13	6	47	165	3.82
2011	Rk	GCL Rays	37	7	8	0	0	216	310	243	553	12	73	0.50	6	1	13	27	2.34
2011	A	Bowling Green	210	28	48	4	21	229	277	343	620	6	60	0.16	6	0	29	114	3.30

Long and strong outfielder with exciting upside, but erratic approach hasn't produced results. Missed time with elbow injury and never got on track. Has excellent talent and tools, including plus raw power and keen glovework in CF. Owns plus arm strength and good speed for range. Strikes out a ton and needs to shorten swing late in count.

Goeddel, Tyler — 5 — Tampa Bay

EXP MLB DEBUT: 2015 | POTENTIAL: Starting 3B | 8D

Bats R Age 19
2011 (1-S) HS (CA)
Pwr + +
BAvg + + +
Spd + + +
Def + +

Year	Lev	Team	AB	R	H	HR	RBI	Avg	OB	Slg	OPS	bb%	ct%	Eye	SB	CS	x/h%	Iso	RC/G
2011		Did not play																	

Tall, speedy, and athletic infielder with plenty of room to add muscle to slender physique, but swing and game more suitable for moderate power. Takes aggressive cuts at pitches and has ample bat speed, but level swing path mutes HR. Secondary skills are OK at present and should improve defense with more reps. Above average arm strength is asset.

Goetzman, Granden — 679 — Tampa Bay

EXP MLB DEBUT: 2015 | POTENTIAL: Starting OF | 8D

Bats R Age 19
2011 (2) HS (FL)
Pwr + + + +
BAvg + +
Spd + + +
Def + +

Year	Lev	Team	AB	R	H	HR	RBI	Avg	OB	Slg	OPS	bb%	ct%	Eye	SB	CS	x/h%	Iso	RC/G
2011	Rk	GCL Rays	75	8	13	0	8	173	253	213	466	10	77	0.47	6	1	23	40	1.26

Tall and powerful prospect who struggled in pro debut, but shows glimpses of being solid offensive performer. Has holes in swing and subpar swing mechanics hinder BA potential, but bat speed and leverage give him plenty of raw natural power. Runs very well for size and can steal bases. Future defensive position is big question mark.

Golden, Reggie — 8 — Chicago (N)

EXP MLB DEBUT: 2014 | POTENTIAL: Starting CF | 8D

Bats R Age 20
2010 (2) HS, (AL)
Pwr + + +
BAvg + + +
6.5/60 Spd + + + +
Def + + + +

Year	Lev	Team	AB	R	H	HR	RBI	Avg	OB	Slg	OPS	bb%	ct%	Eye	SB	CS	x/h%	Iso	RC/G
2010	Rk	AZL Cubs	15	3	5	0	1	333	375	400	775	6	53	0.14	1	0	20	67	6.71
2011	A-	Boise	231	36	56	7	39	242	324	420	744	11	71	0.41	5	2	39	177	4.94

Short, muscular, athletic OF prospect. A legit 5-tool prospect, he struggled offensively in '11. Has good power and bat speed and has above-average speed, and a strong throwing arm. Game is still a very raw, but the tools are there for him to develop into an exciting player.

Gomez, Hector — 6 — Colorado

EXP MLB DEBUT: 2011 | POTENTIAL: Starting SS | 8C

Bats R Age 24
2005 NDFA, D.R.
Pwr +
BAvg + + +
Spd + + + +
Def + + +

Year	Lev	Team	AB	R	H	HR	RBI	Avg	OB	Slg	OPS	bb%	ct%	Eye	SB	CS	x/h%	Iso	RC/G
2009	A+	Modesto	338	39	93	7	46	275	306	423	729	4	80	0.22	10	4	34	148	4.33
2010	A-	Tri-City	69	8	17	2	7	246	297	391	689	7	78	0.33	0	3	29	145	3.89
2010	AA	Tulsa	35	6	11	0	3	314	314	429	743	0	77	0.00	0	0	36	114	4.39
2011	AA	Tulsa	425	46	100	14	50	235	268	416	684	4	78	0.20	16	4	43	181	3.74
2011	MLB	Colorado	6	1	2	0	0	333	429	333	762	14	67	0.50	0	0	0	0	5.49

Wiry, athletic SS with plus defensive skills. Continued to struggle offensively, hitting just .235/.272/.416. Plus range and strong arm mean he can stay at the position long-term. Speed is best asset and makes good contact, but poor plate discipline (19 BB/94 K) and low OB% will hinder both BA and power. Defense will only take him so far.

Gonzalez, Elevys — 5 — Pittsburgh

EXP MLB DEBUT: 2014 | POTENTIAL: Starting 3B | 7C

Bats B Age 22
2008 NDFA Venz.
Pwr + + +
BAvg + + +
Spd + + +
Def + + +

Year	Lev	Team	AB	R	H	HR	RBI	Avg	OB	Slg	OPS	bb%	ct%	Eye	SB	CS	x/h%	Iso	RC/G
2009	Rk	GCL Pirates	107	17	29	1	9	271	304	346	649	4	80	0.24	6	3	14	75	3.34
2009	A-	State College	51	5	11	0	3	216	231	333	564	2	73	0.07	2	1	36	118	2.26
2010	A	West Virginia	236	30	65	6	31	275	360	424	783	12	80	0.65	8	11	29	148	5.39
2011	A+	Bradenton	454	63	146	6	83	322	375	467	842	8	80	0.42	7	5	33	145	6.02

Short, switch-hitting 3B had a nice breakout in the FSL. Has played a variety of positions, but seems to have settled in at 3B. Power is more of the gap variety right now though he did have 36 doubles. Solid defender, but plate discipline will need to improve and will need to prove that '11 wasn't a fluke.

Goodrum, Niko

46 | **Minnesota** | EXP MLB DEBUT: 2014 | POTENTIAL: Starting 2B/3B | **8D**

Bats B Age 20
2010 (2) HS (GA)

- Pwr +++
- BAvg +++
- Spd ++++
- Def +++

Year	Lev	Team	AB	R	H	HR	RBI	Avg	OB	Slg	OPS	bb%	ct%	Eye	SB	CS	x/h%	Iso	RC/G
2010	Rk	GCL Twins	118	10	19	0	5	161	220	195	415	7	71	0.26	4	2	21	34	0.23
2011	Rk	Elizabethton	204	39	56	2	20	275	342	382	725	9	73	0.38	8	1	27	108	4.64

Tall and lean infielder who showed glimpses of positive production in inconsistent season. Covers plate well with long arms and has leverage and swing path to project to average power down the line. May take awhile to develop as he has long swing and needs to add strength. Doesn't have ideal SS actions, but has soft, quick hands and fundamental footwork.

Goodwin, Brian

8 | **Washington** | EXP MLB DEBUT: 2015 | POTENTIAL: Starting LF | **8D**

Bats L Age 21
2011 (1-S) Miami Dade JC

- Pwr +++
- BAvg +++
- Spd +++
- Def +++

Year	Lev	Team	AB	R	H	HR	RBI	Avg	OB	Slg	OPS	bb%	ct%	Eye	SB	CS	x/h%	Iso	RC/G
2010	NCAA	North Carolina	227	47	66	7	63	291	408	511	919	17	78	0.92	7	2	42	220	7.49

Goodwin is a plus athlete who can do a bit of everything. He runs well, has solid strike zone judgment, moderate power, and should hit for average. Defensively he can make all of the plays and should be able to stick in CF. He needs to show more consistency and refine his game, but getting a toolsy OF in the supplemental round is a bonus for WAS.

Gose, Anthony

8 | **Toronto** | EXP MLB DEBUT: 2012 | POTENTIAL: Starting OF | **8B**

Bats L Age 21
2008 (2) HS (CA)

- Pwr +++
- BAvg ++
- Spd ++++
- Def ++++

Year	Lev	Team	AB	R	H	HR	RBI	Avg	OB	Slg	OPS	bb%	ct%	Eye	SB	CS	x/h%	Iso	RC/G
2008	Rk	GCL Phillies	39	4	10	0	3	256	275	359	634	3	69	0.08	3	1	30	103	3.23
2009	A	Lakewood	510	72	132	2	52	259	306	353	659	6	78	0.32	76	20	27	94	3.64
2010	A+	Clearwater	418	67	110	4	20	263	316	385	701	7	75	0.31	36	27	29	122	4.21
2010	A+	Dunedin	94	21	24	3	6	255	346	426	771	12	69	0.45	9	5	33	170	5.40
2011	AA	New Hampshire	509	87	129	16	59	253	335	415	749	11	70	0.40	70	15	33	161	4.99

Speedy and athletic outfielder who easily set career high in HR and led EL in SB, but also finished 2nd in Ks. Has eye-popping tools that project well and power starting to emerge. Generates plus bat speed, but pitch recognition problems have led to lots of strikeouts. He improved his baserunning skills and is a stellar defender with strong arm and plus range.

Grandal, Yasmani

2 | **San Diego** | EXP MLB DEBUT: 2013 | POTENTIAL: Starting C | **9D**

Bats B Age 23
2010 (1) Miami-FL

- Pwr ++++
- BAvg +++
- Spd ++
- Def +++

Year	Lev	Team	AB	R	H	HR	RBI	Avg	OB	Slg	OPS	bb%	ct%	Eye	SB	CS	x/h%	Iso	RC/G
2010	NCAA	Miami	222	56	89	15	60	401	523	721	1244	20	84	1.63	1	1	45	320	11.48
2010	Rk	AZL Reds	28	4	8	0	1	286	375	321	696	13	86	1.00	0	1	13	36	4.51
2011	A+	Bakersfield	206	47	61	10	40	296	413	510	923	17	72	0.72	0	0	39	214	7.55
2011	AA	Carolina	156	20	47	4	26	301	355	474	829	8	75	0.33	0	1	40	173	5.88
2011	AAA	Louisville	12	2	6	0	2	500	647	667	1314	29	92	5.00	0	0	33	167	13.25

Strong, physical catcher had huge breakout in '11. The switch-hitter has good power and is willing to hit ball to all fields. Swing can get a bit long, but has a good idea of what he is doing at the plate. Solid defender but arm is below average with slow trigger. Did a better job limiting running game, throwing out almost 35% of runners.

Green, Grant

8 | **Oakland** | EXP MLB DEBUT: 2012 | POTENTIAL: Starting OF | **8B**

Bats R Age 24
2009 (1) USC

- Pwr +++
- BAvg +++
- Spd +++
- Def +++

Year	Lev	Team	AB	R	H	HR	RBI	Avg	OB	Slg	OPS	bb%	ct%	Eye	SB	CS	x/h%	Iso	RC/G
2008	NCAA	USC	205	46	80	9	46	390	432	644	1076	7	83	0.43	10	4	36	254	8.59
2009	NCAA	USC	211	46	79	4	32	374	429	569	997	9	82	0.53	16	8	35	194	7.94
2009	A+	Stockton	19	2	6	0	3	316	350	368	718	5	74	0.20	1	0	17	53	4.30
2010	A+	Stockton	548	107	174	20	87	318	362	520	882	6	79	0.32	9	5	37	203	6.33
2011	AA	Midland	530	76	154	9	62	291	339	408	747	7	78	0.33	6	8	28	117	4.69

Pure and natural hitter who converted from SS to CF in July. Exhibits instincts at plate and brings mature approach and solid-average bat speed and power potential. Power output declined, but focusing more on contact and controlling swing. Has the athleticism to be good defender, but needs reps to improve jumps, routes, and instincts. Arm is playable.

Green, Taylor

54 | **Milwaukee** | EXP MLB DEBUT: 2011 | POTENTIAL: Starting 3B | **8D**

Bats L Age 25
2005 (26) Cypress JC

- Pwr +++
- BAvg +++
- 4.40 Spd ++
- Def ++

Year	Lev	Team	AB	R	H	HR	RBI	Avg	OB	Slg	OPS	bb%	ct%	Eye	SB	CS	x/h%	Iso	RC/G
2009	AA	Huntsville	306	34	79	5	43	258	330	356	687	10	88	0.89	0	2	25	98	4.23
2010	AA	Huntsville	393	51	102	13	81	260	336	438	773	10	83	0.67	0	2	42	178	5.17
2011	AA	Huntsville	11	2	4	0	3	364	364	455	818	0	73	0.00	0	0	25	91	5.42
2011	AAA	Nashville	420	74	141	22	88	336	413	583	996	12	83	0.76	1	0	42	248	7.89
2011	MLB	Milwaukee	37	2	10	0	1	270	270	351	622	0	84	0.00	0	0	30	81	2.88

Green is strong and has above-average power. He makes consistent contact and has plus bat speed, giving him the ability to hit for average and power. Improved plate discipline fueled his breakout as he started to use the whole field and the power is legit. He has soft hands and an average arm at 3B. Improved defense at 3B gives him a chance to stick.

Greene, Larry

7 | **Philadelphia** | EXP MLB DEBUT: 2015 | POTENTIAL: Starting 1B | **8D**

Bats L Age 19
2011 (1) HS (GA)

- Pwr ++++
- BAvg ++
- Spd ++
- Def ++

Year	Lev	Team	AB	R	H	HR	RBI	Avg	OB	Slg	OPS	bb%	ct%	Eye	SB	CS	x/h%	Iso	RC/G
2011		Did not play																	

Greene showed plus power in high school and at 6'2" 235, he is already physically mature. He was a two-sport star in high school and has nice athleticism. He is still very raw in many aspects of his game, but has the potential to develop into a nice power left-handed bat. He has yet to make his profesional debut.

Gregorius, Didi

6 | **Cincinnati** | EXP MLB DEBUT: 2013 | POTENTIAL: Starting SS | **8D**

Bats L Age 22
2008 NDFA Netherlands

- Pwr ++
- BAvg +++
- Spd +++
- Def +++

Year	Lev	Team	AB	R	H	HR	RBI	Avg	OB	Slg	OPS	bb%	ct%	Eye	SB	CS	x/h%	Iso	RC/G
2009	A+	Sarasota	71	8	18	0	2	254	264	310	574	1	87	0.11	0	0	22	56	2.47
2010	A	Dayton	501	65	137	5	41	273	318	379	698	6	88	0.53	16	7	23	106	4.18
2010	A+	Lynchburg	25	4	6	0	0	240	296	240	536	7	76	0.33	0	0	0	0	1.94
2011	A+	Bakersfield	188	30	57	5	28	303	338	457	796	5	87	0.40	8	8	32	154	5.14
2011	AA	Carolina	148	18	40	2	16	270	312	392	704	6	83	0.36	3	2	28	122	4.15

Slick fielding, strong-armed SS from the Netherlands continues to impress. Has plus speed and range and a good glove. Does has an aggressive approach at the plate with moderate bat speed, but minimal power. Is still raw in some aspects of the game, but has some nice tools and should be able to stick at SS.

Gretzky, Trevor

3 | **Chicago (N)** | EXP MLB DEBUT: 2015 | POTENTIAL: Starting 1B | **7C**

Bats R Age 19
2011 (7) HS (CA)

- Pwr +++
- BAvg +++
- Spd +++
- Def +++

Year	Lev	Team	AB	R	H	HR	RBI	Avg	OB	Slg	OPS	bb%	ct%	Eye	SB	CS	x/h%	Iso	RC/G
2011		Did not play																	

Tall, lanky 1B prospect is the son of former NHL great Wayne Gretzky. Strong athlete with good bat speed and the potential to hit for power. Is still very raw but is a plus athlete and the potential to succeed.

Grichuk, Randal

89 | **Los Angeles (A)** | EXP MLB DEBUT: 2014 | POTENTIAL: Starting OF | **8C**

Bats R Age 20
2009 (1) HS (TX)

- Pwr +++
- BAvg +++
- Spd +++
- Def +++

Year	Lev	Team	AB	R	H	HR	RBI	Avg	OB	Slg	OPS	bb%	ct%	Eye	SB	CS	x/h%	Iso	RC/G
2010	Rk	AZL Angels	49	7	16	4	10	327	365	714	1080	6	82	0.33	0	0	56	388	8.53
2010	A	Cedar Rapids	202	41	59	7	36	292	322	530	852	4	75	0.18	4	0	51	238	6.02
2011	Rk	AZL Angels	24	2	8	0	6	333	385	458	843	8	83	0.50	0	0	25	125	6.05
2011	A	Cedar Rapids	122	12	28	2	13	230	266	402	667	5	76	0.21	0	1	46	172	3.69
2011	A+	Inland Empire	53	13	15	1	6	283	283	491	774	0	75	0.00	0	0	47	208	4.85

Athletic outfielder missed time due to fractured kneecap and struggled upon return. Owns quick, natural swing and plus bat speed and leverage give him power projection. Knows how to battle pitchers from both sides, though rarely works counts and will swing and miss. Solid defender with good range and average arm strength.

Grossman, Robbie

8 | **Pittsburgh** | EXP MLB DEBUT: 2013 | POTENTIAL: Starting CF | **8D**

Bats B Age 22
2008 (6) HS (TX)

- Pwr +++
- BAvg +++
- 4.20 Spd ++++
- Def ++++

Year	Lev	Team	AB	R	H	HR	RBI	Avg	OB	Slg	OPS	bb%	ct%	Eye	SB	CS	x/h%	Iso	RC/G
2008	Rk	GCL Pirates	16	3	3	0	1	188	350	250	600	20	56	0.57	1	0	33	63	3.35
2009	A	West Virginia	451	83	120	5	42	266	371	355	725	14	64	0.46	35	12	23	89	5.07
2010	A+	Bradenton	470	84	115	4	50	245	338	345	682	12	75	0.56	15	8	31	100	4.19
2011	A+	Bradenton	490	127	144	13	56	294	418	451	869	18	77	0.94	24	10	34	157	6.85

Athletic, switch-hitting outfielder with good speed and plus on base ability (104 walks). Has the the tools to be a solid leadoff hitter and showed improved power, both during the regular season and the AFL. Has good range and a strong, accurate throwing arm. Broken hamate bone should be healed by spring.

Gumbs, Angelo — 4 — New York (A)
EXP MLB DEBUT: 2014 | POTENTIAL: Starting 2B | 8C

Bats R | Age 19 | 2010 (2) HS (CA)
Pwr +++ | BAvg ++++ | Spd +++ | Def ++

Year	Lev	Team	AB	R	H	HR	RBI	Avg	OB	Slg	OPS	bb%	ct%	Eye	SB	CS	x/h%	Iso	RC/G
2010	Rk	GCL Yankees	26	1	5	0	0	192	222	231	453	4	88	0.33	3	0	20	38	1.31
2011	A-	Staten Island	197	32	52	3	29	264	332	406	738	9	71	0.35	11	7	35	142	4.87

Quick and athletic infielder who does a variety of things well. Possesses raw strength and hits hard line drives all over field. Bat speed ideal for producing power and has acumen to hit for BA. Can be passive at times and swing can get too loose. Also can be jammed inside. Range and agility are a tad short, but has potential to be solid with good arm strength.

Guyer, Brandon — 789 — Tampa Bay
EXP MLB DEBUT: 2011 | POTENTIAL: Starting OF | 8C

Bats R | Age 26 | 2007 (5) Virginia
Pwr +++ | BAvg ++++ | Spd +++ | Def +++

Year	Lev	Team	AB	R	H	HR	RBI	Avg	OB	Slg	OPS	bb%	ct%	Eye	SB	CS	x/h%	Iso	RC/G
2009	A+	Daytona	265	40	92	2	32	347	401	453	854	8	87	0.71	23	2	23	106	6.11
2009	AA	Tennessee	189	22	36	1	14	190	231	291	522	5	83	0.30	7	5	42	101	1.99
2010	AA	Tennessee	369	76	127	13	58	344	389	588	977	7	86	0.53	30	3	46	244	7.41
2011	AAA	Durham	388	78	121	14	61	312	369	521	889	8	80	0.44	16	6	40	209	6.53
2011	MLB	Tampa Bay	41	7	8	2	3	195	214	366	580	2	78	0.11	0	0	38	171	2.18

Well-rounded outfielder who just needs opportunity at plate, but makes contact and has moderate power to all fields. Fluid, quick swing is method for producing high BA and average pop. Can swing at bad pitches early in count, but shortens swing when needed. Has good speed and can play all OF positions.

Guzman, Ronald — 7 — Texas
EXP MLB DEBUT: 2016 | POTENTIAL: Starting OF | 9E

Bats L | Age 17 | 2011 FA (DR)
Pwr ++++ | BAvg +++ | Spd +++ | Def ++

Year	Lev	Team	AB	R	H	HR	RBI	Avg	OB	Slg	OPS	bb%	ct%	Eye	SB	CS	x/h%	Iso	RC/G
2011		Did not play																	

Tall and very projectable athlete with as much upside as any player in minors. Has loose swing with tremendous strength for age. Shows an advanced approach and ability to put ball in play. Should grow into frame and add even more power. Jury is out on defensive skills as he lacks present arm strength and doesn't run very well.

Gyorko, Jedd — 5 — San Diego
EXP MLB DEBUT: 2012 | POTENTIAL: Starting 3B | 8C

Bats R | Age 23 | 2010 (2) West Virginia
Pwr +++ | BAvg +++ | Spd +++ | Def ++

Year	Lev	Team	AB	R	H	HR	RBI	Avg	OB	Slg	OPS	bb%	ct%	Eye	SB	CS	x/h%	Iso	RC/G
2010	NCAA	West Virginia	236	71	90	19	57	381	477	750	1227	15	90	1.79	1	2	53	369	10.62
2010	A-	Eugene	106	16	35	5	18	330	383	528	911	8	75	0.35	1	1	31	198	6.77
2010	A	Fort Wayne	162	19	46	2	23	284	359	389	748	10	81	0.61	1	0	28	105	4.94
2011	A+	Lake Elsinore	340	78	124	18	74	365	429	638	1067	10	81	0.59	11	3	44	274	8.74
2011	AA	San Antonio	236	41	68	7	40	288	359	428	787	10	79	0.52	1	0	28	140	5.28

Stocky 3B prospect with quick hands, good bat speed, and excellent pitch recognition. Put on an offensive show in '11. Power is above average with 42 doubles and 25 home runs. Improved range and glove on defense, but thick lower half limits range. Will need to continue to improve defensively, but the bat is legit and he could reach the majors by mid-2012.

Hager, Jake — 6 — Tampa Bay
EXP MLB DEBUT: 2015 | POTENTIAL: Reserve 2B/SS | 7C

Bats R | Age 19 | 2011 (1) HS (NV)
Pwr ++ | BAvg +++ | Spd +++ | Def ++

Year	Lev	Team	AB	R	H	HR	RBI	Avg	OB	Slg	OPS	bb%	ct%	Eye	SB	CS	x/h%	Iso	RC/G
2011	Rk	Princeton	193	29	52	4	17	269	302	399	701	4	87	0.35	5	7	31	130	4.03

Lean and fundamentally-sound infielder who plays above average tools. May not be able to stick at SS as range isn't ideal, but makes plays and offers decent arm strength. Could play 2B or 3B just as well. Brings solid approach to plate and makes excellent contact with plus hand-eye coordination and bat control. Won't hit for much pop, but uses whole field.

Hagerty, Jason — 2 — San Diego
EXP MLB DEBUT: 2013 | POTENTIAL: Starting C | 7C

Bats B | Age 24 | 2009 (5) Miami-FL
Pwr +++ | BAvg +++ | Spd ++ | Def +

Year	Lev	Team	AB	R	H	HR	RBI	Avg	OB	Slg	OPS	bb%	ct%	Eye	SB	CS	x/h%	Iso	RC/G
2009	A-	Eugene	173	34	39	6	26	225	327	399	725	13	73	0.55	0	0	46	173	4.68
2009	AAA	Portland	15	3	2	0	1	133	235	200	435	12	73	0.50	0	0	50	67	0.80
2010	A	Fort Wayne	431	74	130	14	74	302	420	494	914	17	76	0.85	2	1	40	193	7.46
2011	A+	Lake Elsinore	257	53	80	8	47	311	375	518	892	9	76	0.42	3	2	44	206	6.77
2011	AA	San Antonio	130	15	30	1	18	231	306	315	621	10	69	0.35	0	1	27	85	3.52

Strong, powerful backstop started well in the CAL, but struggled when promoted to Double-A. Good bat speed and solid power has some nice offensive potential. Will need to make more consistent contact to hit for average, though he does draw walks. Defensively he has a strong arm and receives the ball well, but overall is not a plus defender.

Hague, Rick — 6 — Washington
EXP MLB DEBUT: 2013 | POTENTIAL: Reserve SS/2B | 6C

Bats R | Age 23 | 2010 (3) Rice
Pwr ++ | BAvg +++ | Spd ++ | Def +++

Year	Lev	Team	AB	R	H	HR	RBI	Avg	OB	Slg	OPS	bb%	ct%	Eye	SB	CS	x/h%	Iso	RC/G
2009	NCAA	Rice	254	47	81	9	57	319	373	492	865	8	73	0.32	11	5	32	173	6.35
2010	NCAA	Rice	259	71	88	15	55	340	408	591	999	10	80	0.57	10	2	40	251	7.90
2010	Rk	GCL Nationals	40	7	11	0	6	275	396	300	696	17	78	0.89	3	0	9	25	4.58
2010	A	Hagerstown	159	26	52	3	27	327	382	522	904	8	79	0.41	3	2	38	195	6.86
2011	A+	Potomac	14	4	5	1	4	357	438	714	1152	13	93	2.00	1	0	60	357	9.55

Gritty SS prospect missed almost all of '11 with a shoulder injury. Has good baseball sense, but only average tools and the injury cost him developmental time. When healthy he has a nice bat with a compact stroke and a willingness to use the whole field. Defensively, he doesn't have the range for shortstop, but his footwork and arm are sufficient for 2B.

Hamilton, Billy — 6 — Cincinnati
EXP MLB DEBUT: 2013 | POTENTIAL: Starting SS | 9D

Bats B | Age 21 | 2009 (2) HS (MS)
Pwr ++ | BAvg +++ | Spd +++++ (3.60) | Def +++

Year	Lev	Team	AB	R	H	HR	RBI	Avg	OB	Slg	OPS	bb%	ct%	Eye	SB	CS	x/h%	Iso	RC/G
2009	Rk	GCL Reds	166	19	34	0	11	205	254	277	531	6	72	0.23	14	3	26	72	1.89
2010	Rk	Billings	283	61	90	2	24	318	379	456	835	9	80	0.50	48	9	28	138	6.03
2011	A	Dayton	550	99	153	3	50	278	341	360	701	9	76	0.39	103	20	20	82	4.25

Raw, athletic switch-hitting SS prospect is one of the most dynamic athletes in baseball. Stole 103 bases despite getting just 136 hits. Uses a slash-and-run approach at the plate so power isn't likely going to develop. Still raw defensively and made 39 errors, in part because he got to balls others can't, but also because his mechanics and positioning are not great.

Hamilton, Mark — 3 — St. Louis
EXP MLB DEBUT: 2010 | POTENTIAL: Reserve 1B | 7C

Bats L | Age 27 | 2006 (2) Tulane
Pwr ++++ | BAvg +++ | Spd ++ | Def ++

Year	Lev	Team	AB	R	H	HR	RBI	Avg	OB	Slg	OPS	bb%	ct%	Eye	SB	CS	x/h%	Iso	RC/G
2010	Rk	GCL Cardinals	27	2	8	2	2	296	387	556	943	13	67	0.44	0	0	38	259	7.81
2010	AAA	Memphis	258	53	77	18	60	298	382	585	968	12	73	0.50	0	0	49	287	7.82
2010	MLB	St. Louis	14	0	2	0	0	143	200	143	343	7	64	0.20	0	0	0	0	
2011	AAA	Memphis	252	46	87	2	39	345	439	472	911	14	83	0.95	0	0	32	127	7.26
2011	MLB	St. Louis	47	5	10	0	4	213	275	277	551	8	66	0.25	0	0	30	64	2.19

Tall, strong (6'4" 220 lbs) 1B prospect has solid plate discipline and the ability to hit for average. Power evaporated in '11, but should be good for 10-15 a year in the majors with the potential for a .300 average. Got into 38 games for the Cardinals, but is slow and below average defensively limiting his potential.

Hanson, Alen — 64 — Pittsburgh
EXP MLB DEBUT: 2015 | POTENTIAL: Starting SS/2B | 7C

Bats B | Age 19 | 2009 NDFA D.R.
Pwr +++ | BAvg +++ | Spd ++++ | Def +++

Year	Lev	Team	AB	R	H	HR	RBI	Avg	OB	Slg	OPS	bb%	ct%	Eye	SB	CS	x/h%	Iso	RC/G
2011	Rk	GCL Pirates	198	42	52	2	35	263	333	429	763	10	83	0.62	24	6	42	167	5.19
2011	A-	State College	10	1	2	0	0	200	273	200	473	9	80	0.50	0	0	0	0	1.36

Small, wiry (5'11", 155 lbs) infield prospect has plus speed and good athleticism. Line-drive approach and good plate discipline give him potential to hit for average. Good range, but below-average arm makes 2B his likely destination.

Harper, Bryce — 9 — Washington
EXP MLB DEBUT: 2012 | POTENTIAL: Starting RF | 10D

Bats L | Age 19 | 2010 (1) College of S. Nevada
Pwr +++++ | BAvg ++++ | Spd +++ | Def +++

Year	Lev	Team	AB	R	H	HR	RBI	Avg	OB	Slg	OPS	bb%	ct%	Eye	SB	CS	x/h%	Iso	RC/G
2011	A	Hagerstown	258	49	82	14	46	318	417	554	971	15	76	0.72	19	5	39	236	7.93
2011	AA	Harrisburg	129	14	33	3	12	256	333	395	729	10	80	0.58	7	2	33	140	4.64

Strong, athletic OF has a much raw power as any prospect in baseball. Did nothing in '11 to diminish expectations, reaching Double-A as an 18-year-old. A physically mature LH hitter with mammoth power to all fields. Nice approach at the plate should allow him to hit for average as well. The top prospect in baseball will get a chance to win a starting job in 2012.

Harrilchak, Cory
8 | **Atlanta** | EXP MLB DEBUT: 2013 | POTENTIAL: Reserve OF | **6C**

Bats L Age 24
2009 (14) Elon
Pwr ++
BAvg +++
Spd ++
Def ++

Year	Lev	Team	AB	R	H	HR	RBI	Avg	OB	Slg	OPS	bb%	ct%	Eye	SB	CS	x/h%	Iso	RC/G
2009	NCAA	Elon	256	79	86	16	61	336	426	617	1043	14	84	0.95	10	9	43	281	8.53
2009	Rk	Danville	222	43	72	2	41	324	398	441	839	11	90	1.23	19	2	24	117	6.15
2010	A	Rome	219	31	67	1	22	306	374	393	767	10	89	1.00	18	11	21	87	5.26
2010	A+	Myrtle Beach	234	29	63	2	25	269	329	406	735	8	81	0.47	4	4	37	137	4.74
2011	AA	Mississippi	429	44	114	7	56	266	331	399	730	9	83	0.58	10	7	33	133	4.65

Short, athletic OF prospect took a step back in '11. None of tools stand out, but is a solid player with moderate power, solid BA, moderate speed in CF, and solid plate discipline. A grinder who doesn't wow, but is a solid player who has value due to his versitility.

Harrison, Travis
5 | **Minnesota** | EXP MLB DEBUT: 2015 | POTENTIAL: Starting 3B | **8D**

Bats R Age 19
2011 (1-S) HS (CA)
Pwr ++++
BAvg +++
Spd ++
Def ++

Year	Lev	Team	AB	R	H	HR	RBI	Avg	OB	Slg	OPS	bb%	ct%	Eye	SB	CS	x/h%	Iso	RC/G
2011		Did not play																	

Instinctual and strong infielder whose upside revolves around power potential. Swings for the fences while making hard, consistent contact, but has chance to hit for BA as he shortens swings in situations. Fails to recognize breaking balls and long swing may result in high K totals. Could eventually move across diamond due to subpar range and footwork at 3B.

Hassan, Alex
79 | **Boston** | EXP MLB DEBUT: 2012 | POTENTIAL: Reserve OF | **7C**

Bats R Age 24
2009 (20) Duke
Pwr +++
BAvg +++
Spd ++
Def +++

Year	Lev	Team	AB	R	H	HR	RBI	Avg	OB	Slg	OPS	bb%	ct%	Eye	SB	CS	x/h%	Iso	RC/G
2009	A-	Lowell	93	14	31	1	11	333	386	441	827	8	88	0.73	1	1	23	108	5.76
2009	A	Greenville	32	6	10	1	7	313	353	563	915	6	78	0.29	0	0	50	250	6.87
2010	A+	Salem	342	46	98	8	48	287	388	456	845	14	80	0.83	6	1	40	170	6.37
2010	AAA	Pawtucket	3	0	0	0	1	0	0	0	0	0	100		0	0			
2011	AA	Portland	454	75	132	13	64	291	392	456	848	14	83	0.96	8	2	36	165	6.35

Consistent outfielder who continues to exceed expectations by producing with bat and glove. Set career highs in 2B and HR while showing strong, discerning eye at plate. Makes such easy contact that he is comfortable working deep into counts. Power is merely average and bat speed is a little short for full-time role. Doesn't possess much speed, but has passable range.

Havens, Reese
4 | **New York (N)** | EXP MLB DEBUT: 2012 | POTENTIAL: Starting 2B | **8D**

Bats L Age 25
2008 (1) South Carolina
Pwr +++
BAvg +++
4.40 Spd ++
Def +++

Year	Lev	Team	AB	R	H	HR	RBI	Avg	OB	Slg	OPS	bb%	ct%	Eye	SB	CS	x/h%	Iso	RC/G
2009	A+	St. Lucie	360	53	89	14	52	247	347	422	769	13	80	0.75	3	2	38	175	5.21
2010	A+	St. Lucie	57	9	16	3	7	281	369	509	878	12	68	0.44	0	1	38	228	6.88
2010	AA	Binghamton	68	12	23	6	12	338	392	662	1054	8	78	0.40	0	2	39	324	8.36
2011	A+	St. Lucie	11	1	3	0	2	273	385	455	839	15	55	0.40	0	0	67	182	8.19
2011	AA	Binghamton	211	37	61	6	26	289	370	455	825	11	72	0.46	2	0	36	166	6.06

Strong, athletic SS has seen limited action due to a back/rib injury. When healthy Havens has shown the ability to hit for power and average. He has strong hands, good bat speed, and a solid strike zone. Defensively he moves well, has soft hands, and strong throwing arm. Limited range resulted in a move from SS to 2B where he fits better.

Hawkins, Christopher
7 | **Toronto** | EXP MLB DEBUT: 2015 | POTENTIAL: Starting OF | **8D**

Bats L Age 20
2010 (3) HS (GA)
Pwr +++
BAvg +++
Spd +++
Def +++

Year	Lev	Team	AB	R	H	HR	RBI	Avg	OB	Slg	OPS	bb%	ct%	Eye	SB	CS	x/h%	Iso	RC/G
2010	Rk	GCL Blue Jays	157	29	40	0	15	255	320	350	670	9	76	0.41	8	3	30	96	3.94
2011	Rk	Bluefield	242	49	77	5	52	318	375	492	867	8	81	0.48	14	4	34	174	6.30
2011	A+	Dunedin	4	0	0	0	0	0	0	0	0	0	50	0.00	0	0			

Strong and tall prospect who moved from 3B to OF prior to season. Makes hard contact and drives ball to all fields while offering plus power potential. Can be tied up with good FB and swing mechanics may lead to reduced BA in future. Lacks arm strength for anything other than LF and will need time to work on routes and jumps in OF.

Hawn, Cody
3 | **Milwaukee** | EXP MLB DEBUT: 2014 | POTENTIAL: Backup 1B | **7C**

Bats L Age 23
2010 (6) Tennessee
Pwr +++
BAvg ++++
Spd ++
Def ++

Year	Lev	Team	AB	R	H	HR	RBI	Avg	OB	Slg	OPS	bb%	ct%	Eye	SB	CS	x/h%	Iso	RC/G
2009	NCAA	Tennessee	198	46	72	22	81	364	440	773	1213	12	82	0.75	0	1	51	409	10.33
2010	NCAA	Tennessee	199	40	65	14	61	327	444	593	1037	17	78	0.95	2	2	38	266	8.79
2010	Rk	Helena	253	36	78	13	61	308	392	542	934	12	77	0.60	0	0	42	233	7.29
2011	A	Wisconsin	377	56	111	6	50	294	379	406	784	12	77	0.60	3	4	27	111	5.46

Strong, left handed hitting 1B. Hawn has good bat speed and decent raw power, but projects to more of a high BA hitter than a power hitter. Struggles with left-handed pitching. Runs fairly well, but he isn't likely to steal many bases and defense at 1B is below average. Will need to hit for average to have value.

Hazelbaker, Jeremy
89 | **Boston** | EXP MLB DEBUT: 2013 | POTENTIAL: Starting OF | **7C**

Bats L Age 24
2009 (4) Ball State
Pwr +++
BAvg +++
Spd ++++
Def ++

Year	Lev	Team	AB	R	H	HR	RBI	Avg	OB	Slg	OPS	bb%	ct%	Eye	SB	CS	x/h%	Iso	RC/G
2009	A-	Lowell	8	0	1	0	0	125	417	125	542	33	63	1.33	0	0	0	0	2.18
2009	A	Greenville	150	16	25	1	9	167	277	233	511	13	61	0.40	11	2	28	67	1.61
2010	A	Greenville	442	78	118	12	62	267	353	455	808	12	69	0.44	63	17	42	188	5.99
2011	A+	Salem	122	26	34	5	14	279	380	475	856	14	72	0.59	12	6	41	197	6.54
2011	AA	Portland	354	60	94	12	41	266	343	435	778	11	70	0.40	35	8	35	169	5.38

Tall and athletic outfielder who is among fastest players in org. Despite speed, likes to swing for fences and posted career high in HR. Has solid leadoff skills, but will need to shorten swing and make better contact. Steals bases effectively and average arm and range make him decent defender. Fringy arm strength and questionable routes may move him to LF.

Head, Miles
35 | **Oakland** | EXP MLB DEBUT: 2014 | POTENTIAL: Starting 1B/3B | **8E**

Bats R Age 21
2009 (26) HS (GA)
Pwr ++++
BAvg +++
Spd +
Def ++

Year	Lev	Team	AB	R	H	HR	RBI	Avg	OB	Slg	OPS	bb%	ct%	Eye	SB	CS	x/h%	Iso	RC/G
2009	Rk	GCL Red Sox	29	1	3	0	0	103	188	103	291	9	72	0.38	0	0			
2010	A-	Lowell	229	21	55	1	35	240	328	341	669	12	84	0.83	1	1	35	100	4.15
2011	A	Greenville	263	61	89	15	53	338	406	612	1018	10	80	0.57	4	2	46	274	8.17
2011	A+	Salem	232	27	59	7	29	254	313	405	719	8	76	0.36	0	2	34	151	4.34

Short and strong infielder who has been consistent performer in career. Drives balls to all fields and possesses above average raw power. Has a mature approach, but can let good pitches go by and can be jammed inside due to stiff swing. Lacks speed to steal bases and owns less than ideal footwork at 1B. Arm is strong, though, and after his December trade, OAK is going to try him out at 3B.

Heathcott, Slade
8 | **New York (A)** | EXP MLB DEBUT: 2014 | POTENTIAL: Starting OF | **7B**

Bats L Age 21
2009 (1) HS (TX)
Pwr +++
BAvg +++
Spd ++++
Def +++

Year	Lev	Team	AB	R	H	HR	RBI	Avg	OB	Slg	OPS	bb%	ct%	Eye	SB	CS	x/h%	Iso	RC/G
2009	Rk	GCL Yankees	10	0	1	0	0	100	182	100	282	9	80	0.50	0	0			
2010	A	Charleston (SC)	298	48	77	2	30	258	350	352	702	12	66	0.42	15	10	27	94	4.61
2011	A	Charleston (SC)	210	36	57	4	16	271	332	419	751	8	73	0.33	6	7	33	148	4.93
2011	A+	Tampa	5	2	3	1	1	600	600	1200	1800	0	80	0.00	0	0	33	600	16.14

Strong and aggressive outfielder who plays game with passion. Shut down in June after shoulder injury and has experienced multiple ailments in career. Pitch selectivity is an issue and lacks swing fluidity for present power. Bat speed is more than enough and has good secondary skills. Runs swiftly and ranges well in CF. Arm strength is best tool.

Hechevarria, Adeiny
6 | **Toronto** | EXP MLB DEBUT: 2012 | POTENTIAL: Starting SS | **8D**

Bats R Age 23
2010 FA (Cuba)
Pwr ++
BAvg ++
Spd ++++
Def ++++

Year	Lev	Team	AB	R	H	HR	RBI	Avg	OB	Slg	OPS	bb%	ct%	Eye	SB	CS	x/h%	Iso	RC/G
2010	A+	Dunedin	161	21	31	1	7	193	217	292	509	3	84	0.20	7	0	35	99	1.78
2010	AA	Nw Hampshire	253	36	69	3	34	273	306	360	665	5	84	0.30	6	3	22	87	3.59
2011	AA	Nw Hampshire	464	58	109	6	46	235	274	347	621	5	83	0.32	19	13	31	112	3.13
2011	AAA	Las Vegas	108	16	42	2	11	389	431	537	968	7	81	0.38	1	2	24	148	7.43

Quick and nimble infielder who stands out more for glove than bat. Strong, accurate arm is terrific while soft hands make plays at SS. Has swing path and bat speed to eventually hit for BA, but can lunge at balls out of zone. Could benefit by hitting more balls on ground and making better contact. Power will never be part of game.

Hedges, Austin
2 | **San Diego** | EXP MLB DEBUT: 2015 | POTENTIAL: Starting C | **8D**

Bats R Age 19
2011 (2) HS (CA)
Pwr ++
BAvg +++
Spd +++
Def ++++

Year	Lev	Team	AB	R	H	HR	RBI	Avg	OB	Slg	OPS	bb%	ct%	Eye	SB	CS	x/h%	Iso	RC/G
2011	Rk	AZL Padres	16	3	5	1	4	313	476	500	976	24	94	5.00	1	0	20	188	8.32
2011	A-	Eugene	10	0	1	0	0	100	250	200	450	17	70	0.67	0	0	100	100	1.03

Hedges was the best defensive catcher available in the '11 draft. Fell to the 2nd round due to concerns about signability. Agile, athletic backstop who receives the ball, blocks well, has a quick pop time and a strong throwing arm. Does have good raw power and decent bat speed, but contact ability and pitch recognition are question marks.

Henry, Justin — 789 — Detroit

EXP MLB DEBUT: 2012 | POTENTIAL: Utility player | 6B

Bats L Age 27
2007 (9) Mississippi

- Pwr +
- BAvg + + +
- Spd + + + +
- Def + + +

Year	Lev	Team	AB	R	H	HR	RBI	Avg	OB	Slg	OPS	bb%	ct%	Eye	SB	CS	x/h%	Iso	RC/G
2009	A+	Lakeland	424	56	109	0	43	257	328	309	637	10	91	1.13	22	7	17	52	3.82
2010	AA	Erie	200	28	52	1	15	260	373	355	728	15	80	0.90	9	6	29	95	5.00
2010	AAA	Toledo	156	18	42	0	14	269	345	333	678	10	84	0.72	9	4	21	64	4.16
2011	AA	Erie	376	52	116	0	46	309	406	404	811	14	86	1.19	21	8	26	96	6.06
2011	AAA	Toledo	19	5	8	0	1	421	500	526	1026	14	89	1.50	2	1	25	105	8.54

Tall and athletic outfielder with ideal on base skills to hit atop lineup. Puts balls in play after working counts and uses above average speed to steal sacks. Short swing produces grounders and low liners, but only has three career HR to his credit. Versatile defender who can play all OF positions, but also can play middle infield if needed.

Hernandez, Elier — 79 — Kansas City

EXP MLB DEBUT: 2015 | POTENTIAL: Starting OF | 9E

Bats R Age 17
2011 FA (DR)

- Pwr + + +
- BAvg + + +
- Spd + + +
- Def + + +

Year	Lev	Team	AB	R	H	HR	RBI	Avg	OB	Slg	OPS	bb%	ct%	Eye	SB	CS	x/h%	Iso	RC/G
2011		Did not play																	

Young and athletic international signee with significant upside. Owns swing conducive to hard line drives at present, but has strength and bat speed to project to plus pop down the line. Still very raw with game and will need to learn to hit in situations and recognize pitches. Has athleticism for average speed, but may slow down as he adds muscle to tall frame.

Hernandez, Gorkys — 8 — Pittsburgh

EXP MLB DEBUT: 2012 | POTENTIAL: Starting CF | 7D

Bats R Age 24
2005 NDFA D.R.

- Pwr + +
- BAvg + + +
- 4.00 Spd + + + +
- Def + + +

Year	Lev	Team	AB	R	H	HR	RBI	Avg	OB	Slg	OPS	bb%	ct%	Eye	SB	CS	x/h%	Iso	RC/G
2008	A+	Myrtle Beach	406	75	107	5	42	264	341	387	728	11	81	0.61	20	4	32	123	4.72
2009	AA	Mississippi	212	33	67	0	19	316	361	387	748	7	75	0.28	10	8	19	71	4.80
2009	AA	Altoona	344	45	90	3	31	262	310	340	650	7	78	0.32	9	8	21	78	3.45
2010	AA	Altoona	368	45	98	2	26	266	327	334	661	8	74	0.35	17	3	17	68	3.68
2011	AAA	Indianapolis	424	48	120	1	40	283	338	392	729	8	79	0.38	21	9	29	108	4.63

Lean, athletic OF recovered from down season in '10. Hernandez has plus speed, contact ability, and plate discipline. Power continues to be below average, but he can drive the gaps. Possesses arm strength and range in CF, but will need to improve his routes. Needs to make more consistent contact to allow his slash and run style to play up.

Hernandez, Marco — 4 — Chicago (N)

EXP MLB DEBUT: 2015 | POTENTIAL: Starting SS/2B | 8D

Bats L Age 19
2008 NDFA D.R.

- Pwr + + +
- BAvg + + +
- Spd + + +
- Def + + +

Year	Lev	Team	AB	R	H	HR	RBI	Avg	OB	Slg	OPS	bb%	ct%	Eye	SB	CS	x/h%	Iso	RC/G
2011	Rk	AZL Cubs	210	39	70	2	42	333	381	486	866	7	86	0.55	9	7	33	152	6.22

Lean, athletic SS, Hernandez had an impressive U.S. debut. He played SS and 2B, but has the actions and range to stick at SS. He is a switch-hitter with gap power and decent plate discipline. He has good bat speed and an aggressive line-drive approach. He is very young and has a lot of work to do, but the upside is exciting.

Herrera, Rosell — 6 — Colorado

EXP MLB DEBUT: 2014 | POTENTIAL: Starting SS | 8D

Bats R Age 19
2009 NDFA, D.R.

- Pwr + + + +
- BAvg + + +
- Spd + +
- Def + + +

Year	Lev	Team	AB	R	H	HR	RBI	Avg	OB	Slg	OPS	bb%	ct%	Eye	SB	CS	x/h%	Iso	RC/G
2011	Rk	Casper	243	38	69	6	34	284	356	449	804	10	74	0.44	5	4	29	165	5.67

Toolsy switch-hitting SS had an impressive pro debut. He is better from the LH side where he has good power and makes contact. At 6'4", he might grow out of the position and doesn't have plus range. He might not have enough power for 3B, but does have good bat speed and moves well enough and could play a corner OF spot.

Hewitt, Anthony — 9 — Philadelphia

EXP MLB DEBUT: 2014 | POTENTIAL: Backup OF | 7E

Bats R Age 23
2008 (1) HS (NY)

- Pwr + + +
- BAvg +
- 4.20 Spd + + + +
- Def +

Year	Lev	Team	AB	R	H	HR	RBI	Avg	OB	Slg	OPS	bb%	ct%	Eye	SB	CS	x/h%	Iso	RC/G
2008	Rk	GCL Phillies	117	14	23	1	9	197	242	299	541	6	53	0.13	2	0	39	103	2.42
2009	A-	Williamsport	233	25	52	7	30	223	252	395	647	4	67	0.12	9	5	38	172	3.37
2010	A	Lakewood	440	47	89	11	49	202	225	327	552	3	64	0.08	10	6	34	125	1.95
2011	A	Lakewood	454	62	109	14	55	240	268	405	673	4	67	0.11	36	5	38	165	3.70

Former 1st rounder has plus power but continues to struggle. He has good athleticism, speed, and plus bat speed, but never figured out how to hit and has horrendous plate discipline. Despite being drafted in '08 he has yet to play above Low-A. He did hit 19 home runs, but it is hard to see him getting much better. Looks like this gamble will not pay off.

Hicks, Aaron — 8 — Minnesota

EXP MLB DEBUT: 2013 | POTENTIAL: Starting OF | 8B

Bats B Age 22
2008 (1) HS (CA)

- Pwr + + +
- BAvg + + +
- Spd + + + +
- Def + + + +

Year	Lev	Team	AB	R	H	HR	RBI	Avg	OB	Slg	OPS	bb%	ct%	Eye	SB	CS	x/h%	Iso	RC/G
2008	Rk	GCL Twins	173	32	55	4	27	318	413	491	904	14	82	0.88	12	2	33	173	7.09
2009	A	Beloit	251	43	63	4	29	251	354	382	736	14	78	0.73	10	8	35	131	4.96
2010	A	Beloit	423	86	118	8	49	279	403	428	831	17	74	0.79	21	11	35	149	6.46
2011	A+	Fort Myers	443	79	107	5	38	242	355	368	723	15	75	0.71	17	9	38	126	4.88

Toolsy and athletic outfielder who hasn't lived up to hype, but skills still evident. Can be overly passive at plate and needs to swing with authority at drivable pitches. Quick bat shows promise in realizing power potential and should add more pop with added strength. Struggles from left side. Exhibits plus speed and CF range while showcasing one of top arms in minors.

Hill, Steven — 2 — St. Louis

EXP MLB DEBUT: 2010 | POTENTIAL: Backup C | 6C

Bats R Age 27
2007 (13) SF Austin St

- Pwr + + + +
- BAvg + +
- 4.35 Spd + +
- Def + +

Year	Lev	Team	AB	R	H	HR	RBI	Avg	OB	Slg	OPS	bb%	ct%	Eye	SB	CS	x/h%	Iso	RC/G
2010	AA	Springfield	361	60	101	22	86	280	348	543	891	10	75	0.42	1	0	50	263	6.61
2010	AAA	Memphis	34	2	6	2	6	176	243	382	626	8	71	0.30	0	0	50	206	2.92
2010	MLB	St. Louis	3	1	1	1	1	333	333	1333	1667	0	67	0.00	0	0	100	1000	16.66
2011	AA	Springfield	131	22	37	11	26	282	333	573	906	7	73	0.29	1	0	43	290	6.57
2011	AAA	Memphis	17	3	5	3	6	294	368	824	1192	11	71	0.40	0	0	60	529	10.40

Hill is a strong backstop with nice offensive potential and owns a career minor league line of .289/.340/.518. His plate discipline is below average as he can be overly aggressive. Missed most of the '11 with knee surgery, but was fine by the end of the year. Well below average defensively and is unliikely to see much action behind the plate in the majors.

Hobson, K.C. — 3 — Toronto

EXP MLB DEBUT: 2014 | POTENTIAL: Reserve 1B | 7D

Bats R Age 21
2009 (6) HS (CA)

- Pwr + + +
- BAvg + + +
- Spd + +
- Def + +

Year	Lev	Team	AB	R	H	HR	RBI	Avg	OB	Slg	OPS	bb%	ct%	Eye	SB	CS	x/h%	Iso	RC/G
2010	Rk	GCL Blue Jays	129	17	36	4	17	279	316	411	727	5	87	0.41	1	5	25	132	4.29
2010	A	Lansing	92	14	24	2	9	261	292	391	683	4	82	0.24	0	0	29	130	3.73
2011	A	Lansing	480	65	120	4	53	250	335	333	668	11	85	0.84	1	0	25	83	4.07

Tall and pure-hitting infielder who has frame for power production, but didn't hit for much pop. Takes a lot of pitches and can be tentative at plate, but draws walks and can hit to all fields. Made much better contact with excellent barrel awareness and can lace doubles to gaps. Not much speed evident and defense is barely passable at 1B.

Hoes, L.J. — 47 — Baltimore

EXP MLB DEBUT: 2012 | POTENTIAL: Starting LF | 7B

Bats R Age 22
2008 (3) HS (MD)

- Pwr + +
- BAvg + + +
- Spd + + +
- Def + + +

Year	Lev	Team	AB	R	H	HR	RBI	Avg	OB	Slg	OPS	bb%	ct%	Eye	SB	CS	x/h%	Iso	RC/G
2010	A-	Aberdeen	28	8	13	1	5	464	500	821	1321	7	96	2.00	1	1	54	357	11.03
2010	A+	Frederick	353	52	98	3	44	278	372	368	740	13	80	0.76	10	8	24	91	4.99
2010	AA	Bowie	9	1	2	0	1	222	222	222	444	0	89	0.00	0	0	0	0	0.93
2011	A+	Frederick	158	23	38	3	17	241	286	342	627	6	84	0.40	4	2	26	101	3.20
2011	AA	Bowie	344	47	105	6	54	305	382	413	795	11	84	0.77	16	7	23	108	5.52

Pure hitter with solid, but not spectacular, offensive package. Posted career highs in HR and SB after conversion to LF. Gets better every year with patient approach and level swing. Has enough bat speed to smash doubles and makes good contact with hand-eye coordination. Won't hit for much power and may have to move back to 2B.

Hoffmann, Jamie — 789 — Colorado

EXP MLB DEBUT: 2009 | POTENTIAL: Backup OF | 7C

Bats R Age 27
2003 (8) HS, (MN)

- Pwr + +
- BAvg + + +
- Spd + + +
- Def + + +

Year	Lev	Team	AB	R	H	HR	RBI	Avg	OB	Slg	OPS	bb%	ct%	Eye	SB	CS	x/h%	Iso	RC/G
2009	AAA	Albuquerque	257	44	73	8	48	284	363	455	819	11	86	0.86	10	8	34	171	5.78
2009	MLB	Los Angeles (N)	22	2	4	1	7	182	182	409	591	0	77	0.00	0	0	75	227	2.35
2010	AAA	Albuquerque	545	91	169	8	74	310	361	431	792	7	82	0.44	17	7	28	121	5.28
2011	AAA	Albuquerque	475	91	141	22	84	297	356	497	853	8	79	0.43	14	4	34	200	5.99
2011	MLB	Los Angeles (N)	4	0	0	0	0	0	0	0	0	0	75	0.00	0	0			

Hoffman is an athletic outfielder that combines strength and speed. Hits for BA despite an unorthodox swing, but his stroke limits his power, even though he has sufficient bat speed and strong wrists. Plus strike zone judgement gives him a chance, but at 27 the ship may have already sailed. Time is running out.

Holt, Tyler — 78 — Cleveland

EXP MLB DEBUT: 2013 — POTENTIAL: Reserve OF — 6B

Bats R Age 23
2010 (10) Florida State
Pwr +
BAvg + + +
Spd + + + +
Def + + +

Year	Lev	Team	AB	R	H	HR	RBI	Avg	OB	Slg	OPS	bb%	ct%	Eye	SB	CS	x/h%	Iso	RC/G
2008	NCAA	Florida State	250	83	81	3	41	324	462	416	878	20	82	1.39	15	9	19	92	7.16
2009	NCAA	Florida State	237	87	95	5	28	401	512	578	1090	19	80	1.15	34	5	32	177	9.84
2010	NCAA	Florida State	259	87	92	13	48	355	475	629	1104	19	81	1.23	30	3	46	274	9.80
2010	A	Lake County	70	12	20	0	8	286	412	457	869	18	83	1.25	5	3	50	171	7.08
2011	A+	Kinston	449	66	114	2	26	254	364	325	689	15	76	0.74	34	6	21	71	4.41

Short and athletic outfielder whose game revolves around speed and defense. Plays above tools with polished ability to get on base and wreak havoc on basepaths. Hits hard line drives to all fields, but understands power isn't strength. Possesses good range in CF or LF though arm strength is below average.

Hood, Destin — 8 — Washington

EXP MLB DEBUT: 2013 — POTENTIAL: Starting CF — 8D

Bats R Age 22
2008 (2) HS (AL)
Pwr + + + +
BAvg + +
4.25 Spd + + + +
Def + + +

Year	Lev	Team	AB	R	H	HR	RBI	Avg	OB	Slg	OPS	bb%	ct%	Eye	SB	CS	x/h%	Iso	RC/G
2008	Rk	GCL Nationals	86	18	22	0	14	256	319	349	668	9	78	0.42	5	2	32	93	3.90
2009	Rk	GCL Nationals	88	18	29	3	24	330	385	614	999	8	78	0.42	3	0	55	284	8.11
2009	A-	Vermont	138	12	34	2	24	246	302	333	635	7	67	0.24	2	1	21	87	3.29
2010	A	Hagerstown	492	56	140	5	65	285	330	388	718	6	76	0.28	5	7	27	104	4.34
2011	A+	Potomac	463	61	128	13	83	276	357	445	802	11	79	0.60	21	6	37	168	5.61

Plus athlete with raw abilities. Hood is starting to realize his potenitial and had a solid season, htting for average with speed and power. Has plus bat speed, but can get pull-conscious and can struggle to make contact, though plate discipline was much improved. Good range in CF, but only fringe-average arm strength. Still has some work to do, but the upside is exciting.

House, Tyreace — 789 — Free Agent

EXP MLB DEBUT: 2014 — POTENTIAL: Reserve OF — 7E

Bats R Age 24
2008 (6) Col of the Canyons
Pwr +
BAvg + +
Spd + + + +
Def + + + +

Year	Lev	Team	AB	R	H	HR	RBI	Avg	OB	Slg	OPS	bb%	ct%	Eye	SB	CS	x/h%	Iso	RC/G
2008	Rk	AZL Athletics	99	25	26	0	10	263	376	273	649	15	78	0.82	12	1	4	10	3.87
2009	A-	Vancouver	196	31	57	0	16	291	347	306	654	8	81	0.45	19	10	5	15	3.57
2010	A	Kane County	424	83	104	1	32	245	385	290	675	18	79	1.09	37	13	13	45	4.42
2011	A	Burlington	348	46	66	0	27	190	279	210	489	11	77	0.53	27	6	11	20	1.54

Short and speedy outfielder who lives off legs and athleticism. Repeated Low-A and regressed with bat. Continues to fan while not having ability to turn on pitches and drive balls. Frame and swing lack projection and offense needs overhaul. Outstanding defender with plus-plus range, strong arm, and honed jumps and routes.

Hudson, Kyle — 78 — Baltimore

EXP MLB DEBUT: 2011 — POTENTIAL: Reserve OF — 6C

Bats L Age 25
2008 (4) Illinois
Pwr +
BAvg + + +
Spd + + + +
Def + + + +

Year	Lev	Team	AB	R	H	HR	RBI	Avg	OB	Slg	OPS	bb%	ct%	Eye	SB	CS	x/h%	Iso	RC/G
2011	A+	Frederick	86	12	24	0	2	279	354	314	668	10	81	0.63	8	6	13	35	3.95
2011	AA	Bowie	91	9	28	0	10	308	376	363	739	10	74	0.42	7	2	14	55	4.85
2011	AAA	Norfolk	246	39	73	0	11	297	380	333	713	12	78	0.60	26	8	11	37	4.56
2011	MLB	Baltimore	28	3	4	0	2	143	143	143	286	0	79	0.00	2	0	0	0	-1.43

Athletic outfielder with excellent speed, baserunning, and defensive abilities. Patience at plate along with disciplined eye give him chance to hit atop lineup, but strikes out a lot and fails to line balls for extra base hits. Has yet to hit HR in career. Steals bases easily and uses wheels for plus range in outfield. Possesses strong, accurate arm and keen instincts.

Hudson, Kyrell — 8 — Philadelphia

EXP MLB DEBUT: 2014 — POTENTIAL: Starting CF — 7D

Bats R Age 21
2009 (3) HS (WA)
Pwr + + +
BAvg + +
6.3/60 Spd + + + +
Def + + +

Year	Lev	Team	AB	R	H	HR	RBI	Avg	OB	Slg	OPS	bb%	ct%	Eye	SB	CS	x/h%	Iso	RC/G
2009	Rk	GCL Phillies	37	3	6	0	6	162	225	216	441	8	76	0.33	2	0	33	54	0.81
2010	A-	Williamsport	156	13	27	0	15	173	199	205	404	3	71	0.11	11	3	19	32	-0.06
2011	A-	Williamsport	269	31	74	1	18	275	321	357	677	6	77	0.29	28	11	22	82	3.84

Raw, toolsy OF is starting to put things together. Hudson has good bat speed and plus speed on the bases. He struggles with plate discipline and making consistent contact, but he does drive the ball well. He has limited power, which hurts his long-term value. Strong defender in CF with range and a good arm. There is some upside, but also work to do.

Iglesias, Jose — 6 — Boston

EXP MLB DEBUT: 2011 — POTENTIAL: Starting SS — 8B

Bats R Age 22
2009 FA (Cuba)
Pwr +
BAvg + + +
Spd + + + +
Def + + + + +

Year	Lev	Team	AB	R	H	HR	RBI	Avg	OB	Slg	OPS	bb%	ct%	Eye	SB	CS	x/h%	Iso	RC/G
2010	A-	Lowell	40	8	14	0	7	350	447	500	947	15	80	0.88	2	1	29	150	7.91
2010	AA	Portland	221	29	63	0	13	285	310	357	668	3	78	0.16	5	2	21	72	3.57
2011	AAA	Pawtucket	357	35	84	1	31	235	278	269	547	6	84	0.36	12	4	12	34	2.24
2011	MLB	Boston	6	3	2	0	0	333	333	333	667	0	67	0.00	0	0	0	0	3.37

Defensive standout who struggles with bat currently, but glovework gives him significant value. Hands, feet, and arm are well above average and he ranges well to both sides. Will show glimpses of offensive potential and realizes keeping ball on ground is best for plus speed. Lacks power, but has BA potential once he learns better swing mechanics.

Jackson, Brett — 8 — Chicago (N)

EXP MLB DEBUT: 2012 — POTENTIAL: Staring CF — 9C

Bats L Age 23
2009 (1) UC Berkeley
Pwr + + + +
BAvg + + + +
4.15 Spd + + +
Def + + +

Year	Lev	Team	AB	R	H	HR	RBI	Avg	OB	Slg	OPS	bb%	ct%	Eye	SB	CS	x/h%	Iso	RC/G
2009	A	Peoria	112	30	33	7	17	295	358	545	902	9	71	0.34	11	1	39	250	6.85
2010	A+	Daytona	263	56	83	6	38	316	412	517	929	14	76	0.68	12	7	40	202	7.60
2010	AA	Tennessee	228	47	63	6	28	276	360	465	825	12	72	0.48	18	4	40	189	6.13
2011	AA	Tennessee	246	45	63	10	32	256	371	443	814	15	70	0.61	15	6	37	187	6.06
2011	AAA	Iowa	185	39	55	10	26	297	390	551	941	13	65	0.44	6	1	45	254	8.12

Polished prospect with 5 above-average tools. Another solid season of growth. Showed improved power without sacriificing plate discipline, going 20/20. He still might outgrow CF, but for now is a solid defender with a strong arm. Nice, compact LH stroke and an ability to use the whole field. Smart player who works hard. Contact rate is a concern going forward.

Jackson, Ryan — 6 — St. Louis

EXP MLB DEBUT: 2012 — POTENTIAL: Starting SS — 8C

Bats R Age 24
2009 (5) Miami-FL
Pwr + +
BAvg + +
Spd + + + +
Def + + +

Year	Lev	Team	AB	R	H	HR	RBI	Avg	OB	Slg	OPS	bb%	ct%	Eye	SB	CS	x/h%	Iso	RC/G
2009	NCAA	Miami	194	38	51	4	28	263	367	381	749	14	83	0.97	9	4	27	119	5.12
2009	A-	Batavia	245	29	53	0	14	216	299	241	540	11	85	0.78	4	3	9	24	2.50
2010	A	Quad Cities	302	47	82	2	27	272	371	348	719	14	79	0.76	6	7	21	76	4.75
2010	A+	Palm Beach	148	14	43	1	8	291	340	392	732	7	86	0.52	3	2	28	101	4.60
2011	AA	Springfield	533	65	148	11	73	278	333	415	747	8	83	0.48	2	0	32	137	4.74

Jackson is an athletic SS with good speed and solid defense. A nice spike in power makes him more viable as a starter. He has plus range, soft hands, a strong arm, and is good enough defensively to play on a regular basis. If the offense proves to be legit, he has nice potential. He doesn't get much press, but fits into the Cardinals organizational mode nicely.

Jacobs, Brandon — 7 — Boston

EXP MLB DEBUT: 2014 — POTENTIAL: Starting OF — 8C

Bats R Age 21
2009 (10) HS (GA)
Pwr + + + +
BAvg + + +
Spd + + +
Def +

Year	Lev	Team	AB	R	H	HR	RBI	Avg	OB	Slg	OPS	bb%	ct%	Eye	SB	CS	x/h%	Iso	RC/G
2009	Rk	GCL Red Sox	24	1	6	0	0	250	308	333	641	8	67	0.25	0	0	33	83	3.56
2010	A-	Lowell	236	30	57	6	31	242	304	411	715	8	75	0.36	4	1	46	169	4.38
2011	A	Greenville	442	75	134	17	80	303	365	505	869	9	72	0.35	30	7	39	201	6.51

Strong and powerful athlete who showed off surprising polish in first full season. Controls strike zone with patient appraoch, but long swing can be exploited. Plus bat speed and quick wrists supply pop while good speed can leg out doubles in gaps. Has improved baserunning as well. Defense is subpar currently where his arm and range need attention.

James, Jiwan — 8 — Philadelphia

EXP MLB DEBUT: 2014 — POTENTIAL: Starting CF — 8D

Bats B Age 23
2007 (22) HS (FL)
Pwr + +
BAvg + + +
Spd + + + +
Def + + + +

Year	Lev	Team	AB	R	H	HR	RBI	Avg	OB	Slg	OPS	bb%	ct%	Eye	SB	CS	x/h%	Iso	RC/G
2009	A-	Williamsport	121	15	32	1	13	264	326	372	698	8	82	0.50	7	4	25	107	4.24
2010	A	Lakewood	556	85	150	5	64	270	313	365	678	6	76	0.27	33	20	25	95	3.80
2011	A+	Clearwater	526	76	141	4	38	268	320	363	683	7	77	0.33	31	16	26	95	3.94

Tall, wiry, switch-hitting OF prospect. James has some exciting tools, highlighted by his plus speed. At the pate, he has good bat speed and nice power potential, but struggles with breaking balls. He is currently a slap hitter and uses his speed well. He covers ground well on defense with a strong throwing arm. Plate discipline and pitch recognition will need to improve.

Jensen, Kyle — 79 — Florida

EXP MLB DEBUT: 2012 — POTENTIAL: Starting RF/LF — 8D

Bats R Age 24
2009 (12) St. Mary's
Pwr + + + +
BAvg + +
Spd + + +
Def + +

Year	Lev	Team	AB	R	H	HR	RBI	Avg	OB	Slg	OPS	bb%	ct%	Eye	SB	CS	x/h%	Iso	RC/G
2009	NCAA	St. Mary's Coll	213	45	61	15	40	286	350	587	937	9	73	0.36	4	4	51	300	7.28
2009	A-	Jamestown	182	24	51	4	24	280	345	456	801	9	75	0.39	3	0	37	176	5.62
2010	A	Greensboro	470	61	128	18	86	272	336	447	783	9	75	0.38	5	1	35	174	5.20
2011	A+	Jupiter	391	53	121	22	66	309	382	535	917	11	71	0.40	0	0	36	225	7.18
2011	AA	Jacksonville	80	14	20	5	10	250	310	475	785	8	71	0.30	1	0	35	225	5.14

Big, powerful OF with plus bat speed and solid power. Has all-out swing which results in a low contact rate. Did have a nice season in the FSL, hitting .309/.385/.535 with 22 HR, but also 114 K. Defensively has the speed and arm strength to be an above-average OF. Was not young for High-A, so Double-A in '12 will be a good test.

Jerez, Williams

8 | **Boston** | EXP MLB DEBUT: 2015 | POTENTIAL: Starting OF | **9E**

Bats L Age 20
2011 (2) HS (NY)

- Pwr + + +
- BAvg + +
- Spd + + + +
- Def + + +

Year	Lev	Team	AB	R	H	HR	RBI	Avg	OB	Slg	OPS	bb%	ct%	Eye	SB	CS	x/h%	Iso	RC/G
2011	Rk	GCL Red Sox	129	12	32	0	12	248	281	310	592	4	74	0.18	5	3	16	62	2.62

Tall and lean athlete who has significant upside, though may take a long time to develop. Best current attribute is plus speed which aids range in CF. Strong arm playable at any OF position. Provides average, raw power and bat speed starting to emerge. Has tendency to lengthen swing in hopes for more pop, but can shorten swing for contact as necessary.

Jimenez, A.J.

2 | **Toronto** | EXP MLB DEBUT: 2014 | POTENTIAL: Starting C | **7B**

Bats R Age 22
2008 (9) HS (PR)

- Pwr + +
- BAvg + + +
- Spd + +
- Def + + + +

Year	Lev	Team	AB	R	H	HR	RBI	Avg	OB	Slg	OPS	bb%	ct%	Eye	SB	CS	x/h%	Iso	RC/G
2008	Rk	GCL Blue Jays	47	5	9	0	5	191	240	234	474	6	66	0.19	5	2	22	43	0.94
2009	A	Lansing	278	30	73	3	31	263	281	356	637	2	74	0.10	5	2	26	94	3.07
2010	A	Lansing	262	35	80	4	54	305	350	435	785	6	79	0.32	17	4	33	130	5.18
2010	A+	Dunedin	9	1	1	1	1	111	111	444	556	0	44	0.00	0	0	100	333	2.96
2011	A+	Dunedin	379	49	115	4	52	303	351	417	768	7	84	0.47	11	2	30	113	5.00

Plus defender who had breakout season with bat. Owns plus arm strength with quick release and negates would-be basestealers. Receiving and blocking skills are unmatched in system and exhibits athleticism and agility. Improved swing mechanics led to high BA while possessing enough bat speed to smack doubles. Runs well for catcher.

Jimenez, Luis

5 | **Los Angeles (A)** | EXP MLB DEBUT: 2013 | POTENTIAL: Starting 3B | **8C**

Bats R Age 24
2006 FA (Venezuela)

- Pwr + + +
- BAvg + + +
- Spd + + +
- Def + + +

Year	Lev	Team	AB	R	H	HR	RBI	Avg	OB	Slg	OPS	bb%	ct%	Eye	SB	CS	x/h%	Iso	RC/G
2008	Rk	Orem	284	57	94	15	65	331	356	630	986	4	84	0.24	6	2	52	299	7.29
2010	A	Cedar Rapids	168	32	49	2	38	292	335	476	811	6	84	0.41	6	2	45	185	5.57
2010	A+	Rancho Cucam	318	52	91	12	43	286	314	522	836	4	86	0.30	15	8	52	236	5.57
2011	AA	Arkansas	490	62	142	18	94	290	327	486	813	5	85	0.38	15	6	42	196	5.32

Strong and unheralded infielder who has been injury prone, but produces when healthy. Crushes LHP while recognizing pitches and making easy contact. Strength in arms and wrists give him moderate power, but free-swinging ways need to be tempered. Runs well for size and is solid-average defender with textbook footwork.

Jones, Chuckie

8 | **San Francisco** | EXP MLB DEBUT: 2014 | POTENTIAL: Starting CF | **7D**

Bats R Age 19
2010 (7) HS (MO)

- Pwr + + +
- BAvg + + +
- Spd + + +
- Def + + +

Year	Lev	Team	AB	R	H	HR	RBI	Avg	OB	Slg	OPS	bb%	ct%	Eye	SB	CS	x/h%	Iso	RC/G
2010	Rk	AZL Giants	165	25	46	5	17	279	357	461	817	11	63	0.33	6	2	35	182	6.42
2011	A-	Salem-Keizer	124	19	27	2	9	218	302	315	617	11	61	0.31	4	2	30	97	3.26

Strong, athletic OF struggled in rookie ball, hitting just .218/.322/.315. Inability to make consistent contact undermines his raw tools. Now has 109 K in 289 professional AB. He is still very young and has nice athleticism and above-average speed, but will need to show more soon.

Jones, Duanel

5 | **San Diego** | EXP MLB DEBUT: 2015 | POTENTIAL: Starting 3B | **8D**

Bats R Age 19
2010 NDFA D.R.

- Pwr + + + +
- BAvg + + +
- Spd + +
- Def + + +

Year	Lev	Team	AB	R	H	HR	RBI	Avg	OB	Slg	OPS	bb%	ct%	Eye	SB	CS	x/h%	Iso	RC/G
2011	Rk	AZL Padres	150	38	40	8	23	267	337	500	837	10	71	0.37	1	1	43	233	6.04
2011	A-	Eugene	68	7	14	0	5	206	260	279	540	7	63	0.20	3	0	36	74	2.04

Strong, athletic 3B prospect has some exciting long-term potential. Already has good size (6'3") and should add power as he matures. Needs to make more consistent contact and improve defensively, but has projectable power and posted a .500 SLG% in the AZL. If he can stick at 3B, there is a lot to like.

Jones, James

9 | **Seattle** | EXP MLB DEBUT: 2013 | POTENTIAL: Starting OF | **8E**

Bats R Age 23
2009 (4) Long Island

- Pwr + + +
- BAvg + +
- Spd + + +
- Def + + +

Year	Lev	Team	AB	R	H	HR	RBI	Avg	OB	Slg	OPS	bb%	ct%	Eye	SB	CS	x/h%	Iso	RC/G
2008	NCAA	Long Island U	188	41	58	5	28	309	372	452	824	9	87	0.76	19	4	26	144	5.73
2009	NCAA	Long Island U	173	47	63	9	32	364	450	618	1068	14	86	1.13	20	3	37	254	8.83
2009	A-	Everett	164	28	51	3	24	311	383	463	846	10	76	0.48	0	3	33	152	6.26
2010	A	Clinton	491	87	132	12	65	269	351	432	783	11	75	0.51	24	10	35	163	5.43
2011	A+	High Desert	296	42	73	5	29	247	340	378	719	12	69	0.46	16	3	34	132	4.74

Lean and athletic prospect who exhibits excellent raw power and speed. Covers plate with long arms and adds mature eye for high OBP. Can swing defensively at times and power more evident in batting practice, but could evolve into 20/20 performer. Breaking balls are problematic and LHP can be troublesome.

Jones, Mycal

8 | **Atlanta** | EXP MLB DEBUT: 2013 | POTENTIAL: Backup CF | **7C**

Bats R Age 25
2009 (4) Miami Dade JC

- Pwr + + +
- BAvg + +
- Spd + + + + (6.4/60)
- Def + + + +

Year	Lev	Team	AB	R	H	HR	RBI	Avg	OB	Slg	OPS	bb%	ct%	Eye	SB	CS	x/h%	Iso	RC/G
2009	Rk	Danville	244	50	63	4	27	258	330	430	760	10	77	0.47	19	4	44	172	5.12
2010	A	Rome	199	27	52	6	34	261	300	412	712	5	76	0.23	6	3	35	151	4.11
2010	A+	Myrtle Beach	275	51	74	7	22	269	343	422	765	10	76	0.47	15	4	36	153	5.10
2010	AA	Mississippi	30	5	6	2	5	200	226	467	692	3	70	0.11	1	0	50	267	3.74
2011	AA	Mississippi	373	63	94	7	36	252	350	381	730	13	76	0.62	17	6	35	129	4.82

Athletic, powerful CF prospect regressed a bit in '11. Has plus speed, good range, a strong arm, and good hands. Has speed to burn, but saw his home run output drop from 15 to 7. Move from SS to CF could help, but will need to show more in '12 and time is running out.

Joseph, Corban

4 | **New York (A)** | EXP MLB DEBUT: 2013 | POTENTIAL: Reserve 2B | **7C**

Bats L Age 23
2008 (4) HS (TN)

- Pwr + +
- BAvg + + + +
- Spd + +
- Def + +

Year	Lev	Team	AB	R	H	HR	RBI	Avg	OB	Slg	OPS	bb%	ct%	Eye	SB	CS	x/h%	Iso	RC/G
2008	Rk	GCL Yankees	159	25	44	2	18	277	358	434	792	11	85	0.83	2	5	43	157	5.61
2009	A	Charleston (SC)	380	39	114	4	57	300	380	418	798	11	84	0.80	8	5	25	118	5.66
2010	A+	Tampa	381	52	115	6	52	302	373	436	808	10	81	0.58	5	8	31	134	5.68
2010	AA	Trenton	111	11	24	0	13	216	310	342	652	12	70	0.45	1	0	42	126	3.90
2011	AA	Trenton	499	75	138	5	58	277	353	415	768	11	79	0.57	4	3	37	138	5.27

Instinctual and aggressive infielder with sweet lefty swing and pure hitting ability. Produces gap power with clean, line drive stroke and has bat control to make consistent contact. Doubles are in abundance, but doesn't hit many HR. Lacks quickness to be above average 2B and arm strength doesn't profile well at 3B. Needs to continue to hit to have value.

Joseph, Tommy

2 | **San Francisco** | EXP MLB DEBUT: 2013 | POTENTIAL: Starting 1B | **8D**

Bats R Age 20
2009 (2) HS (AZ)

- Pwr + + + +
- BAvg + + +
- Spd + +
- Def + +

Year	Lev	Team	AB	R	H	HR	RBI	Avg	OB	Slg	OPS	bb%	ct%	Eye	SB	CS	x/h%	Iso	RC/G
2010	A	Augusta	436	46	103	16	68	236	279	401	681	6	73	0.22	0	0	38	165	3.70
2011	A+	San Jose	514	80	139	22	95	270	309	471	780	5	80	0.28	1	0	41	200	4.92

Strong, athletic backstop has impressive raw power. Solid bat speed and raw strength hint at future potential. Defensively he is still below average. His thick frame is not particularly agile; he struggles blocking balls and has a below average throwing arm. Will need to show improved plate discipline if he is going to hit at higher levels.

Kepler, Max

79 | **Minnesota** | EXP MLB DEBUT: 2014 | POTENTIAL: Starting OF | **9E**

Bats L Age 19
2009 FA (Germany)

- Pwr + + +
- BAvg + + +
- Spd + + +
- Def + + +

Year	Lev	Team	AB	R	H	HR	RBI	Avg	OB	Slg	OPS	bb%	ct%	Eye	SB	CS	x/h%	Iso	RC/G
2010	Rk	GCL Twins	140	15	40	0	11	286	346	343	689	8	81	0.48	6	1	18	57	4.12
2011	Rk	Elizabethton	191	29	50	1	24	262	341	366	708	11	72	0.43	1	1	30	105	4.53

Premier athlete who is starting to turn tools into production, though still will still take awhile to develop. Can be a standout defender with ideal range and arm strength. Possesses strong swing and barrel awareness to hit for BA and power. Plate discipline still a tad behind, but needs to trust hands in swing. Power should come later.

Keyes, Kevin

9 | **Washington** | EXP MLB DEBUT: 2014 | POTENTIAL: Reserve OF | **6C**

Bats R Age 23
2010 (7) Texas

- Pwr + + + +
- BAvg + +
- Spd + +
- Def + +

Year	Lev	Team	AB	R	H	HR	RBI	Avg	OB	Slg	OPS	bb%	ct%	Eye	SB	CS	x/h%	Iso	RC/G
2008	NCAA	Texas	59	13	20	4	10	339	381	610	991	6	59	0.17	2	1	35	271	9.24
2009	NCAA	Texas	213	46	65	9	46	305	393	521	915	13	74	0.56	9	3	42	216	7.23
2010	NCAA	Texas	238	49	74	15	59	311	381	550	932	10	81	0.59	14	3	36	239	6.95
2010	A-	Vermont	126	13	22	3	23	175	307	278	584	16	71	0.67	1	2	32	103	2.78
2011	A	Hagerstown	304	49	80	17	65	263	333	510	843	10	74	0.40	6	0	50	247	6.03

Strong, muscular OF has tremendous raw power but is fairly one-dimensional. Does not run well and has all-or-nothing swing that leads to high K totals. Keyes showed some progress in '11, hitting .263 with 17 home runs, but also struck out 80 times in 304 AB.

Kieschnick, Roger | 8 | San Francisco | EXP MLB DEBUT: 2012 | POTENTIAL: Starting CF | 7C

Bats L Age 25
2008 (3) Texas Tech

Ratings	Year	Lev	Team	AB	R	H	HR	RBI	Avg	OB	Slg	OPS	bb%	ct%	Eye	SB	CS	x/h%	Iso	RC/G
Pwr ++++	2007	NCAA	Texas Tech	232	50	70	13	36	302	367	621	988	9	81	0.55	7	4	61	319	7.78
BAvg ++	2008	NCAA	Texas Tech	220	47	67	17	65	305	400	632	1032	14	81	0.83	8	4	52	327	8.42
Spd +++ (4.15)	2009	A+	San Jose	517	86	153	23	110	296	342	532	874	7	75	0.28	9	1	44	236	6.34
Def ++++	2010	AA	Richmond	223	21	56	4	23	251	307	368	675	7	75	0.33	2	3	27	117	3.79
	2011	AA	Richmond	459	71	117	16	65	255	306	429	735	7	74	0.28	13	7	37	174	4.53

Strong, athletic OF prospect with excellent bat speed and power to all fields. Struggled with back problems in '10, but was healthy in '11. Swing can get lengthy and doesn't always stay back, limiting his BA. Plus arm strength and good range, making him an above average fielder. Poor pitch recognition and long swing continue to limit BA. Will need to hit soon.

Knecht, Marcus | 79 | Toronto | EXP MLB DEBUT: 2015 | POTENTIAL: Starting OF | 8D

Bats R Age 22
2010 (3) Connors State JC

Ratings	Year	Lev	Team	AB	R	H	HR	RBI	Avg	OB	Slg	OPS	bb%	ct%	Eye	SB	CS	x/h%	Iso	RC/G
Pwr ++++																				
BAvg ++	2009	NCAA	Oklahoma State	12	3	2	2	4	167	286	667	952	14	58	0.40	0	0	100	500	8.15
Spd +++	2010	A-	Auburn	231	32	62	5	34	268	342	437	780	10	79	0.54	7	1	42	169	5.33
Def +++	2011	A	Lansing	439	77	120	16	86	273	370	474	843	13	72	0.54	4	3	44	200	6.40

Strong and raw outfielder with as many positive tools as any player in system. Possesses plus power potential with quick, strong swing, but has trouble putting bat to ball. Will get on base with patient approach, but swings and misses too frequently to hit for BA. Runs relatively well and offers average range, but instincts haven't yet caught up to tools.

Kobernus, Jeff | 4 | Washington | EXP MLB DEBUT: 2012 | POTENTIAL: Reserve 2B | 7C

Bats R Age 23
2009 (2) UC Berkeley

Ratings	Year	Lev	Team	AB	R	H	HR	RBI	Avg	OB	Slg	OPS	bb%	ct%	Eye	SB	CS	x/h%	Iso	RC/G
	2008	NCAA	U. California	228	34	69	3	27	303	343	417	760	6	84	0.39	11	5	26	114	4.80
Pwr +++	2009	NCAA	U. California	217	43	74	8	40	341	389	544	933	7	88	0.68	20	4	34	203	6.83
BAvg +++	2009	A-	Vermont	41	8	9	0	2	220	256	244	500	5	88	0.40	4	0	11	24	1.82
Spd ++++	2010	A	Hagerstown	312	40	87	1	42	279	316	346	662	5	81	0.29	21	10	22	67	3.59
Def +++	2011	A+	Potomac	489	67	138	7	52	282	312	387	698	4	82	0.24	53	8	24	104	3.93

Strong, athletic 2B had a nice season in '11, hitting .282 with 53 SB. Quick bat and good speed give him the ability to hit for average. Piitch recognition and walk rate could be better, but he does moderate power and a nice line-drive approach. He has good size (6'2", 200), plus speed and plays solid defense.

Komatsu, Erik | 7 | St. Louis | EXP MLB DEBUT: 2012 | POTENTIAL: Reserve OF | 6B

Bats L Age 24
2008 (8) Cal St. Fullerton

Ratings	Year	Lev	Team	AB	R	H	HR	RBI	Avg	OB	Slg	OPS	bb%	ct%	Eye	SB	CS	x/h%	Iso	RC/G
	2009	Rk	AZL Brewers	13	1	4	0	3	308	400	308	708	13	85	1.00	0	0	0	0	4.62
Pwr ++	2009	A	Wisconsin	66	6	16	1	5	242	324	318	643	11	79	0.57	0	2	19	76	3.53
BAvg ++++	2010	A+	Brevard County	486	90	157	5	63	323	406	442	849	12	87	1.11	28	9	27	119	6.33
Spd ++++	2011	AA	Huntsville	320	48	94	6	40	294	394	416	810	14	86	1.20	13	6	28	122	5.93
Def +++	2011	AA	Harrisburg	128	12	30	1	8	234	295	297	592	8	83	0.50	8	3	20	63	2.89

Short, athletic OF prospect has hit at almost every level. He has above-average plate discipline and good speed. At 5'10", 175 lbs. he has limited power, but can play all three OF positions. Was traded from Milwaukee to Washington and then taken by the Cardinals in the Rule 5 draft and has an outside shot of making the club in '12.

Kozma, Peter | 6 | St. Louis | EXP MLB DEBUT: 2011 | POTENTIAL: Platoon SS | 6C

Bats R Age 24
2007 (1) HS (OK)

Ratings	Year	Lev	Team	AB	R	H	HR	RBI	Avg	OB	Slg	OPS	bb%	ct%	Eye	SB	CS	x/h%	Iso	RC/G
	2009	A+	Palm Beach	73	8	23	0	8	315	383	384	766	10	78	0.50	1	0	22	68	5.19
Pwr +	2009	AA	Springfield	407	52	88	6	37	216	290	312	602	9	78	0.48	4	2	27	96	2.97
BAvg ++	2010	AA	Springfield	503	69	122	13	72	243	318	384	702	10	78	0.50	13	2	35	141	4.25
Spd +++ (4.10)	2011	AAA	Memphis	398	48	85	3	47	214	279	289	568	8	77	0.40	2	2	26	75	2.49
Def ++++	2011	MLB	St. Louis	17	2	3	0	1	176	333	235	569	19	76	1.00	0	0	33	59	2.97

Another brutal offensive season for this former 18th overall pick. He remains athletic and fundamentally sound defensively and did make his MLB debut, but his career minor league line is now .237/.311/.342. Makes plays defensively, with above average range and arm strength. With little speed and no offense, it is hard to see how he will make an impact.

Krauss, Marc | 9 | Arizona | EXP MLB DEBUT: 2012 | POTENTIAL: Backup corner OF | 7C

Bats R Age 24
2009 (2) Ohio

Ratings	Year	Lev	Team	AB	R	H	HR	RBI	Avg	OB	Slg	OPS	bb%	ct%	Eye	SB	CS	x/h%	Iso	RC/G
	2008	NCAA	Ohio	229	62	76	10	54	332	448	568	1015	17	86	1.55	5	5	42	236	8.51
Pwr ++	2009	NCAA	Ohio	209	73	84	27	70	402	510	852	1361	18	86	1.59	6	2	48	450	12.24
BAvg +++	2009	A	South Bend	115	14	35	2	17	304	380	478	858	11	82	0.67	0	1	43	174	6.38
Spd ++	2010	A+	Visalia	530	107	160	25	87	302	370	509	879	10	73	0.40	1	3	35	208	6.56
Def ++	2011	AA	Mobile	433	69	105	16	65	242	340	439	779	13	72	0.52	3	3	45	196	5.46

Solidly-built corner OF struggled to repeat breakout of '10. Does have solid power, but failed to make consistent contact at Double-A. Quick LH bat generates good power, handles breaking balls and LHP well, and uses the entire field. Lack of speed and athleticism make it unlikely that he will see much action in the OF and a move to 1B or DH seems likely.

Kuhn, Tyler | 457 | Chicago (A) | EXP MLB DEBUT: 2012 | POTENTIAL: Utility player | 6A

Bats L Age 25
2008 (15) West Virginia

Ratings	Year	Lev	Team	AB	R	H	HR	RBI	Avg	OB	Slg	OPS	bb%	ct%	Eye	SB	CS	x/h%	Iso	RC/G
	2009	A	Kannapolis	221	27	66	0	27	299	351	371	723	8	86	0.60	19	4	20	72	4.56
Pwr ++	2009	A+	Winston-Salem	256	28	72	0	19	281	319	352	670	5	85	0.37	7	7	22	70	3.78
BAvg +++	2010	AA	Birmingham	384	52	107	5	50	279	340	393	734	9	80	0.48	6	5	26	115	4.65
Spd +++	2011	AA	Birmingham	414	61	141	1	55	341	397	464	861	9	85	0.61	16	5	28	123	6.29
Def +++	2011	AAA	Charlotte	91	9	27	0	4	297	333	363	696	5	86	0.38	0	2	19	66	4.07

Versatile infielder who finished 2nd in IL in BA. Contact-oriented bat produces high BA by using entire field and being tough out. Only possesses average speed, but runs bases well. No power projection in short swing, but can leg out doubles. Can play variety of positions and average arm strength plays up due to quick release.

Kvasnicka, Mike | 5 | Houston | EXP MLB DEBUT: 2014 | POTENTIAL: Starting 3B | 7C

Bats R Age 23
2010 (2) Minnesota

Ratings	Year	Lev	Team	AB	R	H	HR	RBI	Avg	OB	Slg	OPS	bb%	ct%	Eye	SB	CS	x/h%	Iso	RC/G
	2008	NCAA	Minnesota	189	23	45	4	25	238	280	365	645	6	74	0.22	2	0	33	127	3.30
Pwr +++	2009	NCAA	Minnesota	249	48	85	10	65	341	376	550	927	5	78	0.26	5	4	35	209	6.80
BAvg +++	2010	NCAA	Minnesota	245	51	87	8	50	355	457	571	1028	16	88	1.59	4	7	40	216	8.61
Spd ++	2010	A-	Tri City	261	31	61	5	36	234	306	337	643	9	82	0.56	2	1	26	103	3.52
Def ++	2011	A	Lexington	484	59	126	4	59	260	325	368	692	9	78	0.43	5	5	32	107	4.17

Strong right-handed 3B had modest success in full-season debut. Kvasnicka caught and played the OF in college but was moved to 3B by the Astros. He has nice athleticism and a good approach at the plate, makes solid contact, and uses the whole field. Defensively he moves well, has soft hands and a strong arm. If his power develops, 3B and LF are options.

Laird, Brandon | 35 | New York (A) | EXP MLB DEBUT: 2011 | POTENTIAL: Reserve 1B | 7C

Bats R Age 24
2007 (27) Cypress JC

Ratings	Year	Lev	Team	AB	R	H	HR	RBI	Avg	OB	Slg	OPS	bb%	ct%	Eye	SB	CS	x/h%	Iso	RC/G
	2009	A+	Tampa	451	53	120	13	75	266	324	415	739	8	83	0.52	1	1	31	149	4.62
Pwr ++++	2010	AA	Trenton	409	73	119	23	90	291	351	523	874	9	79	0.45	2	2	39	232	6.21
BAvg ++	2010	AAA	Scranton/W-B	122	13	30	2	12	246	270	344	614	3	78	0.15	0	0	27	98	2.79
Spd ++	2011	AAA	Scranton/W-B	462	51	120	16	69	260	286	422	708	4	82	0.20	0	0	36	162	3.94
Def +++	2011	MLB	New York (A)	21	3	4	0	1	190	292	190	482	13	81	0.75	0	0	0	0	1.68

Strong infielder who struggled in AAA, though appeared with NYY for short time. Aggressive approach and free-swinging ways hinder BA and OBP while holes in swing can negate above average power to all fields. Has bat speed and leverage to hit 20+ HR annually, but can be beaten by good breaking balls. Speed and range are subpar, but has good hands and arm.

Lake, Junior | 6 | Chicago (N) | EXP MLB DEBUT: 2013 | POTENTIAL: Starting SS/3B | 9E

Bats R Age 22
2008 NDFA D.R.

Ratings	Year	Lev	Team	AB	R	H	HR	RBI	Avg	OB	Slg	OPS	bb%	ct%	Eye	SB	CS	x/h%	Iso	RC/G
	2008	Rk	AZL Cubs	168	24	48	2	23	286	337	417	754	7	75	0.31	12	2	25	131	4.91
Pwr ++	2009	A	Peoria	463	71	115	7	42	248	277	365	642	4	70	0.13	10	7	29	117	3.25
BAvg ++++	2010	A+	Daytona	394	56	104	9	46	264	324	398	722	8	75	0.35	13	9	30	135	4.45
Spd +++	2011	A+	Daytona	203	39	64	6	34	315	335	498	832	3	76	0.12	19	4	33	182	5.59
Def ++++	2011	AA	Tennessee	242	41	60	6	17	248	286	380	666	5	75	0.22	19	2	30	132	3.53

Tall, athletic but raw SS. Lake runs well, has a cannon for an arm, and has good power potential. He is extremely aggressive at the plate with a long, violent swing. The ball jumps off his bat when he makes contact, but he doesn't do that often enough. He is very raw defensively but has good range. Long-term he will likely be moved off SS due to size and inconsistency.

LaMarre, Ryan | 9 | Cincinnati | EXP MLB DEBUT: 2013 | POTENTIAL: Starting RF | 7C

Bats R Age 23
2010 (2) Michigan

Ratings	Year	Lev	Team	AB	R	H	HR	RBI	Avg	OB	Slg	OPS	bb%	ct%	Eye	SB	CS	x/h%	Iso	RC/G
	2010	NCAA	Michigan	148	40	62	5	40	419	438	649	1087	3	86	0.25	7	5	31	230	8.34
Pwr +++	2010	A	Dayton	227	44	64	5	29	282	343	396	739	8	77	0.40	18	7	25	115	4.64
BAvg +++	2010	A+	Lynchburg	27	2	6	1	3	222	276	407	683	7	85	0.50	1	1	50	185	3.92
Spd +++	2011	A+	Bakersfield	445	78	124	6	47	279	341	371	712	9	78	0.43	52	14	21	92	4.33
Def +++	2011	AA	Carolina	15	3	4	0	0	267	389	333	722	17	80	1.00	3	0	25	67	5.01

Speedy and athletic OF. At 6'2", 205 lbs. he has good size, but is more of a burner than a masher. Right now, he has moderate gap power that should play up as he advances. LaMarre has good plate discipline and has plenty of range in CF, but probably not enough power for a corner OF slot. The Reds continue to advance him quickly and like his tools.

Lambo, Andrew — 3 — Pittsburgh

EXP MLB DEBUT: 2012 | POTENTIAL: Backup 1B | 7D

Bats L Age 23
2007 (4) HS (CA)
Pwr ++++
BAvg ++
4.35 Spd ++
Def ++

Year	Lev	Team	AB	R	H	HR	RBI	Avg	OB	Slg	OPS	bb%	ct%	Eye	SB	CS	x/h%	Iso	RC/G
2009	AA	Chattanooga	492	70	126	11	61	256	311	407	717	7	81	0.41	4	3	40	150	4.36
2010	AA	Chattanooga	181	26	49	4	25	271	327	420	746	8	78	0.38	1	1	35	149	4.74
2010	AA	Altoona	91	12	25	2	10	275	340	352	692	9	67	0.30	0	0	12	77	4.09
2011	AA	Altoona	252	35	69	8	41	274	342	437	778	9	77	0.44	4	3	36	163	5.18
2011	AAA	Indianapolis	185	19	34	3	17	184	252	292	544	8	74	0.35	1	0	41	108	2.10

Strong, muscular 1B has good power and bat speed. Hasn't looked the same since 50-game PED suspension in 2010. Struggled at Triple-A to start the season. Looked better back at Double-A, but strike zone judgement is only average and raises concerns about BA. Lambo is below average defensively and looks more like a back-up now.

Landry, Leon — 8 — Los Angeles (N)

EXP MLB DEBUT: 2013 | POTENTIAL: Backup CF | 8D

Bats L Age 22
2010 (3) LSU
Pwr +++
BAvg +++
Spd +++
Def +++

Year	Lev	Team	AB	R	H	HR	RBI	Avg	OB	Slg	OPS	bb%	ct%	Eye	SB	CS	x/h%	Iso	RC/G
2008	NCAA	Louisiana St	214	38	58	5	26	271	297	435	732	4	83	0.22	12	5	34	164	4.34
2009	NCAA	Louisiana St	170	38	51	12	41	300	380	571	951	11	75	0.51	9	6	43	271	7.44
2010	NCAA	Louisiana St	240	55	81	6	45	338	411	513	924	11	90	1.20	16	4	30	175	7.07
2010	Rk	Ogden	249	46	87	4	38	349	398	510	908	7	86	0.56	13	9	32	161	6.69
2011	A	Great Lakes	500	59	125	4	41	250	302	360	662	7	87	0.55	28	12	29	110	3.83

Short, athletic OF. Landry is a good athlete, runs well, and has decent pop in his bat. Poor pitch recognition led to .250 avg and could keep him from reaching his potential. He has some nice tools with good speed/power potential, but will need a repeat of Low-A and that doesn't bode well. 2012 will be key.

LaStella, Tommy — 4 — Atlanta

EXP MLB DEBUT: 2014 | POTENTIAL: Starting 2B | 8D

Bats L Age 23
2011 (8) Coastal Carolina
Pwr +++
BAvg +++
Spd +++
Def +++

Year	Lev	Team	AB	R	H	HR	RBI	Avg	OB	Slg	OPS	bb%	ct%	Eye	SB	CS	x/h%	Iso	RC/G
2008	NCAA	St. John's	25	2	8	0	6	320	393	400	793	11	88	1.00	0	0	25	80	5.62
2010	NCAA	Coastal Carol	246	63	93	14	66	378	450	622	1072	12	94	2.13	6	0	32	244	8.55
2011	NCAA	Coastal Carol	231	59	92	14	70	398	471	680	1151	12	92	1.78	7	4	36	281	9.51
2011	A	Rome	232	46	76	9	40	328	395	543	938	10	88	0.93	2	2	36	216	7.11

Short, athletic 2B prospect was impressive in his pro debut, hitting .328 with 13 doubles and 9 home runs in the SAL. Showed solid plate discipline in college and as a pro. LaStella is a solid hitter, but his speed and defense are only average. He could be moved to the OF, but will stick at 2B for now. Should be able to hit due to plate discipline and moderate power.

Lavarnway, Ryan — 2 — Boston

EXP MLB DEBUT: 2011 | POTENTIAL: Starting C | 7A

Bats R Age 24
2008 (6) Yale
Pwr ++++
BAvg +++
Spd +
Def ++

Year	Lev	Team	AB	R	H	HR	RBI	Avg	OB	Slg	OPS	bb%	ct%	Eye	SB	CS	x/h%	Iso	RC/G
2010	A+	Salem	304	66	88	14	63	289	379	487	866	13	80	0.71	1	0	36	197	6.38
2010	AA	Portland	158	25	45	8	39	285	386	494	880	14	73	0.62	0	0	38	209	6.75
2011	AA	Portland	208	35	59	14	38	284	361	510	870	11	77	0.53	0	0	32	226	6.20
2011	AAA	Pawtucket	227	40	67	18	55	295	382	612	995	12	74	0.53	1	1	54	317	8.13
2011	MLB	Boston	39	5	9	2	8	231	302	436	738	9	74	0.40	0	0	44	205	4.56

Big and strong backstop who continues to hit for consistent power to all fields. Reached BOS due to offensive output, though defense is big concern. Possesses average arm and has quickened release, but receiving, blocking, and agility aren't up to snuff. Disciplined eye at plate is asset and has hit for nice BA despite hard cuts and fringy pitch recognition.

Lavisky, Alex — 2 — Cleveland

EXP MLB DEBUT: 2014 | POTENTIAL: Starting C | 8D

Bats R Age 21
2010 (8) HS (OH)
Pwr ++++
BAvg ++
Spd ++
Def +++

Year	Lev	Team	AB	R	H	HR	RBI	Avg	OB	Slg	OPS	bb%	ct%	Eye	SB	CS	x/h%	Iso	RC/G
2010	Rk	AZL Indians	15	0	3	0	0	200	200	200	400	0	53	0.00	0	0			
2011	A-	Mahoning Vall	259	29	52	5	28	201	258	328	586	7	73	0.28	0	1	44	127	2.60
2011	A	Lake County	184	19	38	8	24	207	244	391	635	5	64	0.14	0	1	47	185	3.19

Strong backstop who struggled with BA in first full season, but secondary skills were impressive. Has good power to all fields and has solid athleticism behind plate. Not a threat to steal and impatient approach hinders OBP, but recognizes pitches. Long release mutes arm strength, but is excellent receiver with nice agility.

Lee, Hak-Ju — 6 — Tampa Bay

EXP MLB DEBUT: 2013 | POTENTIAL: Starting SS | 8B

Bats L Age 21
2008 FA (South Korea)
Pwr ++
BAvg ++++
Spd ++++
Def ++++

Year	Lev	Team	AB	R	H	HR	RBI	Avg	OB	Slg	OPS	bb%	ct%	Eye	SB	CS	x/h%	Iso	RC/G
2009	A-	Boise	264	56	87	2	33	330	400	420	820	11	81	0.62	25	8	21	91	5.85
2010	A	Peoria	485	85	137	1	40	282	348	351	699	9	82	0.57	32	7	20	68	4.30
2011	A+	Charlotte	400	82	127	4	23	318	382	443	825	10	82	0.58	28	14	24	125	5.87
2011	AA	Montgomery	100	16	19	1	7	190	270	310	580	10	78	0.50	5	2	32	120	2.80

Lean and athletic infielder who continues to improve and finished 3rd in FSL in BA. Handles bat well and controls strike zone with quick, repeatable swing. Uses line drive approach for contact and above average speed to leg out doubles and triples. HR power is below average, but game revolves around contact, speed, and plus, rangy defense.

LeMahieu, D.J. — 4 — Colorado

EXP MLB DEBUT: 2011 | POTENTIAL: Utility INF | 6B

Bats R Age 23
2009 (2) LSU
Pwr +++
BAvg +++
Spd ++
Def +++

Year	Lev	Team	AB	R	H	HR	RBI	Avg	OB	Slg	OPS	bb%	ct%	Eye	SB	CS	x/h%	Iso	RC/G
2009	A	Peoria	152	19	48	0	30	316	366	368	734	7	86	0.55	2	2	13	53	4.63
2010	A+	Daytona	554	63	174	2	73	314	348	386	734	5	89	0.48	15	7	18	72	4.53
2011	AA	Tennessee	187	32	67	2	27	358	394	492	886	6	88	0.50	4	3	28	134	6.28
2011	AAA	Iowa	227	23	65	3	23	286	328	366	693	6	88	0.52	5	5	17	79	4.05
2011	MLB	Chicago Cubs	60	3	15	0	4	250	262	283	546	2	80	0.08	0	0	13	33	1.91

Tall, athletic 2B. Good line-drive approach at the plate. Looked good at Triple-A (.319/.354/.423), but lacks the power necessary to provide much offense. He struggled once he reached the majors and his bat didn't look quick enough. Played 2B most of the season, but saw action at 1B in the AFL. Looking more and more like a super-sub without power.

Lemmerman, Jake — 6 — Los Angeles (N)

EXP MLB DEBUT: 2013 | POTENTIAL: Utility INF | 7D

Bats R Age 23
2010 (5) Duke
Pwr +++
BAvg +++
Spd ++
Def +++

Year	Lev	Team	AB	R	H	HR	RBI	Avg	OB	Slg	OPS	bb%	ct%	Eye	SB	CS	x/h%	Iso	RC/G
2009	NCAA	Duke	223	31	64	7	45	287	346	448	794	8	86	0.63	13	3	31	161	5.30
2010	NCAA	Duke	218	47	73	11	45	335	411	569	979	11	85	0.85	9	3	36	234	7.63
2010	Rk	Ogden	259	69	94	12	47	363	431	610	1041	11	78	0.55	5	4	40	247	8.61
2011	A+	Rancho Cucamg	400	71	117	8	54	293	367	420	787	11	78	0.52	9	3	28	128	5.40
2011	AA	Chattanooga	77	11	18	2	11	234	306	390	695	9	71	0.36	1	0	44	156	4.19

Smart, savvy SS gets most of his abilities, but doesn't have the greatest tools. Looked good in the CAL, but struggled when promoted to Double-A. Showed moderate power for position and squares the ball up consistently. Speed is a tick below average, but he's a plus defender with good hands and a plus arm. Nice player who shows some offensive potential.

Leonard, Joe — 5 — Atlanta

EXP MLB DEBUT: 2013 | POTENTIAL: Starting 3B | 7D

Bats R Age 23
2010 (3) Pittsburgh
Pwr +++
BAvg +++
Spd ++
Def +++

Year	Lev	Team	AB	R	H	HR	RBI	Avg	OB	Slg	OPS	bb%	ct%	Eye	SB	CS	x/h%	Iso	RC/G
2009	NCAA	Pittsburgh	171	31	54	5	35	316	361	480	840	7	87	0.52	2	0	30	164	5.74
2010	NCAA	Pittsburgh	240	62	104	8	71	433	481	663	1143	8	88	0.73	6	4	34	229	9.38
2010	Rk	Danville	36	6	10	1	5	278	333	417	750	8	81	0.43	0	0	30	139	4.71
2010	A	Rome	112	11	30	3	19	268	305	446	752	5	80	0.27	0	0	40	179	4.66
2011	A+	Lynchburg	405	43	100	8	63	247	313	378	691	9	78	0.44	1	2	36	131	4.09

Tall/athletic 3B prospect has been slow to develop. Modest power for his size (6'5") but does have the potential to develop more. Solid bat control but K rate spiked in '11. Moves well at 3B and has soft hands and a strong arm. Below average speed.

LePage, Pierre — 4 — Chicago (N)

EXP MLB DEBUT: 2014 | POTENTIAL: Backup 2B | 6C

Bats R Age 23
2010 (13) Connecticut
Pwr ++
BAvg ++
Spd +++
Def ++

Year	Lev	Team	AB	R	H	HR	RBI	Avg	OB	Slg	OPS	bb%	ct%	Eye	SB	CS	x/h%	Iso	RC/G
2010	NCAA	Connecticut	248	63	81	3	57	327	367	468	835	6	99	5.33	29	6	32	141	5.92
2010	Rk	AZL Cubs	10	2	7	0	0	700	700	700	1400	0	100		2	1	0	0	10.63
2010	A-	Boise	254	39	84	1	38	331	358	453	811	4	90	0.42	9	6	30	122	5.40
2011	Rk	AZL Cubs	3	0	2	0	1	667	667	667	1333	0	100		0	1	0	0	9.99
2011	A	Peoria	238	37	60	2	26	252	310	357	667	8	92	1.00	8	2	33	105	4.08

High energy 2B prospect. Doesn't have much power and at 5'8", 170 he isn't likely to develop more, but controls the strike zone, puts the ball in play, and uses his speed well. He is a solid defender at with good speed and soft hands, but 2B is the only position he can play at the next level.

Lewis, Chad — 5 — Oakland

EXP MLB DEBUT: 2014 | POTENTIAL: Starting 3B | 8E

Bats R Age 20
2010 (4) HS (CA)
Pwr +++
BAvg +++
Spd ++
Def ++

Year	Lev	Team	AB	R	H	HR	RBI	Avg	OB	Slg	OPS	bb%	ct%	Eye	SB	CS	x/h%	Iso	RC/G
2010	Rk	AZL Athletics	13	5	3	0	3	231	375	231	606	19	62	0.60	0	0	0	0	3.24
2011	A-	Vermont	265	32	63	4	40	238	273	332	605	5	73	0.18	4	1	25	94	2.73

Athletic and strong infielder with potential to evolve into legitimate prospect. Average power generated by above average bat speed. Focuses more on line drives, but tendency to chase pitches leaves BA muted. Clean swing mechanics gives hope to improved BA output. Limited range at infield corners, but strong arm and quick feet are assets.

Liddi, Alex

5 | **Seattle** | EXP MLB DEBUT: 2011 | POTENTIAL: Starting 1B/3B | **9D**

Bats R Age 23
2005 FA (Italy)
Pwr + + + +
BAvg + + +
Spd + +
Def + +

Year	Lev	Team	AB	R	H	HR	RBI	Avg	OB	Slg	OPS	bb%	ct%	Eye	SB	CS	x/h%	Iso	RC/G
2008	A	Wisconsin	447	65	109	6	53	244	309	360	669	9	74	0.37	17	5	33	116	3.82
2009	A+	High Desert	493	97	170	23	104	345	408	594	1003	10	75	0.43	10	6	42	249	8.21
2010	AA	W. Tennessee	502	78	141	15	92	281	346	476	822	9	71	0.34	5	7	43	195	5.99
2011	AAA	Tacoma	559	121	145	30	104	259	332	488	821	10	70	0.36	5	1	45	229	5.88
2011	MLB	Seattle	40	7	9	3	6	225	279	525	804	7	58	0.18	1	0	67	300	6.34

Powerful and offensive infielder who doubled career-high in HR and finished 3rd in PCL. Offers significant size and strength with natural power to all fields. Draws walks and improved pitch recognition, but lengthens swing and fans frequently (2nd in PCL in Ks). Soft hands at 3B, but lack of speed and range may necessitate move across diamond.

Lin, Che-Hsuan

8 | **Boston** | EXP MLB DEBUT: 2012 | POTENTIAL: Starting OF | **7A**

Bats R Age 23
2007 FA (Taiwan)
Pwr + +
BAvg + + +
Spd + + + +
Def + + + +

Year	Lev	Team	AB	R	H	HR	RBI	Avg	OB	Slg	OPS	bb%	ct%	Eye	SB	CS	x/h%	Iso	RC/G
2008	A	Greenville	362	60	90	5	37	249	328	359	688	11	83	0.69	33	7	27	110	4.22
2009	A+	Salem	479	75	127	7	54	265	354	365	719	12	84	0.88	26	11	25	100	4.70
2010	AA	Portland	458	88	126	2	34	275	374	343	716	14	86	1.14	26	12	18	68	4.83
2011	AA	Portland	138	23	37	0	11	268	361	333	694	13	90	1.43	12	3	19	65	4.65
2011	AAA	Pawtucket	328	49	77	2	25	235	314	293	607	10	84	0.75	16	4	18	58	3.27

Lean and athletic outfielder who showcased exquisite speed and defense in first foray in Triple-A. Not much in the way of power and struggles to hit for BA, but has solid strike zone knowledge and an improved batting eye. Combined with plate discipline, has skill set to hit at top of lineup. Owns one of strongest arms in org and is terrific defender in CF.

Lindor, Francisco

6 | **Cleveland** | EXP MLB DEBUT: 2014 | POTENTIAL: Starting SS | **8A**

Bats B Age 18
2011 (1) HS (PR)
Pwr + + +
BAvg + + + +
Spd + + + +
Def + + + +

Year	Lev	Team	AB	R	H	HR	RBI	Avg	OB	Slg	OPS	bb%	ct%	Eye	SB	CS	x/h%	Iso	RC/G
2011	A-	Mahoning Vall	19	4	6	0	2	316	350	316	666	5	74	0.20	1	0	0	0	3.48

Lean and strong infielder with solid all-around game. Focuses on smashing line drives to gaps, but has enough strength in wrists and arms for moderate power. Should hit for high BA due to barrel awareness and simple stroke. Good runner with quickness and instincts and has the techniques and fundamentals to be standout with glove, including arm and range.

Lindsey, Taylor

4 | **Los Angeles (A)** | EXP MLB DEBUT: 2014 | POTENTIAL: Starting 2B | **8B**

Bats L Age 20
2010 (1-S) HS (AZ)
Pwr + +
BAvg + + + +
Spd + +
Def + + +

Year	Lev	Team	AB	R	H	HR	RBI	Avg	OB	Slg	OPS	bb%	ct%	Eye	SB	CS	x/h%	Iso	RC/G
2010	Rk	AZL Angels	194	26	55	0	18	284	325	407	732	6	83	0.36	8	3	33	124	4.62
2011	Rk	Orem	290	64	105	9	46	362	389	593	983	4	84	0.28	10	4	41	231	7.34

Pioneer League MVP with several solid attributes, led by line drive swing and ability to hit for high BA. Makes consistent contact with clean swing and uses entire field in approach. Doesn't draw many walks and lacks power projection. Hits LHP, but struggles with breaking balls. Good fundamental defender with average arm, range, and hands.

Linton, Ty

7 | **Arizona** | EXP MLB DEBUT: 2014 | POTENTIAL: Starting LF | **8E**

Bats R Age 21
2010 (14) HS, (NC)
Pwr + + +
BAvg + +
Spd + + +
Def + + +

Year	Lev	Team	AB	R	H	HR	RBI	Avg	OB	Slg	OPS	bb%	ct%	Eye	SB	CS	x/h%	Iso	RC/G
2010	Rk	Missoula	0	0	0	0	0					100			0	0			
2011	Rk	Missoula	136	18	35	3	17	257	308	434	742	7	61	0.19	3	6	40	176	5.33

Linton's calling card is above-average power. He has plus bat speed and raw strength, but his swing is long and he struggles with pitch recognition and making consistent contact. He looked over-matched in his pro debut, striking out 53 times in just 138 AB. With only average speed and a below average arm, he is limited to a corner OF slot. Needs better plate discipline.

Lipka, Matt

6 | **Atlanta** | EXP MLB DEBUT: 2014 | POTENTIAL: Starting SS | **7C**

Bats R Age 20
2010 (1-S) HS, (TX)
Pwr + +
BAvg + +
6.3/60 Spd + + + +
Def + +

Year	Lev	Team	AB	R	H	HR	RBI	Avg	OB	Slg	OPS	bb%	ct%	Eye	SB	CS	x/h%	Iso	RC/G
2010	Rk	GCL Braves	192	33	58	1	24	302	350	401	751	7	89	0.64	20	3	22	99	4.86
2010	Rk	Danville	16	1	2	0	1	125	176	125	301	6	88	0.50	1	0			
2011	A	Rome	530	78	131	1	37	247	302	304	606	7	84	0.51	28	14	19	57	3.11

Solid all-around athlete struggled in his full-season debut, hitting just .247 with 1 home run. Lipka has nice bat speed and sprays line-drives to all fields. He has plus-plus speed and a chance to develop moderate power. Stiff hands and actions at SS and he eventually may profile better as a centerfielder. His stock is down, but he still has time.

Liriano, Rymer

9 | **San Diego** | EXP MLB DEBUT: 2014 | POTENTIAL: Starting CF | **9D**

Bats R Age 21
2007 NDFA D.R.
Pwr + + + +
BAvg + +
Spd + + + +
Def + + +

Year	Lev	Team	AB	R	H	HR	RBI	Avg	OB	Slg	OPS	bb%	ct%	Eye	SB	CS	x/h%	Iso	RC/G
2010	A-	Eugene	203	35	55	0	12	271	327	394	721	8	74	0.32	17	7	35	123	4.63
2010	A	Fort Wayne	188	21	36	2	20	191	232	293	525	5	71	0.19	11	6	39	101	1.71
2010	A+	Lake Elsinore	50	3	11	1	6	220	291	320	611	9	76	0.42	3	0	27	100	2.99
2011	A	Fort Wayne	455	81	145	12	62	319	382	499	881	9	79	0.49	65	20	34	180	6.54
2011	A+	Lake Elsinore	55	8	7	0	6	127	213	182	395	10	76	0.46	1	1	29	55	0.32

Strong, athletic international CF struggled to start the year, but had a nice breakout back in the MWL. He has plus power and it is beginning to be game-usable. Also has plus speed and swiped 65 bases in the MWL. Questions about ability to recognize pitches continue. Covers ground well with a strong throwing arm and has enough speed to stay in CF.

Littlewood, Marcus

26 | **Seattle** | EXP MLB DEBUT: 2015 | POTENTIAL: Starting C | **8D**

Bats B Age 20
2010 (2) HS (UT)
Pwr + + +
BAvg + + +
Spd +
Def + +

Year	Lev	Team	AB	R	H	HR	RBI	Avg	OB	Slg	OPS	bb%	ct%	Eye	SB	CS	x/h%	Iso	RC/G
2011	A-	Everett	233	45	48	8	30	206	335	373	708	16	65	0.56	3	3	46	167	4.64
2011	A	Clinton	95	7	15	1	6	158	238	211	449	10	76	0.43	0	1	13	53	0.88

Tall and instinctual prospect who is being converted to catcher in offseason. Has athleticism and arm to be good backstop, but lot of work to do. Hasn't contributed much with bat despite natural skills. Bat speed is below average and power generated more with strength in swing and wrists. Distinguishes between balls and strikes well.

Loewen, Adam

89 | **New York (N)** | EXP MLB DEBUT: 2011 | POTENTIAL: Reserve OF | **6B**

Bats L Age 28
2002 (1) Chipola JC
Pwr + + +
BAvg + + +
Spd + + +
Def + + +

Year	Lev	Team	AB	R	H	HR	RBI	Avg	OB	Slg	OPS	bb%	ct%	Eye	SB	CS	x/h%	Iso	RC/G
2006	MLB	Baltimore	2	0	0	0	0	0	0	0	0	0	100		0	0			
2009	A+	Dunedin	335	47	79	4	31	236	335	355	690	13	66	0.44	5	2	37	119	4.44
2010	AA	New Hampshire	459	70	113	13	70	246	341	412	753	13	69	0.46	17	6	42	166	5.18
2011	AAA	Las Vegas	520	83	159	17	85	306	379	508	886	10	74	0.45	11	7	42	202	6.82
2011	MLB	Toronto	32	4	6	1	4	188	257	313	570	9	59	0.23	0	0	33	125	2.38

Converted pitcher who reached TOR by showcasing power stroke along with size, speed, and strength. Long swing and struggles against breaking balls mute upside, but swings with confidence and authority. Possesses bat speed and has been doubles machine. Strong arm is highlight of defensive game and has average range to play any outfield position.

Lohman, Devin

4 | **Cincinnati** | EXP MLB DEBUT: 2014 | POTENTIAL: Starting 2B | **7C**

Bats R Age 23
2010 (3) Long Beach St
Pwr + +
BAvg + + +
Spd + + +
Def + + +

Year	Lev	Team	AB	R	H	HR	RBI	Avg	OB	Slg	OPS	bb%	ct%	Eye	SB	CS	x/h%	Iso	RC/G
2010	NCAA	Long Beach St	151	31	61	1	24	404	467	550	1017	11	83	0.69	7	8	31	146	8.34
2010	Rk	Billings	230	33	55	1	31	239	311	322	633	9	80	0.51	2	5	27	83	3.46
2011	Rk	Billings	115	23	37	4	21	322	405	461	865	12	81	0.73	6	2	22	139	6.35
2011	A	Dayton	207	14	43	1	31	208	268	256	524	8	77	0.36	9	2	16	48	1.87
2011	A+	Bakersfield	130	25	43	5	17	331	392	554	945	9	82	0.57	4	2	40	223	7.21

Strong player with moderate power was moved from SS to 2B where he profiles much better. Is an offensive-minded player who hits hard line drives to the gaps and has the speed to leg out doubles and triples. Defensively has good hands and range. Arm and actions are better suited at 2B.

Lombardozzi, Steve

4 | **Washington** | EXP MLB DEBUT: 2011 | POTENTIAL: Starting 2B | **7B**

Bats B Age 23
2008 (19) St. Petersburg
Pwr + +
BAvg + + +
Spd + +
Def + + +

Year	Lev	Team	AB	R	H	HR	RBI	Avg	OB	Slg	OPS	bb%	ct%	Eye	SB	CS	x/h%	Iso	RC/G
2010	A+	Potomac	440	71	129	1	38	293	364	409	773	10	86	0.82	20	10	31	116	5.36
2010	AA	Harrisburg	105	19	31	5	11	295	368	524	891	10	86	0.80	4	2	39	229	6.53
2011	AA	Harrisburg	262	40	81	4	23	309	354	454	808	6	85	0.47	16	3	28	145	5.45
2011	AAA	Syracuse	294	46	91	4	29	310	356	408	764	7	86	0.53	14	5	21	99	4.90
2011	MLB	Washington	31	3	6	0	1	194	219	226	445	3	87	0.25	0	0	17	32	1.10

Scrappy, solid, all-around, athlete who is son of former major leaguer Steve Lombardozzi. Doesn't have a real standout tool, but does a little bit of everything. Switch hitter and does a good job of using the whole field and hits RHP and LHP equally. Doesn't project to have much power but he can find the gap just fine. Above-average speed and a smart baserunner.

Lough, David — 789 — Kansas City

EXP MLB DEBUT: 2012 | POTENTIAL: Reserve OF | 6A

Bats L Age 26 — 2007 (11) Mercyhurst
Pwr +++ | BAvg +++ | Spd +++ | Def +++

Year	Lev	Team	AB	R	H	HR	RBI	Avg	OB	Slg	OPS	bb%	ct%	Eye	SB	CS	x/h%	Iso	RC/G
2008	A	Burlington	488	76	131	16	62	268	317	455	772	7	86	0.50	12	11	37	186	4.98
2009	A+	Wilmington	222	28	71	5	30	320	355	473	828	5	85	0.35	6	4	31	153	5.54
2009	AA	NW Arkansas	236	41	78	9	31	331	363	517	880	5	87	0.40	13	4	31	186	6.02
2010	AAA	Omaha	460	65	129	11	58	280	338	437	775	8	84	0.56	14	5	29	157	5.11
2011	AAA	Omaha	456	87	145	9	65	318	368	482	850	7	89	0.73	14	8	32	164	6.00

Fundamentally-sound outfielder who continues to produce, yet hasn't appeared in majors. Produces moderate power to all fields with short, direct swing path. Makes outstanding contact and has enough speed to get infield hits. Likes to use middle of field and can jam one out of park on occasion. Can play all outfield positions, but not above average at any one.

Lowery, Jake — 2 — Cleveland

EXP MLB DEBUT: 2014 | POTENTIAL: Backup C | 7C

Bats L Age 21 — 2011 (4) James Madison
Pwr +++ | BAvg +++ | Spd + | Def ++

Year	Lev	Team	AB	R	H	HR	RBI	Avg	OB	Slg	OPS	bb%	ct%	Eye	SB	CS	x/h%	Iso	RC/G
2009	NCAA	James Madison	115	15	28	1	17	243	331	365	696	12	57	0.30	5	1	36	122	5.05
2010	NCAA	James Madison	186	32	53	8	41	285	361	505	866	11	78	0.54	1	7	42	220	6.36
2011	NCAA	James Madison	251	80	90	24	91	359	443	797	1240	13	81	0.81	9	3	60	438	10.96
2011	A-	Mahoning Vall	253	43	62	6	43	245	378	415	793	18	78	0.96	3	2	48	170	5.88

Short and stocky backstop with fine offensive skills. Combines professional approach with all-fields power. Doesn't recognize pitches well and long swing puts damper on BA potential. Strong, accurate arm is best trait behind plate, but receiving skills a little short for major league role.

Lutz, Zach — 5 — New York (N)

EXP MLB DEBUT: 2012 | POTENTIAL: Reserve 3B/1B | 7D

Bats R Age 26 — 2007 (5) HS, (CA)
Pwr ++++ | BAvg ++ | Spd ++ | Def ++

Year	Lev	Team	AB	R	H	HR	RBI	Avg	OB	Slg	OPS	bb%	ct%	Eye	SB	CS	x/h%	Iso	RC/G
2010	A+	St. Lucie	4	0	0	0	0	0	0	0	0	0	50	0.00	0	0			
2010	AA	Binghamton	225	42	65	17	42	289	380	578	958	13	72	0.52	0	2	48	289	7.72
2010	AAA	Buffalo	20	3	6	1	9	300	364	650	1014	9	85	0.67	0	0	83	350	8.07
2011	A+	St. Lucie	8	0	0	0	1	0	111	0	111	11	75	0.50	0	0			
2011	AAA	Buffalo	220	38	65	11	31	295	372	500	872	11	68	0.39	0	0	35	205	6.74

Strong, stocky 3B prospect has solid power, but can't seem to stay healthy. Broken ankle in '09, and broken foot in '10, and two concusions in '11. When healthy, he has as nice bat and good power. Is below-average defensively with fair arm strength and average range so all value is tied into his bat.

Machado, Dixon — 6 — Detroit

EXP MLB DEBUT: 2014 | POTENTIAL: Starting SS | 7D

Bats R Age 20 — 2008 FA (Venezuela)
Pwr + | BAvg ++ | Spd +++ | Def ++++

Year	Lev	Team	AB	R	H	HR	RBI	Avg	OB	Slg	OPS	bb%	ct%	Eye	SB	CS	x/h%	Iso	RC/G
2010	Rk	GCL Tigers	165	22	43	0	11	261	318	321	640	8	84	0.52	12	3	16	61	3.54
2010	A-	Connecticut	24	4	7	0	1	292	370	333	704	11	79	0.60	1	2	14	42	4.42
2011	A	West Michigan	429	47	101	0	28	235	309	247	557	10	82	0.60	25	5	3	12	2.52

Lean and athletic infielder whose value is his glovework. Possesses nimble feet with quick, smooth actions. Exhibits above average arm strength, but can be lazy with throws. Controls bat well and puts ball in play, but lacks strength to hit for power. Ninety-eight of 101 hits were singles and extra bases reached mostly due to speed than hard contact.

Machado, Manny — 6 — Baltimore

EXP MLB DEBUT: 2013 | POTENTIAL: Starting SS | 9B

Bats R Age 19 — 2010 (1) HS (FL)
Pwr ++++ | BAvg ++++ | Spd +++ | Def ++++

Year	Lev	Team	AB	R	H	HR	RBI	Avg	OB	Slg	OPS	bb%	ct%	Eye	SB	CS	x/h%	Iso	RC/G
2010	Rk	GCL Orioles	7	1	1	1	2	143	143	571	714	0	86	0.00	0	0	100	429	3.45
2010	A-	Aberdeen	29	2	10	0	3	345	406	448	855	9	93	1.50	0	0	20	103	6.31
2011	A	Delmarva	145	24	40	6	24	276	375	483	858	14	83	0.92	3	1	40	207	6.37
2011	A+	Frederick	237	24	58	5	26	245	309	384	693	8	80	0.46	8	5	34	139	4.11

Tall and strong infielder who struggled upon promotion to High-A, but has all-around skill set worthy of praise. Exhibits natural hitting talent and has strength and leverage for plus power. Plus bat speed should allow for high BA and ability to work counts enhances OBP. Strong defender with arm strength, though some talk of moving to 3B due to frame. A future All-Star.

Mahoney, Joseph — 37 — Baltimore

EXP MLB DEBUT: 2012 | POTENTIAL: Starting 1B | 8D

Bats L Age 25 — 2007 (6) Richmond
Pwr ++++ | BAvg +++ | Spd ++ | Def +++

Year	Lev	Team	AB	R	H	HR	RBI	Avg	OB	Slg	OPS	bb%	ct%	Eye	SB	CS	x/h%	Iso	RC/G
2009	A+	Frederick	30	2	8	1	5	267	267	500	767	0	67	0.00	0	1	63	233	5.08
2010	A+	Frederick	271	37	81	9	49	299	352	465	816	8	79	0.39	5	3	33	166	5.52
2010	AA	Bowie	191	30	61	9	29	319	375	545	920	8	80	0.44	8	1	38	225	6.82
2011	A+	Frederick	8	0	4	0	2	500	667	750	1417	33	88	4.00	0	0	50	250	15.08
2011	AA	Bowie	315	43	91	11	67	289	341	502	843	7	73	0.30	7	2	44	213	6.08

Big and strong hitter who missed time with quad injury, but produced with bat when healthy. Offers extensive raw power, but has swing and instincts to hit for BA. Owns good approach against LHP and makes ample contact despite long swing. Can be pull-conscious and swing tentatively at times. Questionable hands at 1B, but has good range and can scoop balls in dirt.

Mahtook, Mikie — 789 — Tampa Bay

EXP MLB DEBUT: 2014 | POTENTIAL: Starting OF | 8C

Bats R Age 22 — 2011 (1) LSU
Pwr +++ | BAvg +++ | Spd +++ | Def +++

Year	Lev	Team	AB	R	H	HR	RBI	Avg	OB	Slg	OPS	bb%	ct%	Eye	SB	CS	x/h%	Iso	RC/G
2009	NCAA	Louisiana State	196	41	62	7	38	316	362	495	857	7	79	0.34	9	4	29	179	5.98
2010	NCAA	Louisiana State	239	68	80	14	50	335	426	623	1049	14	77	0.70	22	10	46	289	8.91
2011	NCAA	Louisiana State	196	61	75	14	56	383	489	709	1199	17	84	1.28	29	9	41	327	10.68

Athletic and strong outfielder with boatload of tools that give him considerable value. Can play any OF position well due to decent range and arm strength. Likely will end up in corner as routes and instincts better served there. Makes consistent, hard contact from simple swing and should develop average pop to go along with BA ability and solid speed.

Malm, Jeff — 3 — Tampa Bay

EXP MLB DEBUT: 2015 | POTENTIAL: Reserve 1B | 8E

Bats L Age 21 — 2009 (5) HS (NV)
Pwr ++++ | BAvg ++ | Spd ++ | Def ++

Year	Lev	Team	AB	R	H	HR	RBI	Avg	OB	Slg	OPS	bb%	ct%	Eye	SB	CS	x/h%	Iso	RC/G
2009	Rk	GCL Rays	25	2	6	0	0	240	269	240	509	4	84	0.25	1	0	0	0	1.67
2010	Rk	Princeton	200	20	44	3	25	220	281	310	591	8	77	0.37	2	1	27	90	2.72
2011	A-	Hudson Valley	249	36	64	12	47	257	355	462	817	13	74	0.58	3	2	42	205	5.85

Big and strong hitter who hasn't yet gotten out of short season ball. Produces mammoth power with above average bat speed and smooth lefty stroke. Draws walks, but lacks secondary skills. Relegated to 1B and will need to increase BA to project as starter. Has decent arm strength, but not enough mobility, agility, or speed to be factor.

Marisnick, Jake — 8 — Toronto

EXP MLB DEBUT: 2014 | POTENTIAL: Starting OF | 9C

Bats R Age 21 — 2009 (3) HS (CA)
Pwr +++ | BAvg ++++ | Spd ++++ | Def ++++

Year	Lev	Team	AB	R	H	HR	RBI	Avg	OB	Slg	OPS	bb%	ct%	Eye	SB	CS	x/h%	Iso	RC/G
2010	Rk	GCL Blue Jays	122	17	35	3	14	287	356	459	815	10	85	0.72	14	1	43	172	5.70
2010	A	Lansing	127	16	28	1	12	220	272	339	611	7	71	0.24	9	2	39	118	3.01
2011	A	Lansing	462	68	148	14	77	320	378	496	874	9	80	0.47	37	8	32	175	6.33

Tall and very athletic outfielder who finished 2nd in MWL in BA. Has all requisite tools to become impact hitter in middle of lineup. Has pure hitting skills and ability to hit for average pop to all parts of park. Possesses smarts and nose for game by running bases effectively and playing outstanding CF with plus arm strength and range.

Marrero, Chris — 3 — Washington

EXP MLB DEBUT: 2011 | POTENTIAL: Starting 1B | 8D

Bats R Age 23 — 2006 (1) HS, (FL)
Pwr +++ | BAvg +++ | 4.40 Spd ++ | Def +++

Year	Lev	Team	AB	R	H	HR	RBI	Avg	OB	Slg	OPS	bb%	ct%	Eye	SB	CS	x/h%	Iso	RC/G
2009	A+	Potomac	414	58	119	16	65	287	353	464	817	9	77	0.43	2	3	33	176	5.64
2009	AA	Harrisburg	75	9	20	1	11	267	337	387	724	10	76	0.44	0	1	35	120	4.60
2010	AA	Harrisburg	524	73	154	18	82	294	347	450	798	8	81	0.42	1	3	30	156	5.26
2011	AAA	Syracuse	483	59	145	14	69	300	375	449	825	11	80	0.60	3	2	30	149	5.82
2011	MLB	Washington	109	6	27	0	10	248	274	294	568	4	75	0.15	0	0	19	46	2.24

Tall, strong OF had another solid season and held his own in extended MLB action. None of his tools standout as plus, but he continues to improve in every aspect of the game. He has good bat speed and the ability to make adjustments. He swings aggressively but makes consistent contact. He has good hands at 1B and is a solid defender.

Marte, Jefry — 5 — New York (N)

EXP MLB DEBUT: 2013 | POTENTIAL: Starting 3B | 8D

Bats R Age 21 — 2007 NDFA D.R.
Pwr ++++ | BAvg +++ | 4.30 Spd ++ | Def ++

Year	Lev	Team	AB	R	H	HR	RBI	Avg	OB	Slg	OPS	bb%	ct%	Eye	SB	CS	x/h%	Iso	RC/G
2008	Rk	GCL Mets	154	29	50	4	24	325	377	532	910	8	81	0.43	2	0	42	208	6.82
2009	A	Savannah	485	58	113	6	41	233	271	338	609	5	76	0.21	5	5	29	105	2.84
2010	A	Savannah	329	40	87	6	44	264	326	401	727	8	80	0.46	4	5	33	137	4.55
2011	A+	St. Lucie	483	56	120	7	55	248	307	346	653	8	82	0.48	14	2	26	97	3.60

Short, stocky third baseman is a potent hitter with a live bat and good raw power. Moderate plate discipline and quick hands give him the potential to hit for average. Struggled as one of the younger players in the FSL, but played in the Futures Game and rebounded nicely in the AFL. Broken wrist in the AFL should be healed by spring.

Marte, Starling
8 | **Pittsburgh** | EXP MLB DEBUT: 2012 | POTENTIAL: Starting CF | **8B**

Bats R Age 23
2006 NDFA D.R.
Pwr +++
BAvg +++
Spd ++++
Def ++++

Year	Lev	Team	AB	R	H	HR	RBI	Avg	OB	Slg	OPS	bb%	ct%	Eye	SB	CS	x/h%	Iso	RC/G
2009	A	West Virginia	221	41	69	3	34	312	348	439	787	5	75	0.22	24	7	25	127	5.19
2009	A+	Lynchburg	2	0	2	0	1	1000	1000	1000	2000	0	100		0	0	0	0	16.32
2010	Rk	GCL Pirates	26	6	9	2	5	346	370	692	1063	4	77	0.17	4	1	56	346	8.40
2010	A+	Bradenton	222	41	70	0	33	315	350	432	783	5	73	0.20	22	8	30	117	5.31
2011	AA	Altoona	536	91	178	12	50	332	358	500	858	4	81	0.22	24	12	33	168	5.88

Toolsy, athletic OF had a nice breakout season. Power uptick is a great sign to go along with plus speed and ability to hit for average. Only red flag is substandard plate discipline. Will need to become more patient and selective to maintain a .300 average. Runs very well, covers ground, and has a strong, accurate throwing arm. Profiles as a top-of-the-order CF.

Martin, Brandon
6 | **Tampa Bay** | EXP MLB DEBUT: 2015 | POTENTIAL: Starting SS | **8D**

Bats R Age 18
2011 (1-S) HS (CA)
Pwr ++
BAvg +++
Spd +++
Def ++

Year	Lev	Team	AB	R	H	HR	RBI	Avg	OB	Slg	OPS	bb%	ct%	Eye	SB	CS	x/h%	Iso	RC/G
2011	Rk	GCL Rays	47	10	12	1	3	255	352	340	692	13	74	0.58	5	3	17	85	4.20

Small and athletic infielder with mature all-around game. Has the tools necessary to be standout defender, but needs time to develop instincts and proper footwork. Arm strength is excellent and ranges well, but makes sloppy errors at times. Uses line drive stroke to make good contact and could hit for average pop as he fills out frame.

Martin, Leonys
8 | **Texas** | EXP MLB DEBUT: 2011 | POTENTIAL: Starting OF | **8C**

Bats L Age 24
2011 FA (Cuba)
Pwr ++
BAvg +++
Spd ++++
Def ++++

Year	Lev	Team	AB	R	H	HR	RBI	Avg	OB	Slg	OPS	bb%	ct%	Eye	SB	CS	x/h%	Iso	RC/G
2011	Rk	AZL Rangers	15	2	4	0	1	267	313	533	846	6	60	0.17	0	1	50	267	7.61
2011	AA	Frisco	112	24	39	4	24	348	425	571	997	12	93	1.88	10	8	38	223	7.91
2011	AAA	Round Rock	175	27	46	0	17	263	306	314	621	6	86	0.46	9	2	17	51	3.25
2011	MLB	Texas	8	2	3	0	0	375	375	500	875	0	88	0.00	0	0	33	125	5.80

Quick and athletic outfielder reached majors in first pro season on basis of speed and defense. Natural hitter who possesses quick, level swing and ability to hit balls to gaps. Has some power potential, but most effective when using speed. Plays excellent defense by ranging well in CF and showcasing strong arm. Power development will dictate upside.

Martinez, Alberth
8 | **San Diego** | EXP MLB DEBUT: 2014 | POTENTIAL: Starting CF | **8C**

Bats R Age 21
2009 NDFA D.R.
Pwr +++
BAvg +++
Spd ++++
Def ++++

Year	Lev	Team	AB	R	H	HR	RBI	Avg	OB	Slg	OPS	bb%	ct%	Eye	SB	CS	x/h%	Iso	RC/G
2011	Rk	AZL Padres	189	31	67	7	24	354	387	593	980	5	86	0.37	14	3	37	238	7.29
2011	A-	Eugene	44	3	8	0	3	182	217	273	490	4	82	0.25	4	0	38	91	1.58
2011	A	Fort Wayne	13	0	0	0	0	0	71	0	71	7	54	0.17	0	1			
2011	AAA	Tucson	17	0	2	0	0	118	118	118	235	0	59	0.00	0	0			

Lean, athletic, toolsy OF has an exciting package of tools. Showed plus bat speed and the potential to hit for average and power. Also stole 18 bases and played outstanding CF defense. Takes good routes, covers ground well, and has a strong throwing arm. He wasn't as young as others in the AZL, but the tools are above-average across the board.

Martinez, Francisco
5 | **Seattle** | EXP MLB DEBUT: 2013 | POTENTIAL: Starting 3B | **8C**

Bats R Age 21
2007 FA (Venezuela)
Pwr ++++
BAvg +++
Spd +++
Def +++

Year	Lev	Team	AB	R	H	HR	RBI	Avg	OB	Slg	OPS	bb%	ct%	Eye	SB	CS	x/h%	Iso	RC/G
2009	Rk	GCL Tigers	153	21	34	2	23	222	247	320	567	3	75	0.13	11	1	32	98	2.20
2009	A+	Lakeland	18	1	3	0	2	167	167	167	333	0	83	0.00	1	0			
2010	A+	Lakeland	340	47	92	3	29	271	326	353	679	8	79	0.39	12	5	23	82	3.89
2011	AA	Erie	348	63	98	7	46	282	319	405	724	5	77	0.24	7	8	26	124	4.29
2011	AA	Jackson	129	20	40	3	23	310	331	481	811	3	81	0.17	3	2	33	171	5.25

Strong and athletic infielder set career high in HR and power starting to emerge. Does everything well, but overall game and approach need polish. Bat speed and plate coverage give him BA and power potential, but is a free swinger with tendency to fan. Good speed and quickness enhance defense where arm and release are sufficient.

Martinez, Jorge
46 | **Cleveland** | EXP MLB DEBUT: 2015 | POTENTIAL: Starting SS | **9E**

Bats B Age 19
2009 FA (DR)
Pwr +++
BAvg +++
Spd +++
Def +++

Year	Lev	Team	AB	R	H	HR	RBI	Avg	OB	Slg	OPS	bb%	ct%	Eye	SB	CS	x/h%	Iso	RC/G
2010	Rk	AZL Indians	190	23	41	2	21	216	255	274	529	5	78	0.24	3	4	17	58	1.80
2011	Rk	AZL Indians	180	25	46	4	30	256	316	400	716	8	81	0.47	4	3	35	144	4.39

Tall and raw infielder who returned to Rookie ball and flashed major upside potential. Consistent improved throughout campaign, particularly with making contact and driving ball to all fields. Offers average power from both sides and mixes in nice plate discipline. Inconsistent defender, though has strong arm and good range.

Martinez, Jose
9 | **Chicago (A)** | EXP MLB DEBUT: 2013 | POTENTIAL: Starting OF | **8E**

Bats R Age 23
2006 FA (Venezuela)
Pwr +++
BAvg +++
Spd ++
Def +++

Year	Lev	Team	AB	R	H	HR	RBI	Avg	OB	Slg	OPS	bb%	ct%	Eye	SB	CS	x/h%	Iso	RC/G
2008	A	Kannapolis	144	19	44	2	18	306	359	382	741	8	82	0.46	7	5	16	76	4.62
2010	Rk	Bristol	22	5	9	1	5	409	458	591	1049	8	86	0.67	1	0	22	182	8.15
2010	A+	Winston-Salem	236	28	57	5	24	242	292	347	640	7	82	0.40	4	1	25	106	3.34
2011	A+	Winston-Salem	315	45	99	5	29	314	341	422	764	4	86	0.30	2	3	21	108	4.70
2011	AA	Birmingham	200	19	59	1	16	295	344	385	729	7	88	0.60	5	2	25	90	4.60

Tall and lean outfielder who has been injury prone, but put together solid season. Doubles power at present, but long arms and bat speed show glimpses of above average pop. Makes good contact with relatively short stroke and covers plate well. Isn't a blazer by any means, but covers ground in RF and possesses very strong arm.

Martinez, Mario
5 | **Seattle** | EXP MLB DEBUT: 2013 | POTENTIAL: Reserve INF | **7C**

Bats R Age 22
2006 FA (DR)
Pwr +++
BAvg +++
Spd ++
Def ++++

Year	Lev	Team	AB	R	H	HR	RBI	Avg	OB	Slg	OPS	bb%	ct%	Eye	SB	CS	x/h%	Iso	RC/G
2008	Rk	Pulaski	251	43	80	5	32	319	345	462	807	4	81	0.21	2	2	29	143	5.23
2009	A-	Everett	302	45	93	3	33	308	332	437	769	4	80	0.19	4	0	30	129	4.83
2009	A	Clinton	229	20	49	2	24	214	250	314	564	5	78	0.22	1	0	35	100	2.32
2010	A	Clinton	440	51	105	12	66	239	267	384	651	4	74	0.15	4	1	35	145	3.27
2011	A+	High Desert	432	64	120	11	56	278	308	419	727	4	68	0.14	2	1	30	141	4.46

Athletic and strong infielder who stands out more for glove than bat. Uses whole field in approach and has above average power potential, though hits gaps with level swing. Strong, fundamentally sound stroke accentuates offensive package, but poor eye diminishes value. Doesn't run well, but has quick feet at 3B with soft, quick hands.

Martinez, Ozzie
456 | **Chicago (A)** | EXP MLB DEBUT: 2010 | POTENTIAL: Reserve 2B/SS | **6B**

Bats R Age 24
2006 (11) Porterville CC
Pwr ++
BAvg +++
Spd +++
Def ++++

Year	Lev	Team	AB	R	H	HR	RBI	Avg	OB	Slg	OPS	bb%	ct%	Eye	SB	CS	x/h%	Iso	RC/G
2009	A+	Jupiter	433	54	110	1	45	254	319	321	640	9	88	0.80	16	4	20	67	3.71
2010	AA	Jacksonville	516	90	156	5	54	302	363	401	764	9	88	0.77	13	9	24	99	5.09
2010	MLB	Florida	43	8	14	0	2	326	383	465	848	9	86	0.67	1	0	36	140	6.18
2011	AAA	New Orleans	339	43	83	3	26	245	289	322	610	6	83	0.37	11	4	23	77	3.01
2011	MLB	Florida	23	0	3	0	1	130	130	130	261	0	61	0.00	0	0			

Smooth and quick infielder who has versatile skills worthy of utility role. Poor batting eye limits offensive upside and lacks power requisite for full-time job. Uses level swing to generate power to gaps and makes contact with plus hand-eye coordination. Supplies solid glove with solid feet, hands, and above average arm strength.

Martinson, Jason
6 | **Washington** | EXP MLB DEBUT: 2014 | POTENTIAL: Starting SS | **7C**

Bats R Age 23
2010 (5) Texas State
Pwr +++
BAvg ++
Spd +++
Def +++

Year	Lev	Team	AB	R	H	HR	RBI	Avg	OB	Slg	OPS	bb%	ct%	Eye	SB	CS	x/h%	Iso	RC/G
2008	NCAA	Texas State	72	11	11	3	10	153	274	319	593	14	65	0.48	3	2	55	167	2.72
2009	NCAA	Texas State	173	42	52	7	39	301	395	520	915	14	80	0.77	4	2	40	220	7.14
2010	NCAA	Texas State	234	44	75	4	55	321	398	479	876	11	82	0.73	10	3	35	158	6.61
2010	A-	Vermont	253	38	61	2	36	241	340	344	684	13	71	0.51	4	2	26	103	4.28
2011	A	Hagerstown	433	64	109	19	64	252	351	448	799	13	67	0.46	26	6	40	196	5.86

Strong, powerful SS uses an aggressive approach at the plate to generate solid power, but does not make consistent contact. He needs to develop better pitch recognition. Defensively he has a plus arm, but his range and speed are better suited for 3B. Did manage to hit 19 home runs and steal 26 bases, so there is some potential.

Mastroianni, Darin
78 | **Toronto** | EXP MLB DEBUT: 2011 | POTENTIAL: Reserve OF | **6B**

Bats R Age 26
2007 (16) Winthrop
Pwr +
BAvg +++
Spd ++++
Def ++

Year	Lev	Team	AB	R	H	HR	RBI	Avg	OB	Slg	OPS	bb%	ct%	Eye	SB	CS	x/h%	Iso	RC/G
2009	AA	New Hampshire	247	39	67	1	25	271	371	340	711	14	82	0.87	38	8	19	69	4.68
2010	AA	New Hampshire	525	101	158	4	46	301	390	398	788	13	82	0.80	46	10	23	97	5.61
2011	AA	New Hampshire	169	29	43	1	13	254	340	355	695	12	86	0.92	14	3	28	101	4.48
2011	AAA	Las Vegas	319	63	88	2	23	276	357	389	745	11	83	0.74	20	7	30	113	5.03
2011	MLB	Toronto	2	0	0	0	0	0	0	0	0	0	50	0.00	0	0			

Short and athletic outfielder who has stolen at least 30 bases every year as pro. Plays small ball well and has ideal leadoff skills. Patient approach and strong eye provide on base ability and flat, level swing path produces doubles. Rarely hits HR and has tendency to expand strike zone. Ranges well in LF or CF, but lacks arm strength and instincts.

Mateo, Danny — 5 — Kansas City

EXP MLB DEBUT: 2014 | POTENTIAL: Starting 3B | 7C

Bats B Age 20 | 2008 FA (DR)
Pwr ++ | BAvg ++++ | Spd ++ | Def +++

Year	Lev	Team	AB	R	H	HR	RBI	Avg	OB	Slg	OPS	bb%	ct%	Eye	SB	CS	x/h%	Iso	RC/G
2010	Rk	AZL Royals	206	19	45	2	25	218	255	350	604	5	77	0.21	7	1	40	131	2.86
2011	Rk	Idaho Falls	224	33	78	4	40	348	394	478	872	7	81	0.40	1	1	22	129	6.23

Instinctual and strong infielder who may not project to big league 3B, but has usable skills. Uses hands well in short, compact stroke and spreads ball to all fields. Hits for high BA due to level swing and natural hitting instincts, but isn't long ball threat. Lacks speed and quickness, but has good enough hands and arm strength to convert to 2B in future if necessary.

Matthes, Kent — 8 — Colorado

EXP MLB DEBUT: 2013 | POTENTIAL: Starting RF | 7D

Bats R Age 25 | 2009 (4) Alabama
Pwr ++++ | BAvg ++ | Spd +++ | Def ++

Year	Lev	Team	AB	R	H	HR	RBI	Avg	OB	Slg	OPS	bb%	ct%	Eye	SB	CS	x/h%	Iso	RC/G
2008	NCAA	Alabama	228	45	69	11	52	303	346	504	850	6	77	0.28	7	0	33	202	5.84
2009	NCAA	Alabama	204	67	73	28	81	358	445	858	1303	14	77	0.70	13	2	60	500	11.78
2009	A-	Tri-City	239	39	69	5	35	289	346	456	802	8	68	0.27	6	4	42	167	5.85
2010	A	Asheville	81	9	15	1	11	185	233	333	566	6	60	0.16	0	0	60	148	2.54
2011	A+	Modesto	371	70	124	23	95	334	372	642	1013	6	78	0.28	7	4	52	307	7.88

Athletic OF prospect was back in action after missing most of 2011 with a back injury. Had a monster year in the CAL, hitting .334/.378/.642 with 39 doubles and 23 home runs. Has moderate speed and legit power, but subpar plate discipline make a .300 average unlikely. Can play both corner OF spots, but at 25 he will need to make rapid progress in 2012.

Maynard, Pratt — 2 — Los Angeles (N)

EXP MLB DEBUT: 2014 | POTENTIAL: Starting C | 7C

Bats L Age 22 | 2011 (3) North Carolina State
Pwr +++ | BAvg +++ | Spd ++ | Def ++

Year	Lev	Team	AB	R	H	HR	RBI	Avg	OB	Slg	OPS	bb%	ct%	Eye	SB	CS	x/h%	Iso	RC/G
2009	NCAA	North Carolina St	188	34	49	6	40	261	365	420	786	14	79	0.78	4	3	37	160	5.51
2010	NCAA	North Carolina St	209	55	57	11	49	273	443	493	936	23	80	1.52	2	3	40	220	7.84
2011	NCAA	North Carolina St	251	46	81	5	41	323	412	474	886	13	82	0.84	1	0	33	151	6.81
2011	Rk	Ogden	88	16	21	2	11	239	337	341	678	13	73	0.54	0	0	24	102	4.01

Strong, physical collegiate backstop. Maynard has average power and a nice LH swing. Struggled in his pro debut, but played only 25 games. Below average defensively and might not stick at the position. Solid plate discipline and makes good contact. A work in progress.

McCann, James — 2 — Detroit

EXP MLB DEBUT: 2013 | POTENTIAL: Starting C | 7C

Bats R Age 22 | 2011 (2) Arkansas
Pwr +++ | BAvg +++ | Spd ++ | Def +++

Year	Lev	Team	AB	R	H	HR	RBI	Avg	OB	Slg	OPS	bb%	ct%	Eye	SB	CS	x/h%	Iso	RC/G
2009	NCAA	Arkansas	128	18	31	1	11	242	276	313	589	4	81	0.25	0	1	23	70	2.63
2010	NCAA	Arkansas	213	32	61	9	34	286	342	441	783	8	87	0.64	3	2	25	155	5.05
2011	NCAA	Arkansas	209	35	64	6	38	306	378	469	847	10	88	0.92	11	6	33	163	6.08
2011	Rk	GCL Tigers	14	1	5	1	6	357	400	643	1043	7	93	1.00	0	0	40	286	7.81
2011	A	West Michigan	34	0	2	0	1	59	111	88	199	6	65	0.17	0	0	50	29	

Consistent and strong backstop with no plus skills, but does everything modestly well. Could reach DET quickly more on basis of glovework than bat. Receives well and blocks balls in dirt. Exhibits mobility and agility along with average arm and release. Should hit for moderate BA as he understands strike zone and exhibits bat control. Mostly a fastball hitter to pull side.

McDade, Mike — 3 — Toronto

EXP MLB DEBUT: 2013 | POTENTIAL: Reserve 1B | 7D

Bats B Age 23 | 2007 (6) HS (NV)
Pwr ++++ | BAvg ++ | Spd ++ | Def ++

Year	Lev	Team	AB	R	H	HR	RBI	Avg	OB	Slg	OPS	bb%	ct%	Eye	SB	CS	x/h%	Iso	RC/G
2008	A-	Auburn	191	18	49	3	27	257	333	356	689	10	72	0.42	1	0	24	99	4.13
2008	A	Lansing	216	15	42	2	19	194	233	282	516	5	71	0.17	0	0	36	88	1.56
2009	A	Lansing	408	50	113	16	57	277	330	466	795	7	73	0.29	0	0	39	189	5.34
2010	A+	Dunedin	480	60	128	21	64	267	306	448	754	5	71	0.19	2	0	34	181	4.70
2011	AA	New Hampshire	484	71	136	16	74	281	320	457	777	5	79	0.27	0	1	39	176	4.94

Large-framed infielder who continues to exceed expectations with excellent power. Despite high K total, reduced amount from prior season enhanced BA. Will always fan due to long, upperct swing, but can hit ball a long way when he makes contact. Lacks speed and quickness which limits him to 1B. If he continues to hit, could be nice bat off bench.

Mendonca, Tommy — 5 — Texas

EXP MLB DEBUT: 2012 | POTENTIAL: Reserve 3B | 6A

Bats L Age 24 | 2009 (2) Fresno State
Pwr ++++ | BAvg ++ | Spd ++ | Def +++

Year	Lev	Team	AB	R	H	HR	RBI	Avg	OB	Slg	OPS	bb%	ct%	Eye	SB	CS	x/h%	Iso	RC/G
2009	NCAA	Fresno State	233	54	79	27	78	339	421	721	1142	12	73	0.52	2	2	44	382	9.98
2009	A-	Spokane	188	33	58	9	26	309	340	537	877	5	65	0.14	0	0	40	229	6.85
2009	A+	Bakersfield	43	5	9	0	2	209	227	279	506	2	72	0.08	1	0	33	70	1.39
2010	A+	Bakersfield	419	62	104	10	47	248	308	391	699	8	70	0.29	1	4	37	143	4.20
2011	AA	Frisco	504	75	140	25	87	278	325	492	817	6	68	0.22	0	1	39	214	5.75

Strong infielder who is converting raw power to usable game power. Aggressive approach and poor contact hinder BA potential, but bat speed, leverage, and brute strength offer all-fields power. Owns instincts at plate, but finished 2nd in TL in Ks. Exhibits strong arm and decent hands, but no speed or first step quickness.

Mercer, Jordy — 6 — Pittsburgh

EXP MLB DEBUT: 2012 | POTENTIAL: Reserve 2B | 6B

Bats R Age 25 | 2008 (3) Oklahoma St
Pwr +++ | BAvg ++ | Spd ++++ | Def +++

Year	Lev	Team	AB	R	H	HR	RBI	Avg	OB	Slg	OPS	bb%	ct%	Eye	SB	CS	x/h%	Iso	RC/G
2008	A	Hickory	192	21	48	4	18	250	294	349	643	6	77	0.27	4	3	23	99	3.24
2009	A+	Lynchburg	513	64	131	10	83	255	310	400	710	7	82	0.44	10	6	38	144	4.30
2010	AA	Altoona	485	67	137	3	65	282	326	373	699	6	86	0.45	7	1	26	91	4.15
2011	AA	Altoona	265	40	71	13	48	268	326	487	813	8	87	0.66	6	3	44	219	5.45
2011	AAA	Indianapolis	226	39	54	6	21	239	280	385	665	5	81	0.30	3	3	37	146	3.58

Tall 2B prospect with above-average power. Can be overly aggressive and sells out for power, making it unlikely he will hit for both average and power. Slightly above-average speed, but not a SB threat. Was moved from SS to 2B due to limited range, but does have sure hands and a strong throwing arm.

Mesoraco, Devin — 2 — Cincinnati

EXP MLB DEBUT: 2011 | POTENTIAL: Starting CA | 9C

Bats R Age 24 | 2007 (1) HS (PA)
Pwr ++++ | BAvg +++ | 4.30 Spd ++ | Def ++++

Year	Lev	Team	AB	R	H	HR	RBI	Avg	OB	Slg	OPS	bb%	ct%	Eye	SB	CS	x/h%	Iso	RC/G
2010	A+	Lynchburg	158	24	53	10	31	335	407	620	1027	11	82	0.66	2	2	43	285	8.21
2010	AA	Carolina	187	42	55	13	31	294	356	594	950	9	80	0.49	1	0	49	299	7.14
2010	AAA	Louisville	52	5	12	3	13	231	310	462	772	10	73	0.43	0	1	50	231	5.07
2011	AAA	Louisville	436	60	126	15	71	289	365	484	849	11	81	0.63	1	1	42	195	6.14
2011	MLB	Cincinnati	50	5	9	2	6	180	226	360	586	6	80	0.30	0	0	56	180	2.56

Strong, athletic receiver had solid follow-up to breakout of '10, hitting for power and average. Mesoraco is stonger and in better shape than before, which helped him improve defensively. Has legit power to all fields. He is a solid defender with a plus arm, quick release, and improved blocking skills. He should get a chance to win the starting role at some point in '12.

Michael, Levi — 6 — Minnesota

EXP MLB DEBUT: 2013 | POTENTIAL: Starting SS | 8C

Bats B Age 21 | 2011 (1) North Carolina
Pwr +++ | BAvg +++ | Spd +++ | Def +++

Year	Lev	Team	AB	R	H	HR	RBI	Avg	OB	Slg	OPS	bb%	ct%	Eye	SB	CS	x/h%	Iso	RC/G
2009	NCAA	North Carolina	262	54	76	13	57	290	354	527	881	9	79	0.46	5	4	42	237	6.41
2010	NCAA	North Carolina	214	76	74	9	54	346	457	575	1032	17	88	1.69	20	2	36	229	8.68
2011	NCAA	North Carolina	242	53	70	5	48	289	409	434	843	17	81	1.04	15	1	31	145	6.48

Short and athletic infielder who has all-around skill set. Has enough punch in bat to keep defense honest, but isn't power hitter. Should hit for BA from both sides of plate as he recognizes pitches, exhibits patience, and hits to all fields. Quick actions enhance play at SS with nice arm, though range might move him to 2B. Could reach majors quickly.

Miclat, Greg — 46 — Texas

EXP MLB DEBUT: 2012 | POTENTIAL: Utility player | 6A

Bats B Age 24 | 2008 (5) Virginia
Pwr + | BAvg +++ | Spd ++++ | Def +++

Year	Lev	Team	AB	R	H	HR	RBI	Avg	OB	Slg	OPS	bb%	ct%	Eye	SB	CS	x/h%	Iso	RC/G
2009	A	Delmarva	400	49	91	0	22	228	301	273	573	10	80	0.53	25	6	18	45	2.72
2009	A+	Frederick	24	4	5	0	1	208	296	250	546	11	83	0.75	1	0	20	42	2.57
2010	A+	Frederick	164	30	51	1	19	311	386	402	788	11	84	0.74	8	2	25	91	5.50
2010	AA	Bowie	228	35	56	1	16	246	317	316	633	10	77	0.46	4	6	21	70	3.41
2011	AA	Bowie	421	78	118	2	24	280	362	347	709	11	78	0.57	50	3	18	67	4.48

Fundamentally-sound infielder who led EL in SB. Has mostly played SS in past, but focused on 2B in '11. Good defender with quickness in hands and feet. Has nose for glove, though arm strength is only ideal for 2B. Takes more of a slap approach and can get on base by being patient and making contact. Power will never be part of game and has swing to prove it.

Middlebrooks, Will — 5 — Boston

EXP MLB DEBUT: 2012 | POTENTIAL: Starting 3B | 8B

Bats R Age 23 | 2007 (5) HS (TX)
Pwr ++++ | BAvg +++ | Spd +++ | Def +++

Year	Lev	Team	AB	R	H	HR	RBI	Avg	OB	Slg	OPS	bb%	ct%	Eye	SB	CS	x/h%	Iso	RC/G
2009	A	Greenville	374	53	99	7	57	265	348	404	752	11	67	0.39	7	4	35	139	5.24
2010	A+	Salem	435	69	120	12	70	276	330	439	769	7	72	0.29	5	3	38	163	5.09
2011	A-	Lowell	12	4	4	3	6	333	429	1167	1595	14	92	2.00	1	0	100	833	13.77
2011	AA	Portland	371	54	112	18	80	302	339	520	860	5	74	0.22	6	0	39	218	6.02
2011	AAA	Pawtucket	56	4	9	2	8	161	203	268	471	5	68	0.17	3	1	22	107	0.65

Tall and strong infielder who posted career high in BA and HR. Has vaulted up prospect charts with solid all-around game. Displays quickness and fundamental glovework at 3B and has enough agility and arm to be asset. Natural hitter with power to all fields, though long swing results in Ks. Could stand to draw more walks, but bat speed and plus power have much value.

Mier, Jiovanni

6 | **Houston** | EXP MLB DEBUT: 2013 | POTENTIAL: Starting SS | **7C**

Bats R Age 21
2009 (1) HS, (CA)
Pwr +++
BAvg +++
Spd ++++
Def ++++

Year	Lev	Team	AB	R	H	HR	RBI	Avg	OB	Slg	OPS	bb%	ct%	Eye	SB	CS	x/h%	Iso	RC/G
2011	A	Lexington	216	39	53	5	29	245	356	380	735	15	73	0.64	6	2	36	134	4.94
2011	A+	Lancaster	206	35	48	2	23	233	328	306	633	12	74	0.54	5	3	21	73	3.46

Former 1st rounder has yet to do anything as a professional. Remains athletic but has shown no aptitude for hitting. Slick fielder with good speed and plus range with true SS actions. Continues to be advanced by the organization without dominating or even being league average offensively. Is only 21 years old, but will need to do something soon.

Miller, Brad

6 | **Seattle** | EXP MLB DEBUT: 2013 | POTENTIAL: Starting SS | **7A**

Bats L Age 22
2011 (2) Clemson
Pwr ++
BAvg ++++
Spd +++
Def +++

Year	Lev	Team	AB	R	H	HR	RBI	Avg	OB	Slg	OPS	bb%	ct%	Eye	SB	CS	x/h%	Iso	RC/G
2009	NCAA	Clemson	238	49	65	3	36	273	405	345	750	18	85	1.51	16	5	15	71	5.43
2010	NCAA	Clemson	252	71	90	8	49	357	464	560	1023	17	83	1.16	9	2	34	202	8.68
2011	NCAA	Clemson	195	53	77	5	50	395	498	559	1057	17	83	1.18	21	5	25	164	9.16
2011	A	Clinton	53	9	22	0	7	415	456	528	984	7	83	0.44	1	0	23	113	7.66

Tall and rangy infielder who lacks high upside, but does enough of everything well to have value. Lacks power and projection with even bat plane, but makes consistent contact. Knows value of getting on base with solid eye and possesses instincts on base and in the infield. Makes lazy errors, but defensive skills are sound.

Milligan, Adam

7 | **Atlanta** | EXP MLB DEBUT: 2013 | POTENTIAL: Staring LF | **7C**

Bats L Age 24
2008 (8) Walters State CC
Pwr +++
BAvg +++
Spd ++
Def ++

Year	Lev	Team	AB	R	H	HR	RBI	Avg	OB	Slg	OPS	bb%	ct%	Eye	SB	CS	x/h%	Iso	RC/G
2009	Rk	Danville	41	9	18	2	10	439	477	756	1233	7	83	0.43	0	0	44	317	10.53
2009	A	Rome	197	28	68	10	33	345	383	589	972	6	78	0.28	4	5	38	244	7.36
2009	A+	Myrtle Beach	24	2	4	1	6	167	167	333	500	0	67	0.00	0	0	50	167	1.00
2010	A+	Myrtle Beach	85	13	17	4	8	200	277	376	653	10	59	0.26	2	0	41	176	3.75
2011	A+	Lynchburg	237	35	69	12	40	291	336	557	893	6	68	0.21	1	0	51	266	6.97

Strong-bodied OF was healthy after missing most of '10 following shoulder surgery. Has potential to hit for average and power, though plate discipline needs improvement (16 BB/76 K). Milligan has average speed and arm strength and should be a competent defender, but the bat will be his ticket to the majors and he will get a good test in 2012.

Mills, Beau

3 | **Cleveland** | EXP MLB DEBUT: 2012 | POTENTIAL: Platoon 1B | **7B**

Bats L Age 25
2007 (1) Lewis & Clark
Pwr +++
BAvg +++
Spd +
Def +++

Year	Lev	Team	AB	R	H	HR	RBI	Avg	OB	Slg	OPS	bb%	ct%	Eye	SB	CS	x/h%	Iso	RC/G
2008	A+	Kinston	482	78	141	21	90	293	364	506	870	10	78	0.51	2	3	41	214	6.36
2009	AA	Akron	516	59	138	14	83	267	309	417	726	6	82	0.33	1	2	35	149	4.32
2010	AA	Akron	427	55	103	10	72	241	309	377	686	9	83	0.59	2	1	36	136	4.07
2011	AA	Akron	230	37	69	11	49	300	361	522	883	9	84	0.59	0	0	41	222	6.33
2011	AAA	Columbus	119	13	32	7	18	269	326	496	821	8	82	0.45	0	0	41	227	5.45

Strong infielder who was much improved and was promoted to Triple-A after two seasons in Double-A. Made much more consistent contact while power returned due to additional leverage and strength in balanced swing. Uses hands well with bat and in field, though footwork around bag is a little sloppy. Lacks secondary skills, but bat works well.

Mitchell, Jared

8 | **Chicago (A)** | EXP MLB DEBUT: 2013 | POTENTIAL: Starting CF | **8D**

Bats L Age 23
2009 (1) LSU
Pwr ++
BAvg +++
Spd ++++
Def +++

Year	Lev	Team	AB	R	H	HR	RBI	Avg	OB	Slg	OPS	bb%	ct%	Eye	SB	CS	x/h%	Iso	RC/G
2007	NCAA	Louisiana St	209	41	54	3	21	258	314	349	663	8	77	0.35	18	2	22	91	3.64
2008	NCAA	Louisiana St	175	44	52	6	29	297	353	463	821	8	72	0.31	16	2	33	171	5.79
2009	NCAA	Louisiana St	226	64	74	11	50	327	463	580	1043	20	72	0.89	36	9	41	252	9.54
2009	A	Kannapolis	115	13	34	0	10	296	413	435	848	17	65	0.58	5	3	41	139	7.23
2011	A+	Winston-Salem	477	74	106	9	58	222	299	377	676	10	62	0.28	14	6	45	155	4.29

Very athletic prospect who missed all of '10 with ankle injury. Led CAR in Ks while game showed little improvement throughout season. Owns impressive tools, but needs time to mesh together. Has plus speed and quickness when healthy, but struggles to make contact and raw power may not materialize. Fringy arm and poor instincts reduce defensive upside.

Mitchell, Jermaine

78 | **Oakland** | EXP MLB DEBUT: 2012 | POTENTIAL: Reserve OF | **7D**

Bats L Age 27
2006 (5) UNC-Greensboro
Pwr +++
BAvg +++
Spd ++++
Def +++

Year	Lev	Team	AB	R	H	HR	RBI	Avg	OB	Slg	OPS	bb%	ct%	Eye	SB	CS	x/h%	Iso	RC/G
2010	A+	Stockton	304	68	94	10	32	309	408	523	931	14	72	0.59	21	9	40	214	7.76
2010	AA	Midland	121	16	27	0	11	223	329	298	626	14	66	0.46	2	6	22	74	3.52
2010	AAA	Sacramento	11	1	2	0	2	182	250	273	523	8	73	0.33	1	0	50	91	1.91
2011	AA	Midland	304	67	108	10	50	355	453	589	1041	15	79	0.83	14	13	35	234	9.00
2011	AAA	Sacramento	232	48	70	5	28	302	402	453	855	14	80	0.83	13	5	31	151	6.50

Athletic outfielder who had career year at plate. Established highs in BA, 2B, HR, SB, and walks by showing improvement in swing mechanics and plate patience. Long swing will lead to Ks, but producing more gap power with confidence. Runs bases very well and can steal bases in bunches. Average defender who fits best in LF.

Montero, Jesus

2 | **New York (A)** | EXP MLB DEBUT: 2011 | POTENTIAL: Starting C | **9B**

Bats R Age 22
2006 FA (Venezuela)
Pwr +++++
BAvg ++++
Spd +
Def +

Year	Lev	Team	AB	R	H	HR	RBI	Avg	OB	Slg	OPS	bb%	ct%	Eye	SB	CS	x/h%	Iso	RC/G
2009	A+	Tampa	180	26	64	8	37	356	402	583	985	7	86	0.54	0	0	38	228	7.43
2009	AA	Trenton	167	19	53	9	33	317	370	539	909	8	87	0.67	0	0	36	222	6.49
2010	AAA	Scranton/W-B	453	66	131	21	75	289	355	517	871	9	80	0.51	0	0	44	227	6.29
2011	AAA	Scranton/W-B	420	52	121	18	67	288	344	467	811	8	77	0.37	0	0	31	179	5.45
2011	MLB	New York (A)	61	9	20	4	12	328	397	590	987	10	72	0.41	0	0	40	262	8.05

Strong and steady backstop who has chance to become monster offensive producer in near-term. Possesses significant power to all fields and has outstanding feel for hitting. Projects to high BA due to excellent hand-eye coordination and clean swing. Obvious shortcoming is with glove. He has plus arm strength, but slow release and crude receiving skills.

Moore, Jeremy

89 | **Los Angeles (A)** | EXP MLB DEBUT: 2011 | POTENTIAL: Starting OF | **8E**

Bats L Age 24
2005 (6) HS (LA)
Pwr +++
BAvg +++
Spd ++++
Def +++

Year	Lev	Team	AB	R	H	HR	RBI	Avg	OB	Slg	OPS	bb%	ct%	Eye	SB	CS	x/h%	Iso	RC/G
2009	A+	Rancho Cucamg	470	61	131	11	58	279	327	443	770	7	69	0.24	17	13	33	164	5.22
2009	AA	Arkansas	21	5	7	2	10	333	417	714	1131	13	67	0.43	1	1	43	381	10.64
2010	AA	Arkansas	456	72	138	13	61	303	358	463	820	8	73	0.32	24	10	27	160	5.77
2011	AAA	Salt Lake	426	76	127	15	66	298	331	545	876	5	73	0.18	21	10	45	246	6.45
2011	MLB	Los Angeles (A)	8	3	1	0	0	125	125	125	250	0	75	0.00	0	0			

Athletic and aggressive player who earned Sept callup after well-rounded campaign. Hits gap-to-gap with free-swinging approach and uses plus speed very well on base and in OF. Doesn't work counts and racks up many Ks, but knows how to hit and offers average pop to all fields. Merely an average defender with moderate arm strength.

Moore, Tyler

3 | **Washington** | EXP MLB DEBUT: 2013 | POTENTIAL: Starting 1B | **8D**

Bats R Age 25
2008 (16) Mississippi St
Pwr ++++
BAvg ++
Spd ++
Def +++

Year	Lev	Team	AB	R	H	HR	RBI	Avg	OB	Slg	OPS	bb%	ct%	Eye	SB	CS	x/h%	Iso	RC/G
2008	NCAA	Mississippi St	204	41	61	14	46	299	364	559	923	9	80	0.51	5	0	41	260	6.79
2008	A-	Vermont	265	17	53	6	28	200	237	306	543	5	75	0.20	1	1	30	106	1.88
2009	A	Hagerstown	421	38	125	9	87	297	358	447	804	9	74	0.36	2	2	34	150	5.64
2010	A+	Potomac	502	78	135	31	111	269	323	552	875	7	75	0.32	0	0	57	283	6.31
2011	AA	Harrisburg	519	70	140	31	90	270	310	532	841	5	73	0.22	2	0	50	262	5.82

Strong and athletic 1B has plus power and put up impressive numbers at Double-A. Sometimes struggles with breaking balls but will punish mistakes up in the zone. Lacks the foot speed or arm strength to play the OF, but is a solid defender at 1B. Contact rate and high K rate will likely prevent him for hitting for average, but he does have legit power.

Morales, Alfredo

9 | **Seattle** | EXP MLB DEBUT: 2015 | POTENTIAL: Starting OF | **8D**

Bats L Age 19
2009 FA (DR)
Pwr ++
BAvg ++++
Spd +++
Def ++

Year	Lev	Team	AB	R	H	HR	RBI	Avg	OB	Slg	OPS	bb%	ct%	Eye	SB	CS	x/h%	Iso	RC/G
2010	Rk	AZL Mariners	174	25	39	1	14	224	282	362	644	7	66	0.24	6	3	51	138	3.67
2011	Rk	Pulaski	143	17	38	2	19	266	348	357	704	11	68	0.39	0	0	24	91	4.46
2011	Rk	AZL Mariners	74	13	30	2	12	405	463	608	1072	10	74	0.42	8	2	33	203	9.30
2011	A+	High Desert	8	4	1	0	2	125	300	125	425	20	88	2.00	0	0	0	0	1.72

Lean and athletic outfielder who showcased impressive skill set in first pro season. Possesses mature hitting acumen with fundamental swing and has ability to use entire field. Can chase breaking balls out of zone, but generally works counts. Power could eventually catch up to speed and defense should evolve with more reps.

Morales, Angel

789 | **Minnesota** | EXP MLB DEBUT: 2014 | POTENTIAL: Starting OF | **7C**

Bats R Age 22
2007 (3) HS (PR)
Pwr +++
BAvg +++
Spd ++++
Def +++

Year	Lev	Team	AB	R	H	HR	RBI	Avg	OB	Slg	OPS	bb%	ct%	Eye	SB	CS	x/h%	Iso	RC/G
2009	A	Beloit	376	63	100	13	62	266	320	455	775	7	72	0.29	19	6	40	189	5.15
2010	A	Beloit	211	34	61	4	36	289	362	474	836	10	69	0.37	18	7	39	185	6.42
2010	A+	Fort Myers	261	35	71	1	19	272	343	349	691	10	71	0.37	11	5	21	77	4.22
2011	Rk	GCL Twins	14	2	3	1	4	214	214	500	714	0	93	0.00	0	0	67	286	3.90
2011	A+	Fort Myers	121	17	32	3	13	264	336	388	724	10	70	0.36	3	2	28	124	4.58

Athletic outfielder who missed most of season due to elbow injury. Aggressive approach and decline in power output have caused prospect status to dim, but upside remains due to above average speed and potential for power. Can be pitched to on outer half of plate and has been FB hitter. Can swing tentatively at pitches and needs to get strength and bat speed to work in tandem.

Morban, Julio — 789 — Seattle

EXP MLB DEBUT: 2014 | POTENTIAL: Starting OF | **8D**

Bats L Age 20 | 2008 FA (DR) | Pwr +++ | BAvg +++ | Spd ++++ | Def ++++

Year	Lev	Team	AB	R	H	HR	RBI	Avg	OB	Slg	OPS	bb%	ct%	Eye	SB	CS	x/h%	Iso	RC/G
2010	Rk	Pulaski	10	1	1	0	0	100	357	100	457	29	70	1.33	0	0	0	0	1.17
2010	Rk	AZL Mariners	5	0	2	0	1	400	400	400	800	0	80	0.00	0	0	0	0	4.75
2010	A-	Everett	4	0	1	0	0	250	250	250	500	0	50	0.00	0	0	0	0	1.64
2010	A+	High Desert	6	0	2	0	1	333	333	333	667	0	67	0.00	0	0	0	0	3.37
2011	A	Clinton	301	44	77	4	28	256	315	382	697	8	67	0.26	10	5	30	126	4.33

Smooth and quick outfielder who returned after missing most of '10 with thumb injury. Inconsistent performer with raw ability, but shows enough natural hitting skills to project well. Raw power produced with bat speed and strength and will need time to improve approach. Has enough range and speed to play any outfield position.

Morla, Ramon — 5 — Seattle

EXP MLB DEBUT: 2014 | POTENTIAL: Reserve INF | **7B**

Bats R Age 22 | 2006 FA (DR) | Pwr +++ | BAvg +++ | Spd +++ | Def +++

Year	Lev	Team	AB	R	H	HR	RBI	Avg	OB	Slg	OPS	bb%	ct%	Eye	SB	CS	x/h%	Iso	RC/G
2009	Rk	AZL Mariners	102	20	30	2	12	294	333	392	725	6	72	0.21	4	2	17	98	4.36
2010	Rk	Pulaski	251	60	81	17	49	323	361	610	970	6	74	0.23	13	4	44	287	7.47
2011	Rk	AZL Mariners	12	1	3	0	1	250	250	333	583	0	83	0.00	1	1	33	83	2.44
2011	A-	Everett	179	24	47	4	21	263	330	380	710	9	75	0.41	10	5	23	117	4.30
2011	A	Clinton	106	7	18	0	7	170	200	255	455	4	74	0.14	5	2	33	85	0.83

Instinctual and strong infielder who had disappointing season including drastic drop off in power production. Uses leverage in swing to generate good bat speed and has all-fields approach for potential high BA. Overswings at times and gets overzealous early in count. Good defender due to range and strong, accurate arm.

Morris, Hunter — 3 — Milwaukee

EXP MLB DEBUT: 2014 | POTENTIAL: Starting 1B | **7C**

Bats L Age 23 | 2010 (4) Auburn | Pwr ++++ | BAvg +++ | Spd ++ | Def ++

Year	Lev	Team	AB	R	H	HR	RBI	Avg	OB	Slg	OPS	bb%	ct%	Eye	SB	CS	x/h%	Iso	RC/G
2009	NCAA	Auburn	195	39	55	12	33	282	375	503	878	13	74	0.58	2	0	35	221	6.54
2010	NCAA	Auburn	272	66	105	23	76	386	440	743	1182	9	82	0.52	6	2	44	357	9.89
2010	A	Wisconsin	291	38	73	9	44	251	299	436	735	6	80	0.34	7	2	44	186	4.52
2011	A+	Brevard County	501	75	136	19	67	271	297	461	758	3	83	0.21	7	3	38	190	4.55
2011	AA	Huntsville	17	6	6	1	2	353	353	706	1059	0	94	0.00	0	0	50	353	7.64

Strong, mobile 1B prospect has solid power and a nice bat. Had a breakout season in '11, hitting .274 with 54 extra-base hits. Decent bat speed allows him to drive the ball. Runs well, but is a below average defender. Plate discipline will need to improve (18 BB/84 K) to keep average his average up. At 23 he will need to make an impact at Double-A in 2012.

Muno, Danny — 6 — New York (N)

EXP MLB DEBUT: 2014 | POTENTIAL: Starting 2B | **8D**

Bats B Age 23 | 2011 (8) Fresno State | Pwr ++ | BAvg ++++ | Spd +++ | Def +++

Year	Lev	Team	AB	R	H	HR	RBI	Avg	OB	Slg	OPS	bb%	ct%	Eye	SB	CS	x/h%	Iso	RC/G
2008	NCAA	Fresno State	283	62	94	3	30	332	441	424	865	16	84	1.20	10	3	19	92	6.74
2009	NCAA	Fresno State	224	74	85	3	41	379	517	540	1058	22	87	2.21	13	3	34	161	9.55
2010	NCAA	Fresno State	246	68	81	7	33	329	439	500	939	16	87	1.45	10	3	32	171	7.58
2011	NCAA	Fresno State	204	47	71	3	52	348	468	471	939	18	87	1.70	14	6	25	123	7.78
2011	A-	Brooklyn	220	45	78	2	24	355	460	514	974	16	82	1.10	9	4	36	159	8.22

Short, athletic 2B had an impressive professional debut. Muno is a professional hitter with a quick bat who sprays the ball to all fields. Plus plate discipline means he should continue to hit as he moves up. Above-average runner with good range and actions. Played SS in college but was moved to 2B when drafted and profiles well there. Nice find in the 8th round.

Murphy, J.R. — 2 — New York (A)

EXP MLB DEBUT: 2014 | POTENTIAL: Starting C | **7C**

Bats B Age 21 | 2009 (2) HS (FL) | Pwr +++ | BAvg +++ | Spd ++ | Def ++

Year	Lev	Team	AB	R	H	HR	RBI	Avg	OB	Slg	OPS	bb%	ct%	Eye	SB	CS	x/h%	Iso	RC/G
2009	Rk	GCL Yankees	33	4	11	1	7	333	389	485	874	8	76	0.38	0	0	27	152	6.38
2010	A	Charleston (SC)	330	46	84	7	54	255	328	376	704	10	81	0.56	4	5	29	121	4.29
2011	A	Charleston (SC)	256	31	76	6	32	297	345	457	802	7	85	0.50	2	0	38	160	5.37
2011	A+	Tampa	85	8	22	1	14	259	276	365	641	2	89	0.22	0	0	32	106	3.32

Athletic catcher with good hitting ability, but less-than-stellar glovework behind dish. Doesn't possess ideal mobility, catch-and-throw skills, or receiving ability, but has strong arm. Runs well for catcher and has quick, smooth swing to produce line drives to gaps. Has bat speed and strength to punch balls out of park, but only has average power potential.

Myers, Wil — 9 — Kansas City

EXP MLB DEBUT: 2012 | POTENTIAL: Starting OF | **9C**

Bats R Age 21 | 2009 (3) HS (NC) | Pwr ++++ | BAvg ++++ | Spd ++ | Def +++

Year	Lev	Team	AB	R	H	HR	RBI	Avg	OB	Slg	OPS	bb%	ct%	Eye	SB	CS	x/h%	Iso	RC/G
2009	Rk	Idaho Falls	68	18	29	4	14	426	494	735	1229	12	78	0.60	2	0	41	309	11.11
2009	Rk	Burlington	16	1	2	1	4	125	125	438	563	0	81	0.00	0	0	100	313	2.11
2010	A	Burlington	242	42	70	10	45	289	407	500	907	17	77	0.87	10	3	43	211	7.24
2010	A+	Wilmington	205	28	71	4	38	346	446	512	958	15	81	0.95	2	3	34	166	7.90
2011	AA	NW Arkansas	354	50	90	8	49	254	350	393	742	13	75	0.60	9	2	36	138	4.95

Natural-hitting outfielder whose stock didn't drop despite ordinary campaign. Outstanding in AFL after knee injury curtailed offensive production during regular season. Possesses plus bat speed and combines mature approach with ability to make hard contact. Could be perennial .300 hitter with 20+ HR. Can be passive at plate and doesn't run or range well.

Nash, Telvin — 39 — Houston

EXP MLB DEBUT: 2013 | POTENTIAL: Reserve OF | **7D**

Bats R Age 21 | 2009 (3) HS, (GA) | Pwr ++++ | BAvg ++ | Spd + | Def ++

Year	Lev	Team	AB	R	H	HR	RBI	Avg	OB	Slg	OPS	bb%	ct%	Eye	SB	CS	x/h%	Iso	RC/G
2009	Rk	GCL Astros	142	15	31	1	20	218	279	324	603	8	68	0.27	1	2	39	106	2.95
2010	Rk	Greeneville	200	30	53	12	39	265	347	515	862	11	68	0.39	1	1	47	250	6.58
2010	A-	Tri City	13	2	4	1	1	308	308	769	1077	0	46	0.00	0	1	75	462	14.53
2011	Rk	GCL Astros	13	5	5	0	0	385	500	538	1038	19	85	1.50	0	0	40	154	9.22
2011	A	Lexington	268	41	72	14	37	269	364	485	849	13	62	0.39	2	0	42	216	6.92

Big, strong, and mature OF starting to realize his plus raw power. Takes long, viscious swings, which generates power, but causes difficulty hitting breaking balls. Will need to improve pitch recognition and learn to make more consistent contact if the power is to fully emerge. Below average runner and on defense.

Navarro, Raul — 6 — Arizona

EXP MLB DEBUT: 2015 | POTENTIAL: Starting SS | **7D**

Bats R Age 20 | 2009 NDFA D.R. | Pwr ++ | BAvg +++ | Spd +++ | Def ++

Year	Lev	Team	AB	R	H	HR	RBI	Avg	OB	Slg	OPS	bb%	ct%	Eye	SB	CS	x/h%	Iso	RC/G
2010	Rk	Missoula	243	39	74	2	28	305	352	416	768	7	83	0.44	2	3	24	111	5.01
2011	A-	Yakima	207	12	41	0	13	198	256	237	492	7	76	0.33	0	2	15	39	1.45
2011	A	South Bend	151	18	31	0	11	205	273	252	524	8	74	0.36	10	2	19	46	1.88

Short, wiry SS prospect looked completely overmatched in the MWL, hitting just .205 with 0 home runs before being sent back to rookie ball. Defensively he is raw, but has nice tools including good speed and range. Will need to prove that '11 was a fluke.

Navarro, Rey — 46 — Kansas City

EXP MLB DEBUT: 2012 | POTENTIAL: Starting 2B | **7B**

Bats B Age 22 | 2007 (3) HS (PR) | Pwr ++ | BAvg +++ | Spd +++ | Def ++++

Year	Lev	Team	AB	R	H	HR	RBI	Avg	OB	Slg	OPS	bb%	ct%	Eye	SB	CS	x/h%	Iso	RC/G
2009	A	South Bend	451	57	118	0	46	262	303	339	643	6	81	0.32	12	4	25	78	3.43
2010	A+	Visalia	79	9	19	1	7	241	310	329	639	9	77	0.44	2	2	21	89	3.43
2010	A+	Wilmington	393	43	93	5	38	237	257	331	588	3	89	0.25	5	5	24	94	2.74
2011	A+	Wilmington	277	34	79	8	41	285	329	484	813	6	86	0.46	5	4	41	199	5.46
2011	AA	NW Arkansas	188	26	51	1	18	271	322	330	652	7	86	0.54	6	3	18	59	3.63

Solid infielder who posted career highs in 2B, HR, BA, and OBP. Owns clean, repeatable swing and makes terrific contact. Offers more gap power than long ball pop, but can reach fences on occasion. Contact-oriented approach works for him, but doesn't work counts or draw many walks. Runs well and makes all plays at 2B or SS. Range may be better served at 2B.

Navarro, Yamaico — 456 — Pittsburgh

EXP MLB DEBUT: 2010 | POTENTIAL: Starting INF | **8D**

Bats R Age 24 | 2005 FA (DR) | Pwr +++ | BAvg +++ | Spd +++ | Def +++

Year	Lev	Team	AB	R	H	HR	RBI	Avg	OB	Slg	OPS	bb%	ct%	Eye	SB	CS	x/h%	Iso	RC/G
2010	MLB	Boston	42	4	6	0	5	143	182	143	325	5	60	0.12	0	0			
2011	AAA	Pawtucket	128	25	33	5	13	258	345	469	814	12	80	0.68	3	2	45	211	5.75
2011	MLB	Boston	37	6	8	1	3	216	275	351	626	8	76	0.33	0	0	38	135	3.11
2011	AAA	Omaha	92	11	25	2	9	272	323	391	715	7	80	0.39	3	4	24	120	4.26
2011	MLB	Kansas City	23	2	7	0	6	304	360	348	708	8	78	0.40	0	0	14	43	4.28

Versatile and fundamentally-sound performer who can play virtually any position on diamond. Strong arm suitable for SS or 3B, but range and quickness may play best at 2B. Merely an average hitter, but understands balls and strikes and offers decent pop for size. Brings consistent approach to plate and draws enough walks to get on base and use moderate speed.

Neal, Thomas — 7 — Cleveland

EXP MLB DEBUT: 2012 | POTENTIAL: Starting OF | **7C**

Bats R Age 24 | 2005 (36) Riverside JC | Pwr +++ | BAvg +++ | Spd ++ | Def +++

Year	Lev	Team	AB	R	H	HR	RBI	Avg	OB	Slg	OPS	bb%	ct%	Eye	SB	CS	x/h%	Iso	RC/G
2008	A	Augusta	428	69	118	15	81	276	349	444	793	10	76	0.47	3	4	35	168	5.40
2009	A+	San Jose	475	102	160	22	90	337	417	579	996	12	79	0.66	3	0	42	242	8.07
2010	AA	Richmond	525	69	153	12	69	291	349	440	789	8	82	0.49	11	5	35	149	5.26
2011	AAA	Fresno	220	35	65	2	25	295	335	409	744	6	77	0.26	7	6	28	114	4.65
2011	AAA	Columbus	36	5	9	0	1	250	270	278	548	3	81	0.14	1	0	11	28	2.00

Tall and strong outfielder whose power disappeared. Had nagging hand injury, but bat slowed and rarely pulled ball. Hits for nice BA and has success against LHP by reading pitches. Doesn't work counts much, but makes easy contact. Possesses below average speed, but is a solid baserunner and usable in outfield corner where arm strength is good.

Nick, David — 6 — Arizona — EXP MLB DEBUT: 2012 — POTENTIAL: Starting SS — 7B

Bats R Age 22
2009 (4) HS, (CA)
Pwr ++
BAvg +++
6.5/60 Spd +++
Def +++

Year	Lev	Team	AB	R	H	HR	RBI	Avg	OB	Slg	OPS	bb%	ct%	Eye	SB	CS	x/h%	Iso	RC/G
2009	Rk	Missoula	273	46	78	6	35	286	339	440	779	7	82	0.45	16	8	35	154	5.12
2010	A	South Bend	495	66	124	7	49	251	308	366	673	8	80	0.42	12	7	29	115	3.85
2011	A+	Visalia	564	99	169	13	68	300	335	449	784	5	86	0.38	5	5	31	149	5.02

Smart, athletic SS with better than anticipated offense. No standout tools, but a smart ballplayer. Unorthodox approach at the plate as he doesn't load up as most players do. Defensively has good hands but not enough speed or range to stick at SS long-term. Scrappy player who gets the most out of his abitlities.

Nieuwenhuis, Kirk — 7 — New York (N) — EXP MLB DEBUT: 2012 — POTENTIAL: Starting CF — 7B

Bats L Age 24
2008 (3) HS, (CA)
Pwr +++
BAvg +++
Spd +++
Def +++

Year	Lev	Team	AB	R	H	HR	RBI	Avg	OB	Slg	OPS	bb%	ct%	Eye	SB	CS	x/h%	Iso	RC/G
2009	A+	St. Lucie	482	91	132	16	71	274	346	467	813	10	76	0.45	16	4	42	193	5.72
2009	AA	Binghamton	32	8	13	1	2	406	472	656	1128	11	72	0.44	1	1	38	250	10.42
2010	AA	Binghamton	394	81	114	16	60	289	340	510	850	7	76	0.32	13	7	46	221	6.01
2010	AAA	Buffalo	120	10	27	2	17	225	290	358	648	8	68	0.28	0	0	41	133	3.60
2011	AAA	Buffalo	188	33	56	6	14	298	400	505	905	15	69	0.54	5	2	45	207	7.57

Strong and athletic CF with good power and the ability to hit for average. Uses a line-drive approach and hits the ball to all fields, but can also turn on pitches and has 15-20 HR potential. Runs the bases well despite not having plus speed. Can play all three OF positions and is a solid defender. Torn labrum in June limted him to 188 AB, but should be ready to go by spring.

Nimmo, Brandon — 7 — New York (N) — EXP MLB DEBUT: 2015 — POTENTIAL: Starting CF — 9D

Bats L Age 19
2011 (1) HS, (WY)
Pwr +++
BAvg ++++
Spd +++
Def +++

Year	Lev	Team	AB	R	H	HR	RBI	Avg	OB	Slg	OPS	bb%	ct%	Eye	SB	CS	x/h%	Iso	RC/G
2011	Rk	Kingsport	9	0	1	0	0	111	333	111	444	25	44	0.60	0	0	0	0	0.02
2011	Rk	GCL Mets	29	5	7	2	4	241	313	448	761	9	69	0.33	0	0	29	207	4.81

Nimmo is athletic OF from Wyoming. The Mets took a gamble on him with the 13th overall pick. He projects to have good power and puts the ball into play regularly with a compact left-handed stroke. He is a good runner and covers ground well with a strong throwing arm. He has a strong, powerful frame and the potential to develop into a plus CF.

Noriega, Gabriel — 46 — Seattle — EXP MLB DEBUT: 2013 — POTENTIAL: Reserve INF — 7D

Bats B Age 21
2007 FA (Venezuela)
Pwr ++
BAvg ++
Spd +++
Def ++++

Year	Lev	Team	AB	R	H	HR	RBI	Avg	OB	Slg	OPS	bb%	ct%	Eye	SB	CS	x/h%	Iso	RC/G
2008	Rk	AZL Mariners	38	7	16	0	2	421	436	421	857	3	84	0.17	3	0	0	0	5.57
2009	Rk	Pulaski	206	27	64	4	26	311	360	456	817	7	71	0.27	8	6	31	146	5.84
2010	A	Clinton	374	47	85	2	28	227	266	283	550	5	71	0.19	6	4	20	56	2.00
2011	A+	High Desert	383	45	102	3	50	266	299	363	662	4	72	0.17	4	11	25	97	3.57
2011	AA	Jackson	93	8	22	0	7	237	260	280	540	3	78	0.15	1	0	18	43	1.91

Lean and athletic infielder who won't provide much offensive production, but is a defensive standout due to quick, nimble feet, smooth actions, and plenty of range. Would carry more value with bat if not for high Ks and lack of strike zone familiarity. Lacks power projection, but runs relatively well. Should get to majors at least as backup MIF.

Norris, Derek — 2 — Oakland — EXP MLB DEBUT: 2012 — POTENTIAL: Starting C — 8C

Bats R Age 23
2007 (4) HS, (KS)
Pwr ++++
BAvg +++
Spd +
Def +++

Year	Lev	Team	AB	R	H	HR	RBI	Avg	OB	Slg	OPS	bb%	ct%	Eye	SB	CS	x/h%	Iso	RC/G
2007	Rk	GCL Nationals	123	16	25	4	15	203	338	382	720	17	69	0.66	2	1	48	179	4.81
2008	A-	Vermont	227	42	63	10	38	278	434	463	897	22	75	1.13	11	9	35	185	7.34
2009	A	Hagerstown	437	78	125	23	84	286	408	513	921	17	73	0.78	6	3	42	227	7.47
2010	A+	Potomac	298	67	70	12	49	235	411	419	830	23	68	0.95	6	3	44	185	6.61
2011	AA	Harrisburg	334	75	70	20	46	210	358	446	804	19	65	0.66	13	4	54	237	6.05

Strong, durable backstop had another subpar offensive season. Norris is a solid defender with a strong throwing arm. Receives the ball and moves well behind the plate. Judges the strike zone well but struggles with breaking balls and fails to make consistent contact. Does have good power, giving him added value on offense. There is a breakout coming at some point.

Nunez, Gustavo — 6 — Detroit — EXP MLB DEBUT: 2012 — POTENTIAL: Starting SS — 7C

Bats B Age 24
2006 FA (DR)
Pwr ++
BAvg ++
Spd ++++
Def ++++

Year	Lev	Team	AB	R	H	HR	RBI	Avg	OB	Slg	OPS	bb%	ct%	Eye	SB	CS	x/h%	Iso	RC/G
2009	Rk	GCL Tigers	21	5	4	1	4	190	227	333	561	5	76	0.20	3	0	25	143	1.95
2009	A	West Michigan	464	82	146	5	40	315	350	425	774	5	87	0.40	45	25	21	110	4.95
2010	A+	Lakeland	523	66	116	2	33	222	252	281	533	4	82	0.23	33	8	18	59	1.97
2011	A+	Lakeland	260	46	79	3	18	304	365	431	796	9	85	0.63	14	10	25	127	5.46
2011	AA	Erie	121	13	26	2	8	215	246	289	535	4	78	0.19	4	3	19	74	1.79

Short and quick infielder with Gold Glove-caliber defense. Very athletic and quick middle infield actions provide plus range to both sides. Hands and feet work well together and makes as many spectacular plays as routine ones. Possesses some offensive skills, but aggressive approach and lack of strength limit upside. Can leg out infield grounders with good speed.

Nunez, Renato — 5 — Oakland — EXP MLB DEBUT: 2015 — POTENTIAL: Starting 3B — 9E

Bats R Age 18
2010 FA (Venezuela)
Pwr ++++
BAvg ++
Spd ++
Def +++

Year	Lev	Team	AB	R	H	HR	RBI	Avg	OB	Slg	OPS	bb%	ct%	Eye	SB	CS	x/h%	Iso	RC/G
2011		Did not play																	

Ultra-raw infielder is far away from majors and has yet to play in U.S. All about projection with excellent tools. Powerful swing and leverage give him power potential, but expands strike zone consistently in overzealous approach. Is an OK runner and isn't likely to be basestealer. Should become at least average with glove due to good hands and arm strength.

O'Conner, Justin — 2 — Tampa Bay — EXP MLB DEBUT: 2015 — POTENTIAL: Starting C — 8E

Bats R Age 20
2010 (1) HS (IN)
Pwr +++
BAvg ++
Spd ++
Def +++

Year	Lev	Team	AB	R	H	HR	RBI	Avg	OB	Slg	OPS	bb%	ct%	Eye	SB	CS	x/h%	Iso	RC/G
2010	Rk	GCL Rays	161	18	34	3	29	211	291	348	638	10	71	0.39	1	0	47	137	3.46
2011	Rk	Princeton	178	18	28	9	29	157	231	354	585	9	56	0.22	4	1	61	197	2.70

Agile and strong catcher who was ineffective with bat, but still has solid upside due to defensive and power potential. Owns strong arm with quick feet and release. Receiving should continually get better as he learns nuances of position. Very poor BA a result of inability to make contact. Swing can get long and can be jammed inside.

Odor, Rougned — 46 — Texas — EXP MLB DEBUT: 2014 — POTENTIAL: Starting 2B — 8D

Bats L Age 18
2011 FA (Venezuela)
Pwr ++
BAvg ++++
Spd +++
Def +++

Year	Lev	Team	AB	R	H	HR	RBI	Avg	OB	Slg	OPS	bb%	ct%	Eye	SB	CS	x/h%	Iso	RC/G
2011	A-	Spokane	233	33	61	2	29	262	301	352	653	5	84	0.35	10	4	23	90	3.52

Small and lean infielder with interesting game and tools. Possesses above average instincts and does little things well. Controls bat with simple, quick swing and gets on base. Offers good power for size, but may need more strength. Owns average speed, while hands and feet work well in middle infield. Glut of quality SS in org may move him to 2B.

Olt, Mike — 5 — Texas — EXP MLB DEBUT: 2012 — POTENTIAL: Starting 3B — 9C

Bats R Age 23
2010 (1-S) Connecticut
Pwr ++++
BAvg +++
Spd ++
Def ++++

Year	Lev	Team	AB	R	H	HR	RBI	Avg	OB	Slg	OPS	bb%	ct%	Eye	SB	CS	x/h%	Iso	RC/G
2009	NCAA	Connecticut	146	33	44	8	40	301	389	527	917	13	69	0.47	10	3	34	226	7.39
2010	NCAA	Connecticut	264	67	84	23	76	318	396	659	1055	11	80	0.63	7	2	48	341	8.55
2010	A-	Spokane	263	57	77	9	43	293	386	464	850	13	71	0.52	6	0	34	171	6.50
2011	Rk	AZL Rangers	14	2	3	1	4	214	267	429	695	7	64	0.20	0	0	33	214	3.90
2011	A+	Myrtle Beach	240	39	64	14	42	267	389	504	893	17	71	0.69	0	1	45	238	7.12

Tall and strong infielder missed two months with broken collarbone, but performed admirably when healthy. All-fields power continues to emerge and offense enhanced by strength and leverage in swing. Lacks foot speed to be threat on base, but is among top defenders at 3B in minors. Has potential Gold Glove in future due to smooth, quick actions and strong arm.

Ortega, Rafael — 8 — Colorado — EXP MLB DEBUT: 2015 — POTENTIAL: Starting CF — 8D

Bats L Age 21
2008 NDFA Venz.
Pwr +++
BAvg +++
Spd +++
Def +++

Year	Lev	Team	AB	R	H	HR	RBI	Avg	OB	Slg	OPS	bb%	ct%	Eye	SB	CS	x/h%	Iso	RC/G
2010	Rk	Casper	288	69	103	7	45	358	415	510	925	9	85	0.67	23	9	26	153	6.91
2011	A	Asheville	479	77	141	9	66	294	333	438	772	6	81	0.31	32	19	30	144	4.93

Short but athletic OF prospect with a nice power/speed package. Power is starting to emerge as he knocked 26 doubles and 9 home runs while stealing 32 bases. Needs to become more consistent and improve plate discipline (28 BB/90 K), but he is young and has some nice tools.

Ortiz, Ryan — 2 — Oakland

EXP MLB DEBUT: 2012 | POTENTIAL: Backup C | **7D**

Bats R Age 24
2009 (6) Oregon State
Pwr +++
BAvg +++
Spd +
Def +++

Year	Lev	Team	AB	R	H	HR	RBI	Avg	OB	Slg	OPS	bb%	ct%	Eye	SB	CS	x/h%	Iso	RC/G
2009	NCAA	Oregon State	216	55	76	5	45	352	451	509	960	15	84	1.15	2	0	30	157	7.82
2009	A-	Vancouver	151	25	39	4	24	258	367	430	798	15	81	0.90	3	0	44	172	5.77
2010	A+	Stockton	188	35	52	8	35	277	393	479	872	16	75	0.77	1	0	40	202	6.76
2011	A+	Stockton	97	17	33	4	21	340	458	515	973	18	77	0.95	2	0	27	175	8.15
2011	AA	Midland	152	19	36	2	14	237	329	303	632	12	74	0.53	2	0	17	66	3.39

Tall and muscular catcher who impresses with bat and glove. Limited at bats in career due to myriad injuries. Bat produces moderate power due to strength more than bat speed, but has chance to hit for BA by driving balls to gaps. Knows strike zone and can shorten swing for contact. Receiving and blocking need work, but has average, accurate arm.

Osuna, Jose — 9 — Pittsburgh

EXP MLB DEBUT: 2015 | POTENTIAL: Starting RF | **8D**

Bats R Age 19
2009 NDFA Venz.
Pwr ++++
BAvg +++
Spd ++
Def ++

Year	Lev	Team	AB	R	H	HR	RBI	Avg	OB	Slg	OPS	bb%	ct%	Eye	SB	CS	x/h%	Iso	RC/G
2011	Rk	GCL Pirates	178	28	59	4	32	331	393	511	904	9	88	0.86	3	2	36	180	6.74
2011	A-	State College	8	2	2	0	1	250	333	375	708	11	100		0	0	50	125	5.15

Tall, physically mature Venezuelan prospect has plus power potential. He drives the ball well and has power to all fields. Plus plate discipline and a .300 average with power suggests he is ready to make his full season debut in '12. Converted from pitching to the OF, so has a plus arm, but is still somewhat raw defensively. Doesn't get much attention, but that could change soon.

Ovando, Ariel — 9 — Houston

EXP MLB DEBUT: 2015 | POTENTIAL: Starting OF | **8D**

Bats L Age 18
2010 NDFA (D.R.)
Pwr +++
BAvg ++
Spd ++
Def ++

Year	Lev	Team	AB	R	H	HR	RBI	Avg	OB	Slg	OPS	bb%	ct%	Eye	SB	CS	x/h%	Iso	RC/G
2011	Rk	Greeneville	170	16	40	2	30	235	286	365	650	7	70	0.24	0	0	38	129	3.56

Strong, physically mature OF was one of the biggest international signings in 2011. Raw even by international standards, but has plus power potential. He currently has a long swing and tends to be a pull hitter. Not a plus runner, but does have a solid arm and plays good defense. He has time, but also much work to do.

Owings, Chris — 6 — Arizona

EXP MLB DEBUT: 2013 | POTENTIAL: Starting SS | **8D**

Bats R Age 20
2009 (1) HS, (SC)
Pwr ++
BAvg +++
4.15 Spd +++
Def +++

Year	Lev	Team	AB	R	H	HR	RBI	Avg	OB	Slg	OPS	bb%	ct%	Eye	SB	CS	x/h%	Iso	RC/G
2009	Rk	Missoula	108	20	33	2	10	306	324	426	750	3	77	0.12	3	0	24	120	4.48
2010	A	South Bend	255	39	76	5	28	298	322	447	769	3	80	0.18	1	3	34	149	4.77
2011	A+	Visalia	521	67	128	11	50	246	267	388	655	3	75	0.12	10	4	36	142	3.32

Raw but toolsy SS prospect. Has plus potential, but has yet to put it together. Short, compact stroke and moderate power. Drives the ball to all fields, but below average plate discipline limits his offense. Defensively has good range and a strong arm, but is inconsistent and made 32 errors in '11. Scouts love the tools and athleticism, but the results are just not there yet.

Ozuna, Marcell — 9 — Florida

EXP MLB DEBUT: 2013 | POTENTIAL: Starting RF | **8D**

Bats R Age 21
2008 NDFA D.R.
Pwr ++++
BAvg +++
Spd ++
Def ++

Year	Lev	Team	AB	R	H	HR	RBI	Avg	OB	Slg	OPS	bb%	ct%	Eye	SB	CS	x/h%	Iso	RC/G
2009	Rk	GCL Marlins	214	32	67	5	39	313	377	486	863	9	76	0.42	4	2	40	173	6.41
2010	A-	Jamestown	270	53	72	21	60	267	310	556	866	6	65	0.18	3	1	47	289	6.51
2010	A	Greensboro	25	3	4	1	2	160	222	280	502	7	60	0.20	0	0	25	120	1.12
2011	A	Greensboro	496	87	132	23	71	266	328	482	810	8	76	0.38	17	2	42	216	5.53

Lean and athletic OF prospect has a nice mix of power and speed, but also strikes out too much, though he did improve. Showed solid growth in the 2nd half. Has good speed and a strong arm so should be able to stay in the OF down the road. Swing can get long at times and he remains a bit raw, but the power/speed upside is legit.

Pacheco, Jordan — 2 — Colorado

EXP MLB DEBUT: 2011 | POTENTIAL: Backup C | **7C**

Bats R Age 26
2007 (9) HS, (NM)
Pwr ++
BAvg ++++
Spd ++
Def ++

Year	Lev	Team	AB	R	H	HR	RBI	Avg	OB	Slg	OPS	bb%	ct%	Eye	SB	CS	x/h%	Iso	RC/G
2009	A	Asheville	451	67	145	13	79	322	374	492	866	8	90	0.86	12	2	32	171	6.15
2010	A+	Modesto	390	59	125	5	70	321	403	444	847	12	91	1.50	5	6	28	123	6.32
2010	AA	Tulsa	78	11	26	1	19	333	381	436	817	7	92	1.00	1	1	23	103	5.61
2011	AAA	Colorado Spgs	363	57	101	3	50	278	333	377	711	8	87	0.63	2	2	27	99	4.41
2011	MLB	Colorado	84	5	24	2	14	286	310	369	679	3	89	0.33	0	0	13	83	3.67

Solid bodied backstop has some nice offensive upside and hit .278/.343/.377 prior to making his MLB debut. Has solid plate discipline and a short, compact line drive stroke so should hit for average. Only moderate power limits his future value. Defensively he makes a good 1B and will likely only catch as a 3rd option.

Pan, Chih-Fang — 46 — Oakland

EXP MLB DEBUT: 2014 | POTENTIAL: Starting 2B | **7D**

Bats L Age 21
2010 FA (Taiwan)
Pwr +
BAvg ++++
Spd +++
Def +++

Year	Lev	Team	AB	R	H	HR	RBI	Avg	OB	Slg	OPS	bb%	ct%	Eye	SB	CS	x/h%	Iso	RC/G
2011	A-	Vermont	143	22	48	1	22	336	387	385	772	8	81	0.44	8	4	10	49	5.00

Lean and athletic infielder who is developing slowly, but has potential to play excellent small ball. Power potential is limited due to lack of strength and erratic swing. Puts ball in play with quick bat and uses plus speed for infield hits and SB. Lively defender with quick, textbook footwork and sufficient arm for either middle infield position.

Panik, Joe — 4 — San Francisco

EXP MLB DEBUT: 2013 | POTENTIAL: Starting 2B | **8C**

Bats L Age 21
2011 (1) St. Johns
Pwr +++
BAvg +++
Spd +++
Def +++

Year	Lev	Team	AB	R	H	HR	RBI	Avg	OB	Slg	OPS	bb%	ct%	Eye	SB	CS	x/h%	Iso	RC/G
2009	NCAA	St. John's	187	38	62	5	47	332	421	513	935	13	91	1.81	6	1	32	182	7.36
2010	NCAA	St. John's	227	66	85	10	53	374	464	621	1085	14	93	2.24	6	3	38	247	9.04
2011	NCAA	St. John's	226	60	90	10	57	398	496	642	1138	16	89	1.83	21	6	36	243	9.83
2011	A-	Salem-Keizer	270	49	92	6	54	341	403	467	869	9	91	1.12	13	5	21	126	6.29

Athletic grinder gets the most of his abilities. Offense is ahead of his defense. Has good bat speed, battles every AB, and has moderate gap-to-gap power. Squares the ball up consistently with compact LH stroke. Is a below average runner and doesn't have great range or a strong arm. Played SS in pro debut, but was moved 2B in AFL, a position where he profiles better.

Parker, Jarrett — 7 — San Francisco

EXP MLB DEBUT: 2014 | POTENTIAL: Starting RF | **8D**

Bats L Age 23
2010 (2) U. of Virginia
Pwr +++
BAvg +++
Spd +++
Def +++

Year	Lev	Team	AB	R	H	HR	RBI	Avg	OB	Slg	OPS	bb%	ct%	Eye	SB	CS	x/h%	Iso	RC/G
2008	NCAA	Virginia	148	29	39	0	16	264	347	331	678	11	72	0.46	14	2	18	68	4.13
2009	NCAA	Virginia	265	76	94	16	65	355	438	664	1102	13	70	0.49	20	5	46	309	10.14
2010	NCAA	Virginia	243	56	81	10	56	333	413	593	1006	12	77	0.59	12	2	43	259	8.37
2011	A+	San Jose	486	81	123	13	61	253	352	397	749	13	70	0.51	20	5	33	144	5.09

Tall, lean, athletic OF had a disappointing pro debut, but still has potential. Parker has good speed and athleticism, but at 6'4" his swing can get long and while he is good raw power, he doesn't have plus bat speed. Defensively he runs well and while his arm is below average, he should be able to stick at CF and projects more as a top-of-the order hitter.

Parker, Kyle — 9 — Colorado

EXP MLB DEBUT: 2014 | POTENTIAL: Starting RF | **9D**

Bats R Age 22
2010 (1) Clemson
Pwr ++++
BAvg +++
Spd ++
Def ++

Year	Lev	Team	AB	R	H	HR	RBI	Avg	OB	Slg	OPS	bb%	ct%	Eye	SB	CS	x/h%	Iso	RC/G
2008	NCAA	Clemson	211	44	64	14	50	303	395	559	954	13	77	0.67	2	1	41	256	7.50
2009	NCAA	Clemson	231	48	59	12	52	255	338	442	780	11	77	0.56	6	0	32	186	5.14
2010	NCAA	Clemson	247	85	85	20	64	344	465	656	1121	18	76	0.93	4	2	42	312	10.06
2011	A	Asheville	445	75	127	21	95	285	355	483	838	10	70	0.36	2	0	35	198	6.11

Wiry and athletic OF with good speed and developing power. Improved across the board in '11, hitting 33 home runs and 67 extra-base hits. Needs to make more consistent contact (145 whiffs) and improve vs. LHP. Size and moderate speed make it unlikely he will stick in CF, but does have enough power and batting average for a corner slot.

Parker, Stephen — 5 — Oakland

EXP MLB DEBUT: 2012 | POTENTIAL: Starting 3B | **8D**

Bats L Age 24
2009 (5) BYU
Pwr +++
BAvg +++
Spd ++
Def +++

Year	Lev	Team	AB	R	H	HR	RBI	Avg	OB	Slg	OPS	bb%	ct%	Eye	SB	CS	x/h%	Iso	RC/G
2009	Rk	AZL Athletics	14	2	3	0	2	214	267	357	624	7	57	0.17	0	0	67	143	3.84
2009	A	Kane County	254	27	62	5	39	244	312	362	674	9	78	0.45	1	4	29	118	3.86

Sweet-swinging infielder thriving as sleeper with fundamental approach to hitting. Quick bat produces solid BA and has discerning eye to get on base. Power is more of doubles variety, but can reach seats on occasion. Has improved range and footwork, but makes fair share of errors and throws can be inaccurate. Don't expect much in the way of stolen bases.

Parmelee, Chris — 39 — Minnesota

EXP MLB DEBUT: 2011 | POTENTIAL: Starting 1B | **8C**

Bats L Age 24
2006 (1) HS (CA)
Pwr ++++
BAvg +++
Spd +
Def ++

Year	Lev	Team	AB	R	H	HR	RBI	Avg	OB	Slg	OPS	bb%	ct%	Eye	SB	CS	x/h%	Iso	RC/G
2009	A+	Fort Myers	422	61	109	16	73	258	357	441	798	13	74	0.60	2	2	40	182	5.66
2010	A+	Fort Myers	80	9	27	2	17	338	430	463	893	14	86	1.18	0	1	19	125	6.84
2010	AA	New Britain	411	51	113	6	44	275	344	389	733	9	83	0.61	3	2	29	114	4.70
2011	AA	New Britain	530	76	152	13	83	287	368	436	804	11	82	0.72	0	1	32	149	5.64
2011	MLB	Minnesota	76	8	27	4	14	355	443	592	1035	14	83	0.92	0	0	37	237	8.49

Patient and powerful natural hitter who showed improvement across board. Becoming a complete hitter by using entire field and making much better contact. Has reduced K rate in last two seasons and demolishes RHP. Doesn't have athleticism or agility to be SB artist or top defender, but has enough bat to be weapon.

Pastornicky, Tyler — 6 — Atlanta

EXP MLB DEBUT: 2012 | POTENTIAL: Starting SS | **8B**

Bats R Age 22
2008 (5) HS, (FL)
Pwr +++
BAvg +++
Spd +++
Def +++

Year	Lev	Team	AB	R	H	HR	RBI	Avg	OB	Slg	OPS	bb%	ct%	Eye	SB	CS	x/h%	Iso	RC/G
2009	A+	Dunedin	63	9	17	0	3	270	303	317	620	5	89	0.43	6	3	18	48	3.23
2010	A+	Dunedin	287	50	74	6	35	258	347	376	723	12	83	0.80	24	7	30	118	4.68
2010	AA	Mississippi	134	22	34	2	15	254	333	366	699	11	84	0.73	11	2	26	112	4.37
2011	AA	Mississippi	355	50	106	6	36	299	343	414	757	6	90	0.71	20	8	23	115	4.86
2011	AAA	Gwinnett	104	15	38	1	9	365	411	413	824	7	89	0.73	7	3	8	48	5.59

Well-rounded, athletic SS had a breakout season in '11. Doesn't get a ton of power from his line-drive stroke, but makes solid and consistent contact. When coupled with good plate discipline and plus speed, he has nice offensive potential. Can make routine plays at SS and has a chance to stick. Not a flashy player, but gets the most of his ability.

Paulino, Dorssys — 6 — Cleveland

EXP MLB DEBUT: 2016 | POTENTIAL: Starting SS | **8D**

Bats R Age 17
2011 FA (DR)
Pwr +++
BAvg +++
Spd +++
Def +++

Year	Lev	Team	AB	R	H	HR	RBI	Avg	OB	Slg	OPS	bb%	ct%	Eye	SB	CS	x/h%	Iso	RC/G
2011		Did not play																	

Lean and athletic infielder who signed in July and has yet to appear in pro ball. Projects as more of a doubles hitter for near term, but offers some power potential when he adds strength and leverage in short swing. Intent on using whole field with quick bat. Hands work well at SS while arm strength works at any position.

Paulsen, Ben — 3 — Colorado

EXP MLB DEBUT: 2013 | POTENTIAL: Starting 1B | **7D**

Bats L Age 24
2009 (3) Clemson
Pwr +++
BAvg +++
Spd ++
Def ++

Year	Lev	Team	AB	R	H	HR	RBI	Avg	OB	Slg	OPS	bb%	ct%	Eye	SB	CS	x/h%	Iso	RC/G
2008	NCAA	Clemson	226	46	70	13	49	310	383	571	954	11	76	0.50	1	0	46	261	7.50
2009	NCAA	Clemson	259	56	95	13	61	367	438	618	1056	11	85	0.85	3	1	37	251	8.56
2009	A-	Tri-City	175	28	49	1	25	280	326	377	703	6	82	0.38	2	1	27	97	4.20
2010	A+	Modesto	498	65	155	12	83	311	354	474	828	6	77	0.29	5	4	32	163	5.71
2011	AA	Tulsa	547	69	132	19	78	241	293	413	706	7	76	0.30	2	3	39	172	4.11

Solid 1B prospect has a nice LH swing, but does not have great plate discipline and needs to put the ball into play more. Decent power, but not enough to make up for low BA. Solid defender with soft hands and decent range. He can make the plays, but is not going to be a gold-glover.

Pederson, Joc — 7 — Los Angeles (N)

EXP MLB DEBUT: 2015 | POTENTIAL: Starting LF | **8C**

Bats L Age 20
2010 (11) HS, (CA)
Pwr +++
BAvg +++
4.20 Spd +++
Def +++

Year	Lev	Team	AB	R	H	HR	RBI	Avg	OB	Slg	OPS	bb%	ct%	Eye	SB	CS	x/h%	Iso	RC/G
2010	Rk	AZL Dodgers	7	1	0	0	0	0	364	0	364	36	29	0.80	0	0			
2011	Rk	Ogden	266	54	94	11	64	353	430	568	998	12	80	0.67	24	5	35	214	8.08
2011	A	Great Lakes	50	4	8	0	1	160	263	160	423	12	82	0.78	2	0	0	0	0.99

Can do a bit of everything and quickly emerged as one of the top position players in the system. Former 11th round pick was a one-man wrecking crew in the Pioneer League. Solid approach from the LH side with good strike zone judgment and plus bat speed. Also has above-average speed and solid defense. Is only 19 so still has some projection left. Worth keeping an eye on.

Pedroza, Jaime — 6 — Los Angeles (N)

EXP MLB DEBUT: 2012 | POTENTIAL: Backup 2B | **6C**

Bats B Age 25
2007 (9) UC Riverside
Pwr ++
BAvg ++
Spd ++++
Def +++

Year	Lev	Team	AB	R	H	HR	RBI	Avg	OB	Slg	OPS	bb%	ct%	Eye	SB	CS	x/h%	Iso	RC/G
2008	A+	Inland Empire	479	78	139	9	57	290	336	441	776	6	75	0.28	25	11	34	150	5.14
2009	A	Great Lakes	520	100	135	15	78	260	356	433	789	13	69	0.48	36	14	40	173	5.74
2010	AA	Chattanooga	411	53	115	7	37	280	374	401	776	13	75	0.61	11	8	28	122	5.44
2011	A+	Rancho Cucamg	108	18	30	4	26	278	350	472	822	10	80	0.55	2	0	40	194	5.76
2011	AA	Chattanooga	268	28	67	6	24	250	347	399	747	13	72	0.53	9	6	37	149	5.08

Athletic infielder with solid defense and some offensive potential. Moderate power with good bat speed and hits for BA despite marginal plate discipline. Above average speed doesn't net steals. Average range resulted in a move to 2B where he profiles better. Will need to show more to be a regular in the majors.

Peguero, Francisco — 7 — San Francisco

EXP MLB DEBUT: 2012 | POTENTIAL: Starting LF | **9D**

Bats R Age 24
2006 NDFA D.R.
Pwr +++
BAvg +++
4.00 Spd ++++
Def ++++

Year	Lev	Team	AB	R	H	HR	RBI	Avg	OB	Slg	OPS	bb%	ct%	Eye	SB	CS	x/h%	Iso	RC/G
2009	A-	Salem-Keizer	71	14	28	0	12	394	419	465	884	4	87	0.33	7	0	14	70	6.11
2009	A	Augusta	238	28	81	1	34	340	354	437	791	2	84	0.13	15	5	21	97	4.95
2010	A+	San Jose	510	78	168	10	77	329	352	488	841	3	83	0.20	40	22	27	159	5.62
2011	A+	San Jose	68	12	22	2	9	324	387	441	828	9	88	0.88	4	0	18	118	5.73
2011	AA	Richmond	285	34	88	5	37	309	321	446	766	2	84	0.11	8	1	26	137	4.61

Lean, athletic speedster puts the ball into play and uses his plus speed. Likely to have moderate, gap power but can turn on the ball. Can be overly aggressive at the plate. Knee injury limited him to 353 AB, but was productive when healthy. Has hit over .300 the past three seasons. Plus defender in CF with good range above-average arm.

Peguero, Martin — 6 — Seattle

EXP MLB DEBUT: 2015 | POTENTIAL: Starting SS | **9E**

Bats R Age 18
2010 FA (DR)
Pwr +++
BAvg ++++
Spd +++
Def +++

Year	Lev	Team	AB	R	H	HR	RBI	Avg	OB	Slg	OPS	bb%	ct%	Eye	SB	CS	x/h%	Iso	RC/G
2011	Rk	AZL Mariners	165	23	46	1	25	279	304	382	686	4	87	0.27	17	5	30	103	3.88

Athletic infielder succeeded in first pro experience, but is years from majors. Skills need time to develop including power and speed. Owns short swing capable of making contact and shoots gaps with line drive approach. Should grow into more power as he learns to read pitches. Defense is adequate, but could become plus due to hands and instincts.

Penalver, Carlos — 4 — Chicago (N)

EXP MLB DEBUT: 2016 | POTENTIAL: Starting 2B | **8D**

Bats R Age 18
2011 NDFA Venz.
Pwr +++
BAvg +++
Spd +++
Def ++++

Year	Lev	Team	AB	R	H	HR	RBI	Avg	OB	Slg	OPS	bb%	ct%	Eye	SB	CS	x/h%	Iso	RC/G
2011		Did not play																	

Lean, athletic 2B prospect put up solid numbers in the DSL, hitting .272/.364/.341 despite being just 17. Has plus speed and an advanced approach at the plate. Penalver stole 21 bases and has a ton of potential. Raw, but with tons of upside.

Perez, Carlos — 2 — Toronto

EXP MLB DEBUT: 2014 | POTENTIAL: Starting C | **8D**

Bats R Age 21
2007 FA (DR)
Pwr ++
BAvg +++
Spd ++
Def ++++

Year	Lev	Team	AB	R	H	HR	RBI	Avg	OB	Slg	OPS	bb%	ct%	Eye	SB	CS	x/h%	Iso	RC/G
2009	Rk	GCL Blue Jays	141	17	41	1	21	291	363	433	796	10	84	0.70	2	5	37	142	5.62
2010	A-	Auburn	235	44	70	2	41	298	387	438	825	13	83	0.83	7	3	30	140	6.11
2011	A	Lansing	383	58	98	3	41	256	321	355	677	9	81	0.50	6	2	27	99	3.99

Athletic and fundamentally-sound backstop who didn't match '10 campaign, but still possesses upside. Knows the strike zone and is patient hitter with some pop. Plate coverage and poor pitch recognition was exploited, but has acumen to improve in time. Has outstanding catch-and-throw skills to go along with mature receiving and leadership abilities.

Perez, Eury — 8 — Washington

EXP MLB DEBUT: 2013 | POTENTIAL: Starting OF | **7C**

Bats R Age 22
2007 NDFA (D.R.)
Pwr ++
BAvg ++++
Spd ++++
Def +++

Year	Lev	Team	AB	R	H	HR	RBI	Avg	OB	Slg	OPS	bb%	ct%	Eye	SB	CS	x/h%	Iso	RC/G
2009	Rk	GCL Nationals	181	38	69	3	24	381	429	503	931	8	89	0.75	16	8	16	122	6.88
2010	A	Hagerstown	438	88	131	3	42	299	334	381	715	5	83	0.31	64	13	19	82	4.22
2011	A+	Potomac	424	54	120	1	41	283	318	321	639	5	85	0.35	45	15	10	38	3.32

Speedy OF continues to make steady progess, notching 45 steals in '11 and 64 in '10. Quick bat and solid contact ability allows him to put the ball in play and then use his plus speed. Defensively he covers ground well and has a strong, accurate throwing arm, so should be able to stay in CF. Power is not part of his game, but is worth keeping an eye on.

Perez, Hernan — 46 — Detroit

EXP MLB DEBUT: 2014 — POTENTIAL: Reserve INF — 6B

Bats R Age 21 — 2007 FA (Venezuela)
Pwr ++ | BAvg ++ | Spd +++ | Def +++

Year	Lev	Team	AB	R	H	HR	RBI	Avg	OB	Slg	OPS	bb%	ct%	Eye	SB	CS	x/h%	Iso	RC/G
2009	Rk	GCL Tigers	81	9	18	1	9	222	250	395	645	4	83	0.21	2	0	61	173	3.44
2009	A	West Michigan	44	0	10	0	5	227	227	273	500	0	82	0.00	2	1	10	45	1.36
2009	A+	Lakeland	72	7	19	0	10	264	293	347	641	4	71	0.14	0	0	26	83	3.32
2010	A	West Michigan	473	45	111	5	50	235	273	298	571	5	79	0.26	5	1	18	63	2.36
2011	A	West Michigan	503	69	130	8	42	258	311	364	674	7	83	0.44	23	6	26	105	3.82

Lean and athletic infielder who repeated Low-A and improved across board. Offensive output increased as he swung with confidence and authority. Makes contact with compact swing and has improved strength to hit line drives to all fields. Has tidied up approach and more willing to work counts. Solid defender with athleticism and quickness. Hands and arm may work best at 2B.

Perez, Nelson — 9 — Chicago (N)

EXP MLB DEBUT: 2013 — POTENTIAL: Backup OF — 7D

Bats L Age 24 — 2007 NDFA D.R.
Pwr ++++ | BAvg +++ | 4.20 Spd +++ | Def ++++

Year	Lev	Team	AB	R	H	HR	RBI	Avg	OB	Slg	OPS	bb%	ct%	Eye	SB	CS	x/h%	Iso	RC/G
2009	A	Peoria	427	48	107	11	65	251	286	391	677	5	70	0.16	2	0	32	141	3.73
2010	A	Peoria	305	43	88	11	48	289	326	462	788	5	70	0.18	2	1	33	174	5.27
2010	A+	Daytona	80	10	13	1	7	163	212	288	499	6	64	0.17	0	1	54	125	1.37
2011	A+	Daytona	101	17	33	4	17	327	364	505	869	6	66	0.18	1	0	27	178	6.63
2011	AA	Tennessee	237	28	59	8	32	249	307	430	738	8	63	0.23	1	2	44	181	5.01

Tall/athletic outfielder with impressive bat speed and power to all fields. Swings aggressively and doesn't walk, so will likely continue to struggle to maintain BA against advanced pitching (26 BB/121 K). Possesses plus arm strength and adequate range, which could make him a prototypical rightfielder. Nice athleticism, but results continue to be mediorce.

Perio, Noah — 4 — Florida

EXP MLB DEBUT: 2015 — POTENTIAL: Starting 2B — 8D

Bats L Age 20 — 2009 (39) HS, (CA)
Pwr +++ | BAvg +++ | Spd +++ | Def ++

Year	Lev	Team	AB	R	H	HR	RBI	Avg	OB	Slg	OPS	bb%	ct%	Eye	SB	CS	x/h%	Iso	RC/G
2009	Rk	GCL Marlins	14	2	6	0	5	429	429	643	1071	0	100	0.00	1	0	33	214	7.91
2010	A-	Jamestown	225	30	58	0	31	258	310	302	612	7	89	0.68	7	0	17	44	3.30
2011	A	Greensboro	488	76	144	6	52	295	321	406	727	4	87	0.30	15	6	27	111	4.32

Lean, wiry, athletic 2B prospect is quickly emerging as one of the Marlins better prospects. Has good bat speed and moderate power potential, but below average plate discipline will need to be addressed. Has good speed, but is only average defensively and will need to be more consistent.

Perkins, Kendrick — 7 — Boston

EXP MLB DEBUT: 2015 — POTENTIAL: Starting OF — 8E

Bats L Age 20 — 2010 (6) HS (TX)
Pwr ++++ | BAvg ++ | Spd ++++ | Def ++

Year	Lev	Team	AB	R	H	HR	RBI	Avg	OB	Slg	OPS	bb%	ct%	Eye	SB	CS	x/h%	Iso	RC/G
2010	Rk	GCL Red Sox	7	1	0	0	1	0	125	0	125	13	0	0.14	0	0			
2011	Rk	GCL Red Sox	171	24	44	3	19	257	359	386	745	14	64	0.44	1	2	34	129	5.35

Tall and athletic outfielder with very high upside, but hasn't played past rookie ball. Org is impressed with potential for above average power and speed. Swings at anything near strike zone at present and will need to tighten approach and read breaking balls better. Very raw in most aspects of game, including defense, and will likely take several years to develop.

Peterson, Jace — 6 — San Diego

EXP MLB DEBUT: 2014 — POTENTIAL: Starting SS/CF — 8C

Bats L Age 22 — 2011 (1-S) McNeese State
Pwr +++ | BAvg +++ | Spd ++++ | Def ++++

Year	Lev	Team	AB	R	H	HR	RBI	Avg	OB	Slg	OPS	bb%	ct%	Eye	SB	CS	x/h%	Iso	RC/G
2009	NCAA	McNeese St	71	14	26	0	9	366	438	437	874	11	92	1.50	13	1	15	70	6.60
2010	NCAA	McNeese St	232	68	82	4	49	353	451	491	942	15	85	1.17	35	5	26	138	7.59
2011	NCAA	McNeese St	224	67	75	2	34	335	442	473	915	16	88	1.54	30	10	25	138	7.41
2011	A-	Eugene	276	48	67	2	27	243	359	333	692	15	81	0.94	39	10	24	91	4.53

Strong, athletic, but raw SS prospect. At 6'0", 200 lbs. he is already physically mature and should hit 15-20 home runs down the road. Has plus speed and solid plate discipline (50 BB/53 K) so should be a stolen base threat regardless of position. Has good range, but is raw defensively and will need to work hard to stay at SS.

Pham, Tommy — 8 — St. Louis

EXP MLB DEBUT: 2012 — POTENTIAL: Starting CF — 8D

Bats R Age 24 — 2006 (16) HS, (NV)
Pwr +++ | BAvg +++ | Spd ++++ | Def +++

Year	Lev	Team	AB	R	H	HR	RBI	Avg	OB	Slg	OPS	bb%	ct%	Eye	SB	CS	x/h%	Iso	RC/G
2008	A+	Palm Beach	82	9	12	1	7	146	213	220	433	8	63	0.23	1	1	33	73	0.26
2009	A+	Palm Beach	336	47	78	8	44	232	306	378	684	10	70	0.35	18	6	36	146	4.07
2010	A+	Palm Beach	237	42	62	3	27	262	373	392	765	15	75	0.71	13	4	34	131	5.45
2010	AA	Springfield	121	19	41	3	18	339	424	537	962	13	77	0.64	4	2	41	198	7.92
2011	AA	Springfield	143	31	42	5	16	294	373	517	890	11	72	0.45	3	3	45	224	7.00

Lean, toolsy OF was in the midst of a breakout season when he broke his hand in July. Pham is still raw, but has a nice swing and emerging power. He also has a good arm, solid speed, and covers ground well in CF. Pham still has some work to do, but if everything comes together he could have a nice career.

Phegley, Josh — 2 — Chicago (A)

EXP MLB DEBUT: 2013 — POTENTIAL: Backup C — 7D

Bats R Age 24 — 2009 (1-S) Indiana
Pwr ++++ | BAvg ++ | Spd ++ | Def ++

Year	Lev	Team	AB	R	H	HR	RBI	Avg	OB	Slg	OPS	bb%	ct%	Eye	SB	CS	x/h%	Iso	RC/G
2010	Rk	Bristol	15	1	3	0	1	200	294	267	561	12	73	0.50	0	0	33	67	2.53
2010	A+	Winston-Salem	89	16	26	3	12	292	344	427	771	7	75	0.32	0	0	23	135	4.92
2010	AA	Birmingham	72	7	21	2	13	292	311	431	741	3	69	0.09	0	0	29	139	4.51
2011	AA	Birmingham	364	43	88	7	50	242	287	368	655	6	83	0.38	1	2	34	126	3.55
2011	AAA	Charlotte	79	9	19	2	6	241	310	367	677	9	77	0.44	0	0	32	127	3.87

Short and powerful receiver whose game built more around bat than glove. Has chance to realize power potential due to exemplary bat speed and strong swing. Struggles to hit for BA dut to long swing and poor pitch recognition. Receiving and blocking are below average, though strong arm with quick release help aid pitching staff.

Phelps, Cord — 456 — Cleveland

EXP MLB DEBUT: 2011 — POTENTIAL: Utility player — 7B

Bats B Age 25 — 2008 (3) Stanford
Pwr ++ | BAvg +++ | Spd ++ | Def +++

Year	Lev	Team	AB	R	H	HR	RBI	Avg	OB	Slg	OPS	bb%	ct%	Eye	SB	CS	x/h%	Iso	RC/G
2009	A+	Kinston	479	72	125	4	53	261	381	363	744	16	80	0.96	17	14	29	102	5.24
2010	AA	Akron	199	25	59	2	23	296	346	397	743	7	85	0.52	1	4	22	101	4.70
2010	AAA	Columbus	243	41	77	6	31	317	378	506	884	9	84	0.62	3	2	39	189	6.51
2011	AAA	Columbus	378	51	111	14	63	294	378	492	870	12	76	0.57	3	6	39	198	6.53
2011	MLB	Cleveland	71	10	11	1	6	155	241	254	494	10	76	0.47	1	0	36	99	1.56

Tall and versatile infielder who set career high in HR. Reached majors on basis of ability to make contact and play variety of positions. Focuses on hard line drives and working counts to get on base consistently. Posssesses instincts and bat control for #2 hitter in lineup, but he doesn't run well and lacks ideal strength for MLB pop.

Pill, Brett — 3 — San Francisco

EXP MLB DEBUT: 2011 — POTENTIAL: Starting 1B — 7C

Bats R Age 27 — 2006 (7) Cal State Fullerton
Pwr +++ | BAvg +++ | Spd ++ | Def ++

Year	Lev	Team	AB	R	H	HR	RBI	Avg	OB	Slg	OPS	bb%	ct%	Eye	SB	CS	x/h%	Iso	RC/G
2008	A+	San Jose	458	73	122	9	65	266	316	395	711	7	81	0.39	5	2	34	129	4.24
2009	AA	Connecticut	527	71	157	19	109	298	344	480	824	7	86	0.51	6	3	36	182	5.53
2010	AAA	Fresno	520	63	143	16	84	275	315	433	747	5	88	0.46	7	2	35	158	4.60
2011	AAA	Fresno	536	82	167	25	107	312	342	530	872	4	90	0.46	6	6	38	218	5.90
2011	MLB	San Francisco	50	7	15	2	9	300	327	560	887	4	84	0.25	0	1	47	260	6.19

The 6'4" 210 pound right-hander played nearly half of his games at 2B to increase his versatility and value and a had a nice breakout. He has excellent, soft hands and solid glovework, but he lacks athleticism and arm strength. He makes outstanding contact and uses the entire field, but has only moderate bat speed. Will need to prove '11 was not a fluke.

Pimentel, Guillermo — 79 — Seattle

EXP MLB DEBUT: 2014 — POTENTIAL: Starting OF — 9D

Bats L Age 19 — 2009 FA (DR)
Pwr ++++ | BAvg +++ | Spd ++ | Def +++

Year	Lev	Team	AB	R	H	HR	RBI	Avg	OB	Slg	OPS	bb%	ct%	Eye	SB	CS	x/h%	Iso	RC/G
2010	Rk	AZL Mariners	184	20	46	6	31	250	270	451	721	3	68	0.09	5	1	41	201	4.37
2011	Rk	Pulaski	245	33	65	11	46	265	308	441	749	6	70	0.21	4	1	32	176	4.64

Athletic and strong outfielder has significant upside predicated on power potential. Swings a quick bat and has strength in hands and wrists for all-fields pop. Crushes FB, but free-swinging ways conducive to high K totals. Has secondary tools, but speed and range weren't apparent and arm strength could use improvement.

Polanco, Jorge — 456 — Minnesota

EXP MLB DEBUT: 2015 — POTENTIAL: Starting SS — 8E

Bats B Age 18 — 2009 FA (DR)
Pwr + | BAvg +++ | Spd +++ | Def ++++

Year	Lev	Team	AB	R	H	HR	RBI	Avg	OB	Slg	OPS	bb%	ct%	Eye	SB	CS	x/h%	Iso	RC/G
2010	Rk	GCL Twins	103	12	23	1	12	223	304	301	605	10	91	1.33	2	4	26	78	3.51
2011	Rk	GCL Twins	172	21	43	1	16	250	310	349	659	8	86	0.63	6	4	28	99	3.85

Quick and lean-framed infielder who provides exquisite versatility. Played virtually every position in '11, but projects as quality middle infielder. Plus range and quick hands highlight glovework and has strong arm to make eye-opening plays. Size, lack of strength, and swing path don't provide much power potential, but has chance to hit for BA.

Pollock, A.J. — 8 — Arizona

EXP MLB DEBUT: 2012 | POTENTIAL: Starting CF | 8C

Bats R Age 24
2009 (1) Notre Dame
Pwr +++
BAvg +++
Spd +++
Def +++

Year	Lev	Team	AB	R	H	HR	RBI	Avg	OB	Slg	OPS	bb%	ct%	Eye	SB	CS	x/h%	Iso	RC/G
2007	NCAA	Notre Dame	196	39	73	3	28	372	461	474	935	14	91	1.78	11	2	16	102	7.40
2008	NCAA	Notre Dame	216	49	76	4	42	352	417	505	921	10	95	2.40	28	3	29	153	7.02
2009	NCAA	Notre Dame	241	69	88	10	52	365	435	610	1045	11	90	1.25	21	4	39	245	8.39
2009	A	South Bend	255	36	69	3	22	271	314	376	690	6	86	0.44	10	4	26	106	4.03
2011	AA	Mobile	550	103	169	8	73	307	359	444	802	7	84	0.51	36	7	32	136	5.44

Solid all-around performer. Has a smooth, level swing and good bat speed that produces doubles power and has moderate long ball potential. Pollock has good speed to go along with mature instincts and a strong arm. Was among league leaders in all offensive catagories except HR.

Poythress, Rich — 3 — Seattle

EXP MLB DEBUT: 2012 | POTENTIAL: Platoon 1B | 7C

Bats R Age 24
2009 (2) Georgia
Pwr +++
BAvg +++
Spd +
Def ++

Year	Lev	Team	AB	R	H	HR	RBI	Avg	OB	Slg	OPS	bb%	ct%	Eye	SB	CS	x/h%	Iso	RC/G
2009	NCAA	Georgia	237	69	89	25	86	376	470	764	1233	15	84	1.08	4	5	47	388	10.73
2009	Rk	AZL Mariners	20	4	6	1	6	300	440	450	890	20	70	0.83	0	0	17	150	7.22
2009	AA	W. Tennessee	87	11	20	1	9	230	343	287	630	15	72	0.63	1	0	15	57	3.46
2010	A+	High Desert	476	88	150	31	130	315	383	580	962	10	79	0.52	3	2	43	265	7.38
2011	AA	Jackson	450	50	120	11	64	267	340	416	756	10	82	0.61	2	3	35	149	4.97

Big and strong infielder whose value wholly revolves around offense. Power output declined sharply and may lack sufficient load and trigger in swing to project to big league pop. Manages strike zone with keen eye and makes good contact despite long swing. Range, speed, and athleticism are below average, but hands work well at 1B.

Profar, Jurickson — 6 — Texas

EXP MLB DEBUT: 2013 | POTENTIAL: Starting SS | 9B

Bats B Age 19
2009 FA (Curacao)
Pwr +++
BAvg ++++
Spd ++++
Def ++++

Year	Lev	Team	AB	R	H	HR	RBI	Avg	OB	Slg	OPS	bb%	ct%	Eye	SB	CS	x/h%	Iso	RC/G
2010	A-	Spokane	252	42	63	4	23	250	325	373	698	10	82	0.61	8	3	37	123	4.30
2011	A	Hickory	430	86	123	12	65	286	380	493	873	13	85	1.03	23	9	46	207	6.64

Fundamentally-sound infielder who was SAL MVP after solid all-around season. Does everything well and best tools include speed and defense. No apparent weakness and even can hit for power despite slight frame. Generates plus bat speed from both sides and disciplined eye leads to high OBP. Possesses plus range and arm strength.

Puello, Cesar — 9 — New York (N)

EXP MLB DEBUT: 2015 | POTENTIAL: Starting RF | 9E

Bats R Age 21
2007 NDFA D.R.
Pwr +++
BAvg +++
Spd ++++
Def +++

Year	Lev	Team	AB	R	H	HR	RBI	Avg	OB	Slg	OPS	bb%	ct%	Eye	SB	CS	x/h%	Iso	RC/G
2008	Rk	GCL Mets	151	24	46	1	17	305	327	364	691	3	79	0.16	14	5	15	60	3.75
2009	Rk	Kingsport	196	37	58	5	23	296	330	423	754	5	74	0.20	15	5	26	128	4.65
2010	A	Savannah	404	80	118	1	34	292	344	359	703	7	80	0.39	45	10	20	67	4.21
2011	A+	St. Lucie	441	67	114	10	50	259	288	397	684	4	77	0.17	19	9	32	138	3.73

Tall, strong, projectable OF. Looked overmatched at times in the FSL, hitting for decent power, but also showing horrible plate discipline. Will need to make progress quickly to live up to his potential. Covers ground well in the OF and has a strong, accurate throwing arm. Starting to tap into his power and it should continue to develop as he matures.

Quinn, Roman — 6 — Philadelphia

EXP MLB DEBUT: 2015 | POTENTIAL: Starting SS/CF | 7C

Bats R Age 19
2011 (2) HS, (FL)
Pwr ++
BAvg +++
Spd ++++
Def +++

Year	Lev	Team	AB	R	H	HR	RBI	Avg	OB	Slg	OPS	bb%	ct%	Eye	SB	CS	x/h%	Iso	RC/G
2011		Did not play																	

Short, speedy SS was considered one of the fastest players in the 2011 draft. He has moderate pop for his size (5'9", 165 lbs.) and has a decent approach at the plate. Defensively he moves well and could hold his own at SS, 2B, or even CF. He has yet to make his professional debut and will likely start in rookie ball in '12.

Raben, Dennis — 3 — Seattle

EXP MLB DEBUT: 2013 | POTENTIAL: Reserve 1B/LF | 7C

Bats L Age 24
2008 (2) Miami-FL
Pwr ++++
BAvg +++
Spd +
Def ++

Year	Lev	Team	AB	R	H	HR	RBI	Avg	OB	Slg	OPS	bb%	ct%	Eye	SB	CS	x/h%	Iso	RC/G
2008	NCAA	Miami	192	51	56	10	51	292	406	521	927	16	78	0.88	5	1	43	229	7.38
2008	A-	Everett	91	24	25	5	14	275	400	560	960	17	74	0.79	1	1	64	286	8.10
2010	A	Clinton	149	26	33	8	23	221	293	450	742	9	67	0.31	0	1	52	228	4.81
2010	A+	High Desert	160	35	57	12	43	356	411	681	1093	9	71	0.32	0	0	44	325	9.57
2011	A+	High Desert	309	61	102	18	75	330	386	599	984	8	75	0.37	2	1	43	269	7.80

Tall and strong infielder who was healthy most of season and cut down on Ks while showcasing impressive power and ability to hit LHP and RHP. Uses entire field and knows strike zone, but takes vicious hacks that can be exploited. Does not run well and lack of fluidity prompted move from OF to 1B. Prospect on bat alone.

Ramirez, Carlos — 2 — Los Angeles (A)

EXP MLB DEBUT: 2013 | POTENTIAL: Platoon C | 7D

Bats R Age 24
2009 (8) Arizona State
Pwr ++
BAvg +++
Spd +
Def +++

Year	Lev	Team	AB	R	H	HR	RBI	Avg	OB	Slg	OPS	bb%	ct%	Eye	SB	CS	x/h%	Iso	RC/G
2009	Rk	Orem	149	34	56	7	36	376	495	638	1132	19	83	1.35	0	0	45	262	10.17
2010	A	Cedar Rapids	257	39	58	9	34	226	318	381	700	12	72	0.49	3	2	34	156	4.25
2011	A	Cedar Rapids	108	20	28	3	12	259	350	370	720	12	84	0.88	1	2	21	111	4.60
2011	A+	Inland Empire	181	28	63	4	28	348	401	530	931	8	82	0.48	1	0	40	182	7.06
2011	AA	Arkansas	9	1	2	0	1	222	222	222	444	0	89	0.00	1	0	0	0	0.93

Short and strong receiver who makes easy contact and gets on base due to strike zone knowledge and patient approach. Quick bat and wrists produce results, though sacrifices power for contact. Has struggled with RHP and lacks athleticism to be standout with glove. Has average, accurate arm that is enhanced by quick release.

Ramos, Henry — 89 — Boston

EXP MLB DEBUT: 2014 | POTENTIAL: Starting OF | 8D

Bats B Age 20
2010 (5) HS (PR)
Pwr +++
BAvg ++
Spd +++
Def +++

Year	Lev	Team	AB	R	H	HR	RBI	Avg	OB	Slg	OPS	bb%	ct%	Eye	SB	CS	x/h%	Iso	RC/G
2010	Rk	GCL Red Sox	136	18	42	3	26	309	365	449	813	8	79	0.43	12	6	29	140	5.58
2010	A-	Lowell	24	1	3	0	2	125	160	125	285	4	67	0.13	0	0			
2011	A	Greenville	332	40	87	5	43	262	298	383	681	5	77	0.22	15	6	30	120	3.77

Strong and athletic outfielder who suffered through poor season in aggressive placement in Low-A. Normally patient approach regressed and bat speed wasn't as evident. Only exhibits average speed, but runs bases more on solid instincts and feel. Lots of length in swing and can be beaten on outer half. Lots of work to do to recapture declining tools, but still hope.

Ray, Andrew — 7 — Los Angeles (A)

EXP MLB DEBUT: 2014 | POTENTIAL: Reserve OF | 7D

Bats R Age 21
2011 (5) NE Texas CC
Pwr ++
BAvg +++
Spd +++
Def +++

Year	Lev	Team	AB	R	H	HR	RBI	Avg	OB	Slg	OPS	bb%	ct%	Eye	SB	CS	x/h%	Iso	RC/G
2011	Rk	Orem	126	18	22	2	13	175	257	254	511	10	65	0.32	3	0	27	79	1.49

Athletic and contact-oriented outfielder who projects to hit for a solid BA due to above average instincts and line drive approach. Power a little on short side, but could tap into strength and pull balls out of park. Strong arm enhances OF play while range and jumps are sufficient for corner OF. Not a burner, but can steal bases.

Realmuto, J.T. — 2 — Florida

EXP MLB DEBUT: 2015 | POTENTIAL: Starting C | 8C

Bats R Age 21
2010 (3) HS, (OK)
Pwr ++
BAvg +++
Spd +++
Def ++

Year	Lev	Team	AB	R	H	HR	RBI	Avg	OB	Slg	OPS	bb%	ct%	Eye	SB	CS	x/h%	Iso	RC/G
2010	Rk	GCL Marlins	40	2	7	0	4	175	298	175	473	15	73	0.64	0	1	0	0	1.27
2011	A	Greensboro	348	46	100	12	49	287	337	454	791	7	78	0.33	13	6	31	167	5.18

Strong, athletic catching prospect. Has excellent bat speed, power potential, and solid offensive value. Improved approach hints at better things to come. Defensively is more mobile than your average backstop and has a strong throwing arm - nailed over 40% of runners in '11. Still somewhat raw, but made as much progress as anyone in the Marlins system in 2011.

Recker, Anthony — 2 — Oakland

EXP MLB DEBUT: 2011 | POTENTIAL: Backup C | 6B

Bats R Age 28
2005 (18) Alvernia
Pwr +++
BAvg ++
Spd ++
Def ++

Year	Lev	Team	AB	R	H	HR	RBI	Avg	OB	Slg	OPS	bb%	ct%	Eye	SB	CS	x/h%	Iso	RC/G
2009	AAA	Sacramento	272	30	71	12	45	261	330	449	779	9	71	0.35	2	0	35	188	5.24
2010	AA	Midland	38	8	8	1	3	211	333	316	649	16	68	0.58	1	0	25	105	3.67
2010	AAA	Sacramento	250	36	72	10	42	288	346	496	842	8	75	0.35	0	1	42	208	5.98
2011	AAA	Sacramento	345	61	99	16	48	287	387	501	888	14	77	0.69	7	5	41	214	6.82
2011	MLB	Oakland	17	3	3	0	0	176	333	235	569	19	59	0.57	0	0	33	59	2.72

Big and strong catcher with all-fields power and ability to crush LHP. Overall package is short for starting role, but exhibiting patience at plate and getting on base consistently. Subpar bat speed hinders BA potential and will struggle with fastballs up in zone. Not the most agile defender behind plate, but has average arm and release.

Rendon, Anthony — 5 — Washington

EXP MLB DEBUT: 2013 | POTENTIAL: Starting 3B/2B | 9C

Bats R Age 22
2011 (1) Rice
Pwr ++++
BAvg ++++
Spd +++
Def ++++

Year	Lev	Team	AB	R	H	HR	RBI	Avg	OB	Slg	OPS	bb%	ct%	Eye	SB	CS	x/h%	Iso	RC/G
2009	NCAA	Rice	242	60	94	20	72	388	458	702	1160	11	90	1.35	9	2	37	314	9.44
2010	NCAA	Rice	226	83	89	26	85	394	529	801	1330	22	90	2.95	14	4	44	407	12.09
2011	NCAA	Rice	214	58	70	6	37	327	510	523	1034	27	85	2.42	13	5	40	196	9.50

Strong, athletic 3B was the best position player in the '11 draft. He slipped due to concerns about a lingering shoulder injury, but should be 100% by spring. Rendon has good power, hits for average, has solid plate discipline, and gold glove defense. He could be moved to 2B or the OF and has enough skill, both offensively and defensively, to be an asset at any position.

Richardson, D'Vontrey — 8 — Milwaukee

EXP MLB DEBUT: 2014 | POTENTIAL: Starting CF | 8E

Bats R Age 23
2009 (5) Florida State
Pwr +++
BAvg ++
Spd ++++
Def +++

Year	Lev	Team	AB	R	H	HR	RBI	Avg	OB	Slg	OPS	bb%	ct%	Eye	SB	CS	x/h%	Iso	RC/G
2010	A	Wisconsin	522	78	127	7	51	243	319	368	687	10	69	0.35	17	15	34	125	4.21
2011	A+	Brevard County	359	47	102	3	41	284	325	384	710	6	81	0.31	9	13	23	100	4.21

Held his own in the FSL, hitting .284/.327/.384. Has some nice tools, but is still somewhat raw. Has plus speed, but stole only 9 bases in 13 attempts. Good raw power, but lack of plate discipline and troubles with breaking balls limits ceiling.

Rincon, Edinson — 5 — San Diego

EXP MLB DEBUT: 2013 | POTENTIAL: Starting 3B | 8D

Bats R Age 21
2007 NDFA D.R.
Pwr +++
BAvg +++
Spd +++
Def ++

Year	Lev	Team	AB	R	H	HR	RBI	Avg	OB	Slg	OPS	bb%	ct%	Eye	SB	CS	x/h%	Iso	RC/G
2008	Rk	AZL Padres	65	8	20	0	19	308	430	354	784	18	72	0.78	0	0	10	46	5.89
2009	A-	Eugene	267	47	80	7	47	300	403	468	871	15	78	0.77	5	0	35	169	6.74
2010	A	Fort Wayne	511	72	128	13	69	250	310	399	709	8	81	0.46	1	2	38	149	4.27
2011	Rk	AZL Padres	10	0	3	0	1	300	364	300	664	9	90	1.00	0	0	0	0	3.98
2011	A+	Lake Elsinore	298	54	98	8	50	329	394	497	891	10	80	0.54	1	1	34	168	6.63

Strong, aggressive hitter with moderate power and decent plate discipline. Should continue to hit for average due to strike zone judgment and contact ability. SB and power have not developed but he is still young. Still learning the OF and taking routes in outfield. True test will come once he reaches Double-A in 2012.

Rivera, Yadiel — 6 — Milwaukee

EXP MLB DEBUT: 2014 | POTENTIAL: Backup SS | 7D

Bats R Age 20
2010 (9) HS, P.R.
Pwr ++
BAvg +++
Spd +++
Def +++

Year	Lev	Team	AB	R	H	HR	RBI	Avg	OB	Slg	OPS	bb%	ct%	Eye	SB	CS	x/h%	Iso	RC/G
2010	Rk	AZL Brewers	206	22	43	0	23	209	242	257	499	4	65	0.13	6	2	21	49	1.27
2011	Rk	Helena	330	47	82	8	38	248	279	406	685	4	72	0.15	7	3	35	158	3.82
2011	A	Wisconsin	103	6	20	1	5	194	224	262	486	4	67	0.12	0	0	20	68	1.01

Tall but skinny SS has potential but needs to gain more strength. Did have 9 home runs in '11, but hit only .236 on the year. Was overmatched in the MWL and was sent back to rookie ball. Has true SS actions and nice range with good speed. Will need to prove he can hit and have some semblance of plate discipline (18 BB/125 K) before he has much value.

Rizzo, Anthony — 3 — Chicago (N)

EXP MLB DEBUT: 2011 | POTENTIAL: Starting 1B | 9C

Bats L Age 22
2007 (6) HS, (FL)
Pwr ++++
BAvg ++++
Spd ++
Def +++

Year	Lev	Team	AB	R	H	HR	RBI	Avg	OB	Slg	OPS	bb%	ct%	Eye	SB	CS	x/h%	Iso	RC/G
2009	A+	Salem	200	23	59	3	24	295	373	420	793	11	81	0.64	2	0	32	125	5.54
2010	A+	Salem	117	26	29	5	20	248	338	479	817	12	73	0.50	3	0	59	231	5.93
2010	AA	Portland	414	66	109	20	80	263	336	481	816	10	76	0.45	7	1	46	217	5.65
2011	AAA	Tucson	356	64	118	26	101	331	404	652	1055	11	75	0.48	7	6	52	320	8.85
2011	MLB	San Diego	128	9	18	1	9	141	262	242	504	14	64	0.46	2	1	56	102	1.58

Tall, strong, athletic 1B with plus power. Drives the ball well to all fields with good bat speed and a short stroke. Solid plate discipline should allow him to hit for average. Dominated at Triple-A Tucson, but struggled when promoted to the majors. Doesn't offer much speed, but runs the bases well. Solid defender at 1B with soft hands and a good glove.

Rizzotti, Matt — 3 — Philadelphia

EXP MLB DEBUT: 2012 | POTENTIAL: Backup 1B | 7C

Bats L Age 26
2007 (6) Manhattan
Pwr ++++
BAvg +++
Spd +
Def ++

Year	Lev	Team	AB	R	H	HR	RBI	Avg	OB	Slg	OPS	bb%	ct%	Eye	SB	CS	x/h%	Iso	RC/G
2009	A+	Clearwater	350	44	92	13	58	263	352	454	806	12	74	0.53	0	0	43	191	5.73
2010	A+	Clearwater	109	18	39	1	10	358	426	477	903	11	80	0.59	0	0	26	119	6.95
2010	AA	Reading	266	48	96	16	62	361	444	635	1080	13	79	0.71	1	1	43	274	9.15
2010	AAA	Lehigh Valley	45	0	9	0	4	200	294	267	561	12	69	0.43	0	0	33	67	2.47
2011	AA	Reading	499	73	147	24	84	295	391	511	902	14	75	0.63	4	1	40	216	7.03

Tall, muscular 1B with plus power. Rizzotti had an impressive season in '11, folllowing up on his breakout from 2010. Rizzotti has demonstrated and ability to hit for power and average with solid plate disciipline. Defensively he is well below average and does not run well. He will need to hit to have value and at 26 will need to do so soon.

Roberts, Nate — 7 — Minnesota

EXP MLB DEBUT: 2013 | POTENTIAL: Reserve OF | 7C

Bats L Age 23
2010 (5) High Point
Pwr +++
BAvg +++
Spd +++
Def +++

Year	Lev	Team	AB	R	H	HR	RBI	Avg	OB	Slg	OPS	bb%	ct%	Eye	SB	CS	x/h%	Iso	RC/G
2010	NCAA	High Point	209	88	87	19	69	416	534	746	1281	20	83	1.51	36	3	34	330	11.77
2010	Rk	Elizabethton	128	30	43	5	17	336	430	547	976	14	77	0.72	5	2	37	211	8.04
2011	A	Beloit	222	55	67	4	34	302	380	446	826	11	78	0.58	9	4	30	144	5.98

Tall and strong outfielder with impactful first full season. Brings mature approach to plate and clean swing to produce BA/OBP. Likes to work counts and can differentiate between balls and drivable pitches. Bat speed isn't ideal for power hitter and doesn't possess much in the way of speed. Relegated to LF as instincts are short, but has strong arm to be an asset.

Roberts, Tyler — 2 — Milwaukee

EXP MLB DEBUT: 2014 | POTENTIAL: Starting C | 7D

Bats R Age 21
2010 (10) HS, (GA)
Pwr ++
BAvg +++
Spd ++
Def ++

Year	Lev	Team	AB	R	H	HR	RBI	Avg	OB	Slg	OPS	bb%	ct%	Eye	SB	CS	x/h%	Iso	RC/G
2009	Rk	AZL Brewers	72	11	21	1	8	292	400	375	775	15	74	0.68	2	0	14	83	5.53
2010	Rk	Helena	3	0	0	0	0	0	250	0	250	25	67	1.00	0	0			
2010	Rk	AZL Brewers	156	30	45	6	23	288	351	513	864	9	81	0.50	0	0	51	224	6.22
2011	Rk	Helena	133	20	35	2	14	263	342	391	733	11	71	0.41	0	0	37	128	4.85
2011	A	Wisconsin	152	14	32	4	27	211	268	349	617	7	62	0.21	1	0	41	138	3.15

Strong, stocky backstop. Struggled offensively in the MWL and was sent back to rookie ball. Has some pop in his bat, but needs to make more consistent contact (97 K in 285 AB). Is still a work in progress defensively. Needs to improve ability to block balls, but does have a decent throwing arm.

Robinson, Clint — 3 — Kansas City

EXP MLB DEBUT: 2012 | POTENTIAL: Reserve 1B | 7C

Bats L Age 27
2007 (25) Troy
Pwr ++++
BAvg ++
Spd +
Def +

Year	Lev	Team	AB	R	H	HR	RBI	Avg	OB	Slg	OPS	bb%	ct%	Eye	SB	CS	x/h%	Iso	RC/G
2007	Rk	Idaho Falls	253	39	85	15	66	336	382	593	975	7	83	0.45	2	0	40	257	7.27
2008	A	Burlington	379	53	100	17	64	264	329	472	802	9	82	0.55	0	3	42	208	5.38
2009	A+	Wilmington	436	65	130	13	57	298	350	463	814	7	82	0.44	4	3	35	165	5.49
2010	AA	NW Arkansas	477	90	160	29	98	335	407	625	1032	11	82	0.67	4	3	47	289	8.30
2011	AAA	Omaha	503	86	164	23	100	326	396	533	929	10	83	0.66	2	1	35	207	6.99

Tall and strong hitter who won Triple Crown in Double-A in '10 and produced another offensive onslaught in Triple-A. Mashes fastballs and mistakes to all parts of park, but long, uppercut stroke may be exploited in big leagues. Doesn't read breaking balls, but puts bat to ball very well. Offers absolutely no speed or defensive value and could be used as PH or DH.

Robinson, Trayvon — 78 — Seattle

EXP MLB DEBUT: 2011 | POTENTIAL: Starting OF | 8B

Bats B Age 24
2005 (10) HS (CA)
Pwr ++++
BAvg +++
Spd +++
Def ++++

Year	Lev	Team	AB	R	H	HR	RBI	Avg	OB	Slg	OPS	bb%	ct%	Eye	SB	CS	x/h%	Iso	RC/G
2009	AA	Chattanooga	57	8	14	2	10	246	358	439	797	15	68	0.56	4	2	36	193	5.91
2010	AA	Chattanooga	434	80	130	9	57	300	400	438	838	14	71	0.58	38	15	28	138	6.46
2011	AAA	Albuquerque	368	70	108	26	71	293	370	563	933	11	67	0.37	8	6	38	269	7.63
2011	AAA	Tacoma	9	1	1	0	0	111	333	111	444	25	56	0.75	1	0	0	0	0.23
2011	MLB	Seattle	143	12	30	2	14	210	252	336	587	5	57	0.13	1	0	47	126	2.96

Athletic outfielder turned raw abilities into production en route to career high in HR. Reached majors with variety of skills including plus power, speed, pitch recognition, and defense. Projects to double digits in HR and SB, but can also hit for BA despite high K totals. SB declined, but has plus speed and significant range.

Rodriguez, Aderlin — 5 — New York (N)

EXP MLB DEBUT: 2013 | POTENTIAL: Starting 3B | 7D

Bats R Age 20
2008 NDFA D.R.
Pwr ++++
BAvg ++
Spd ++
Def ++

Year	Lev	Team	AB	R	H	HR	RBI	Avg	OB	Slg	OPS	bb%	ct%	Eye	SB	CS	x/h%	Iso	RC/G
2009	Rk	GCL Mets	62	5	18	1	10	290	380	387	767	13	76	0.60	1	1	22	97	5.27
2010	Rk	Kingsport	250	44	78	13	48	312	351	556	907	6	83	0.35	3	1	45	244	6.42
2010	A	Savannah	30	3	6	1	11	200	333	333	667	17	67	0.60	0	0	33	133	3.94
2011	A	Savannah	516	59	114	17	78	221	262	372	634	5	79	0.27	2	1	37	151	3.12

Strong, solidly built 3B has plus bat speed and advanced power for his age. Plate discipline eroded badly in '11 and resulted in a .227 average. Doesn't run well and despite having a strong arm, defense will need to improve if he is to stay at 3B long-term. Likely needs another season at this level, but the power potential is plus.

Rodriguez, Javier — 9 — New York (N)

Bats R | Age 22 | EXP MLB DEBUT: 2014 | POTENTIAL: Starting RF/LF | 8D

2008 (2) HS P.R.

	Pwr	++++
BAvg	++
4.35	Spd	++
Def	++

Year	Lev	Team	AB	R	H	HR	RBI	Avg	OB	Slg	OPS	bb%	ct%	Eye	SB	CS	x/h%	Iso	RC/G
2008	Rk	GCL Mets	135	17	26	1	20	193	248	237	485	7	80	0.37	0	2	15	44	1.42
2009	Rk	GCL Mets	139	9	32	2	19	230	282	338	620	7	72	0.26	2	1	31	108	3.05
2010	Rk	Kingsport	160	29	51	4	24	319	343	513	856	4	83	0.21	1	2	41	194	5.84
2011	A-	Brooklyn	249	32	64	4	43	257	346	410	756	12	75	0.55	5	0	44	153	5.18
2011	A	Savannah	86	10	18	4	4	209	284	407	691	9	83	0.60	0	1	44	198	4.04

Raw, projectable OF failed to follow up on his breakout of '10. Rodriguez has plus bat speed and good raw tools, but his swing can get long. Has decent pitch recognition and acceptable plate discipline. He is a below average runner and doesn't get the greatest jumps, but has good arm strength in the OF. There is good potential, but his development has been slow.

Rodriguez, Julio — 2 — Kansas City

Bats R | Age 22 | EXP MLB DEBUT: 2013 | POTENTIAL: Backup C | 6B

2006 FA (DR)

	Pwr	++
BAvg	++
Spd	++
Def	+++

Year	Lev	Team	AB	R	H	HR	RBI	Avg	OB	Slg	OPS	bb%	ct%	Eye	SB	CS	x/h%	Iso	RC/G
2010	A-	Connecticut	189	19	51	1	14	270	307	360	666	5	83	0.31	2	0	25	90	3.68
2010	A	West Michigan	8	0	2	0	1	250	250	250	500	0	88	0.00	0	0	0	0	1.47
2010	A+	Lakeland	101	9	21	2	13	208	223	307	530	2	89	0.18	0	0	29	99	2.02
2011	A+	Lakeland	226	20	64	1	27	283	314	354	668	4	88	0.36	0	0	20	71	3.70
2011	A+	Wilmington	73	3	16	1	8	219	240	329	569	3	88	0.22	0	0	38	110	2.51

Strong and mobile backstop who was acquired midseason and should provide value with nifty glovework and game-calling. Strong arm accentuated by quick release to neutralize would-be basestealers. Considered a solid leader of pitching staff, though receiving could be upgraded. Not much of a hitter, but makes good contact and shoot balls to the opposite field.

Rodriguez, Luigi — 78 — Cleveland

Bats B | Age 19 | EXP MLB DEBUT: 2014 | POTENTIAL: Starting OF | 9D

2009 FA (DR)

	Pwr	+++
BAvg	++++
Spd	++++
Def	++

Year	Lev	Team	AB	R	H	HR	RBI	Avg	OB	Slg	OPS	bb%	ct%	Eye	SB	CS	x/h%	Iso	RC/G
2011	Rk	AZL Indians	95	18	36	3	14	379	410	579	989	5	80	0.26	12	5	31	200	7.54
2011	A	Lake County	132	10	33	0	5	250	322	311	633	10	73	0.39	6	5	18	61	3.40

Short and quick outfielder who was standout performer in first year in U.S. Converted from 2B to CF and showed good skills. Has sufficient range to stick in CF while having good arm strength, but needs time to learn jumps and reads. Possesses well above average speed and should hit for high BA and moderate pop due to strike zone knowledge and quick bat.

Rodriguez, Rafael — 8 — San Francisco

Bats R | Age 19 | EXP MLB DEBUT: 2014 | POTENTIAL: Starting CF | 9E

2008 NDFA D.R.

	Pwr	+++
BAvg	+++
Spd	++++
Def	++++

Year	Lev	Team	AB	R	H	HR	RBI	Avg	OB	Slg	OPS	bb%	ct%	Eye	SB	CS	x/h%	Iso	RC/G
2009	Rk	AZL Giants	127	25	38	0	19	299	378	362	740	11	82	0.70	5	4	21	63	4.93
2010	Rk	AZL Giants	123	20	37	2	14	301	328	398	726	4	81	0.22	4	2	22	98	4.21
2010	A-	Salem-Keizer	43	3	7	0	4	163	217	209	427	7	72	0.25	1	0	14	47	0.43
2011	A	Augusta	364	39	86	1	30	236	284	297	580	6	81	0.35	1	6	21	60	2.65

Tall/athletic OF struggled in his full-season debut. Still, Rodriguez has true 5-tool potential. He should be able develop power to go along with his plus speed and strong arm. He is still very raw and was one of the youngest players in the SAL and his power should develop as he matures. Look for more in 2012.

Rodriguez, Ronny — 6 — Cleveland

Bats R | Age 20 | EXP MLB DEBUT: 2014 | POTENTIAL: Starting SS | 8E

2010 FA (DR)

	Pwr	+++
BAvg	+++
Spd	+++
Def	+++

Year	Lev	Team	AB	R	H	HR	RBI	Avg	OB	Slg	OPS	bb%	ct%	Eye	SB	CS	x/h%	Iso	RC/G
2011	A	Lake County	370	41	91	11	42	246	272	449	720	3	78	0.16	10	7	51	203	4.22

Tall and lean infielder who progressed nicely in first year in U.S. Uses clean, textbook swing mechanics to provide BA potential while having enough strength for average power. Offers nice upside with bat and could have breakout with better approach. Rarely draws walks and will need to get on base in order to use speed and quickness.

Rodriguez, Yorman — 8 — Cincinnati

Bats R | Age 19 | EXP MLB DEBUT: 2014 | POTENTIAL: Starting CF | 9E

2008 NDFA Venz.

	Pwr	++++
BAvg	++
Spd	++++
Def	++++

Year	Lev	Team	AB	R	H	HR	RBI	Avg	OB	Slg	OPS	bb%	ct%	Eye	SB	CS	x/h%	Iso	RC/G
2009	Rk	GCL Reds	84	9	23	0	2	274	351	321	672	11	73	0.43	5	0	13	48	3.98
2009	Rk	Billings	183	21	40	3	17	219	255	344	599	5	67	0.15	5	2	38	126	2.76
2010	Rk	Billings	171	25	58	2	39	339	369	456	825	4	82	0.27	12	2	22	117	5.50
2011	A	Dayton	280	38	71	7	40	254	315	393	708	8	70	0.30	20	8	30	139	4.31

Power/speed prospect with good bat speed and power to all fields who struggled in full-season debut. Still hasn't shown much power, but has the size and bat speed for it to develop. Needs to show better pitch recognition. Plus speed should allow him to steal bases and plays solid defense with plus arm strength. Age was questioned in the past, but the Reds say he is 19.

Rojas, Mel — 7 — Pittsburgh

Bats B | Age 22 | EXP MLB DEBUT: 2014 | POTENTIAL: Starting CF | 7D

2010 (3) Wabash Valley CC, IL

	Pwr	++
BAvg	+++
6.6/60	Spd	++++
Def	+++

Year	Lev	Team	AB	R	H	HR	RBI	Avg	OB	Slg	OPS	bb%	ct%	Eye	SB	CS	x/h%	Iso	RC/G
2010	A-	State College	164	19	34	0	14	207	297	250	547	11	74	0.50	7	3	21	43	2.31
2011	A	West Virginia	508	66	125	5	46	246	309	335	643	8	77	0.39	23	14	22	89	3.46

Fleet-footed CF prospect is the son of former major leaguer Mel Rojas. He struggles with pitch recognition and plate discipline. His flat, slashing swing makes it unlikely he will hit for much power. For now, Rojas will stick in CF and has a strong throwing arm with good range, but needs to take better routes.

Rojas, Miguel — 6 — Cincinnati

Bats R | Age 23 | EXP MLB DEBUT: 2013 | POTENTIAL: Backup SS | 6B

2005 NDFA (Venz)

	Pwr	++
BAvg	++
Spd	+++
Def	++++

Year	Lev	Team	AB	R	H	HR	RBI	Avg	OB	Slg	OPS	bb%	ct%	Eye	SB	CS	x/h%	Iso	RC/G
2010	Rk	AZL Reds	4	1	3	0	1	750	750	750	1500	0	100		1	0	0	0	11.58
2010	A+	Lynchburg	244	28	56	1	14	230	263	270	533	4	84	0.29	12	4	11	41	2.04
2010	AA	Carolina	27	1	6	0	4	222	276	222	498	7	85	0.50	1	1	0	0	1.77
2011	Rk	AZL Reds	17	6	8	0	6	471	609	647	1256	26	94	6.00	4	1	38	176	12.22
2011	AA	Carolina	239	26	62	0	24	259	306	285	590	6	84	0.41	11	7	10	25	2.80

Graceful, athlete is one of the best defensive SS in the minors. Moves well, has solid range, and plus hands. Makes even tough plays look easy. Offensively there isn't much going on. Lacks power and doesn't make enough contact or drive the ball well enough to be a threat. Still the defense is good enough that he will play in the majors, but most likely as a defensive backup.

Romine, Andrew — 6 — Los Angeles (A)

Bats B | Age 26 | EXP MLB DEBUT: 2010 | POTENTIAL: Starting SS | 7C

2007 (5) Arizona St

	Pwr	+
BAvg	+++
Spd	++++
Def	++++

Year	Lev	Team	AB	R	H	HR	RBI	Avg	OB	Slg	OPS	bb%	ct%	Eye	SB	CS	x/h%	Iso	RC/G
2009	A+	Rancho Cucamg	479	68	133	1	36	278	347	349	696	10	83	0.61	26	11	17	71	4.30
2010	AA	Arkansas	383	55	108	3	34	282	365	366	730	12	83	0.76	21	9	20	84	4.81
2010	MLB	Los Angeles (A)	11	0	1	0	0	91	91	91	182	0	64	0.00	0	0			
2011	AAA	Salt Lake	381	67	107	4	35	281	357	346	703	11	77	0.52	23	6	14	66	4.31
2011	MLB	Los Angeles (A)	16	2	2	0	0	125	176	125	301	6	63	0.17	1	0			

Versatile and athletic infielder who is among top defensive prospects in minors. Earned Sept callups last two seasons for nimble and quick glovework. Possesses ample hands, range, and arm strength and can play any infield position. Ideal #2 hitter by combining patient approach with level swing. Makes contact and is good situational hitter.

Romine, Austin — 2 — New York (A)

Bats R | Age 23 | EXP MLB DEBUT: 2011 | POTENTIAL: Starting C | 8D

2007 (2) HS (CA)

	Pwr	+++
BAvg	+++
Spd	++
Def	++++

Year	Lev	Team	AB	R	H	HR	RBI	Avg	OB	Slg	OPS	bb%	ct%	Eye	SB	CS	x/h%	Iso	RC/G
2009	A+	Tampa	442	61	122	13	72	276	321	441	762	6	82	0.37	11	5	36	165	4.79
2010	AA	Trenton	455	61	122	10	69	268	323	402	725	8	79	0.39	2	0	34	134	4.44
2011	AA	Trenton	336	43	96	6	47	286	348	378	726	9	82	0.53	2	2	20	92	4.49
2011	AAA	Scranton/W-B	15	1	2	0	1	133	133	133	267	0	80	0.00	0	0			
2011	MLB	New York (A)	19	2	3	0	0	158	200	158	358	5	74	0.20	0	0			

Athletic backstop who does many things relatively well, but has a few shortcomings. Power hasn't developed as much as hoped, but makes contact with short, simple stroke. Hands work well and has quick wrists and bat. May not be power-hitter, but should hit for nice BA. Agility and receiving are up to snuff, though shoddy footwork hinders arm.

Rosa, Gabriel — 95 — Cincinnati

Bats R | Age 18 | EXP MLB DEBUT: 2015 | POTENTIAL: Starting CF/3B | 8D

2011 (2) HS, P.R.

	Pwr	++++
BAvg	++
Spd	+++
Def	+++

Year	Lev	Team	AB	R	H	HR	RBI	Avg	OB	Slg	OPS	bb%	ct%	Eye	SB	CS	x/h%	Iso	RC/G
2011	Rk	AZL Reds	106	17	26	2	10	245	298	406	704	7	74	0.29	6	3	38	160	4.25

Tall, wiry, athletic OF has good raw power with plus bat speed, but is still very raw. Swing needs refinement and is all-or-nothing right now. Loose athleticism and plus and power potential mean he could play 3B or the OF. Much will depend upon how quickly he can tone done with swing and become more consistent.

Rosario, Eddie — 4 — Minnesota

Bats L | Age 20 | 2010 (4) HS (PR)

EXP MLB DEBUT: 2014 | POTENTIAL: Starting 2B | 8B

Pwr ++++ | BAvg ++++ | Spd +++ | Def ++

Year	Lev	Team	AB	R	H	HR	RBI	Avg	OB	Slg	OPS	bb%	ct%	Eye	SB	CS	x/h%	Iso	RC/G
2010	Rk	GCL Twins	194	34	57	5	26	294	348	438	786	8	86	0.57	22	5	28	144	5.18
2011	Rk	Elizabethton	270	71	91	21	60	337	397	670	1068	9	78	0.45	17	6	43	333	8.73

Instinctual and savvy hitter who led Appy in HR en route to MVP year. Has acumen to be top hitter based upon batting eye and ability to read pitches. Hits with power to entire field and has leverage and strength to hit at upper levels. Though showed good skill in OF, was moved to 2B in instructional league. Has decent arm and natural quickness to be an asset.

Rosario, Wilin — 2 — Colorado

Bats R | Age 23 | 2007 NDFA D.R.

EXP MLB DEBUT: 2011 | POTENTIAL: Starting C | 9D

Pwr ++++ | BAvg ++++ | Spd ++ | Def +++

Year	Lev	Team	AB	R	H	HR	RBI	Avg	OB	Slg	OPS	bb%	ct%	Eye	SB	CS	x/h%	Iso	RC/G
2008	Rk	Casper	263	48	83	12	49	316	373	532	905	8	78	0.42	4	3	36	217	6.68
2009	A+	Modesto	203	17	54	4	33	266	300	404	704	5	73	0.18	2	1	33	138	4.10
2010	AA	Tulsa	270	42	77	19	52	285	337	552	889	7	79	0.37	1	0	43	267	6.25
2011	AA	Tulsa	405	52	101	21	48	249	283	457	740	4	78	0.21	1	2	39	207	4.32
2011	MLB	Colorado	54	6	11	3	8	204	232	463	695	4	63	0.10	0	0	64	259	4.18

Athletic catcher with plus power and solid defensive skills who put up respectable numbers and made his MLB debut. Plate discipline and contact ability regressed due to overly aggressive approach and long swing. Continues to improve defensively and limits running game with quick release and plus arm. The power is legit and he could hit 30 HR in the majors.

Rupp, Cameron — 2 — Philadelphia

Bats R | Age 23 | 2010 (3) Texas

EXP MLB DEBUT: 2013 | POTENTIAL: Starting C | 7C

Pwr ++++ | BAvg ++ | Spd ++ | Def ++++

Year	Lev	Team	AB	R	H	HR	RBI	Avg	OB	Slg	OPS	bb%	ct%	Eye	SB	CS	x/h%	Iso	RC/G
2008	NCAA	Texas	194	34	60	4	32	309	362	479	841	8	77	0.36	0	0	38	170	6.01
2009	NCAA	Texas	216	46	63	11	46	292	381	505	885	13	75	0.58	0	1	38	213	6.69
2010	NCAA	Texas	240	50	73	10	54	304	386	483	869	12	75	0.52	0	0	32	179	6.50
2010	A-	Williamsport	193	20	42	5	28	218	307	378	686	11	74	0.49	0	0	50	161	4.13
2011	A	Lakewood	324	33	88	4	44	272	335	373	709	9	70	0.32	0	0	27	102	4.40

Strong, stocky backstop had a nice offensive season at Low-A. Doesn't really have a plus tool, but is average across the board. Swing mechanics are not great and plate discipline is below average. Rupp is solid defensively with a strong throwing arm, but is not quick and struggles limiting the running game. He has some work to do, but will play in the majors.

Russell, Kyle — 9 — Los Angeles (N)

Bats L | Age 26 | 2008 (3) Texas

EXP MLB DEBUT: 2012 | POTENTIAL: Staring RF | 8D

Pwr ++++ | BAvg ++ | Spd +++ | Def +++

Year	Lev	Team	AB	R	H	HR	RBI	Avg	OB	Slg	OPS	bb%	ct%	Eye	SB	CS	x/h%	Iso	RC/G
2009	A	Great Lakes	481	90	131	26	102	272	367	545	912	13	63	0.40	20	2	55	272	7.94
2010	A+	Inland Empire	198	42	70	16	53	354	443	692	1135	14	68	0.50	8	3	44	338	10.75
2010	AA	Chattanooga	273	36	67	10	28	245	318	462	779	10	59	0.26	3	2	54	216	6.14
2011	AA	Chattanooga	394	61	102	19	69	259	335	497	832	10	63	0.31	5	1	51	239	6.51
2011	AAA	Albuquerque	38	6	8	1	3	211	348	395	743	17	74	0.80	1	0	50	184	5.18

Tall/lanky outfielder has plus power, but low contact rate and poor pitch recognition limits potential. Plus bat speed and all-around athleticism. All-out swing results in extremely high K total (154), but does draw walks and hit 31 doubles and 20 home runs in '11. Nothing fancy, just an old-fashioned masher with a severe upper-cut and solid defense.

Rutledge, Josh — 64 — Colorado

Bats R | Age 23 | 2010 (3) Alabama

EXP MLB DEBUT: 2014 | POTENTIAL: Starting SS/2B | 8C

Pwr ++ | BAvg +++ | Spd +++ | Def +++

Year	Lev	Team	AB	R	H	HR	RBI	Avg	OB	Slg	OPS	bb%	ct%	Eye	SB	CS	x/h%	Iso	RC/G
2008	NCAA	Alabama	268	62	99	0	31	369	407	418	825	6	85	0.44	16	3	11	49	5.56
2009	NCAA	Alabama	239	64	73	5	44	305	371	444	815	9	79	0.50	8	3	29	138	5.69
2010	NCAA	Alabama	297	65	107	10	69	360	389	529	918	5	85	0.31	15	3	26	168	6.45
2010	A-	Tri-City	39	6	5	0	4	128	209	128	338	9	74	0.40	1	0			
2011	A+	Modesto	460	91	160	9	71	348	401	517	919	8	80	0.45	16	3	32	170	6.95

Polished collegiate SS was very impressive in full season debut. Has good speed and solid range, but some scouts question his arm strength. If he can stay at the position has the potential to hit for average and moderate power. Could end up moving to 2B as he moves up as SS is not an option in Colorado.

Saladino, Tyler — 6 — Chicago (A)

Bats R | Age 22 | 2010 (7) Oral Roberts

EXP MLB DEBUT: 2014 | POTENTIAL: Starting SS | 7B

Pwr +++ | BAvg +++ | Spd ++ | Def +++

Year	Lev	Team	AB	R	H	HR	RBI	Avg	OB	Slg	OPS	bb%	ct%	Eye	SB	CS	x/h%	Iso	RC/G
2010	NCAA	Oral Roberts	239	72	91	17	73	381	454	678	1132	12	78	0.62	16	2	38	297	9.70
2010	Rk	Bristol	48	7	14	1	6	292	358	417	775	9	75	0.42	1	2	29	125	5.21
2010	A	Kannapolis	165	40	51	2	18	309	390	442	833	12	73	0.50	4	2	33	133	6.26
2011	A+	Winston-Salem	397	75	107	16	55	270	353	501	854	11	77	0.57	7	7	48	232	6.31

Short and smart infielder with breakout season, particularly in power department. Solid defender with athleticism, strong arm, and ample range. Short swing path and quick bat produce gap power and could develop more pop with added strength. Plate coverage needs attention and can swing and miss at good breaking balls. Could be utility player at worst.

Salcedo, Edward — 5 — Atlanta

Bats R | Age 20 | 2010 NDFA D.R.

EXP MLB DEBUT: 2014 | POTENTIAL: Starting SS/3B | 8E

Pwr ++++ | BAvg +++ | Spd ++ | Def ++

Year	Lev	Team	AB	R	H	HR	RBI	Avg	OB	Slg	OPS	bb%	ct%	Eye	SB	CS	x/h%	Iso	RC/G
2010	A	Rome	193	23	38	2	16	197	240	295	536	5	71	0.20	6	5	29	98	1.86
2011	A	Rome	508	83	126	12	68	248	304	396	700	7	79	0.39	23	10	36	148	4.13

Strong bodied 3B had mixed results in his first full season. Good bat speed gives him the ability to drive the ball and he has the potential for above-average power. Below average speed and range resulted in move from SS to 3B, which seems permanent. Showed soft hands and a strong arm so should be able to stick at 3B.

Sale, Josh — 7 — Tampa Bay

Bats L | Age 20 | 2010 (1) HS (WA)

EXP MLB DEBUT: 2014 | POTENTIAL: Starting OF | 8C

Pwr ++++ | BAvg ++ | Spd ++ | Def ++

Year	Lev	Team	AB	R	H	HR	RBI	Avg	OB	Slg	OPS	bb%	ct%	Eye	SB	CS	x/h%	Iso	RC/G
2011	Rk	Princeton	214	24	45	4	15	210	287	346	633	10	81	0.56	4	3	40	136	3.46

Strong outfielder who struggled in short-season ball despite one of the quickest bat speeds in org. Brings patient and mature approach to plate and can launch balls into orbit. Knows strike zone, but strikes out abundantly due to poor swings against breaking balls. Limited to LF where arm strength and range are below average. High upside, but needs time to develop.

Sanchez, Gary — 2 — New York (A)

Bats R | Age 19 | 2009 FA (DR)

EXP MLB DEBUT: 2014 | POTENTIAL: Starting C | 9D

Pwr ++++ | BAvg +++ | Spd ++ | Def ++

Year	Lev	Team	AB	R	H	HR	RBI	Avg	OB	Slg	OPS	bb%	ct%	Eye	SB	CS	x/h%	Iso	RC/G
2010	Rk	GCL Yankees	119	25	42	6	36	353	408	597	1004	8	76	0.39	1	1	40	244	8.04
2010	A-	Staten Island	54	8	15	2	7	278	316	426	742	5	70	0.19	1	1	27	148	4.53
2011	A	Charleston (SC)	301	49	77	17	52	256	335	485	820	11	69	0.39	2	1	44	229	5.90

Power-hitting catcher who missed time due to maturity issues, but returned and feasted on lower level pitching. Owns high ceiling with ability to smash balls to all parts of park. Plus bat speed and strength generate pop, but can expand strike zone by flailing at breaking balls. Blocking and receiving need attention, while strong arm is asset.

Sanchez, Hector — 2 — San Francisco

Bats B | Age 22 | 2007 NDFA Venz.

EXP MLB DEBUT: 2011 | POTENTIAL: Starting C | 8C

Pwr ++++ | BAvg +++ | Spd ++ | Def ++

Year	Lev	Team	AB	R	H	HR	RBI	Avg	OB	Slg	OPS	bb%	ct%	Eye	SB	CS	x/h%	Iso	RC/G
2009	Rk	AZL Giants	117	13	35	1	22	299	383	410	794	12	82	0.76	0	0	29	111	5.64
2010	A	Augusta	310	29	85	5	31	274	334	394	728	8	84	0.56	0	2	31	119	4.57
2011	A+	San Jose	212	31	64	11	58	302	336	533	869	5	77	0.22	0	1	41	231	6.03
2011	AAA	Fresno	153	15	40	1	26	261	319	340	659	8	86	0.59	0	1	25	78	3.79
2011	MLB	San Francisco	31	0	8	0	1	258	324	323	646	9	81	0.50	0	0	25	65	3.62

Strong, athletic backstop with impressive raw power. Power started to develop and is now more game usable. Good bat speed and moderate plate discipline give him some nice offensive potential. Has a strong arm and quick release that limits running game, but needs to improve his receiving and blocking skills where he is still somewhat raw.

Sanchez, Tony — 2 — Pittsburgh

Bats R | Age 24 | 2009 (1) Boston College

EXP MLB DEBUT: 2013 | POTENTIAL: Starting C | 7B

Pwr +++ | BAvg ++++ | Spd ++ | Def ++++

Year	Lev	Team	AB	R	H	HR	RBI	Avg	OB	Slg	OPS	bb%	ct%	Eye	SB	CS	x/h%	Iso	RC/G
2009	A-	State College	13	2	4	0	1	308	357	385	742	7	85	0.50	0	0	25	77	4.74
2009	A	West Virginia	155	29	49	7	46	316	398	561	959	12	78	0.62	1	0	47	245	7.65
2009	A+	Lynchburg	10	2	2	0	1	200	273	400	673	9	60	0.25	0	0	100	200	4.66
2010	A+	Bradenton	207	31	65	4	35	314	396	454	850	12	80	0.68	2	1	32	140	6.29
2011	AA	Altoona	402	46	97	5	44	241	321	318	639	10	81	0.62	5	5	21	77	3.54

Athletic backstop was the 4th pick in the '09, but struggled in '11. Moderate bat speed limits power potential. Does have decent pitch recognition and should be able to hit for average, though he struggles with breaking balls. Solid defensive catcher with a good arm, but threw out just 22% of baserunners and made 18 errors. Catchers sometimes develop later, so don't give up yet.

Sano, Miguel — 5 — Minnesota — EXP MLB DEBUT: 2014 — POTENTIAL: Starting 3B — 9B

Bats R Age 19 | 2009 FA (DR) | Pwr ++++ | BAvg ++++ | Spd ++ | Def ++

Year	Lev	Team	AB	R	H	HR	RBI	Avg	OB	Slg	OPS	bb%	ct%	Eye	SB	CS	x/h%	Iso	RC/G
2010	Rk	GCL Twins	148	23	43	4	19	291	335	466	802	6	71	0.23	2	2	42	176	5.56
2011	Rk	Elizabethton	267	58	78	20	59	292	348	637	985	8	71	0.30	5	4	58	345	8.03

Natural-hitting infielder with as much power potential as any in minors. Generates incredible bat speed with quick, strong wrists. Makes hard contact to all fields and punches balls out with ease. Swing can get long and pull-oriented at times. Should be able to hit for BA with improved pitch recognition. Footwork and throwing accuracy need attention and runs OK.

Santana, Alex — 5 — Los Angeles (N) — EXP MLB DEBUT: 2015 — POTENTIAL: Starting 3B — 9E

Bats R Age 18 | 2011 (2) HS, (FL) | Pwr +++ | BAvg +++ | Spd +++ | Def +++

Year	Lev	Team	AB	R	H	HR	RBI	Avg	OB	Slg	OPS	bb%	ct%	Eye	SB	CS	x/h%	Iso	RC/G
2011	Rk	AZL Dodgers	189	30	45	1	19	238	276	339	615	5	66	0.16	8	1	31	101	3.07

Tall, strong, projectable 3B is son of former major leaguer Rafael Santana. Santana is very raw both on offense and defense at 3B is a new position. Hit just .238 in the AZL but showed nice athleticism and was the youngest player on the team. He should improve with experience and has nice long-term potential.

Santana, Domingo — 9 — Houston — EXP MLB DEBUT: 2014 — POTENTIAL: Starting RF — 8D

Bats R Age 19 | 2009 NDFA D.R. | Pwr +++ | BAvg +++ | Spd ++++ | Def +++

Year	Lev	Team	AB	R	H	HR	RBI	Avg	OB	Slg	OPS	bb%	ct%	Eye	SB	CS	x/h%	Iso	RC/G
2009	Rk	GCL Phillies	118	17	34	6	28	288	368	508	877	11	63	0.34	3	1	38	220	7.25
2010	A-	Williamsport	186	28	44	5	20	237	321	366	686	11	61	0.32	4	4	32	129	4.37
2010	A	Lakewood	165	27	30	3	16	182	304	297	601	15	54	0.38	5	6	43	115	3.35
2011	A	Lakewood	350	45	94	7	32	269	319	434	753	7	66	0.22	4	1	43	166	5.20
2011	A	Lexington	68	13	26	5	21	382	432	662	1094	8	78	0.40	1	0	35	279	8.93

Tall, strong OF had a mini-breakout in '11. Santana came over to the Astros as part of the H. Pence trade. He has a nice mix of speed and power, though speed could fade as he fills out his 6'5", 200 lb. frame. Puts on an impressive display in batting practice, but needs to put the power into game action. Needs to improve plate discipline and tone down his swing.

Santana, Ravel — 8 — New York (A) — EXP MLB DEBUT: 2015 — POTENTIAL: Starting OF — 9D

Bats R Age 20 | 2008 FA (DR) | Pwr ++++ | BAvg +++ | Spd ++++ | Def ++++

Year	Lev	Team	AB	R	H	HR	RBI	Avg	OB	Slg	OPS	bb%	ct%	Eye	SB	CS	x/h%	Iso	RC/G
2011	Rk	GCL Yankees	162	43	48	9	29	296	363	568	931	9	75	0.43	10	3	48	272	7.20

Plus athlete enjoyed solid debut in US and showcased promising tools across board. May eventually become top prospect in org. Possesses excellent strength despite lean physique and has more than ample arm strength, speed, and range to be potential plus defender in CF. Bat speed and mature approach should lead to hit BA and HR outputs.

Sappelt, Dave — 8 — Chicago (N) — EXP MLB DEBUT: 2011 — POTENTIAL: Starting OF — 7C

Bats R Age 25 | 2008 (9) Coastal Carolina | Pwr +++ | BAvg ++++ | Spd ++ | Def +++

Year	Lev	Team	AB	R	H	HR	RBI	Avg	OB	Slg	OPS	bb%	ct%	Eye	SB	CS	x/h%	Iso	RC/G
2010	A+	Lynchburg	71	7	20	0	4	282	329	352	681	7	79	0.33	6	4	25	70	3.92
2010	AA	Carolina	330	53	119	9	62	361	416	548	964	9	86	0.67	15	13	30	188	7.36
2010	AAA	Louisville	108	12	35	1	8	324	360	481	841	5	88	0.46	4	1	34	157	5.82
2011	AAA	Louisville	297	40	93	7	29	313	376	458	834	9	87	0.77	4	4	28	145	5.87
2011	MLB	Cincinnati	107	14	26	0	5	243	289	318	607	6	84	0.41	1	1	31	75	3.10

Short, powerful OF had a solid follow-up to his breakout in '10. Hard charging player who has surprising pop for size (5'9"). Covers ground well in CF, but arm strength is below average. Solid plate discipline and good contact rate should allow him to hit for average as he advances. Likely profiles better as a 4th OF but could have a some solid seasons in the majors.

Sardinas, Luis — 6 — Texas — EXP MLB DEBUT: 2014 — POTENTIAL: Starting SS — 8C

Bats B Age 19 | 2009 FA (Venezuela) | Pwr ++ | BAvg ++++ | Spd ++++ | Def ++++

Year	Lev	Team	AB	R	H	HR	RBI	Avg	OB	Slg	OPS	bb%	ct%	Eye	SB	CS	x/h%	Iso	RC/G
2010	Rk	AZL Rangers	103	22	32	0	8	311	355	350	704	6	85	0.47	8	2	13	39	4.19
2011	Rk	AZL Rangers	52	11	16	0	7	308	357	385	742	7	81	0.40	2	1	19	77	4.72

Long and lean infielder has been victim of injuries past two seasons. Does all the little things well. Has well above average wheels and high SB potential. Makes contact with simple swing from both sides and hits high amount of groundballs to use speed. Ranges well to both sides and owns plus arm. Very little power potential.

Schafer, Logan — 8 — Milwaukee — EXP MLB DEBUT: 2011 — POTENTIAL: Starting CF — 7B

Bats L Age 25 | 2008 (3) Cal Poly | Pwr ++ | BAvg +++ | Spd +++ | Def +++

Year	Lev	Team	AB	R	H	HR	RBI	Avg	OB	Slg	OPS	bb%	ct%	Eye	SB	CS	x/h%	Iso	RC/G
2010	A+	Brevard County	23	7	4	0	1	174	296	261	557	15	74	0.67	0	0	50	87	2.63
2011	A+	Brevard County	36	4	11	0	1	306	390	306	696	12	89	1.25	1	1	0	0	4.52
2011	AA	Huntsville	189	31	57	0	19	302	359	392	751	8	87	0.68	10	5	23	90	4.97
2011	AAA	Nashville	169	31	56	5	23	331	392	521	913	9	89	0.94	5	3	36	189	6.79
2011	MLB	Milwaukee	3	1	1	0	0	333	500	333	833	25	67	1.00	0	0	0	0	7.07

Lean, athletic LH CF had his best season as a pro and got a cup of coffee in the majors. He was finally healthy after missing most of '10 due to injury. Schafer has plus plate discipline and uses a line-drive approach to make consistent contact. Power is more of the gap variety, but he uses his speed well. Defensively he covers ground well and has a strong throwing arm.

Schoop, Jonathan — 456 — Baltimore — EXP MLB DEBUT: 2014 — POTENTIAL: Starting 3B — 8B

Bats R Age 20 | 2008 FA (Curacao) | Pwr +++ | BAvg +++ | Spd +++ | Def ++++

Year	Lev	Team	AB	R	H	HR	RBI	Avg	OB	Slg	OPS	bb%	ct%	Eye	SB	CS	x/h%	Iso	RC/G
2010	Rk	GCL Orioles	60	11	15	3	16	250	328	467	795	10	88	1.00	0	0	47	217	5.41
2010	Rk	Bluefield	133	16	42	2	16	316	372	459	831	8	89	0.86	1	1	33	143	5.86
2010	A+	Frederick	21	5	5	0	3	238	273	381	654	5	81	0.25	0	0	60	143	3.63
2011	A	Delmarva	212	45	67	8	34	316	375	514	889	9	85	0.63	6	4	34	198	6.43
2011	A+	Frederick	299	37	81	5	37	271	321	375	695	7	85	0.50	6	3	23	104	4.09

Advanced natural hitter who had breakout season. Can play any infield position, but spent most of '11 as 2B. Combines discerning eye with quick swing to produce gap power and high BA. Should grow into more power with additional strength and leverage. Just an average runner, but has instincts. Range short at SS, but has quick hands and strong arm.

Scott, Jordan — 7 — Houston — EXP MLB DEBUT: 2014 — POTENTIAL: Starting CF — 7C

Bats Age 20 | 2010 (14) HS, (SC) | Pwr ++ | BAvg +++ | Spd ++++ | Def +++

Year	Lev	Team	AB	R	H	HR	RBI	Avg	OB	Slg	OPS	bb%	ct%	Eye	SB	CS	x/h%	Iso	RC/G
2010	Rk	GCL Astros	146	19	44	0	10	301	363	370	732	9	77	0.42	6	4	18	68	4.69
2011	Rk	Greeneville	246	41	83	1	31	337	385	423	808	7	85	0.51	11	5	19	85	5.49
2011	A-	Tri City	17	4	4	0	6	235	409	353	762	23	88	2.50	1	1	25	118	6.06
2011	A	Lexington	47	6	13	0	6	277	320	340	660	6	83	0.38	0	1	23	64	3.66

Surprised in the APPY, hitting or average with a bit of speed. At 6'2" 180 lbs., this lefty has a nice line-drive stroke, good strike zone judgment, and a bit of speed. For now has the speed to stick in CF, but not enough arm to play a corner spot. In a thin system he could move up quickly.

Segedin, Rob — 579 — New York (A) — EXP MLB DEBUT: 2014 — POTENTIAL: Reserve 3B — 7D

Bats R Age 23 | 2010 (3) Tulane | Pwr +++ | BAvg +++ | Spd ++ | Def ++

Year	Lev	Team	AB	R	H	HR	RBI	Avg	OB	Slg	OPS	bb%	ct%	Eye	SB	CS	x/h%	Iso	RC/G
2010	NCAA	Tulane	212	55	92	14	54	434	510	788	1298	13	91	1.65	4	1	49	354	11.35
2010	Rk	GCL Yankees	8	3	2	1	3	250	250	625	875	0	88	0.00	0	0	50	375	5.26
2010	A-	Staten Island	70	13	17	1	7	243	312	400	712	9	90	1.00	0	1	47	157	4.64
2011	A	Charleston (SC)	226	33	73	5	34	323	386	482	868	9	83	0.59	3	2	32	159	6.32
2011	A+	Tampa	188	32	46	2	21	245	300	309	609	7	79	0.38	4	1	15	64	2.95

Tall and strong infielder who makes consistent, hard contact from short, line drive swing. May not be prototypical 3B due to lack of power, but has hit for BA. Needs to address deficiencies with strike zone and will need loft in swing for additional pop. Footwork can be sloppy, but arm strength has value and seems to make routine plays.

Segura, Jean — 46 — Los Angeles (A) — EXP MLB DEBUT: 2013 — POTENTIAL: Starting 2B/SS — 8B

Bats R Age 22 | 2007 FA (DR) | Pwr ++ | BAvg ++++ | Spd ++++ | Def +++

Year	Lev	Team	AB	R	H	HR	RBI	Avg	OB	Slg	OPS	bb%	ct%	Eye	SB	CS	x/h%	Iso	RC/G
2009	Rk	Orem	162	33	56	3	21	346	387	512	900	6	93	1.00	11	3	30	167	6.50
2009	AAA	Salt Lake	19	2	8	0	2	421	421	526	947	0	79	0.00	0	0	25	105	6.80
2010	A	Cedar Rapids	515	89	161	10	79	313	368	464	832	8	86	0.63	50	10	29	151	5.81
2011	Rk	AZL Angels	30	5	11	1	5	367	367	600	967	0	90	0.00	0	0	45	233	6.71
2011	A+	Inland Empire	185	26	52	3	21	281	335	422	757	8	86	0.58	18	6	31	141	4.92

Athletic infielder missed three months with hamstring injury, but showed positive traits when healthy. Makes exemplary contact from short swing and has good bat speed and pop for someone his size. Swings aggressively and may need to draw more walks to utilize speed. Converted from 2B to SS where strong arm and hands work, but may lack range.

Shields, Robbie — 6 — New York (N)

EXP MLB DEBUT: 2012 | POTENTIAL: Reserve SS/2B | **6B**

Bats R Age 24
2009 (3) Florida Southern
Pwr +
BAvg + +
Spd + + +
Def + + +

Year	Lev	Team	AB	R	H	HR	RBI	Avg	OB	Slg	OPS	bb%	ct%	Eye	SB	CS	x/h%	Iso	RC/G
2010	Rk	GCL Mets	82	11	20	1	7	244	333	341	675	12	88	1.10	3	1	30	98	4.26
2010	A	Savannah	162	26	47	5	26	290	331	457	788	6	79	0.29	4	0	34	167	5.10
2010	A+	St. Lucie	7	0	2	0	1	286	375	286	661	13	100		1	0	0	0	4.61
2011	A	Savannah	226	30	62	2	26	274	357	425	782	11	84	0.81	9	4	42	150	5.52
2011	A+	St. Lucie	67	14	18	1	12	269	347	388	735	11	87	0.89	0	0	33	119	4.86

Steady, but not flashy SS. Shields has a nice bat with good pitch recognition and plus plate discipline. His power is more of the gap variety and will likely keep him from starting in the majors. He is a good defender with sound middle infield actions. Good feet and steady hands to match. Strong arm that could fit anywhere in the infield.

Shipman, Aaron — 78 — Oakland

EXP MLB DEBUT: 2014 | POTENTIAL: Starting OF | **8D**

Bats L Age 20
2010 (3) HS (GA)
Pwr + +
BAvg + + +
Spd + + + +
Def + + +

Year	Lev	Team	AB	R	H	HR	RBI	Avg	OB	Slg	OPS	bb%	ct%	Eye	SB	CS	x/h%	Iso	RC/G
2010	Rk	AZL Athletics	17	2	2	0	2	118	118	118	235	0	65	0.00	3	0			
2011	A-	Vermont	201	34	51	0	19	254	383	303	686	17	81	1.08	17	3	18	50	4.56

Athletic and spry outfielder has all requisite tools to be star with exception of power. Very raw, but exhibits good hitting skills including ability to put bat to ball with short stroke and disciplined approach. Possesses good strength, but prefers to put ball in play and use plus speed. Could become plus defender with excellent speed, range, and arm strength.

Short, Brandon — 789 — Chicago (A)

EXP MLB DEBUT: 2012 | POTENTIAL: Starting OF | **8C**

Bats R Age 23
2008 (28) St. John's River CC
Pwr + + +
BAvg + + +
Spd + + +
Def + + +

Year	Lev	Team	AB	R	H	HR	RBI	Avg	OB	Slg	OPS	bb%	ct%	Eye	SB	CS	x/h%	Iso	RC/G
2008	Rk	Bristol	183	30	50	1	23	273	332	383	714	8	80	0.43	14	7	32	109	4.44
2009	A	Kannapolis	345	56	98	7	55	284	336	417	753	7	77	0.35	12	1	30	133	4.80
2010	A+	Winston-Salem	491	77	155	15	79	316	353	491	843	5	78	0.26	7	10	33	175	5.79
2011	AA	Birmingham	526	75	138	13	60	262	310	411	720	6	76	0.29	21	9	34	148	4.32

Multi-tooled outfielder does a number of things well, but owns no plus tools. Established career high in SB, but more predicated on better pitcher reads than speed. Continuous improvement in career with power, speed, and instincts. Free swinger at plate, but has quick enough bat to catch up to good FB. Good platoon option at worst.

Shuck, JB — 8 — Houston

EXP MLB DEBUT: 2011 | POTENTIAL: Reserve CF/LF | **7D**

Bats L Age 25
2008 (6) Ohio St
Pwr +
BAvg + + +
4.10 Spd + + + +
Def + + + +

Year	Lev	Team	AB	R	H	HR	RBI	Avg	OB	Slg	OPS	bb%	ct%	Eye	SB	CS	x/h%	Iso	RC/G
2009	A+	Lancaster	556	98	175	1	36	315	385	414	799	10	90	1.16	18	9	24	99	5.71
2010	AA	Corpus Christi	389	52	116	2	28	298	372	360	732	11	86	0.82	9	9	16	62	4.80
2010	AAA	Round Rock	139	15	38	0	7	273	348	317	665	10	89	1.07	7	3	11	43	4.12
2011	AAA	Oklahoma City	354	60	105	0	30	297	393	367	760	14	92	1.87	20	11	17	71	5.51
2011	MLB	Houston	81	9	22	0	3	272	359	321	680	12	91	1.57	2	0	14	49	4.47

Wiry athlete whose skills are well-suited for leadoff role, possessing on-base ability and aggressive baserunning. He uses whole field and hits for BA with a line-drive stroke. There is still no power development, but that isn't part of his game. Features excellent range and a throwing arm that is strong and accurate.

Sierra, Moises — 9 — Toronto

EXP MLB DEBUT: 2013 | POTENTIAL: Reserve OF | **7C**

Bats R Age 23
2005 FA (DR)
Pwr + + +
BAvg + +
Spd + + +
Def + + +

Year	Lev	Team	AB	R	H	HR	RBI	Avg	OB	Slg	OPS	bb%	ct%	Eye	SB	CS	x/h%	Iso	RC/G
2009	A+	Dunedin	405	56	116	5	56	286	342	393	734	8	84	0.52	10	2	27	106	4.62
2009	AA	New Hampshire	34	1	12	1	6	353	371	471	842	3	76	0.13	0	1	17	118	5.54
2010	Rk	GCL Blue Jays	34	4	9	1	3	265	342	412	754	11	76	0.50	0	0	33	147	4.92
2010	A+	Dunedin	37	4	6	1	5	162	184	270	454	3	70	0.09	0	1	33	108	0.48
2011	AA	New Hampshire	495	81	137	18	67	277	330	436	766	7	81	0.42	16	14	29	160	4.84

Physically mature hitter with terrific size and strength. Set easy career high in HR after missing most of '10 campaign. Has very good speed for large frame, but gets caught too often. Has some semblance of OBP to provide SB potential. Very rough around edges, but has raw skills to produce. Has among best arms in entire minors with average range in RF.

Silva, Juan — 8 — Cincinnati

EXP MLB DEBUT: 2014 | POTENTIAL: Starting OF | **8D**

Bats L Age 21
2009 (8) HS (P.R.)
Pwr + + +
BAvg + + +
Spd + + +
Def + + +

Year	Lev	Team	AB	R	H	HR	RBI	Avg	OB	Slg	OPS	bb%	ct%	Eye	SB	CS	x/h%	Iso	RC/G
2009	Rk	GCL Reds	143	26	40	1	16	280	372	462	833	13	69	0.47	7	4	43	182	6.66
2010	Rk	AZL Reds	178	26	41	3	24	230	318	371	689	11	73	0.48	4	1	34	140	4.24
2011	Rk	Billings	150	30	44	4	21	293	404	413	818	16	71	0.65	4	6	18	120	6.13

Strong, athletic OF prospect had a solid season in the PIO. Was much better against LHP, has decent strike zone judgment, and some power potential from the LH side. Silva runs well, but is not likely to be a SB threat. He moves well in RF and has a strong throwing arm. Still young and has some upside.

Silverio, Alfredo — 8 — Los Angeles (N)

EXP MLB DEBUT: 2012 | POTENTIAL: Starter RF/LF | **8D**

Bats R Age 25
2003 NDFA D.R.
Pwr + + + +
BAvg + + +
Spd + + + +
Def + + +

Year	Lev	Team	AB	R	H	HR	RBI	Avg	OB	Slg	OPS	bb%	ct%	Eye	SB	CS	x/h%	Iso	RC/G
2008	A	Great Lakes	376	37	99	10	45	263	277	404	681	2	78	0.08	6	3	29	141	3.53
2009	A	Great Lakes	490	75	139	13	61	284	320	457	777	5	79	0.25	2	5	38	173	4.97
2010	A+	Inland Empire	387	66	113	12	43	292	323	486	809	4	84	0.29	17	7	40	194	5.28
2010	AA	Chattanooga	16	1	1	0	0	63	63	63	125	0	81	0.00	0	0			
2011	AA	Chattanooga	533	90	163	16	85	306	343	542	885	5	83	0.33	11	12	47	236	6.33

Strong, powerful, athletic OF has all the tools to star and had a breakout season at Double-A and played in the Futures game. Has plus bat speed, drives the ball with authority, and is a bit of a late bloomer. Moderate plate discipline and good pitch recognition should enable him to hit for average.

Simmons, Andrelton — 6 — Atlanta

EXP MLB DEBUT: 2013 | POTENTIAL: Starting SS | **8C**

Bats R Age 22
2010 (2) Western Okl St. Col
Pwr + +
BAvg + + +
7.0/60 Spd + +
Def + + +

Year	Lev	Team	AB	R	H	HR	RBI	Avg	OB	Slg	OPS	bb%	ct%	Eye	SB	CS	x/h%	Iso	RC/G
2010	Rk	Danville	239	36	66	2	26	276	322	356	677	6	94	1.14	18	4	21	79	4.12
2011	A+	Lynchburg	517	69	161	1	52	311	348	408	756	5	92	0.67	26	18	26	97	4.90

Raw, athletic SS had an impressive full-season debut. Plays SS with outstanding range, fluid actions, and quick hands. Arm is plus (can hit 98 mph and he possesses mature instincts for the position. Runs well and may be able to hit enough to project as an everyday player. His power is below average, but he does have good speed.

Singleton, Jonathan — 3 — Houston

EXP MLB DEBUT: 2013 | POTENTIAL: Starting 1B | **9D**

Bats L Age 20
2009 (8) HS (CA)
Pwr + + + +
BAvg + + + +
Spd + + +
Def + +

Year	Lev	Team	AB	R	H	HR	RBI	Avg	OB	Slg	OPS	bb%	ct%	Eye	SB	CS	x/h%	Iso	RC/G
2009	Rk	GCL Phillies	100	12	29	2	12	290	398	440	838	15	87	1.38	1	0	38	150	6.37
2010	A	Lakewood	376	64	109	14	77	290	390	479	869	14	80	0.84	9	7	38	189	6.57
2011	A+	Clearwater	320	48	91	9	47	284	391	413	803	15	74	0.67	3	3	25	128	5.82
2011	A+	Lancaster	129	20	43	4	16	333	399	512	910	10	69	0.35	0	0	33	178	7.34

Strong, athletic prospect cointinues to make rapid progress. Trade from Philly to Houston means he can play his natural position. Polished hitter with a sweet LH stroke and plus bat speed that leads to good power and BA. Plate discipline is solid, though he did strke out 123 times in '11. Top propsect in a weak Astros system means he will move up rapidly.

Skipworth, Kyle — 2 — Florida

EXP MLB DEBUT: 2013 | POTENTIAL: Starting CA | **8E**

Bats L Age 22
2008 (1) HS (CA)
Pwr + + + +
BAvg + +
Spd + +
Def + + +

Year	Lev	Team	AB	R	H	HR	RBI	Avg	OB	Slg	OPS	bb%	ct%	Eye	SB	CS	x/h%	Iso	RC/G
2008	Rk	GCL Marlins	159	22	33	5	21	208	267	340	607	8	71	0.28	2	2	33	132	2.78
2009	A	Greensboro	264	28	55	7	37	208	259	348	607	6	66	0.20	1	2	40	140	2.87
2010	A	Greensboro	397	55	99	17	59	249	305	426	731	7	67	0.24	1	2	35	176	4.61
2010	AA	Jacksonville	7	1	0	0	0	0	125	0	125	13	57	0.33	0	0			
2011	AA	Jacksonville	396	35	82	11	49	207	270	331	601	8	64	0.24	0	4	30	124	2.79

Tall/strong-framed catcher has failed to develop. Catchers do sometimes develop more slowly, but there just isn't any sign of growth on either side of the ball. Struggled with bat in 2011 and played lackluster defense. Does have good power and a strong throwing arm, but does not block balls well and still looks uncomforatable. Does not turn 21 until March so there is still time.

Skole, Jake — 78 — Texas

EXP MLB DEBUT: 2014 | POTENTIAL: Starting OF | **8D**

Bats L Age 20
2010 (1) HS (GA)
Pwr + + +
BAvg + + +
Spd + + +
Def + + +

Year	Lev	Team	AB	R	H	HR	RBI	Avg	OB	Slg	OPS	bb%	ct%	Eye	SB	CS	x/h%	Iso	RC/G
2010	Rk	AZL Rangers	28	7	8	0	5	286	394	357	751	15	82	1.00	3	0	25	71	5.32
2010	A-	Spokane	201	29	51	2	27	254	330	348	679	10	74	0.44	6	4	25	95	4.02
2011	A	Hickory	424	76	112	9	62	264	362	389	751	13	67	0.47	21	14	26	125	5.23

Plus athlete who had ups and downs in first full season, but showed glimpses of greatness. Has potential to be power-speed producer with smooth lefty stroke and solid wheels. Makes hard contact with clean, repeatable swing and is patient enough to draw walks. Range and arm may be best served in LF, but is good defender.

Skole, Matt — 5 — Washington

EXP MLB DEBUT: 2015 | POTENTIAL: Starting 3B | 7D

Bats L Age 22
2011 (5) Georgia Tech
Pwr +++
BAvg ++
Spd ++
Def ++

Year	Lev	Team	AB	R	H	HR	RBI	Avg	OB	Sig	OPS	bb%	ct%	Eye	SB	CS	x/h%	Iso	RC/G
2009	NCAA	Georgia Tech	215	41	65	17	58	302	380	600	980	11	68	0.39	2	1	46	298	8.22
2010	NCAA	Georgia Tech	233	62	78	20	63	335	442	682	1125	16	85	1.32	1	1	49	348	9.53
2011	NCAA	Georgia Tech	233	56	81	10	58	348	451	545	996	16	86	1.33	1	3	32	197	8.15
2011	A-	Auburn	272	43	79	5	48	290	385	438	823	13	81	0.81	2	1	37	147	6.05

Strong, muscular third baseman had a solid professional debut. He has nice raw power from the left-hand side. Also has good plate discipline and an improved approach at the plate. Defensively he is below average with stiff hands and limited range. He will need to continue to hit to have value.

Smith, Blake — 7 — Los Angeles (N)

EXP MLB DEBUT: 2012 | POTENTIAL: Platoon RF | 6C

Bats L Age 24
2009 (2) California
Pwr +++
BAvg ++
Spd ++
Def +++

Year	Lev	Team	AB	R	H	HR	RBI	Avg	OB	Sig	OPS	bb%	ct%	Eye	SB	CS	x/h%	Iso	RC/G
2009	Rk	Ogden	104	14	22	1	12	212	299	308	607	11	63	0.34	0	0	36	96	3.13
2009	Rk	AZL Dodgers	22	3	5	0	2	227	292	273	564	8	59	0.22	0	0	20	45	2.50
2010	A	Great Lakes	430	77	121	19	76	281	355	488	843	10	69	0.36	2	3	40	207	6.33
2011	Rk	AZL Dodgers	20	7	9	4	10	450	522	1150	1672	13	95	3.00	0	0	67	700	14.54
2011	A+	Rancho Cucamg	293	59	86	16	63	294	363	539	902	10	72	0.39	3	2	47	246	6.96

23-year-old OF had a solid season in the CAL. Showed good power, but strikes out too frequently. Swing has some length and will need to be shortened, but has considerable power potential. Plus arm strength and range to play RF. Speed is below average and given age, he will need to move up quickly.

Smith, Dwight — 7 — Toronto

EXP MLB DEBUT: 2015 | POTENTIAL: Starting OF | 8D

Bats L Age 19
2011 (1-S) HS (GA)
Pwr +++
BAvg +++
Spd +++
Def +++

Year	Lev	Team	AB	R	H	HR	RBI	Avg	OB	Sig	OPS	bb%	ct%	Eye	SB	CS	x/h%	Iso	RC/G
2011		Did not play																	

Toolsy and strong outfielder with solid bat control and clean, simple swing. Has potential to hit for high BA once he learns to read pitches better and should provide at least average pop when he adds muscle to frame. Possesses very strong arm and excellent instincts in OF. Could play CF despite average speed.

Smith, Kevan — 2 — Chicago (A)

EXP MLB DEBUT: 2014 | POTENTIAL: Starting C | 8D

Bats R Age 23
2011 (7) Pittsburgh
Pwr ++++
BAvg ++
Spd ++
Def +++

Year	Lev	Team	AB	R	H	HR	RBI	Avg	OB	Sig	OPS	bb%	ct%	Eye	SB	CS	x/h%	Iso	RC/G
2009	NCAA	Pittsburgh	102	19	37	3	21	363	414	520	934	8	87	0.69	3	1	24	157	6.90
2010	NCAA	Pittsburgh	233	59	84	5	46	361	411	511	922	8	94	1.33	3	4	29	150	6.81
2011	NCAA	Pittsburgh	209	59	83	11	56	397	455	675	1129	10	90	1.10	10	1	39	278	9.15
2011	Rk	Great Falls	107	22	34	2	16	318	397	523	920	12	85	0.88	1	0	47	206	7.18
2011	Rk	Bristol	96	24	38	7	32	396	473	740	1212	13	85	1.00	1	2	47	344	10.44

Strong and athletic catcher who shocked with terrific pro debut. Unpolished defensively, but has potential to be good backstop. Good athlete for size and has arm and footwork to be passable. Recognizes pitches and uses short, simple stroke to make contact. Hits for power at present, though moderate bat speed and swing path don't project to BA.

Smolinski, Jake — 4 — Florida

EXP MLB DEBUT: 2012 | POTENTIAL: Backup OF/INF | 6C

Bats R Age 23
2007 (2) HS (IL)
Pwr ++++
BAvg +++
Spd ++
Def +++

Year	Lev	Team	AB	R	H	HR	RBI	Avg	OB	Sig	OPS	bb%	ct%	Eye	SB	CS	x/h%	Iso	RC/G
2008	A-	Vermont	98	17	30	0	9	306	364	408	773	8	83	0.53	4	0	30	102	5.22
2008	A	Hagerstown	184	28	48	4	22	261	330	402	732	9	82	0.58	1	2	35	141	4.66
2009	A	Greensboro	279	50	79	7	31	283	369	448	817	12	84	0.84	2	5	41	165	5.86
2010	A+	Jupiter	405	45	107	5	51	264	317	383	699	7	85	0.50	8	5	33	119	4.21
2011	AA	Jacksonville	396	42	97	7	36	245	343	364	706	13	86	1.04	6	5	34	119	4.62

Short, athletic OF with solid plate discipline. His power has yet to develop and looks to be moderate at best. Instinctive runner who will take the extra base, despite below average speed. Arm strength is enough to stay corner OF or 3B. At best, he looks to be a super utility type.

Snyder, Brandon — 35 — Texas

EXP MLB DEBUT: 2010 | POTENTIAL: Starting 1B | 7C

Bats R Age 25
2005 (1) HS (VA)
Pwr +++
BAvg +++
Spd ++
Def ++

Year	Lev	Team	AB	R	H	HR	RBI	Avg	OB	Sig	OPS	bb%	ct%	Eye	SB	CS	x/h%	Iso	RC/G
2010	A-	Aberdeen	13	2	3	1	4	231	231	538	769	0	85	0.00	0	0	67	308	4.37
2010	AAA	Norfolk	339	36	87	9	43	257	313	407	720	8	70	0.28	4	1	37	150	4.47
2010	MLB	Baltimore	20	1	6	0	3	300	300	400	700	0	85	0.00	0	1	33	100	3.82
2011	AAA	Norfolk	448	55	117	14	71	261	310	406	717	7	80	0.35	1	2	31	145	4.21
2011	MLB	Baltimore	13	2	3	0	1	231	375	308	683	19	69	0.75	0	0	33	77	4.52

Natural hitting infielder who has spent most of last three seasons in AAA. Has morphed from potential plus power-hitter to moderate BA hitter with occasional pop. Has strength in arms and wrists along with ample bat speed, but making contact has been issue. Is overly aggressive at plate, but covers plate well and recognizes pitches. Only a fringe-average defender.

Sogard, Eric — 456 — Oakland

EXP MLB DEBUT: 2010 | POTENTIAL: Utility player | 6B

Bats L Age 26
2007 (2) Arizona State
Pwr ++
BAvg +++
Spd +++
Def +++

Year	Lev	Team	AB	R	H	HR	RBI	Avg	OB	Sig	OPS	bb%	ct%	Eye	SB	CS	x/h%	Iso	RC/G
2009	AA	San Antonio	457	79	134	6	51	293	373	400	773	11	90	1.23	10	6	25	107	5.39
2010	AAA	Sacramento	514	82	154	5	65	300	389	407	795	13	87	1.10	14	9	25	107	5.73
2010	MLB	Oakland	7	0	3	0	0	429	556	429	984	22	86	2.00	0	1	0	0	8.64
2011	AAA	Sacramento	315	55	94	5	37	298	377	410	787	11	89	1.18	13	3	24	111	5.52
2011	MLB	Oakland	70	7	14	2	4	200	243	329	572	5	81	0.31	0	0	36	129	2.41

Short and athletic infielder who brings mature approach and short stroke to plate to produce moderate gap power and BA skills. Hits LHP and RHP consistently and draws walks while limiting Ks. Bat speed and strength not conducive to long balls. Plays 2B, SS, and 3B, though not a standout. Hands are soft and quick while range is average.

Solarte, Yangervis — 457 — Texas

EXP MLB DEBUT: 2012 | POTENTIAL: Utility player | 6B

Bats B Age 24
2005 FA (Venezuela)
Pwr ++
BAvg +++
Spd +++
Def ++

Year	Lev	Team	AB	R	H	HR	RBI	Avg	OB	Sig	OPS	bb%	ct%	Eye	SB	CS	x/h%	Iso	RC/G
2009	AA	New Britain	7	0	1	0	0	143	143	143	286	0	86	0.00	0	0			
2010	Rk	GCL Twins	23	3	4	0	0	174	208	174	382	4	83	0.25	0	0	0	0	0.15
2010	A+	Fort Myers	172	19	55	2	15	320	368	419	786	7	92	1.00	3	0	22	99	5.28
2010	AA	New Britain	127	14	35	3	19	276	292	417	710	2	86	0.17	1	1	34	142	3.98
2011	AA	New Britain	459	64	151	7	49	329	362	466	829	5	92	0.63	5	4	30	137	5.60

Athletic and versatile infielder who finished in 2nd in EL in BA while posting career high in HR. Exhibits solid batting eye, but makes such easy contact that he can swing and succeed early in count. Not much power projection in short, simple swing, but can leg out doubles with average speed. Lack of plus skill on defense likely will lead to utility role at best.

Solorzano, Jesus — 8 — Florida

EXP MLB DEBUT: 2015 | POTENTIAL: Starting CF | 8D

Bats R Age 21
2009 NDFA Venz.
Pwr ++
BAvg +++
Spd ++++
Def +++

Year	Lev	Team	AB	R	H	HR	RBI	Avg	OB	Sig	OPS	bb%	ct%	Eye	SB	CS	x/h%	Iso	RC/G
2011	Rk	GCL Marlins	194	34	58	3	31	299	343	454	797	6	85	0.43	18	7	34	155	5.32

Toolsy, athletic OF prospect from Venezuela had nice U.S. debut. Runs very well with a strong throwing arm and has the potential to hit for average/moderate power. Has the tools to stick in CF, but will be more of a leadoff hitter who gets on base and not a run producer.

Songco, Angelo — 7 — Los Angeles (N)

EXP MLB DEBUT: 2014 | POTENTIAL: Starting LF | 8D

Bats L Age 23
2009 (5) Loyola Marymnt
Pwr ++++
BAvg +++
Spd ++
Def ++

Year	Lev	Team	AB	R	H	HR	RBI	Avg	OB	Sig	OPS	bb%	ct%	Eye	SB	CS	x/h%	Iso	RC/G
2009	NCAA	Loyola Marymnt	214	65	77	15	63	360	463	678	1140	16	76	0.80	5	3	45	318	10.27
2009	Rk	Ogden	144	27	44	9	29	306	351	583	934	6	72	0.24	0	1	48	278	7.21
2009	A	Great Lakes	120	8	18	1	16	150	215	258	474	8	77	0.36	1	0	50	108	1.30
2010	A	Great Lakes	507	87	139	15	71	274	341	446	786	9	82	0.56	6	1	37	172	5.28
2011	A+	Rancho Cucamg	534	110	167	29	114	313	363	581	943	7	77	0.35	4	3	49	268	7.15

Strong, aggressive hitter dominated in the CAL. Struggles some against LHP, but has legit power and an all-out swing. Dead pull hitter who swings and misses a lot (121 K). Swing can get long and could struggle against advanced breaking balls. Average defender so value comes only from his bat. He will be interesting to watch, but at 23 he doesn't have a ton of time.

Soto, Neftali — 3 — Cincinnati

EXP MLB DEBUT: 2013 | POTENTIAL: Starting 1B | 8D

Bats R Age 23
2007 (3) HS P.R.
Pwr ++++
BAvg ++
4.30 Spd +++
Def +++

Year	Lev	Team	AB	R	H	HR	RBI	Avg	OB	Sig	OPS	bb%	ct%	Eye	SB	CS	x/h%	Iso	RC/G
2008	A	Dayton	218	26	71	7	36	326	347	500	847	3	83	0.19	1	1	32	174	5.58
2009	A+	Sarasota	505	53	125	11	57	248	280	362	643	4	81	0.24	1	3	27	115	3.23
2010	A+	Lynchburg	522	73	140	21	73	268	310	460	770	6	80	0.30	0	0	40	192	4.83
2011	AA	Carolina	379	70	103	30	76	272	317	575	892	6	75	0.26	0	1	50	303	6.36
2011	AAA	Louisville	17	1	7	1	4	412	444	588	1033	6	88	0.50	0	0	14	176	7.57

Lean, athletic hitter with a grip-it-and-rip-it approach and solid bat speed, giving him excellent power. Good bad-ball hitter, but lack of plate discipline continues to cut into BA ability, though did hit 31 HR. Defensively Soto has good arm strength and soft hands, but limited range caused him to move to 1B, which hurts his long-term value behind Votto.

Spangenberg, Cory — 4 — San Diego

EXP MLB DEBUT: 2013 | POTENTIAL: Starting 2B | 8C

Bats L Age 21
2011 (1) Indian River JC, FL

Pwr	+++	
BAvg	+++	
Spd	+++	
Def	+++	

Year	Lev	Team	AB	R	H	HR	RBI	Avg	OB	Slg	OPS	bb%	ct%	Eye	SB	CS	x/h%	Iso	RC/G
2011	A-	Eugene	86	20	33	1	20	384	547	535	1082	26	83	2.07	10	4	33	151	10.25
2011	A	Fort Wayne	189	35	54	2	24	286	335	365	700	7	78	0.33	15	4	19	79	4.09

Natural, athletic 2B was impressive in his debut after being drafted 10th overall in '11. Patient approach at the plate allows him to get on base and use his plus speed to his advantage. The left-handed hitter has a textbook swing and can put bat to ball consistently. Uses the entire field and has some power potential. Played 3B at JuCo, but was moved to 2B when drafted.

Springer, George — 8 — Houston

EXP MLB DEBUT: 2014 | POTENTIAL: Starting OF | 8B

Bats R Age 22
2011 (1) Connecticut

Pwr	+++	
BAvg	+++	
Spd	+++	
Def	+++	

Year	Lev	Team	AB	R	H	HR	RBI	Avg	OB	Slg	OPS	bb%	ct%	Eye	SB	CS	x/h%	Iso	RC/G
2009	NCAA	Connecticut	212	75	76	16	57	358	443	679	1122	13	75	0.60	12	3	43	321	9.87
2010	NCAA	Connecticut	243	84	82	18	62	337	469	658	1127	20	71	0.86	33	2	46	321	10.62
2011	NCAA	Connecticut	237	60	83	12	77	350	436	624	1060	13	84	0.95	31	7	46	274	8.81
2011	A-	Tri City	28	8	5	1	3	179	233	393	626	7	93	1.00	4	0	80	214	3.57

Strong, athletic 5-tool OF was the 11th overall pick in '11. Springer has a strong throwing arm, some nice pop, and hits for average. His swing can get lengthy but plus bat speed and quick hands allows him to get away with it. Similar in build and athleticism to H. Pence. He covers ground well and gives the Astros a young, athletic OF with good upside.

Stanley, Cody — 2 — St. Louis

EXP MLB DEBUT: 2015 | POTENTIAL: Platoon C | 7D

Bats L Age 23
2010 (4) NC - Wilmington

Pwr	+++	
BAvg	+++	
Spd	++	
Def	++	

Year	Lev	Team	AB	R	H	HR	RBI	Avg	OB	Slg	OPS	bb%	ct%	Eye	SB	CS	x/h%	Iso	RC/G
2009	NCAA	NC Wilmington	223	54	74	12	56	332	411	605	1016	12	83	0.81	10	2	42	274	8.17
2010	NCAA	NC Wilmington	226	53	73	11	40	323	429	540	969	16	90	1.83	13	2	37	217	7.77
2010	Rk	Johnson City	209	34	67	5	39	321	383	498	880	9	86	0.70	8	1	33	177	6.45
2010	A	Quad Cities	4	1	1	1	2	250	250	1000	1250	0	50	0.00	0	0	100	750	14.93
2011	A	Quad Cities	379	54	100	11	66	264	313	425	738	7	76	0.29	4	2	37	161	4.55

Strong, stocky left-handed catcher has nice offensive potential. Had a solid full-season debut, holding his own in the MWL. Barrels the ball well, but below-average plate discipline will limit BA potential. Is an average defender who can make all of the plays, but at this point the offense is ahead of the defense.

Starling, Bubba — 8 — Kansas City

EXP MLB DEBUT: 2014 | POTENTIAL: Starting OF | 9C

Bats R Age 19
2011 (1) HS (KS)

Pwr	++++	
BAvg	+++	
Spd	++++	
Def	++++	

Year	Lev	Team
2011		Did not play

Multi-talented, tall and strong athlete with terrific upside. Owns ideal frame for plus-plus power and athleticism. Runs extremely well and should stick in CF with nice arm strength and range. Swing mechanics and instincts are a bit raw, but has ability to shine. Pro debut will be watched closely, but has skill set to advance multiple levels.

Stassi, Max — 2 — Oakland

EXP MLB DEBUT: 2013 | POTENTIAL: Starting C | 8D

Bats R Age 21
2009 (4) HS (CA)

Pwr	+++	
BAvg	+++	
Spd	++	
Def	+++	

Year	Lev	Team	AB	R	H	HR	RBI	Avg	OB	Slg	OPS	bb%	ct%	Eye	SB	CS	x/h%	Iso	RC/G
2009	Rk	AZL Athletics	1	0	0	0	0	0	500	0	500	50	0	1.00	0	0			
2009	A-	Vancouver	49	3	14	0	8	286	314	367	681	4	78	0.18	0	0	29	82	3.78
2010	A	Kane County	411	54	94	13	51	229	305	380	684	10	66	0.32	3	3	37	151	4.10
2011	A+	Stockton	121	22	28	2	19	231	321	331	652	12	82	0.73	1	1	29	99	3.78

Short and stocky backstop missed most of campaign with shoulder injury. Hasn't produced with bat when healthy, displaying bat speed and strength, but lacking pitch selectivity and recognition. Produces average power to pull side with short swing. Possesses good hands and agility behind dish, though long release neutralizes strong arm.

Stock, Robert — 2 — St. Louis

EXP MLB DEBUT: 2014 | POTENTIAL: Platoon C | 7C

Bats L Age 22
2009 (2) USC

Pwr	+++	
BAvg	++	
Spd	++	
Def	+++	

Year	Lev	Team	AB	R	H	HR	RBI	Avg	OB	Slg	OPS	bb%	ct%	Eye	SB	CS	x/h%	Iso	RC/G
2009	Rk	Johnson City	149	25	48	7	24	322	369	550	919	7	81	0.39	0	1	38	228	6.70
2009	A	Quad Cities	21	1	2	0	0	95	174	95	269	9	76	0.40	0	0			
2010	A	Quad Cities	310	32	66	1	31	213	301	277	578	11	82	0.70	2	2	27	65	2.92
2011	A	Quad Cities	51	4	9	1	6	176	250	275	525	9	88	0.83	1	0	33	98	2.33
2011	A+	Palm Beach	149	16	39	1	9	262	341	349	690	11	89	1.06	0	1	26	87	4.42

Strong, athletic backstop has failed to live up to expectations. Solid approach at the plate and controls the strike zone well, but average bat speed leaves him with below average power. Moves well defensively and has a plus arm, but has yet to have a breakout. Knee injury limited him to 58 games in '11 and he will likely repeat High-A in '12.

Story, Trevor — 6 — Colorado

EXP MLB DEBUT: 2014 | POTENTIAL: Starting SS | 8D

Bats R Age 19
2011 (1-S) HS (TX)

Pwr	+++	
BAvg	+++	
Spd	+++	
Def	+++	

Year	Lev	Team	AB	R	H	HR	RBI	Avg	OB	Slg	OPS	bb%	ct%	Eye	SB	CS	x/h%	Iso	RC/G
2011	Rk	Casper	179	37	48	6	28	268	361	436	797	13	77	0.63	13	1	33	168	5.59

Athletic, toolsy SS had a solid professional debut. Story can make all of the plays on defense and shows good range and a plus arm. At the plate, he has quick hands, decent bat speed, and surprising pop. There are some concerns about his ability to hit for average, but if his hit tool develops, he has the skills to turn into a legitimate 5-tool player.

Strieby, Ryan — 37 — Detroit

EXP MLB DEBUT: 2012 | POTENTIAL: Starting 1B | 8D

Bats R Age 26
2006 (4) Kentucky

Pwr	+++++	
BAvg	++	
Spd	+	
Def	++	

Year	Lev	Team	AB	R	H	HR	RBI	Avg	OB	Slg	OPS	bb%	ct%	Eye	SB	CS	x/h%	Iso	RC/G
2007	A	West Michigan	443	65	112	16	76	253	346	422	768	12	82	0.81	6	5	37	169	5.19
2008	A+	Lakeland	421	65	117	29	94	278	349	563	912	10	76	0.46	0	1	47	285	6.83
2009	AA	Erie	294	64	89	19	58	303	416	565	981	16	73	0.71	2	0	43	262	8.24
2010	AAA	Toledo	290	29	71	10	49	245	322	400	722	10	71	0.39	1	1	35	155	4.51
2011	AAA	Toledo	487	66	124	19	76	255	336	429	766	11	65	0.35	5	2	38	175	5.37

Tall and powerful hitter with history of injuries. Ended year on positive note after slow start, though led IL in Ks. Uses entire field in approach and recognizes pitches to drive. Works counts and has prolific power when he makes contact. Speed and defense are well below average and may be best served as DH. Has bat to play everyday, but needs to find opportunity.

Susac, Andrew — 2 — San Francisco

EXP MLB DEBUT: 2014 | POTENTIAL: Starting C | 8C

Bats R Age 22
2011 (2) Oregon State

Pwr	+++	
BAvg	+++	
Spd	+++	
Def	++++	

Year	Lev	Team	AB	R	H	HR	RBI	Avg	OB	Slg	OPS	bb%	ct%	Eye	SB	CS	x/h%	Iso	RC/G
2010	NCAA	Oregon State	96	15	25	2	13	260	360	365	725	14	76	0.65	0	1	24	104	4.71
2011	NCAA	Oregon State	134	31	42	5	32	313	429	552	981	17	76	0.84	0	1	43	239	8.36

Was arguably the best collegiate backstop in the '11 draft. Broken wrist in April cost him a month of action. Good athlete and a solid defender with a strong throwing arm. Should be able to stay behind the plate as he progresses. Offensively has moderate power because of high leg kick not all scouts are convinced he will hit for average. If he does, he will move up quickly.

Swanner, Will — 2 — Colorado

EXP MLB DEBUT: 2015 | POTENTIAL: Starting C | 8D

Bats R Age 20
2010 (15) HS (CA)

Pwr	++++	
BAvg	+++	
Spd	++	
Def	++	

Year	Lev	Team	AB	R	H	HR	RBI	Avg	OB	Slg	OPS	bb%	ct%	Eye	SB	CS	x/h%	Iso	RC/G
2010	Rk	Casper	76	14	23	7	13	303	303	632	934	0	57	0.00	0	1	48	329	8.37
2011	Rk	Casper	159	33	42	10	24	264	346	553	900	11	62	0.33	1	2	60	289	7.65

2010 15th rounder looks to be a steal. Swanner is strong and athletic with good bat speed and solid power. Swing can be long at times and pitch recognition needs work, leading to high K rate (60 K), but did draw some walks. Still raw behind the plate, so there is work to do, but there is some nice upside as well.

Swihart, Blake — 2 — Boston

EXP MLB DEBUT: 2015 | POTENTIAL: Starting C | 8D

Bats B Age 20
2011 (1) HS (NM)

Pwr	+++	
BAvg	+++	
Spd	++	
Def	++	

Year	Lev	Team	AB	R	H	HR	RBI	Avg	OB	Slg	OPS	bb%	ct%	Eye	SB	CS	x/h%	Iso	RC/G
2011	Rk	GCL Red Sox	6	0	0	0	0	0	0	0	0	0	67	0.00	0	0			

Mobile and athletic backstop who has chance to become all-around performer. Still relatively raw behind plate, but shows maturity, strength, and marked improvement. Exhibits clean footwork and nice receiving skills, but blocking and release need to be improved. Ultimate power potential in question, but should be able to hit for BA as he understands swing and strike zone.

Szczur, Matt

8 | Chicago (N) | EXP MLB DEBUT: 2014 | POTENTIAL: Starting CF | 8D

Bats R Age 22 — 2010 (5) Villanova — 6.4/60
Pwr ++ | BAvg +++ | Spd ++++ | Def ++

Year	Lev	Team	AB	R	H	HR	RBI	Avg	OB	Slg	OPS	bb%	ct%	Eye	SB	CS	x/h%	Iso	RC/G
2010	Rk	AZL Cubs	2	1	1	0	0	500	667	500	1167	33	100		1	0	0	0	11.77
2010	A-	Boise	73	17	29	0	8	397	443	521	964	8	85	0.55	1	0	31	123	7.43
2010	A	Peoria	26	6	5	0	2	192	276	308	584	10	81	0.60	0	0	40	115	3.02
2011	A	Peoria	274	55	86	5	27	314	363	431	793	7	90	0.75	17	5	24	117	5.30
2011	A+	Daytona	173	20	45	5	19	260	281	410	691	3	88	0.25	7	0	31	150	3.83

Strong, athletic OF had solid full-season debut. Blazing speed but still raw in some aspects. He needs to take better routes in the OF and learn how to use his speed. Szczur has a slashing approach at the plate that limits current power, but does have raw strength. Scouts are divided on his long-term potential, but he is a plus athlete who can create havoc with his plus speed.

Tate, Donavan

8 | San Diego | EXP MLB DEBUT: 2014 | POTENTIAL: Starting CF | 9E

Bats R Age 21 — 2009 (1) HS (GA) — 6.3/60
Pwr +++ | BAvg +++ | Spd ++++ | Def +++

Year	Lev	Team	AB	R	H	HR	RBI	Avg	OB	Slg	OPS	bb%	ct%	Eye	SB	CS	x/h%	Iso	RC/G
2010	Rk	AZL Padres	90	19	20	2	10	222	333	344	678	14	54	0.37	7	1	35	122	4.72
2011	A-	Eugene	127	24	36	0	20	283	401	409	811	16	75	0.78	17	5	33	126	6.27
2011	A	Fort Wayne	19	3	6	0	2	316	435	421	856	17	84	1.33	2	2	33	105	6.82

Legitimate 5-tool guy who can't seem to stay on the field. Missed the first 50 games due to PED violation, then broke his wrist in August. He still has solid across-the-board tools, but has only 2 professional home runs. Defensively he covers tons of ground and has a strong throwing arm. Still very raw and needs to learn how to hit, but the upside is substantial.

Taveras, Oscar

9 | St. Louis | EXP MLB DEBUT: 2014 | POTENTIAL: Starting CF | 9D

Bats L Age 20 — 2008 NDFA D.R.
Pwr +++ | BAvg +++ | Spd +++ | Def ++++

Year	Lev	Team	AB	R	H	HR	RBI	Avg	OB	Slg	OPS	bb%	ct%	Eye	SB	CS	x/h%	Iso	RC/G
2010	Rk	Johnson City	211	39	68	8	43	322	359	526	885	5	81	0.29	8	5	35	204	6.24
2010	Rk	GCL Cardinals	30	1	5	0	2	167	194	200	394	3	83	0.20	1	0	20	33	0.34
2011	A	Quad Cities	308	52	119	8	62	386	444	584	1029	9	83	0.62	1	4	34	198	8.28

Lean, quick, toolsy OF had a breakout season. He has good balance and makes consistent hard contact. He is working on getting more backspin and loft from his swing and the results are encouraging. Solid speed and solid arm allow him to play all three OF positions. Good plate discipline and plus speed give him the potential to hit for average with moderate power.

Taylor, Beau

2 | Oakland | EXP MLB DEBUT: 2014 | POTENTIAL: Backup C | 7D

Bats L Age 22 — 2011 (5) Central Florida
Pwr ++ | BAvg +++ | Spd ++ | Def ++

Year	Lev	Team	AB	R	H	HR	RBI	Avg	OB	Slg	OPS	bb%	ct%	Eye	SB	CS	x/h%	Iso	RC/G
2009	NCAA	Central Florida	164	28	55	4	23	335	374	500	874	6	85	0.42	0	1	35	165	6.11
2010	NCAA	Central Florida	198	45	70	7	35	354	421	561	981	10	84	0.74	1	1	36	207	7.69
2011	NCAA	Central Florida	231	51	75	5	47	325	386	455	840	9	88	0.85	0	3	24	130	5.93
2011	A-	Vermont	18	1	2	0	1	111	111	111	222	0	78	0.00	0	0			
2011	A	Burlington	147	16	43	0	17	293	370	367	737	11	77	0.53	1	3	21	75	4.89

Short and powerful catcher who could advance rapidly on basis of solid defense and polished hitting skills. Doesn't project to much power despite strength, but knows strike zone and swings with level swing path. Makes contact and can use entire field. Possesses solid, accurate arm, but agility and speed are fringe-average at best.

Taylor, Michael

78 | Oakland | EXP MLB DEBUT: 2011 | POTENTIAL: Starting OF | 8C

Bats R Age 26 — 2007 (5) Stanford
Pwr ++++ | BAvg ++ | Spd +++ | Def +++

Year	Lev	Team	AB	R	H	HR	RBI	Avg	OB	Slg	OPS	bb%	ct%	Eye	SB	CS	x/h%	Iso	RC/G
2009	AA	Reading	318	59	106	15	65	333	399	569	969	10	84	0.69	18	4	39	236	7.45
2009	AAA	Lehigh Valley	110	15	31	5	19	282	358	491	849	11	83	0.68	3	1	39	209	6.04
2010	AAA	Sacramento	464	79	126	6	78	272	344	392	736	10	80	0.55	16	5	30	121	4.77
2011	AAA	Sacramento	349	51	95	16	64	272	357	456	813	12	77	0.58	14	5	34	183	5.65
2011	MLB	Oakland	30	4	6	1	1	200	314	300	614	14	63	0.45	0	0	17	100	3.04

Strong and athletic outfielder regained lost power from '10 and bat speed returned. Has potential to be double-double (HR/SB) player who draws walks with patient approach. BA projects to be low unless he shortens swing and uses whole field. Doesn't range well, though arm strength is asset in corner or CF. Exhibits plus athleticism for size.

Tejeda, Isaias

2 | New York (A) | EXP MLB DEBUT: 2015 | POTENTIAL: Starting C | 8E

Bats R Age 20 — 2009 FA (DR)
Pwr +++ | BAvg +++ | Spd ++ | Def +++

Year	Lev	Team	AB	R	H	HR	RBI	Avg	OB	Slg	OPS	bb%	ct%	Eye	SB	CS	x/h%	Iso	RC/G
2011	Rk	GCL Yankees	148	34	49	6	27	331	377	568	945	7	86	0.55	5	3	41	236	6.99
2011	A-	Staten Island	3	1	1	0	0	333	333	333	667	0	100		0	0	0	0	3.67

Patient and natural hitter who enjoyed solid season on both sides of ball. Uses whole field in professional approach and swings with quickness and authority to produce power. Lacks upside of other catchers in org, but exhibits good glove and catch-and-throw skills. Can be overly aggressive with stick and should develop pitch recognition in time.

Tejeda, Oscar

4 | Boston | EXP MLB DEBUT: 2012 | POTENTIAL: Utility player | 7C

Bats R Age 22 — 2006 FA (DR)
Pwr +++ | BAvg ++ | Spd +++ | Def ++++

Year	Lev	Team	AB	R	H	HR	RBI	Avg	OB	Slg	OPS	bb%	ct%	Eye	SB	CS	x/h%	Iso	RC/G
2007	A-	Lowell	94	14	28	0	12	298	340	394	734	6	72	0.23	4	1	25	96	4.68
2008	A	Greenville	372	44	97	4	38	261	298	347	645	5	80	0.26	11	5	24	86	3.32
2009	A	Greenville	370	50	95	3	50	257	313	332	645	8	76	0.34	3	5	20	76	3.42
2010	A+	Salem	508	76	156	11	69	307	348	455	803	6	81	0.33	17	7	31	148	5.31
2011	AA	Portland	457	50	114	5	41	249	294	339	633	6	78	0.29	13	4	26	90	3.21

Lean, but strong infielder with consistent and dependable defensive skills. Owns good range, hands, and arm strength to play any infield position, though org prefers at 2B. Bat control has regressed in attempt to realize power potential and BA has suffered. Lengthens swing frequently, but makes hard contact when bat put to ball. Has strong wrists and swings hard.

Tekotte, Blake

8 | San Diego | EXP MLB DEBUT: 2011 | POTENTIAL: Platoon CF/LF | 7B

Bats L Age 25 — 2008 (3) Miami-FL — 4.10
Pwr ++ | BAvg +++ | Spd ++++ | Def +++

Year	Lev	Team	AB	R	H	HR	RBI	Avg	OB	Slg	OPS	bb%	ct%	Eye	SB	CS	x/h%	Iso	RC/G
2009	A	Fort Wayne	530	83	137	13	56	258	343	396	739	11	82	0.70	30	12	31	138	4.82
2010	A+	Lake Elsinore	203	41	63	8	27	310	414	522	936	15	77	0.78	22	8	41	212	7.57
2010	AA	San Antonio	268	44	67	10	37	250	316	444	760	9	76	0.41	6	9	37	194	4.93
2011	AA	San Antonio	414	77	118	19	67	285	385	498	882	14	74	0.62	36	12	41	213	6.82
2011	MLB	San Diego	34	1	6	0	1	176	263	265	528	11	38	0.19	2	1	33	88	3.88

Athletic OF with nice of speed and the ability to use it. Uses the whole field and makes solid contact. Had another solid season and made his MLB debut. Showed improved power, but likely projects more as a 4th OF. Possesses outstanding range and makes-up for below average arm strength with accuracy and getting to the ball quickly.

Telis, Tomas

2 | Texas | EXP MLB DEBUT: 2014 | POTENTIAL: Starting C | 7C

Bats B Age 21 — 2007 FA (Venezuela)
Pwr ++ | BAvg +++ | Spd +++ | Def ++

Year	Lev	Team	AB	R	H	HR	RBI	Avg	OB	Slg	OPS	bb%	ct%	Eye	SB	CS	x/h%	Iso	RC/G
2009	Rk	AZL Rangers	183	30	59	2	28	322	337	470	807	2	92	0.27	8	1	31	148	5.21
2009	A-	Spokane	20	4	8	2	2	400	400	750	1150	0	80	0.00	0	0	38	350	8.79
2010	Rk	AZL Rangers	144	22	47	2	35	326	353	431	784	4	89	0.38	4	1	21	104	4.96
2011	A	Hickory	461	67	137	11	69	297	324	430	753	4	92	0.51	12	6	28	132	4.65

Short and stocky backstop who is sleeper is system. Produces hard line drives to gaps and rarely strikes out due to extreme contact approach. Doesn't draw many walks and lacks true offensive upside, but should hit for moderate BA. Average arm accentuated by quick release, though receiving and blocking could be improved.

Terdoslavich, Joe

3 | Atlanta | EXP MLB DEBUT: 2014 | POTENTIAL: Starting 1B | 8D

Bats B Age 23 — 2010 (6) Long Beach State
Pwr ++++ | BAvg +++ | Spd + | Def ++

Year	Lev	Team	AB	R	H	HR	RBI	Avg	OB	Slg	OPS	bb%	ct%	Eye	SB	CS	x/h%	Iso	RC/G
2008	NCAA	Miami	123	22	36	5	25	293	365	472	837	10	80	0.58	2	0	33	179	5.88
2010	NCAA	Long Beach St	224	34	73	7	46	326	379	491	870	8	84	0.53	3	6	29	165	6.16
2010	Rk	Danville	189	27	56	2	24	296	348	402	750	7	86	0.56	3	3	25	106	4.82
2010	A	Rome	79	7	25	0	10	316	357	430	788	6	77	0.28	0	0	36	114	5.32
2011	A+	Lynchburg	483	72	138	20	82	286	342	526	867	8	78	0.38	2	0	54	240	6.27

Short, but athletic switch-hitting 1B had a breakout season. Power spike came on quickly but is legit. Has a simple, compact swing and drives the ball with surprising power. Moderate plate discpline will likely keep his average below .300. Solid defender at 1B. Defense is average at best, this blue-collar slugger works hard and has some nice upside.

Thompson, Trayce

8 | Chicago (A) | EXP MLB DEBUT: 2014 | POTENTIAL: Starting CF | 9E

Bats R Age 21 — 2009 (2) HS (CA)
Pwr ++++ | BAvg ++ | Spd +++ | Def +++

Year	Lev	Team	AB	R	H	HR	RBI	Avg	OB	Slg	OPS	bb%	ct%	Eye	SB	CS	x/h%	Iso	RC/G
2009	Rk	Great Falls	21	2	5	0	0	238	333	238	571	13	62	0.38	1	0	0	0	2.54
2009	Rk	Bristol	85	8	16	0	10	188	225	247	472	4	61	0.12	2	0	25	59	0.91
2010	A	Kannapolis	210	28	48	8	31	229	299	433	732	9	67	0.30	6	4	50	205	4.78
2011	A	Kannapolis	519	95	125	24	87	241	320	457	776	10	67	0.35	8	4	50	216	5.42

Tall and athletic outfielder turning raw tools into production and finished 3rd in SAL in HR. Repeated Low-A and also led league in Ks. Improved approach led to more walks, but long swing and struggles with breaking balls don't provide much BA hope. Average speed enhanced by good instincts and smarts on base. Owns plus CF range with average arm strength.

Thon, Dickie — 6 — Toronto

Bats R Age 20 — 2010 (5) HS (PR)

Pwr ++ | BAvg +++ | Spd +++ | Def +++

EXP MLB DEBUT: 2015 — POTENTIAL: Starting SS — 8E

Year	Lev	Team	AB	R	H	HR	RBI	Avg	OB	Slg	OPS	bb%	ct%	Eye	SB	CS	x/h%	Iso	RC/G
2011	Rk	GCL Blue Jays	121	23	27	3	15	223	347	322	670	16	64	0.52	6	2	22	99	4.07

Tall and athletic infielder who struggled in first taste of pro ball, but offers interesting attributes that project well. Could either become top-of-order hitter with keen eye or middle-of-order guy with doubles power. Swing can get long and needs to drive ball better, but has strength and bat speed. Footwork is excellent while strong arm enhances defensive package.

Tilson, Charlie — 8 — St. Louis

Bats L Age 19 — 2011 (2) HS (IL)

Pwr ++ | BAvg +++ | Spd +++ | Def +++

EXP MLB DEBUT: 2015 — POTENTIAL: Starting CF — 7C

Year	Lev	Team	AB	R	H	HR	RBI	Avg	OB	Slg	OPS	bb%	ct%	Eye	SB	CS	x/h%	Iso	RC/G
2011	Rk	Johnson City	15	2	7	0	4	467	500	600	1100	6	93	1.00	0	0	29	133	8.69
2011	Rk	GCL Cardinals	12	2	2	0	1	167	286	167	452	14	75	0.67	1	0	0	0	1.08

Short, athletic, high-energy OF has a smooth compact stroke and is willing to drive the ball the opposite way. He has gap power, above-average speed, and good plate discipline. Projects as a solid CF with some speed and good OB ability.

Toney, D'Andre — 78 — Kansas City

Bats R Age 20 — 2011 (14) Gulf Coast CC

Pwr +++ | BAvg +++ | Spd ++++ | Def ++

EXP MLB DEBUT: 2015 — POTENTIAL: Starting OF — 8D

Year	Lev	Team	AB	R	H	HR	RBI	Avg	OB	Slg	OPS	bb%	ct%	Eye	SB	CS	x/h%	Iso	RC/G
2011	Rk	AZL Royals	150	32	51	5	29	340	396	587	983	9	81	0.50	7	11	43	247	7.74

Short and athletic outfielder who tore up Rookie ball after being ignored in draft. Presents good tools, including average power potential and plus speed. Doesn't look part of slugger with short frame, but has above average bat speed and good batting eye. Instincts are a little short on base and poor range, jumps, and routes will likely relegate him to LF.

Torreyes, Ronald — 4 — Chicago (N)

Bats R Age 19 — 2010 NDFA Venz.

Pwr ++ | BAvg ++++ | Spd +++ | Def +++

EXP MLB DEBUT: 2014 — POTENTIAL: Starting 2B — 7B

Year	Lev	Team	AB	R	H	HR	RBI	Avg	OB	Slg	OPS	bb%	ct%	Eye	SB	CS	x/h%	Iso	RC/G
2010	Rk	AZL Reds	83	13	29	1	11	349	357	494	851	1	94	0.20	2	2	31	145	5.60
2010	A	Dayton	25	3	6	0	2	240	240	400	640	0	88	0.00	0	0	50	160	3.34
2011	A	Dayton	278	53	99	3	41	356	387	457	844	5	93	0.74	12	7	17	101	5.74

Short, speedy 2B prospect was one of the better prospects in the MWL. Similar in size and profile to the Astros Jose Altuve. Listed at 5'9" he is probably more like 5'7" 140 lbs. He has surprising pop, solid strike zone judgment, and a bit of speed. Range and arm strength limit him to 2B. An interesting player, but his upside is limited by size.

Townsend, Tyler — 3 — Baltimore

Bats L Age 24 — 2009 (3) Florida Int'l

Pwr ++++ | BAvg +++ | Spd + | Def ++

EXP MLB DEBUT: 2013 — POTENTIAL: Starting 1B — 8D

Year	Lev	Team	AB	R	H	HR	RBI	Avg	OB	Slg	OPS	bb%	ct%	Eye	SB	CS	x/h%	Iso	RC/G
2010	Rk	GCL Orioles	13	3	5	0	5	385	429	692	1121	7	85	0.50	0	0	80	308	9.57
2010	A	Delmarva	117	16	40	3	26	342	389	556	944	7	85	0.50	0	1	43	214	7.12
2010	A+	Frederick	67	6	19	3	14	284	377	552	929	13	78	0.67	1	0	53	269	7.38
2011	Rk	GCL Orioles	17	3	4	1	8	235	350	529	879	15	76	0.75	0	0	75	294	6.76
2011	A+	Frederick	252	43	80	13	50	317	346	583	929	4	75	0.17	2	2	49	266	6.93

Strong and smart hitter with pure lefty stroke and strength in wrists and arms. Hits for BA due to acute strike zone knowledge and clean, level swing. Has ability to jolt balls out of park, but more focused on hitting hard line drives. Doesn't draw many walks despite pitch recognition and plate coverage. Does not run well and lack of agility keeps him at 1B.

Triunfel, Carlos — 46 — Seattle

Bats R Age 22 — 2006 FA (DR)

Pwr +++ | BAvg ++++ | Spd ++ | Def +++

EXP MLB DEBUT: 2012 — POTENTIAL: Starting INF — 8D

Year	Lev	Team	AB	R	H	HR	RBI	Avg	OB	Slg	OPS	bb%	ct%	Eye	SB	CS	x/h%	Iso	RC/G
2009	Rk	AZL Mariners	16	0	4	0	4	250	250	313	563	0	88	0.00	1	0	25	63	2.28
2009	AA	W. Tennessee	26	2	6	0	4	231	259	269	528	4	92	0.50	0	0	17	38	2.31
2010	AA	W. Tennessee	470	51	121	7	42	257	277	332	609	3	89	0.24	2	8	17	74	2.90
2011	AA	Jackson	395	45	111	6	35	281	324	392	716	6	82	0.35	5	7	27	111	4.26
2011	AAA	Tacoma	111	7	31	0	10	279	292	351	643	2	85	0.12	1	0	23	72	3.24

Strong and compact infielder who had productive season with bat and glove. Hands and arm are assets in field, though lacks fluid actions and overall athleticism. Quick bat allows him to make consistent, hard contact and should be able to hit for high BA due to natural swing and strength. Power potential still remains, but may not develop without more disciplined eye.

Trout, Mike — 8 — Los Angeles (A)

Bats R Age 20 — 2009 (1) HS (NJ)

Pwr +++ | BAvg ++++ | Spd ++++ | Def ++++

EXP MLB DEBUT: 2011 — POTENTIAL: Starting CF — 9A

Year	Lev	Team	AB	R	H	HR	RBI	Avg	OB	Slg	OPS	bb%	ct%	Eye	SB	CS	x/h%	Iso	RC/G
2009	A	Cedar Rapids	15	1	4	0	0	267	421	267	688	21	60	0.67	0	0	0	0	4.74
2010	A	Cedar Rapids	312	76	113	6	39	362	444	526	970	13	83	0.88	45	9	28	163	7.82
2010	A+	Rancho Cucamg	196	30	60	4	19	306	390	434	824	12	83	0.82	11	6	25	128	5.93
2011	AA	Arkansas	353	82	115	11	38	326	402	544	946	11	78	0.59	33	10	37	218	7.52
2011	MLB	Los Angeles (A)	123	20	27	5	16	220	273	390	663	7	76	0.30	4	0	41	171	3.49

Athletic and instinctual outfielder with ability to impact game on all levels. Saw quality action in majors and held his own. Led TL in BA and projects to high BA with good power and plus-plus speed. Can be dynamic defender with plus range and improved arm strength. Adept in all phases of game, including situational hitting. Should be perennial All-Star.

Valaika, Chris — 4 — Cincinnati

Bats R Age 26 — 2006 (3) UCSB

Pwr ++++ | BAvg +++ | Spd ++ (4.40) | Def +

EXP MLB DEBUT: 2009 — POTENTIAL: Starting 3B/2B — 7C

Year	Lev	Team	AB	R	H	HR	RBI	Avg	OB	Slg	OPS	bb%	ct%	Eye	SB	CS	x/h%	Iso	RC/G
2009	AAA	Louisville	366	32	86	6	36	235	267	344	611	4	79	0.21	1	0	31	109	2.85
2010	AAA	Louisville	424	49	129	4	53	304	334	408	742	4	83	0.26	3	3	26	104	4.51
2010	MLB	Cincinnati	38	3	10	1	2	263	282	368	650	3	76	0.11	0	0	20	105	3.12
2011	AAA	Louisville	417	39	109	7	37	261	297	355	652	5	84	0.32	1	0	23	94	3.42
2011	MLB	Cincinnati	25	3	7	0	0	280	333	400	733	7	88	0.67	0	0	29	120	4.78

Valaika is a strong, athletic hitter with solid bat speed. He put up decent numbers at Triple-A and saw limited action in the majors. He can be overly aggressive at the plate and his power has not developed. He has a stocky build that limits his range, but has quick hands and arm strength. The move to 2B now looks permanent, but he is stuck behind Brandon Phillips for now.

Valdespin, Jordany — 6 — New York (N)

Bats L Age 24 — 2007 NDFA D.R.

Pwr ++++ | BAvg ++ | Spd +++ | Def ++

EXP MLB DEBUT: 2012 — POTENTIAL: Starting 2B — 9E

Year	Lev	Team	AB	R	H	HR	RBI	Avg	OB	Slg	OPS	bb%	ct%	Eye	SB	CS	x/h%	Iso	RC/G
2009	A	Savannah	152	30	49	3	18	322	368	480	848	7	79	0.34	7	2	31	158	5.99
2010	A+	St. Lucie	270	40	78	6	33	289	309	437	746	3	83	0.18	13	10	32	148	4.44
2010	AA	Binghamton	112	8	26	0	8	232	246	304	549	2	79	0.09	4	2	31	71	2.04
2011	AA	Binghamton	404	62	120	15	51	297	332	483	814	5	83	0.31	33	14	35	186	5.31
2011	AAA	Buffalo	107	7	30	2	9	280	306	411	718	4	77	0.16	4	4	33	131	4.15

Lean, strong, and athletic 2B. Plays an aggressive brand of baseball with a firery temper. Aggressive approach at the plate results in good power, but below average plate discipline. Combines power with plus speed for an exciting package from the left side. He has good tools on defense, but is inconsistent and has not always had the best attitude.

Valle, Sebastian — 2 — Philadelphia

Bats R Age 22 — 2006 NDFA Mexico

Pwr +++ | BAvg ++++ | Spd + | Def +++

EXP MLB DEBUT: 2013 — POTENTIAL: Starting CA — 8D

Year	Lev	Team	AB	R	H	HR	RBI	Avg	OB	Slg	OPS	bb%	ct%	Eye	SB	CS	x/h%	Iso	RC/G
2008	Rk	GCL Phillies	167	27	47	2	18	281	330	407	737	7	81	0.39	0	0	36	126	4.61
2009	A-	Williamsport	192	25	59	6	40	307	342	531	873	5	79	0.24	0	0	44	224	6.21
2009	A	Lakewood	157	16	35	1	15	223	295	331	626	9	76	0.43	1	2	40	108	3.35
2010	A	Lakewood	447	51	114	16	74	255	297	430	727	6	77	0.27	3	2	39	174	4.31
2011	A+	Clearwater	348	34	99	5	40	284	310	394	704	4	76	0.15	0	0	26	109	3.98

A strong, aggressive backstop, Valle continues to improve on both sides of the ball. Defensively he is strong with an accurate throwing arm and moves well. Offensively he has good bat speed and raw power. His power production was well down in '11, but the FSL can be a tough. He needs better plate discipline, but has the tools to become one of the better catchers in the NL.

Van Slyke, Scott — 3 — Los Angeles (N)

Bats R Age 25 — 2005 (14) HS (MO)

Pwr +++ | BAvg +++ | Spd ++ | Def ++

EXP MLB DEBUT: 2012 — POTENTIAL: Starting 1B — 7C

Year	Lev	Team	AB	R	H	HR	RBI	Avg	OB	Slg	OPS	bb%	ct%	Eye	SB	CS	x/h%	Iso	RC/G
2009	AAA	Albuquerque	6	1	1	0	0	167	375	167	542	25	83	2.00	0	0	0	0	3.11
2010	A+	Inland Empire	189	34	58	9	35	307	364	534	898	8	79	0.44	3	1	40	228	6.57
2010	AA	Chattanooga	217	28	51	4	29	235	294	350	644	8	83	0.49	4	2	27	115	3.50
2010	AAA	Albuquerque	38	5	11	1	5	289	289	474	763	0	82	0.00	0	0	45	184	4.49
2011	AA	Chattanooga	457	81	159	20	92	348	429	595	1024	12	78	0.65	6	5	43	247	8.55

Son of former major leaguer Andy Van Slyke had a nice breakout in '11. Worked to shorten swing with good results. Moderate plate discipline suggests some ability to hit. Not a liability on defense. Potential opening at 1B gives him a window, but will need to seize it quickly. RH/1B only players are a dime a dozen, so power will need to be plus and might fall short.

Vasquez, Danry

9 | **Detroit** | EXP MLB DEBUT: 2015 | POTENTIAL: Starting OF | **9E**

Bats L Age 18
2010 FA (Venezuela)
Pwr +++
BAvg +++
Spd ++
Def +++

Year	Lev	Team	AB	R	H	HR	RBI	Avg	OB	Slg	OPS	bb%	ct%	Eye	SB	CS	x/h%	Iso	RC/G
2011	Rk	GCL Tigers	206	25	56	2	30	272	296	350	645	3	83	0.21	3	2	20	78	3.26

Tall and natural-hitting outfielder who showcased plentiful tools despite mediocre performance in first stint in U.S. Oozes athleticism in lean frame and smashes line drives to gaps with clean swing mechanics. Will need to add strength to physique to realize plus power potential. Fringy speed plays up due to baserunning and is a fine OF despite limited arm strength.

Vaughn, Cory

7 | **New York (N)** | EXP MLB DEBUT: 2013 | POTENTIAL: Starting RF/LF | **8D**

Bats R Age 23
2010 (4) San Diego State
Pwr ++++
BAvg +++
Spd +++
Def +++

Year	Lev	Team	AB	R	H	HR	RBI	Avg	OB	Slg	OPS	bb%	ct%	Eye	SB	CS	x/h%	Iso	RC/G
2009	NCAA	San Diego St.	235	54	77	10	51	328	392	549	941	10	74	0.40	15	4	36	221	7.46
2010	NCAA	San Diego St.	188	42	71	9	55	378	440	606	1047	10	71	0.38	15	1	34	229	9.09
2010	A-	Brooklyn	264	45	81	14	56	307	386	557	943	11	76	0.54	12	5	41	250	7.41
2011	A	Savannah	245	33	70	4	30	286	377	408	785	13	74	0.56	8	5	29	122	5.59
2011	A+	St. Lucie	210	29	46	9	29	219	296	395	691	10	75	0.43	2	3	39	176	3.99

Strong, powerful OF is the son of Greg Vaughn. Has plus power, but struggles with pitch recognition and making consistent contact. He is athletic, but also fairly stiff at the plate and doesn't have a fluid swing. He has good speed and defensively covers ground well with a strong arm. Remains raw and needs to refine his approach at the plate.

Vazquez, Christian

2 | **Boston** | EXP MLB DEBUT: 2014 | POTENTIAL: Backup C | **6B**

Bats R Age 21
2008 (9) HS (PR)
Pwr +++
BAvg ++
Spd ++
Def +++

Year	Lev	Team	AB	R	H	HR	RBI	Avg	OB	Slg	OPS	bb%	ct%	Eye	SB	CS	x/h%	Iso	RC/G
2008	Rk	GCL Red Sox	58	7	11	0	5	190	266	207	473	9	71	0.35	0	0	9	17	1.06
2009	Rk	GCL Red Sox	36	5	10	0	7	278	350	417	767	10	81	0.57	0	0	50	139	5.31
2009	A-	Lowell	65	4	8	2	9	123	250	246	496	14	75	0.69	0	0	50	123	1.58
2010	A	Greenville	270	34	71	3	32	263	321	337	658	8	77	0.37	3	1	20	74	3.58
2011	A	Greenville	392	71	111	18	84	283	354	505	859	10	79	0.51	1	1	43	222	6.19

Short and solidly-built catcher who repeated Low-A and had breakout season. HR and 2B output increased significantly while BA also improved. Has learned to read breaking balls and make adjustments within an at bat. Still doesn't project well with bat as bat speed is fringe-average. Slow release mutes arm strength, but is athletic and agile behind plate.

Vettleson, Drew

9 | **Tampa Bay** | EXP MLB DEBUT: 2014 | POTENTIAL: Starting OF | **9D**

Bats L Age 20
2010 (1-S) HS (WA)
Pwr +++
BAvg +++
Spd +++
Def +++

Year	Lev	Team	AB	R	H	HR	RBI	Avg	OB	Slg	OPS	bb%	ct%	Eye	SB	CS	x/h%	Iso	RC/G
2011	Rk	Princeton	234	33	66	7	40	282	356	462	818	10	77	0.51	20	6	36	179	5.79

Thin and athletic outfielder who enjoyed solid season with bat thanks to better bat control and willingness to use the entire field with quick, line-drive stroke. Should eventually produce at least average pop once he adds strength to lean frame. Steals bases, but more on instincts than speed. Average defender at best with suitable arm and range for RF.

Villanueva, Christian

5 | **Texas** | EXP MLB DEBUT: 2014 | POTENTIAL: Starting 3B | **8D**

Bats R Age 21
2009 FA (Mexico)
Pwr +++
BAvg +++
Spd +++
Def ++++

Year	Lev	Team	AB	R	H	HR	RBI	Avg	OB	Slg	OPS	bb%	ct%	Eye	SB	CS	x/h%	Iso	RC/G
2010	Rk	AZL Rangers	188	30	59	2	35	314	358	431	789	6	78	0.31	6	2	29	117	5.26
2011	A	Hickory	467	78	130	17	84	278	331	465	796	7	82	0.43	32	6	38	186	5.25

Short and lean infielder who can be enigma due to inconsistency, but has good overall bat and glove. Offensive output better than tools suggest, though has strong, clean swing with ample gap power. Developing more HR power as he learns to read pitches better. Has average speed, but is a good baserunner and solid defender.

Villar, Jonathan

6 | **Houston** | EXP MLB DEBUT: 2014 | POTENTIAL: Starting SS | **7B**

Bats B Age 21
2008 NDFA D.R.
Pwr ++
BAvg +++
Spd ++++
Def ++++

Year	Lev	Team	AB	R	H	HR	RBI	Avg	OB	Slg	OPS	bb%	ct%	Eye	SB	CS	x/h%	Iso	RC/G
2009	A-	Williamsport	39	6	9	0	5	231	302	308	610	9	64	0.29	6	0	22	77	3.19
2010	A	Lakewood	371	61	101	2	36	272	320	358	678	7	72	0.25	38	13	24	86	3.88
2010	A+	Lancaster	129	18	29	3	19	225	291	372	663	9	61	0.24	7	2	38	147	4.00
2011	A+	Lancaster	174	26	45	4	26	259	352	414	766	13	68	0.45	20	6	33	155	5.45
2011	AA	Corpus Christi	324	52	75	10	26	231	295	386	680	8	69	0.29	14	6	37	154	3.91

Quick, athletic SS has plus tools, but is still raw. Villar has plus speed and is a plus defender with a strong, accurate arm. He can make all of the plays and is the best defender in the system. Offensively he still has some work to do. He doesn't project to hit for much power and plate discipline is below average. He does draws walks and will get his fair share of stolen bases.

Vinicio, Jose

6 | **Boston** | EXP MLB DEBUT: 2015 | POTENTIAL: Starting SS | **7D**

Bats B Age 18
2009 FA (DR)
Pwr ++
BAvg ++
Spd ++++
Def ++++

Year	Lev	Team	AB	R	H	HR	RBI	Avg	OB	Slg	OPS	bb%	ct%	Eye	SB	CS	x/h%	Iso	RC/G
2010	Rk	GCL Red Sox	158	23	40	1	22	253	285	373	658	4	84	0.27	13	1	28	120	3.59
2011	Rk	GCL Red Sox	179	22	52	2	18	291	317	419	736	4	82	0.21	19	10	27	128	4.43

Short and lean infielder who repeated rookie ball and showed off exciting skills. Plays outstanding defense at SS with smooth, quick actions and soft hands. Gets to balls that others wouldn't by getting good reads off bat. Has strong arm too. Has impressive bat speed for lack of strength, but impatient approach has hindered OBP. Bunts well and likely won't hit for much pop.

Vitek, Kolbrin

5 | **Boston** | EXP MLB DEBUT: 2013 | POTENTIAL: Starting 3B | **8D**

Bats R Age 23
2010 (1) Ball State
Pwr +++
BAvg +++
Spd +++
Def ++

Year	Lev	Team	AB	R	H	HR	RBI	Avg	OB	Slg	OPS	bb%	ct%	Eye	SB	CS	x/h%	Iso	RC/G
2009	NCAA	Ball State	208	57	81	13	67	389	462	736	1197	12	84	0.82	17	9	52	346	10.38
2010	NCAA	Ball State	233	73	84	17	68	361	440	691	1131	12	85	0.92	16	4	48	330	9.46
2010	A-	Lowell	204	30	55	4	30	270	352	422	774	11	70	0.43	13	2	36	152	5.47
2010	A	Greenville	40	7	11	0	3	275	383	400	783	15	68	0.54	4	1	36	125	6.01
2011	A+	Salem	473	78	133	3	43	281	344	372	716	9	78	0.44	12	3	23	91	4.45

Tall and savvy infielder who struggled to hit for power, but has other impressive attributes. Has natural hitting skills and swing mechanics thru line drive approach. Makes hard contact and exhibits mature eye at plate. Has average power potential, but lacks load and trigger in swing. Possesses strong arm, but poor hands and footwork caused very high error totals.

Vitters, Josh

5 | **Chicago (N)** | EXP MLB DEBUT: 2012 | POTENTIAL: Starting 3B | **8D**

Bats R Age 22
2007 (1) HS (CA)
Pwr +++
BAvg +++
Spd ++
Def ++

Year	Lev	Team	AB	R	H	HR	RBI	Avg	OB	Slg	OPS	bb%	ct%	Eye	SB	CS	x/h%	Iso	RC/G
2009	A	Peoria	269	42	85	15	46	316	333	535	869	3	84	0.17	4	0	33	219	5.66
2009	A+	Daytona	189	21	45	3	22	238	258	344	602	3	88	0.22	2	1	27	106	2.84
2010	A+	Daytona	110	16	32	3	13	291	339	445	784	7	80	0.36	4	1	34	155	5.11
2010	AA	Tennessee	206	28	46	7	26	223	269	383	653	6	80	0.32	2	0	41	160	3.40
2011	AA	Tennessee	449	56	127	14	81	283	316	448	764	5	88	0.41	4	10	35	165	4.75

Lean, athletic 3B has yet to have a breakout. Vitters still has potential, but has not shown an ability to adjust. Until he does, his development is stuck in neutral. He can hit anything, but is not selective and doesn't wait for his pitch. Is now only an average defender. Vitters has decent power potential and has the frame to develop more, but the clock is ticking.

Vogelbach, Dan

3 | **Chicago (N)** | EXP MLB DEBUT: 2015 | POTENTIAL: Starting 1B | **8D**

Bats R Age 19
2011 (2) HS (FL)
Pwr ++++
BAvg +++
Spd +
Def ++

Year	Lev	Team	AB	R	H	HR	RBI	Avg	OB	Slg	OPS	bb%	ct%	Eye	SB	CS	x/h%	Iso	RC/G
2011		Did not play																	

Strong, physically mature 1B prospect with advanced power. At 6'0", 250 lbs. he has strength and size, but is a below average runner. At the plate, has a nice LH power stroke and hit 17 HR in 32 games in HS. Below average athleticism and will need to work on conditioning, but a power-hitting LH/1B does have some value.

Vogt, Stephen

237 | **Tampa Bay** | EXP MLB DEBUT: 2012 | POTENTIAL: Utility player | **7D**

Bats L Age 27
2007 (12) Azusa Pacific
Pwr +++
BAvg +++
Spd +
Def ++

Year	Lev	Team	AB	R	H	HR	RBI	Avg	OB	Slg	OPS	bb%	ct%	Eye	SB	CS	x/h%	Iso	RC/G
2008	A	Columbus	392	57	114	6	54	291	367	408	775	11	88	0.98	6	1	27	117	5.33
2009	A+	Charlotte	35	0	6	0	3	171	216	229	445	5	89	0.50	0	1	33	57	1.36
2010	A+	Charlotte	368	56	127	8	47	345	396	511	907	8	88	0.67	3	1	33	166	6.65
2011	AA	Montgomery	386	52	116	13	85	301	351	487	838	7	87	0.59	4	2	34	187	5.76
2011	AAA	Durham	124	15	36	4	20	290	313	516	829	3	77	0.14	0	0	53	226	5.60

Versatile and strong player who has played a variety of position, though more time at C the last two seasons. Good fastball hitter and posted career high in HR and doubles. Makes consistent, hard contact, though swings early in count and doesn't draw many walks. Can produce with bat, but defense is suspect. Not agile enough to be C in big leagues.

Vollmuth, B.A. — 5 — Oakland
EXP MLB DEBUT: 2013 | POTENTIAL: Starting 3B | 8D

Bats R Age 22
2011 (3) Southern Miss
- Pwr ++++
- BAvg ++
- Spd ++
- Def +++

Year	Lev	Team	AB	R	H	HR	RBI	Avg	OB	Slg	OPS	bb%	ct%	Eye	SB	CS	x/h%	Iso	RC/G
2009	NCAA	S. Mississippi	97	16	23	8	28	237	315	515	830	10	70	0.38	1	1	48	278	5.79
2010	NCAA	S. Mississippi	236	72	91	20	76	386	480	729	1209	15	78	0.84	4	2	43	343	10.88
2011	NCAA	S. Mississippi	219	48	66	12	49	301	402	548	950	14	73	0.62	2	0	41	247	7.81
2011	Rk	AZL Athletics	27	3	4	1	2	148	233	259	493	10	78	0.50	0	0	25	111	1.39
2011	A-	Vermont	14	8	7	0	6	500	563	929	1491	13	79	0.67	0	1	71	429	15.26

Tall and strong infielder impressed in short season with multitude of skills. Exhibits good nose for the game and power projects well. Swings with authority early in the count and can hit long balls to all fields. BA could be issue unless he shortens swing and makes more consistent contact. Owns strong arm, but lacks speed and range.

Walding, Mitch — 654 — Philadelphia
EXP MLB DEBUT: 2015 | POTENTIAL: Starting 3B/2B | 7D

Bats L Age 19
2011 (5) HS (CA)
- Pwr +++
- BAvg ++
- Spd ++
- Def ++

Year	Lev	Team	AB	R	H	HR	RBI	Avg	OB	Slg	OPS	bb%	ct%	Eye	SB	CS	x/h%	Iso	RC/G
2011		Did not play																	

Athletic, two-sport star in high school is 6'4", 185 lbs., and probably too big to stick at SS. He projects to have moderate power, so a move to 3B or even 2B is possible. Walding has good bat speed and makes solid contact. He is an average runner with a solid arm and will make his pro debut in '12.

Waldrop, Kyle — 9 — Cincinnati
EXP MLB DEBUT: 2015 | POTENTIAL: Starting OF | 8D

Bats L Age 20
2010 (12) HS (FL)
- Pwr +++
- BAvg +++
- Spd +++
- Def +++

Year	Lev	Team	AB	R	H	HR	RBI	Avg	OB	Slg	OPS	bb%	ct%	Eye	SB	CS	x/h%	Iso	RC/G
2010	Rk	AZL Reds	28	1	6	0	1	214	241	250	491	3	68	0.11	0	0	17	36	1.11
2011	Rk	Billings	278	38	76	5	29	273	299	471	770	3	77	0.15	4	4	47	198	4.96

Waldrop is an athletic OF. Has a smooth LH stroke, makes consistent contact, and has the potential to develop moderate power. Has good speed, plays solid defense, and has a strong throwing arm. Showed solid results in '11. Needs better plate discipline. <ight not stick in CF, but he should have the power needed to play a corner slot.

Walker, Keenyn — 89 — Chicago (A)
EXP MLB DEBUT: 2014 | POTENTIAL: Starting OF | 8D

Bats B Age 21
2011 (1-S) Central AZ JC
- Pwr ++
- BAvg +++
- Spd ++++
- Def +++

Year	Lev	Team	AB	R	H	HR	RBI	Avg	OB	Slg	OPS	bb%	ct%	Eye	SB	CS	x/h%	Iso	RC/G
2011	Rk	Great Falls	60	16	20	0	9	333	403	483	886	10	72	0.41	11	5	40	150	7.16
2011	A	Kannapolis	162	25	37	0	15	228	290	259	549	8	60	0.22	10	4	8	31	2.16

Athletic and speedy hitter with intriguing set of tools. Plus-plus speed among tops in minors, but could slow down with age. Other tools aren't as developed, though have potential. Offers some pop from both sides of plate and gap-hitting could lead to leadoff slot. Strikes out too much for skill set. Plays sufficient CF defense with average arm.

Waring, Brandon — 35 — Baltimore
EXP MLB DEBUT: 2012 | POTENTIAL: Reserve INF | 7D

Bats R Age 26
2007 (7) Wofford
- Pwr ++++
- BAvg ++
- Spd +
- Def ++

Year	Lev	Team	AB	R	H	HR	RBI	Avg	OB	Slg	OPS	bb%	ct%	Eye	SB	CS	x/h%	Iso	RC/G
2008	A	Dayton	441	63	119	20	71	270	335	467	802	9	65	0.28	1	0	38	197	5.85
2009	A+	Frederick	473	70	129	26	90	273	344	520	864	10	74	0.42	5	3	49	247	6.31
2009	AA	Bowie	24	4	7	1	6	292	370	542	912	11	63	0.33	0	0	57	250	8.00
2010	AA	Bowie	472	70	114	22	70	242	326	458	783	11	62	0.33	0	1	49	216	5.83
2011	AA	Bowie	406	60	90	21	59	222	280	443	724	8	69	0.26	0	0	50	222	4.43

Tall and lean infielder who repeated Double-A and regressed in most categories. Continues to hit for power to all fields, but aggressive approach has hindered BA development. Expands strike zone with pull-conscious tendencies, though drastically reduced K rate. Bat speed remains, but will need to hit as feet and glove are not sufficient for full-time role.

Washington, LeVon — 8 — Cleveland
EXP MLB DEBUT: 2014 | POTENTIAL: Starting CF | 8C

Bats L Age 20
2010 (2) Chipola JC
- Pwr ++
- BAvg +++
- Spd ++++
- Def +++

Year	Lev	Team	AB	R	H	HR	RBI	Avg	OB	Slg	OPS	bb%	ct%	Eye	SB	CS	x/h%	Iso	RC/G
2010	Rk	AZL Indians	9	0	4	0	3	444	583	444	1028	25	89	3.00	1	0	0	0	9.38
2011	A	Lake County	298	35	65	4	20	218	329	315	644	14	70	0.55	15	6	26	97	3.67

Ultra-athletic outfielder who missed time early with knee injury. Never got going and struggled in all phases of game. Speed is best tool and could be top SB guy. Shows ability to work counts and has enough bat speed and pitch recognition to hit for BA. Power may take awhile to develop and will need to add strength to wiry frame.

Wates, Austin — 8 — Houston
EXP MLB DEBUT: 2013 | POTENTIAL: Starting CF | 8D

Bats R Age 23
2010 (3) Virginia Tech
- Pwr +
- BAvg +++
- Spd ++++
- Def +++

Year	Lev	Team	AB	R	H	HR	RBI	Avg	OB	Slg	OPS	bb%	ct%	Eye	SB	CS	x/h%	Iso	RC/G
2009	NCAA	Virginia Tech	194	50	77	5	42	397	435	608	1043	6	84	0.41	16	1	36	211	8.23
2010	NCAA	Virginia Tech	225	61	86	8	54	382	467	604	1072	14	87	1.20	18	3	34	222	8.98
2010	Rk	GCL Astros	3	1	0	0	0	0	0	0	0	0	33	0.00	0	0			
2010	A-	Tri City	38	11	12	1	6	316	435	500	935	17	84	1.33	9	0	33	184	7.65
2011	A+	Lancaster	526	85	158	6	75	300	358	413	770	8	84	0.55	26	7	24	112	5.10

Athletic, toolsy OF prospect had a solid season in the CAL. Has plus speed and the potential for moderate power as he matures. Wates has the potential to be a top of the order table setter who can steal bases. Defensively he is a fringy in CF with a below average arm. His value take a huge hit if he has to move off CF.

Watkins, Logan — 4 — Chicago (N)
EXP MLB DEBUT: 2013 | POTENTIAL: Backup 2B | 7D

Bats L Age 22
2008 (21) HS KS
- Pwr ++
- BAvg ++++
- Spd +++
- Def +++

Year	Lev	Team	AB	R	H	HR	RBI	Avg	OB	Slg	OPS	bb%	ct%	Eye	SB	CS	x/h%	Iso	RC/G
2008	Rk	AZL Cubs	80	15	26	0	14	325	460	363	823	20	76	1.05	2	0	12	38	6.49
2009	A-	Boise	279	48	91	0	29	326	386	391	776	9	89	0.87	14	7	18	65	5.28
2010	A	Peoria	440	69	115	1	30	261	347	339	686	12	78	0.60	19	10	21	77	4.25
2011	A+	Daytona	441	70	124	5	45	281	346	404	750	9	78	0.45	21	5	26	122	4.92

Scrappy, no-nonsense player put up solid numbers in the FSL. Watkins has good bat control and puts the ball into play, but a lack of power limits his long-term potential. He is a solid defender with soft hand and good turn at 2B. Profiles as a solild UT guy with nice speed and a good glove.

Weglarz, Nick — 7 — Cleveland
EXP MLB DEBUT: 2012 | POTENTIAL: Starting LF | 8C

Bats L Age 24
2005 (3) HS (Canada)
- Pwr ++++
- BAvg ++
- Spd ++
- Def ++

Year	Lev	Team	AB	R	H	HR	RBI	Avg	OB	Slg	OPS	bb%	ct%	Eye	SB	CS	x/h%	Iso	RC/G
2008	A+	Kinston	375	68	102	10	41	272	388	432	820	16	79	0.91	9	5	34	160	6.10
2009	AA	Akron	339	69	77	16	65	227	367	431	798	18	77	0.96	2	3	45	204	5.78
2010	AA	Akron	137	21	39	7	27	285	384	511	895	14	81	0.85	1	0	44	226	6.79
2010	AAA	Columbus	175	30	50	6	20	286	384	497	881	14	75	0.65	2	2	48	211	6.87
2011	AA	Akron	134	25	24	3	12	179	353	306	659	21	68	0.84	0	1	46	127	4.03

Strong and patient outfielder who started late due to knee surgery. History of injuries has dampened status, but still offers upside. Covers plate with long arms and can hit to any part of ballpark when extended. Disciplined eye and plus pitch recognition give him chance for BA, though can be too passive. No other skills beyond bat as he lacks speed, arm and defense.

Welty, Ronnie — 9 — Baltimore
EXP MLB DEBUT: 2013 | POTENTIAL: Reserve OF | 7D

Bats R Age 24
2008 (20) Chandler-Gilbert
- Pwr +++
- BAvg ++
- Spd +++
- Def +++

Year	Lev	Team	AB	R	H	HR	RBI	Avg	OB	Slg	OPS	bb%	ct%	Eye	SB	CS	x/h%	Iso	RC/G
2008	Rk	Bluefield	207	26	65	3	34	314	343	440	782	4	76	0.18	6	3	28	126	5.04
2009	A	Delmarva	431	60	125	10	67	290	358	425	783	10	72	0.38	13	5	29	135	5.39
2010	A+	Frederick	504	86	142	18	82	282	343	464	807	9	68	0.30	11	4	37	183	5.78
2011	AA	Bowie	391	47	89	13	45	228	317	394	711	12	68	0.41	11	3	40	166	4.49

Tall and athletic outfielder who has advanced one level per year in quiet, consistent career. No tool stands out, but is a natural hitter who can hit for power on occasion. Has bat plane and free-swinging approach that will result in strikeouts, but can show off pop when contact made. Average foot speed and arm strength give him value with glove.

Westlake, Aaron — 3 — Detroit
EXP MLB DEBUT: 2013 | POTENTIAL: Starting 1B | 8D

Bats L Age 23
2011 (3) Vanderbilt
- Pwr ++++
- BAvg +++
- Spd ++
- Def ++

Year	Lev	Team	AB	R	H	HR	RBI	Avg	OB	Slg	OPS	bb%	ct%	Eye	SB	CS	x/h%	Iso	RC/G
2009	NCAA	Vanderbilt	239	53	90	10	57	377	433	565	998	9	82	0.57	5	3	28	188	7.75
2010	NCAA	Vanderbilt	260	66	80	14	61	308	384	538	922	11	82	0.68	6	0	39	231	6.92
2011	NCAA	Vanderbilt	250	59	86	18	56	344	448	640	1088	16	78	0.87	2	5	43	296	9.37
2011	Rk	GCL Tigers	18	2	3	1	4	167	250	389	639	10	67	0.33	0	0	67	222	3.27
2011	A-	Connecticut	106	14	28	2	15	264	328	377	705	9	78	0.43	1	0	25	113	4.23

Big and strong infielder who has chance to become all-around hitter. Possesses good patience at plate, which combined with barrel awareness, provide BA ability. Has power to all fields, though may be more of doubles hitter in big leagues due to level swing path. May be too passive at plate at times. Lacks foot speed and agility, but owns good glove at 1B.

Wheeler, Ryan — 5 — Arizona

EXP MLB DEBUT: 2012 | POTENTIAL: Starting 1B | 8D

Bats L | Age 23 | 2009 (5) Loyola Marymnt

Pwr ++++ | BAvg +++ | Spd ++ | Def +

Year	Lev	Team	AB	R	H	HR	RBI	Avg	OB	Slg	OPS	bb%	ct%	Eye	SB	CS	x/h%	Iso	RC/G
2009	A-	Yakima	234	44	85	5	36	363	450	538	989	14	88	1.32	7	4	33	175	8.03
2009	A	South Bend	29	4	10	1	5	345	441	552	993	15	86	1.25	0	1	30	207	8.11
2010	A+	Visalia	465	62	132	9	57	284	334	404	738	7	79	0.36	3	1	27	120	4.57
2010	AA	Mobile	67	8	17	3	10	254	306	433	738	7	76	0.31	0	0	35	179	4.45
2011	AA	Mobile	480	69	141	16	89	294	354	465	819	9	79	0.44	3	4	34	171	5.63

Big/strong offensive-minded player showed solid progress at the plate. He worked hard to shorten his stroke and can hit breaking balls and uses the whole field. For now it is not clear if he will hit for both power and average. He is stiff and slow on defense with limited range at 3B and a corner OF slot is unlikely. If he can only play 1B that limits his long-term potential, but the bat is good.

Wheeler, Tim — 8 — Colorado

EXP MLB DEBUT: 2013 | POTENTIAL: Starting CF | 8C

Bats L | Age 24 | 2009 (1) Cal State Sac

Pwr +++ | BAvg ++++ | Spd +++ | Def +++

Year	Lev	Team	AB	R	H	HR	RBI	Avg	OB	Slg	OPS	bb%	ct%	Eye	SB	CS	x/h%	Iso	RC/G
2008	NCAA	Sacramento St	218	38	72	3	43	330	365	436	801	5	84	0.35	10	2	22	106	5.22
2009	NCAA	Sacramento St	200	59	77	18	72	385	463	765	1228	13	86	1.04	15	2	48	380	10.50
2009	A-	Tri-City	273	44	70	5	35	256	328	381	709	10	78	0.48	10	4	30	125	4.36
2010	A+	Modesto	510	88	127	12	63	249	328	384	712	11	78	0.53	22	8	31	135	4.42
2011	AA	Tulsa	561	105	161	33	86	287	355	535	890	10	75	0.42	21	12	42	248	6.59

Wiry and athletic OF with speed and developing power. Improved across the board in '11, hitting 33 home runs and 67 extra-base hits. Needs to make more consistent contact (145 whiffs) and improve vs. LHP. Size and moderate speed make it unlikely he will stick in CF, but does have enough power and batting average for a corner slot. Not a slam dunk, but could be very good.

Wilkins, Andy — 3 — Chicago (A)

EXP MLB DEBUT: 2013 | POTENTIAL: Backup 1B | 7C

Bats L | Age 23 | 2010 (5) Arkansas

Pwr +++ | BAvg ++ | Spd + | Def +++

Year	Lev	Team	AB	R	H	HR	RBI	Avg	OB	Slg	OPS	bb%	ct%	Eye	SB	CS	x/h%	Iso	RC/G
2008	NCAA	Arkansas	136	29	45	8	38	331	417	588	1005	13	79	0.69	1	0	42	257	8.16
2009	NCAA	Arkansas	235	53	75	19	58	319	435	638	1073	17	78	0.94	8	1	49	319	9.19
2010	NCAA	Arkansas	235	49	66	15	69	281	394	540	935	16	81	1.00	4	1	45	260	7.33
2010	Rk	Great Falls	218	37	67	6	40	307	398	463	862	13	86	1.06	7	2	31	156	6.44
2011	A+	Winston-Salem	493	72	137	23	89	278	352	485	836	10	82	0.62	2	2	41	207	5.86

Tall and strong infielder who finished 2nd in CAR in HR. Exhibits plenty of strength and raw power with moderate bat speed. Can be too pull-conscious and beaten by quick FB. Long swing results in Ks and low BA and he doesn't run well. Has been a passable defender with good range and agility. Arm strength is an asset.

Williams, Everett — 8 — San Diego

EXP MLB DEBUT: 2013 | POTENTIAL: Starting CF | 8E

Bats L | Age 21 | 2009 (2) HS (TX)

Pwr ++++ | BAvg ++ | Spd ++++ | Def ++++

Year	Lev	Team	AB	R	H	HR	RBI	Avg	OB	Slg	OPS	bb%	ct%	Eye	SB	CS	x/h%	Iso	RC/G
2009	Rk	AZL Padres	18	1	7	0	6	389	421	611	1032	5	61	0.14	2	1	43	222	10.30
2009	A-	Eugene	25	1	5	1	3	200	310	400	710	14	56	0.36	0	0	60	200	5.12
2010	A	Fort Wayne	390	53	95	5	59	244	331	372	703	12	66	0.39	10	5	37	128	4.58
2011	A	Fort Wayne	20	5	6	0	1	300	364	300	664	9	85	0.67	3	0	0	0	3.83

Proto-typical CF prospect who is fast and toolsy. Tore his ACL in May and was limited to 20 AB in '11. Prior to the injury showed plus speed and covered ground well in CF. Moderate power potential though for now it is not game useable. Has the potential to develop into one of the better power/speed prospects in the NL. But will need to prove he is healthy.

Williams, Mason — 8 — New York (A)

EXP MLB DEBUT: 2014 | POTENTIAL: Starting OF | 8C

Bats L | Age 20 | 2010 (4) HS (FL)

Pwr ++ | BAvg ++++ | Spd ++++ | Def ++++

Year	Lev	Team	AB	R	H	HR	RBI	Avg	OB	Slg	OPS	bb%	ct%	Eye	SB	CS	x/h%	Iso	RC/G
2010	Rk	GCL Yankees	18	0	4	0	0	222	263	222	485	5	78	0.25	1	2	0	0	1.24
2011	A-	Staten Island	269	42	94	3	31	349	394	468	863	7	85	0.49	28	12	21	119	6.11

Lean and athletic outfielder who finished 2nd in NYP in BA. Has keen eye at plate which coupled with advanced feel for hitting provide exciting leadoff capabilities. Has above average speed and knows how to run bases. Quick hands produce bat speed, but doesn't project well for power. Routes aren't crisp in CF, but has solid arm strength and plus range.

Wilson, Russell — 8 — Colorado

EXP MLB DEBUT: 2014 | POTENTIAL: Starting CF | 8E

Bats R | Age 23 | 2010 (4) NC State

Pwr +++ | BAvg ++ | Spd ++++ (6.5/60) | Def +++

Year	Lev	Team	AB	R	H	HR	RBI	Avg	OB	Slg	OPS	bb%	ct%	Eye	SB	CS	x/h%	Iso	RC/G
2008	NCAA	North Carolina St	71	9	21	2	8	296	351	437	787	8	80	0.43	6	1	24	141	5.17
2009	NCAA	North Carolina St	72	13	17	0	10	236	329	292	621	12	78	0.63	2	2	18	56	3.41
2010	NCAA	North Carolina St	98	25	30	3	12	306	414	490	904	16	74	0.72	9	1	33	184	7.29
2010	A-	Tri-City	122	18	28	2	11	230	319	377	696	12	70	0.44	4	6	36	148	4.38
2011	A	Asheville	193	40	44	3	15	228	346	342	688	15	58	0.43	15	2	27	114	4.78

Strong, athletic OF has yet to hit as a pro. His status is in limbo for now as the Rockies allowed him to return to college football where he is playing QB for Wisconsin. Long-term prospects are probably better on the gridiron, but we will have to wait and see. Still very raw at the plate.

Witherspoon, Travis — 8 — Los Angeles (A)

EXP MLB DEBUT: 2014 | POTENTIAL: Starting OF | 8D

Bats R | Age 23 | 2009 (12) Spartanburg

Pwr +++ | BAvg +++ | Spd ++++ | Def ++++

Year	Lev	Team	AB	R	H	HR	RBI	Avg	OB	Slg	OPS	bb%	ct%	Eye	SB	CS	x/h%	Iso	RC/G
2009	Rk	Orem	194	37	44	6	26	227	265	397	662	5	69	0.16	10	1	34	170	3.56
2009	Rk	AZL Angels	13	2	3	0	0	231	286	308	593	7	77	0.33	0	0	33	77	2.84
2010	Rk	Orem	288	57	89	10	45	309	362	472	834	8	75	0.33	20	0	27	163	5.84
2011	A	Cedar Rapids	404	60	99	12	42	245	307	394	700	8	75	0.35	44	9	32	149	4.12
2011	A+	Inland Empire	68	15	19	1	10	279	329	382	711	7	79	0.36	2	2	26	103	4.23

Tall and strong outfielder with good upside due to variety of raw tools. Steals bases with plus speed and improved instincts. Learning to recognize pitches and using entire field in approach. Long swing can be exploited and needs to shorten swing in situations. Provides average power, especially against LHP. Potential to be plus CF with range and strong arm.

Wolters, Tony — 46 — Cleveland

EXP MLB DEBUT: 2014 | POTENTIAL: Starting 2B | 7A

Bats L | Age 20 | 2010 (3) HS (CA)

Pwr ++ | BAvg +++ | Spd +++ | Def ++++

Year	Lev	Team	AB	R	H	HR	RBI	Avg	OB	Slg	OPS	bb%	ct%	Eye	SB	CS	x/h%	Iso	RC/G
2010	Rk	AZL Indians	19	2	4	0	3	211	286	211	496	10	74	0.40	2	0	0	0	1.44
2011	A-	Mahoning Vall	267	50	78	1	20	292	364	363	727	10	82	0.61	19	4	18	71	4.68

Short and polished infielder with few weaknesses in package. Tough to pitch to due to disciplined eye and contact-oriented approach. Puts bat to ball easily and offers gap power with level swing path. Proven ability to hit LHP with knack for situational hitting. Range is only fringe-average, but has quick hands and solid defensive instincts.

Wong, Kolten — 4 — St. Louis

EXP MLB DEBUT: 2014 | POTENTIAL: Starting 2B | 8C

Bats L | Age 21 | 2011 (1) University of Hawaii

Pwr ++ | BAvg ++++ | Spd +++ | Def +++

Year	Lev	Team	AB	R	H	HR	RBI	Avg	OB	Slg	OPS	bb%	ct%	Eye	SB	CS	x/h%	Iso	RC/G
2009	NCAA	Hawaii	226	46	77	11	52	341	406	597	1004	10	90	1.09	11	4	44	257	7.80
2010	NCAA	Hawaii	249	57	89	7	40	357	439	534	973	13	92	1.80	19	7	29	177	7.71
2011	NCAA	Hawaii	209	48	79	7	53	378	482	560	1042	17	90	2.10	23	7	27	182	8.77
2011	A	Quad Cities	194	39	65	5	25	335	400	510	910	10	88	0.88	9	5	34	175	6.81

Wong is a short, athletic 2B with a compact stroke and the ability to make consistent contact. He uses the entire field and has enough pop to project to at least an average big league hitter. He has a disciplined eye and is a good situational hitter. Wong is a passable defender with a good arm and average speed. His nice professional debut moves up his time-table.

Wright, Ryan — 4 — Cincinnati

EXP MLB DEBUT: 2014 | POTENTIAL: Starting 2B | 8D

Bats R | Age 22 | 2011 (5) Louisville

Pwr +++ | BAvg ++ | Spd +++ | Def +++

Year	Lev	Team	AB	R	H	HR	RBI	Avg	OB	Slg	OPS	bb%	ct%	Eye	SB	CS	x/h%	Iso	RC/G
2009	NCAA	Louisville	257	43	86	5	66	335	376	471	847	6	89	0.59	12	4	27	136	5.83
2010	NCAA	Louisville	254	61	93	16	80	366	412	638	1050	7	90	0.77	10	1	38	272	8.01
2011	NCAA	Louisville	234	49	81	12	52	346	427	598	1025	12	86	1.03	16	2	38	252	8.24
2011	Rk	Billings	161	28	48	7	32	298	335	522	857	5	83	0.33	6	1	42	224	5.84
2011	Rk	AZL Reds	22	4	7	1	5	318	318	636	955	0	77	0.00	1	2	57	318	7.04

Solid, offensive-minded 2B had an impressive pro debut. Has a solid stroke and puts the ball into play. He has only average speed, but has good instincts on the bases. Plays solid defense with good positioning, soft hands, and a decent arm. Not Brandon Phillips, but you could do worse.

Yelich, Christian — 78 — Florida

EXP MLB DEBUT: 2013 | POTENTIAL: Starting OF | 8C

Bats L | Age 20 | 2010 (1) HS (CA)

Pwr +++ | BAvg +++ | Spd +++ | Def +++

Year	Lev	Team	AB	R	H	HR	RBI	Avg	OB	Slg	OPS	bb%	ct%	Eye	SB	CS	x/h%	Iso	RC/G
2010	Rk	GCL Marlins	24	3	9	0	3	375	423	500	923	8	71	0.29	1	0	22	125	7.51
2010	A	Greensboro	23	2	8	0	2	348	375	435	810	4	74	0.17	0	0	25	87	5.52
2011	A	Greensboro	461	73	144	15	77	312	386	484	869	11	78	0.54	32	5	33	171	6.42

Tall, strong lefty OF is easily the best prospect in the system. Yelich makes consistent contact with lots of line drives and is beginning to tap into raw power. Solid swing plane enables him to hit for average, and he has good speed. Good defender who moves well. If the power continues to develop, he could beat this ranking and will be fun to watch.

Pitchers are classified as Starters (SP) or Relievers (RP).

THROWS: Handedness — right (RH) or left (LH).

AGE: Pitcher's age, as of April 1, 2012.

DRAFTED: The year, round, and school that the pitcher performed at as an amateur if drafted, or the year and country where the player was signed from, if a free agent.

EXP MLB DEBUT: The year a player is expected to debut in the major leagues.

PROJ ROLE: The role that the pitcher is expected to have for the majority of his major league career, not necessarily his greatest upside.

PITCHES: Each pitch that a pitcher throws is graded and designated with a "+", indicating the quality of the pitch, taking into context the pitcher's age and level pitched. Pitches are graded for their velocity, movement, and command. An average pitch will receive three "+" marks. If known, a pitcher's velocity for each pitch is indicated.

FB	fastball
CB	curveball
SP	split-fingered fastball
SL	slider
CU	change-up
CT	cut-fastball
KC	knuckle-curve
KB	knuckle-ball
SC	screwball
SU	slurve

PLAYER STAT LINES: Pitchers receive statistics for the last five teams that they played for (if applicable), including college and the major leagues.

TEAM DESIGNATIONS: Each team that the pitcher performed for during a given year is included.

LEVEL DESIGNATIONS: The level for each team a player performed is included. "AAA" means Triple-A, "AA" means Double-A, "A+" means high Class-A, "A-" means low Class-A and "Rk" means rookie level.

SABERMETRIC CATEGORIES: Descriptions of all the sabermetric categories appear in the glossary.

CAPSULE COMMENTARIES: For each pitcher, a brief analysis of their skills/statistics, and their future potential is provided.

ELIGIBILITY: Eligibility for inclusion is the standard for which Major League Baseball adheres to; 50 innings pitched or 45 days on the 25-man roster, not including the month of September.

POTENTIAL RATINGS: The Potential Ratings are a two-part system in which a player is assigned a number rating based on his upside potential (1-10) and a letter rating based on the probability of reaching that potential (A-E).

Potential

10:	Hall of Famer	5:	MLB reserve
9:	Elite player	4:	Top minor leaguer
8:	Solid regular	3:	Average minor leaguer
7:	Average regular	2:	Minor league reserve
6:	Platoon player	1:	Minor league roster filler

Probability Rating

A: 90% probability of reaching potential
B: 70% probability of reaching potential
C: 50% probability of reaching potential
D: 30% probability of reaching potential
E: 10% probability of reaching potential

FASTBALL: Scouts grade a fastball in terms of both velocity and movement. Movement of a pitch is purely subjective, but one can always watch the hitter to see how he reacts to a pitch or if he swings and misses. Pitchers throw four types of fastballs with varying movement. A two-seam fastball is often referred to as a sinker. A four-seam fastball appears to maintain its plane at high velocities. A cutter can move in different directions and is caused by the pitcher both cutting-off his extension out front and by varying the grip. A split-fingered fastball (forkball) is thrown with the fingers spread apart against the seams and demonstrates violent downward movement. Velocity is often graded on the 20-80 scale and is indicated by the chart below.

Scout Grade	Velocity (mph)
80	96+
70	94-95
60	92-93
50 (avg)	89-91
40	87-88
30	85-86
20	82-84

PITCHER RELEASE TIMES: The speed (in seconds) that a pitcher releases a pitch from the stretch is extremely important in terms of halting the running game and establishing good pitching mechanics. Pitchers are timed from the movement of the front leg until the baseball reaches the catcher's mitt. The phrases "slow to the plate" or "quick to the plate" may often appear in the capsule commentary box.

1.0-1.2	+
1.3-1.4	MLB average
1.5+	-

Abreu, Juan — RP — Houston

EXP MLB DEBUT: 2011 | POTENTIAL: Setup reliever | **8C**

Thrws R Age 27
2003 NDFA D.R.

Velo	Pitch	Grade
94-97	FB	++++
78-80	CB	+++
		++

Year	Lev	Team	W	L	Sv	IP	K	ERA	WHIP	BF/G	OBA	H%	S%	xERA	Ctl	Dom	Cmd	hr/9	BPV
2010	A+	Myrtle Beach	0	0	1	15	15	8.34	1.46	8.1	247	25	47	6.08	4.8	8.9	1.9	3.0	9
2010	AA	Mississippi	4	2	11	44	47	3.05	1.43	4.8	248	33	79	3.57	4.5	9.6	2.1	0.4	96
2011	AAA	Gwinnett	4	2	1	48	68	2.25	1.27	4.8	201	30	88	3.07	5.1	12.8	2.5	0.9	116
2011	AAA	Oklahoma City	1	0	3	9	9	1.96	1.63	5.8	236	32	87	3.56	6.8	8.8	1.3	0.0	88
2011	MLB	Houston	0	0	0	6	12	2.90	1.45	3.8	255	48	88	4.65	4.4	17.4	4.0	1.5	149

Short, athletic reliever with a blazing fastball had a nice breakout in '11 and made his MLB debut. Also features a plus curve and a decent change-up. Control and inconsistent mechanics continue to be problems, but Dom and ability to miss bats are plus. He held his own in the majors and should get a chance to win a spot on the Opening Day roster in '12.

Adam, Jason — SP — Kansas City

EXP MLB DEBUT: 2014 | POTENTIAL: #3 starter | **8D**

Thrws R Age 20
2010 (5) HS (KS)

Velo	Pitch	Grade
88-95	FB	++++
76-81	CB	+++
80-84	CU	++

Year	Lev	Team	W	L	Sv	IP	K	ERA	WHIP	BF/G	OBA	H%	S%	xERA	Ctl	Dom	Cmd	hr/9	BPV
2011	A	Kane County	6	9	0	104	76	4.24	1.14	19.6	243	28	64	3.17	2.2	6.6	3.0	0.8	86

Tall and powerful pitcher who relies on above average FB and potentially plus CB. Has shown continuous improvement since signing; next step is consistency of CU -- his arm speed slows, but has enough separation from FB to be effective in lower levels. Registers Ks with CB, but needs to stay on top of it and trust it more often.

Adams, Austin — SP — Cleveland

EXP MLB DEBUT: 2012 | POTENTIAL: #4 starter | **7C**

Thrws R Age 25
2009 (5) Faulkner

Velo	Pitch	Grade
89-95	FB	+++
81-83	SL	++
80-82	CB	+++
	CU	++

Year	Lev	Team	W	L	Sv	IP	K	ERA	WHIP	BF/G	OBA	H%	S%	xERA	Ctl	Dom	Cmd	hr/9	BPV
2009	A-	Mahoning Vall	3	1	1	37	29	4.86	1.46	9.3	272	32	68	4.55	3.6	7.1	1.9	1.0	54
2010	A	Lake County	2	4	1	53	61	3.56	1.15	16.2	211	27	74	3.14	3.6	10.3	2.9	1.2	100
2010	A+	Kinston	6	1	0	58	51	1.55	1.12	17.6	234	28	92	2.97	2.3	7.9	3.4	0.8	104
2011	AA	Akron	11	10	0	136	131	3.77	1.54	22.8	277	36	75	4.28	4.2	8.7	2.1	0.4	83

Small pitcher with power arm who attacks hitters with hard stuff. He has a compact delivery and quick arm to produce solid FB and hard CB. Uses two breaking balls, but doesn't sequence pitches well and struggles to find the strike zone. Inconsistent FB command forces him to pitch behind in count and makes him hittable. Needs better CU to combat LHH.

Alcantara, Raul — SP — Oakland

EXP MLB DEBUT: 2015 | POTENTIAL: #3 starter | **8D**

Thrws R Age 19
2009 FA (DR)

Velo	Pitch	Grade
88-95	FB	+++
77-80	CB	+++
	CU	++

Year	Lev	Team	W	L	Sv	IP	K	ERA	WHIP	BF/G	OBA	H%	S%	xERA	Ctl	Dom	Cmd	hr/9	BPV
2011	Rk	GCL Red Sox	1	1	0	48	36	0.75	0.60	18.3	145	19	86		1.1	6.8	6.0	0.0	192
2011	A-	Lowell	0	3	0	17	14	6.32	1.81	19.8	341	42	61	5.61	3.2	7.4	2.3	0.0	80

Tall, lean pitcher whose first U.S. season led GCL in ERA. GB specialist who pitches off commandable FB and locates effectively to all strike zone quadrants. Quick, clean arm produces pitch movement, and his CB can be a knockout pitch. CU has potential to be average. He needs to add strength to pitch deep into games.

Alderson, Tim — RP — Pittsburgh

EXP MLB DEBUT: 2012 | POTENTIAL: Reliever | **6C**

Thrws R Age 23
2007 (1-C) HS, (AZ)

Velo	Pitch	Grade
88-92	FB	++++
78-81	CB	++++
80-82	CU	++

Year	Lev	Team	W	L	Sv	IP	K	ERA	WHIP	BF/G	OBA	H%	S%	xERA	Ctl	Dom	Cmd	hr/9	BPV
2009	AA	Connecticut	6	1	0	72	46	3.49	1.25	22.6	272	31	73	3.69	1.7	5.7	3.3	0.6	85
2009	AA	Altoona	3	1	0	38	18	4.71	1.36	22.8	266	28	67	4.21	3.1	4.2	1.4	0.9	28
2010	A+	Bradenton	4	3	0	38	25	7.07	1.57	18.6	304	34	55	5.50	3.1	5.9	1.9	1.2	35
2010	AA	Altoona	7	6	0	89	59	5.65	1.56	21.7	308	35	64	5.38	2.7	6.0	2.2	1.0	45
2011	AA	Altoona	0	4	0	74	57	4.13	1.31	7.3	251	30	69	3.65	3.3	6.9	2.1	0.7	69

Tall, thin hurler has yet to live up to expectations. At one time, this 22nd overall pick had a nice low-90s FB, but his velocity dropped and he was moved to relief; he now looks like a middle reliever. FB is back in the low-90s and he does have a good curve and plus control. He is still young and could make his MLB debut in 2012.

Allie, Stetson — SP — Pittsburgh

EXP MLB DEBUT: 2015 | POTENTIAL: #1 starter | **9E**

Thrws R Age 21
2010 (2) HS, (OH)

Velo	Pitch	Grade
94-98	FB	++++
87-91	SL	++++
	CU	++

Year	Lev	Team	W	L	Sv	IP	K	ERA	WHIP	BF/G	OBA	H%	S%	xERA	Ctl	Dom	Cmd	hr/9	BPV
2011	A-	State College	0	2	0	26	28	6.58	1.88	8.2	214	30	63	4.25	10.0	9.7	1.0	0.3	80

Strong, but raw. His 94-98 FB has good movement, but he struggles with control and walked more than he struck out. Complements the FB with a nasty 87-91 mph slider and a CU that has nice potential. He was moved to relief to try to get him on track, but the results were no better. Too soon to give up.

Ames, Jeff — SP — Tampa Bay

EXP MLB DEBUT: 2014 | POTENTIAL: #3 starter/Closer | **8E**

Thrws R Age 21
2011 (1-S) Lower Columbia JC

Velo	Pitch	Grade
90-96	FB	++++
80-84	SL	+++
	CU	+

Year	Lev	Team	W	L	Sv	IP	K	ERA	WHIP	BF/G	OBA	H%	S%	xERA	Ctl	Dom	Cmd	hr/9	BPV
2011	Rk	Princeton	4	2	1	30	39	7.18	1.56	12.0	320	44	53	5.70	2.1	11.7	5.6	1.2	142

Tall and strong pitcher with pitch mix and ability to start, but he could be better off in the pen, where his extreme arm strength plays up. Peppers the strike zone with lively FB and counters heater with solid-average hard SL. Lots of movement with FB, but hangs SL from time to time. Doesn't change speeds enough and needs to tame max-effort delivery.

Ames, Steve — RP — Los Angeles (N)

EXP MLB DEBUT: 2012 | POTENTIAL: Setup reliever | **7C**

Thrws R Age 24
2009 (17) Gonzaga

Velo	Pitch	Grade
90-93	FB	+++
81-83	SL	+++

Year	Lev	Team	W	L	Sv	IP	K	ERA	WHIP	BF/G	OBA	H%	S%	xERA	Ctl	Dom	Cmd	hr/9	BPV
2009	Rk	Ogden	1	1	7	30	47	2.10	0.87	6.5	191	32	79	1.61	1.8	14.1	7.8	0.6	248
2010	Rk	AZL Dodgers	0	0	0	3	4	0.00	0.67	3.5	191	31	100	0.56	0.0	12.0		0.0	
2010	A	Great Lakes	0	2	16	28	44	2.56	0.85	4.5	209	37	67	1.23	1.0	14.1	14.7	0.0	406
2011	A+	Rancho Cucam	0	0	9	15	28	1.19	0.79	3.6	190	38	91	1.38	1.2	16.7	14.0	0.6	393
2011	AA	Chattanooga	2	2	5	32	41	2.52	1.34	4.8	261	37	85	3.91	3.1	11.5	3.7	0.8	125

Short, athletic reliever from Gonzaga continues to put up impressive numbers, showing the ability to dominate with good control. Ames attacks hitters with a low-90s FB and a plus SL. He should reach LA in '12 and profiles as a solid late-inning reliever.

Anderson, Tyler — SP — Colorado

EXP MLB DEBUT: 2014 | POTENTIAL: #3 starter/reliever | **8D**

Thrws L Age 22
2011 (1) Oregon

Velo	Pitch	Grade
88-92	FB	+++
77-80	SL	+++
74-77	CB	+++
81-83	CU	

Year	Lev	Team	W	L	Sv	IP	K	ERA	WHIP	BF/G	OBA	H%	S%	xERA	Ctl	Dom	Cmd	hr/9	BPV
2009	NCAA	Oregon	2	9	0	82	66	6.26	1.67	24.5	298	35	63	5.47	4.3	7.2	1.7	1.0	45
2010	NCAA	Oregon	7	5	0	102	105	2.99	1.14	23.8	226	28	78	3.12	2.9	9.2	3.2	1.0	103
2011	NCAA	Oregon	8	3	0	107	114	2.35	1.03	27.5	199	28	76	1.74	2.9	9.6	3.3	0.2	136

Polished college lefty complements an 89-92 mph FB with a good SL and CB, and an above-average CU. He has good command of all of his pitches and has some nice deception from his funky delivery. Repeats his delivery well and has clean, consistent mechanics.

Andriese, Matt — SP — San Diego

EXP MLB DEBUT: 2014 | POTENTIAL: #3 starter | **8D**

Thrws R Age 22
2011 (3) UC Riverside

Velo	Pitch	Grade
91-94	FB	++++
	CB	+++
	CU	++

Year	Lev	Team	W	L	Sv	IP	K	ERA	WHIP	BF/G	OBA	H%	S%	xERA	Ctl	Dom	Cmd	hr/9	BPV
2009	NCAA	Cal-Riverside	5	4	0	66	37	3.95	1.29	19.4	259	30	67	3.29	2.7	5.0	1.9	0.3	64
2010	NCAA	Cal-Riverside	5	5	0	103	69	4.97	1.43	29.3	309	36	63	4.46	1.6	6.0	3.8	0.3	99
2011	NCAA	Cal-Riverside	4	5	0	95	74	2.65	1.23	27.5	255	32	76	2.82	2.4	7.0	3.0	0.0	108
2011	A-	Eugene	5	1	0	41	42	1.53	0.95	12.9	200	28	82	1.39	2.2	9.2	4.2	0.0	158

2011 3rd rounder had a nice professional debut. He shows good command of a nice three-pitch mix: a 90-94 mph sinking fastball, a power CB, and a decent CU. At 6'3", 210, he has ideal size, but he needs to improve his stamina. If he can get stronger, he has a bright future.

Araujo, Elvis — SP — Cleveland

EXP MLB DEBUT: 2014 | POTENTIAL: #3 starter | **8C**

Thrws L Age 20
2007 FA (Venezuela)

Velo	Pitch	Grade
90-96	FB	++++
82-85	SL	+++
	CU	++

Year	Lev	Team	W	L	Sv	IP	K	ERA	WHIP	BF/G	OBA	H%	S%	xERA	Ctl	Dom	Cmd	hr/9	BPV
2011	Rk	AZL Indians	9	1	0	63	58	2.86	1.14	19.2	233	30	74	2.57	2.6	8.3	3.2	0.3	117
2011	A-	Mahoning Vall	0	0	0	6	5	8.71	2.90	17.7	386	47	67	9.18	10.2	7.3	0.7	0.0	36

Tall, projectable pitcher who returned after missing two seasons from TJ surgery. First year in the U.S. went well, with command of a three-pitch arsenal. Gets ahead of hitters with a quick FB, then polishes them off with good SL and okay CU. Varies his arm slot at times and can overthrow. Could be quickly promoted due to advanced pitchability.

Archer, Chris — SP — Tampa Bay

EXP MLB DEBUT: 2012 | POTENTIAL: #2 starter | **9E**

Thrws R Age 23
2006 (5) HS (NC)

- 90-97 FB ++++
- 83-88 SL ++++
- CU ++

Year	Lev	Team	W	L	Sv	IP	K	ERA	WHIP	BF/G	OBA	H%	S%	xERA	Ctl	Dom	Cmd	hr/9	BPV
2009	A	Peoria	6	4	0	109	119	2.81	1.32	16.7	202	29	76	2.36	5.4	9.8	1.8	0.0	111
2010	A+	Daytona	7	1	0	72	82	2.87	1.11	18.9	210	29	75	2.38	3.2	10.2	3.2	0.5	126
2010	AA	Tennessee	8	2	0	70	67	1.80	1.24	21.9	196	26	86	2.34	5.0	8.6	1.7	0.3	96
2011	AA	Montgomery	8	7	0	134	118	4.43	1.61	23.8	265	32	73	4.60	5.4	7.9	1.5	0.7	58
2011	AAA	Durham	1	0	0	13	12	0.69	1.31	26.8	231	31	94	2.69	4.2	8.3	2.0	0.0	101

Excellent FB/SL combo generates weak contact and can get swings and misses. Good, natural stuff with plus FB and hard SL. Control problems have been major issue, and the tall, athletic RHP will need to upgrade CU to sustain prospect status. Relies on SL too much and could stand to be more aggressive with FB early in count.

Arguelles, Noel — SP — Kansas City

EXP MLB DEBUT: 2013 | POTENTIAL: #4 starter | **7B**

Thrws L Age 22
2010 FA (Cuba)

- 86-92 FB +++
- 74-78 CB +++
- CU +++

Year	Lev	Team	W	L	Sv	IP	K	ERA	WHIP	BF/G	OBA	H%	S%	xERA	Ctl	Dom	Cmd	hr/9	BPV
2011	A+	Wilmington	4	5	0	104	64	3.20	1.13	19.5	241	28	72	2.87	2.1	5.5	2.7	0.5	81

Command-oriented starter did not pitch in '10, but was deceptively strong upon return. Throws with a live arm, but thrives on command and location more than stuff. Commands plate with average FB and can get hitters to chase CB. Velocity is inconsistent from game to game, and he has been flyball pitcher. Not much upside, but a safe bet to succeed.

Armstrong, Jack — SP — Houston

EXP MLB DEBUT: 2014 | POTENTIAL: #4 starter | **7C**

Thrws R Age 22
2011 (3) Vanderbilt

- 90-93 FB +++
- CB ++
- CU ++

Year	Lev	Team	W	L	Sv	IP	K	ERA	WHIP	BF/G	OBA	H%	S%	xERA	Ctl	Dom	Cmd	hr/9	BPV
2009	NCAA	Vanderbilt	0	0	1	7	8	13.75	2.22	6.1	256	36	31	5.31	11.3	10.0	0.9	0.0	82
2010	NCAA	Vanderbilt	7	4	0	78	50	4.72	1.65	21.8	290	33	72	5.15	4.5	5.8	1.3	0.8	34
2011	NCAA	Vanderbilt	0	1	0	17	17	2.65	1.41	5.5	111	16	79	1.63	9.5	9.0	0.9	0.0	107

A third round pick in '11. At 6'7", 230, he is strong and durable. FB is not overpowering at 90-93, but he pairs it with an average CB and CU. Control struggles caused him to drop despite size and stuff. He will make his professional debut in 2012 and has potential, but lots of work to do.

Arnett, Eric — SP — Milwaukee

EXP MLB DEBUT: 2013 | POTENTIAL: #4 starter | **7C**

Thrws R Age 24
2009 (1) Indiana

- 87-90 FB ++++
- 80-82 SL +++
- CU ++

Year	Lev	Team	W	L	Sv	IP	K	ERA	WHIP	BF/G	OBA	H%	S%	xERA	Ctl	Dom	Cmd	hr/9	BPV
2009	Rk	Helena	0	4	0	34	35	4.47	1.58	10.7	255	34	70	3.93	5.5	9.2	1.7	0.3	86
2010	Rk	AZL Brewers	2	0	1	16	19	7.31	1.69	14.4	307	42	54	5.22	3.9	10.7	2.7	0.6	98
2010	A	Wisconsin	1	9	1	84	60	6.73	1.63	18.7	292	32	60	5.76	4.2	6.4	1.5	1.5	22
2011	Rk	Helena	4	2	0	52	49	5.19	1.40	24.4	304	37	65	5.09	1.6	8.5	5.4	1.2	123
2011	A	Wisconsin	0	4	0	27	25	5.00	1.44	23.0	289	37	63	4.15	2.7	8.3	3.1	0.3	103

Solid bodied SP has yet to live up to expectations (26th pick in '09). When he is going well, he can dominate with a solid FB and hard SL. Velocity on his FB is down from college. Uses his height well to pitch downhill, but his delivery will need to be tweaked. SL can be tough to hit, but is very inconsistent. At 23, his time is now.

Aumont, Phillippe — RP — Philadelphia

EXP MLB DEBUT: 2012 | POTENTIAL: Potential Closer | **8B**

Thrws R Age 23
2007 (1) Gatinueau, QC

- 95-97 FB ++++
- 77-82 CB +++
- 81-84 CU +

Year	Lev	Team	W	L	Sv	IP	K	ERA	WHIP	BF/G	OBA	H%	S%	xERA	Ctl	Dom	Cmd	hr/9	BPV
2009	AA	W.Tennessee	1	4	4	17	24	5.23	1.86	5.4	302	45	71	5.53	5.8	12.6	2.2	0.5	100
2010	A+	Clearwater	2	5	1	72	77	4.49	1.61	20.0	267	35	73	4.62	5.2	9.6	1.8	0.7	75
2010	AA	Reading	1	6	0	49	38	7.50	1.89	21.1	284	34	58	5.58	7.0	7.0	1.0	0.7	39
2011	AA	Reading	1	5	4	31	41	2.32	1.10	4.9	208	31	81	2.39	3.2	11.9	3.7	0.6	146
2011	AAA	Lehigh Valley	1	0	3	22	37	3.24	1.58	5.4	251	45	77	3.56	5.7	15.0	2.6	0.0	150

Aumont struggled in a starting role, then the Phillies moved him back to relief, with good results, after he came over in the Cliff Lee trade. He showed better velocity and improved control. He gets nice sink from his 95-97 FB. He also throws a plus power CB. He did have a three week stint on the DL, so durability is a concern, but he has the stuff to close.

Axelrod, Dylan — SP — Chicago (A)

EXP MLB DEBUT: 2011 | POTENTIAL: #5 starter | **6B**

Thrws R Age 26
2007 (30) UC-Irvine

- 85-92 FB +++
- 79-81 SL +++
- CU +++

Year	Lev	Team	W	L	Sv	IP	K	ERA	WHIP	BF/G	OBA	H%	S%	xERA	Ctl	Dom	Cmd	hr/9	BPV
2010	A+	Winston-Salem	8	3	0	99	84	2.00	1.08	16.8	254	32	81	2.59	1.1	7.6	7.0	0.2	192
2010	AA	Birmingham	0	1	0	10	8	2.70	1.10	19.6	221	28	73	2.05	2.7	7.2	2.7	0.0	110
2011	AA	Birmingham	3	2	0	59	57	3.35	1.12	21.2	238	32	68	2.44	2.1	8.7	4.1	0.2	140
2011	AAA	Charlotte	6	1	0	91	75	2.27	1.04	23.5	224	28	77	2.13	2.1	7.4	3.6	0.2	124
2011	MLB	Chicago Wsox	1	0	0	18	19	2.97	1.48	19.6	260	34	81	3.97	4.5	9.4	2.1	0.5	89

Short and durable, he pitches to contact, but allows few HR despite flyball tendencies. Lacks frontline velocity and a swing-and-miss pitch, but his average stuff plays up due to ability to command and locate. Gets tailing action on FB and throws CU with same arm speed. Low upside, but has versatility in roles.

Balcom-Miller, Chris — SP — Boston

EXP MLB DEBUT: 2013 | POTENTIAL: #5 starter | **7D**

Thrws R Age 23
2009 (6) West Valley College

- 87-92 FB +++
- 79-82 SL ++
- 80-82 CU +++

Year	Lev	Team	W	L	Sv	IP	K	ERA	WHIP	BF/G	OBA	H%	S%	xERA	Ctl	Dom	Cmd	hr/9	BPV
2009	Rk	Casper	4	0	0	57	60	1.58	0.82	18.9	187	25	84	1.38	1.6	9.5	6.0	0.5	186
2010	A	Asheville	6	7	0	108	117	3.33	0.97	21.6	220	31	64	1.92	1.6	9.7	6.2	0.2	191
2010	A	Greenville	1	0	0	6	3	3.00	0.83	21.9	228	22	75	2.91	0.0	4.5		1.5	
2011	A+	Salem	3	1	0	34	37	2.37	1.02	18.8	199	27	79	2.07	2.9	9.7	3.4	0.5	128
2011	AA	Portland	3	6	0	82	75	4.82	1.64	22.9	308	39	69	5.03	3.5	8.2	2.3	0.4	79

Strong sinkerballer with deceptive delivery and ability to keep ball on ground. Dom is high, though should continue to fall in upper levels as he lacks velocity or a true out pitch. FB exhibits lots of sink and balls rarely get into the air. He hasn't been able to throw a below-average breaking ball for strikes. Effort in delivery and poor results against LHH may lead to bullpen.

Bandilla, Bryce — RP — San Francisco

EXP MLB DEBUT: 2014 | POTENTIAL: reliever | **7D**

Thrws L Age 22
2011 (4) Arizona

- 92-96 FB ++++
- SL ++
- CU +++

Year	Lev	Team	W	L	Sv	IP	K	ERA	WHIP	BF/G	OBA	H%	S%	xERA	Ctl	Dom	Cmd	hr/9	BPV
2009	NCAA	Arizona	3	3	0	49	30	6.23	1.69	8.5	269	31	60	4.54	5.9	5.5	0.9	0.4	43
2010	NCAA	Arizona	6	4	1	77	70	4.09	1.61	11.8	293	37	74	4.74	4.0	8.2	2.1	0.5	75
2011	NCAA	Arizona	5	3	1	46	48	3.70	1.52	6.3	207	29	74	3.09	7.0	9.4	1.3	0.2	92

Strong, athletic lefty with a heavy, plus mid-90s FB that tops out at 97. Also has a SL and a solid CU. Both will need to improve before he can have success as a professional. Has yet to make his debut, but when he does it will be in relief. Struggled with control and consistency in college.

Banuelos, Manny — SP — New York (A)

EXP MLB DEBUT: 2012 | POTENTIAL: #2 starter | **8B**

Thrws L Age 21
2008 FA (Mexico)

- 88-95 FB ++++
- 80-82 CB +++
- CU +++

Year	Lev	Team	W	L	Sv	IP	K	ERA	WHIP	BF/G	OBA	H%	S%	xERA	Ctl	Dom	Cmd	hr/9	BPV
2010	Rk	GCL Yankees	0	0	0	5	6	1.80	0.80	9.1	66	11	75		5.4	10.8	2.0	0.0	149
2010	A+	Tampa	0	3	0	44	62	2.24	1.18	17.6	234	37	80	2.55	2.9	12.7	4.4	0.2	171
2010	AA	Trenton	0	1	0	15	17	3.58	1.52	21.9	260	34	81	4.73	4.8	10.1	2.1	1.2	73
2011	AA	Trenton	4	5	0	95	94	3.60	1.54	20.7	260	33	78	4.26	4.9	8.9	1.8	0.7	75
2011	AAA	Scranton/W-B	2	2	0	34	31	4.22	1.61	21.6	272	34	74	4.51	5.0	8.2	1.6	0.5	68

Short, quick-armed pitcher who was inconsistent, but had periods of dominance. Produces pitch movement and high number of GBs. Has clean delivery, which enhances deception, and a plus FB and nice CU. Power CB with bite can get Ks. FB command could be better and has tendency to overthrow and vary release point.

Barbato, John — SP — San Diego

EXP MLB DEBUT: 2015 | POTENTIAL: #4 starter | **7D**

Thrws R Age 19
2010 (6) Miami, FL

- 90-94 FB +++
- SL ++
- CU +

Year	Lev	Team	W	L	Sv	IP	K	ERA	WHIP	BF/G	OBA	H%	S%	xERA	Ctl	Dom	Cmd	hr/9	BPV
2011	A-	Eugene	1	4	0	57	50	4.89	1.46	16.2	244	30	66	3.84	4.9	7.9	1.6	0.6	68

Strong, athletic high school righty held his own in professional debut. He complements a 90-94 FB with a good overhand CB. He needs to develop a solid third pitch and to throw more strikes. He showed some command and easy velocity in high school, but at this point is very raw.

Barnes, Matt — SP — Boston

EXP MLB DEBUT: 2013 | POTENTIAL: #2 starter | **8B**

Thrws R Age 22
2011 (1) Connecticut

- 90-98 FB ++++
- 77-81 CB +++
- 80-83 SL ++
- 79-82 CU +++

Year	Lev	Team	W	L	Sv	IP	K	ERA	WHIP	BF/G	OBA	H%	S%	xERA	Ctl	Dom	Cmd	hr/9	BPV
2009	NCAA	Connecticut	5	3	1	53	55	5.43	1.45	17.4	265	36	60	3.82	3.9	9.3	2.4	0.3	98
2010	NCAA	Connecticut	8	3	0	82	75	3.94	1.27	22.4	254	32	69	3.51	2.7	8.2	3.0	0.7	97
2011	NCAA	Connecticut	11	4	0	116	111	1.70	0.88	26.9	178	24	82	1.27	2.4	8.6	3.6	0.3	137

Projectable, durable righty with potential to become a tough starter. Throws hard with quick arm speed and action, while being able to spin a hard CB that hitters will chase out of the zone, and to change speeds. Lacks deception in delivery and varies release point, but not by design. He might eventually shelve SL, but core remains FB/CB combo.

Barnes, Scott — SP — Cleveland

EXP MLB DEBUT: 2012 | POTENTIAL: #4 starter | **7B**

Thrws L Age 24
2008 (8) St. John's

Velocity	Pitch	Grade
86-91	FB	+++
80-83	SL	+++
75-79	CB	+++
81-84	CU	+++

Year	Lev	Team	W	L	Sv	IP	K	ERA	WHIP	BF/G	OBA	H%	S%	xERA	Ctl	Dom	Cmd	hr/9	BPV
2009	A+	Kinston	0	0	0	12	10	2.21	1.64	18.1	289	35	89	5.03	4.4	7.4	1.7	0.7	54
2009	AA	Akron	2	2	0	31	29	5.77	1.57	22.8	285	32	69	5.98	4.0	8.4	2.1	2.0	31
2010	AA	Akron	6	11	0	138	127	5.22	1.33	22.0	245	30	62	3.85	3.8	8.3	2.2	1.0	72
2011	AA	Akron	1	0	0	11	17	1.64	0.64	19.0	139	26	71		1.6	13.9	8.5	0.0	289
2011	AAA	Columbus	7	4	0	88	90	3.68	1.30	22.6	244	30	76	3.97	3.5	9.2	2.6	1.2	80

Tall, projectable starter with high-quality and dependable pitch mix. Hides the ball in deceptive delivery and fires a sneaky quick FB into the zone. Changes speeds with precision and has two average breaking balls. Lacks upside because FB lacks velocity and can be straight and hittable. Little margin for error, but can be a back-of-rotation option.

Barnese, Nick — SP — Tampa Bay

EXP MLB DEBUT: 2013 | POTENTIAL: #3 starter | **8C**

Thrws R Age 23
2007 (3) HS (CA)

Velocity	Pitch	Grade
87-94	FB	+++
80-83	SL	+++
78-81	CU	+++

Year	Lev	Team	W	L	Sv	IP	K	ERA	WHIP	BF/G	OBA	H%	S%	xERA	Ctl	Dom	Cmd	hr/9	BPV
2007	Rk	Princeton	2	2	0	36	37	3.24	0.94	15.1	228	31	64	1.95	1.0	9.2	9.3	0.2	252
2008	A-	Hudson Valley	5	3	0	66	84	2.45	1.15	20.2	218	33	77	2.24	3.3	11.5	3.5	0.1	149
2009	A	Bowling Green	6	5	0	74	62	2.55	1.09	19.3	211	26	77	2.25	3.0	7.5	2.5	0.4	99
2010	A+	Charlotte	8	4	0	122	100	3.02	1.15	23.1	249	31	73	2.87	1.9	7.4	3.8	0.4	119
2011	AA	Montgomery	6	8	0	117	91	3.77	1.42	20.7	248	30	74	3.78	4.4	7.0	1.6	0.6	62

The pinnacle of consistency in progressing one level per year, though control wasn't as strong as years past. Lean and athletic RHP has a whip-like arm action from 3/4 slot, producing FB that induces GBs. Hard SL and CU are effective against RHH and LHH. Dom decreased, which could be problematic in future.

Bashore, Matt — SP — Minnesota

EXP MLB DEBUT: 2014 | POTENTIAL: #4 starter | **8E**

Thrws L Age 24
2009 (1-S) Indiana

Velocity	Pitch	Grade
88-93	FB	+++
76-80	CB	++++
79-82	CU	++

Year	Lev	Team	W	L	Sv	IP	K	ERA	WHIP	BF/G	OBA	H%	S%	xERA	Ctl	Dom	Cmd	hr/9	BPV
2007	NCAA	Indiana	4	7	0	70	50	4.36	1.41	22.8	261	31	69	3.97	3.7	6.4	1.7	0.6	58
2008	NCAA	Indiana	7	3	0	82	86	3.61	1.45	25.1	239	32	75	3.55	5.0	9.4	1.9	0.4	90
2009	NCAA	Indiana	7	5	0	95	108	4.07	1.35	24.7	268	37	69	3.62	2.8	10.2	3.6	0.4	127
2009	Rk	Elizabethton	0	0	0	2	2	0.00	1.50	8.6	347	45	100	4.90	0.0	9.0		0.0	
2011	Rk	Elizabethton	0	0	0	16	15	3.33	1.30	5.6	222	26	79	3.59	4.4	8.3	1.9	1.1	67

Injuries have let him pitch only 18 innings since signing. Missed '10 after TJS, and velocity is coming back slowly. When healthy, uses athletic delivery of and deep arsenal to retire hitters. Best pitch is CB with a nasty late break. Can be good against LHH and RHH. Needs to upgrade CU, and repeating arm speed would help.

Bauer, Trevor — SP — Arizona

EXP MLB DEBUT: 2012 | POTENTIAL: #1 starter | **9B**

Thrws R Age 21
2011 (1) UCLA

Velocity	Pitch	Grade
92-96	FB	++++
85-86	SL	++++
77-79	CB	+++
82-85	CU	+++

Year	Lev	Team	W	L	Sv	IP	K	ERA	WHIP	BF/G	OBA	H%	S%	xERA	Ctl	Dom	Cmd	hr/9	BPV
2009	NCAA	UCLA	9	3	2	105	92	3.00	1.07	20.4	223	28	73	2.55	2.3	7.9	3.4	0.6	111
2010	NCAA	UCLA	12	3	0	131	165	3.02	1.24	29.5	247	35	78	3.33	2.8	11.3	4.0	0.7	138
2011	NCAA	UCLA	13	2	0	136	203	1.26	0.80	30.8	160	27	87	0.91	2.4	13.4	5.6	0.4	210
2011	A+	Visalia	0	1	0	9	17	3.00	1.22	12.1	216	42	80	3.15	4.0	17.0	4.3	1.0	173
2011	AA	Mobile	1	1	0	16	26	7.78	1.73	18.4	304	48	54	5.76	4.4	14.4	3.3	1.1	116

Third overall pick in '11 generates torque and arm speed from a small frame (6'1", 175). FB is 89-96 and he mixes in a plus CB, above-average CU, SL, and splitter. Because he has so many pitches, he can be inefficient. Has top of the rotation stuff, knows how to pitch, and is fun to watch. Should be in the majors soon.

Bedrosian, Cam — SP — Los Angeles (A)

EXP MLB DEBUT: 2014 | POTENTIAL: #3 starter | **8D**

Thrws R Age 20
2010 (1) HS (GA)

Velocity	Pitch	Grade
89-96	FB	++++
80-83	SL	+++
77-80	CB	++
78-80	CU	++

Year	Lev	Team	W	L	Sv	IP	K	ERA	WHIP	BF/G	OBA	H%	S%	xERA	Ctl	Dom	Cmd	hr/9	BPV
2010	Rk	AZL Angels	0	2	0	12	10	4.50	1.67	10.8	278	35	70	4.23	5.3	7.5	1.4	0.0	74

Strong-framed but missed the entire season after TJS in May. When healthy, he uses a power repertoire including plus FB and solid-average hard SL that hitters chase. Repeats delivery well, though CU needs work. Throws with effort, but should stick as SP due to potential four average to plus pitches.

Belfiore, Mike — SP — Arizona

EXP MLB DEBUT: 2013 | POTENTIAL: #5 starter | **7D**

Thrws L Age 23
2009 (1-S) Boston College

Velocity	Pitch	Grade
90-93	FB	+++
80-83	SL	+++
77-79	CU	++++

Year	Lev	Team	W	L	Sv	IP	K	ERA	WHIP	BF/G	OBA	H%	S%	xERA	Ctl	Dom	Cmd	hr/9	BPV
2008	NCAA	Boston College	2	0	8	18	19	2.49	1.22	4.1	250	33	81	3.16	2.5	9.4	3.8	0.5	127
2009	NCAA	Boston College	5	1	9	48	59	2.06	1.16	7.7	245	35	83	2.83	2.2	11.0	4.9	0.4	164
2009	Rk	Missoula	2	2	0	58	55	2.17	1.24	16.8	265	34	83	3.27	2.0	8.5	4.2	0.3	133
2010	A	South Bend	3	10	0	126	105	4.00	1.44	21.5	281	35	71	4.10	3.0	7.5	2.5	0.4	83
2011	A+	Visalia	4	4	0	79	79	5.92	1.81	10.5	279	32	72	6.41	6.5	9.0	1.4	1.9	24

Solid-bodied lefty moved back into starting, where he struggled with his command, walking 57 in 79 IP in the CAL. When he's on, he generates easy velocity and nice movement on a 90-93 heater. He complements the FB with a solid SL and CU. Will need to show that '11 was a fluke.

Bellamy, Kyle — RP — Chicago (A)

EXP MLB DEBUT: 2013 | POTENTIAL: Setup reliever | **6B**

Thrws R Age 24
2009 (5) Miami

Velocity	Pitch	Grade
84-91	FB	+++
79-82	SL	++
77-81	CU	+++

Year	Lev	Team	W	L	Sv	IP	K	ERA	WHIP	BF/G	OBA	H%	S%	xERA	Ctl	Dom	Cmd	hr/9	BPV
2009	Rk	Bristol	0	0	1	3	2	0.00	0.00	2.8	0	0			0.0	6.0		0.0	
2009	A	Kannapolis	2	0	2	19	30	1.42	0.84	4.1	207	36	87	1.61	0.9	14.2	15.0	0.5	400
2010	A	Kannapolis	0	0	0	5	6	1.80	1.00	4.8	124	20	80	0.70	5.4	10.8	2.0	0.0	137
2010	A+	Winston-Salem	5	0	5	47	59	1.53	1.10	6.0	222	33	86	2.22	2.7	11.3	4.2	0.2	161
2010	AA	Birmingham	2	2	0	25	19	6.43	2.10	6.2	304	37	67	6.06	7.9	6.8	0.9	0.4	42

Tall sidearming reliever missed the entire season due to an arm injury. He's spent his entire career in bullpen and can serve as righty specialist. Precisely commands average, sinking FB and arm angle and slot provide plenty of deception. SL and CU are nothing special and has trouble consistently throwing strikes with them.

Berger, Eric — RP — Cleveland

EXP MLB DEBUT: 2012 | POTENTIAL: Setup reliever | **7C**

Thrws L Age 26
2008 (8) Arizona

Velocity	Pitch	Grade
88-95	FB	++++
75-79	CB	+++
79-82	CU	++

Year	Lev	Team	W	L	Sv	IP	K	ERA	WHIP	BF/G	OBA	H%	S%	xERA	Ctl	Dom	Cmd	hr/9	BPV
2009	AA	Akron	3	1	0	33	33	2.71	1.45	23.6	255	34	81	3.60	4.3	8.9	2.1	0.3	93
2010	AA	Akron	5	5	0	87	73	4.65	1.49	20.9	241	29	70	4.17	5.4	7.5	1.4	0.9	54
2010	AAA	Columbus	0	1	0	24	17	5.95	2.11	23.8	312	36	71	6.58	7.4	6.3	0.9	0.7	26
2011	AA	Akron	2	0	0	57	67	2.53	1.16	7.3	215	30	81	2.69	3.5	10.6	3.0	0.6	120
2011	AAA	Columbus	0	1	0	14	20	10.21	2.84	7.3	395	55	63	10.35	8.9	12.8	1.4	1.3	44

Quick-armed lefty moved to bullpen after career as starter. Posted much higher Dom in the pen, where his FB plays up and he doesn't need to develop CU. Keeps the ball down with a high arm slot and keen arm speed. Has been a menace to LHH and could be situational reliever at worst. Has pitchability to return to SP, but relief may be best.

Berry, Ryan — SP — Baltimore

EXP MLB DEBUT: 2013 | POTENTIAL: #4 starter | **7B**

Thrws R Age 23
2009 (9) Rice

Velocity	Pitch	Grade
86-91	FB	+++
76-80	CB	++++
76-83	CU	+++

Year	Lev	Team	W	L	Sv	IP	K	ERA	WHIP	BF/G	OBA	H%	S%	xERA	Ctl	Dom	Cmd	hr/9	BPV
2010	A	Delmarva	0	3	0	46	43	3.51	1.30	23.8	274	34	75	3.98	2.1	8.4	3.9	0.8	109
2010	A+	Frederick	2	2	2	71	63	3.04	1.15	16.6	222	27	75	2.79	3.2	8.0	2.5	0.6	93
2011	Rk	GCL Orioles	0	0	0	10	9	1.80	1.20	8.0	151	17	91	2.35	6.3	8.1	1.3	0.9	73
2011	A-	Aberdeen	1	1	0	22	19	4.89	1.58	9.7	302	37	70	5.15	3.3	7.7	2.4	0.8	66
2011	A+	Frederick	0	0	0	4	4	0.00	0.75	14.3	210	29	100	1.02	0.0	9.0		0.0	

Live-armed pitcher who underwent minor shoulder surgery and returned in June. Has been ideal GBer with a heavy FB with nasty late movement. Plus CB has big breaking action and serves as K pitch. Pitches play up due to deceptive, max-effort delivery, but injury history is concern. Might eventually move to bullpen, but will stay as SP for now.

Betances, Dellin — SP — New York (A)

EXP MLB DEBUT: 2011 | POTENTIAL: #2 starter | **9D**

Thrws R Age 24
2006 (8) HS (NJ)

Velocity	Pitch	Grade
88-96	FB	++++
80-82	CB	++++
84-88	SL	++
	CU	++

Year	Lev	Team	W	L	Sv	IP	K	ERA	WHIP	BF/G	OBA	H%	S%	xERA	Ctl	Dom	Cmd	hr/9	BPV
2010	A+	Tampa	8	1	0	71	88	1.77	0.87	18.7	177	27	79	1.05	2.4	11.2	4.6	0.1	180
2010	AA	Trenton	0	0	0	14	20	3.83	0.92	17.6	201	26	70	3.11	1.9	12.8	6.7	1.9	174
2011	AA	Trenton	4	6	0	105	115	3.43	1.34	20.8	225	30	75	3.25	4.7	9.8	2.1	0.6	95
2011	AAA	Scranton/W-B	0	3	0	21	27	5.14	1.48	22.6	213	30	66	3.66	6.4	11.6	1.8	0.9	94
2011	MLB	New York (A)	0	0	0	2	2	8.18	3.18	6.6	139	19	71	6.37	24.5	8.2	0.3	0.0	83

A high ceiling with excellent pure stuff led by explosive, hard FB and CB. But the big-framed power pitcher has often been unable to throw strikes, and good hitters have laid off. Also uses hard SL and CU, though both are fringy at best. Can overthrow at times, but can be dynamite when spotting pitches to both sides of plate.

Bettis, Chad — SP — Colorado

EXP MLB DEBUT: 2014 | POTENTIAL: #2 starter/reliever | **9D**

Thrws R Age 23
2010 (3) Texas Tech

Velocity	Pitch	Grade
88-94	FB	++++
81-84	SL	+++
		++

Year	Lev	Team	W	L	Sv	IP	K	ERA	WHIP	BF/G	OBA	H%	S%	xERA	Ctl	Dom	Cmd	hr/9	BPV
2009	NCAA	Texas Tech	6	1	7	72	58	3.61	1.47	13.5	272	32	77	4.36	3.7	7.2	1.9	0.7	62
2010	NCAA	Texas Tech	7	4	10	85	102	4.44	1.53	15.4	288	39	72	4.78	3.5	10.8	3.1	0.8	102
2010	A-	Tri-City	4	1	0	48	39	1.12	1.12	19.0	245	31	89	2.41	1.9	7.3	3.9	0.0	132
2010	A	Asheville	2	0	0	18	17	0.99	0.93	22.8	214	27	94	2.01	1.5	8.4	5.7	0.5	167
2011	A+	Modesto	12	5	0	169	184	3.35	1.11	24.6	229	31	70	2.65	2.4	9.8	4.1	0.5	138

Strong-armed, mature righty dominated in a full season in the CAL. Features an 89-94 FB that tops out around 98. He also has a good 81-84 SL but an inconsistent CU. Low 3/4 delivery gives his FB solid sinking action. Was 8-1 with a 2.51 ERA in the second half. If the CU can improve, he should be a solid #2 starter.

Biddle, Jesse — SP — Philadelphia

EXP MLB DEBUT: 2014 | POTENTIAL: #2 starter | 8D

Thrws L Age 20
2010 (1) HS (PA)

Velo	Pitch	Grade
89-93	FB	+ + +
70-73	CB	+ + + +
77-80	CU	+ +

Year	Lev	Team	W	L	Sv	IP	K	ERA	WHIP	BF/G	OBA	H%	S%	xERA	Ctl	Dom	Cmd	hr/9	BPV
2010	Rk	GCL Phillies	3	1	0	33	41	4.35	1.33	15.3	273	39	67	3.79	2.4	11.1	4.6	0.5	147
2010	A-	Williamsport	1	0	0	10	9	2.67	1.58	14.8	149	20	81	2.46	9.8	8.0	0.8	0.0	90
2011	A	Lakewood	7	8	0	133	124	2.98	1.28	21.8	217	28	76	2.76	4.5	8.4	1.9	0.3	91

Durable 6'4" left-hander had a nice breakout. A 92-94 FB in high school, but 88-92 since. Progressed because of improved CB and CU. His FB remains his bread and butter and features late, sinking action. If he can improve his command, he has the stuff to be a solid #2 starter.

Billo, Greg — SP — Kansas City

EXP MLB DEBUT: 2014 | POTENTIAL: #4 starter | 7C

Thrws R Age 21
2008 (28) HS (IL)

Velo	Pitch	Grade
86-92	FB	+ + +
78-82	CB	+ + +
	CU	+ +

Year	Lev	Team	W	L	Sv	IP	K	ERA	WHIP	BF/G	OBA	H%	S%	xERA	Ctl	Dom	Cmd	hr/9	BPV
2008	Rk	AZL Royals	0	1	1	14	13	5.74	2.06	9.8	346	43	71	6.88	5.1	8.3	1.6	0.6	51
2009	Rk	Burlington	2	2	1	54	51	1.83	1.03	16.1	207	26	87	2.33	2.7	8.5	3.2	0.7	111
2010	Rk	Idaho Falls	4	8	0	78	79	5.19	1.47	19.7	295	36	67	5.17	2.7	9.1	3.4	1.3	85
2011	A	Kane County	9	5	1	135	119	1.93	1.02	19.2	229	29	83	2.33	1.7	7.9	4.8	0.4	145

Tall control-oriented pitcher who led MWL in ERA in his first full season in minors. Toyed with hitters by locating average stuff on outer and inner parts of plate. Keeps the ball on the ground with a quality sinker and can get hitters to chase an effective breaking ball. Not a Dom pitcher, as he lacks frontline velocity, and upper level hitters are unlikely to be deceived.

Black, Victor — SP — Pittsburgh

EXP MLB DEBUT: 2013 | POTENTIAL: Reliever | 7C

Thrws R Age 24
2009 (1-S) Dallas Baptist

Velo	Pitch	Grade
92-94	FB	+ + +
82-84	SL	+ +
	CU	+ +

Year	Lev	Team	W	L	Sv	IP	K	ERA	WHIP	BF/G	OBA	H%	S%	xERA	Ctl	Dom	Cmd	hr/9	BPV
2008	NCAA	Dallas Baptist	1	6	0	70	56	5.00	1.60	22.1	250	29	70	4.52	5.9	7.2	1.2	0.9	47
2009	A-	State College	1	2	1	31	33	3.47	1.32	9.9	229	32	71	2.68	4.3	9.5	2.2	0.0	113
2010	A	West Virginia	0	0	0	4	8	10.71	1.90	9.9	202	34	43	5.77	10.7	17.1	1.6	2.1	87
2011	A	West Virginia	2	1	1	29	23	5.28	1.59	5.8	268	34	63	3.90	5.0	7.1	1.4	0.0	74
2011	A+	Bradenton	1	0	0	6	5	4.35	1.94	5.9	314	36	82	6.83	5.8	7.3	1.3	1.5	18

Strong-armed, athletic RHP pitches off a 92-94 FB that tops out at 97. Also has a SL and a below-average CU. Uses a low 3/4 arm slot to get movement, but inconsistent mechanics result in subpar control. Was moved to relief to try and keep him healthy and made 22 appearances in '11, but durability concerns linger.

Blackburn, Clayton — SP — San Francisco

EXP MLB DEBUT: 2015 | POTENTIAL: #2 starter | 8D

Thrws R Age 19
2011 (16) HS, (OK)

Velo	Pitch	Grade
90-93	FB	+ + +
	CB	+ +
	SL	+ +
	CU	+ +

Year	Lev	Team	W	L	Sv	IP	K	ERA	WHIP	BF/G	OBA	H%	S%	xERA	Ctl	Dom	Cmd	hr/9	BPV
2011	Rk	AZL Giants	3	1	0	33	30	1.09	0.57	9.4	146	18	88	0.39	0.8	8.2	10.0	0.5	268

Had an impressive pro debut, walking 3 while striking out 30. He could move up quickly with a solid four-pitch mix: A 90-93 FB, a good CB, SL, and CU. His breaking balls need refinement, but he has good size, consistent mechanics, and throws strikes.

Blair, Kyle — SP — Cleveland

EXP MLB DEBUT: 2013 | POTENTIAL: #4 starter | 7C

Thrws R Age 23
2010 (4) San Diego

Velo	Pitch	Grade
88-93	FB	+ +
77-80	SL	+ + +
81-85	CB	+ + +
	CU	+ + +

Year	Lev	Team	W	L	Sv	IP	K	ERA	WHIP	BF/G	OBA	H%	S%	xERA	Ctl	Dom	Cmd	hr/9	BPV
2008	NCAA	San Diego	8	4	0	74	99	3.88	1.29	19.1	229	35	69	2.93	4.1	12.0	2.9	0.4	132
2009	NCAA	San Diego	3	2	2	54	62	3.15	1.20	21.8	235	33	73	2.76	3.0	10.3	3.4	0.3	132
2010	NCAA	San Diego	8	4	0	98	126	2.84	1.09	25.6	222	33	74	2.35	2.6	11.6	4.5	0.4	163
2011	Rk	AZL Indians	0	0	0	1	2	16.36	2.73	6.1	492	73	33	11.18	0.0	16.4		0.0	
2011	A	Lake County	3	5	0	80	70	5.05	1.47	15.0	256	31	66	4.18	4.5	7.9	1.8	0.8	64

Big, strong, durable pitcher with enough versatility and stamina for a variety of roles. Not much projection left in frame or arm, but can find success with sinker and a decent assortment of secondary pitches. SL serves as K pitch, but pitches backwards due to lack of top FB. Can be hit hard, particularly by LHH, and needs to reduce walks to realize potential.

Blair, Seth — SP — St. Louis

EXP MLB DEBUT: 2013 | POTENTIAL: #3 starter | 8D

Thrws R Age 23
2010 (1-S) Arizona State

Velo	Pitch	Grade
90-94	FB	+ + +
78-81	CB	+ +
78-81	SL	+ +
80-82	CU	+ +

Year	Lev	Team	W	L	Sv	IP	K	ERA	WHIP	BF/G	OBA	H%	S%	xERA	Ctl	Dom	Cmd	hr/9	BPV
2008	NCAA	Arizona State	4	2	1	54	34	6.99	1.87	13.3	341	38	63	6.85	3.7	5.7	1.5	1.2	18
2009	NCAA	Arizona State	7	2	1	77	78	3.39	1.30	18.7	244	32	75	3.37	3.5	9.1	2.6	0.6	98
2010	NCAA	Arizona State	12	1	0	106	108	3.65	1.33	24.5	272	35	75	4.17	2.5	9.2	3.7	0.9	106
2011	A	Quad Cities	6	3	0	81	70	5.32	1.74	17.6	257	31	70	5.05	6.9	7.8	1.1	1.0	44

Polished college starter struggled mightily in his debut. He has a nice four-pitch mix featuring a 90-93 sinking FB, a 12-6 CB, a SL, and a CU. Both breaking balls need work and he struggled to throw strikes all season. Does have some recoil on his low 3/4 delivery and an inconsistent arm slot, but look for better results in '12.

Boer, Madison — SP — Minnesota

EXP MLB DEBUT: 2014 | POTENTIAL: #3 starter | 8C

Thrws R Age 22
2011 (2) Oregon

Velo	Pitch	Grade
89-94	FB	+ + +
83-87	SL	+ + +
	CU	+ +

Year	Lev	Team	W	L	Sv	IP	K	ERA	WHIP	BF/G	OBA	H%	S%	xERA	Ctl	Dom	Cmd	hr/9	BPV
2009	NCAA	Oregon	1	8	0	62	37	6.97	1.58	16.0	277	31	53	4.57	4.5	5.4	1.2	0.6	39
2010	NCAA	Oregon	3	1	5	51	48	2.46	1.17	8.9	261	34	78	2.91	1.6	8.4	5.3	0.2	160
2011	NCAA	Oregon	3	6	3	99	74	2.27	1.17	22.0	225	28	80	2.46	3.2	6.7	2.1	0.2	89
2011	Rk	Elizabethton	2	1	9	17	31	2.63	0.88	4.2	212	41	71	1.79	1.1	16.3	15.5	0.5	420
2011	A	Beloit	0	0	2	8	12	6.75	1.63	4.4	347	53	54	5.17	1.1	13.5	12.0	0.0	319

Athletic pitcher who came out of the bullpen upon signing, but will be a SP. Pitches with easy, quick arm that produces velocity and sinking action down in the zone. Developing a CU is vital for future success, though he pitches efficiently. Could move quickly if CU comes around, especially if control and command continue to be strengths.

Boxberger, Brad — RP — San Diego

EXP MLB DEBUT: 2012 | POTENTIAL: Potential Closer | 8B

Thrws R Age 24
2009 (2) USC

Velo	Pitch	Grade
90-95	SL	+ + +
84-86	CB	+ + +
74-76	CU	+ + +
		+ +

Year	Lev	Team	W	L	Sv	IP	K	ERA	WHIP	BF/G	OBA	H%	S%	xERA	Ctl	Dom	Cmd	hr/9	BPV
2009	NCAA	USC	6	3	0	94	99	3.16	1.27	27.4	207	28	75	2.63	4.8	9.5	2.0	0.4	101
2010	A+	Lynchburg	4	6	0	62	70	3.19	1.24	18.0	246	34	74	3.11	2.9	10.2	3.5	0.4	127
2010	AA	Carolina	1	4	0	29	40	8.63	1.95	6.3	298	42	55	6.37	6.8	12.3	1.8	1.2	71
2011	AA	Carolina	1	2	4	34	57	1.32	0.85	4.2	143	26	89	0.96	3.4	15.0	4.4	0.5	193
2011	AAA	Louisville	1	2	7	27	36	2.98	1.14	4.3	173	26	76	2.17	5.0	11.9	2.4	0.7	122

Strong, athletic reliever has four good pitches: a 90-95 FB, SL, CB, and CU. A deceptive delivery enhances the look of his off-speed stuff, and he changes speeds effectively. Impressive Dom at every level, and has the stuff to close (11 saves). Should see extensive time in the Padres' pens in '12.

Boyd, Hudson — SP — Minnesota

EXP MLB DEBUT: 2015 | POTENTIAL: #3 starter | 8D

Thrws R Age 19
2011 (1-S) HS (FL)

Velo	Pitch	Grade
88-95	FB	+ + + +
77-80	CB	+ + +
	CU	+

Year	Lev	Team	W	L	Sv	IP	K	ERA	WHIP	BF/G	OBA	H%	S%	xERA	Ctl	Dom	Cmd	hr/9	BPV
2011		Did not play																	

Big, strong pitcher with the ideal frame to become a bulldog SP soon. He's all about arm strength at present, but can spin a CB that shows potential to be above average. Needs consistent velocity and mechanics, but can generate high heat by rearing back and firing. CU lacks movement and needs to be upgraded for him to last as starter.

Brackman, Andrew — SP — Cincinnati

EXP MLB DEBUT: 2011 | POTENTIAL: #3 starter/Setup reliever | 8D

Thrws R Age 26
2007 (1) North Carolina State

Velo	Pitch	Grade
88-95	FB	+ + + +
72-81	CB	+ + +
83-87	CU	+

Year	Lev	Team	W	L	Sv	IP	K	ERA	WHIP	BF/G	OBA	H%	S%	xERA	Ctl	Dom	Cmd	hr/9	BPV
2009	A	Charleston (SC)	2	12	0	106	103	5.93	1.71	16.6	261	33	64	4.75	6.4	8.7	1.4	0.7	63
2010	A+	Tampa	5	4	0	60	56	5.10	1.27	20.4	284	35	59	4.01	1.4	8.4	6.2	0.8	157
2010	AA	Trenton	5	7	0	80	70	3.03	1.33	22.2	254	32	77	3.38	3.4	7.9	2.3	0.3	90
2011	AAA	Scranton/W-B	3	6	1	96	75	6.00	1.64	13.0	232	27	63	4.43	7.0	7.0	1.0	0.9	44
2011	MLB	New York (A)	0	0	0	2	0	0.00	1.90	3.3	144	14	100	3.29	12.9	0.0	0.0	0.0	26

Outstanding pure stuff, but he hasn't lived up to expectations due to poor command. Lots of moving parts in an inconsistent delivery have led to major control problems, and he doesn't pitch aggressively despite a tall, menacing figure. When he's on, has big FB that he throws on downward angle, and he can wipe out hitters with nasty CB.

Bradley, Archie — SP — Arizona

EXP MLB DEBUT: 2014 | POTENTIAL: #1 Starter | 9D

Thrws R Age 19
2011 (1) HS, (OK)

Velo	Pitch	Grade
93-96	FB	+ + + +
80-83	CB	+ + +
	CU	+ +

Year	Lev	Team	W	L	Sv	IP	K	ERA	WHIP	BF/G	OBA	H%	S%	xERA	Ctl	Dom	Cmd	hr/9	BPV
2011	Rk	Missoula	0	0	0	2	4	0.00	0.50	3.3	151	38	100		0.0	18.0		0.0	

Tall, athletic Oklahoman was one of the best power arms in the '11 draft. He has a plus 93-96 FB that tops out at 100. He also has a plus CB and a CU with potential. The arm strength and stuff to be a true #1 starter are here; he just needs more reps and to refine his CU. The sky is the limit.

Bradley, J.R. — SP — Arizona

EXP MLB DEBUT: 2014 | POTENTIAL: #4 starter | 7D

Thrws R | Age 20
2010 (2) South Carleston WV

Velo	Pitch	Grade
88-93	FB	+++
77-80	CU	++
73-75	CB	++
	SL	++

Year	Lev	Team	W	L	Sv	IP	K	ERA	WHIP	BF/G	OBA	H%	S%	xERA	Ctl	Dom	Cmd	hr/9	BPV
2010	Rk	Missoula	1	7	0	54	40	5.98	1.66	17.3	302	34	65	5.67	4.0	6.6	1.7	1.2	35
2011	A	South Bend	6	16	0	142	88	5.00	1.55	23.0	296	33	69	5.18	3.2	5.6	1.7	1.0	35

Tall, projectable RHP throws his 90-93 FB for strikes, but remains hittable because his secondary pitches are raw. Still, he has a clean, smooth delivery and maintains arm speed on his CU. He will need to make significant strides to remain a prospect, but it is too soon to give up.

Bradley, Jed — SP — Milwaukee

EXP MLB DEBUT: 2014 | POTENTIAL: #2 starter | 9D

Thrws L | Age 22
2011 (1) Georgia Tech

Velo	Pitch	Grade
90-93	FB	++++
80-83	SL	+++
78-80	CB	+++
	CU	+++

Year	Lev	Team	W	L	Sv	IP	K	ERA	WHIP	BF/G	OBA	H%	S%	xERA	Ctl	Dom	Cmd	hr/9	BPV
2009	NCAA	Georgia Tech	2	3	0	44	49	6.72	1.61	16.3	302	37	61	6.14	3.5	10.0	2.9	1.8	60
2010	NCAA	Georgia Tech	9	5	0	91	99	4.84	1.45	24.3	294	39	66	4.46	2.5	9.8	4.0	0.6	120
2011	NCAA	Georgia Tech	7	3	0	98	106	3.49	1.22	24.8	244	34	69	2.72	2.8	9.7	3.4	0.1	134

Solid college lefty commands a nice four-pitch mix, with a good 90-93 FB that tops out at 95, a two-seam FB, an 80-83 SL, a CB, and a 78-80 CU. He isn't a flamethrower, but he has some nice deception and a bit of projection left and is a quality starter.

Brasier, Ryan — RP — Los Angeles (A)

EXP MLB DEBUT: 2012 | POTENTIAL: Middle reliever | 7D

Thrws R | Age 24
2007 (6) Weatherford JC

Velo	Pitch	Grade
89-96	FB	+++
79-84	SL	+++
	CU	+

Year	Lev	Team	W	L	Sv	IP	K	ERA	WHIP	BF/G	OBA	H%	S%	xERA	Ctl	Dom	Cmd	hr/9	BPV
2009	A+	Rancho Cucam	5	4	0	98	93	5.23	1.38	15.2	272	32	66	4.87	2.9	8.5	2.9	1.6	66
2009	AA	Arkansas	2	1	2	11	6	5.68	1.80	6.4	293	32	68	5.59	5.7	4.9	0.9	0.8	19
2010	AA	Arkansas	7	12	0	142	94	5.07	1.37	21.3	241	24	69	4.67	4.3	6.0	1.4	1.8	18
2011	AA	Arkansas	0	1	16	25	26	0.72	1.27	4.1	203	28	97	2.59	5.0	9.3	1.9	0.4	99
2011	AAA	Salt Lake	2	1	3	27	26	5.00	1.30	4.4	255	32	61	3.59	3.0	8.7	2.9	0.7	97

Short, stocky reliever who finished second in TL in saves. A SP in '10, but Cmd fell and he went back to pen for '11, where he restored Dom and Ctl. Batters can find it tough to square up his quick FB, which he complements with a SL that shows flashes of being dependable. He lacks feel for changing speeds, and needs to spot FB early in count.

Brewer, Charles — SP — Arizona

EXP MLB DEBUT: 2013 | POTENTIAL: #5 starter | 7B

Thrws R | Age 24
2009 (12) UCLA

Velo	Pitch	Grade
90-93	FB	+++
72-74	CB	+++
78-80	CU	+++
	SL	++

Year	Lev	Team	W	L	Sv	IP	K	ERA	WHIP	BF/G	OBA	H%	S%	xERA	Ctl	Dom	Cmd	hr/9	BPV
2009	Rk	Missoula	7	2	0	54	61	2.49	1.07	12.4	220	30	80	2.56	2.5	10.1	4.1	0.7	137
2010	A	South Bend	4	5	0	69	78	1.83	1.09	20.7	220	31	85	2.35	2.6	10.2	3.9	0.4	142
2010	A+	Visalia	7	3	0	81	75	2.99	1.10	22.7	244	31	74	2.85	1.7	8.3	5.0	0.6	144
2011	Rk	Arizona	0	0	0	3	4	0.00	1.00	11.5	262	40	100	2.29	0.0	12.0		0.0	
2011	AA	Mobile	5	1	0	52	48	2.59	1.29	19.4	246	32	80	3.16	3.3	8.3	2.5	0.3	98

A tall, athletic righty with a nice four-pitch mix. His bread and butter is a 90-93 FB that has some nice movement. He also throws a tight 72-74 CB and an improved CU. A concussion from a foul ball limited him to just 12 starts in '11, but he was healthy and moderately successful in the AFL.

Brice, Austin — SP — Florida

EXP MLB DEBUT: 2014 | POTENTIAL: #4 starter | 7D

Thrws R | Age 20
2010 (9) HS, (NC)

Velo	Pitch	Grade
92-94	FB	+++
	CB	++
	CU	++

Year	Lev	Team	W	L	Sv	IP	K	ERA	WHIP	BF/G	OBA	H%	S%	xERA	Ctl	Dom	Cmd	hr/9	BPV
2010	Rk	GCL Marlins	0	1	0	8	8	4.44	1.73	6.1	235	32	71	3.79	7.8	8.9	1.1	0.0	85
2011	Rk	GCL Marlins	6	0	0	48	55	2.99	1.35	18.3	191	27	78	2.64	6.2	10.3	1.7	0.4	102

Tall, projectable righty was impressive in the GCL. He attacks hitters with a lively 92-94 FB. Also has the makings of an above-average CB and CU, but both need considerable work. Poor front-side mechanics lead to flying open on delivery and inconsistent control. Needs significant work, but there is potential.

Brickhouse, Bryan — SP — Kansas City

EXP MLB DEBUT: 2015 | POTENTIAL: #3 starter | 8E

Thrws R | Age 20
2011 (3) HS (TX)

Velo	Pitch	Grade
87-95	FB	++++
75-79	CB	+++
	CU	+

Year	Lev	Team	W	L	Sv	IP	K	ERA	WHIP	BF/G	OBA	H%	S%	xERA	Ctl	Dom	Cmd	hr/9	BPV
2011		Did not play																	

Short, strong pitcher with chance to be a mid-rotation starter. Pitches aggressively with plenty of effort in delivery. Gets ahead with a plus FB and complements it with a good CB. Stamina is a question due to effort, and he lacks athleticism to repeat delivery and arm slot. Needs coaching, but has good ingredients to work with.

Bridwell, Parker — SP — Baltimore

EXP MLB DEBUT: 2014 | POTENTIAL: #2 starter | 9E

Thrws R | Age 20
2010 (9) HS (TX)

Velo	Pitch	Grade
87-95	FB	++++
84-87	SL	+++
	CU	++

Year	Lev	Team	W	L	Sv	IP	K	ERA	WHIP	BF/G	OBA	H%	S%	xERA	Ctl	Dom	Cmd	hr/9	BPV
2010	Rk	GCL Orioles	0	0	0	1	4	7.50	3.33	3.7	228	260	75	7.54	22.5	30.0	1.3	0.0	217
2010	A-	Aberdeen	0	0	0	4	2	0.00	1.00	7.6	210	24	100	1.70	2.3	4.5	2.0	0.0	82
2011	A-	Aberdeen	2	5	0	53	57	4.57	1.47	19.0	272	37	67	3.94	3.7	9.6	2.6	0.3	103
2011	A	Delmarva	0	3	0	21	13	7.22	1.70	19.2	278	33	53	4.33	5.5	5.5	1.0	0.0	54

Long and athletic pitcher with better skills than his numbers suggest. Plus FB is best pitch and could add a few ticks with mechanical adjustments. Throws with quick arm, but doesn't repeat delivery, which affects command. Uses hard SL as an out pitch, but must improve CU to advance quickly through the minors. Pitch sequencing needs attention.

Brigham, Jake — SP — Texas

EXP MLB DEBUT: 2013 | POTENTIAL: #4 starter | 8E

Thrws R | Age 24
2006 (6) HS (FL)

Velo	Pitch	Grade
90-96	FB	++++
80-82	CB	+++
	CU	+

Year	Lev	Team	W	L	Sv	IP	K	ERA	WHIP	BF/G	OBA	H%	S%	xERA	Ctl	Dom	Cmd	hr/9	BPV
2007	A-	Spokane	5	4	0	77	65	3.16	1.34	21.3	241	28	81	3.89	4.0	7.6	1.9	1.1	61
2009	A	Hickory	2	11	1	89	81	5.55	1.59	15.7	293	36	66	5.20	3.8	8.2	2.1	1.0	60
2010	A	Hickory	6	5	0	83	67	3.36	1.08	23.1	220	27	69	2.51	2.6	7.3	2.8	0.5	97
2010	A+	Bakersfield	1	5	0	49	39	6.97	1.89	21.0	326	38	63	6.42	4.8	7.1	1.5	0.9	37
2011	AA	Frisco	6	6	0	114	114	4.50	1.42	13.8	250	31	70	4.17	4.3	9.0	2.1	1.0	72

Both SP and RP en route to breakout season. Repeats clean and simple delivery to pepper strike zone with a hard FB and a CB that exhibits quality break. Durable and athletic, he maintains velocity as games wear on and has high K rate. Slows arm speed on CU and needs to improve erratic command of CB.

Britton, Drake — SP — Boston

EXP MLB DEBUT: 2014 | POTENTIAL: #3 starter | 8D

Thrws L | Age 23
2007 (23) HS (TX)

Velo	Pitch	Grade
89-95	FB	+++
74-79	CB	++++
79-82	CU	+++

Year	Lev	Team	W	L	Sv	IP	K	ERA	WHIP	BF/G	OBA	H%	S%	xERA	Ctl	Dom	Cmd	hr/9	BPV
2008	A-	Lowell	1	2	0	33	26	4.34	1.39	17.5	243	29	70	3.81	4.3	7.0	1.6	0.8	58
2009	Rk	GCL Red Sox	0	0	0	7	11	0.00	0.86	6.4	92	19	100	0.01	5.1	14.1	2.8	0.0	179
2009	A-	Lowell	0	0	0	4	8	2.14	1.67	6.3	252	51	86	3.79	6.4	17.1	2.7	0.0	163
2010	A	Greenville	2	3	0	75	78	2.99	1.22	14.5	245	32	77	3.22	2.8	9.3	3.4	0.6	115
2011	A+	Salem	1	13	0	97	89	6.94	1.71	16.9	288	35	59	5.53	5.1	8.2	1.6	1.1	47

Self-combusted in miserable season. Earned kudos for attitude and work ethic, but failed to string together quality outings. Generally works off sinking FB from high 3/4 slot, but didn't repeat delivery consistently, and control fell completely apart. Wasn't able to use plus CB and solid-average CU because he was always behind in the count. Allowed too many HR.

Bromberg, David — SP — Minnesota

EXP MLB DEBUT: 2013 | POTENTIAL: #4 starter | 7C

Thrws R | Age 24
2006 (32) HS (CA)

Velo	Pitch	Grade
87-94	FB	+++
77-80	CB	+++
78-82	SL	++
79-81	CU	++

Year	Lev	Team	W	L	Sv	IP	K	ERA	WHIP	BF/G	OBA	H%	S%	xERA	Ctl	Dom	Cmd	hr/9	BPV
2009	A+	Fort Myers	13	4	0	153	148	2.70	1.23	23.0	225	30	78	2.74	3.7	8.7	2.3	0.4	101
2010	AA	New Britain	5	5	0	99	65	3.63	1.41	24.7	273	32	74	3.89	3.2	5.9	1.9	0.4	64
2010	AAA	Rochester	1	4	0	52	47	3.98	1.15	23.0	243	28	73	3.92	2.3	8.1	3.6	1.6	84
2011	Rk	GCL Twins	0	0	0	5	5	9.00	1.60	7.4	262	35	38	3.83	5.4	9.0	1.7	0.0	92
2011	AA	New Britain	1	3	0	37	23	6.08	1.76	21.2	324	37	65	5.87	3.6	5.6	1.5	0.7	34

Durable-framed pitcher who missed time with a broken forearm after being hit by batted ball. Tall, he uses height well and uses sharp, downer CB to get hitters to chase. Struggles with LHH and needs to establish better FB command early. SL and CU are below average, but still have potential to produce. Dom has dropped significantly at upper levels of minors.

Bryson, Rob — RP — Cleveland

EXP MLB DEBUT: 2012 | POTENTIAL: Closer | 8D

Thrws R | Age 24
2006 (31) HS (DE)

Velo	Pitch	Grade
88-95	FB	++++
78-82	SL	++++
77-81	CU	+

Year	Lev	Team	W	L	Sv	IP	K	ERA	WHIP	BF/G	OBA	H%	S%	xERA	Ctl	Dom	Cmd	hr/9	BPV
2010	A+	Kinston	2	1	1	20	38	2.25	0.75	5.5	110	21	77	0.72	3.6	17.1	4.8	0.9	208
2010	AA	Akron	1	1	0	20	21	1.80	1.10	6.5	163	22	86	1.79	5.0	9.5	1.9	0.5	106
2011	A	Lake County	0	1	0	4	5	4.50	1.50	4.3	307	39	80	6.33	2.3	11.3	5.0	2.3	99
2011	A+	Kinston	0	0	1	14	20	0.64	0.64	4.8	132	20	100	0.46	1.9	12.9	6.7	0.6	226
2011	AA	Akron	2	0	0	21	23	2.99	1.37	5.5	222	30	79	3.14	5.1	9.8	1.9	0.4	97

Aggressive reliever with closer mentality and skills. Throws an explosive FB with lightning-quick arm speed and commands it to all strike zone quadrants. Deceives with drop-and-drive delivery, though can leave balls up. Good SL complements heater, but no CU. He has been beset by injuries in recent years and needs work to improve.

Bucci, Nick — SP — Milwaukee

Thrws R Age 21
2008 (18) Ontario, CAN

EXP MLB DEBUT: 2014 | POTENTIAL: #4 starter | **7C**

Velo	Pitch	Grade
88-92	FB	+++
	CB	++
	CU	++

Year	Lev	Team	W	L	Sv	IP	K	ERA	WHIP	BF/G	OBA	H%	S%	xERA	Ctl	Dom	Cmd	hr/9	BPV
2008	Rk	AZL Brewers	0	3	0	11	14	7.36	1.27	9.0	279	37	42	4.76	1.6	11.5	7.0	1.6	166
2009	Rk	Helena	6	3	0	69	66	4.43	1.16	21.1	232	29	63	3.19	2.7	8.6	3.1	0.9	99
2009	AA	Huntsville	1	0	0	4	3	6.75	1.25	5.4	210	11	67	6.53	4.5	6.8	1.5	4.5	-50
2010	A	Wisconsin	6	7	1	120	100	3.52	1.36	19.3	221	26	77	3.56	5.1	7.5	1.5	0.9	60
2011	A+	Brevard County	8	11	0	150	119	3.84	1.29	23.7	253	30	71	3.63	3.1	7.1	2.3	0.7	75

Athletic Canadian righty has solid pitchability and knows how to keep hitters off balance. He throws an 88-92 FB, a CB, and a solid CU. Throws strikes and isn't afraid to pitch to contact. Works hard at his craft and has shown steady progress. He's not going to be a star, but has solid back-end starter potential.

Buckel, Cody — SP — Texas

Thrws R Age 20
2010 (2) HS (CA)

EXP MLB DEBUT: 2014 | POTENTIAL: #3 starter | **8C**

Velo	Pitch	Grade
88-94	FB	++++
77-80	CB	++
86-89	CT	+++
	CU	+++

Year	Lev	Team	W	L	Sv	IP	K	ERA	WHIP	BF/G	OBA	H%	S%	xERA	Ctl	Dom	Cmd	hr/9	BPV
2010	Rk	AZL Rangers	0	0	0	5	9	0.00	0.60	4.3	124	28	100		1.8	16.2	9.0	0.0	316
2011	A	Hickory	8	3	0	96	120	2.62	1.14	16.6	234	33	80	2.91	2.5	11.2	4.4	0.7	149

Aggressive and athletic pitcher who showed surprising Dom ability with four-pitch mix. Spots FB well for youth and has good feel for secondary offerings. CU is second-best pitch, disrupting hitters' timing. CT and CB round out the set, though both need work. There is some concern about his size and his ability to maintain velocity deep into games.

Bundy, Bobby — SP — Baltimore

Thrws R Age 22
2008 (8) HS (OK)

EXP MLB DEBUT: 2013 | POTENTIAL: #4 starter | **7A**

Velo	Pitch	Grade
91-93	FB	+++
74-78	CB	+++
80-81	SL	++
	CU	++

Year	Lev	Team	W	L	Sv	IP	K	ERA	WHIP	BF/G	OBA	H%	S%	xERA	Ctl	Dom	Cmd	hr/9	BPV
2008	Rk	GCL Orioles	0	0	0	2	4	9.00	2.50	5.3	470	71	75	14.22	0.0	18.0		4.5	
2009	Rk	Bluefield	2	7	0	54	38	5.15	1.22	18.2	235	26	58	3.47	3.2	6.3	2.0	1.0	58
2010	A	Delmarva	4	6	0	116	91	3.65	1.22	16.8	234	27	73	3.41	3.3	7.1	2.2	0.9	68
2011	A+	Frederick	11	5	0	121	100	2.75	1.10	23.7	230	28	77	2.72	2.3	7.4	3.2	0.6	103
2011	AA	Bowie	1	3	0	15	13	9.60	2.40	15.7	371	43	61	9.32	6.6	7.8	1.2	1.8	-2

Aggressive pitcher who finished third in CAR in ERA before getting hit hard in Double-A. Lacks upside of brother Dylan, but consistently locates FB down in zone and mixes four pitches effectively. Durable frame offers ability to maintain velocity deep into games, but below-average CU might mean a move to the pen. Likely no high Dom with no plus pitch.

Bundy, Dylan — SP — Baltimore

Thrws R Age 19
2011 (1) HS (OK)

EXP MLB DEBUT: 2013 | POTENTIAL: #1 starter | **9B**

Velo	Pitch	Grade
93-99	FB	+++++
77-80	CB	++++
83-85	CU	++

Year	Lev	Team	W	L	Sv	IP	K	ERA	WHIP	BF/G	OBA	H%	S%	xERA	Ctl	Dom	Cmd	hr/9	BPV
2011		Did not play																	

Live, strong-armed pitcher with a very high ceiling. Plus-plus FB with location down in the zone and explosive movement. Complements the heater with a crisp CB. Repeats delivery, which enhances secondary pitches. Displays feel well beyond his youth. CU is below average, but flashes potential and should become solid-average.

Burgos, Alex — SP — Detroit

Thrws L Age 21
2010 (5) State JC of Florida

EXP MLB DEBUT: 2014 | POTENTIAL: #4 starter | **7C**

Velo	Pitch	Grade
88-92	FB	+++
74-77	CB	+++
79-83	SL	++
	CU	+++

Year	Lev	Team	W	L	Sv	IP	K	ERA	WHIP	BF/G	OBA	H%	S%	xERA	Ctl	Dom	Cmd	hr/9	BPV
2010	Rk	GCL Tigers	0	0	1	11	15	1.61	1.16	5.6	240	35	92	3.16	2.4	12.1	5.0	0.8	160
2011	A	West Michigan	6	5	0	94	89	2.20	1.02	22.6	192	25	79	1.85	3.2	8.5	2.7	0.4	113

Short and strong pitcher has limited upside, but hitters have had a tough time squaring balls up. He limits the long ball by burying four pitches in the lower half of the zone. Cuts the FB well and has polished secondary offerings, though none is a plus, swing-and-miss pitch. Can effectively work backwards, but doesn't have the velocity or projection to be a future stud.

Bush, Matt — RP — Tampa Bay

Thrws R Age 26
2004 (1) HS (CA)

EXP MLB DEBUT: 2013 | POTENTIAL: Setup reliever | **7C**

Velo	Pitch	Grade
92-98	FB	++++
84-87	CB	++
	CU	+

Year	Lev	Team	W	L	Sv	IP	K	ERA	WHIP	BF/G	OBA	H%	S%	xERA	Ctl	Dom	Cmd	hr/9	BPV
2007	Rk	AZL Padres	1	0	0	7	16	1.27	0.99	4.5	200	55	86	1.38	2.5	20.3	8.0	0.0	305
2007	A	Fort Wayne	0	0	0	0	0			0.3									
2010	Rk	GCL Rays	1	0	0	5	8	1.76	0.59	4.3	122	24	67		1.8	14.1	8.0	0.0	283
2010	A+	Charlotte	0	0	1	8	12	4.44	1.11	5.3	235	36	63	3.24	2.2	13.3	6.0	1.1	181
2011	AA	Montgomery	5	3	5	50	77	4.85	1.44	5.9	254	40	67	4.10	4.3	13.8	3.2	0.9	128

Converted infielder who has one of the quickest arms in minors. Top overall pick in '04 has transformed into solid RP prospect with hard FB and SL and ability to dominate hitters. Shows inexperience at times with inconsistent mechanics and control. Development of SL is integral to future role and has stamina issues.

Bushue, Tanner — SP — Houston

Thrws R Age 21
2009 (2) HS, (IL)

EXP MLB DEBUT: 2013 | POTENTIAL: #4 starter | **7D**

Velo	Pitch	Grade
88-92	FB	+++
75-77	CB	+++
	CU	++
	SL	++

Year	Lev	Team	W	L	Sv	IP	K	ERA	WHIP	BF/G	OBA	H%	S%	xERA	Ctl	Dom	Cmd	hr/9	BPV
2009	Rk	GCL Astros	1	0	0	22	19	2.44	1.04	17.1	224	27	81	2.70	2.0	7.7	3.8	0.8	112
2010	A	Lexington	7	8	0	133	114	4.12	1.33	22.1	256	30	73	4.22	3.2	7.7	2.4	1.2	63
2011	Rk	GCL Astros	0	2	0	8	7	7.88	1.75	12.2	383	47	50	6.21	0.0	7.9		0.0	
2011	A	Lexington	6	6	0	77	51	4.67	1.37	20.2	290	31	71	5.13	2.0	6.0	3.0	1.5	50

Lacking the stuff to dominate, this athletic RHP needs to get stronger and more durable. His nice, smooth arm action generates easy velocity -- a 90-93 FB -- and he has a nice 12-6 CB, but he needs to be more consistent with CB and CU.

Cabrera, Edwar — SP — Colorado

Thrws L Age 24
2008 NDFA D.R.

EXP MLB DEBUT: 2013 | POTENTIAL: #4 starter | **8D**

Velo	Pitch	Grade
90-92	FB	+++
	CU	++++
	SL	++

Year	Lev	Team	W	L	Sv	IP	K	ERA	WHIP	BF/G	OBA	H%	S%	xERA	Ctl	Dom	Cmd	hr/9	BPV
2008	Rk	Casper	0	4	0	30	38	7.80	1.77	15.3	310	40	59	6.91	4.5	11.4	2.5	2.1	52
2009	Rk	Casper	0	0	0	21	28	3.41	1.47	10.1	242	35	79	4.01	5.1	11.9	2.3	0.9	102
2010	A-	Tri-City	1	8	0	73	87	3.08	1.30	21.5	256	37	75	3.21	3.0	10.7	3.6	0.2	137
2011	A	Asheville	4	2	0	86	110	3.14	1.10	26.0	241	34	76	3.26	1.9	11.5	6.1	1.0	173
2011	A+	Modesto	4	1	0	81	107	3.56	1.25	25.3	255	37	74	3.65	2.6	11.9	4.7	0.9	146

Lefty doesn't have a blazing FB, but it is enough to keep hitters honest, and he led the minors in Ks (217) on the strength of a true swing-and-miss plus CU that really sets him apart. He has solid control and gets plenty of GB outs. Definitely worth watching.

Cain, Colton — SP — Pittsburgh

Thrws R Age 21
2009 (8) HS, (TX)

EXP MLB DEBUT: 2014 | POTENTIAL: #3 starter | **8D**

Velo	Pitch	Grade
90-94	FB	++++
	CB	+++
	CU	+++

Year	Lev	Team	W	L	Sv	IP	K	ERA	WHIP	BF/G	OBA	H%	S%	xERA	Ctl	Dom	Cmd	hr/9	BPV
2010	Rk	GCL Pirates	0	1	0	14	15	3.83	1.21	14.2	232	31	69	3.03	3.2	9.6	3.0	0.6	110
2010	A-	State College	1	1	0	34	32	5.03	1.09	12.1	193	25	51	2.18	3.7	8.5	2.3	0.5	99
2011	A	West Virginia	6	8	0	106	81	3.65	1.16	17.6	235	28	68	2.86	2.6	6.9	2.6	0.5	89

Athletic lefty has a nice 90-94 sinking FB, a decent CB and CU, and throws strikes. He did not dominate as much as his raw stuff would suggest, and went on the DL in August. He still leaves the ball up in the zone too frequently, but gave up only six HR. He controls the strike zone well and long-term has the raw stuff to make an impact in the majors.

Campos, Albert — SP — Colorado

Thrws R Age 21
2007 NDFA Venz.

EXP MLB DEBUT: 2014 | POTENTIAL: #3 starter | **8D**

Velo	Pitch	Grade
89-93	FB	+++
75-77	CB	+++
	CU	++

Year	Lev	Team	W	L	Sv	IP	K	ERA	WHIP	BF/G	OBA	H%	S%	xERA	Ctl	Dom	Cmd	hr/9	BPV
2010	Rk	Casper	4	4	0	88	68	2.05	1.10	23.0	244	29	84	2.83	1.7	7.0	4.0	0.5	117
2011	A	Asheville	6	4	0	86	64	5.22	1.51	24.9	313	37	64	4.87	2.0	6.7	3.4	0.5	87

Tall, athletic Venezuelan righty took a step back in his full-season debut. He has an 88-93 sinking FB, a plus mid-70s CB, and a CU that needs work. He needs to miss more bats, but does have good Cmd and induced plenty of GB outs with power sinker. Should rebound in '12, as he is better than 2011 showed.

Campos, Vicente — SP — Seattle

Thrws R Age 19
2009 FA (Venezuela)

EXP MLB DEBUT: 2014 | POTENTIAL: #2 starter | **9D**

Velo	Pitch	Grade
90-96	FB	++++
79-83	CB	+++
80-83	CU	++

Year	Lev	Team	W	L	Sv	IP	K	ERA	WHIP	BF/G	OBA	H%	S%	xERA	Ctl	Dom	Cmd	hr/9	BPV
2011	Rk	Everett	5	5	0	81	85	2.33	0.98	22.0	224	30	77	2.17	1.4	9.4	6.5	0.4	191

Significant success in his first year in U.S., leading the NWL in ERA and K by exhibiting plus control and using a lively FB effectively early in count. He repeats a deceptive delivery that fools inexperienced hitters, but he will need to polish secondary offerings to succeed at higher levels. Has projectable arm, and already gets good movement at lesser velocity.

Capps, Carter

RP | **Seattle** | EXP MLB DEBUT: 2013 | POTENTIAL: Setup reliever/Closer | **8D**

Thrws R Age 21
2011 (3-S) Mount Olive

90-96	FB	++++
76-82	SL	++++
	CB	++
	CU	+

Year	Lev	Team	W	L	Sv	IP	K	ERA	WHIP	BF/G	OBA	H%	S%	xERA	Ctl	Dom	Cmd	hr/9	BPV
2011	A	Clinton	1	1	0	18	21	6.00	1.61	19.9	272	38	61	4.46	5.0	10.5	2.1	0.5	93

Strong pitcher who has a quick arm action and the ability to use his height and mid-3/4 slot to throw on a downward plane. Throws with significant effort to generate very hard FB and solid SL, but his mechanics can be erratic, and his delivery might force a move to bullpen. To have any chance as SP, he needs to upgrade his CU.

Cardona, Adonys

SP | **Toronto** | EXP MLB DEBUT: 2015 | POTENTIAL: #2 starter | **9D**

Thrws R Age 18
2010 FA (VZ)

88-95	FB	+++
77-80	CB	++
	CU	++++

Year	Lev	Team	W	L	Sv	IP	K	ERA	WHIP	BF/G	OBA	H%	S%	xERA	Ctl	Dom	Cmd	hr/9	BPV
2011	Rk	GCL Blue Jays	1	3	0	31	35	4.62	1.38	13.1	261	35	66	3.78	3.5	10.1	2.9	0.6	107

Cleaner mechanics led to velocity gains for this young, projectable Venezuelan. He keeps hitters off balance with an outstanding CU, a excellent complement to his hard FB, which he buries low in the zone to keep the ball on the ground. He needs consistency and better spin on a below average CB. Some concerns his delivery suits him for the pen.

Carignan, Andrew

RP | **Oakland** | EXP MLB DEBUT: 2011 | POTENTIAL: Setup reliever | **7B**

Thrws R Age 25
2007 (5) North Carolina

88-95	FB	++++
82-84	SL	++
83-84	CT	+++

Year	Lev	Team	W	L	Sv	IP	K	ERA	WHIP	BF/G	OBA	H%	S%	xERA	Ctl	Dom	Cmd	hr/9	BPV
2010	A+	Stockton	3	3	0	33	44	6.27	1.88	5.2	231	35	65	4.61	9.3	12.0	1.3	0.5	92
2011	A+	Stockton	1	0	5	11	12	0.00	0.55	4.1	114	17	100		1.6	9.8	6.0	0.0	217
2011	AA	Midland	0	0	3	11	15	3.24	1.17	4.0	242	36	75	3.21	2.4	12.2	5.0	0.8	160
2011	AAA	Sacramento	0	0	0	16	19	2.22	1.11	4.9	194	27	82	2.25	3.9	10.6	2.7	0.6	120
2011	MLB	Oakland	0	0	0	6	5	4.43	1.64	4.5	317	36	78	6.16	3.0	7.4	2.5	1.5	44

Short, stocky reliever who reached MLB after pitching on three levels of minors. He showed drastic improvement in control by locating an electric FB in strike zone. He pitches aggressively off deceptive 3/4 delivery and uses CT as dependable second pitch. Also has SL at disposal, but it's far from polished. His injury history is cause of concern.

Carpenter, Chris

SP | **Chicago (N)** | EXP MLB DEBUT: 2011 | POTENTIAL: Setup reliever/closer | **8D**

Thrws R Age 26
2008 (3) Kent St

95-99	FB	++++
79-82	SL	+++
81-83	CU	++

Year	Lev	Team	W	L	Sv	IP	K	ERA	WHIP	BF/G	OBA	H%	S%	xERA	Ctl	Dom	Cmd	hr/9	BPV
2010	AA	Tennessee	8	6	0	119	100	3.17	1.39	21.8	260	32	77	3.65	3.6	7.6	2.1	0.4	81
2010	AAA	Iowa	0	0	0	15	12	5.40	1.87	23.4	310	35	76	6.92	5.4	7.2	1.3	1.8	10
2011	AA	Tennessee	1	1	1	12	6	4.46	1.16	4.8	227	22	67	3.69	3.0	4.5	1.5	1.5	23
2011	AAA	Iowa	2	3	1	30	28	6.58	1.83	6.4	274	34	63	5.42	6.9	8.4	1.2	0.9	49
2011	MLB	Chi Cubs	0	0	0	9	8	2.93	2.07	4.5	316	38	89	6.74	6.8	7.8	1.1	1.0	33

Strong-armed, athletic hurler pitched exclusively in relief in '11. Was healthy all year in that role and FB velocity jumped to the upper 90s. Also has a slurvy SL and a decent CU, though the FB/SL combo is his bread and butter. He must resolve struggles with command before he can be reliable, but he has a big-time arm.

Carpenter, David

RP | **Los Angeles (A)** | EXP MLB DEBUT: 2012 | POTENTIAL: Middle reliever | **6B**

Thrws R Age 24
2009 (9) Paris JC

87-93	FB	+++
77-80	SL	+++
	CU	+

Year	Lev	Team	W	L	Sv	IP	K	ERA	WHIP	BF/G	OBA	H%	S%	xERA	Ctl	Dom	Cmd	hr/9	BPV
2009	Rk	Orem	2	2	8	34	42	2.38	1.09	5.3	213	31	80	2.37	2.9	11.1	3.8	0.5	143
2010	A	Cedar Rapids	2	4	8	45	52	2.59	1.22	4.9	221	31	79	2.69	3.8	10.4	2.7	0.4	119
2011	A+	Inland Empire	0	1	11	29	36	0.93	1.10	4.6	220	32	94	2.30	2.8	11.2	4.0	0.3	153
2011	AA	Arkansas	1	0	5	18	16	0.00	0.93	3.6	190	25	100	1.26	2.5	7.9	3.2	0.0	132

Tall, lean righty has spent his entire career in the pen. His quick arm produces pitch movement, but he has outstanding control of a good FB with legitimate sink and tail and a SL that he locates well. He gets GBs by throwing down in the strike zone, but lacks a true K offering. Registers Ks more on deception than natural stuff.

Carpenter, Ryan

SP | **Tampa Bay** | EXP MLB DEBUT: 2014 | POTENTIAL: #3 starter | **8D**

Thrws L Age 21
2011 (7) Gonzaga

87-98	FB	+++
74-78	CB	+++
79-83	SL	++
	CU	+++

Year	Lev	Team	W	L	Sv	IP	K	ERA	WHIP	BF/G	OBA	H%	S%	xERA	Ctl	Dom	Cmd	hr/9	BPV
2009	NCAA	Gonzaga	6	4	0	65	68	5.26	1.57	19.0	285	37	66	4.72	4.0	9.4	2.3	0.7	83
2010	NCAA	Gonzaga	4	4	0	60	53	5.69	1.56	22.0	277	35	61	4.25	4.3	7.9	1.8	0.3	77
2011	NCAA	Gonzaga	8	2	0	96	107	2.63	1.09	26.8	210	30	75	2.05	3.1	10.0	3.2	0.2	136
2011	A-	Hudson Valley	2	1	0	23	26	0.78	0.56	9.8	121	19	85		1.6	10.1	6.5	0.0	228

Tall, inconsistent pitcher who projects well with loose, quick arm action. He passes the eyeball test with quality offerings and excellent size and durability. He was very tough to hit in his pro debut, with a hard FB and big-breaking CB. He might shelve SL in favor of using CB more frequently. CU is good, though he will need to repeat arm speed more consistently.

Carreno, Joel

SP | **Toronto** | EXP MLB DEBUT: 2011 | POTENTIAL: #4 starter | **7B**

Thrws R Age 25
2004 FA (DR)

87-93	FB	+++
80-83	SL	+++
75-78	CB	+++
80-83	CU	+++

Year	Lev	Team	W	L	Sv	IP	K	ERA	WHIP	BF/G	OBA	H%	S%	xERA	Ctl	Dom	Cmd	hr/9	BPV
2009	A-	Auburn	1	0	0	11	12	0.82	0.82	20.0	162	24	89	0.64	2.5	9.8	4.0	0.0	165
2009	A	Lansing	2	4	0	79	62	3.64	1.33	23.5	254	31	73	3.58	3.3	7.0	2.1	0.6	74
2010	A+	Dunedin	9	6	0	137	173	3.74	1.29	20.9	275	39	71	3.71	2.0	11.3	5.8	0.5	173
2011	AA	New Hampshire	7	9	0	134	152	3.42	1.25	22.8	209	28	75	3.02	4.6	10.2	2.2	0.8	97
2011	MLB	Toronto	1	0	0	15	14	1.18	0.99	5.3	204	26	93	2.11	2.4	8.3	3.5	0.6	120

Polished pitcher finished third in EL in Ks despite average pitches, which play up due to command, deception, and moxie. He has confidence to throw any pitch in any count and messes with timing by dropping in a nice CU for strikes. Held RHH to fine .188 oppBA, but exhibited the worst control of career and can leave too many balls up.

Carreno, Josue

SP | **Detroit** | EXP MLB DEBUT: 2014 | POTENTIAL: #4 starter | **7C**

Thrws R Age 21
2007 FA (Venezuela)

87-94	FB	+++
75-79	CB	+++
	CU	+++

Year	Lev	Team	W	L	Sv	IP	K	ERA	WHIP	BF/G	OBA	H%	S%	xERA	Ctl	Dom	Cmd	hr/9	BPV
2010	A-	Connecticut	5	6	0	64	59	4.77	1.51	19.8	261	33	68	4.27	4.6	8.3	1.8	0.7	69
2011	A	West Michigan	7	10	1	124	115	4.57	1.39	21.8	274	35	66	3.96	3.0	8.3	2.8	0.5	94

Thin, athletic pitcher works off a lively FB to set up decent slow CB and CU. He needs to add strength to enrich the feel of his FB, and CB has potential to be legitimate put-away pitch at higher levels. Repeats arm speed on CU, but movement is too limited to be a weapon against LHH. Locates FB well and limits walks, but could be better served in the pen.

Carter, Anthony

RP | **Chicago (A)** | EXP MLB DEBUT: 2012 | POTENTIAL: Closer | **7C**

Thrws R Age 26
2005 (26) Georgia Perimeter

90-95	FB	++++
80-84	SL	+++
	CU	+

Year	Lev	Team	W	L	Sv	IP	K	ERA	WHIP	BF/G	OBA	H%	S%	xERA	Ctl	Dom	Cmd	hr/9	BPV
2008	A+	Winston-Salem	6	5	0	82	41	4.93	1.47	20.8	282	30	69	4.97	3.3	4.5	1.4	1.2	18
2009	A+	Winston-Salem	11	7	0	154	119	4.38	1.25	23.2	255	29	68	4.02	2.5	6.9	2.8	1.2	67
2010	AA	Birmingham	1	4	22	57	58	3.94	1.21	5.0	226	28	70	3.26	3.5	9.1	2.6	0.9	92
2011	AA	Birmingham	1	0	5	14	14	1.28	0.78	4.2	131	19	82	0.24	3.2	8.9	2.8	0.0	141
2011	AAA	Charlotte	0	2	3	47	48	7.26	1.83	6.3	311	39	60	6.20	5.0	9.2	1.8	1.1	52

Reliever struggled in Triple-A and was demoted to Double-A. Provides deception with high 3/4 delivery and has been tough on LHH. Primarily uses FB and SL, and has moments of dominance despite inconsistency. Pitches up frequently, leaving him vulnerable to HR and doesn't change speeds well.

Cash, Ralston

SP | **Los Angeles (N)** | EXP MLB DEBUT: 2014 | POTENTIAL: #3 starter | **8D**

Thrws R Age 20
2010 (2) HS, (GA)

88-93	FB	+++
75-77	CB	+++
	CU	+++

Year	Lev	Team	W	L	Sv	IP	K	ERA	WHIP	BF/G	OBA	H%	S%	xERA	Ctl	Dom	Cmd	hr/9	BPV
2010	Rk	Ogden	0	0	0	6	5	12.00	2.33	15.5	394	43	50	10.72	4.5	7.5	1.7	3.0	-34
2010	Rk	AZL Dodgers	2	2	0	30	25	3.60	1.33	13.8	255	33	70	3.08	3.3	7.5	2.3	0.0	97

Short, athletic RH missed all of '11 with a hip injury, but should be ready to go in '12. Before the injury, he showed a nice 88-93 FB, a slow CB, and a decent CU. Gets downward sink on FB and lots of GB outs. Has good feel and command of all three offerings. Off-speed stuff needs to be sharper. Look for a breakout in '12.

Castillo, Richard

SP | **St. Louis** | EXP MLB DEBUT: 2012 | POTENTIAL: Spot starter/reliever | **6C**

Thrws R. Age 22
2007 NDFA Venz.

87-92	FB	++
	CB	++
	CU	++

Year	Lev	Team	W	L	Sv	IP	K	ERA	WHIP	BF/G	OBA	H%	S%	xERA	Ctl	Dom	Cmd	hr/9	BPV
2008	A+	Palm Beach	1	0	0	16	19	1.13	1.25	10.9	210	31	90	2.26	4.5	10.7	2.4	0.0	127
2009	A+	Palm Beach	6	13	0	148	105	3.89	1.49	22.0	271	33	72	3.93	4.0	6.4	1.6	0.2	65
2010	A+	Palm Beach	7	12	0	133	75	5.21	1.72	22.4	310	35	69	5.52	4.1	5.1	1.3	0.7	29
2011	A+	Palm Beach	5	4	0	59	47	3.65	1.42	19.3	271	33	74	3.94	3.3	7.1	2.1	0.5	75
2011	AA	Springfield	1	1	0	44	42	4.30	1.86	8.6	330	41	78	6.29	4.3	8.6	2.0	0.8	58

Short, athletic (5'11", 165) RHP worked both in relief and as a starter. His quick arm action generates plus pitch movement. He has decent control, but does not miss enough bats to remain a starter. Also has a CB and a CU, but neither is plus. He could develop into a solid swingman.

Castro, Simon — SP — Chicago (A)

Thrws R Age 24
2006 NDFA D.R.

90-96	FB	+ + + +
82-85	SL	+ + +
79-84	CU	+ +

EXP MLB DEBUT: 2012 POTENTIAL: #2 starter **8D**

Year	Lev	Team	W	L	Sv	IP	K	ERA	WHIP	BF/G	OBA	H%	S%	xERA	Ctl	Dom	Cmd	hr/9	BPV
2009	A	Fort Wayne	10	6	0	140	157	3.34	1.11	19.6	230	31	71	2.70	2.4	10.1	4.2	0.6	141
2010	AA	San Antonio	7	6	0	129	107	2.93	1.11	21.1	227	28	75	2.67	2.5	7.5	3.0	0.6	100
2010	AAA	Portland	0	1	0	10	6	8.02	2.18	25.2	360	40	62	7.71	5.3	5.3	1.0	0.9	9
2011	AA	San Antonio	5	6	0	89	73	4.34	1.25	22.6	274	33	67	3.98	1.6	7.4	4.6	0.9	113
2011	AAA	Tucson	2	2	0	25	21	10.36	2.18	21.0	342	39	52	8.23	6.4	7.5	1.2	1.8	2

Tall, strong-armed hurler had a disastrous season at Triple-A. He has a nice 90-93 FB that tops out at 96 with movement, and complements it with a plus SL and a decent CU. Castro showed better results when sent back to Double-A, but will need to prove that '11 was a fluke.

Cates, Zack — SP — Chicago (N)

Thrws R Age 22
2010 (3) NE Texas CC, TX

92-95	FB	+ + + +
	CB	+ + + +
	CU	+ +

EXP MLB DEBUT: 2014 POTENTIAL: #3 starter **8D**

Year	Lev	Team	W	L	Sv	IP	K	ERA	WHIP	BF/G	OBA	H%	S%	xERA	Ctl	Dom	Cmd	hr/9	BPV
2011	A	Fort Wayne	4	10	0	118	111	4.73	1.36	19.7	243	32	63	3.26	4.0	8.5	2.1	0.3	92

Tall, athletic hurler has a mid-90s FB, a CU, and a CB. He had mixed results in debut, struggling with command, walking 53 and throwing 15 WP. CB and CU both need to be better and more consistent. Still has some potential, but also some work to do.

Chafin, Andrew — SP — Arizona

Thrws L Age 22
2011 (1-S) Kent State

90-95	FB	+ + + +
79-[illegible]	SL	+ + + +
83-[illegible]	CU	+ +

EXP MLB DEBUT: 2013 POTENTIAL: #2 starter/Power reliever **8C**

Year	Lev	Team	W	L	Sv	IP	K	ERA	WHIP	BF/G	OBA	H%	S%	xERA	Ctl	Dom	Cmd	hr/9	BPV
2009	NCAA	Kent State	4	1	8	35	55	1.28	1.16	8.3	201				4.1	14.1	3.4		
2011	NCAA	Kent State	8	1	0	89	105	2.02	0.92	23.8	190	28	78	1.40	2.3	10.6	4.6	0.2	170
2011	Rk	Arizona	0	0	0	1	2	0.00	1.00	3.8	262	55	100	2.23	0.0	18.0		0.0	

Was healthy after having TJS in '10. He features a quality 90-95 FB, a plus SL, a CB, and a below average CU. At 6'2", 205, he has a nice, strong frame, but doesn't have a lot of projection left. Competes on the mound, even when he isn't 100%. Durability will determine whether he starts or works in relief.

Christenson, Ryan — SP — Los Angeles (N)

Thrws L Age 23
2010 (7) South Mountain CC

88-90	FB	+ +
	CB	+ +
	CU	+ +

EXP MLB DEBUT: 2014 POTENTIAL: #4 starter **7C**

Year	Lev	Team	W	L	Sv	IP	K	ERA	WHIP	BF/G	OBA	H%	S%	xERA	Ctl	Dom	Cmd	hr/9	BPV
2010	Rk	AZL Dodgers	0	0	0	14	16	0.63	0.92	10.6	200	29	92	1.31	1.9	10.1	5.3	0.0	188
2010	A	Great Lakes	3	1	0	36	26	6.75	1.75	20.6	330	39	58	5.50	3.3	6.5	2.0	0.3	63
2011	A	Great Lakes	7	8	0	119	98	5.06	1.49	19.8	303	37	65	4.60	2.4	7.4	3.1	0.5	90

Short, athletic lefty was not particularly effective in his full-season debut, but does have potential. He commands his 88-90 FB well, works both sides of the plate and throws strikes. Found too much of the strike zone in '11. CB and CU will need to improve to compensate for average velocity on FB.

Cingrani, Tony — SP — Cincinnati

Thrws L Age 22
2011 (3) Rice

92-95	FB	+ + + +
	SL	+ +
	CU	+ +

EXP MLB DEBUT: 2014 POTENTIAL: #3 stater/power reliever **8D**

Year	Lev	Team	W	L	Sv	IP	K	ERA	WHIP	BF/G	OBA	H%	S%	xERA	Ctl	Dom	Cmd	hr/9	BPV
2010	NCAA	Rice	1	0	0	22	13	8.59	1.95	17.5	303	34	54	6.13	6.5	5.3	0.8	0.8	19
2011	NCAA	Rice	4	2	12	57	66	1.74	1.00	6.4	226	33	81	1.84	1.6	10.4	6.6	0.0	211
2011	Rk	Billings	3	2	0	51	80	1.76	0.80	14.2	195	35	78	1.10	1.1	14.1	13.3	0.2	375

A third round pick in '11, the Rice lefty has a plus 92-95 FB with a long arm action and a low 3/4 slot that give him nice deception but raise long-term concerns about durability. The Reds worked to shorten his arm action. He also has a decent CU and a below average SL. A work in progress.

Clemens, Paul — SP — Houston

Thrws R Age 24
2008 (7) Louisburg JC

92-95	FB	+ + + +
	SL	+ +
	CB	+ + +
	CU	+ +

EXP MLB DEBUT: 2012 POTENTIAL: #3 starter **8D**

Year	Lev	Team	W	L	Sv	IP	K	ERA	WHIP	BF/G	OBA	H%	S%	xERA	Ctl	Dom	Cmd	hr/9	BPV
2010	A	Rome	2	0	1	19	16	1.42	1.00	9.1	170	21	89	1.66	3.8	7.6	2.0	0.5	94
2010	A+	Myrtle Beach	0	4	2	75	65	3.71	1.48	12.0	281	35	75	4.36	3.4	7.8	2.3	0.6	76
2011	AA	Mississippi	6	5	0	108	93	3.74	1.36	22.6	252	31	73	3.73	3.7	7.7	2.1	0.7	75
2011	AA	Corpus Christi	2	1	0	30	26	2.38	1.16	24.0	213	25	84	2.94	3.6	7.7	2.2	0.9	78
2011	AAA	Oklahoma City	0	1	0	4	6	17.14	2.38	21.8	252	34	22	7.64	12.9	12.9	1.0	2.1	38

A chip in the Michael Bourn deal, Clemens (no relation) has a quick arm action with good front-side mechanics. He sometimes throws with max effort, but has a nice 92-95 sinking FB. Complements the heat with a decent CB, a SL, and a below-average CU. He can overthrow at times, causing his pitches to flatten out.

Cleto, Maikel — SP — St. Louis

Thrws R Age 23
2006 NDFA D.R.

94-97	FB	+ + + +
78-81	SL	+ + +
82-86	CU	+ +

EXP MLB DEBUT: 2011 POTENTIAL: Power reliever **7C**

Year	Lev	Team	W	L	Sv	IP	K	ERA	WHIP	BF/G	OBA	H%	S%	xERA	Ctl	Dom	Cmd	hr/9	BPV
2010	A+	High Desert	4	9	0	102	83	6.17	1.66	19.9	303	36	62	5.41	3.9	7.3	1.9	0.9	52
2011	A+	Palm Beach	1	1	0	29	33	2.48	1.03	22.4	197	27	79	2.15	3.1	10.2	3.3	0.6	128
2011	AA	Springfield	2	2	0	34	36	3.96	1.52	21.2	294	39	74	4.59	3.2	9.5	3.0	0.5	100
2011	AAA	Memphis	5	3	0	71	66	4.30	1.41	23.1	221	27	70	3.53	5.4	8.4	1.5	0.8	70
2011	MLB	St. Louis	0	0	0	4	6	13.17	2.68	7.5	377	47	56	12.52	8.8	13.2	1.5	4.4	-42

Tall, stocky righty has a live 94-97 FB that tops out at 101. He adds a CB and a CU that are good but inconsistent. The Cards have worked to get him to tone down his FB and keep his front side closed longer. For now he remains a starter, but the bullpen seems most likely.

Cloyd, Tyler — SP — Philadelphia

Thrws R Age 25
2008 (18) Bellevue, NE

87-90	FB	+ +
73-75	CB	+ +
80-82	CU	+ +

EXP MLB DEBUT: 2012 POTENTIAL: #5 starer/reliever **6B**

Year	Lev	Team	W	L	Sv	IP	K	ERA	WHIP	BF/G	OBA	H%	S%	xERA	Ctl	Dom	Cmd	hr/9	BPV
2009	A+	Clearwater	5	6	0	76	39	4.13	1.39	24.7	279	31	70	4.03	2.7	4.6	1.7	0.5	48
2010	A+	Clearwater	4	3	0	69	67	5.34	1.46	8.5	304	38	65	5.07	2.1	8.7	4.2	1.0	103
2010	AA	Reading	1	1	0	9	6	4.00	0.67	15.7	165	9	67	3.15	1.0	6.0	6.0	3.0	94
2011	A+	Clearwater	3	1	0	39	39	2.76	0.97	11.4	219	28	74	2.34	1.6	9.0	5.6	0.7	161
2011	AA	Reading	6	3	0	106	99	2.80	1.09	23.1	252	32	76	2.98	1.3	8.4	6.6	0.6	176

Tall, strong-armed RHP continues a successful transition from relief. He's not overpowering -- his FB is 87-90 and tops out at 92 -- but he has a decent breaking ball and CU, and locates all his offerings well. He doesn't get much attention, but he does get hitters out and could reach Philly soon.

Coffey, Cameron — SP — Baltimore

Thrws L Age 21
2009 (22) HS (TX)

88-94	FB	+ + +
81-83	SL	+ +
	CU	+ + +

EXP MLB DEBUT: 2014 POTENTIAL: #3 starter **8E**

Year	Lev	Team	W	L	Sv	IP	K	ERA	WHIP	BF/G	OBA	H%	S%	xERA	Ctl	Dom	Cmd	hr/9	BPV
2010	Rk	GCL Orioles	0	1	0	11	8	5.73	1.91	7.4	380	44	70	7.33	1.6	6.5	4.0	0.8	78
2011	Rk	GCL Orioles	4	3	0	36	26	2.24	1.19	14.5	255	32	79	2.73	2.0	6.5	3.3	0.0	111

Health has kept this tall, projectable lefty in Rookie ball for two years, but he's potent when he pitches. He has been dynamite against LHH, working off a hard FB with quick arm action. His velocity should continue to increase with cleaner delivery. SL hasn't developed as hoped, but he has shown some touch for changing speeds. He didn't allow HR despite flyball tendencies.

Cohoon, Mark — SP — New York (N)

Thrws L Age 24
2008 (12) N. Central Texas JC

87-90	FB	+ + +
70-74	CB	+ +
81-83	CU	+ +

EXP MLB DEBUT: 2012 POTENTIAL: #5 starter **6C**

Year	Lev	Team	W	L	Sv	IP	K	ERA	WHIP	BF/G	OBA	H%	S%	xERA	Ctl	Dom	Cmd	hr/9	BPV
2009	A-	Brooklyn	9	2	0	92	70	2.15	0.97	24.9	210	26	79	1.96	2.0	6.8	3.5	0.4	116
2010	A	Savannah	7	1	0	90	75	1.30	0.94	26.1	211	27	87	1.72	1.7	7.5	4.4	0.2	144
2010	AA	Binghamton	5	4	0	71	56	4.18	1.25	22.2	270	32	67	3.68	1.9	7.1	3.7	0.6	103
2011	AA	Binghamton	1	3	0	52	44	3.81	1.46	24.7	287	34	78	4.99	2.9	7.6	2.6	1.2	61
2011	AAA	Buffalo	4	11	0	94	51	6.12	1.68	23.5	311	34	64	5.79	3.6	4.9	1.3	1.1	19

Finesse lefty started the season well at Double-A, but struggled after promotion to Triple-A. He has a decent 87-90 FB, a backdoor CB, and a nice CU, but none is a plus pitch. He struggles at times with control, and with such below-average stuff, his margin for error is small. Has good mound presence and knows what he can do. Profiles as a back-end starter or swingman.

Cole, A.J. — SP — Oakland

Thrws R Age 20
2010 (4) Winter Springs, FL

92-96	FB	+ + + +
75-78	CB	+ + +
	CU	+ +

EXP MLB DEBUT: 2013 POTENTIAL: #1 starter **9D**

Year	Lev	Team	W	L	Sv	IP	K	ERA	WHIP	BF/G	OBA	H%	S%	xERA	Ctl	Dom	Cmd	hr/9	BPV
2010	A-	Vermont	0	0	0	1	1	0.00	2.00	4.8	262	35	100	4.84	9.0	9.0	1.0	0.0	78
2011	A	Hagerstown	4	7	0	89	108	4.04	1.25	18.1	257	36	68	3.43	2.4	10.9	4.5	0.6	145

Tall, lanky right-hander has a plus arm and gets plus movement from a 92-96 FB that tops out at 98. Also throws a good CB and a CU that has potential. Cole gets good downhill tilt from his delivery and proved willing to attack hitters to both sides of the plate. Just scratching the surface of what he can do and the upside is substantial.

Cole, Gerrit — SP — Pittsburgh

EXP MLB DEBUT: 2013 | POTENTIAL: #1 starter | 9C

Thrws R Age 21
2011 (1) UCLA

- 93-97 FB ++++
- 86-88 SL ++++
- 83-85 CU +++

Year	Lev	Team	W	L	Sv	IP	K	ERA	WHIP	BF/G	OBA	H%	S%	xERA	Ctl	Dom	Cmd	hr/9	BPV
2009	NCAA	UCLA	4	8	0	85	104	3.49	1.12	22.3	192	26	73	2.71	4.0	11.0	2.7	1.1	108
2010	NCAA	UCLA	11	4	0	123	153	3.37	1.17	25.8	210	31	70	2.33	3.8	11.2	2.9	0.3	133
2011	NCAA	UCLA	6	8	0	114	119	3.31	1.11	28.0	242	32	71	2.93	1.9	9.4	5.0	0.6	148

Hard-throwing righty with 93-97 FB that tops out at 100. Also has a two-seam FB, sharp SL, and CU that could develop into a plus offering. Above-average command while pitching with a clean, loose arm. Can leave FB up in the zone, which can make it hittable. Has upside, but Stephen Strasburg comps are premature.

Colome, Alexander — SP — Tampa Bay

EXP MLB DEBUT: 2012 | POTENTIAL: #2 starter | 9D

Thrws R Age 23
2007 FA (DR)

- 89-97 FB ++++
- 79-83 CB +++
- 81-86 SL +++
- CU +++

Year	Lev	Team	W	L	Sv	IP	K	ERA	WHIP	BF/G	OBA	H%	S%	xERA	Ctl	Dom	Cmd	hr/9	BPV
2009	A-	Hudson Valley	7	4	0	76	94	1.66	1.03	19.5	177	28	82	1.31	3.8	11.1	2.9	0.0	148
2010	A	Bowling Green	6	6	0	114	118	3.95	1.25	21.1	234	29	72	3.62	3.6	9.3	2.6	1.1	86
2010	A+	Charlotte	0	0	0	4	8	2.25	1.25	16.3	307	60	80	3.52	0.0	18.0		0.0	
2011	A+	Charlotte	9	5	0	105	92	3.68	1.16	22.0	208	25	69	2.69	3.8	7.9	2.1	0.7	84
2011	AA	Montgomery	3	4	0	52	31	4.15	1.33	24.0	219	24	70	3.43	4.8	5.4	1.1	0.9	41

Loose-armed hurler didn't post high Dom despite outstanding set of average-to-plus offerings: an explosive FB, thrown with ease; two solid-average breaking balls in hard SL and big-breaking CB; and a CU with late movement. Overthrows and loses arm slot, which affects command, but his ceiling is as high as any pitcher in a loaded system.

Colvin, Brody — SP — Philadelphia

EXP MLB DEBUT: 2013 | POTENTIAL: #2 starter | 8D

Thrws R Age 21
2009 (7) Layfayette, LA

- 92-96 FB ++++
- 75-77 CU +++
- CB +++

Year	Lev	Team	W	L	Sv	IP	K	ERA	WHIP	BF/G	OBA	H%	S%	xERA	Ctl	Dom	Cmd	hr/9	BPV
2009	Rk	GCL Phillies	0	0	0	2	2	0.00	0.50	6.6	0	0	100		4.5	9.0	2.0	0.0	151
2010	A	Lakewood	6	8	0	138	120	3.39	1.30	21.1	262	33	74	3.52	2.7	7.8	2.9	0.5	96
2011	A+	Clearwater	3	8	0	116	78	4.72	1.49	22.8	286	33	69	4.64	3.3	6.0	1.9	0.8	50

Tall, power-armed RHP had mixed results. At times, he looked dominant, mixing his plus 92-95 FB with a sharp CB and CU. At other times, he looked lost and struggled to find the zone. Back and groin injuries nagged him all year. Throws across his body, so mechanics need work. CB and CU will be key to development.

Comer, Kevin — SP — Toronto

EXP MLB DEBUT: 2015 | POTENTIAL: #3 starter | 8E

Thrws R Age 19
2011 (1-S) HS (NJ)

- 86-92 FB +++
- 74-78 CB +++
- CU +++

Year	Lev	Team	W	L	Sv	IP	K	ERA	WHIP	BF/G	OBA	H%	S%	xERA	Ctl	Dom	Cmd	hr/9	BPV
2011		Did not play																	

Tall and strong pitcher has a chance for future success, but likely will take a while to develop. He has average pitches now, but velocity could grow with cleaner delivery. He throws from a high 3/4 slot which bodes well for sinker. Shows good spin on decent CB and has touch and feel for changing speeds.

Conley, Adam — SP — Florida

EXP MLB DEBUT: 2014 | POTENTIAL: #3 starter | 8D

Thrws L Age 22
2011 (2) Washington State

- 88-93 FB +++
- SL ++
- CU +++

Year	Lev	Team	W	L	Sv	IP	K	ERA	WHIP	BF/G	OBA	H%	S%	xERA	Ctl	Dom	Cmd	hr/9	BPV
2009	NCAA	Washington St	1	1	1	37	26	6.05	1.69	6.7	323	36	67	6.37	3.1	6.3	2.0	1.5	27
2010	NCAA	Washington St	5	4	12	67	47	3.35	1.29	9.5	261	31	75	3.58	2.7	6.3	2.4	0.5	74
2011	NCAA	Washington St	6	7	0	108	83	3.50	1.30	27.8	271	33	72	3.44	2.3	6.9	3.1	0.3	99
2011	Rk	GCL Marlins	0	0	0	2	2	0.00	0.50	3.3	151	22	100		0.0	9.0		0.0	

Tall, lanky lefty was a reliever/closer in his first two years in college before being converted to a SP. Has a nice 88-93 FB that can hit 95, an average SL with some potential, and a good CU. SL will need to make progress, and he will need to prove he is durable enough to start, otherwise a move back to relief is likely.

Cook, Ryan — RP — Oakland

EXP MLB DEBUT: 2011 | POTENTIAL: Setup reliever | 7B

Thrws R Age 24
2008 (27) USC

- 95-98 FB ++++
- SL +++
- CU +

Year	Lev	Team	W	L	Sv	IP	K	ERA	WHIP	BF/G	OBA	H%	S%	xERA	Ctl	Dom	Cmd	hr/9	BPV
2010	AA	Mobile	1	1	0	18	12	2.97	1.26	24.8	202	23	77	2.72	4.9	5.9	1.2	0.5	61
2010	AAA	Reno	0	0	0	5	5	10.80	1.80	23.1	332	40	38	7.09	3.6	9.0	2.5	1.8	41
2011	AA	Mobile	1	4	13	44	50	2.25	0.95	4.9	184	26	78	1.61	2.9	10.2	3.6	0.4	142
2011	AAA	Reno	0	1	6	17	12	2.12	1.24	4.9	213	27	81	2.31	4.2	6.4	1.5	0.0	82
2011	MLB	Arizona	0	1	0	7	7	7.50	2.64	3.3	351	45	68	7.85	10.0	8.8	0.9	0.0	56

USC 27th rounder continues to excel in relief. Fared well at two levels with 62 K/22 BB in 62 IP. FB velocity is now 95-98 and tops out at 100 with good sink. He mixes FB with solid SL to give him a nice one-two punch that works well in relief. Below-average change means the move is likely permanent.

Corbin, Pat — SP — Arizona

EXP MLB DEBUT: 2013 | POTENTIAL: #3 starter | 8C

Thrws L Age 22
2009 (2) HS, (FL)

- 88-92 FB ++++
- 78-83 SL +++
- CU +++

Year	Lev	Team	W	L	Sv	IP	K	ERA	WHIP	BF/G	OBA	H%	S%	xERA	Ctl	Dom	Cmd	hr/9	BPV
2009	Rk	Orem	4	2	0	46	46	5.08	1.52	15.4	312	39	69	5.47	2.1	9.0	4.2	1.2	99
2010	A	Cedar Rapids	8	0	0	58	42	3.87	1.07	25.1	241	29	62	2.52	1.5	6.5	4.2	0.3	125
2010	A+	Rancho Cucam	5	3	0	60	64	3.89	1.25	22.2	252	32	72	3.78	2.7	9.6	3.6	1.0	105
2010	A+	Visalia	0	1	0	26	30	1.38	1.00	12.4	188	27	88	1.71	3.1	10.4	3.3	0.3	139
2011	AA	Mobile	9	8	0	160	142	4.22	1.32	25.5	276	34	70	4.13	2.2	8.0	3.6	0.8	97

Part of the Dan Haren trade, his FB has good movement and he attacks hitters to both sides of the plate. Complements the FB with an improved SL and a CU that has good potential but is still a work in progress. Has fairly polished mechanics and could add more velocity as he fills out a tall, athletic frame.

Corcino, Daniel — SP — Cincinnati

EXP MLB DEBUT: 2014 | POTENTIAL: #3 starter | 9D

Thrws R Age 21
2008 NDFA D.R.

- 91-95 FB ++++
- 75-78 SL ++++
- 84-85 CU +++

Year	Lev	Team	W	L	Sv	IP	K	ERA	WHIP	BF/G	OBA	H%	S%	xERA	Ctl	Dom	Cmd	hr/9	BPV
2009	Rk	GCL Reds	0	1	0	2	2	0.00	2.73	6.1	446	54	100	10.06	4.1	8.2	2.0	0.0	57
2009	Rk	Billings	1	4	3	25	30	5.00	1.51	5.5	245	34	67	4.02	5.4	10.7	2.0	0.7	91
2010	Rk	Billings	1	3	0	39	31	3.44	1.40	18.4	256	31	75	3.70	3.9	7.1	1.8	0.5	71
2010	A	Dayton	1	1	0	31	29	4.34	1.48	22.3	261	34	69	3.79	4.3	8.4	1.9	0.3	85
2011	A	Dayton	11	7	0	139	156	3.43	1.16	21.3	246	33	72	3.12	2.2	10.1	4.6	0.6	143

Corncino had a breakout season in the MWL. He uses a 90-96 FB with good late tailing action, complementing it with a 75-78 SL and an improved CU. He'll need to answer questions about his size -- he's short, but athletic -- and durability, but for now he has good dominance and clean mechanics.

Cortes, Dan — RP — Washington

EXP MLB DEBUT: 2010 | POTENTIAL: Closer | 8C

Thrws R Age 25
2005 (7) HS (CA)

- 90-97 FB ++++
- 83-85 SL +++
- 80-83 CB ++
- CU +

Year	Lev	Team	W	L	Sv	IP	K	ERA	WHIP	BF/G	OBA	H%	S%	xERA	Ctl	Dom	Cmd	hr/9	BPV
2010	AA	W. Tennessee	6	4	1	83	85	5.30	1.56	14.6	247	33	64	3.94	5.7	9.2	1.6	0.4	81
2010	AAA	Tacoma	1	2	1	12	13	5.16	1.39	5.7	274	36	63	4.17	3.0	9.6	3.3	0.7	104
2010	MLB	Seattle	0	1	0	5	6	3.53	1.18	5.1	173	26	67	1.65	5.3	10.6	2.0	0.0	126
2011	AAA	Tacoma	1	2	3	39	46	5.08	1.85	5.7	281	38	72	5.35	6.7	10.6	1.6	0.7	75
2011	MLB	Seattle	0	2	0	10	3	6.18	1.86	4.8	311	32	67	6.11	5.3	2.6	0.5	0.9	-7

Tall, strong pitcher converted to relief in '10. Game is all about arm strength as he regularly delivers explosive FB. Uses height and arm slot to throw on downward angle, and a hard SL gives him a second pitch that gets hitters to swing and miss. Lack of repeatable delivery hinders command and control, and he lacks feel for changing speeds.

Cosart, Jarred — SP — Houston

EXP MLB DEBUT: 2013 | POTENTIAL: #2 starter | 9D

Thrws R Age 22
2008 (38) HS, (TX)

- 93-96 FB ++++
- 75-78 CB +++
- CU +++

Year	Lev	Team	W	L	Sv	IP	K	ERA	WHIP	BF/G	OBA	H%	S%	xERA	Ctl	Dom	Cmd	hr/9	BPV
2009	Rk	GCL Phillies	2	2	0	24	25	2.24	0.79	12.4	150	22	68	0.45	2.6	9.3	3.6	0.0	156
2010	A	Lakewood	7	3	0	71	77	3.80	1.07	19.8	230	32	63	2.42	2.0	9.7	4.8	0.4	157
2011	A+	Clearwater	9	8	0	108	79	3.92	1.31	22.3	243	29	70	3.41	3.6	6.6	1.8	0.6	67
2011	AA	Corpus Christi	1	2	0	36	22	4.74	1.27	21.1	245	27	64	3.75	3.2	5.5	1.7	1.0	45

There are some red flags due to max-effort delivery, but earlier elbow problems were not an issue and he logged a career high 144.1 innings. Strong-armed hurler has plus stuff, starting with a 93-96 FB that tops out at 99, and backs it up with a good 11-5 CB and a potentially plus CU. He is one of the best arms in a thin system, so will move up quickly.

Crick, Kyle — SP — San Francisco

EXP MLB DEBUT: 2015 | POTENTIAL: #3 starter | 8D

Thrws R Age 19
2011 (1-S) HS, (TX)

- 90-94 FB +++
- 72-74 CB +++
- 81-83 SL ++
- 78-82 CU ++

Year	Lev	Team	W	L	Sv	IP	K	ERA	WHIP	BF/G	OBA	H%	S%	xERA	Ctl	Dom	Cmd	hr/9	BPV
2011	Rk	AZL Giants	1	0	0	7	8	6.43	2.43	5.2	313	43	71	6.66	10.3	10.3	1.0	0.0	75

Late bloomer with some nice projection. Big, athletic righty with a nice 90-94 FB that tops out at 97. He complements the FB with a CB, a SL, and a CU. Crick needs to develop these secondary offerings. If he does, he has the raw stuff and ideal frame to develop into a front-line starter.

Crosby, Casey — SP — Detroit

EXP MLB DEBUT: 2012 | POTENTIAL: #2 starter | **9D**

Thrws L Age 23
2007 (5) HS (IL)

Velo	Pitch	Grade
89-98	FB	++++
80-84	CB	++++
77-80	CU	+++

Year	Lev	Team	W	L	Sv	IP	K	ERA	WHIP	BF/G	OBA	H%	S%	xERA	Ctl	Dom	Cmd	hr/9	BPV
2008	Rk	GCL Tigers	0	0	0	4	2	0.00	1.67	6.3	252	29	100	3.92	6.4	4.3	0.7	0.0	44
2009	A	West Michigan	10	4	0	104	117	2.42	1.13	17.2	192	27	78	2.01	4.1	10.1	2.4	0.3	121
2010	Rk	GCL Tigers	0	1	0	12	10	8.93	2.07	19.7	381	45	54	7.67	3.0	7.4	2.5	0.7	54
2011	AA	Erie	9	7	0	131	121	4.12	1.52	22.8	248	31	74	4.15	5.3	8.3	1.6	0.8	66

Tall, athletic lefty who returned to action after limited time in '10. Bypassed High-A despite hiatus and showed poise, moxie, and good stuff. Uses a deceptive high 3/4 slot and peppers the zone with quick FB and plus CB. Walks were up due to pitch movement. He needs to trust his stuff, especially CU. Could reach MLB quickly if he's healthy in '12.

Cruz, Antonio — RP — Kansas City

EXP MLB DEBUT: 2014 | POTENTIAL: Setup reliever | **7D**

Thrws L Age 20
2009 FA (DR)

Velo	Pitch	Grade
88-93	FB	+++
74-78	CB	+++
	CU	++

Year	Lev	Team	W	L	Sv	IP	K	ERA	WHIP	BF/G	OBA	H%	S%	xERA	Ctl	Dom	Cmd	hr/9	BPV
2010	Rk	GCL Tigers	0	0	0	5	3	7.20	1.80	4.6	262	31	56	4.37	7.2	5.4	0.8	0.0	51
2010	A-	Connecticut	0	1	0	13	12	2.08	1.23	5.9	214	29	81	2.29	4.2	8.3	2.0	0.0	104
2010	A	West Michigan	2	0	0	19	13	2.83	1.52	8.3	261	32	79	3.64	4.7	6.1	1.3	0.0	67
2011	A	West Michigan	2	6	1	75	58	3.12	1.28	14.0	243	29	77	3.35	3.4	7.0	2.1	0.6	74
2011	A	Kane County	1	0	0	30	39	1.80	1.20	11.0	214	32	88	2.74	3.9	11.7	3.0	0.6	127

Short, strong reliever whose quick arm offers projection. Needs to find a consistent slot and release point to realize his potential as a short-innings RP. FB has room to grow, while tight CB can get hitters to swing and miss. Not much of a CU as his slow arm speed telegraphs it. May need to focus on FB/CB combo to advance in a deep organization.

Cruz, Joe — SP — Tampa Bay

EXP MLB DEBUT: 2014 | POTENTIAL: #4 starter | **7D**

Thrws R Age 23
2007 (30) E Los Angeles JC

Velo	Pitch	Grade
87-94	FB	+++
74-78	CB	+++
80-84	CU	++

Year	Lev	Team	W	L	Sv	IP	K	ERA	WHIP	BF/G	OBA	H%	S%	xERA	Ctl	Dom	Cmd	hr/9	BPV
2009	A	Bowling Green	5	8	0	98	99	4.04	1.39	19.6	285	37	70	4.05	2.4	9.1	3.8	0.5	119
2010	A+	Charlotte	13	6	0	142	131	2.85	1.24	23.1	255	33	77	3.19	2.5	8.3	3.4	0.4	113
2011	Rk	GCL Rays	2	0	0	13	16	0.00	0.61	11.3	139	22	100		1.4	10.9	8.0	0.0	261
2011	A+	Charlotte	1	0	0	14	6	5.14	1.29	19.2	233	25	59	3.31	3.9	3.9	1.0	0.6	33
2011	AA	Montgomery	3	5	0	47	42	8.43	2.02	20.7	361	43	59	7.92	3.8	8.0	2.1	1.5	29

Tall, projectable righty was dreadful in shortened season after shoulder injury. Proved to be very hittable by tipping pitches and overusing FB. Pitched tentatively with secondary pitches and his methodical delivery wasn't deceptive. Still has plus arm strength and generally throws strikes. Must improve CU to remain as starter.

Darnell, Logan — SP — Minnesota

EXP MLB DEBUT: 2013 | POTENTIAL: #4 starter | **7C**

Thrws L Age 23
2010 (6) Kentucky

Velo	Pitch	Grade
87-93	FB	+++
82-84	SL	+++
	CU	+++

Year	Lev	Team	W	L	Sv	IP	K	ERA	WHIP	BF/G	OBA	H%	S%	xERA	Ctl	Dom	Cmd	hr/9	BPV
2010	NCAA	Kentucky	5	3	1	73	55	5.66	1.64	23.3	308	36	66	5.56	3.4	6.8	2.0	1.0	46
2010	Rk	Elizabethton	2	3	0	34	32	2.11	0.99	11.9	225	29	81	2.32	1.6	8.4	5.3	0.5	157
2011	A	Beloit	2	2	0	33	24	3.81	0.97	20.9	205	25	58	1.78	2.2	6.5	3.0	0.3	108
2011	A+	Fort Myers	8	3	0	86	46	4.18	1.39	24.2	281	31	70	4.21	2.6	4.8	1.8	0.6	47
2011	AA	New Britain	1	1	0	30	20	5.66	1.39	25.4	309	35	59	4.86	1.2	6.0	5.0	0.9	107

Savvy pitcher might move to bullpen due to short arm action and max-effort delivery. He pounds the zone with an average pitch mix and aggressively commands FB to lower half of strike zone. CU can be very effective, but reliance on pitching to contact hinders his ability to tally Ks. Could throw harder in short outings and SL could play up.

De Fratus, Justin — RP — Philadelphia

EXP MLB DEBUT: 2011 | POTENTIAL: Power reliever | **7B**

Thrws R Age 24
2007 (11) Ventura JC

Velo	Pitch	Grade
89-93	FB	++++
79-82	SL	+++
80-81	CU	++

Year	Lev	Team	W	L	Sv	IP	K	ERA	WHIP	BF/G	OBA	H%	S%	xERA	Ctl	Dom	Cmd	hr/9	BPV
2010	A+	Clearwater	2	0	15	40	43	1.80	1.05	5.3	215	30	83	2.04	2.5	9.7	3.9	0.2	145
2010	AA	Reading	1	0	6	24	28	2.23	0.91	4.5	199	27	80	1.98	1.9	10.4	5.6	0.7	173
2011	AA	Reading	4	0	8	34	43	2.11	1.23	6.0	226	34	83	2.65	3.7	11.3	3.1	0.3	135
2011	AAA	Lehigh Valley	2	3	7	41	56	3.73	1.12	5.8	232	35	67	2.82	2.4	12.3	5.1	0.7	169
2011	MLB	Philadelphia	1	0	0	4	3	2.25	1.00	3.1	81	11	75	0.35	6.8	6.8	1.0	0.0	100

Tall, strong right-handed reliever continues to master hitters. De Fratus blows hitters away with a 93-96 FB that tops out at 98. He also throws a nasty, late-breaking SL. He keeps ball low with nice sinking action on his FB and is tough on RH batters. He should factor prominently in the Phillies' pen in '12.

De La Cruz, Kelvin — SP — Cleveland

EXP MLB DEBUT: 2013 | POTENTIAL: #3 starter | **8D**

Thrws L Age 23
2004 FA (DR)

Velo	Pitch	Grade
87-94	FB	+++
78-81	CB	++++
74-77	CU	++

Year	Lev	Team	W	L	Sv	IP	K	ERA	WHIP	BF/G	OBA	H%	S%	xERA	Ctl	Dom	Cmd	hr/9	BPV
2008	AA	Akron	1	0	0	5	4	7.20	1.40	21.1	221	23	50	4.50	5.4	7.2	1.3	1.8	28
2009	A+	Kinston	2	0	0	12	19	1.50	0.67	20.9	151	25	86	0.80	1.5	14.3	9.5	0.8	287
2010	A+	Kinston	2	2	0	34	28	2.91	0.88	21.0	187	22	70	1.84	2.1	7.4	3.5	0.8	112
2010	AA	Akron	5	6	0	93	77	5.79	1.74	21.2	272	32	68	5.42	6.2	7.4	1.2	1.2	36
2011	AA	Akron	5	6	2	86	95	4.19	1.48	16.1	224	31	70	3.31	6.0	9.9	1.7	0.3	95

Tall, projectable lefty was much better in his second stint at AA. Batters found it hard to make hard contact against his nice FB and excellent CB. He pitches aggressively with quick arm action and adds solid movement to pitches, but struggles to repeat delivery and needs better CU. Was much better keeping the ball in the park.

De Leon, Victor — SP — St. Louis

EXP MLB DEBUT: 2015 | POTENTIAL: Power reliever | **8E**

Thrws R Age 20
2009 NDFA D. R.

Velo	Pitch	Grade
94-97	FB	++++
	CB	++
	CU	++

Year	Lev	Team	W	L	Sv	IP	K	ERA	WHIP	BF/G	OBA	H%	S%	xERA	Ctl	Dom	Cmd	hr/9	BPV
2011	Rk	GCL Cardinals	0	6	0	50	30	4.49	1.60	22.1	284	33	71	4.51	4.3	5.4	1.3	0.4	46

Strong-armed Dominican had a solid debut. Features a live 93-96 FB that tops out at 97. Also has a CU and a SL, but both are well below average. De Leon is very raw right now, and struggles with command and control. At 19, he was not particularly young for the GCL and '12 will give a better idea of his long-term potential.

De Los Santos, Miguel — SP — Texas

EXP MLB DEBUT: 2013 | POTENTIAL: #3 starter | **8D**

Thrws L Age 23
2006 FA (DR)

Velo	Pitch	Grade
86-94	FB	+++
80-82	CB	+++
81-84	CU	++++

Year	Lev	Team	W	L	Sv	IP	K	ERA	WHIP	BF/G	OBA	H%	S%	xERA	Ctl	Dom	Cmd	hr/9	BPV
2010	A-	Spokane	2	0	0	32	50	1.69	1.03	17.6	126	24	82	0.77	5.6	14.1	2.5	0.0	167
2010	A	Hickory	2	2	0	38	62	4.02	1.34	13.2	201	35	71	3.00	5.7	14.6	2.6	0.7	136
2011	Rk	AZL Rangers	0	0	0	3	7	3.00	1.67	13.5	321	73	80	4.76	3.0	21.0	7.0	0.0	264
2011	A+	Myrtle Beach	6	3	0	63	97	3.84	1.17	19.4	205	35	65	2.24	4.0	13.8	3.5	0.3	161
2011	AA	Frisco	1	3	0	28	38	8.04	1.57	20.5	255	36	48	4.84	5.5	12.2	2.2	1.3	86

Versatile pitcher has taken a while to develop, and missed two months with shoulder issues. He got rocked in AA, but continues to post high Dom at every level. FB command is subpar, but he throws with fine velocity, and plus CU keeps hitters off-guard. Mixes in solid-average CB, though it is very inconsistent.

Dean, Pat — SP — Minnesota

EXP MLB DEBUT: 2013 | POTENTIAL: #5 starter | **7D**

Thrws L Age 23
2010 (3) Boston College

Velo	Pitch	Grade
86-92	FB	+++
76-80	CB	+++
79-82	CU	+++

Year	Lev	Team	W	L	Sv	IP	K	ERA	WHIP	BF/G	OBA	H%	S%	xERA	Ctl	Dom	Cmd	hr/9	BPV
2010	Rk	GCL Twins	0	0	0	5	5	0.00	0.60	4.3	175	25	100	0.25	0.0	9.0		0.0	
2010	Rk	Elizabethton	2	2	0	24	32	2.61	0.75	17.2	200	28	73	1.92	0.4	12.0	32.0	1.1	725
2011	A	Beloit	2	0	0	44	37	2.86	1.11	21.6	244	29	78	3.14	1.8	7.6	4.1	0.8	113
2011	A+	Fort Myers	3	6	0	58	36	6.67	1.69	23.8	337	37	61	6.40	2.3	5.6	2.4	1.2	34
2011	AA	New Britain	0	1	0	6	3	4.50	1.67	26.9	347	39	70	5.37	1.5	4.5	3.0	0.0	76

Durable, polished pitcher who consistently works ahead in the count by pitching off FB and mixing in solid-average CU. Lacks the velocity to pitch up in the zone and has been victimized by HR. Can also hang the breaking ball, though he has confidence to throw it in any count. Has ability to notch strikeouts with CB and CU and has the stamina to pitch deep into games.

Delgado, Dimaster — SP — Atlanta

EXP MLB DEBUT: 2013 | POTENTIAL: #4 starter/reliever | **7D**

Thrws L Age 23
2007 NDFA Panama

Velo	Pitch	Grade
85-90	FB	+++
71-74	CB	++
76-78	CU	++

Year	Lev	Team	W	L	Sv	IP	K	ERA	WHIP	BF/G	OBA	H%	S%	xERA	Ctl	Dom	Cmd	hr/9	BPV
2008	Rk	GCL Braves	5	1	0	39	39	4.36	1.53	15.5	316	41	71	4.88	2.1	9.0	4.3	0.5	123
2009	A	Rome	5	7	0	99	104	3.63	1.16	23.2	241	33	68	2.78	2.4	9.4	4.0	0.4	136
2011	A+	Lynchburg	9	6	0	96	77	3.94	1.40	17.6	241	29	73	3.76	4.5	7.2	1.6	0.8	61

Athletic Panamanian has a nice low-90s FB, but his velocity can be inconsistent and keeps him from dominating. Big, looping CB can be effective, but spin needs to be tighter to remain effective. Still some work to do and will get a good test when he reaches Double-A.

Delgado, Randall — SP — Atlanta

EXP MLB DEBUT: 2011 | POTENTIAL: #3 starter | **8B**

Thrws R Age 22
2006 NDFA Panama

Velo	Pitch	Grade
92-94	FB	+++
75-77	CB	++++
80-83	CU	+++

Year	Lev	Team	W	L	Sv	IP	K	ERA	WHIP	BF/G	OBA	H%	S%	xERA	Ctl	Dom	Cmd	hr/9	BPV
2010	A+	Myrtle Beach	4	7	0	117	120	2.77	1.03	22.6	212	28	75	2.27	2.5	9.2	3.8	0.5	130
2010	AA	Mississippi	3	5	0	43	42	4.79	1.30	22.2	228	30	61	3.01	4.2	8.8	2.1	0.4	93
2011	AA	Mississippi	5	5	0	117	110	3.84	1.38	23.4	260	32	74	4.06	3.5	8.5	2.4	0.8	79
2011	AAA	Gwinnett	2	2	0	21	25	4.25	1.42	22.4	241	30	77	4.67	4.7	10.6	2.3	1.7	67
2011	MLB	Atlanta	1	1	0	35	18	2.83	1.23	20.2	227	23	84	3.69	3.6	4.6	1.3	1.3	26

Tall, athletic pitcher has solid arm action that gives outstanding movement to his FB and CB. High 3/4 slot lets him pitch on a downhill plane. He overthrows at times, leading to control issues. His CB might be the best in the system, and a decent CU gives him three above-average offerings.

Dodson, Zack — SP — Pittsburgh — EXP MLB DEBUT: 2014 — POTENTIAL: #4 starter — 7C

Thrws L Age 21 — 2009 (4) HS (TX)

89-92 FB ++ / CB +++ / CU ++

Year	Lev	Team	W	L	Sv	IP	K	ERA	WHIP	BF/G	OBA	H%	S%	xERA	Ctl	Dom	Cmd	hr/9	BPV
2009	Rk	GCL Pirates	0	0	0	1	1	0.00	0.00	2.8	0	0			0.0	9.0		0.0	
2010	A-	State College	2	6	0	57	41	4.88	1.47	16.4	261	31	65	3.81	4.2	6.5	1.5	0.3	64
2011	Rk	GCL Pirates	0	1	0	8	7	4.39	1.34	11.4	257	30	70	4.16	3.3	7.7	2.3	1.1	66
2011	A-	State College	0	1	0	17	13	4.71	1.51	18.6	312	36	71	5.35	2.1	6.8	3.3	1.0	70
2011	A	West Virginia	6	4	0	66	46	2.58	1.15	20.2	246	29	78	2.89	2.0	6.3	3.1	0.4	95

Athletic finesse lefty has a nice 89-92 FB and a good 12-6 CB, but a below average CU. A broken hand in May cost him a month, but he still managed 20 starts. Improved GB/FB ratio gives him a chance to succeed if CU improves. FB is not good enough to dominate, but he competes well.

Dolis, Rafael — RP — Chicago (N) — EXP MLB DEBUT: 2011 — POTENTIAL: reliever — 8D

Thrws R Age 24 — 2004 NDFA D.R.

92-96 FB +++ / 85-87 SL +++ / CU ++

Year	Lev	Team	W	L	Sv	IP	K	ERA	WHIP	BF/G	OBA	H%	S%	xERA	Ctl	Dom	Cmd	hr/9	BPV
2009	A+	Daytona	3	9	0	99	75	3.81	1.32	15.2	218	27	70	2.92	4.8	6.8	1.4	0.4	71
2010	A+	Daytona	4	5	0	71	48	2.92	1.31	20.9	239	28	78	3.18	3.8	6.1	1.6	0.4	66
2010	AA	Tennessee	5	4	0	55	45	4.08	1.67	20.6	295	36	75	4.96	4.4	7.4	1.7	0.5	60
2011	AA	Tennessee	8	5	17	72	48	3.24	1.33	5.9	231	27	74	3.00	4.4	6.0	1.4	0.2	66
2011	MLB	Chi Cubs	0	0	0	1	1	0.00	0.91	4.1	0	0	100		8.2	8.2	1.0	0.0	125

Converted infielder has a strong arm and gets tons of GB outs (2.07 GB/FB ratio). Was used primarily in relief, and the results were encouraging. His control and command are inconsistent and he doesn't miss as many bats as he should. Has a plus FB/SL combination and the stuff to contribute at the MLB level.

Doubront, Felix — SP — Boston — EXP MLB DEBUT: 2010 — POTENTIAL: #4 starter — 7B

Thrws L Age 24 — 2004 FA (Venezuela)

88-94 FB +++ / 74-79 CB ++ / 78-80 CU ++++

Year	Lev	Team	W	L	Sv	IP	K	ERA	WHIP	BF/G	OBA	H%	S%	xERA	Ctl	Dom	Cmd	hr/9	BPV
2010	MLB	Boston	2	2	2	25	23	4.32	1.48	9.0	277	34	74	4.76	3.6	8.3	2.3	1.1	65
2011	A-	Lowell	0	0	0	2	4	0.00	0.00	5.6	0	0			0.0	18.0		0.0	
2011	AA	Portland	1	0	0	5	9	1.80	0.80	18.1	221	44	75	1.21	0.0	16.2		0.0	
2011	AAA	Pawtucket	2	5	0	70	61	4.24	1.30	16.0	247	29	72	4.09	3.3	7.8	2.3	1.3	63
2011	MLB	Boston	0	0	1	10	6	6.24	1.98	4.4	296	33	68	6.16	7.1	5.3	0.8	0.9	17

Aggressive pitcher who was used as RP in BOS, but still could become a SP. Repeats a high 3/4 delivery that gives him good command of FB and secondary offerings. CU and cut FB have been effective against RHH, and his CB continues to improve. Has tendency to pitch up, but doesn't have electric FB to get away with it.

Dunning, Jake — RP — San Francisco — EXP MLB DEBUT: 2013 — POTENTIAL: reliever — 7D

Thrws R Age 23 — 2009 (33) Indiana

92-95 FB +++ / SL +++ / CB ++ / CU +

Year	Lev	Team	W	L	Sv	IP	K	ERA	WHIP	BF/G	OBA	H%	S%	xERA	Ctl	Dom	Cmd	hr/9	BPV
2009	NCAA	Indiana	0	2	1	7	6	7.71	1.86	5.5	358	44	54	6.01	2.6	7.7	3.0	0.0	93
2009	Rk	AZL Giants	0	0	0	1	2	9.00	3.00	5.8	415	71	67	9.92	9.0	18.0	2.0	0.0	122
2010	A-	Salem-Keizer	1	0	2	36	46	2.98	1.05	7.8	227	33	72	2.43	2.0	11.4	5.8	0.5	184
2011	A+	San Jose	6	3	10	76	71	4.74	1.45	7.9	286	36	68	4.58	2.8	8.4	3.0	0.8	85

Tall, wiry righty held his own in the CAL. Has a 93-95 FB and a nice four-pitch mix that includes a SL, CB, FB, and CU. He is still raw on the mound after playing mostly SS in college. Worked in relief in '11, but was more hittable than before. Very much a work in progress.

Dwyer, Chris — SP — Kansas City — EXP MLB DEBUT: 2012 — POTENTIAL: #2 starter — 9D

Thrws L Age 24 — 2009 (4) Clemson

88-95 FB +++ / 81-83 CB ++++ / 80-82 CU +++

Year	Lev	Team	W	L	Sv	IP	K	ERA	WHIP	BF/G	OBA	H%	S%	xERA	Ctl	Dom	Cmd	hr/9	BPV
2009	NCAA	Clemson	5	6	0	86	95	4.92	1.27	20.7	239	31	63	3.75	3.5	9.9	2.9	1.2	93
2009	Rk	Idaho Falls	0	0	0	8	15	4.39	2.44	10.8	342	58	84	8.13	8.8	16.5	1.9	1.1	92
2010	A+	Wilmington	6	3	0	84	93	3.00	1.33	23.3	250	35	77	3.28	3.5	10.0	2.8	0.3	114
2010	AA	NW Arkansas	2	1	0	17	20	3.14	1.22	17.4	185	24	79	2.88	5.2	10.5	2.0	1.0	91
2011	AA	NW Arkansas	8	10	0	141	126	5.61	1.43	22.2	238	29	61	3.93	5.0	8.0	1.6	0.9	63

Durable pitcher who pitched better than his stats. Finished third in TL in Ks, but also had a high walk rate. Hitters still struggle to make hard contact against him, due to his velocity and knockout CB. He can use any pitch in all counts, but delivery and arm slot vary, frequently leading to command issues. Has enough stuff to be a dynamite starter.

Eichhorn, Kevin — SP — Detroit — EXP MLB DEBUT: 2014 — POTENTIAL: #4 starter — 7D

Thrws R Age 22 — 2008 (3) HS (CA)

87-92 FB +++ / 73-75 CB +++ / 78-81 CU +++

Year	Lev	Team	W	L	Sv	IP	K	ERA	WHIP	BF/G	OBA	H%	S%	xERA	Ctl	Dom	Cmd	hr/9	BPV
2009	Rk	Missoula	0	2	0	16	25	3.38	1.38	6.7	224	37	76	3.24	5.1	14.1	2.8	0.6	136
2010	Rk	Missoula	5	5	0	74	71	4.97	1.28	23.4	277	33	65	4.60	1.8	8.6	4.7	1.5	107
2010	A-	Yakima	0	1	0	6	5	4.50	1.50	25.9	262	33	67	3.59	4.5	7.5	1.7	0.0	83
2010	A+	Visalia	0	0	0	5	5	6.92	1.73	23.7	380	48	56	6.10	0.0	8.7		0.0	
2011	A	West Michigan	11	5	0	152	109	3.61	1.19	24.4	257	30	70	3.31	2.0	6.5	3.3	0.6	94

Athletic pitcher with plus control and feel. Body and arm action don't provide much projection or velocity, but he pitches to contact and lets defenses do their work. FB has enough movement to be effective against RHH and LHH, while he can drop slow CB and CU for strikes. Has been hittable and can be guilty of rearing back and overthrowing.

Eovaldi, Nathan — SP — Los Angeles (N) — EXP MLB DEBUT: 2011 — POTENTIAL: #3 starter/reliever — 9D

Thrws R Age 22 — 2008 (11) HS, (TX)

88-92 FB ++++ / 70-71 CB +++ / 75-77 CU +

Year	Lev	Team	W	L	Sv	IP	K	ERA	WHIP	BF/G	OBA	H%	S%	xERA	Ctl	Dom	Cmd	hr/9	BPV
2010	Rk	Ogden	1	0	0	5	4	1.80	0.60	17.1	175	23	67	0.26	0.0	7.2		0.0	
2010	Rk	AZL Dodgers	0	1	0	8	10	4.44	1.23	10.9	208	32	60	2.20	4.4	11.1	2.5	0.0	133
2010	A+	Inland Empire	3	5	0	85	58	4.45	1.55	23.2	292	35	70	4.47	3.5	6.1	1.8	0.3	61
2011	AA	Chattanooga	6	5	0	103	99	2.62	1.18	20.6	207	28	77	2.33	4.0	8.7	2.2	0.3	103
2011	MLB	Los Angeles (N)	1	2	0	34	23	3.68	1.40	14.4	225	26	74	3.37	5.3	6.1	1.2	0.5	55

Strong-armed hurler has good arm action that provides movement and velocity on a plus 92-96 FB; he also has a SL and a below-average CU. Can be effectively wild, but is living on borrowed time if Cmd doesn't improve. Delivery is deceptive, with high leg kick and jerky motion. Dominated at Double-A and will get a chance to start in '12.

Eppley, Cody — RP — Texas — EXP MLB DEBUT: 2011 — POTENTIAL: Setup reliever — 6B

Thrws R Age 26 — 2008 (43) VCU

85-89 FB +++ / SL ++ / CU ++

Year	Lev	Team	W	L	Sv	IP	K	ERA	WHIP	BF/G	OBA	H%	S%	xERA	Ctl	Dom	Cmd	hr/9	BPV
2010	A+	Bakersfield	2	0	6	18	24	0.00	0.56	4.3	151	25	100	0.00	0.5	12.0	24.0	0.0	601
2010	AA	Frisco	1	1	9	22	27	1.22	0.95	4.4	161	25	86	0.94	3.6	10.9	3.0	0.0	152
2010	AAA	Oklahoma City	2	1	1	28	31	4.15	1.60	6.9	287	37	76	5.07	4.1	9.9	2.4	1.0	78
2011	AAA	Round Rock	4	2	10	55	55	3.92	1.54	5.6	247	32	74	3.95	5.6	9.0	1.6	0.5	79
2011	MLB	Texas	1	1	0	9	6	8.00	1.78	4.1	302	29	62	7.72	5.0	6.0	1.2	3.0	-34

Tall, deceptive sidearmer who reached MLB briefly and has a chance to be solid situational or setup guy. Gets a lot of GBs and is very effective against RHH, but he lacks velocity and a dependable second pitch. Needs to develop something to battle LHH. Peripheral numbers (Ctl, Dom) are going in wrong direction.

Erlin, Robbie — SP — San Diego — EXP MLB DEBUT: 2012 — POTENTIAL: #3 starter — 8A

Thrws L Age 21 — 2009 (3) HS, (CA)

88-93 FB ++++ / 72-75 CB ++++ / 71-72 CU +++

Year	Lev	Team	W	L	Sv	IP	K	ERA	WHIP	BF/G	OBA	H%	S%	xERA	Ctl	Dom	Cmd	hr/9	BPV
2009	Rk	AZL Rangers	0	0	0	4	9	2.25	1.50	5.8	307	69	83	4.13	2.3	20.3	9.0	0.0	304
2010	A	Hickory	6	3	1	114	125	2.13	0.93	15.3	217	29	81	2.21	1.3	9.9	7.4	0.7	204
2011	A+	Myrtle Beach	3	2	0	54	62	2.16	0.55	20.3	141	17	74	0.84	0.8	10.3	12.4	1.2	314
2011	AA	Frisco	5	2	0	66	61	4.35	1.21	24.2	281	34	68	4.27	1.0	8.3	8.7	1.2	195
2011	AA	San Antonio	1	0	0	26	31	1.38	1.15	17.2	262	36	93	3.34	1.4	10.7	7.8	0.7	209

Short, athletic lefty with extreme pitchability and mature approach. Dominated in '11 by getting ahead and then attacking hitters with a plus CB and CU. FB is not overpowering (88-92), but he locates everything well and understands how to pitch. Does give up some HR, but pitching in PETCO will help that.

Espinosa, Abraham — SP — Atlanta — EXP MLB DEBUT: 2015 — POTENTIAL: #3 starter — 8D

Thrws R Age 19 — 2009 NDFA Panama

86-89 FB +++ / CB +++ / CU ++

Year	Lev	Team	W	L	Sv	IP	K	ERA	WHIP	BF/G	OBA	H%	S%	xERA	Ctl	Dom	Cmd	hr/9	BPV
2011		Did not play																	

Exciting, highly touted youngster from Panama has yet to make his pro debut. He put up a solid season in the DSL. FB is currently in the upper 80s, but should add velocity as he matures. He does a good job inducing GB outs, and has given up only three HR in two seasons. Still raw, but a player who could break out in 2012.

Familia, Jeurys — SP — New York (N) — EXP MLB DEBUT: 2013 — POTENTIAL: #1 starter — 9D

Thrws R Age 22 — 2007 NDFA D.R.

93-96 FB ++++ / 83-85 SL +++ / CU ++

Year	Lev	Team	W	L	Sv	IP	K	ERA	WHIP	BF/G	OBA	H%	S%	xERA	Ctl	Dom	Cmd	hr/9	BPV
2008	Rk	GCL Mets	2	2	0	51	38	2.81	1.15	18.5	242	29	75	2.78	2.3	6.7	2.9	0.4	98
2009	A	Savannah	10	6	0	134	109	2.69	1.16	22.2	224	28	76	2.42	3.1	7.3	2.4	0.2	98
2010	A+	St. Lucie	6	9	0	121	137	5.58	1.58	22.2	255	35	63	4.16	5.5	10.2	1.9	0.5	88
2011	A+	St. Lucie	1	1	0	36	36	1.50	0.80	21.8	171	23	82	0.94	2.0	9.0	4.5	0.2	162
2011	AA	Binghamton	4	4	0	87	96	3.51	1.38	21.5	257	33	78	4.16	3.6	9.9	2.7	1.0	90

Strong, athletic RHP dominated at two different levels with a plus 93-96 FB that tops out at 99, a plus SL and a developing CU. Improved velocity keyed his breakout, as did improved control -- he cut his walk rate almost in half, though he still has work to do. If progress continues, he has the stuff to be an elite starter.

Faulkner, Andrew — SP — Texas
EXP MLB DEBUT: 2015 | POTENTIAL: #3 starter | 8E

Thrws L Age 19
2011 (14) HS (SC)

Velo	Pitch	Grade
86-92	FB	+++
69-74	CB	+++
	CU	+

Year	Lev	Team	W	L	Sv	IP	K	ERA	WHIP	BF/G	OBA	H%	S%	xERA	Ctl	Dom	Cmd	hr/9	BPV
2011	Rk	AZL Rangers	0	2	0	25	27	2.16	0.84	7.6	194	27	75	1.39	1.4	9.7	6.8	0.4	205

Tall and athletic pitcher with loads of projection. Loose, quick arm action produces decent velocity, with more to come. He commands heavy FB to both sides of plate and mixes in solid, slow CB. Has effort in delivery and needs to be smoothed out to reach potential. Enhancing his CU is paramount for future success.

Fernandez, Jose — SP — Florida
EXP MLB DEBUT: 2014 | POTENTIAL: #1 starter | 9D

Thrws R Age 19
2011 (1) HS, (FL)

Velo	Pitch	Grade
90-95	FB	++++
80-83	SL	+++
	CB	++
	CU	++

Year	Lev	Team	W	L	Sv	IP	K	ERA	WHIP	BF/G	OBA	H%	S%	xERA	Ctl	Dom	Cmd	hr/9	BPV
2011	Rk	GCL Marlins	0	0	0	2	3	0.00	1.00	7.6	151	27	100	0.94	4.5	13.5	3.0	0.0	169
2011	A-	Jamestown	0	1	0	2	4	21.43	3.33	12.9	403	68	29	10.52	12.9	17.1	1.3	0.0	105

Cuban defector is an intriguing power pitcher with a nice set of pitches and good durability. Plus FB has good sinking action at 90-95, topping out at 97. He also throws a late-breaking SL and slow CB. Also has the makings of a good CU. If that develops, he has the stuff and the make-up to be a top-of-the-rotation starter.

Ferrara, Anthony — SP — St. Louis
EXP MLB DEBUT: 2013 | POTENTIAL: #3 starter | 7D

Thrws L Age 22
2008 (7) HS (FL)

Velo	Pitch	Grade
86-91	FB	+++
75-78	CB	+++
77-79	CU	+++

Year	Lev	Team	W	L	Sv	IP	K	ERA	WHIP	BF/G	OBA	H%	S%	xERA	Ctl	Dom	Cmd	hr/9	BPV
2008	Rk	GCL Cardinals	2	1	0	30	36	4.50	1.37	12.6	242	33	68	3.80	4.2	10.8	2.6	0.9	98
2009	Rk	Johnson City	4	1	0	50	40	3.24	1.32	15.9	258	32	74	3.26	3.1	7.2	2.4	0.2	91
2010	A-	Batavia	1	0	2	18	17	6.00	1.50	9.7	312	38	60	5.26	2.0	8.5	4.3	1.0	103
2011	A	Quad Cities	13	7	0	127	93	3.04	1.23	22.4	223	27	76	2.87	3.8	6.6	1.8	0.5	72

Athletic southpaw does a nice job of mixing pitches and features quick arm action that generates movement and allows him to miss bats. CB breaks well, being thrown on and off plate. Solid season of growth in 22 starts in the MWL but a lack of overpowering FB limits his upside.

Fiers, Michael — SP — Milwaukee
EXP MLB DEBUT: 2011 | POTENTIAL: #4 starter | 7C

Thrws R Age 27
2009 (22) Nova Southeastern

Velo	Pitch	Grade
88-92	FB	+++
80-83	CB	++
73-75	SL	+++
	CU	+++

Year	Lev	Team	W	L	Sv	IP	K	ERA	WHIP	BF/G	OBA	H%	S%	xERA	Ctl	Dom	Cmd	hr/9	BPV
2010	A+	Brevard County	4	8	0	93	94	3.48	1.08	21.4	229	30	68	2.64	2.2	9.1	4.1	0.6	132
2010	AA	Huntsville	1	1	1	31	36	3.75	1.19	12.5	241	32	71	3.31	2.6	10.4	4.0	0.9	127
2011	AA	Huntsville	5	3	5	61	63	2.65	0.92	10.4	196	24	78	2.24	2.1	9.3	4.5	1.0	135
2011	AAA	Nashville	8	0	0	64	69	1.12	0.98	20.3	185	25	93	1.83	3.1	9.7	3.1	0.6	125
2011	MLB	Milwaukee	0	0	0	2	2	0.00	2.50	5.3	262	35	100	6.10	13.5	9.0	0.7	0.0	71

A monster season in AA/AAA led to a late callup. He lacks an overpowering FB -- 88-92 -- but it has nice movement and he locates it well for strikes. He complements the FB by locating a plus CU, a SL, and a CB with consistent arm action and mechanics that make all of his offerings play up.

Filak, David — SP — Atlanta
EXP MLB DEBUT: 2014 | POTENTIAL: #4 starter/reliever | 7D

Thrws R Age 22
2010 (4) HS, (NY)

Velo	Pitch	Grade
90-93	FB	+++
77-80	CB	++++
	CU	++

Year	Lev	Team	W	L	Sv	IP	K	ERA	WHIP	BF/G	OBA	H%	S%	xERA	Ctl	Dom	Cmd	hr/9	BPV
2010	Rk	Danville	0	2	0	26	27	2.42	1.12	10.2	197	27	79	2.11	3.8	9.3	2.5	0.3	113
2011	Rk	Danville	1	6	0	58	47	5.10	1.56	19.6	305	37	65	4.67	2.9	7.3	2.5	0.3	80
2011	A	Rome	2	5	0	45	32	7.58	1.97	19.7	306	34	61	6.56	6.6	6.4	1.0	1.2	17

A converted catcher who struggled in his full-season debut on the mound. He has a nice 90-93 mph FB that tops out at 96 and a plus 70-73 mph CB, but the ability to throw strikes abandoned him in '11. He will need to regroup and become more consistent, and he will need to develop a CU to remain a starter. He could be moved to relief.

Fleming, Marquis — RP — Tampa Bay
EXP MLB DEBUT: 2012 | POTENTIAL: Setup reliever | 6A

Thrws R Age 25
2008 (24) Cal St Stanislaus

Velo	Pitch	Grade
88-93	FB	++
77-79	CB	++
74-77	CU	++++

Year	Lev	Team	W	L	Sv	IP	K	ERA	WHIP	BF/G	OBA	H%	S%	xERA	Ctl	Dom	Cmd	hr/9	BPV
2009	A	Bowling Green	2	7	5	63	68	2.86	1.32	6.2	230	32	78	2.96	4.3	9.7	2.3	0.3	106
2009	A+	Charlotte	0	0	0	2	5	9.00	2.00	4.8	347	82	50	6.03	4.5	22.5	5.0	0.0	226
2010	A+	Charlotte	5	0	5	72	96	2.50	1.04	6.6	181	28	76	1.74	3.7	12.0	3.2	0.4	147
2011	AA	Montgomery	5	4	4	80	104	3.60	1.24	7.9	201	30	71	2.65	4.7	11.7	2.5	0.6	120
2011	AAA	Durham	0	0	0	2	1	0.00	2.38	5.5	403	45	100	8.24	4.3	4.3	1.0	0.0	21

Unheralded reliever who has among top CU in minors. Dom is a bit deceptive as he doesn't have very good FB and CB is more of show-me pitch. Messes with hitters timing by using fast arm speed on CU. Has been effective against RHH and LHH. Lacks upside due to poor FB velocity and command. He could be intriguing option in late innings.

Flynn, Brian — SP — Detroit
EXP MLB DEBUT: 2014 | POTENTIAL: #3 starter | 8E

Thrws L Age 22
2011 (7) Wichita State

Velo	Pitch	Grade
87-94	FB	+++
80-82	SL	+++
	CU	++

Year	Lev	Team	W	L	Sv	IP	K	ERA	WHIP	BF/G	OBA	H%	S%	xERA	Ctl	Dom	Cmd	hr/9	BPV
2011	NCAA	Wichita State	6	4	2	83	77	4.65	1.42	17.6	252	32	66	3.65	4.2	8.3	2.0	0.4	83
2011	A	West Michigan	7	2	0	67	57	3.48	1.21	20.8	234	29	71	2.86	3.1	7.6	2.5	0.4	94

Tall, large-bodied lefty who uses his height well and pitches downhill. FB has potential to be top offering due to heavy action. He throws with some effort, but should last as SP due to durability. Mixes in an improving SL, though CU must improve to be effective against LHH. Inconsistent control and spotty FB command limit his upside.

Foltynewicz, Mike — SP — Houston
EXP MLB DEBUT: 2014 | POTENTIAL: #3 starter | 8D

Thrws R Age 20
2010 (1) HS, (SC)

Velo	Pitch	Grade
90-94	FB	++++
80-83	SL	+++
75-77	CB	+++
80-82	CU	

Year	Lev	Team	W	L	Sv	IP	K	ERA	WHIP	BF/G	OBA	H%	S%	xERA	Ctl	Dom	Cmd	hr/9	BPV
2010	Rk	Greeneville	0	3	0	44	39	4.07	1.38	15.5	270	33	71	3.97	3.1	7.9	2.6	0.6	85
2011	A	Lexington	5	11	0	134	88	4.97	1.49	22.2	283	32	66	4.52	3.4	5.9	1.7	0.7	50

Tall, athletic, righty struggled in his full-season debut. He has good raw stuff with a 90-94 sinking FB that tops out at 96. Also has the makings of a good CB and a decent CU. The key to his development will be his breaking ball. He has a hammer CB, but he doesn't command it well. Still, at 6'4" he has good size and a live arm.

Font, Wilmer — SP — Texas
EXP MLB DEBUT: 2014 | POTENTIAL: #3 starter | 8E

Thrws R Age 22
2006 FA (DR)

Velo	Pitch	Grade
90-98	FB	++++
74-79	CB	++
80-82	CU	+++

Year	Lev	Team	W	L	Sv	IP	K	ERA	WHIP	BF/G	OBA	H%	S%	xERA	Ctl	Dom	Cmd	hr/9	BPV
2007	Rk	AZL Rangers	2	3	0	45	61	4.58	1.44	13.7	243	37	67	3.52	4.8	12.1	2.5	0.4	121
2008	Rk	AZL Rangers	1	0	0	4	6	10.98	0.49	4.5	80	0		1.04	2.2	13.2	6.0	2.2	178
2009	A	Hickory	8	3	0	108	105	3.50	1.41	15.8	234	31	74	3.28	4.9	8.7	1.8	0.3	88
2010	A	Hickory	4	1	0	29	33	5.24	1.64	18.6	298	39	69	5.32	4.0	10.2	2.5	0.9	82
2010	A+	Bakersfield	1	2	0	49	52	3.86	1.43	23.1	216	28	75	3.66	5.9	9.6	1.6	0.9	76

Tall righty has the stuff to be a knockout performer, but has been plagued by injuries and inconsistency. He hasn't pitched since July '10 and has lots of work to do to reach potential. He has an explosive FB with heavy life, thrown with fluid arm action, and a potentially above-average CU, though he often slows arm speed.

Frazier, Parker — SP — Colorado
EXP MLB DEBUT: 2014 | POTENTIAL: #5 starter/reliever | 7D

Thrws R Age 23
2007 (8) HS, (OK)

Velo	Pitch	Grade
88-93	FB	+++
79-84	SL	++
	CU	+

Year	Lev	Team	W	L	Sv	IP	K	ERA	WHIP	BF/G	OBA	H%	S%	xERA	Ctl	Dom	Cmd	hr/9	BPV
2008	A-	Tri-City	5	5	0	87	47	3.83	1.31	24.0	277	31	69	3.64	2.1	4.9	2.4	0.3	69
2009	A	Asheville	10	7	0	130	98	4.49	1.47	24.3	301	36	68	4.54	2.3	6.8	3.0	0.5	83
2010	A-	Tri-City	1	3	0	20	15	7.61	1.79	18.5	331	39	54	5.80	3.6	6.7	1.9	0.4	55
2010	A+	Modesto	2	2	0	46	38	4.70	1.30	21.1	274	34	61	3.45	2.2	7.4	3.5	0.2	111
2011	A+	Modesto	11	11	0	154	105	4.50	1.41	24.1	283	32	69	4.49	2.7	6.1	2.3	0.9	57

Tall, lean righty survived a full-season in the CAL. Has one of the better breaking balls in the system to go along with a plus mid-80s SL and an upper-80s FB. His below average velocity (for his 6'5" size) means he doesn't have a lot of upside and will need to show better Dom as he moves forward.

Friedrich, Christian — SP — Colorado
EXP MLB DEBUT: 2012 | POTENTIAL: #3 starter | 8D

Thrws L Age 24
2008 (1) E. Kentucky

Velo	Pitch	Grade
87-92	FB	+++
79-82	SL	++++
70-74	CB	++++
75-80	CU	++

Year	Lev	Team	W	L	Sv	IP	K	ERA	WHIP	BF/G	OBA	H%	S%	xERA	Ctl	Dom	Cmd	hr/9	BPV
2008	A	Asheville	0	1	0	12	15	7.50	1.75	18.3	293	39	58	6.04	5.3	11.3	2.1	1.5	64
2009	A	Asheville	3	3	0	45	66	2.20	1.11	22.1	216	35	81	2.33	3.0	13.2	4.4	0.4	171
2009	A+	Modesto	3	2	0	74	93	2.55	1.17	21.1	220	33	79	2.53	3.4	11.3	3.3	0.4	138
2010	AA	Tulsa	3	6	0	87	78	5.06	1.55	21.1	289	35	69	5.07	3.6	8.1	2.2	1.0	61
2011	AA	Tulsa	6	10	0	133	103	5.00	1.50	23.0	294	33	70	5.31	2.9	7.0	2.4	1.4	48

His '09 breakout is starting to look like an outlier, as the tall lefty continued to struggle. Features a nice four-pitch mix including a 90-93 FB, solid CU, a plus CB, and a decent SL. Velocity is deceptive, though will need to repeat delivery better to improve overall command, as his control and lack of dominance make him very hittable. Time is running out.

Fulmer, Michael — SP — New York (N) — EXP MLB DEBUT: 2015 — POTENTIAL: #2 starter — 9D

Thrws R Age 19
2011 (1-S) HS, (OK)

Velo	Pitch	Grade
92-95	FB	++++
83-85	SL	++++
	CU	+

Year	Lev	Team	W	L	Sv	IP	K	ERA	WHIP	BF/G	OBA	H%	S%	xERA	Ctl	Dom	Cmd	hr/9	BPV
2011	Rk	GCL Mets	0	1	0	5	10	10.59	2.55	6.8	385	67	54	8.16	7.1	17.6	2.5	0.0	136

Strong, polished righty with a solid 92-95 FB that tops out at 97. He also throws a plus 83-85 mph SL with good late break. His CU is undeveloped and needs work. At 6'3", 200, he is already physically mature. If his CU develops, he has the raw stuff to be a top-end starter.

Gardner, Joe — SP — Colorado — EXP MLB DEBUT: 2012 — POTENTIAL: #4 starter — 7B

Thrws R Age 24
2009 (3) UC Santa Barbara

Velo	Pitch	Grade
88-93	FB	++++
74-78	SL	+++
78-82	CU	++

Year	Lev	Team	W	L	Sv	IP	K	ERA	WHIP	BF/G	OBA	H%	S%	xERA	Ctl	Dom	Cmd	hr/9	BPV
2009	NCAA	Cal-SantaBarb	7	1	0	84	69	3.42	1.31	26.7	250	31	73	3.24	3.3	7.4	2.2	0.3	86
2010	A	Lake County	1	0	0	25	38	3.24	1.12	16.4	194	32	73	2.40	4.0	13.7	3.5	0.7	149
2010	A+	Kinston	12	6	0	122	104	2.65	1.11	21.8	198	25	76	2.09	3.8	7.7	2.0	0.3	95
2011	AA	Akron	7	8	0	97	60	5.01	1.60	22.6	283	32	68	4.67	4.4	5.6	1.3	0.6	42
2011	AA	Tulsa	3	3	0	36	22	2.49	1.08	23.5	233	27	76	2.41	2.0	5.5	2.8	0.2	91

Part of the Jimenez deal. Generates GB outs (2.30 GB/FB) by spotting a sinking 89-93 mph FB in the lower half of strike zone from a low 3/4 slot. All his offerings have good movement and he throws free and easy. Must improve CU and SL to remain a starter, but he's tall, he's strong, and he does have potential.

Garner, Perci — SP — Philadelphia — EXP MLB DEBUT: 2013 — POTENTIAL: #3 starter — 8D

Thrws R Age 23
2010 (2) Ball State

Velo	Pitch	Grade
92-95	FB	++++
83-85	CB	+++
	CU	++
	SL	++

Year	Lev	Team	W	L	Sv	IP	K	ERA	WHIP	BF/G	OBA	H%	S%	xERA	Ctl	Dom	Cmd	hr/9	BPV
2009	NCAA	Ball State	1	0	1	20	24	4.95	1.80	5.4	262	38	69	4.31	7.2	10.8	1.5	0.0	99
2010	NCAA	Ball State	5	3	0	74	83	4.62	1.50	18.8	262	36	68	4.02	4.5	10.1	2.2	0.5	96
2010	A-	Williamsport	0	2	0	4	1	18.00	2.25	10.1	415	41	13	10.30	2.3	2.3	1.0	2.3	-61
2011	A-	Williamsport	1	1	1	30	30	1.20	1.27	15.3	255	35	89	2.90	2.7	9.0	3.3	0.0	128

Tall, physically imposing righty had an impressive season, working both as a starter and in relief. Garner has a plus 92-95 mph FB that has good life. He also throws a CB, SL, and a CU. While his CB and CU show potential, neither is a plus offering. Mechanics and command will need to improve if he is to reach his potential.

Garrett, Amir — SP — Cincinnati — EXP MLB DEBUT: 2015 — POTENTIAL: #3 starter — 7D

Thrws L Age 20
2011 (22) HS, (NV)

Velo	Pitch	Grade
92-95	FB	+++
	CB	+
	CU	+

Year	Lev	Team	W	L	Sv	IP	K	ERA	WHIP	BF/G	OBA	H%	S%	xERA	Ctl	Dom	Cmd	hr/9	BPV
2011		Did not play																	

Possibly a late round nugget. He already has a 92-95 mph FB and could see more once he grows into his 6'6" frame. Also has the makings of a decent change and CB. Was a two-sport standout in high school and so is still raw. The Reds gave him $1 million to steal him away from St. John's. At this point he is a big, strong project, but has potential.

Garvin, Grayson — SP — Tampa Bay — EXP MLB DEBUT: 2014 — POTENTIAL: #4 starter — 7B

Thrws L Age 22
2011 (1-S) Vanderbilt

Velo	Pitch	Grade
86-92	FB	+++
80-82	SL	++
	CU	+++

Year	Lev	Team	W	L	Sv	IP	K	ERA	WHIP	BF/G	OBA	H%	S%	xERA	Ctl	Dom	Cmd	hr/9	BPV
2009	NCAA	Vanderbilt	0	1	0	12	18	8.11	2.13	6.7	343	52	58	6.38	5.9	13.3	2.3	0.0	113
2010	NCAA	Vanderbilt	1	1	1	36	38	1.25	1.17	11.0	240	32	93	2.91	2.5	9.5	3.8	0.5	129
2011	NCAA	Vanderbilt	13	2	0	112	101	2.49	1.10	24.4	236	29	81	2.98	2.0	8.1	4.0	0.8	117

Tall and durable lefty who uses height well to pitch on downward plane. Uses FB to get ahead of hitters and mixes in nice CU. He doesn't have a pitch to get swings and misses, and lacks upside to front rotation. Will need to use smarts and moxie to succeed, as he has little margin for error. Not much projection left due to short arm action.

Gast, John — SP — St. Louis — EXP MLB DEBUT: 2014 — POTENTIAL: #3 starter/reliever — 7C

Thrws L Age 23
2010 (6) Florida State

Velo	Pitch	Grade
90-93	FB	+++
76-78	CB	+++
	CU	++

Year	Lev	Team	W	L	Sv	IP	K	ERA	WHIP	BF/G	OBA	H%	S%	xERA	Ctl	Dom	Cmd	hr/9	BPV
2009	NCAA	Florida State	5	3	0	38	24	5.18	1.68	6.1	285	32	70	5.27	4.9	5.7	1.1	0.9	28
2010	NCAA	Florida State	7	3	0	71	64	5.32	1.56	14.8	293	36	65	4.78	3.5	8.1	2.3	0.6	74
2010	A-	Batavia	6	0	0	35	36	1.54	1.00	16.7	215	29	85	1.95	2.1	9.3	4.5	0.3	154
2011	A+	Palm Beach	5	4	0	82	59	3.95	1.38	26.5	269	31	73	4.11	3.1	6.5	2.1	0.8	61
2011	AA	Springfield	4	4	0	79	54	4.10	1.43	25.9	264	30	74	4.42	3.8	6.1	1.6	1.0	43

Short power lefty works off a nice 90-93 mph FB with good movement. Also features a solid CB and a decent CU. Delivery is close to max-effort and he has already had TJS. Wore down in the second half of '11, raising concerns about durability. Still has three nice offerings, and a move to relief isn't out of the question.

Geltz, Steve — RP — Los Angeles (A) — EXP MLB DEBUT: 2012 — POTENTIAL: Setup reliever — 6B

Thrws R Age 24
2008 FA (SUNY)

Velo	Pitch	Grade
90-96	FB	++++
79-83	CB	+++
	CU	+

Year	Lev	Team	W	L	Sv	IP	K	ERA	WHIP	BF/G	OBA	H%	S%	xERA	Ctl	Dom	Cmd	hr/9	BPV
2009	A+	Rancho Cucam	7	1	0	64	73	3.79	1.31	7.8	223	29	74	3.50	4.5	10.2	2.3	1.0	90
2010	A+	Rancho Cucam	3	1	2	34	51	3.44	0.88	5.7	173	26	65	1.88	2.6	13.5	5.1	1.1	177
2010	AA	Arkansas	1	0	0	18	36	2.47	1.37	4.8	149	37	80	1.83	7.9	17.8	2.3	0.0	179
2011	AA	Arkansas	3	3	0	46	67	3.12	0.97	5.5	192	29	73	2.25	2.7	13.1	4.8	1.0	166
2011	AAA	Salt Lake	0	0	0	1	1	30.00	5.00	4.7	542	63	33	18.61	15.0	7.5	0.5	0.0	2

Short, athletic reliever with high Dom. Establishes himself with a sneaky quick FB thrown with plus arm speed, and can get swings and misses with hard CB. Improved control enhances overall package, but FB command comes and goes. Lots of moving parts in delivery and short stature give him low upside, but he has value.

Gibson, Kyle — SP — Minnesota — EXP MLB DEBUT: 2013 — POTENTIAL: #2 starter — 9D

Thrws R Age 24
2009 (1) Missouri

Velo	Pitch	Grade
86-94	FB	++++
82-85	SL	+++
78-82	CU	+++

Year	Lev	Team	W	L	Sv	IP	K	ERA	WHIP	BF/G	OBA	H%	S%	xERA	Ctl	Dom	Cmd	hr/9	BPV
2009	NCAA	Missouri	11	3	0	106	131	3.22	1.07	25.8	241				1.6	11.1	6.9		
2010	A+	Fort Myers	4	1	0	43	40	1.88	1.04	23.8	214	28	84	2.20	2.5	8.4	3.3	0.4	120
2010	AA	New Britain	7	5	0	93	77	3.68	1.22	23.5	258	32	69	3.27	2.1	7.5	3.5	0.5	107
2010	AAA	Rochester	0	0	0	15	9	1.78	1.12	20.0	219	26	82	2.09	3.0	5.3	1.8	0.0	81
2011	AAA	Rochester	3	8	0	95	91	4.83	1.43	22.5	289	36	68	4.77	2.6	8.6	3.4	1.0	88

Tall, lean pitcher who had TJS in September and will likely miss '12. Commands lively FB to both sides of plate and induces GBs. Pitchability is best in organization, and he knows how to sequence pitches. Cuts and sinks FB at will and pitches aggressively with SL and sinking CU. Health certainly a question mark, but should return strong.

Gilmartin, Sean — SP — Atlanta — EXP MLB DEBUT: 2012 — POTENTIAL: #3 or #4 starter — 8C

Thrws L Age 22
2011 (1) Florida St

Velo	Pitch	Grade
88-92	FB	+++
	CU	++++
	SL	+++
	CB	++

Year	Lev	Team	W	L	Sv	IP	K	ERA	WHIP	BF/G	OBA	H%	S%	xERA	Ctl	Dom	Cmd	hr/9	BPV
2009	NCAA	Florida State	12	3	1	98	83	3.49	1.20	21.9	227	26	77	3.59	3.4	7.6	2.2	1.3	64
2010	NCAA	Florida State	9	8	0	111	108	5.26	1.51	24.1	299	37	67	5.29	2.8	8.7	3.2	1.2	78
2011	NCAA	Florida State	12	1	0	113	122	1.83	0.94	25.0	212	29	82	1.89	1.6	9.7	6.1	0.4	187
2011	Rk	GCL Braves	0	1	0	2	1	9.00	1.50	8.6	347	39	33	4.95	0.0	4.5		0.0	
2011	A	Rome	2	1	0	21	30	2.56	0.95	15.9	232	34	82	2.96	0.9	12.8	15.0	1.3	362

Was one of the more polished pitchers in the '11 draft. He won't lead MLB in strikeouts, but has good control of an 88-92 mph FB, a plus CU, CB, and a SL. He has smooth, repeatable mechanics and is a strike-throwing machine. Attacks both sides of the plate, knows how to pitch, and keeps hitters off balance.

Glasnow, Tyler — SP — Pittsburgh — EXP MLB DEBUT: 2015 — POTENTIAL: #3 starter — 8E

Thrws R Age 18
2011 (5) HS, (CA)

Velo	Pitch	Grade
88-92	FB	+++
	SL	++
	CB	++
	CU	+

Year	Lev	Team	W	L	Sv	IP	K	ERA	WHIP	BF/G	OBA	H%	S%	xERA	Ctl	Dom	Cmd	hr/9	BPV
2011		Did not play																	

Lanky projectable California high schooler will make his professional debut in '12. He already features a FB that peaks in the low 90s, and at 6'7", 200, he has room to grow. Also throws a SL, CB, and a CU, though none is very polished. Very raw, but also has significant upside.

Godfrey, Graham — SP — Oakland — EXP MLB DEBUT: 2011 — POTENTIAL: #4 starter — 7D

Thrws R Age 27
2006 (34) Coll of Charleston

Velo	Pitch	Grade
87-93	FB	+++
80-83	SL	+++
	CU	+++

Year	Lev	Team	W	L	Sv	IP	K	ERA	WHIP	BF/G	OBA	H%	S%	xERA	Ctl	Dom	Cmd	hr/9	BPV
2010	AA	Midland	0	1	0	18	16	3.96	1.70	16.5	300	38	74	4.65	4.5	7.9	1.8	0.0	80
2010	AAA	Sacramento	4	7	0	106	87	5.60	1.52	19.2	265	32	63	4.40	4.5	7.4	1.6	0.8	58
2011	AA	Midland	0	0	0	4	6	0.00	1.00	15.3	210	36	100	1.61	2.3	13.5	6.0	0.0	220
2011	AAA	Sacramento	14	3	0	107	89	2.69	1.14	22.3	233	29	78	2.78	2.5	7.5	3.0	0.5	100
2011	MLB	Oakland	1	2	0	25	13	3.96	1.48	21.5	312	34	76	5.33	1.8	4.7	2.6	1.1	43

Durable pitcher who reached MLB after leading the PCL in wins. Exhibited much better control by locating his quality sinker down in the zone. Delivers pitches with good height and arm angle. Overuses FB and can be subject to HRs despite sinker. Limited upside based upon okay velocity and lack of any potent secondary offerings.

Goeddel, Erik — RP — New York (N)

EXP MLB DEBUT: 2014 | POTENTIAL: #3 starter | **7D**

Thrws R Age 23
2010 (24) UCLA

90-93	FB	+++
84-86	SL	++++
	CU	++

Year	Lev	Team	W	L	Sv	IP	K	ERA	WHIP	BF/G	OBA	H%	S%	xERA	Ctl	Dom	Cmd	hr/9	BPV
2009	NCAA	UCLA	0	0	0	8	6	3.38	1.75	4.1	307	35	85	5.95	4.5	6.8	1.5	1.1	32
2010	NCAA	UCLA	2	0	1	50	59	3.06	1.34	5.8	238	33	79	3.51	4.1	10.6	2.6	0.7	103
2010	Rk	GCL Mets	0	0	0	1	1	0.00	1.00	3.8	262	35	100	2.32	0.0	9.0		0.0	
2011	Rk	GCL Mets	0	0	0	6	2	1.50	0.83	7.3	228	25	80	1.51	0.0	3.0		0.0	
2011	A	Savannah	3	5	0	71	67	3.41	1.15	18.9	224	28	71	2.80	3.0	8.5	2.8	0.6	101

Tall, strong-armed RHP was used primarily as a reliever in college. The Mets moved him into a starting role and the results have been promising. His FB hits 90-93 with good downward tilt. He uses the sinker effectively to get plenty of GB outs. He also throws a decent CU and a plus SL that has good late break.

Goforth, David — RP — Milwaukee

EXP MLB DEBUT: 2013 | POTENTIAL: Power reliever | **8C**

Thrws R Age 23
2011 (7) Mississippi

96-98	FB	++++
90-93	CT	++
	SL	++

Year	Lev	Team	W	L	Sv	IP	K	ERA	WHIP	BF/G	OBA	H%	S%	xERA	Ctl	Dom	Cmd	hr/9	BPV
2009	NCAA	Mississippi	1	1	3	35	36	2.82	1.28	5.8	202	26	81	2.98	5.1	9.2	1.8	0.8	85
2010	NCAA	Mississippi	1	6	3	56	43	9.47	2.28	13.0	363	39	61	9.43	6.1	6.9	1.1	2.4	-25
2011	NCAA	Mississippi	4	8	0	83	63	4.88	1.37	24.9	271	32	63	3.92	2.9	6.8	2.3	0.5	75
2011	Rk	Helena	0	4	2	40	42	4.48	1.34	8.8	280	35	69	4.48	2.2	9.4	4.2	1.1	110

Seventh rounder looks like a bargain. A SP in college, but he will work in relief as a pro, which lets his plus mid-to-upper-90s FB play up. As a SP, FB was 90-94 mph, but in relief was 95-98. He is working on developing a cutter to go with a below-average SL. Could be an impact reliever.

Goodnight, Michael — SP — Cleveland

EXP MLB DEBUT: 2013 | POTENTIAL: #4 starter | **7B**

Thrws R Age 23
2010 (13) Houston

87-94	FB	+++
80-82	SL	+++
	CU	++

Year	Lev	Team	W	L	Sv	IP	K	ERA	WHIP	BF/G	OBA	H%	S%	xERA	Ctl	Dom	Cmd	hr/9	BPV
2009	NCAA	Houston	5	5	0	65	58	4.43	1.52	18.8	271	34	70	4.16	4.3	8.0	1.9	0.4	76
2010	NCAA	Houston	7	7	0	85	90	5.39	1.69	24.0	273	34	71	5.49	5.7	9.5	1.7	1.4	51
2010	A-	Mahoning Vall	0	2	0	13	12	4.12	1.53	14.2	213	29	70	3.02	6.9	8.2	1.2	0.0	87
2011	A	Lake County	5	12	0	130	117	4.15	1.31	19.9	221	28	68	3.15	4.6	8.1	1.8	0.6	78
2011	A+	Kinston	1	0	0	5	6	1.76	0.59	17.4	173	26	67	0.17	0.0	10.6		0.0	

Durable, physical pitcher is not widely known despite a nifty FB/SL combination. He might move to the pen due to inconsistency and cross-body delivery. He sets up hitters by using FB with late life early in the count. Can wipe out RHH with a sharp SL, but fails to throw it for strikes when he has to. CU has potential, but he doesn't trust it yet.

Gould, Garrett — SP — Los Angeles (N)

EXP MLB DEBUT: 2014 | POTENTIAL: #3 starter | **8D**

Thrws R Age 20
2009 (2) HS, (KS)

88-93	FB	++++
80-83	CB	++++
80-82	CU	++

Year	Lev	Team	W	L	Sv	IP	K	ERA	WHIP	BF/G	OBA	H%	S%	xERA	Ctl	Dom	Cmd	hr/9	BPV
2009	Rk	Ogden	0	1	0	2	4	12.27	2.73	4.1	392	58	60	12.61	8.2	16.4	2.0	4.1	-6
2010	Rk	Ogden	1	4	0	57	52	4.09	1.54	19.2	297	37	74	4.77	3.1	8.2	2.6	0.6	80
2011	A	Great Lakes	11	6	0	123	104	2.41	1.13	18.0	227	28	81	2.74	2.7	7.6	2.8	0.6	97

Nice strong-armed RHP. Has good size and some projectability left. Was one of the better starters in the MWL. Has a nice 88-93 mph sinking FB, a plus 12-6 CB, and a decent CU. Gould locates well, knows how to pitch and throws tons of strikes. He isn't overpowering and so projects more as a solid #3 or #4 starter.

Graham, J.R. — SP — Atlanta

EXP MLB DEBUT: 2014 | POTENTIAL: #2 starter/Power Reliever | **9D**

Thrws R Age 22
2011 (4) Santa Clara

95-98	FB	++++
	SL	+++
	CU	++

Year	Lev	Team	W	L	Sv	IP	K	ERA	WHIP	BF/G	OBA	H%	S%	xERA	Ctl	Dom	Cmd	hr/9	BPV
2009	NCAA	Santa Clara	0	3	1	34	35	7.15	1.97	8.6	360	45	63	7.32	3.4	9.3	2.7	1.1	63
2010	NCAA	Santa Clara	1	1	4	27	21	5.31	2.03	5.7	371	44	72	7.00	3.3	7.0	2.1	0.3	57
2011	NCAA	Santa Clara	3	5	3	62	45	3.34	1.00	10.3	233	29	64	2.09	1.3	6.5	5.0	0.1	148
2011	Rk	Danville	5	2	0	57	52	1.73	1.14	17.4	244	32	83	2.43	2.0	8.2	4.0	0.0	139

Short, lean, athletic righty had a nice pro debut. FB reaches 95-98 mph, and can hit 100. He also features a nice SL and a decent CU. He was a closer in college, but has worked primarily as a starter once drafted. He will need to improve his secondary offerings to remain in that role, but is a player to keep an eye on.

Gray, Sonny — SP — Oakland

EXP MLB DEBUT: 2012 | POTENTIAL: #2 starter | **8B**

Thrws R Age 22
2011 (1) Vanderbilt

89-95	FB	+++
82-84	CB	++++
	CU	++

Year	Lev	Team	W	L	Sv	IP	K	ERA	WHIP	BF/G	OBA	H%	S%	xERA	Ctl	Dom	Cmd	hr/9	BPV
2009	NCAA	Vanderbilt	5	1	5	58	72	4.33	1.46	11.3	284	39	72	4.64	3.1	11.1	3.6	0.9	113
2010	NCAA	Vanderbilt	10	5	1	108	113	3.49	1.38	23.9	249	34	74	3.40	4.0	9.4	2.4	0.3	101
2011	NCAA	Vanderbilt	12	4	0	126	132	2.43	1.17	26.5	214	29	79	2.41	3.6	9.4	2.6	0.3	114
2011	Rk	AZL Athletics	0	1	0	2	2	4.50	2.00	9.6	415	52	75	7.49	0.0	9.0		0.0	
2011	AA	Midland	1	0	0	20	18	0.45	1.05	15.5	210	28	95	1.79	2.7	8.1	3.0	0.0	125

Smart pitcher who should succeed despite lack of size. He has a big arm with impressive pitchability. Gets good velocity on FB and mixes in a big-breaking CB that is tough for RHH and LHH to hit hard. He locates his pitches well, but lacks deception. CU is in early stage, and he will need it to sustain success as a starter.

Green, Tyler — SP — Arizona

EXP MLB DEBUT: 2015 | POTENTIAL: Power reliever | **7D**

Thrws R Age 20
2010 (8) HS, (TX)

90-94	FB	++++
78-80	CB	+++
80-81	CU	++

Year	Lev	Team	W	L	Sv	IP	K	ERA	WHIP	BF/G	OBA	H%	S%	xERA	Ctl	Dom	Cmd	hr/9	BPV
2011	A	South Bend	6	8	1	114	79	4.97	1.46	19.5	268	31	66	4.35	3.9	6.2	1.6	0.8	49

Short, athletic, projectable righty struggled in his full-season debut. He does have a solid 90-93 mph FB that touches 95, but needs to improve his CB -- and throw more strikes. He has a CU, but rarely uses it, relying instead on his two main pitches. Mechanics remain inconsistent, and a move to relief seems likely.

Gregorio, Joan — SP — San Francisco

EXP MLB DEBUT: 2015 | POTENTIAL: #2 starter | **9E**

Thrws R Age 20
2010 NDFA D.R.

88-93	FB	+++
	SL	++
	CU	+

Year	Lev	Team	W	L	Sv	IP	K	ERA	WHIP	BF/G	OBA	H%	S%	xERA	Ctl	Dom	Cmd	hr/9	BPV
2011	Rk	AZL Giants	3	0	0	50	43	2.34	1.18	16.7	233	30	79	2.57	2.9	7.7	2.7	0.2	106

Tall, lean, athletic hurler from the D.R. has a big arm and room for projection. At 6'7", 180, he has lots of room to fill out and add velocity to a FB already 88-93 and as high as 95. His breaking ball and CU are still very raw, but the SL has shown potential. He keeps the ball down and gave up just 1 HR to go along with a 1.20 GB/FB.

Griffin, A.J. — SP — Oakland

EXP MLB DEBUT: 2012 | POTENTIAL: #4 starter | **7C**

Thrws R Age 24
2010 (13) San Diego

86-92	FB	+++
80-82	SL	++
77-79	CB	++
	CU	+++

Year	Lev	Team	W	L	Sv	IP	K	ERA	WHIP	BF/G	OBA	H%	S%	xERA	Ctl	Dom	Cmd	hr/9	BPV
2010	A-	Vancouver	1	1	15	21	27	2.99	1.00	4.0	190	30	67	1.38	3.0	11.5	3.9	0.0	167
2011	A	Burlington	4	0	0	52	46	1.56	0.79	23.5	197	25	82	1.30	0.9	8.0	9.2	0.3	246
2011	A+	Stockton	5	3	0	70	82	3.59	1.11	23.0	244	33	71	3.31	1.8	10.5	5.9	1.0	161
2011	AA	Midland	2	3	0	32	20	6.47	1.56	23.4	302	32	61	5.93	3.1	5.6	1.8	1.7	16
2011	AAA	Sacramento	0	1	0	6	8	3.00	1.33	24.9	262	36	86	4.54	3.0	12.0	4.0	1.5	114

Tall, lean closer converted to SP. Throws his four-pitch mix with a clean, quick arm action that produces good deception and movement. Rarely beats himself and changes speeds effectively early in the count. He needs to develop a breaking ball to keep hitters honest, and he can be guilty of pitching up in the zone despite average velocity.

Griffith, Nevin — SP — Chicago (A)

EXP MLB DEBUT: 2013 | POTENTIAL: #3 starter | **8E**

Thrws R Age 23
2007 (2) HS (FL)

88-96	FB	++++
75-80	CB	+++
80-82	CU	+

Year	Lev	Team	W	L	Sv	IP	K	ERA	WHIP	BF/G	OBA	H%	S%	xERA	Ctl	Dom	Cmd	hr/9	BPV
2008	Rk	Great Falls	0	0	0	12	12	2.21	1.48	17.5	274	37	83	3.69	3.7	8.9	2.4	0.0	104
2009	Rk	Bristol	0	1	0	9	7	5.00	1.89	21.2	283	35	71	4.87	7.0	7.0	1.0	0.0	61
2009	A	Kannapolis	5	5	0	67	35	3.88	1.41	21.9	267	30	73	3.98	3.5	4.7	1.3	0.5	42
2010	A+	Winston-Salem	4	2	0	63	41	3.13	1.39	22.2	255	30	77	3.51	3.8	5.8	1.5	0.3	62
2011	AA	Birmingham	5	9	0	108	85	6.24	1.82	20.1	249	30	65	4.86	8.0	7.1	0.9	0.7	46

Tall athletic RHP induces GBs with a hard, sinking FB and can be tough to hit. But he has major control problems. CB has at least developed into average offering, but CU is poor with slowed arm speed. Missed most of '08 and '09 after TJS and hasn't progressed as hoped. Still young with upside, but time is running out.

Grimm, Justin — SP — Texas

EXP MLB DEBUT: 2013 | POTENTIAL: #4 starter | **7C**

Thrws R Age 23
2010 (5) Georgia

88-94	FB	+++
80-82	CB	+++
	CU	++

Year	Lev	Team	W	L	Sv	IP	K	ERA	WHIP	BF/G	OBA	H%	S%	xERA	Ctl	Dom	Cmd	hr/9	BPV
2008	NCAA	Georgia	0	1	0	31	27	11.00	2.06	8.0	313	38	43	6.57	6.9	7.8	1.1	0.9	37
2009	NCAA	Georgia	4	4	0	78	72	4.15	1.38	21.9	272	34	71	4.08	3.0	8.3	2.8	0.7	88
2010	NCAA	Georgia	3	7	0	77	73	5.49	1.52	22.3	274	33	65	4.90	4.1	8.5	2.1	1.2	60
2011	A	Hickory	2	1	0	50	54	3.41	1.26	22.7	242	31	76	3.53	3.2	9.7	3.0	0.9	101
2011	A+	Myrtle Beach	5	2	0	90	73	3.40	1.27	23.0	248	31	71	3.01	3.0	7.3	2.4	0.2	94

Enjoyed a nice High-A season after cleaning up his delivery and command. FB exhibits late life and hard CB is excellent complement. CU lags behind other offerings. He's athletic and tall, but doesn't use his height well and often rushes his delivery. Still, his ideal frame oozes projection and he could be solid late reliever. A sleeper indeed.

Guerra, Deolis
RP | **Minnesota** | **EXP MLB DEBUT:** 2012 | **POTENTIAL:** Middle reliever | **7D**

Thrws R Age 23
2005 FA (Venezuela)

Velo	Pitch	Grade
86-94	FB	+++
70-74	CB	+++
77-80	CU	++

Year	Lev	Team	W	L	Sv	IP	K	ERA	WHIP	BF/G	OBA	H%	S%	xERA	Ctl	Dom	Cmd	hr/9	BPV
2009	A+	Fort Myers	6	8	0	86	57	4.70	1.39	22.7	281	32	66	4.20	2.6	6.0	2.3	0.6	64
2009	AA	New Britain	6	3	0	62	49	5.21	1.27	21.2	261	31	57	3.55	2.5	7.1	2.9	0.6	88
2010	AA	New Britain	2	10	0	102	67	6.26	1.61	23.8	306	34	62	5.68	3.3	5.9	1.8	1.2	30
2010	AAA	Rochester	0	3	0	25	18	6.84	1.72	22.7	332	36	63	6.91	2.9	6.5	2.3	1.8	21
2011	AA	New Britain	8	7	1	95	95	5.59	1.37	10.8	276	34	60	4.42	2.7	9.0	3.4	1.0	94

Tall, hefty righty has spent most of the past three seasons in Double-A, but was moved to bullpen and succeeded. Dom increased as reliever and he might have regained prospect status. Has been more aggressive and still spins nasty CB. Uses smooth arm action to produce nice FB, but still relies on CU which is fringe-average at best.

Guerrieri, Taylor
SP | **Tampa Bay** | **EXP MLB DEBUT:** 2015 | **POTENTIAL:** #2 starter | **9D**

Thrws R Age 19
2011 (1) HS (SC)

Velo	Pitch	Grade
90-96	FB	++++
80-83	CB	+++
	CU	+

Year	Lev	Team	W	L	Sv	IP	K	ERA	WHIP	BF/G	OBA	H%	S%	xERA	Ctl	Dom	Cmd	hr/9	BPV
2011		Did not play																	

Tall and athletic pitcher with all the ingredients to become a top-flight starter. He'll need to improve command and CU for future success, but has plus arm strength and nasty breaking pitch. Throws with a bit of effort currently, but mechanics could be cleaned up to throw harder. FB is already plus pitch and could get better.

Guillon, Ismael
SP | **Cincinnati** | **EXP MLB DEBUT:** 2015 | **POTENTIAL:** #3 starter | **7D**

Thrws L Age 20
2008 NDFA Venz.

Velo	Pitch	Grade
90-93	FB	++++
	CU	+++
	CB	++

Year	Lev	Team	W	L	Sv	IP	K	ERA	WHIP	BF/G	OBA	H%	S%	xERA	Ctl	Dom	Cmd	hr/9	BPV
2010	Rk	AZL Reds	3	3	0	57	73	3.32	1.09	18.6	195	30	67	1.82	3.6	11.5	3.2	0.2	147
2011	Rk	Billings	3	6	0	63	61	6.57	1.97	20.1	305	36	69	6.87	6.6	8.7	1.3	1.6	27

Long, lean lefty had TJS at 16, but has been healthy since then. Has a dominant arm, but really struggled with consistency and control in '11. Struck out almost a batter an inning, but also walked nearly as many. Relies on a 90-93 mph FB and a plus CU. He needs to develop a quality breaking ball and improve his control.

Gutierrez, Carlos
RP | **Minnesota** | **EXP MLB DEBUT:** 2012 | **POTENTIAL:** Closer | **7A**

Thrws R Age 25
2008 (1-C) Miami-FL

Velo	Pitch	Grade
89-97	FB	++++
79-83	SL	+++
80-82	CU	+

Year	Lev	Team	W	L	Sv	IP	K	ERA	WHIP	BF/G	OBA	H%	S%	xERA	Ctl	Dom	Cmd	hr/9	BPV
2009	A+	Fort Myers	2	3	0	54	33	1.33	1.09	19.3	195	23	88	1.89	3.7	5.5	1.5	0.2	75
2009	AA	New Britain	1	3	0	52	32	6.22	1.65	10.6	297	33	63	5.47	4.1	5.5	1.3	1.0	26
2010	AA	New Britain	5	8	2	122	81	4.57	1.52	16.6	283	33	69	4.46	3.7	6.0	1.6	0.5	53
2010	AAA	Rochester	0	0	0	4	6	2.25	1.75	9.1	307	49	86	4.82	4.5	13.5	3.0	0.0	138
2011	AAA	Rochester	2	3	0	62	57	4.64	1.47	6.2	255	33	66	3.68	4.5	8.3	1.8	0.3	83

Big, strong reliever who relishes late innings. Could be a one-pitch closer with a repeatable, dominant sinker that made him one of the top GBers in the minors; hitters rarely lifted the ball and HRs were rare. Increased K rate helped status, but he must cut walks and command secondary pitches better. Lacks touch and feel for changing speeds.

Hagadone, Nick
RP | **Cleveland** | **EXP MLB DEBUT:** 2011 | **POTENTIAL:** Closer | **9D**

Thrws L Age 26
2007 (1-S) Washington

Velo	Pitch	Grade
88-96	FB	++++
82-85	SL	++++
79-82	CU	++

Year	Lev	Team	W	L	Sv	IP	K	ERA	WHIP	BF/G	OBA	H%	S%	xERA	Ctl	Dom	Cmd	hr/9	BPV
2010	A+	Kinston	1	3	0	37	45	2.42	1.53	16.2	211	30	85	3.44	7.0	10.9	1.6	0.5	96
2010	AA	Akron	2	2	1	48	44	4.50	1.63	11.2	245	30	74	4.56	6.4	8.3	1.3	0.9	54
2011	AA	Akron	2	1	0	22	24	1.62	0.95	7.0	183	27	81	1.19	2.8	9.7	3.4	0.0	149
2011	AAA	Columbus	4	3	4	48	53	3.37	1.19	5.7	236	31	75	3.31	2.8	9.9	3.5	0.9	113
2011	MLB	Cleveland	1	0	0	11	11	4.09	0.91	4.6	114	17	50	0.40	4.9	9.0	1.8	0.0	125

Strong-bodied reliever who reached MLB once CLE let him cut loose after a few seasons of careful monitoring. He has trouble repeating his delivery, and throws with maximum effort, but he can be intimidating and works fine in the bullpen. Quick FB and plus, hard SL can register Ks while he uses occasional CU. FB can be straight and often overthrown.

Haley, Trey
RP | **Cleveland** | **EXP MLB DEBUT:** 2013 | **POTENTIAL:** #3 starter/Setup reliever | **8E**

Thrws R Age 22
2008 (2) HS (TX)

Velo	Pitch	Grade
88-94	FB	+++
77-81	CB	+++
82-84	CU	++

Year	Lev	Team	W	L	Sv	IP	K	ERA	WHIP	BF/G	OBA	H%	S%	xERA	Ctl	Dom	Cmd	hr/9	BPV
2009	A	Lake County	4	8	0	77	57	5.60	1.75	18.6	243	28	67	4.64	7.6	6.6	0.9	0.7	44
2010	A	Lake County	5	11	0	116	97	5.97	1.79	19.8	272	32	67	5.41	6.7	7.5	1.1	1.0	39
2011	Rk	AZL Indians	0	0	0	3	4	0.00	0.00	4.2	0	0			0.0	12.0		0.0	
2011	A	Lake County	0	0	1	12	17	2.95	1.07	5.9	127	22	69	0.88	5.9	12.5	2.1	0.0	149
2011	A+	Kinston	1	1	1	28	27	3.83	1.49	6.4	239	31	73	3.55	5.4	8.6	1.6	0.3	83

Tall, projectable pitcher posted career high in Dom after move to pen. Continues to miss the zone and put hitters on base, but his raw arm strength works best in short stints. Uses two-seam FB with movement along with a harder four-seamer. Big-breaking CB gives him an out pitch, though he slows arm speed for CU. Maintains low oppBA and could be setup guy.

Harden, Trevor
SP | **Arizona** | **EXP MLB DEBUT:** 2014 | **POTENTIAL:** #4 starter | **6C**

Thrws R Age 24
2008 (14) New Mexico JC

Velo	Pitch	Grade
88-93	FB	+++
80-83	SL	+++
	CU	++

Year	Lev	Team	W	L	Sv	IP	K	ERA	WHIP	BF/G	OBA	H%	S%	xERA	Ctl	Dom	Cmd	hr/9	BPV
2008	Rk	Missoula	1	3	2	42	64	1.92	1.07	13.6	223	37	84	2.33	2.4	13.7	5.8	0.4	202
2009	A	South Bend	5	1	0	37	31	2.42	0.94	23.3	211	25	78	2.21	1.7	7.5	4.4	0.7	129
2009	A+	Visalia	2	9	0	91	63	4.45	1.51	23.2	309	35	73	5.36	2.3	6.2	2.7	1.1	55
2010	A+	Visalia	0	2	0	9	7	8.00	1.56	19.7	339	33	60	8.68	1.0	7.0	7.0	4.0	56
2011	A+	Visalia	2	8	0	100	77	6.38	1.78	24.2	302	34	66	6.31	5.0	6.9	1.4	1.5	19

Strong-armed righty got torched in 18 CAL starts despite being healthy all year. Has a nice low-90s sinking FB that tops out at 94 MPH. His SL can also be plus at times. FB/SL combination give him some potential, but not much is going on right now.

Harvey, Matt
SP | **New York (N)** | **EXP MLB DEBUT:** 2012 | **POTENTIAL:** #1 starter | **9D**

Thrws R Age 23
2010 (1) North Carolina

Velo	Pitch	Grade
92-95	FB	++++
83-85	SL	+++
79-83	CU	+++
	CB	+++

Year	Lev	Team	W	L	Sv	IP	K	ERA	WHIP	BF/G	OBA	H%	S%	xERA	Ctl	Dom	Cmd	hr/9	BPV
2008	NCAA	North Carolina	7	2	0	67	80	2.81	1.47	15.2	215	32	80	3.02	6.3	10.7	1.7	0.1	108
2009	NCAA	North Carolina	7	2	1	75	81	5.40	1.73	16.3	294	38	70	5.52	5.0	9.7	1.9	1.0	66
2010	NCAA	North Carolina	8	3	0	96	102	3.09	1.20	27.6	228	30	75	2.89	3.3	9.6	2.9	0.6	111
2011	A+	St. Lucie	8	2	0	76	92	2.37	1.20	21.8	238	34	83	3.04	2.8	10.9	3.8	0.6	135
2011	AA	Binghamton	5	3	0	59	64	4.56	1.37	20.7	258	34	66	3.75	3.5	9.7	2.8	0.6	102

Strong, athletic righty was the seventh pick in the '10 draft. He has a plus 92-95 mph FB that tops out at 98 with good life. He also throws a plus 82-84 mph SL, a CU, and a CB. He has worked hard to develop a more consistent release point and his command improved. Continued progress could mean top-of-the-rotation stuff.

Hauser, Matt
RP | **Minnesota** | **EXP MLB DEBUT:** 2013 | **POTENTIAL:** Setup reliever | **7C**

Thrws R Age 24
2010 (7) San Diego

Velo	Pitch	Grade
89-92	FB	+++
82-84	SL	+++
	SP	+++

Year	Lev	Team	W	L	Sv	IP	K	ERA	WHIP	BF/G	OBA	H%	S%	xERA	Ctl	Dom	Cmd	hr/9	BPV
2010	Rk	Elizabethton	0	0	3	9	13	1.00	1.00	4.3	216	36	89	1.69	2.0	13.0	6.5	0.0	226
2010	A	Beloit	1	0	1	6	4	0.00	0.97	5.9	222	27	100	1.75	1.5	5.8	4.0	0.0	129
2011	A	Beloit	3	0	5	19	27	1.41	1.36	4.7	194	31	92	2.78	6.1	12.7	2.1	0.5	122
2011	A+	Fort Myers	2	6	7	41	44	2.18	1.29	7.0	242	32	86	3.38	3.5	9.6	2.8	0.7	102
2011	AA	New Britain	0	0	0	2	4	4.09	1.36	9.2	326	58	67	4.12	0.0	16.4		0.0	

Athletic reliever has the aggressiveness to close, and his SL/splitter mix has been tough to hit, messing with hitters' timing and making them chase in the lower zone. But inconsistent control and lack of FB command might keep him from sticking as a late-inning RP. He also needs to smooth his mechanics, which might reduce his deceptiveness.

Heath, Deunte
RP | **Chicago (A)** | **EXP MLB DEBUT:** 2012 | **POTENTIAL:** Setup reliever | **7D**

Thrws R Age 26
2006 (19) Tennessee

Velo	Pitch	Grade
89-94	FB	+++
79-83	CB	+++
	CU	++

Year	Lev	Team	W	L	Sv	IP	K	ERA	WHIP	BF/G	OBA	H%	S%	xERA	Ctl	Dom	Cmd	hr/9	BPV
2008	AA	Mississippi	4	5	0	66	46	5.58	1.63	22.6	290	34	65	4.98	4.4	6.3	1.4	0.7	44
2009	AA	Mississippi	2	5	1	80	70	4.16	1.48	13.7	262	33	71	3.95	4.3	7.9	1.8	0.5	75
2009	AAA	Gwinnett	0	1	0	18	18	9.89	2.14	12.9	345	43	51	7.41	5.9	8.9	1.5	1.0	41
2010	AA	Birmingham	2	4	2	57	84	3.15	1.42	6.2	233	37	79	3.53	5.0	13.2	2.6	0.6	124
2011	AAA	Charlotte	4	7	1	102	117	4.76	1.57	14.9	254	33	72	4.61	5.5	10.3	1.9	1.1	74

Big, strong reliever has showed versatility in variety of roles. Mostly SP in career, though moved to RP in '10. His Dom was much higher in bullpen as good, hard FB plays up in short stints. Must improve control and enhance his CB to land a prominent role. Can register Ks with FB, but he has been inefficient in pitch mix.

Heckathorn, Kyle
SP | **Milwaukee** | **EXP MLB DEBUT:** 2012 | **POTENTIAL:** #4 starter/power reliever | **8D**

Thrws R Age 24
2009 (1-S) Kennesaw St

Velo	Pitch	Grade
88-93	FB	+++
86-88	SL	+++
	CU	++

Year	Lev	Team	W	L	Sv	IP	K	ERA	WHIP	BF/G	OBA	H%	S%	xERA	Ctl	Dom	Cmd	hr/9	BPV
2009	Rk	Helena	0	1	0	22	15	6.11	1.54	16.1	325	35	63	6.18	1.6	6.1	3.8	1.6	57
2010	A	Wisconsin	6	6	0	85	67	2.96	1.24	20.3	255	32	75	3.03	2.4	7.1	2.9	0.2	101
2010	A+	Brevard County	4	0	0	39	23	3.00	1.28	20.0	267	31	76	3.35	2.3	5.3	2.3	0.2	75
2011	A+	Brevard County	5	6	0	79	65	3.98	1.30	21.8	269	32	72	4.04	2.4	7.4	3.1	0.9	83
2011	AA	Huntsville	0	4	0	36	24	7.23	1.72	23.4	307	33	60	6.45	4.2	6.0	1.4	1.7	7

Solid workhorse starter scuffled after a mid-season promotion. Above-average arm strength and control give him a chance to pitch effectively at the next level. Can reach the mid-to-high 90s with FB, but also uses a cutter, hard SL and CU. Struggled to put hitters away despite plus stuff. Some scouts see him being more effective in relief.

Heidenreich, Matt — SP — Chicago (A)

Thrws R Age 21
2009 (4) HS (CA)

EXP MLB DEBUT: 2014 | POTENTIAL: #3 starter | 8E

87-93	FB	+++
80-83	SL	++
79-82	CU	+++

Year	Lev	Team	W	L	Sv	IP	K	ERA	WHIP	BF/G	OBA	H%	S%	xERA	Ctl	Dom	Cmd	hr/9	BPV
2009	Rk	Bristol	0	1	0	22	12	4.50	1.55	6.0	262	30	70	4.12	4.9	4.9	1.0	0.4	41
2010	Rk	Bristol	6	2	0	76	58	2.49	1.11	22.9	254	31	77	2.72	1.3	6.9	5.3	0.2	149
2010	A	Kannapolis	0	0	0	1	2	18.00	3.00	5.8	515	79	33	12.58	0.0	18.0		0.0	
2011	A	Kannapolis	10	10	0	154	101	4.32	1.33	23.7	286	33	68	4.23	1.8	5.9	3.3	0.8	79

Tall and lean pitcher has a projectable frame, but passively pitches to contact. Uses height well to induces GBs with sinker down in zone. Thrives by throwing strikes with quick arm action. Hasn't been a strikeout pitcher and likely won't become one without better velocity and SL. He has some upside, but he's not likely to reach it.

Hellweg, John — SP — Los Angeles (A)

Thrws R Age 23
2008 (16) Florida CC

EXP MLB DEBUT: 2013 | POTENTIAL: #3 starter | 8D

90-99	FB	++++
77-81	CB	+++
77-80	CU	++

Year	Lev	Team	W	L	Sv	IP	K	ERA	WHIP	BF/G	OBA	H%	S%	xERA	Ctl	Dom	Cmd	hr/9	BPV
2008	Rk	AZL Angels	1	0	0	21	25	5.09	2.69	8.3	241	34	80	6.68	16.1	10.6	0.7	0.4	72
2009	Rk	AZL Angels	2	1	6	24	25	2.99	1.00	5.1	191	27	67	1.41	3.0	9.3	3.1	0.0	139
2009	A	Cedar Rapids	0	0	2	6	7	1.45	1.77	5.7	186	28	91	3.31	10.2	10.2	1.0	0.0	100
2010	A	Cedar Rapids	2	4	16	43	66	4.38	1.50	4.6	141	24	70	2.51	9.4	13.8	1.5	0.4	128
2011	A+	Inland Empire	6	4	0	89	113	3.74	1.50	13.8	230	35	73	3.33	6.0	11.4	1.9	0.2	112

Can be tough to hit with stellar FB with plus sink. Induces GBs due to height (6'9") and downward angle. Tall and lean, his easy arm action produces velocity and movement. Secondary pitches and command need attention, but the raw skills are there for a promising future. A mid-season move to the rotation led to improved results.

Hembree, Heath — RP — San Francisco

Thrws R Age 23
2010 (5) College of Charleston

EXP MLB DEBUT: 2012 | POTENTIAL: power reliever | 8C

93-97	FB	++++
84-86	SL	++++

Year	Lev	Team	W	L	Sv	IP	K	ERA	WHIP	BF/G	OBA	H%	S%	xERA	Ctl	Dom	Cmd	hr/9	BPV
2008	NCAA	South Carolina	0	0	0	0	1			2.3							0.5		
2010	NCAA	Charleston	5	3	4	29	42	6.52	1.76	4.9	288	43	63	5.43	5.6	13.0	2.3	0.9	97
2010	Rk	AZL Giants	0	0	3	11	22	0.82	0.82	3.3	225	50	89	1.28	0.0	18.0		0.0	
2011	A+	San Jose	0	0	21	24	44	0.74	1.16	3.7	190	38	96	2.09	4.5	16.4	3.7	0.4	181
2011	AA	Richmond	1	1	17	28	34	2.87	1.17	4.0	201	29	75	2.25	4.1	10.9	2.6	0.3	125

RP emerged as one of the dominant closers in the minors. As many tall pitchers do, he struggled with control at times, but FB/SL combination can be overpowering. FB sits at 93-98, topping out at 99. He overthrows at times, which leaves his FB up and straight. He has smoothed out his mechanics and the Giants have to be thrilled with the results so far.

Hendricks, Kyle — SP — Texas

Thrws R Age 22
2011 (8) Dartmouth

EXP MLB DEBUT: 2014 | POTENTIAL: #4 starter | 7A

88-94	FB	+++
78-82	CB	++
83-87	SL	+++
	CU	++++

Year	Lev	Team	W	L	Sv	IP	K	ERA	WHIP	BF/G	OBA	H%	S%	xERA	Ctl	Dom	Cmd	hr/9	BPV
2009	NCAA	Dartmouth	6	3	0	67	50	4.84	1.48	24.0	308	36	68	4.97	2.0	6.7	3.3	0.8	80
2010	NCAA	Dartmouth	4	6	0	57	54	7.55	1.64	23.2	332	39	56	6.77	2.2	8.5	3.9	1.9	64
2011	NCAA	Dartmouth	5	3	0	62	70	2.47	1.03	26.5	233	32	77	2.41	1.6	10.2	6.4	0.4	190
2011	A-	Spokane	2	2	3	32	36	1.96	0.75	5.7	180	27	71	0.66	1.1	10.1	9.0	0.0	268
2011	AA	Frisco	0	0	0	3	2	3.00	2.00	14.5	321	38	83	5.75	6.0	6.0	1.0	0.0	48

Lean and athletic hurler who pitched out of pen, but is likely to be used as SP. Mixes four pitches well, including plus CU that he has confidence to throw in any count. Overall good stuff, but lacks a true swing-and-miss offering. FB velocity and SL are sufficient for him to move quickly, but he lacks upside due to arm action and low projected Dom.

Hendriks, Liam — SP — Minnesota

Thrws R Age 23
2007 FA (Australia)

EXP MLB DEBUT: 2011 | POTENTIAL: #3 starter | 8C

86-93	FB	+++
80-83	SL	+++
	CB	+++
	CU	+++

Year	Lev	Team	W	L	Sv	IP	K	ERA	WHIP	BF/G	OBA	H%	S%	xERA	Ctl	Dom	Cmd	hr/9	BPV
2010	A	Beloit	2	1	0	34	39	1.32	0.59	19.3	143	22	75		1.1	10.3	9.8	0.0	293
2010	A+	Fort Myers	6	3	0	74	66	1.94	0.96	21.6	231	30	80	2.04	1.0	8.0	8.3	0.2	223
2011	AA	New Britain	8	2	0	90	81	2.70	1.14	22.3	251	32	78	3.01	1.8	8.1	4.5	0.5	133
2011	AAA	Rochester	4	4	0	49	30	4.58	1.12	21.5	273	32	55	2.81	0.5	5.5	10.0	0.0	243
2011	MLB	Minnesota	0	2	0	23	16	6.23	1.52	25.0	308	35	59	5.42	2.3	6.2	2.7	1.2	52

Command and control pitcher who reached MIN by throwing four pitches for strikes. Locates FB to any quadrant and mixes in SL and a solid-average CU that uses the same arm speed. He repeats a clean delivery, but lacks a plus knockout pitch, and can be guilty of throwing too many hittable strikes. Won't become a dominator, but could become a true mid-rotation SP.

Heredia, Jairo — SP — New York (A)

Thrws R Age 22
2006 FA (DR)

EXP MLB DEBUT: 2014 | POTENTIAL: #3 starter | 8E

89-94	FB	++++
80-84	SL	++
	CU	++

Year	Lev	Team	W	L	Sv	IP	K	ERA	WHIP	BF/G	OBA	H%	S%	xERA	Ctl	Dom	Cmd	hr/9	BPV
2009	A	Charleston (SC)	1	1	0	19	17	2.37	0.79	17.1	207	26	71	1.54	0.5	8.1	17.0	0.5	405
2009	A+	Tampa	2	2	0	14	10	7.02	2.13	17.4	386	44	68	8.44	3.2	6.4	2.0	1.3	20
2010	A	Charleston (SC)	4	2	0	70	65	3.47	1.33	14.5	272	35	74	3.78	2.4	8.3	3.4	0.5	107
2010	A+	Tampa	0	6	0	24	14	7.07	1.98	19.4	352	39	63	6.93	4.1	5.2	1.3	0.7	20
2011	A+	Tampa	8	2	0	68	68	3.30	1.12	20.6	238	30	75	3.29	2.1	9.0	4.3	1.1	119

Strong, wiry pitcher who has flown under the radar. Uses loose, easy delivery to pepper his FB into both sides of the strike zone, and adds and subtracts speed to keep hitters off guard. FB has enough downward action to generate GBs. SL needs to be tighter. He has lacked the stamina to maintain his velocity deep into games.

Heredia, Luis — SP — Pittsburgh

Thrws R Age 17
2010 NDFA Mexico

EXP MLB DEBUT: 2015 | POTENTIAL: #1 starter | 9E

92-94	FB	++++
	CB	++
	SL	++
	CU	+++

Year	Lev	Team	W	L	Sv	IP	K	ERA	WHIP	BF/G	OBA	H%	S%	xERA	Ctl	Dom	Cmd	hr/9	BPV
2011	Rk	GCL Pirates	1	2	0	30	23	4.78	1.56	11.0	248	29	70	4.41	5.7	6.9	1.2	0.9	45

Tall, lanky teen has tons of projectability. Already features a 92-94 mph FB that tops out at 96 mph, with room for more. Also has a SL, CB, and a CU that showed signs of improvement, but all his pitches need refinement. Still much work to do, but the upside remains substantial.

Hermsen, B.J. — SP — Minnesota

Thrws R Age 22
2008 (6) HS (IA)

EXP MLB DEBUT: 2013 | POTENTIAL: #4 starter | 7C

86-92	FB	+++
80-83	SL	++
78-80	CU	+++

Year	Lev	Team	W	L	Sv	IP	K	ERA	WHIP	BF/G	OBA	H%	S%	xERA	Ctl	Dom	Cmd	hr/9	BPV
2009	Rk	GCL Twins	6	2	0	53	42	1.36	0.68	18.6	176	23	78	0.47	0.7	7.1	10.5	0.0	283
2010	Rk	Elizabethton	2	2	0	38	39	3.32	1.13	18.8	267	35	71	3.16	0.9	9.2	9.8	0.5	248
2010	A	Beloit	4	6	0	72	46	5.00	1.39	25.3	295	33	64	4.51	1.9	5.8	3.1	0.8	72
2011	A	Beloit	11	7	0	124	81	3.12	1.30	24.4	272	31	78	3.94	2.2	5.9	2.6	0.7	69
2011	A+	Fort Myers	2	1	0	26	20	4.47	1.53	22.8	315	38	69	4.78	2.1	6.9	3.3	0.3	93

Large-framed pitcher with commandable FB thanks to ability to repeat delivery and arm slot. Throws downhill consistently and buries a heavy FB low in the zone. Still offers some projection, but can be slow to plate with a stiff arm action. Has pitch mix to register higher Dom, but effectiveness of SL comes and goes. CU has improved, but he still struggles to retire LHH.

Herrera, Kelvin — RP — Kansas City

Thrws R Age 22
2006 FA (DR)

EXP MLB DEBUT: 2011 | POTENTIAL: Closer | 8C

93-98	FB	++++
80-82	CB	++
79-83	CU	++++

Year	Lev	Team	W	L	Sv	IP	K	ERA	WHIP	BF/G	OBA	H%	S%	xERA	Ctl	Dom	Cmd	hr/9	BPV
2010	A	Burlington	2	3	0	41	40	4.38	1.29	21.1	247	32	65	3.26	3.3	8.8	2.7	0.4	101
2011	A+	Wilmington	2	1	1	14	12	0.63	0.70	6.3	167	20	100	1.02	1.3	7.6	6.0	0.6	174
2011	AA	NW Arkansas	4	0	7	36	40	1.75	0.78	5.6	178	23	88	1.65	1.5	10.0	6.7	1.0	189
2011	AAA	Omaha	1	0	6	17	18	2.12	1.12	4.8	200	27	83	2.32	3.7	9.5	2.6	0.5	110
2011	MLB	Kansas City	0	1	0	2	0	13.50	1.00	3.8	262	15		6.64	0.0	0.0		4.5	

Short and strong reliever with closer-type mentality and stuff, he surprised with Futures Game appearance and eventual promotion to KC. Commands a plus-plus FB with velocity and movement, and mixes in plus CU with fade. His CB remains below average, but he generally pitches with FB and CU. Has some effort in delivery, and has had an elbow injury in past.

Hobgood, Matt — SP — Baltimore

Thrws R Age 21
2009 (1) HS (CA)

EXP MLB DEBUT: 2014 | POTENTIAL: #3 starter | 8E

88-95	FB	+++
76-80	CB	+++
81-84	SL	++
77-80	CU	+

Year	Lev	Team	W	L	Sv	IP	K	ERA	WHIP	BF/G	OBA	H%	S%	xERA	Ctl	Dom	Cmd	hr/9	BPV
2009	Rk	Bluefield	1	2	0	26	16	4.81	1.53	14.2	302	36	65	4.27	2.7	5.5	2.0	0.0	70
2010	A	Delmarva	3	7	0	94	59	4.40	1.36	18.7	253	29	67	3.69	3.6	5.6	1.6	0.6	54
2011	Rk	GCL Orioles	0	0	0	10	9	4.46	1.29	8.3	260	32	67	3.86	2.7	8.0	3.0	0.9	87
2011	A-	Aberdeen	0	6	0	26	13	10.65	2.44	17.2	357	39	53	8.14	7.9	4.5	0.6	0.7	2

Burly pitcher has been enigma since early selection in '09. Has been slow to return from shoulder strain and velocity has declined precipitously. Control has fallen apart and mechanics have been out of whack. Still hope of returning to previous success with potential for plus FB and CB. Uses height to throw downhill and induce GBs.

Hoehn, Connor — RP — Oakland

Thrws R Age 22
2009 (12) St. Petersburg JC

EXP MLB DEBUT: 2013 | POTENTIAL: Setup reliever | 7C

90-94	FB	++++
81-84	SL	++
	CU	++

Year	Lev	Team	W	L	Sv	IP	K	ERA	WHIP	BF/G	OBA	H%	S%	xERA	Ctl	Dom	Cmd	hr/9	BPV
2008	NCAA	Alabama	0	0	0	6	10	7.50	1.50	5.2	191	37	44	2.63	7.5	15.0	2.0	0.0	149
2009	Rk	AZL Athletics	0	1	0	2	3	4.50	1.50	4.3	151	27	67	2.20	9.0	13.5	1.5	0.0	137
2009	A-	Vancouver	0	1	7	18	25	1.00	0.89	4.5	151	26	88	0.67	3.5	12.5	3.6	0.0	175
2010	A	Kane County	7	4	1	87	101	3.82	1.24	8.0	219	30	70	2.93	4.0	10.4	2.6	0.6	110
2011	A+	Stockton	2	3	7	48	59	5.24	1.06	5.2	223	27	58	3.88	2.2	11.0	4.9	2.1	118

Durable and live-armed reliever was subject to HR, though home park may have been cause. Impressive secondary numbers with ability to register Ks and improved control. Works primarily off above-average FB and messes with hitters' timing with deceptive, repeatable delivery. SL has moments, but is inconsistent along with middling CU.

Hoffman, Matt — RP — Detroit

EXP MLB DEBUT: 2012 | POTENTIAL: Setup reliever | 7C

Thrws L Age 23
2007 (26) HS (OK)

- 88-95 FB ++++
- 80-84 SL ++
- CU ++

Year	Lev	Team	W	L	Sv	IP	K	ERA	WHIP	BF/G	OBA	H%	S%	xERA	Ctl	Dom	Cmd	hr/9	BPV
2010	A+	Lakeland	0	1	3	22	18	1.62	0.86	5.1	214	26	83	1.73	0.8	7.3	9.0	0.4	233
2010	AA	Erie	1	2	0	26	22	7.56	2.14	5.0	328	39	64	7.16	6.9	7.6	1.1	1.0	27
2010	AAA	Toledo	0	0	0	4	4	10.98	3.17	8.2	438	51	67	13.02	8.8	8.8	1.0	2.2	-25
2011	AA	Erie	0	0	0	0	0			2.3							0.0		
2011	AAA	Toledo	2	5	0	62	46	3.19	1.34	5.3	255	31	76	3.51	3.3	6.7	2.0	0.4	73

Tall, athletic LH reliever who can dominate with excellent velocity. More or less a FB pitcher, which limits possibilities in late innings. Potent against LHH and buries hard sinker low in zone. Lots of moving parts in his delivery, which hinders his ability to spin the breaking ball consistently, and he lacks touch and feel for changing speeds.

Holmberg, David — SP — Arizona

EXP MLB DEBUT: 2014 | POTENTIAL: #3 starter | 8C

Thrws L Age 20
2009 (2) HS, (FL)

- 86-90 FB +++
- CB ++++
- CU +++

Year	Lev	Team	W	L	Sv	IP	K	ERA	WHIP	BF/G	OBA	H%	S%	xERA	Ctl	Dom	Cmd	hr/9	BPV
2009	Rk	Bristol	2	2	0	40	37	4.73	1.45	12.2	262	32	70	4.51	4.1	8.3	2.1	1.1	62
2010	Rk	Great Falls	1	1	0	40	29	4.49	1.52	21.8	315	37	69	4.86	2.0	6.5	3.2	0.4	85
2010	Rk	Missoula	1	4	0	37	47	3.88	1.46	22.7	310	44	73	4.60	1.7	11.4	6.7	0.5	188
2011	A	South Bend	8	3	0	83	81	2.39	0.94	22.3	217	29	75	1.90	1.4	8.8	6.2	0.3	185
2011	A+	Visalia	4	6	0	71	76	4.68	1.52	23.7	267	35	69	4.28	4.4	9.6	2.2	0.6	86

Big, physical lefty had a solid full-season debut. Uptick in FB velocity and ability to throw strikes gives him a chance. Plus CB and above average changeup to go along with an 88-92 mph FB. Uses height effectively along with overhand delivery to pitch downhill. Repeats delivery consistently and is willing to pound the strike zone.

Holmes, Clay — SP — Pittsburgh

EXP MLB DEBUT: 2015 | POTENTIAL: #2 starter | 8D

Thrws R Age 19
2011 (9) HS, (AL)

- 90-93 FB ++++
- SL ++
- CU ++

Year	Lev	Team	W	L	Sv	IP	K	ERA	WHIP	BF/G	OBA	H%	S%	xERA	Ctl	Dom	Cmd	hr/9	BPV
2011		Did not play																	

Tall, mature righty from Alabama. The Pirates paid him $1.2 million to buy him out of a scholarship to Auburn. Already has a 90-93 mph FB that he throws with nice downhill tilt. Also has a good SL that needs to become more consistent. Overall he is very raw, but has plenty of upside and could be a bargain.

Holt, Brad — SP — New York (N)

EXP MLB DEBUT: 2012 | POTENTIAL: Power reliever | 7D

Thrws R Age 25
2008 (1-S) UNC-Wilmington

- 88-93 FB +++
- 80-83 SL +++
- 79-82 CU ++

Year	Lev	Team	W	L	Sv	IP	K	ERA	WHIP	BF/G	OBA	H%	S%	xERA	Ctl	Dom	Cmd	hr/9	BPV
2009	A+	St. Lucie	4	1	0	43	54	3.13	1.09	18.7	219	30	76	2.94	2.7	11.3	4.2	1.0	135
2009	AA	Binghamton	3	6	0	58	45	6.21	1.40	22.2	262	29	57	4.65	3.6	7.0	2.0	1.4	44
2010	A+	St. Lucie	2	9	0	65	62	7.48	1.91	22.0	271	35	58	5.25	7.8	8.6	1.1	0.6	59
2010	AA	Binghamton	1	5	0	30	25	10.20	2.20	15.1	337	41	50	7.07	6.9	7.5	1.1	0.6	37
2011	AA	Binghamton	8	8	0	93	74	4.73	1.42	11.6	222	26	66	3.50	5.5	7.1	1.3	0.7	60

Tall, strong righthander rebounded slightly from a disastrous '10. Has a good 90-93 mph FB, a decent SL, and a CU, but continues to struggle locating. In addition, Holt relies too much on his FB, which simply isn't good enough. Was moved from the starting rotation to a relief where he showed better control.

Hoover, J.J. — RP — Atlanta

EXP MLB DEBUT: 2012 | POTENTIAL: Reliever | 7B

Thrws R Age 24
2008 (10) Calhoun CC

- 88-92 FB +++
- CB +++
- CU +++
- SL +++

Year	Lev	Team	W	L	Sv	IP	K	ERA	WHIP	BF/G	OBA	H%	S%	xERA	Ctl	Dom	Cmd	hr/9	BPV
2009	A+	Myrtle Beach	0	0	0	3	2	9.00	2.67	16.5	262	24	71	9.37	15.0	6.0	0.4	3.0	-43
2010	A+	Myrtle Beach	11	6	0	132	118	3.27	1.22	22.2	253	32	73	3.20	2.4	8.0	3.4	0.5	109
2010	AA	Mississippi	3	1	0	20	34	3.56	1.49	21.7	208	38	76	3.21	6.7	15.1	2.3	0.4	138
2011	AA	Mississippi	2	5	1	87	86	2.48	1.07	10.9	209	27	78	2.30	2.9	8.9	3.1	0.5	115
2011	AAA	Gwinnett	1	1	1	18	31	3.46	1.32	6.3	190	37	71	2.15	5.9	15.3	2.6	0.0	163

Was moved to the pen in '11. As a result, he shelved his CB and CU to focus on FB/SL combo. His results were good, but he would likely remain a starter in another organization. FB hits 90-93, but lacks movement. Also features an above-average CB, but the SL and CU remain below average.

Hope, Mason — SP — Florida

EXP MLB DEBUT: 2015 | POTENTIAL: #3 starter | 8D

Thrws R Age 19
2011 (5) HS, (OK)

- 88-92 FB +++
- 71-73 SL ++
- 74-76 CB ++
- 70-72 CU ++

Year	Lev	Team	W	L	Sv	IP	K	ERA	WHIP	BF/G	OBA	H%	S%	xERA	Ctl	Dom	Cmd	hr/9	BPV
2011	Rk	GCL Marlins	2	0	0	27	31	3.32	1.25	15.8	261	37	71	2.93	2.3	10.3	4.4	0.0	158

Lean and lanky HS righty has a live arm with an 88-92 mph FB that tops out at 94 mph. Gets good downhill movement on his pitches. Also has a decent CB with nice 12-6 break and mixed in an upper 70s SL that needs work. Well rounded hurler with some projection left. Could be a nice pick in the 5th round.

House, T.J. — SP — Cleveland

EXP MLB DEBUT: 2013 | POTENTIAL: #3 starter | 8E

Thrws L Age 22
2008 (16) HS (MS)

- 88-92 FB +++
- 82-85 SL +++
- 80-82 CU +++

Year	Lev	Team	W	L	Sv	IP	K	ERA	WHIP	BF/G	OBA	H%	S%	xERA	Ctl	Dom	Cmd	hr/9	BPV
2009	A	Lake County	6	11	0	134	109	3.15	1.31	21.3	251	31	77	3.48	3.3	7.3	2.2	0.5	79
2010	A+	Kinston	6	10	0	135	106	3.93	1.45	21.4	261	32	72	3.90	4.1	7.1	1.7	0.5	68
2011	A+	Kinston	6	12	0	130	89	5.19	1.53	22.6	266	30	66	4.52	4.6	6.2	1.3	0.8	42

Raw and strong pitcher who regressed in stuff and production while repeating High-A. CU remains his best pitch, but he needs to establish strike zone to enhance the look. Owns sufficient velocity, but pitches up and is subject to flyballs. Lacks polish and consistency and delivery a bit crude to maintain stuff. Upside depends on improving FB command.

Houser, Adrian — SP — Houston

EXP MLB DEBUT: 2015 | POTENTIAL: #3 starter | 8D

Thrws R Age 19
2011 (2) HS, (OK)

- 90-93 FB +++
- 76-78 CB +++
- CU ++

Year	Lev	Team	W	L	Sv	IP	K	ERA	WHIP	BF/G	OBA	H%	S%	xERA	Ctl	Dom	Cmd	hr/9	BPV
2011	Rk	GCL Astros	1	2	0	22	25	4.07	1.54	16.1	278	39	71	3.89	4.1	10.2	2.5	0.0	113
2011	Rk	Greeneville	1	2	0	25	19	4.64	1.59	18.5	260	32	69	4.13	5.4	6.8	1.3	0.4	60

Tall, athletic second rounder. Has a solid 90-93 mph FB that tops out at 95 mph. Also has the makings of a good CB and CU. He has a quick arm and nice athleticism. He has some work to do - he throws across his body a bit, and needs more consistent mechanics -- but also has some projection left and the potential to be a #2 or #3 starter.

Howard, Dillon — SP — Cleveland

EXP MLB DEBUT: 2015 | POTENTIAL: #2 starter | 9D

Thrws R Age 19
2011 (2) HS (AR)

- 88-95 FB ++++
- CB ++
- CU ++

Year	Lev	Team	W	L	Sv	IP	K	ERA	WHIP	BF/G	OBA	H%	S%	xERA	Ctl	Dom	Cmd	hr/9	BPV
2011		Did not play																	

Tall, athletic pitcher who generates easy velocity with quick, loose arm action. Spots sinking FB to both sides of plate and shows advanced command for his age. Needs to develop secondary pitches including CB and CU, though both project to at least solid-average. Might take him a while to reach MLB, but he has very high upside.

Hultzen, Danny — SP — Seattle

EXP MLB DEBUT: 2012 | POTENTIAL: #2 starter | 8A

Thrws L Age 22
2011 (1) Virginia

- 90-95 FB ++++
- 80-82 SL +++
- CU ++++

Year	Lev	Team	W	L	Sv	IP	K	ERA	WHIP	BF/G	OBA	H%	S%	xERA	Ctl	Dom	Cmd	hr/9	BPV
2009	NCAA	Virginia	9	1	0	95	107	2.18	1.22	22.6	247	34	83	3.02	2.6	10.1	3.8	0.4	135
2010	NCAA	Virginia	11	1	0	106	123	2.80	0.93	24.9	200	27	73	2.07	2.0	10.4	5.1	0.8	162
2011	NCAA	Virginia	12	3	0	118	165	1.37	0.84	24.0	186	30	84	1.14	1.8	12.6	7.2	0.2	237

Strong, durable pitcher who debuted in AFL and has an outside shot of winning a rotation slot in Spring Training. Mature approach includes mixing pitches effectively and commanding FB to both sides of the plate. His above-average FB moves to all quadrants of strike zone. CU is next best pitch and SL provides good action at times.

Hutchison, Drew — SP — Toronto

EXP MLB DEBUT: 2014 | POTENTIAL: #3 starter | 8B

Thrws R Age 21
2009 (15) HS (FL)

- 88-93 FB +++
- 84-88 SL +++
- 81-84 CU ++++

Year	Lev	Team	W	L	Sv	IP	K	ERA	WHIP	BF/G	OBA	H%	S%	xERA	Ctl	Dom	Cmd	hr/9	BPV
2010	A-	Auburn	1	1	0	45	44	3.00	1.02	17.3	211	28	69	1.91	2.4	8.8	3.7	0.2	137
2010	A	Lansing	1	2	0	23	19	1.55	1.03	17.9	206	26	87	2.07	2.7	7.4	2.7	0.4	103
2011	A	Lansing	6	2	0	72	84	2.63	1.21	20.7	251	36	77	2.80	2.4	10.5	4.4	0.1	157
2011	A+	Dunedin	5	3	0	62	66	2.75	0.90	21.0	193	26	70	1.61	2.0	9.6	4.7	0.4	160
2011	AA	New Hampshire	3	0	0	15	21	1.20	0.80	18.1	191	32	83	0.89	1.2	12.6	10.5	0.0	313

Tall, lean pitcher who made hitters look foolish by showcasing well above-average command of quality pitches, thanks to consistent arm speed, slot, and release point. FB shows outstanding life low in the zone, and CU creates havoc for hitters from both sides. Ability to spot FB has been key to success at lower levels.

Hyatt, Austin — SP — Philadelphia

EXP MLB DEBUT: 2013 | POTENTIAL: #5 starter/reliever | **6C**

Thrws R Age 26
2009 (15) Alabama

Velo	Pitch	Grade
88-92	FB	+++
	SL	++
	CU	++++

Year	Lev	Team	W	L	Sv	IP	K	ERA	WHIP	BF/G	OBA	H%	S%	xERA	Ctl	Dom	Cmd	hr/9	BPV
2009	A-	Williamsport	3	0	6	54	81	0.67	0.70	11.2	146	26	92	0.30	2.0	13.5	6.8	0.2	243
2009	A	Lakewood	0	0	0	4	8	8.57	1.67	18.8	297	57	43	4.42	4.3	17.1	4.0	0.0	182
2010	A+	Clearwater	11	5	0	124	156	3.05	1.09	21.1	222	33	72	2.34	2.5	11.3	4.5	0.4	161
2010	AA	Reading	1	0	0	22	25	4.91	1.36	23.0	253	31	69	4.64	3.7	10.2	2.8	1.6	75
2011	AA	Reading	12	6	0	154	171	3.85	1.20	22.1	238	31	72	3.60	2.9	10.0	3.5	1.2	105

Polished right-hander relies on command and control. He has posted impressive Cmd ratios by throwing strikes with a nice 88-92 mph FB, a plus CU, and a so-so SL and by understanding how to keep hitters off-balance. But pitchers with plus CUs and little else sometimes hit a wall at Double-A.

Infante, Gregori — RP — Chicago (A)

EXP MLB DEBUT: 2010 | POTENTIAL: Closer | **8C**

Thrws R Age 24
2006 FA (Venezuela)

Velo	Pitch	Grade
89-98	FB	++++
81-84	CB	++++
81-85	CU	++

Year	Lev	Team	W	L	Sv	IP	K	ERA	WHIP	BF/G	OBA	H%	S%	xERA	Ctl	Dom	Cmd	hr/9	BPV
2010	A+	Winston-Salem	1	2	9	33	35	3.52	1.42	4.5	255	35	72	3.26	4.1	9.5	2.3	0.0	110
2010	AA	Birmingham	2	2	3	26	34	3.45	1.34	4.5	238	37	71	2.83	4.1	11.7	2.8	0.0	137
2010	MLB	Chicago Wsox	0	0	0	4	5	0.00	1.43	3.6	144	23	100	1.99	8.6	10.7	1.3	0.0	117
2011	AA	Birmingham	2	0	7	15	14	0.00	0.93	4.7	141	20	100	0.71	4.2	8.3	2.0	0.0	119
2011	AAA	Charlotte	1	4	4	48	40	3.37	1.48	6.1	269	32	80	4.51	3.9	7.5	1.9	0.9	58

Projectable reliever with power arsenal capable of high strikeouts, but he falls behind too often. He has smooth arm action and clean delivery, but often overthrows and leaves balls up. Needs to firm up CB, but it can be a wipeout pitch at times. If he enhances his FB command, he could become a dynamic closer with durability and stamina.

Jackson, Jay — RP — Chicago (N)

EXP MLB DEBUT: 2012 | POTENTIAL: reliever | **7D**

Thrws R Age 24
2008 (9) Furman

Velo	Pitch	Grade
89-93	FB	++++
81-84	SL	+++
75-77	CB	+++
	CU	++

Year	Lev	Team	W	L	Sv	IP	K	ERA	WHIP	BF/G	OBA	H%	S%	xERA	Ctl	Dom	Cmd	hr/9	BPV
2009	A+	Daytona	2	2	0	38	46	1.65	0.92	20.3	224	31	88	2.26	0.9	10.9	11.5	0.7	296
2009	AA	Tennessee	5	5	0	82	77	3.72	1.36	21.5	239	30	74	3.66	4.3	8.4	2.0	0.8	76
2009	AAA	Iowa	1	0	0	6	4	1.50	1.33	24.9	228	24	100	4.15	4.5	6.0	1.3	1.5	28
2010	AAA	Iowa	11	8	0	157	119	4.64	1.28	20.1	257	29	66	4.05	2.7	6.8	2.5	1.1	62
2011	AAA	Iowa	8	14	0	146	97	5.36	1.55	24.5	304	35	64	4.91	2.8	6.0	2.1	0.6	56

A talented righty who showed no signs of progress. He struggles finding the strike zone, then, when he does, he gets lit up. Lack of a quality breaking ball meant that lefties ate him up. In the past, he showed an ability to miss bats and pound the strike zone, but that seems like a distant memory. A move to relief might be the only option, as time is running out.

Jackson, Luke — SP — Texas

EXP MLB DEBUT: 2014 | POTENTIAL: #3 starter | **8D**

Thrws R Age 20
2010 (1-S) HS (FL)

Velo	Pitch	Grade
88-95	FB	+++
79-83	CB	++
	CU	++

Year	Lev	Team	W	L	Sv	IP	K	ERA	WHIP	BF/G	OBA	H%	S%	xERA	Ctl	Dom	Cmd	hr/9	BPV
2011	A	Hickory	5	6	0	75	78	5.64	1.75	18.0	282	36	69	5.49	5.8	9.4	1.6	1.1	57

Athletic, projectable pitcher whose loose, quick arm leads to natural, electric stuff and potential for three average to above average offerings. But inconsistent mechanics hinder his command: He struggled to limit walks and got lit up as flyballer, and he has been inefficient with pitches. He will need to add strength to his frame.

James, Chad — SP — Florida

EXP MLB DEBUT: 2012 | POTENTIAL: #2 starter | **9D**

Thrws L Age 21
2009 (1) HS, (OK)

Velo	Pitch	Grade
90-95	FB	++++
75-78	CB	+++
78-80	CU	+++

Year	Lev	Team	W	L	Sv	IP	K	ERA	WHIP	BF/G	OBA	H%	S%	xERA	Ctl	Dom	Cmd	hr/9	BPV
2010	A	Greensboro	5	10	0	114	105	5.13	1.59	20.9	265	34	65	4.07	5.1	8.3	1.6	0.2	79
2011	A+	Jupiter	5	15	0	149	124	3.80	1.50	23.9	292	35	76	4.70	3.1	7.5	2.4	0.7	71

Tall, lanky LHP had mixed results in '11. Good velocity on a plus 90-95 mph FB. Also throws a good SL and a plus CU. His mechanics can be inconsistent and he throws across his body a bit, so he continues to struggle with command and will need to make progress to succeed at higher levels. Still somewhat raw, but there is a lot of upside here.

Jeffress, Jeremy — RP — Kansas City

EXP MLB DEBUT: 2010 | POTENTIAL: Closer | **9D**

Thrws R Age 24
2006 (1) HS (VA)

Velo	Pitch	Grade
92-99	FB	++++
78-83	CB	+++
80-82	CU	+

Year	Lev	Team	W	L	Sv	IP	K	ERA	WHIP	BF/G	OBA	H%	S%	xERA	Ctl	Dom	Cmd	hr/9	BPV
2010	AA	Huntsville	1	1	3	14	15	1.28	0.71	4.5	167	24	80	0.43	1.3	9.6	7.5	0.0	236
2010	MLB	Milwaukee	1	0	0	10	8	2.70	1.40	4.2	221	28	79	2.81	5.4	7.2	1.3	0.0	82
2011	AA	NW Arkansas	1	3	0	31	20	4.33	1.73	15.8	267	31	75	4.80	6.3	5.8	0.9	0.6	38
2011	AAA	Omaha	2	3	3	24	24	7.13	1.88	7.0	285	33	65	6.61	6.8	9.0	1.3	1.9	24
2011	MLB	Kansas City	1	1	1	15	13	4.77	1.52	4.7	220	27	68	3.66	6.6	7.7	1.2	0.6	64

Loose-armed reliever has been among the top fireballers, but command and control problems have hindered his development. He throws with an easy arm action and mixes in a solid-average CB which serves as out pitch. FB has a tendency to come out of his hand straight, and he might need to take a few ticks off to add movement. No feel for changing speeds.

Jenkins, Chad — SP — Toronto

EXP MLB DEBUT: 2013 | POTENTIAL: #4 starter | **7C**

Thrws R Age 24
2009 (1) Kennesaw State

Velo	Pitch	Grade
88-94	FB	+++
81-86	SL	+++
82-84	CU	++

Year	Lev	Team	W	L	Sv	IP	K	ERA	WHIP	BF/G	OBA	H%	S%	xERA	Ctl	Dom	Cmd	hr/9	BPV
2009	NCAA	Kennesaw St	8	1	0	92	98	2.54	1.03	27.3	236	32	75	2.32	1.5	9.6	6.5	0.3	194
2010	A	Lansing	5	4	0	79	64	3.64	1.26	24.9	281	34	72	3.80	1.5	7.3	4.9	0.6	129
2010	A+	Dunedin	2	6	0	62	42	4.35	1.47	20.5	294	33	72	4.80	2.6	6.1	2.3	0.9	56
2011	A+	Dunedin	4	5	0	67	44	3.08	1.27	24.9	273	32	76	3.55	1.9	5.9	3.1	0.4	90
2011	AA	New Hampshire	5	7	0	100	74	4.14	1.20	25.1	248	29	66	3.33	2.4	6.7	2.7	0.7	81

Big, strong, durable pitcher who might lack the dominant offering to front a rotation, but he has the arm strength and bulldog mentality to be asset at the back end. Consistently generates GBs by keeping ball down with lively FB. Can drop hard SL in for strikes or use as a chase pitch. Not much of a CU and can be hittable, but repeats delivery well.

Jenkins, Tyrell — SP — St. Louis

EXP MLB DEBUT: 2015 | POTENTIAL: #2 starter | **9D**

Thrws R Age 19
2010 (1-@) Henderson, TX

Velo	Pitch	Grade
90-94	FB	++++
	CB	+++
74-76	CU	+++

Year	Lev	Team	W	L	Sv	IP	K	ERA	WHIP	BF/G	OBA	H%	S%	xERA	Ctl	Dom	Cmd	hr/9	BPV
2010	Rk	Johnson City	0	0	0	3	2	0.00	1.33	6.2	191	24	100	2.30	6.0	6.0	1.0	0.0	74
2011	Rk	Johnson City	4	2	0	56	55	3.86	1.36	21.3	285	37	71	4.00	2.1	8.8	4.2	0.5	125

Lively, athletic righty features a plus 90-94 mph FB that tops out at 96, mixing in a good 1-7 CB and a nice CU. At 6'4", 180 he is tall, lean, and projectable. Low 3/4 delivery gives some deception and good movement on his FB. He should make his full-season debut in '12 and is a player to watch.

Johnson, Erik — SP — Chicago (A)

EXP MLB DEBUT: 2013 | POTENTIAL: #3 starter | **8C**

Thrws R Age 22
2011 (2) California

Velo	Pitch	Grade
88-95	FB	++++
85-87	SL	+++
77-80	CB	++
	CU	++

Year	Lev	Team	W	L	Sv	IP	K	ERA	WHIP	BF/G	OBA	H%	S%	xERA	Ctl	Dom	Cmd	hr/9	BPV
2009	NCAA	California	3	6	4	67	55	4.43	1.48	15.2	273	31	74	4.94	3.8	7.4	2.0	1.3	46
2010	NCAA	California	6	3	1	77	73	4.09	1.55	21.0	281	36	73	4.41	4.0	8.5	2.1	0.5	81
2011	NCAA	California	7	4	0	105	102	2.83	1.21	23.5	187	25	76	2.15	5.1	8.7	1.7	0.3	99
2011	Rk	Great Falls	0	0	0	2	2	4.50	2.50	5.3	415	52	80	8.75	4.5	9.0	2.0	0.0	68

Big, durable pitcher uses crude mechanics, but his potentially above-average FB/SL combo could neutralize hitters from both sides of the plate. Spotty FB command is an issue and leads to walks, while his slow CB is below average. CU has potential, but he will need to find a consistent release point and throw strikes to realize his upside.

Jones, Beau — RP — Florida

EXP MLB DEBUT: 2012 | POTENTIAL: Setup reliever | **6B**

Thrws L Age 25
2005 (1-S) HS (LA)

Velo	Pitch	Grade
87-95	FB	+++
76-78	CB	++++
	CU	+

Year	Lev	Team	W	L	Sv	IP	K	ERA	WHIP	BF/G	OBA	H%	S%	xERA	Ctl	Dom	Cmd	hr/9	BPV
2009	A+	Bakersfield	1	0	0	16	26	0.56	0.62	6.2	150	27	100	0.49	1.1	14.5	13.0	0.6	368
2009	AA	Frisco	3	4	2	54	57	4.49	1.66	6.7	279	37	72	4.54	5.2	9.5	1.8	0.3	85
2010	AA	Frisco	3	0	3	52	62	2.93	1.28	6.3	201	30	75	2.24	5.2	10.7	2.1	0.0	122
2011	AA	Frisco	0	0	0	6	5	0.00	1.15	6.1	189	25	100	1.79	4.4	7.4	1.7	0.0	97
2011	AAA	Round Rock	0	1	1	62	54	3.63	1.37	6.7	252	30	78	4.22	3.8	7.8	2.1	1.2	60

Short, strong reliever who has the FB velocity to pitch up in zone despite his size and arm slot, then retires hitters with a plus CB. He can be hit when he is behind in the count, which occurs often, and he has been affected by reverse splits. Increased velocity and deception, but doesn't change speeds well. Did not allow HR in '10 or '11 at AA, but HRs were an issue in AAA in '11.

Jones, Nate — RP — Chicago (A)

EXP MLB DEBUT: 2012 | POTENTIAL: Setup reliever | **7C**

Thrws R Age 26
2007 (5) Northern Kentucky

Velo	Pitch	Grade
89-96	FB	+++
79-84	CB	++++
	CU	+

Year	Lev	Team	W	L	Sv	IP	K	ERA	WHIP	BF/G	OBA	H%	S%	xERA	Ctl	Dom	Cmd	hr/9	BPV
2008	A+	Winston-Salem	0	0	0	2	1	4.09	1.36	4.6	139	16	67	1.83	8.2	4.1	0.5	0.0	62
2009	A	Kannapolis	2	0	1	18	25	2.47	0.93	5.3	135	23	71	0.63	4.5	12.4	2.8	0.0	161
2009	A+	Winston-Salem	2	1	0	49	43	3.67	1.16	6.1	241	30	70	3.15	2.4	7.9	3.3	0.7	102
2010	A+	Winston-Salem	11	6	0	152	109	4.08	1.53	23.6	291	34	73	4.64	3.3	6.4	1.9	0.6	59
2011	AA	Birmingham	2	3	12	63	67	3.28	1.35	6.3	246	33	76	3.37	3.9	9.6	2.5	0.4	102

Tall, lean reliever who converted to bullpen and had tale of two halves. 1H was rough, with shaky command and inability to retire LHH, but 2H brought consistency and better secondary stuff. Velocity plays up in bullpen, though FB can be straight. Uses height well to get GB outs, and excellent CB can get hitters to swing and miss. No CU in arsenal.

Joseph, Donnie — RP — Cincinnati

EXP MLB DEBUT: 2012 | POTENTIAL: Setup reliever | **7D**

Thrws L Age 24
2009 (3) Houston

Velo	Pitch	Grade
90-94	FB	+++
82-85	SL	++

Year	Lev	Team	W	L	Sv	IP	K	ERA	WHIP	BF/G	OBA	H%	S%	xERA	Ctl	Dom	Cmd	hr/9	BPV
2009	A	Dayton	2	2	4	20	31	4.46	1.14	5.0	186	33	57	1.67	4.5	13.8	3.1	0.0	166
2010	A	Dayton	2	1	6	23	40	0.78	0.87	4.5	167	34	90	0.77	2.7	15.7	5.7	0.0	236
2010	A+	Lynchburg	0	4	17	35	56	2.31	1.11	4.4	189	33	81	2.12	4.1	14.4	3.5	0.5	162
2010	AA	Carolina	1	0	1	7	7	5.14	1.29	4.1	262	35	56	3.04	2.6	9.0	3.5	0.0	130
2011	AA	Carolina	1	3	8	58	66	6.97	1.67	4.6	290	38	58	5.56	4.6	10.2	2.2	1.2	67

Strong-armed LH reliever has plus stuff and the ability to dominate. Classic FB/SL guy: FB sits 90-94, and the SL is potentially nasty. He pitches from a high 3/4 arm slot and throws across his body, which gives some nice deception but also leads to below-average control that has hurt him in past seasons. He will need to do more in '12.

Judy, Josh — RP — Cincinnati

EXP MLB DEBUT: 2011 | POTENTIAL: Setup reliever | **7B**

Thrws R Age 26
2007 (34) Indiana Inst Tech

Velo	Pitch	Grade
89-95	FB	+++
83-86	SL	++++
80-84	CU	++

Year	Lev	Team	W	L	Sv	IP	K	ERA	WHIP	BF/G	OBA	H%	S%	xERA	Ctl	Dom	Cmd	hr/9	BPV
2009	AA	Akron	4	3	11	49	63	3.12	1.08	5.3	202	30	71	2.07	3.3	11.5	3.5	0.4	146
2010	AA	Akron	0	0	0	2	2	9.00	3.00	5.8	515	62	67	12.67	0.0	9.0		0.0	
2010	AAA	Columbus	3	0	2	47	55	2.68	1.32	5.1	266	36	84	4.06	2.7	10.5	3.9	1.0	119
2011	AAA	Columbus	6	2	23	52	60	3.12	1.33	4.3	231	31	80	3.53	4.3	10.4	2.4	0.9	96
2011	MLB	Cleveland	0	0	0	14	10	7.07	1.57	5.1	313	32	61	6.96	2.6	6.4	2.5	2.6	6

Tall, aggressive reliever served as closer and reached the big leagues. He has spent his entire career as RP, where his arm strength plays up. Generally throws strikes with explosive FB with good life and uses SL as weapon against hitters from both sides. Overthrowing has been a problem and CU lacks depth and fade. Can be a high-Dom pitcher if given opportunity.

Jungmann, Taylor — SP — Milwaukee

EXP MLB DEBUT: 2014 | POTENTIAL: #2 starter | **9D**

Thrws R Age 22
2011 (1) Texas

Velo	Pitch	Grade
93-95	FB	++++
80-83	SL	++
74-77	CB	+++
81-85	CU	+++

Year	Lev	Team	W	L	Sv	IP	K	ERA	WHIP	BF/G	OBA	H%	S%	xERA	Ctl	Dom	Cmd	hr/9	BPV
2009	NCAA	Texas	11	3	0	94	101	2.01	1.06	14.6	197	28	80	1.73	3.3	9.6	2.9	0.1	131
2010	NCAA	Texas	8	3	0	120	129	2.03	1.08	27.5	206	28	84	2.35	3.1	9.7	3.1	0.6	120
2011	NCAA	Texas	13	3	0	141	126	1.60	0.83	27.1	169	22	81	1.01	2.3	8.0	3.5	0.3	135

Tall, lean righty with good pitch movement. He has a nice low-to-mid 90s FB and uses his height to his advantage. Throws strikes and has improved his slurvy SL to the point where it is a legitimate strikeout pitch. If he can improve his CU and clean up his delivery, he could become a durable starter with excellent stamina.

Kahnle, Tommy — RP — New York (A)

EXP MLB DEBUT: 2014 | POTENTIAL: #4 starter | **7C**

Thrws R Age 22
2010 (5) Lynn

Velo	Pitch	Grade
90-97	FB	++++
78-84	CB	++
	CU	+++

Year	Lev	Team	W	L	Sv	IP	K	ERA	WHIP	BF/G	OBA	H%	S%	xERA	Ctl	Dom	Cmd	hr/9	BPV
2010	A-	Staten Island	0	0	3	16	25	0.56	0.50	4.8	62	13	88		2.8	14.1	5.0	0.0	232
2011	A	Charleston (SC)	3	5	2	81	112	4.22	1.46	8.7	232	37	68	3.14	5.4	12.4	2.3	0.1	128

Stocky, strong reliever with power arm and huge FB. He has trouble locating the heater, but can blow the ball by hitters up in the zone. Throws with maximum effort, but has enough durability to pitch multiple innings on back-to-back days. Breaking ball lacks spin and consistency, though CU can be quite good. He needs to throw strikes and find ways to retire LHH.

Kelly, Casey — SP — San Diego

EXP MLB DEBUT: 2012 | POTENTIAL: #3 starter | **8C**

Thrws R Age 22
2008 (1) HS, (FL)

Velo	Pitch	Grade
89-94	FB	+++
76-79	CB	+++
80-84	CU	++++

Year	Lev	Team	W	L	Sv	IP	K	ERA	WHIP	BF/G	OBA	H%	S%	xERA	Ctl	Dom	Cmd	hr/9	BPV
2009	A	Greenville	6	1	0	48	39	1.12	0.85	19.6	191	25	85	1.07	1.7	7.3	4.3	0.0	152
2009	A+	Salem	1	4	0	46	35	3.12	0.87	21.3	202	23	67	1.97	1.4	6.8	5.0	0.8	137
2010	AA	Portland	3	5	0	95	81	5.31	1.61	20.0	306	37	68	5.40	3.3	7.7	2.3	0.9	60
2011	AA	San Antonio	11	6	0	142	105	3.99	1.40	22.2	276	33	71	4.03	2.9	6.7	2.3	0.5	72

Young righty has plus stuff that includes a 90-94 sinking FB, a good CB, and above-average CU. Scouts continue to rave about his stuff, but the results have yet to materialize and he seems more like a mid-rotation starter than a front-of-rotation stud. Has potential, but will need to show he can miss more bats to live up to the hype.

Kelly, Joe — RP — St. Louis

EXP MLB DEBUT: 2012 | POTENTIAL: #4 starter | **7C**

Thrws R Age 24
2009 (3) UC Riverside

Velo	Pitch	Grade
93-97	FB	+++
83-85	SL	+++
	CU	

Year	Lev	Team	W	L	Sv	IP	K	ERA	WHIP	BF/G	OBA	H%	S%	xERA	Ctl	Dom	Cmd	hr/9	BPV
2009	NCAA	Cal-Riverside	1	1	12	28	23	5.74	1.38	5.2	293	35	57	4.35	1.9	7.3	3.8	0.6	102
2009	A-	Batavia	2	3	1	30	30	4.78	1.46	8.1	280	38	64	3.73	3.3	9.0	2.7	0.0	110
2010	A	Quad Cities	6	8	1	103	92	4.63	1.44	16.9	262	33	66	3.67	3.9	8.0	2.0	0.3	86
2011	A+	Palm Beach	5	2	0	72	62	2.62	1.25	24.5	216	28	78	2.47	4.2	7.7	1.8	0.1	93
2011	AA	Springfield	6	4	0	59	51	5.03	1.61	23.8	296	35	70	5.35	3.8	7.8	2.0	1.1	53

Undersized righty was used exclusively as a SP in '11. Can pump his FB in at 93-97 in shorter stints, but is 90-93 as a SP. FB has good sinking action that allows him to keep the ball in the park and get tons of GB outs. Complements the FB with a nice SL and a below-average CU.

Kelly, Michael — SP — San Diego

EXP MLB DEBUT: 2015 | POTENTIAL: #3 starter | **8D**

Thrws Age 19
2011 (1-S) HS, (FL)

Velo	Pitch	Grade
88-93	FB	+++
	CB	++
	CU	++

Year	Lev	Team	W	L	Sv	IP	K	ERA	WHIP	BF/G	OBA	H%	S%	xERA	Ctl	Dom	Cmd	hr/9	BPV
2011		Did not play																	

Lean and projectable high school righty with a power arm. At 6'5", has a nice low-90s FB with room for more as he matures. He gets good movement from a low 3/4 arm slot but needs to refine his breaking ball and CU and learn how to pitch. Has some work to do, but has tons of potential and will make his professional debut in 2012.

Kickham, Mike — SP — San Francisco

EXP MLB DEBUT: 2014 | POTENTIAL: #5 Starter/reliever | **7D**

Thrws L Age 23
2010 (6) Missouri State

Velo	Pitch	Grade
90-92	FB	+++
	SL	+++
	CU	+

Year	Lev	Team	W	L	Sv	IP	K	ERA	WHIP	BF/G	OBA	H%	S%	xERA	Ctl	Dom	Cmd	hr/9	BPV
2010	NCAA	Missouri State	4	9	0	96	103	5.25	1.36	26.8	272	34	64	4.60	2.8	9.7	3.4	1.3	91
2010	Rk	AZL Giants	0	0	0	2	3	12.86	2.86	4.0	403	58	50	9.36	8.6	12.9	1.5	0.0	83
2011	A	Augusta	5	10	0	111	103	4.13	1.34	22.0	263	33	70	3.88	3.0	8.3	2.8	0.7	89

Tall, physical lefty from Missouri State has a solid 90-92 FB that tops out at 94. Had mixed results in '11, but struck out 103 while walking just 37, with plenty of GB outs. Also has a nice SL, but will need a solid third pitch to remain a starter.

Kimball, Cole — RP — Washington

EXP MLB DEBUT: 2011 | POTENTIAL: Setup reliever | **7C**

Thrws R Age 26
2006 (12) Centenary College

Velo	Pitch	Grade
94-98	FB	++++
	SL	+++
	CU	++

Year	Lev	Team	W	L	Sv	IP	K	ERA	WHIP	BF/G	OBA	H%	S%	xERA	Ctl	Dom	Cmd	hr/9	BPV
2009	A+	Potomac	4	5	9	46	52	6.43	1.67	5.3	273	37	60	4.88	5.5	10.1	1.9	0.8	77
2010	A+	Potomac	3	0	6	24	27	1.86	1.03	4.9	199	29	80	1.60	3.0	10.0	3.4	0.0	146
2010	AA	Harrisburg	5	1	12	54	74	2.33	1.19	5.7	178	27	83	2.34	5.2	12.3	2.4	0.7	124
2011	AAA	Syracuse	1	0	5	13	14	0.00	1.21	4.4	177	26	100	1.80	5.5	9.5	1.8	0.0	114
2011	MLB	Washington	1	0	0	14	11	1.93	1.36	4.9	168	22	84	2.10	7.1	7.1	1.0	0.0	85

Tall, strong-armed reliever was effective again in '11 and made his MLB debut before being shut down with a shoulder injury in June. Kimball had rotator cuff surgery in July and was claimed off waivers by the Blue Jays, but was returned to the Nationals in December. Kimball will miss the start of '12, but should return by mid-season.

Kingham, Nick — SP — Pittsburgh

EXP MLB DEBUT: 2015 | POTENTIAL: #3 starter | **8D**

Thrws R Age 20
2010 (4) HS, (NV)

Velo	Pitch	Grade
90-93	FB	+++
	CB	++
	CU	++

Year	Lev	Team	W	L	Sv	IP	K	ERA	WHIP	BF/G	OBA	H%	S%	xERA	Ctl	Dom	Cmd	hr/9	BPV
2010	Rk	GCL Pirates	0	0	0	3	2	0.00	1.00	5.7	262	32	100	2.35	0.0	6.0		0.0	
2011	A-	State College	6	2	0	71	47	2.15	1.10	18.5	239	27	84	2.89	1.9	6.0	3.1	0.6	90

Tall (6'5"), lean collegiate hurler continues to make impressive progress. Could add velocity to 90-93 FB as he fills out. Also throws an above-average CU and an inconsistent CB. Gets good downhill tilt on his FB, limited hitters to a .238 BAA, and gave up just 5 home runs.

Kirk, Austin — SP — Chicago (N)

EXP MLB DEBUT: 2013 | POTENTIAL: Setup reliever | **7D**

Thrws L Age 22
2009 (3) HS, (OK)

Velo	Pitch	Grade
88-91	FB	+++
75-78	CB	+++

Year	Lev	Team	W	L	Sv	IP	K	ERA	WHIP	BF/G	OBA	H%	S%	xERA	Ctl	Dom	Cmd	hr/9	BPV
2009	Rk	AZL Cubs	1	0	0	8	10	3.29	1.46	7.0	257	38	75	3.40	4.4	11.0	2.5	0.0	122
2009	A-	Boise	1	1	0	5	5	5.40	1.00	9.6	124	10	50	2.41	5.4	9.0	1.7	1.8	65
2010	A-	Boise	4	5	0	51	48	3.34	1.23	17.3	261	32	77	3.88	2.1	8.4	4.0	1.1	106
2010	A	Peoria	1	1	0	12	17	3.69	1.39	17.1	189	29	75	3.05	6.6	12.5	1.9	0.7	110
2011	A	Peoria	5	12	0	151	122	4.29	1.20	20.9	251	29	66	3.64	2.3	7.3	3.2	1.0	85

Short, athletic lefty had a solid season in the MWL. Throws strikes and commands the zone well (122 K/38 BB), but doesn't have overpowering stuff, and lack of third offering could force him to the pen. Nice 88-91 FB gets in on hitters quickly due to some deception in delivery. Fell apart in the second half (1-9/6.19).

Klein, Dan — RP — Baltimore

Thrws R Age 23 | 2010 (3) UCLA | EXP MLB DEBUT: 2013 | POTENTIAL: Setup reliever | 7A

Velo	Pitch	Grade
88-94	FB	+++
80-82	CB	+++
81-84	SL	+++
78-80	CU	++

Year	Lev	Team	W	L	Sv	IP	K	ERA	WHIP	BF/G	OBA	H%	S%	xERA	Ctl	Dom	Cmd	hr/9	BPV
2008	NCAA	UCLA	2	2	0	17	13	7.85	1.80	11.4	366	44	52	6.03	1.6	6.8	4.3	0.0	114
2010	NCAA	UCLA	6	1	10	52	55	1.90	0.96	5.0	210	28	83	2.04	1.9	9.5	5.0	0.5	160
2010	A-	Aberdeen	1	0	1	6	10	0.00	0.33	3.8	55	12	100		1.5	14.8	10.0	0.0	343
2011	A+	Frederick	0	1	0	15	21	1.18	0.79	7.8	174	24	100	1.78	1.8	12.4	7.0	1.2	206
2011	AA	Bowie	3	0	0	16	16	1.11	1.05	7.0	235	32	88	2.08	1.7	8.9	5.3	0.0	173

Tall and athletic reliever who can't stay healthy despite clean, loose delivery. Underwent shoulder surgery in August, and should return once season starts. Pitches off lively, not overpowering, FB. Mixes in two breaking balls. Effective against RHH and LHH. CU exhibits nice movement, but he doesn't use it often. Needs to maintain health to advance.

Kluber, Corey — SP — Cleveland

Thrws R Age 26 | 2007 (4) Stetson | EXP MLB DEBUT: 2011 | POTENTIAL: #4 starter | 7C

Velo	Pitch	Grade
88-92	FB	+++
80-83	SL	+++
72-75	CB	++
78-81	CU	+++

Year	Lev	Team	W	L	Sv	IP	K	ERA	WHIP	BF/G	OBA	H%	S%	xERA	Ctl	Dom	Cmd	hr/9	BPV
2010	AA	San Antonio	6	6	0	122	136	3.46	1.32	23.0	260	35	74	3.56	2.9	10.0	3.4	0.5	119
2010	AA	Akron	2	2	0	26	21	3.79	1.84	24.3	340	42	77	5.66	3.4	7.2	2.1	0.0	74
2010	AAA	Columbus	1	1	0	11	8	3.27	1.45	23.5	244	28	80	4.01	4.9	6.5	1.3	0.8	49
2011	AAA	Columbus	7	11	0	150	143	5.57	1.48	23.9	265	32	64	4.66	4.2	8.6	2.0	1.1	62
2011	MLB	Cleveland	0	0	0	4	5	8.78	2.20	6.9	342	48	56	6.54	6.6	11.0	1.7	0.0	88

Big, strong RHP who finished third in IL in Ks. Promoted to CLE during season, despite inability to keep ball in yard. Lacks athleticism, and his delivery doesn't generate top velocity. Straight FB at lesser velocities hasn't been fruitful against good hitters. A plethora of secondary pitches and deceptive arm action give him shot at success.

Knapp, Jason — SP — Cleveland

Thrws R Age 21 | 2008 (2) HS (NJ) | EXP MLB DEBUT: 2014 | POTENTIAL: #1 starter | 9D

Velo	Pitch	Grade
91-98	FB	+++++
79-83	CB	++++
78-81	CU	+

Year	Lev	Team	W	L	Sv	IP	K	ERA	WHIP	BF/G	OBA	H%	S%	xERA	Ctl	Dom	Cmd	hr/9	BPV
2008	Rk	GCL Phillies	3	1	0	31	38	2.61	1.23	17.9	229	34	78	2.71	3.5	11.0	3.2	0.3	133
2009	A	Lakewood	2	7	0	85	111	4.02	1.20	20.1	208	32	65	2.40	4.1	11.7	2.8	0.3	134
2009	A	Lake County	0	0	0	11	12	5.63	1.61	12.4	240	34	61	3.55	6.4	9.6	1.5	0.0	96
2010	Rk	AZL Indians	0	2	0	12	18	1.49	0.74	8.6	128	24	78	0.07	3.0	13.4	4.5	0.0	204
2010	A	Lake County	1	0	0	16	29	3.94	1.25	16.3	210	43	65	2.21	4.5	16.3	3.6	0.0	187

Missed entire season after shoulder surgery, and missed most of '10 as well. When healthy, uses a deceptive delivery and very effective high 3/4 slot to fire electric FB past hitters and spins solid CB into zone. Mechanics can get out of whack at times, and he throws with maximum effort. Could move to bullpen full-time.

Koehler, Tom — SP — Florida

Thrws R Age 25 | 2008 (18) SUNY Stoney Brook | EXP MLB DEBUT: 2012 | POTENTIAL: #4 starter | 7C

Velo	Pitch	Grade
88-92	FB	+++
82-84	SL	++++
	CB	++
	CU	++

Year	Lev	Team	W	L	Sv	IP	K	ERA	WHIP	BF/G	OBA	H%	S%	xERA	Ctl	Dom	Cmd	hr/9	BPV
2008	A-	Jamestown	5	5	0	66	58	3.68	1.44	18.7	262	34	72	3.43	4.0	7.9	2.0	0.0	92
2009	A	Greensboro	5	5	0	98	82	3.21	1.29	22.4	241	29	78	3.57	3.6	7.5	2.1	0.8	71
2009	A+	Jupiter	4	1	0	34	25	3.42	1.29	23.4	266	33	70	3.12	2.4	6.6	2.8	0.0	100
2010	AA	Jacksonville	16	2	0	158	145	2.62	1.18	22.6	239	30	80	3.05	2.6	8.2	3.2	0.6	104
2011	AAA	New Orleans	12	7	0	150	116	4.98	1.49	23.1	254	29	68	4.47	4.7	7.0	1.5	1.1	44

Righty took a step back. He is not overpowering, but does throw strikes and has four solid pitches: an 88-92 FB that can hit 94, a plus SL, a CB, and a good CU. SL is his best, and he does a good job of keeping hitters off-balance. Control was not good in '11 and he will need to regroup.

Kontos, George — RP — New York (A)

Thrws R Age 27 | 2006 (5) Northwestern | EXP MLB DEBUT: 2011 | POTENTIAL: Middle reliever | 7C

Velo	Pitch	Grade
88-94	FB	+++
82-85	SL	+++
78-82	CB	++
78-80	CU	++

Year	Lev	Team	W	L	Sv	IP	K	ERA	WHIP	BF/G	OBA	H%	S%	xERA	Ctl	Dom	Cmd	hr/9	BPV
2010	A+	Tampa	0	1	0	10	8	2.67	0.99	7.7	197	25	70	1.49	2.7	7.1	2.7	0.0	114
2010	AA	Trenton	0	2	0	32	28	3.38	1.28	7.7	250	31	74	3.40	3.1	7.9	2.5	0.6	89
2010	AAA	Scranton/W-B	0	1	0	2	2	12.27	2.73	6.1	446	49	60	13.90	4.1	8.2	2.0	4.1	-66
2011	AAA	Scranton/W-B	4	4	2	89	91	2.63	1.10	8.7	223	27	84	3.19	2.6	9.2	3.5	1.2	103
2011	MLB	New York (A)	0	0	0	6	6	3.00	1.17	3.4	191	22	83	3.26	4.5	9.0	2.0	1.5	68

Found his niche in '10 after converting to RP. Had TJS in '09, but he's big and strong, and is healthy and throwing harder in short stints. Has been flyball pitcher and has given up fair share of HR, however. Toys with RHH by locating FB early in count and wiping out with hard SL. Uses CB and CU, but hasn't found success against LHH.

Krol, Ian — SP — Oakland

Thrws L Age 21 | 2009 (7) HS (IL) | EXP MLB DEBUT: 2014 | POTENTIAL: #3 starter | 8D

Velo	Pitch	Grade
86-92	FB	+++
78-82	CB	+++
78-81	CU	+++

Year	Lev	Team	W	L	Sv	IP	K	ERA	WHIP	BF/G	OBA	H%	S%	xERA	Ctl	Dom	Cmd	hr/9	BPV
2009	Rk	AZL Athletics	0	0	0	1	0	0.00	0.00	2.8	0	0			0.0	0.0		0.0	
2009	A-	Vancouver	0	1	0	3	4	8.71	2.26	5.2	407	56	57	7.94	2.9	11.6	4.0	0.0	127
2010	A	Kane County	9	4	0	118	91	2.66	0.99	18.8	227	28	73	2.21	1.4	6.9	4.8	0.4	140
2010	A+	Stockton	1	0	0	19	20	3.75	1.41	20.3	250	31	79	4.49	4.2	9.4	2.2	1.4	66
2011	Rk	AZL Athletics	0	0	0	5	6	0.00	0.00	4.7	0	0			0.0	10.8		0.0	

Athletic LHP rarely saw the mound due to forearm injury and an off-field issue. Low ceiling due to lack of velocity and size, but has polished secondary pitches to keep hitters off guard. Commands both sides of plate with average FB and can register Ks with deceptive CU and potential plus CB. Throws consistent strikes and won't beat himself.

Kukuk, Cody — SP — Boston

Thrws L Age 19 | 2011 (7) HS (KS) | EXP MLB DEBUT: 2015 | POTENTIAL: #3 starter | 8E

Velo	Pitch	Grade
86-92	FB	+++
81-84	SL	+++
	CU	++

Year	Lev	Team	W	L	Sv	IP	K	ERA	WHIP	BF/G	OBA	H%	S%	xERA	Ctl	Dom	Cmd	hr/9	BPV
2011		Did not play																	

Tall, loose lefty with projection, but could be years away from making impact in BOS. Only average velocity, but could improve grow as he adds strength and learns to use quick arm. Shows off a hard SL, but struggles to stay on top of it due to varying release points. Has below average control and needs CU to survive.

Lamb, John — SP — Kansas City

Thrws L Age 22 | 2008 (5) HS (CA) | EXP MLB DEBUT: 2013 | POTENTIAL: #2 starter | 9C

Velo	Pitch	Grade
88-95	FB	+++
77-79	CB	+++
78-81	CU	++++

Year	Lev	Team	W	L	Sv	IP	K	ERA	WHIP	BF/G	OBA	H%	S%	xERA	Ctl	Dom	Cmd	hr/9	BPV
2009	Rk	Burlington	2	2	0	27	25	3.99	1.22	18.2	239	28	72	3.82	3.0	8.3	2.8	1.3	75
2010	A	Burlington	2	3	0	40	43	1.58	1.08	19.5	187	26	88	1.99	3.8	9.7	2.5	0.5	115
2010	A+	Wilmington	6	3	0	74	90	1.46	1.00	21.8	220	33	85	1.86	1.8	10.9	6.0	0.1	199
2010	AA	NW Arkansas	2	1	0	33	26	5.45	1.52	20.4	284	34	63	4.47	3.5	7.1	2.0	0.5	66
2011	AA	NW Arkansas	1	2	0	35	22	3.09	1.31	18.1	251	28	79	3.71	3.3	5.7	1.7	0.8	51

Aggressive, physical lefty will miss part of '12 after TJS in June '11. Velocity dropped pre-injury, but he threw with good arm speed when healthy. Best pitch is CU that gets swings and misses. FB and CB both can be above average, but FB often lacks movement at higher velocities. Will likely be handled cautiously upon return.

Lamb, Will — SP — Texas

Thrws L Age 21 | 2011 (2) Clemson | EXP MLB DEBUT: 2014 | POTENTIAL: #3 starter | 8D

Velo	Pitch	Grade
89-94	FB	+++
80-83	CB	+++
	CU	+++

Year	Lev	Team	W	L	Sv	IP	K	ERA	WHIP	BF/G	OBA	H%	S%	xERA	Ctl	Dom	Cmd	hr/9	BPV
2009	NCAA	Clemson	0	0	1	22	15	2.45	1.36	6.1	262	30	86	4.03	3.3	6.1	1.9	0.8	54
2010	NCAA	Clemson	4	4	2	52	30	5.02	1.58	12.7	280	30	70	5.04	4.3	5.2	1.2	1.0	24
2011	NCAA	Clemson	1	1	0	24	29	5.21	1.45	10.3	260	37	62	3.75	4.1	10.8	2.6	0.4	112
2011	A-	Spokane	1	1	0	37	42	3.89	1.57	13.5	251	34	76	4.28	5.6	10.2	1.8	0.7	83
2011	A	Hickory	2	0	0	18	20	0.49	0.99	17.3	163	24	94	1.08	4.0	9.9	2.5	0.0	134

Tall, slender pitcher who has been better in the pros than in college. Arm speed and frame project to more velocity while power CB can be a nice wipeout option. Has shown touch for changing speeds, while mixing three pitches well. Will need time to develop and learn nuances of craft, but has legitimate upside.

Lara, Braulio — SP — Tampa Bay

Thrws L Age 23 | 2008 FA (DR) | EXP MLB DEBUT: 2014 | POTENTIAL: #3 starter | 8D

Velo	Pitch	Grade
91-96	FB	++++
81-84	CB	++
82-85	CU	++

Year	Lev	Team	W	L	Sv	IP	K	ERA	WHIP	BF/G	OBA	H%	S%	xERA	Ctl	Dom	Cmd	hr/9	BPV
2010	Rk	Princeton	6	4	0	66	58	2.18	1.12	20.0	208	27	81	2.20	3.4	7.9	2.3	0.3	101
2011	A	Bowling Green	5	11	0	120	111	4.95	1.43	20.4	257	32	65	4.05	4.1	8.3	2.0	0.7	73

Keeps the ball on the ground and is very tough on LHH but RHH have hit him hard. Uses above-average FB early in count, but inconsistent secondary pitches have hindered. Must upgrade FB command, which might enhance CB and CU in turn. Slows arm speed on CU. Athletic and aggressive pitcher had a disappointing season, but still has potential.

Lee, Chen — RP — Cleveland

Thrws R Age 25 | 2009 FA (Taiwan) | EXP MLB DEBUT: 2012 | POTENTIAL: Setup reliever | 7A

Velo	Pitch	Grade
88-95	FB	+++
80-82	SL	+++
	SP	++

Year	Lev	Team	W	L	Sv	IP	K	ERA	WHIP	BF/G	OBA	H%	S%	xERA	Ctl	Dom	Cmd	hr/9	BPV
2009	A+	Kinston	4	6	2	83	97	3.36	1.14	7.3	222	31	71	2.66	3.0	10.5	3.5	0.5	130
2010	AA	Akron	5	4	0	72	82	3.24	1.12	6.5	225	30	73	2.83	2.7	10.2	3.7	0.7	127
2011	AA	Akron	2	1	0	39	56	2.53	0.97	6.5	196	32	73	1.59	2.5	12.9	5.1	0.2	193
2011	AAA	Columbus	4	0	1	31	43	2.31	1.22	6.0	228	35	83	2.93	3.5	12.4	3.6	0.6	142

Short, quick-armed reliever consistently performs with low 3/4 slot. Succeeds by consistently throwing strikes with all his pitches, spotting FB down, and getting hitters to chase SL -- his go-to K pitch -- and mixing in a good CU. Lacks strength and durability, and projects to dependable setup RP.

Lee, Zach — SP — Los Angeles (N)

EXP MLB DEBUT: 2014 **POTENTIAL:** #2 starter **9D**

Thrws R Age 20
2010 (1) HS, (TX)

90-93 FB	++++
75-78 CB	+++
CU	+++

Year	Lev	Team	W	L	Sv	IP	K	ERA	WHIP	BF/G	OBA	H%	S%	xERA	Ctl	Dom	Cmd	hr/9	BPV
2011	A	Great Lakes	9	6	0	109	91	3.47	1.22	18.3	247	30	73	3.39	2.6	7.5	2.8	0.7	88

Lively, tall, strong athlete flashes a good 89-93 mph FB that touches 95. Also has a nice cutter and an improved change-up that could be plus down the road. Has simple, repeatable mechanics produce good control. If breaking ball and change-up continue to improve, he has nice long-term potential.

Leesman, Charles — SP — Chicago (A)

EXP MLB DEBUT: 2012 **POTENTIAL:** #4 starter **7C**

Thrws L Age 25
2008 (11) Xavier

88-92 FB	++++
79-83 SL	++
75-78 CB	++
79-82 CU	++

Year	Lev	Team	W	L	Sv	IP	K	ERA	WHIP	BF/G	OBA	H%	S%	xERA	Ctl	Dom	Cmd	hr/9	BPV
2008	A	Kannapolis	0	0	0	4	5	0.00	1.19	16.8	202	30	100	2.02	4.3	10.7	2.5	0.0	131
2009	A	Kannapolis	13	5	0	157	117	3.09	1.42	24.7	271	33	77	3.74	3.3	6.7	2.0	0.2	76
2010	A+	Winston-Salem	9	4	0	84	39	5.13	1.69	22.3	292	32	69	5.13	4.7	4.2	0.9	0.6	21
2010	AA	Birmingham	5	2	0	63	51	2.71	1.06	22.3	209	27	73	1.94	2.8	7.3	2.6	0.1	106
2011	AA	Birmingham	10	7	0	152	113	4.03	1.53	24.5	259	32	72	3.87	4.9	6.7	1.4	0.2	65

Tall and durable pitcher with penchant for keeping balls on ground. Plus sinker is tough for hitters to elevate, but hasn't yet developed formidable breaking ball or CU. Could be in majors quickly, but struggles to throw consistent strikes. Doesn't project to a high Dom pitcher, but sinker offers hope. Can battle LHH adeptly, but lacks pitch against RHH.

Lehman, Patrick — SP — Washington

EXP MLB DEBUT: 2012 **POTENTIAL:** Reliever **6B**

Thrws R Age 25
2009 (13) George Washington

88-92 FB	+++
SL	++
CU	++

Year	Lev	Team	W	L	Sv	IP	K	ERA	WHIP	BF/G	OBA	H%	S%	xERA	Ctl	Dom	Cmd	hr/9	BPV
2009	A	Hagerstown	1	1	0	32	28	2.25	0.72	18.9	196	24	71	1.32	0.3	7.9	28.0	0.6	634
2010	Rk	GCL Nationals	1	0	0	10	10	1.80	0.80	9.1	221	31	75	1.28	0.0	9.0		0.0	
2010	A+	Potomac	5	4	0	87	88	4.86	1.32	17.2	262	32	67	4.48	2.9	9.1	3.1	1.4	80
2011	A+	Potomac	2	0	7	15	11	1.78	0.59	4.0	174	22	67	0.23	0.0	6.5		0.0	
2011	AA	Harrisburg	1	2	6	34	34	3.71	0.76	4.2	187	24	50	1.28	1.1	9.0	8.5	0.5	234

Crafty, but not overpowering hurler worked exclusively in relief in '11. Lehman throws a low-90s fastball, an average slider, and decent change-up. He has nice polish and is a strike throwing machine (just 4 BB/ 45 K in 49.2 IP). Not overpowering, but throws strikes, gets plenty of groundball outs (1.44 GB/FB), and can be effective.

Lindsay, Shane — RP — Los Angeles (N)

EXP MLB DEBUT: 2011 **POTENTIAL:** Closer **8E**

Thrws R Age 27
2003 FA (Australia)

92-98 FB	++++
83-85 CB	+++
CU	+

Year	Lev	Team	W	L	Sv	IP	K	ERA	WHIP	BF/G	OBA	H%	S%	xERA	Ctl	Dom	Cmd	hr/9	BPV
2010	AAA	Colorado Spgs	0	1	0	13	19	6.82	2.42	4.9	287	45	69	6.23	11.6	13.0	1.1	0.0	99
2010	AAA	Columbus	0	1	0	11	12	8.18	2.64	8.6	295	39	68	7.68	13.1	9.8	0.8	0.8	46
2011	AA	Birmingham	1	1	0	6	12	4.35	1.94	5.9	186	42	75	3.65	11.6	17.4	1.5	0.0	154
2011	AAA	Charlotte	2	2	4	63	78	1.99	1.25	5.7	136	21	84	1.71	7.3	11.1	1.5	0.3	118
2011	MLB	Chicago Wsox	0	0	0	6	6	12.00	2.67	8.2	394	48	53	10.14	7.5	9.0	1.2	1.5	10

Hard-throwing reliever who earned promotion to big leagues on basis of pure arm strength and ability to induce weak contact. Plus FB thrown from violent, max-effort delivery, but has major problems commanding it. Sharp CB can get hitters to flail, but doesn't stay on top of it. Polished hitters wait him out and challenge him to throw strikes.

Linsky, Lenny — RP — Tampa Bay

EXP MLB DEBUT: 2013 **POTENTIAL:** Closer **7A**

Thrws R Age 22
2011 (2) Hawaii

87-95 FB	++++
82-86 SL	+++
CU	+

Year	Lev	Team	W	L	Sv	IP	K	ERA	WHIP	BF/G	OBA	H%	S%	xERA	Ctl	Dom	Cmd	hr/9	BPV
2009	NCAA	Hawaii	1	1	1	17	16	8.47	2.12	7.0	315	37	61	7.42	7.4	7.9	1.1	1.6	15
2010	NCAA	Hawaii	4	0	12	44	28	1.64	1.18	6.1	244	28	88	2.95	2.5	5.7	2.3	0.4	77
2011	NCAA	Hawaii	1	1	14	34	34	1.32	0.99	4.8	206	29	85	1.59	2.4	8.9	3.8	0.0	147
2011	A-	Hudson Valley	3	0	3	24	27	1.49	1.03	7.8	218	29	91	2.52	2.2	10.0	4.5	0.7	144
2011	A	Bowling Green	0	0	0	4	3	0.00	0.95	4.0	202	25	100	1.46	2.1	6.4	3.0	0.0	116

Durable and polished reliever who should reach TAM quickly with unique low 3/4 slot that induces very high amount of groundballs. Plus sinker plays up due to slot and velocity and can set up wicked SL to put away hitters. Pitches aggressively, though can work against him when he speeds up delivery. Rarely uses CU, but top two pitches are enough.

Lintz, Seth — SP — Milwaukee

EXP MLB DEBUT: 2012 **POTENTIAL:** #4 starter **8E**

Thrws R Age 22
2008 (2) HS, (TN)

87-92 FB	+++
71-74 CB	+++
79-81 CU	++

Year	Lev	Team	W	L	Sv	IP	K	ERA	WHIP	BF/G	OBA	H%	S%	xERA	Ctl	Dom	Cmd	hr/9	BPV
2008	Rk	AZL Brewers	0	3	0	18	26	6.96	2.10	9.9	301	43	69	7.02	8.0	12.9	1.6	1.5	62
2009	Rk	AZL Brewers	0	5	2	40	41	4.94	1.90	12.6	252	31	76	5.48	8.5	9.2	1.1	1.1	49
2010	Rk	Helena	1	3	0	39	27	10.13	2.20	13.1	356	40	53	8.15	5.8	6.2	1.1	1.4	2
2011	Rk	Helena	0	1	0	12	12	6.64	2.30	10.4	368	45	73	8.66	5.9	8.9	1.5	1.5	22
2011	A	Wisconsin	1	0	0	10	12	2.65	1.18	5.1	196	29	75	1.91	4.4	10.6	2.4	0.0	130

Athletic pitcher with fluid mechanics and pitchability beyond experience level. Achieves sinking movement from FB and can notch Ks with CB. Repeating three-quarters delivery would improve deception and command, but that did not happen. Drop in Dom and poor Ctl not a good combination.

Lo, Chia-Jen — RP — Houston

EXP MLB DEBUT: 2013 **POTENTIAL:** Power reliever **8C**

Thrws R Age 26
2008 NDFA (Taiwan)

93-96 FB	++++
CB	++
CU	++

Year	Lev	Team	W	L	Sv	IP	K	ERA	WHIP	BF/G	OBA	H%	S%	xERA	Ctl	Dom	Cmd	hr/9	BPV
2009	A+	Lancaster	1	0	1	25	36	1.79	0.92	7.8	124	21	82	0.80	4.7	12.9	2.8	0.4	155
2009	AA	Corpus Christi	0	2	2	39	39	2.31	1.28	5.3	214	29	82	2.63	4.6	9.0	2.0	0.2	100
2010	AA	Corpus Christi	0	1	0	15	13	1.80	1.27	8.8	175	23	84	1.94	6.0	7.8	1.3	0.0	94
2011	A	Lexington	0	0	0	2	3	13.50	2.00	4.8	262	27	33	9.02	9.0	13.5	1.5	4.5	-20

Short/slender reliever from Taiwan missed almost all of '11 with elbow problems. Prior to the injury, had an easy mid-90s velocity with good movement and some late deception. Secondary pitches were only average, but projects as a serviceable reliever. Showed nice Dom in relief, but will need to prove he is healthy and can get back on the mound.

Lobstein, Kyle — SP — Tampa Bay

EXP MLB DEBUT: 2013 **POTENTIAL:** #4 starter **7C**

Thrws L Age 22
2008 (2) HS (AZ)

88-93 FB	+++
75-78 CB	+++
78-81 CU	++

Year	Lev	Team	W	L	Sv	IP	K	ERA	WHIP	BF/G	OBA	H%	S%	xERA	Ctl	Dom	Cmd	hr/9	BPV
2009	A-	Hudson Valley	3	5	0	73	74	2.59	1.07	20.3	211	28	77	2.29	3.4	9.1	3.2	0.5	120
2010	A	Bowling Green	9	8	0	148	128	4.14	1.31	22.6	251	30	70	3.77	3.3	7.8	2.4	0.9	76
2011	A+	Charlotte	9	9	0	121	85	3.72	1.24	22.3	260	30	72	3.69	2.2	6.3	2.8	0.8	76
2011	AA	Montgomery	1	1	0	11	11	7.36	1.82	25.5	311	33	69	8.18	4.9	9.0	1.8	3.3	-13

Tall and projectable pitcher who has yet to break out despite myriad pitches and skills. Average FB plays up due to lively, late movement and he spots it well to all quadrants of strike zone. Though may not have plus velocity, generates Ks with easy arm action and loose delivery. Still developing CU and could be average in time.

Locke, Jeff — SP — Pittsburgh

EXP MLB DEBUT: 2011 **POTENTIAL:** #3 starter **7B**

Thrws L Age 24
2006 (2-S) HS, (NH)

87-93 FB	+++
72-78 CB	+++
79-81 CU	++

Year	Lev	Team	W	L	Sv	IP	K	ERA	WHIP	BF/G	OBA	H%	S%	xERA	Ctl	Dom	Cmd	hr/9	BPV
2010	A+	Bradenton	9	3	0	86	83	3.55	1.11	19.9	252	32	69	3.07	1.5	8.7	5.9	0.6	162
2010	AA	Altoona	3	2	0	57	56	3.62	1.21	23.0	261	33	72	3.57	1.9	8.8	4.7	0.8	130
2011	AA	Altoona	7	8	0	125	114	4.03	1.31	22.5	251	31	70	3.57	3.3	8.2	2.5	0.6	87
2011	AAA	Indianapolis	1	2	0	28	25	2.24	1.21	22.6	240	31	82	2.86	2.9	8.0	2.8	0.3	104
2011	MLB	Pittsburgh	0	3	0	16	5	6.67	1.91	19.2	315	31	68	7.03	5.6	2.8	0.5	1.7	-31

Short (6'1") lefty has solid stuff and made his MLB debut in '11. Features an 87-91 mph fastball that works because of his ability to locate. Complements it with a good curve and a plus change-up. Knows how to pitch and keeps hitters off-balance. Keeps the ball down and gets plenty of ground ball outs. Back of the rotation starter should be able to contribute.

Lollis, Matt — SP — San Diego

EXP MLB DEBUT: 2013 **POTENTIAL:** #3 starter **8D**

Thrws L Age 21
2009 (15) HS (CA)

90-93 FB	+++
SL	+++
CB	++
CU	++

Year	Lev	Team	W	L	Sv	IP	K	ERA	WHIP	BF/G	OBA	H%	S%	xERA	Ctl	Dom	Cmd	hr/9	BPV
2009	Rk	AZL Padres	0	0	0	8	7	5.49	1.59	6.0	322	38	67	5.74	2.2	7.7	3.5	1.1	77
2010	A-	Eugene	2	2	0	34	24	2.89	0.85	20.9	179	22	62	0.93	2.1	6.3	3.0	0.0	120
2010	A	Fort Wayne	5	2	0	54	45	1.66	1.11	23.6	236	29	88	2.73	2.2	7.5	3.5	0.5	111
2011	A+	Lake Elsinore	4	8	1	119	114	5.37	1.51	16.6	287	36	65	4.81	3.4	8.6	2.5	0.9	75

Tall, projectable righty saw the wheels come off in '11. Lack of dominance caught up with him. Possess a decent 90-92 mph fastball and also has a nice four pitch mix that includes a curve, slider, and change-up. None of them are swing-and-miss offerings, but he knows how to pitch and could carve out a back of the rotation role down the road.

Lopez, Jorge — SP — Milwaukee

EXP MLB DEBUT: 2016 **POTENTIAL:** #3 starter **8D**

Thrws R Age 19
2011 (2) P.R.

88-92 FB	+++
CB	+++
CU	+

Year	Lev	Team	W	L	Sv	IP	K	ERA	WHIP	BF/G	OBA	H%	S%	xERA	Ctl	Dom	Cmd	hr/9	BPV
2011	Rk	AZL Brewers	0	0	0	12	10	2.25	1.33	12.5	278	35	81	3.39	2.3	7.5	3.3	0.0	114

Tall and skinny (6'4", 165 lbs.), Lopez features an 88-92 mph fastball, a potentially plus 1-7 curveball, and a rarely used change-up. He has a loose, easy arm action and should add additional velocity. He will need to work on developing consistent mechanics and refining his off-speed pitches. He is raw right now, but has some interesting upside.

Lorin, Brett — SP — Arizona

EXP MLB DEBUT: 2014 | POTENTIAL: #5 starter/reliever | 7C

Thrws R Age 25
2008 (5) Long Beach St

- 88-92 FB +++
- SL ++++
- CU ++

Year	Lev	Team	W	L	Sv	IP	K	ERA	WHIP	BF/G	OBA	H%	S%	xERA	Ctl	Dom	Cmd	hr/9	BPV
2009	A	Clinton	5	4	0	88	87	2.45	0.98	20.9	197	24	81	2.30	2.6	8.9	3.5	0.9	114
2009	A	West Virginia	3	1	0	34	29	1.58	1.26	19.9	255	32	90	3.40	2.6	7.7	2.9	0.5	95
2010	Rk	GCL Pirates	0	0	0	7	10	1.29	0.57	7.9	48	0	100	0.13	3.9	12.9	3.3	1.3	154
2010	A	West Virginia	2	3	0	41	32	5.24	1.43	14.6	301	35	65	5.02	2.0	7.0	3.6	1.1	79
2011	A+	Bradenton	7	6	1	117	99	2.84	1.04	18.1	238	29	74	2.62	1.5	7.6	5.2	0.5	146

Tall, strong-bodied hurler (6'7", 245 lbs.) had his best season as a pro. Throws a nice 90-92 mph sinking fastball. It tops out at 94 with good movement, but isn't overpowering. Complements the fastball with a good slider and an average change-up. Throws plenty of strikes and gets lots of groundball outs with the sinker/slider mix.

Lotzkar, Kyle — SP — Cincinnati

EXP MLB DEBUT: 2013 | POTENTIAL: #3 starter | 7C

Thrws R Age 22
2007 (1-S) HS (Canada)

- 88-93 FB ++++
- 79-82 SU +++
- 79-83 CU +

Year	Lev	Team	W	L	Sv	IP	K	ERA	WHIP	BF/G	OBA	H%	S%	xERA	Ctl	Dom	Cmd	hr/9	BPV
2007	Rk	Billings	0	0	0	8	12	1.13	0.50	13.3	42	0	100		3.4	13.5	4.0	1.1	178
2008	A	Dayton	2	3	0	37	50	3.63	1.42	15.8	217	33	75	3.22	5.8	12.1	2.1	0.5	113
2010	Rk	Billings	2	0	0	20	33	0.45	0.50	16.6	124	23	100		0.9	14.9	16.5	0.5	452
2010	Rk	AZL Reds	1	1	0	24	27	3.36	1.33	12.5	227	32	74	3.03	4.5	10.1	2.3	0.4	106
2011	A	Dayton	3	2	0	66	72	4.35	1.15	18.8	215	27	65	3.09	3.4	9.8	2.9	1.1	99

The 22-year-old continues to battle health problems. He had elbow surgery in '09 and missed the start of the '11 season with forearm tightness. When he rertumed to action, the results were encouraging. Quick arm action provides plus movement to fastball and slider. Low-90s FB has solid movement, but he needs to stay healthy.

Loux, Barret — SP — Texas

EXP MLB DEBUT: 2013 | POTENTIAL: #3 starter | 8C

Thrws R Age 23
2011 FA (Texas A&M)

- 87-95 FB +++
- 78-81 CB ++
- 80-83 SL +++
- CU +++

Year	Lev	Team	W	L	Sv	IP	K	ERA	WHIP	BF/G	OBA	H%	S%	xERA	Ctl	Dom	Cmd	hr/9	BPV
2008	NCAA	Texas A&M	6	2	0	90	81	4.20	1.23	22.8	230	28	68	3.43	3.5	8.1	2.3	1.0	76
2009	NCAA	Texas A&M	3	3	0	48	62	4.13	1.33	16.6	241	36	68	3.20	3.9	11.6	3.0	0.4	127
2010	NCAA	Texas A&M	11	2	0	105	136	2.83	1.07	24.0	209	31	75	2.34	2.9	11.7	4.0	0.6	149
2011	A+	Myrtle Beach	8	5	0	109	127	3.80	1.28	21.3	256	36	70	3.41	2.8	10.5	3.7	0.5	130

Tall and athletic pitcher finished 2nd in CAR in Ks by showing polish and mixing four pitches. No offering projects as plus, but knows how to set up hitters. Adds and subtracts with easy FB that he locates precisely. Pitches downhill and allows few HR. SL and CB are both thrown for strikes and commands plate despite moving parts in delivery.

Lueke, Josh — RP — Tampa Bay

EXP MLB DEBUT: 2011 | POTENTIAL: Closer | 8D

Thrws R Age 27
2007 (16) Northern Kentucky

- 91-98 FB ++++
- 84-86 SL ++++
- SP +++

Year	Lev	Team	W	L	Sv	IP	K	ERA	WHIP	BF/G	OBA	H%	S%	xERA	Ctl	Dom	Cmd	hr/9	BPV
2010	AA	Frisco	1	1	2	18	26	3.96	1.26	5.0	260	39	71	3.84	2.5	12.9	5.2	1.0	160
2010	AA	W. Tennessee	1	0	3	7	14	0.00	0.56	4.0	167	40	100		0.0	17.7		0.0	
2010	AAA	Tacoma	1	0	2	17	18	2.11	1.11	5.6	225	32	79	2.11	2.6	9.5	3.6	0.0	142
2011	AAA	Tacoma	2	4	11	42	35	2.78	1.09	5.5	223	28	73	2.25	2.6	7.5	2.9	0.2	110
2011	MLB	Seattle	1	1	0	32	29	6.15	1.46	5.5	272	34	56	4.16	3.6	8.1	2.2	0.6	79

Tall and slender reliever with legitimate late-innings stuff. Pitches aggressively with quick FB and potent SL and SP. Throws consistent strikes and has potential to be dynamite short reliever in majors. Dom declined despite stuff and was inconsistent from game to game. Makeup issues in past, but appears to have righted the ship.

Lynn, Lance — SP — St. Louis

EXP MLB DEBUT: 2011 | POTENTIAL: Power reliever | 8C

Thrws R Age 25
2008 (1-S) Mississippi

- 94-96 FB +++
- 80-84 SL ++
- 72-77 CB +++
- 80-81 CU ++

Year	Lev	Team	W	L	Sv	IP	K	ERA	WHIP	BF/G	OBA	H%	S%	xERA	Ctl	Dom	Cmd	hr/9	BPV
2009	AA	Springfield	11	4	0	126	98	2.93	1.33	23.8	248	30	78	3.32	3.6	7.0	1.9	0.4	77
2009	AAA	Memphis	0	0	0	6	9	2.90	1.29	25.5	222	37	75	2.49	4.4	13.1	3.0	0.0	152
2010	AAA	Memphis	13	10	0	164	141	4.77	1.38	23.7	262	31	68	4.36	3.4	7.7	2.3	1.2	62
2011	AAA	Memphis	7	3	0	75	64	3.84	1.39	26.3	272	34	71	3.67	3.0	7.7	2.6	0.2	93
2011	MLB	St. Louis	1	1	1	34	40	3.16	1.05	7.4	206	28	73	2.46	2.9	10.5	3.6	0.8	130

Lynn is a tall, strong-framed pitcher with a plus power sinker and a power curveball that he locates well. He has worked as both a starer and a reliever in the minors, but pitched primarily in relief once he reached the Cardinals. The move to relief allowed his fastball velocity to jump into the 94-96 range with good life. His future role is likely in relief.

Magnuson, Trystan — RP — Oakland

EXP MLB DEBUT: 2011 | POTENTIAL: Setup reliever | 7C

Thrws R Age 27
2007 (1-S) Louisville

- 87-94 FB ++++
- 81-85 SL +++
- 79-83 CU +

Year	Lev	Team	W	L	Sv	IP	K	ERA	WHIP	BF/G	OBA	H%	S%	xERA	Ctl	Dom	Cmd	hr/9	BPV
2009	A+	Dunedin	4	1	1	61	45	2.79	1.36	6.7	245	30	79	3.29	4.0	6.6	1.7	0.3	72
2009	AA	New Hampshire	1	0	0	10	7	0.00	0.50	6.6	124	16	100	0.00	0.9	6.3	7.0	0.0	215
2010	AA	New Hampshire	3	0	5	73	63	2.59	1.09	6.2	253	33	75	2.57	1.2	7.8	6.3	0.1	179
2011	AAA	Sacramento	4	2	5	45	46	2.99	1.18	6.0	211	27	78	2.85	3.8	9.2	2.4	0.8	95
2011	MLB	Oakland	0	0	0	14	11	6.34	1.41	6.7	273	29	59	5.30	3.2	7.0	2.2	1.9	31

Tall and slender reliever with increasing K rate. Uses height well and slings ball from low three-quarters slot to create deception. Primarily pitches off FB and mixes in average SL. Hasn't been effective against LHH and doesn't pitch aggressively despite good velocity. Has worked on CU with SP action, but doesn't use often.

Main, Michael — SP — San Francisco

EXP MLB DEBUT: 2012 | POTENTIAL: reliever | 7D

Thrws R Age 23
2007 (1) HS, (FL)

- 89-95 FB +++
- CB +++
- CU ++

Year	Lev	Team	W	L	Sv	IP	K	ERA	WHIP	BF/G	OBA	H%	S%	xERA	Ctl	Dom	Cmd	hr/9	BPV
2009	Rk	AZL Rangers	0	0	0	3	5	0.00	1.00	5.7	262	46	100	2.26	0.0	15.0		0.0	
2009	A+	Bakersfield	4	6	0	58	49	6.83	1.88	19.5	306	35	65	6.50	5.7	7.6	1.3	1.4	25
2010	A+	Bakersfield	5	3	0	91	72	3.46	1.19	24.3	253	28	78	3.98	2.1	7.1	3.4	1.4	78
2010	AA	Richmond	0	3	0	13	7	14.32	2.65	14.4	361	37	44	10.01	9.5	4.8	0.5	2.0	-39
2011	A+	San Jose	2	4	0	52	46	6.90	1.88	11.1	296	34	67	6.82	6.2	7.9	1.3	1.9	13

Former 1st rounder continues to scuffle. Control desserted him, as he walked 36 in 52.2 IP. Was moved to relief, but if anything, he was worse. Is athletic and pitches aggressively with plus fastball/curveball combo. Puts hitters away with both pitches and can effectively pitch backwards. 2012 might be his last chance.

Maine, Scott — RP — Chicago (N)

EXP MLB DEBUT: 2010 | POTENTIAL: Situational reliever | 7B

Thrws L Age 27
2007 (6) Miami-FL

- 86-91 FB +++
- 73-76 CB +++
- 75-80 CU +++

Year	Lev	Team	W	L	Sv	IP	K	ERA	WHIP	BF/G	OBA	H%	S%	xERA	Ctl	Dom	Cmd	hr/9	BPV
2010	AA	Tennessee	1	1	5	16	15	2.24	0.99	5.1	209	27	80	2.15	2.2	8.4	3.8	0.6	125
2010	AAA	Iowa	3	1	5	41	47	3.51	1.32	5.1	222	30	76	3.41	4.6	10.3	2.2	0.9	93
2010	MLB	Chi Cubs	0	0	0	13	11	2.08	1.08	3.9	197	24	85	2.36	3.5	7.6	2.2	0.7	87
2011	AAA	Iowa	3	4	12	51	72	3.70	1.23	5.5	209	33	70	2.68	4.4	12.7	2.9	0.5	134
2011	MLB	Chi Cubs	0	0	0	7	5	10.29	2.29	5.1	358	32	67	11.93	6.4	6.4	1.0	5.1	-111

Strong-armed lefty reliever lacks overpowering stuff, but continues to be effective. He generates strikeouts by repeating three-quarters delivery and achieving movement via quick arm action. He keeps ball low and gets great fade on CU. Worked effectively in relief and should see extended action in the Cubs pen in '12.

Manzanillo, Santo — RP — Milwaukee

EXP MLB DEBUT: 2012 | POTENTIAL: Power reliever | 8C

Thrws R Age 23
2005 NDFA (Dominican Republic)

- 95-98 FB ++++
- SL +++

Year	Lev	Team	W	L	Sv	IP	K	ERA	WHIP	BF/G	OBA	H%	S%	xERA	Ctl	Dom	Cmd	hr/9	BPV
2007	Rk	AZL Brewers	4	4	1	27	18	3.97	1.88	9.1	223	26	78	4.35	9.6	6.0	0.6	0.3	49
2008	Rk	Helena	0	1	1	32	27	9.28	2.09	12.1	312	38	53	6.63	7.3	7.6	1.0	0.8	35
2010	A	Wisconsin	1	1	0	53	40	5.77	1.66	9.1	280	33	64	4.73	5.1	6.8	1.3	0.5	53
2011	A+	Brevard County	1	0	10	41	43	1.53	1.09	5.7	211	28	88	2.31	3.1	9.4	3.1	0.4	121
2011	AA	Huntsville	0	1	7	20	19	2.24	1.24	4.1	187	23	87	2.84	5.4	8.5	1.6	0.9	75

Short, strong-armed reliever is a bit of a late bloomer. A huge improvement in control fueled this breakout and he was simply dominant at High-A and Double-A. Attacks hitters with a 95-98 mph fastball that tops out at 100 mph. His breaking ball will need to improve if he is to make an impact in the majors, but the potential to be a power reliever is definitely there.

Maples, Dillon — SP — Chicago (N)

EXP MLB DEBUT: 2014 | POTENTIAL: #3 starter | 8D

Thrws R Age 20
2011 (14) HS, (SC)

- 91-93 FB +++
- 75-78 CB +++
- 80-83 CU +++

Year	Lev	Team	W	L	Sv	IP	K	ERA	WHIP	BF/G	OBA	H%	S%	xERA	Ctl	Dom	Cmd	hr/9	BPV
2011		Did not play																	

Strong-armed righty fell to the 14th round due to signability concerns. Cubs ponied up $2.5 million to buy him out of scholarship to UNC. Features 91-93 mph fastball. He throws both a two- and four-seamer with good movement. Also has a nice curveball and a potentially plus change-up. Mechanics need some work, but has nice athleticism and lots of potential.

Marinez, Jhan — RP — Chicago (A)

EXP MLB DEBUT: 2010 | POTENTIAL: Closer | 9D

Thrws R Age 23
2006 FA (DR)

- 92-96 FB ++++
- 86-89 SL +++
- CU +

Year	Lev	Team	W	L	Sv	IP	K	ERA	WHIP	BF/G	OBA	H%	S%	xERA	Ctl	Dom	Cmd	hr/9	BPV
2009	A+	Jupiter	1	1	1	43	42	3.14	1.12	5.8	188	23	75	2.47	4.2	8.8	2.1	0.8	89
2010	A+	Jupiter	0	1	4	25	44	1.43	1.04	4.6	145	29	88	1.29	5.0	15.8	3.1	0.4	176
2010	AA	Jacksonville	1	0	6	16	20	2.22	0.99	4.1	165	24	80	1.61	3.9	11.1	2.9	0.6	132
2010	MLB	Florida	1	1	0	2	3	8.18	2.73	3.1	326	38	80	11.45	12.3	12.3	1.0	4.1	-38
2011	AA	Jacksonville	3	8	3	58	74	3.57	1.53	4.5	223	31	80	4.15	6.5	11.5	1.8	1.1	84

Thin, but explosive pitcher who can dominate with two solid offerings. FB can touch high-90s and thrown with easy, loose arm. Hard SL shows flashes of becoming second plus pitch, but can get on the side of it. Erratic control needs to be cleaned up and he often leaves his SL too far up in zone. Lacks strength for durability, but has significant upside.

Markel, Parker — SP — Tampa Bay

EXP MLB DEBUT: 2013 | POTENTIAL: #3 starter | 8C

Thrws R Age 21
2010 (39) Yavapai JC

- 90-96 FB ++++
- 82-86 SL +++
- CU +++

Year	Lev	Team	W	L	Sv	IP	K	ERA	WHIP	BF/G	OBA	H%	S%	xERA	Ctl	Dom	Cmd	hr/9	BPV
2010	Rk	GCL Rays	2	0	0	10	13	1.78	1.09	5.6	219	34	82	1.96	2.7	11.6	4.3	0.0	172
2011	A-	Hudson Valley	3	4	0	57	44	3.15	1.14	17.4	207	25	73	2.43	3.6	6.9	1.9	0.5	81

Tall sinkerballer who found success by mixing plus, sinking FB and hard SL in pro debut. Has trouble locating FB due to late movement, but can get hitters to look silly by flailing outside of zone. Doesn't repeat delivery consistently and can slow arm speed on CU at times. SL can get Ks, but likes to use sinker to induce contact.

Marks, Justin — SP — Kansas City

EXP MLB DEBUT: 2013 | POTENTIAL: #4 starter | 7C

Thrws L Age 24
2009 (3) Louisville

- 85-90 FB +++
- 80-82 SL +++
- 74-78 CB ++
- 77-80 CU +++

Year	Lev	Team	W	L	Sv	IP	K	ERA	WHIP	BF/G	OBA	H%	S%	xERA	Ctl	Dom	Cmd	hr/9	BPV
2009	NCAA	Louisville	11	3	1	105	129	3.77	1.15	23.2	225	33	66	2.60	3.0	11.1	3.7	0.4	141
2009	Rk	AZL Athletics	0	1	0	0	0			7.0							0.0		
2010	A	Kane County	3	12	0	109	119	4.95	1.37	22.9	261	34	65	4.10	3.4	9.8	2.9	0.9	95
2010	A+	Stockton	3	1	0	19	17	4.69	1.30	15.8	239	26	71	4.54	3.8	8.0	2.1	1.9	43
2011	A+	Wilmington	8	8	0	144	140	3.99	1.34	21.4	262	33	72	3.99	3.1	8.7	2.9	0.9	89

Tall and light-throwing pitcher who led CAR in Ks despite lack of frontline velocity and flat CB. Has proven effective against RHH and LHH by mixing deep repertoire of offerings. Establishes control early in count and teases hitters with varying velocities and breaking balls. Likes to sink and cut FB while throwing strikes with nice CU.

Marlowe, Chris — SP — San Francisco

EXP MLB DEBUT: 2013 | POTENTIAL: Power reliever | 8C

Thrws R Age 22
2011 (5) Oklahoma State

- 92-95 FB ++++
- 81-84 CB +++

Year	Lev	Team	W	L	Sv	IP	K	ERA	WHIP	BF/G	OBA	H%	S%	xERA	Ctl	Dom	Cmd	hr/9	BPV
2011	NCAA	Oklahoma St	3	3	4	41	71	5.05	1.44	7.3	178	33	64	2.94	7.5	15.6	2.1	0.7	137
2011	Rk	AZL Giants	1	0	0	3	5	0.00	1.33	4.2	262	46	100	3.10	3.0	15.0	5.0	0.0	198

Short, strong-armed reliever. Has a plus 92-95 mph FB that he locates well. Complements the heat with a plus 81-84 mph power curveball that can be a true out pitch. Logged only 3 innings as a pro and will likely start at A-ball in 2012. As a polished two-pitch college reliever, he could move up quickly.

Maronde, Nick — SP — Los Angeles (A)

EXP MLB DEBUT: 2014 | POTENTIAL: #3 starter | 8D

Thrws L Age 22
2011 (3) Florida

- 89-95 FB +++
- 80-85 SL +++
- 80-82 CU +++

Year	Lev	Team	W	L	Sv	IP	K	ERA	WHIP	BF/G	OBA	H%	S%	xERA	Ctl	Dom	Cmd	hr/9	BPV
2009	NCAA	Florida	3	1	0	61	59	4.42	1.31	12.0	265	31	71	4.52	2.7	8.7	3.3	1.5	79
2010	NCAA	Florida	2	0	1	26	37	6.21	1.76	5.4	230	36	62	4.11	8.3	12.8	1.5	0.3	108
2011	NCAA	Florida	0	1	3	43	55	2.09	0.84	4.4	182	27	79	1.48	1.9	11.5	6.1	0.6	197
2011	Rk	Orem	5	0	0	46	50	2.15	1.11	16.5	217	28	87	2.91	2.9	9.8	3.3	1.0	111

Tall and athletic pitcher was RP in college, but moved to starter as a pro. Thrives with sneaky quick FB and improved SL. Possesses quick arm that generates late movement and is aggressive up in zone. Can overuse FB and needs to sequence pitches better. Needs to repeat arm speed on CU, but can be effective when on.

Marshall, Brett — SP — New York (A)

EXP MLB DEBUT: 2014 | POTENTIAL: #4 starter | 7B

Thrws R Age 22
2008 (6) HS (TX)

- 87-95 FB ++++
- 80-84 SL +++
- 80-82 CU +++

Year	Lev	Team	W	L	Sv	IP	K	ERA	WHIP	BF/G	OBA	H%	S%	xERA	Ctl	Dom	Cmd	hr/9	BPV
2009	A	Charleston (SC)	3	6	0	87	60	5.58	1.55	22.4	285	33	63	4.74	3.8	6.2	1.6	0.7	48
2010	Rk	GCL Yankees	0	0	0	8	8	2.25	1.25	16.3	210	29	80	2.28	4.5	9.0	2.0	0.0	109
2010	A	Charleston (SC)	4	2	0	72	56	2.50	1.03	21.3	204	25	75	1.90	2.8	7.0	2.5	0.3	102
2010	A+	Tampa	0	0	0	4	6	4.50	1.25	16.3	307	49	60	3.56	0.0	13.5		0.0	
2011	A+	Tampa	9	7	0	140	114	3.79	1.36	21.7	264	33	71	3.63	3.1	7.3	2.4	0.4	84

Short and athletic pitcher who lacks ideal size, but has extreme pitchability and can be successful when he doesn't have best stuff. Uses hard sinker to keep ball in yard and works off of it to stay ahead in count. SL and CU are nothing special, but can get hitters to chase breaking ball at times. Could be excellent in bullpen if given shot.

Marshall, Evan — RP — Arizona

EXP MLB DEBUT: 2012 | POTENTIAL: Setup reliever | 8C

Thrws R Age 22
2011 (4) Kansas State

- 91-95 FB +++
- 86-87 SL +++
- CU

Year	Lev	Team	W	L	Sv	IP	K	ERA	WHIP	BF/G	OBA	H%	S%	xERA	Ctl	Dom	Cmd	hr/9	BPV
2010	NCAA	Kansas State	5	5	1	83	51	3.90	1.19	12.3	252	29	66	3.12	2.2	5.5	2.6	0.4	78
2011	NCAA	Kansas State	5	5	1	61	55	1.62	1.03	7.8	215	29	83	1.80	2.4	8.1	3.4	0.0	133
2011	A-	Yakima	0	0	2	12	13	0.75	1.00	4.2	228	32	92	1.87	1.5	9.8	6.5	0.0	204
2011	A+	Visalia	0	1	4	17	18	1.59	1.12	4.5	226	29	94	3.13	2.6	9.5	3.6	1.1	111
2011	AA	Mobile	0	0	0	2	0	0.00	1.00	7.6	262	26	100	2.41	0.0	0.0		0.0	

Strong collegiate reliever has a plus 94-96 mph fastball and a workable slider. Marshall comes right after hitters with the fastball/slider combination and his fastball explodes on hitters. He was very impressive in his pro debut, posting a 1.16 ERA with 7 BB/31 K in 31 IP at three different levels. Look for Evans to continue to move up quickly.

Marte, Luis — RP — Detroit

EXP MLB DEBUT: 2011 | POTENTIAL: Middle reliever | 6B

Thrws R Age 25
2005 FA (DR)

- 89-95 FB +++
- 82-86 SL +++
- CU ++

Year	Lev	Team	W	L	Sv	IP	K	ERA	WHIP	BF/G	OBA	H%	S%	xERA	Ctl	Dom	Cmd	hr/9	BPV
2010	AA	Erie	2	2	7	48	53	5.06	1.46	5.4	245	32	66	4.12	4.9	9.9	2.0	0.9	80
2010	AAA	Toledo	0	0	0	1	0	0.00	2.00	4.8	262	26	100	4.93	9.0	0.0	0.0	0.0	3
2011	AA	Erie	3	0	3	53	68	1.70	0.89	8.5	163	24	84	1.28	3.1	11.5	3.8	0.5	156
2011	AAA	Toledo	1	0	0	3	2	5.81	2.26	7.9	255	31	71	5.43	11.6	5.8	0.5	0.0	49
2011	MLB	Detroit	1	0	0	3	3	2.81	2.19	4.0	399	50	86	7.64	2.8	8.4	3.0	0.0	89

Short and stocky reliever with terrific arm strength and a lively FB to match. Posts high Dom due to hard stuff, but an unwillingness to work down in zone limits effectiveness. Hard SL serves as knockout offering, but CU lags far behind. Hasn't been victim of too many long balls, but good MLB hitters may take advantage of pitches up in zone.

Martin, Ethan — SP — Los Angeles (N)

EXP MLB DEBUT: 2012 | POTENTIAL: #2 starter | 8D

Thrws R Age 23
2008 (1) HS, (GA)

- 90-95 FB ++++
- 79-81 CB ++++
- 80-84 SP +++

Year	Lev	Team	W	L	Sv	IP	K	ERA	WHIP	BF/G	OBA	H%	S%	xERA	Ctl	Dom	Cmd	hr/9	BPV
2009	A	Great Lakes	6	8	1	100	120	3.87	1.46	15.9	232	33	73	3.40	5.5	10.8	2.0	0.4	104
2010	A+	Inland Empire	9	14	0	113	105	6.37	1.78	20.8	273	34	63	5.19	6.4	8.4	1.3	0.8	54
2011	A+	Rancho Cucam	4	4	0	55	61	7.36	1.85	16.1	295	38	61	6.17	6.1	10.0	1.6	1.3	51
2011	AA	Chattanooga	5	3	2	40	43	4.04	1.50	8.2	215	29	74	3.59	6.5	9.7	1.5	0.7	81

Stocky, athletic starter floundered in '11. Lack of control was the main problem. Has a 90-95 mph fastball, but it tends to be straight and has difficulty locating it. Curveball is sometimes plus pitch and change-up is still a work in progress. Inconsistent mechanics and delivery resulted in struggles locating FB, but has the athletic build to improve his mechanics.

Martin, Rafael — RP — Washington

EXP MLB DEBUT: 2012 | POTENTIAL: Reliever | 7C

Thrws R Age 28
2010 NDFA, HS, (CA)

- 92-94 FB ++++

Year	Lev	Team	W	L	Sv	IP	K	ERA	WHIP	BF/G	OBA	H%	S%	xERA	Ctl	Dom	Cmd	hr/9	BPV
2010	AA	Harrisburg	5	4	0	67	58	3.62	1.21	5.7	225	28	71	3.00	3.5	7.8	2.2	0.7	83
2011	A+	Potomac	1	0	0	8	10	1.13	1.00	5.1	210	32	88	1.63	2.3	11.3	5.0	0.0	185
2011	AA	Harrisburg	4	1	13	35	44	1.79	0.99	4.2	208	31	82	1.82	2.3	11.3	4.9	0.3	176

Righty reliever had the best year of his career. An undrafted free agent from the Mexican League, Martin landed a spot with the Nationals. He throws a good 92-94 mph fastball that tops out at 96 mph, he also throws a good sinker. Martin was solid in the AFL and could be in the majors by '12.

Martinez, Carlos — SP — St. Louis

EXP MLB DEBUT: 2014 | POTENTIAL: #1 starter | 9D

Thrws R Age 20
2010 NDFA D.R.

- 94-96 FB ++++
- CB ++++
- CU +++

Year	Lev	Team	W	L	Sv	IP	K	ERA	WHIP	BF/G	OBA	H%	S%	xERA	Ctl	Dom	Cmd	hr/9	BPV
2011	A	Quad Cities	3	2	0	38	50	2.36	1.07	18.6	200	31	78	1.91	3.3	11.8	3.6	0.2	154
2011	A+	Palm Beach	3	3	0	46	48	5.28	1.72	20.9	274	37	68	4.66	5.9	9.4	1.6	0.4	78

A short, powerful hurler, Martinez uses a 94-96 mph four seam fastball, a 90-93 mph sinker, a plus curveball, and a decent change-up to dominante. Uses a high leg kick to generate torque and deception. His backside mechanics are not conventional and he does have some recoil on release, but he is athletic and aggressive and should be fun to watch.

Martinez, Fabio — SP — Los Angeles (A)

EXP MLB DEBUT: 2013 | POTENTIAL: #2 starter | 9D

Thrws R Age 22
2007 FA (DR)

- 89-98 FB ++++
- 80-83 SL ++++
- 79-83 CU ++

Year	Lev	Team	W	L	Sv	IP	K	ERA	WHIP	BF/G	OBA	H%	S%	xERA	Ctl	Dom	Cmd	hr/9	BPV
2009	Rk	Orem	1	0	0	7	10	3.86	1.00	13.4	202	24	80	3.94	2.6	12.9	5.0	2.6	120
2009	Rk	AZL Angels	3	2	0	60	92	3.29	1.35	17.9	210	36	74	2.61	5.4	13.8	2.6	0.1	145
2010	A	Cedar Rapids	7	3	0	103	141	3.93	1.51	22.3	216	33	74	3.47	6.6	12.3	1.9	0.5	109
2011	Rk	AZL Angels	0	0	0	2	2	0.00	1.43	4.5	252	34	100	3.27	4.3	8.6	2.0	0.0	98

Tall/projectable pitcher who only pitched 2 innings due to shoulder issues. Potential to be dynamic frontline SP with two plus pitches - FB and hard SL. Has high arm slot and pitches with downward angle. Often overthrows and struggles with FB location. Needs to repeat arm speed on CU, but has ingredients to be high Dom performer.

Mathieson, Scott — RP — Free agent

EXP MLB DEBUT: 2006 | POTENTIAL: Spot starter/reliever | **7B**

Thrws R Age 28
2002 (17) Vancouver, BC

Velo	Pitch	Grade
89-95	FB	++++
80-82	CU	+++
79-82	CB	++
83-86	SL	++

Year	Lev	Team	W	L	Sv	IP	K	ERA	WHIP	BF/G	OBA	H%	S%	xERA	Ctl	Dom	Cmd	hr/9	BPV
2009	AA	Reading	2	0	1	19	17	1.41	0.89	5.5	157	20	88	1.23	3.3	8.0	2.4	0.5	109
2010	AAA	Lehigh Valley	3	6	26	64	83	2.81	1.14	4.7	213	30	82	3.07	3.4	11.7	3.5	1.1	121
2010	MLB	Philadelphia	0	0	0	1	1	15.00	5.83	5.2	596	68	71	22.92	15.0	7.5	0.5	0.0	-9
2011	AAA	Lehigh Valley	2	2	5	82	83	3.29	1.47	11.8	235	29	81	4.08	5.5	9.1	1.7	1.0	68
2011	MLB	Philadelphia	0	0	0	5	5	0.00	2.40	6.5	390	50	100	7.97	5.4	9.0	1.7	0.0	66

Mathieson continues his comback from three elbow surgeries. He worked both in relief and as a starter and put up solid numbers. His fastball is still in the 90-95 mph range and he has a nice change-up and a decent splitter. He has solid control and an ability to miss plenty of bats. Released from his MLB contract to play in Japan in 2012.

Matthews, Kevin — SP — Texas

EXP MLB DEBUT: 2014 | POTENTIAL: #3 starter | **8C**

Thrws L Age 19
2011 (1) HS (GA)

Velo	Pitch	Grade
86-93	FB	+++
79-83	CB	+++
	CU	+++

Year	Lev	Team	W	L	Sv	IP	K	ERA	WHIP	BF/G	OBA	H%	S%	xERA	Ctl	Dom	Cmd	hr/9	BPV
2011	Rk	AZL Rangers	1	0	0	12	12	1.50	1.25	7.0	228	29	93	3.21	3.8	9.0	2.4	0.8	91
2011	A-	Spokane	0	3	0	16	18	2.78	1.67	14.5	235	34	81	3.62	7.2	10.0	1.4	0.0	97

Short and athletic hurler with extreme pitchability and poise. Concerns about size are evident and velocity is erratic, but has quick arm action and solid-average three pitch arsenal. FB features sinking, late movement and CB can elicit swings and misses. CU has moments of brilliance, particularly when he repeats arm speed.

Matz, Steven — SP — New York (N)

EXP MLB DEBUT: 2015 | POTENTIAL: #3 starter | **8E**

Thrws L Age 21
2009 (2) HS, (NY)

Velo	Pitch	Grade
88-92	FB	++++
	SL	+++
	CB	++
73-75	CU	++

Year	Lev	Team	W	L	Sv	IP	K	ERA	WHIP	BF/G	OBA	H%	S%	xERA	Ctl	Dom	Cmd	hr/9	BPV
2011		Did not play																	

Matz is a tall, projectable right-hander who was the Mets top pick in '09. He had Tommy John surgery and has yet to pitch as a pro. Prior to the surgery he had a nice low-90s fastball with good tailing action. He also had a decent slider, a curveball, and a change-up. Just getting Matz back on the mound would be progress at this point.

Matzek, Tyler — SP — Colorado

EXP MLB DEBUT: 2013 | POTENTIAL: #1 starter | **8D**

Thrws L Age 21
2009 (1) HS, (CA)

Velo	Pitch	Grade
91-95	FB	++++
80-83	SL	++++
74-76	CB	+++
	CU	++

Year	Lev	Team	W	L	Sv	IP	K	ERA	WHIP	BF/G	OBA	H%	S%	xERA	Ctl	Dom	Cmd	hr/9	BPV
2010	A	Asheville	5	1	0	89	88	2.93	1.39	20.8	198	26	81	3.07	6.3	8.9	1.4	0.6	80
2011	A	Asheville	5	4	0	64	74	4.36	1.48	23.0	200	28	70	3.13	7.0	10.4	1.5	0.4	96
2011	A+	Modesto	0	3	0	33	37	9.82	2.42	17.3	268	34	59	7.26	12.5	10.1	0.8	1.4	38

Tall, physical lefty stumbled out of the gate and simply could not throw strikes. Asked for a leave of absence to clear his head and find his mechanics. Did right the ship a bit in August, but on the year posted a 6.22 ERA. In addition to fastball that sits at 89-93 mph, he also flashes an 80-83 mph slider, curveball, and a change-up that needs work.

May, Trevor — SP — Philadelphia

EXP MLB DEBUT: 2013 | POTENTIAL: #1 starter | **9C**

Thrws R Age 22
2008 (4) Kelso, WA

Velo	Pitch	Grade
92-95	FB	++++
74-78	CB	++++
80-82	CU	+++

Year	Lev	Team	W	L	Sv	IP	K	ERA	WHIP	BF/G	OBA	H%	S%	xERA	Ctl	Dom	Cmd	hr/9	BPV
2008	Rk	GCL Phillies	1	1	0	12	11	3.75	1.50	10.4	245	33	72	3.36	5.3	8.3	1.6	0.0	88
2009	A	Lakewood	4	1	0	77	95	2.57	1.31	21.2	211	31	81	2.75	5.0	11.1	2.2	0.4	115
2010	A	Lakewood	7	3	0	65	92	2.91	1.09	23.1	218	34	74	2.33	2.8	12.7	4.6	0.4	172
2010	A+	Clearwater	5	5	0	70	90	5.01	1.63	19.5	212	30	70	4.07	7.8	11.6	1.5	0.9	86
2011	A+	Clearwater	10	8	0	151	208	3.63	1.24	22.7	221	34	71	2.82	4.0	12.4	3.1	0.5	136

May had a huge breakout season. He struggled with control in '10, but was much better in his second stint in the FSL. May attacks hitters with a plus 92-95 mph fastball that has good life. He also features a nice upper-70s power curve that can be a swing-and-miss pitch. He has a strong pitching frame and holds his velocity deep into games.

Mazzoni, Cory — RP — New York (N)

EXP MLB DEBUT: 2014 | POTENTIAL: Power reliever | **7C**

Thrws R Age 22
2011 (2) NC State

Velo	Pitch	Grade
90-94	FB	+++
72-75	CB	+++
	CU	++

Year	Lev	Team	W	L	Sv	IP	K	ERA	WHIP	BF/G	OBA	H%	S%	xERA	Ctl	Dom	Cmd	hr/9	BPV
2009	NCAA	N. Carolina St	1	5	1	38	30	6.61	1.44	9.6	276	33	52	4.32	3.3	7.1	2.1	0.7	66
2010	NCAA	N. Carolina St	7	3	0	91	89	5.23	1.48	24.5	270	34	65	4.38	3.9	8.8	2.2	0.8	77
2011	NCAA	N. Carolina St	6	6	0	114	137	3.31	1.05	27.6	220	31	70	2.48	2.3	10.8	4.7	0.6	156
2011	A-	Brooklyn	1	0	0	6	10	0.00	1.17	4.0	228	42	100	2.23	3.0	15.0	5.0	0.0	204
2011	A+	St. Lucie	1	1	0	7	8	2.57	1.14	4.6	262	34	86	3.87	1.3	10.3	8.0	1.3	194

Short, strong-armed pitcher. Mazzoni has a good 90-94 mph fastball that tops out at 97 mph. He complements it with a decent curveball and a split-change. His fastball tends to be flat and can be elevated. He did have good command in college and in his pro debut, but his secondary offerings need to improve. He will likely work as a starter in '12.

McAllister, Zach — SP — Cleveland

EXP MLB DEBUT: 2011 | POTENTIAL: #4 starter | **7C**

Thrws R Age 24
2006 (3) Illinois Valley

Velo	Pitch	Grade
87-92	FB	+++
78-81	SL	+++
77-80	CB	+++
78-82	CU	+++

Year	Lev	Team	W	L	Sv	IP	K	ERA	WHIP	BF/G	OBA	H%	S%	xERA	Ctl	Dom	Cmd	hr/9	BPV
2009	AA	Trenton	7	5	0	121	96	2.23	1.08	21.5	223	28	80	2.32	2.5	7.1	2.9	0.3	105
2010	AAA	Scranton/W-B	8	10	0	132	88	5.11	1.54	24.0	307	34	70	5.63	2.6	6.0	2.3	1.4	37
2010	AAA	Columbus	1	2	0	17	11	6.88	1.59	25.0	294	34	54	4.80	3.7	5.8	1.6	0.5	48
2011	AAA	Columbus	12	3	0	154	128	3.33	1.21	24.8	263	32	74	3.47	1.8	7.5	4.1	0.6	115
2011	MLB	Cleveland	0	1	0	17	14	6.28	1.92	20.4	349	42	66	6.50	3.7	7.3	2.0	0.5	55

Tall and strong pitcher who has pitches he can trust to throw in any count. None of pitches are above average, but all play up when he sequences them properly. Exquisite control has been paramount to success, especially due to his preference to pitch to contact. Low Dom has been trend while quick arm provides some deception. Cuts and sinks FB and has nice CU.

McGeary, Jack — SP — Washington

EXP MLB DEBUT: 2014 | POTENTIAL: #4 starter | **7D**

Thrws L Age 23
2007 (6) HS (MA)

Velo	Pitch	Grade
86-91	FB	+++
74-77	CB	+++
77-80	CU	++

Year	Lev	Team	W	L	Sv	IP	K	ERA	WHIP	BF/G	OBA	H%	S%	xERA	Ctl	Dom	Cmd	hr/9	BPV
2008	A-	Vermont	0	0	0	4	5	4.50	2.25	20.3	347	49	78	6.77	6.8	11.3	1.7	0.0	88
2009	A-	Vermont	2	6	0	56	45	4.33	1.82	20.0	278	33	77	5.38	6.6	7.2	1.1	0.8	42
2009	A	Hagerstown	0	6	0	55	44	6.85	1.87	19.9	271	33	62	5.26	7.3	7.2	1.0	0.7	45
2010	A	Hagerstown	4	1	0	39	32	4.62	1.36	20.4	257	30	67	4.04	3.5	7.4	2.1	0.9	65
2011	Rk	GCL Nationals	0	1	0	16	12	2.81	1.25	13.0	224	28	75	2.47	3.9	6.8	1.7	0.0	87

McGeary is a tall, athletic lefty who had Tommy John surgery in 2010 and finally made his way back for five late season starts in the GCL. Prior to the surgery, McGeary had a low-90s fastball, a curveball, and a change-up. At this point, just getting back on the field is a step in the right direction. McGeary should be 100% come next spring and could start back at High-A.

McGough, Scott — RP — Los Angeles (N)

EXP MLB DEBUT: 2013 | POTENTIAL: reliever | **7C**

Thrws R Age 22
2011 (5) Oregon

Velo	Pitch	Grade
90-94	FB	+++
77-80	CB	+++
	CU	++

Year	Lev	Team	W	L	Sv	IP	K	ERA	WHIP	BF/G	OBA	H%	S%	xERA	Ctl	Dom	Cmd	hr/9	BPV
2009	NCAA	Oregon	1	0	0	19	15	5.21	1.53	4.6	309	36	67	5.25	2.4	7.1	3.0	0.9	70
2010	NCAA	Oregon	5	2	4	58	56	2.47	1.25	9.5	264	34	81	3.43	2.2	8.7	4.0	0.5	124
2011	NCAA	Oregon	3	6	5	57	62	3.62	1.35	7.7	244	34	70	2.94	3.9	9.8	2.5	0.0	117
2011	Rk	Ogden	1	1	2	5	8	5.19	1.54	3.8	353	55	63	5.05	0.0	13.8		0.0	
2011	A	Great Lakes	0	4	8	20	25	2.24	1.19	4.0	241	35	83	2.93	2.7	11.2	4.2	0.4	148

Short, strong-armed reliever. Has a 90-94 mph fastball, a good power curve, and decent change-up. He competes well and throws all three offerings for strikes. Had a solid pro debut and uses plus arm speed to get good velocity from small frame. Given his collegiate experience and ability to throw strikes, he could move up quickly.

McGuire, Deck — SP — Toronto

EXP MLB DEBUT: 2013 | POTENTIAL: #3 starter | **8B**

Thrws R Age 23
2010 (1) Georgia Tech

Velo	Pitch	Grade
88-94	FB	+++
82-85	SL	+++
77-80	CB	++
	CU	+++

Year	Lev	Team	W	L	Sv	IP	K	ERA	WHIP	BF/G	OBA	H%	S%	xERA	Ctl	Dom	Cmd	hr/9	BPV
2008	NCAA	Georgia Tech	8	1	0	78	70	3.46	1.31	18.9	241	29	77	3.70	3.7	8.1	2.2	0.9	73
2009	NCAA	Georgia Tech	11	2	0	100	118	3.51	1.27	25.6	234	32	74	3.28	3.7	10.6	2.9	0.7	111
2010	NCAA	Georgia Tech	9	4	0	112	118	2.97	1.13	27.7	229	29	79	3.19	2.6	9.5	3.6	1.0	110
2011	A+	Dunedin	7	4	0	104	102	2.76	1.22	22.1	232	29	81	3.21	3.3	8.8	2.7	0.8	94
2011	AA	New Hampshire	2	1	0	20	22	4.46	1.34	21.0	260	31	74	4.80	3.1	9.8	3.1	1.8	74

Tall and durable starter with polished mix of pitches. Sequences pitches as well as any in system and uses height to throw effectively downhill. Maintains velocity deep into games and uses solid-average CU to deter LHH. Has flyball tendencies, but shouldn't be issue as he induces weak contact. Throws strikes and rarely beats himself.

McNutt, Trey — SP — Chicago (N)

EXP MLB DEBUT: 2012 | POTENTIAL: #2 starter/closer | **8D**

Thrws R Age 22
2009 (32) Shelton State CC

Velo	Pitch	Grade
90-98	FB	++++
	CB	+++
	CU	++

Year	Lev	Team	W	L	Sv	IP	K	ERA	WHIP	BF/G	OBA	H%	S%	xERA	Ctl	Dom	Cmd	hr/9	BPV
2009	A-	Boise	3	0	0	20	21	1.34	1.04	11.1	137	18	90	1.38	5.4	9.4	1.8	0.4	107
2010	A	Peoria	6	0	0	59	70	1.52	1.13	18.0	205	31	85	1.90	3.6	10.6	2.9	0.0	139
2010	A+	Daytona	4	0	0	41	49	2.63	0.93	17.1	201	28	74	1.96	2.0	10.8	5.4	0.7	174
2010	AA	Tennessee	0	1	0	15	13	5.92	1.64	22.6	329	39	65	6.08	2.4	7.7	3.3	1.2	68
2011	AA	Tennessee	5	6	0	95	65	4.55	1.67	18.6	309	36	72	5.19	3.7	6.2	1.7	0.5	51

Tall, athletic hurler took a step back in '11. Can dominate with a nice two-pitch mix that includes a 90-97 MPH fastball and a power curveball. Sometimes reverts to being a thrower and needs to refine his craft and improve his so-so change-up. Fastball can flatten out when he overthrows. Still he has the stuff to be a frontline starter.

McPherson, Kyle

SP | **Pittsburgh** | EXP MLB DEBUT: 2013 | POTENTIAL: #3 starter | **8D**

Thrws R Age 24
2007 (14) Mobile

88-92	FB	+++
73-75	CB	+++
80-83	CU	+++

Year	Lev	Team	W	L	Sv	IP	K	ERA	WHIP	BF/G	OBA	H%	S%	xERA	Ctl	Dom	Cmd	hr/9	BPV
2009	A	West Virginia	5	2	0	51	32	4.94	1.16	15.6	269	31	55	3.35	1.1	5.6	5.3	0.5	131
2010	A	West Virginia	9	9	0	117	124	3.61	1.08	17.6	225	28	71	3.05	2.4	9.5	4.0	1.1	119
2010	A+	Bradenton	0	0	0	4	7	0.00	0.50	6.6	151	32	100		0.0	15.8		0.0	
2011	A+	Bradenton	4	1	0	71	60	2.91	0.96	22.4	236	29	70	2.35	0.8	7.6	10.0	0.5	248
2011	AA	Altoona	8	5	0	89	82	3.03	1.08	21.7	230	29	74	2.76	2.1	8.3	3.9	0.7	120

Tall, athletic pitcher has emerged as one of the more polished arms in the system. Features an 87-92 mph fastball that hits 95. Also has a 11-5 curveball, but it tends to be inconsistent, and an effective change-up. His real value is that he locates his fastball and is able to hit all parts of the zone. Strong durable frame and consistent mechanics give him potential.

Melville, Tim

SP | **Kansas City** | EXP MLB DEBUT: 2013 | POTENTIAL: #4 starter | **8D**

Thrws R Age 22
2008 (4) HS (MO)

88-95	FB	+++
75-79	CB	+++
82-85	SL	+++
	CU	+++

Year	Lev	Team	W	L	Sv	IP	K	ERA	WHIP	BF/G	OBA	H%	S%	xERA	Ctl	Dom	Cmd	hr/9	BPV
2009	A	Burlington	7	7	0	97	96	3.80	1.36	19.3	245	31	75	3.87	4.0	8.9	2.2	0.9	78
2010	Rk	AZL Royals	0	1	0	4	6	4.29	1.43	8.9	252	41	67	3.23	4.3	12.9	3.0	0.0	145
2010	A+	Wilmington	2	12	0	112	90	4.98	1.38	21.4	242	29	64	3.79	4.3	7.2	1.7	0.8	61
2011	A+	Wilmington	11	10	0	135	108	4.33	1.52	20.2	285	35	71	4.41	3.5	7.2	2.0	0.5	70

Tall and durable starter who repeated High-A and showed slight improvement. Possesses the ingredients requisite of mid-rotation guy, but has been plagued by inconsistency with control and command. Prefers to pitch to contact, but has a good enough CB and SL to register Ks. Holds velocity deep into games and uses height well from high three-quarters slot.

Mendez, Roman

SP | **Texas** | EXP MLB DEBUT: 2013 | POTENTIAL: #2 starter | **9E**

Thrws R Age 21
2007 FA (DR)

90-98	FB	++++
82-87	SL	+++
80-83	CU	++

Year	Lev	Team	W	L	Sv	IP	K	ERA	WHIP	BF/G	OBA	H%	S%	xERA	Ctl	Dom	Cmd	hr/9	BPV
2009	Rk	GCL Red Sox	2	3	0	49	47	2.01	0.83	15.0	192	26	75	1.20	1.5	8.6	5.9	0.2	186
2010	A-	Lowell	2	3	0	33	35	4.36	1.52	17.9	250	31	76	4.73	5.2	9.5	1.8	1.4	60
2010	A	Greenville	0	2	0	15	18	11.40	2.60	13.6	407	50	59	11.63	6.0	10.8	1.8	3.0	-14
2010	A-	Spokane	1	1	0	11	13	2.41	1.96	17.9	376	48	95	8.09	2.4	10.4	4.3	1.6	85
2011	A	Hickory	9	1	1	117	130	3.31	1.38	18.9	262	35	77	3.78	3.5	10.0	2.9	0.5	107

Loose and quick-armed hurler who finished 2nd in SAL in Ks. Owns very high ceiling, but has work to do. Explosive FB with velocity and movement complemented by hard SL with potential to be second plus pitch. Erratic command due to inconsistent arm slot and release point. Effort in delivery, but has arm strength and velocity to project well in any role.

Meo, Anthony

SP | **Arizona** | EXP MLB DEBUT: 2014 | POTENTIAL: #4 starter/setup reliever | **8D**

Thrws R Age 22
2011 (2) Coastal Carolina

92-95	FB	+++
87-98	SL	+++
81-83	CB	++
83-85	CU	++

Year	Lev	Team	W	L	Sv	IP	K	ERA	WHIP	BF/G	OBA	H%	S%	xERA	Ctl	Dom	Cmd	hr/9	BPV
2009	NCAA	Coastal Carolina	9	2	0	76	68	2.95	1.30	18.5	238	31	76	2.98	3.8	8.0	2.1	0.2	93
2010	NCAA	Coastal Carolina	13	2	0	96	94	2.62	1.21	21.5	232	30	80	2.97	3.2	8.8	2.8	0.6	103
2011	NCAA	Coastal Carolina	10	3	0	108	115	2.16	1.13	26.7	230	31	82	2.60	2.6	9.6	3.7	0.4	132
2011	Rk	Missoula	0	0	0	2	1	0.00	0.00	5.6	0	0			0.0	4.5		0.0	
2011	Rk	Arizona	0	0	0	1	2	0.00	0.00	2.8	0	0			0.0	18.0		0.0	

Lean, wiry righty features a good 92-94 mph fastball that tops out at 96. He also throws a plus slider that can be a swing-and-miss pitch and a decent change. His curveball is below average and will likely be scrapped in the pros. His mechanics are not smooth and he throws with effort and recoil. If that can't be corrected, he'll end up in relief.

Meyer, Alex

SP | **Washington** | EXP MLB DEBUT: 2015 | POTENTIAL: #1 starter | **9D**

Thrws R Age 22
2011 (1) Kentucky

94-97	FB	++++
82-85	SL	+++
	CB	++
83-85	CU	++

Year	Lev	Team	W	L	Sv	IP	K	ERA	WHIP	BF/G	OBA	H%	S%	xERA	Ctl	Dom	Cmd	hr/9	BPV
2009	NCAA	Kentucky	1	4	1	59	80	5.78	1.66	20.4	241	33	68	5.09	6.8	12.2	1.8	1.5	72
2010	NCAA	Kentucky	5	3	0	51	63	7.06	1.86	19.9	291	40	61	5.71	6.4	11.1	1.8	0.9	74
2011	NCAA	Kentucky	7	5	0	101	110	2.94	1.23	29.2	215	30	75	2.44	4.1	9.8	2.4	0.2	116

Meyer is a tall, lanky 6'9" righty with a big arm. His fastball is in the 94-96 range and topped out at 100 mph. His velocity was down post-draft but should be back to normal next spring. He compliments the fastball with a power slider, a knuckle-curve, and a decent change-up. He sometimes struggles with control but has the stuff to dominate.

Meyers, Brad

SP | **New York (A)** | EXP MLB DEBUT: 2011 | POTENTIAL: #4 starter | **7C**

Thrws R Age 26
2007 (5) Loyola-Mary

88-92	FB	+++
78-81	SL	+++
78-81	CU	+++

Year	Lev	Team	W	L	Sv	IP	K	ERA	WHIP	BF/G	OBA	H%	S%	xERA	Ctl	Dom	Cmd	hr/9	BPV
2009	AA	Harrisburg	5	1	0	48	43	2.25	1.06	20.7	228	29	80	2.39	2.1	8.1	3.9	0.4	129
2010	AA	Harrisburg	1	0	0	30	35	1.49	0.99	19.2	213	29	93	2.49	2.1	10.4	5.0	0.9	153
2011	A-	Auburn	0	0	0	6	4	2.90	0.81	11.2	222	27	60	1.35	0.0	5.8		0.0	
2011	AA	Harrisburg	3	2	0	36	38	2.49	0.97	22.8	256	34	76	2.62	0.0	9.5		0.5	
2011	AAA	Syracuse	6	5	0	95	74	3.50	1.31	23.1	291	34	75	4.25	1.4	7.0	4.9	0.8	120

The 26-year-old rebounded nicely after missing much of the '10 season. Features a fringy 88-92 mph fastball, a slider, and a change-up. He keeps the ball down and has some nice deception. While his stuff if fringy, it plays up because he throws strikes and attacks hitters. He was claimed by the Yankees in the Rule 5 draft, but it is hard to see how he would stick.

Miley, Wade

SP | **Arizona** | EXP MLB DEBUT: 2011 | POTENTIAL: #5 starter | **7C**

Thrws L Age 25
2008 (1-S) SE Louisiana

88-93	FB	+++
78-83	SL	+++
79-82	CB	+++
75-77	CU	+++

Year	Lev	Team	W	L	Sv	IP	K	ERA	WHIP	BF/G	OBA	H%	S%	xERA	Ctl	Dom	Cmd	hr/9	BPV
2010	A+	Visalia	4	5	0	80	50	3.26	1.47	24.6	264	31	76	3.68	4.2	5.6	1.4	0.1	61
2010	AA	Mobile	5	2	0	72	63	1.99	1.22	22.4	228	28	87	3.02	3.5	7.9	2.3	0.6	85
2011	AA	Mobile	4	2	0	75	46	4.79	1.36	22.4	259	29	65	3.89	3.4	5.5	1.6	0.7	49
2011	AAA	Reno	4	1	0	54	56	3.66	1.28	27.7	258	34	72	3.58	2.7	9.3	3.5	0.7	113
2011	MLB	Arizona	4	2	0	40	25	4.50	1.65	22.4	299	32	77	5.79	4.1	5.6	1.4	1.4	18

Miley is an athletic lefty who had a surprising season and made his MLB debut. Throws an 88-92 mph fastball, a slider, a curveball, and a change-up. He showed a bit more velocity this year and has the ability to mix his pitches effectively. Command is still an issue given his fringy fastball and he will need to locate better in '12 to avoid taking a step back.

Miller, Aaron

SP | **Los Angeles (N)** | EXP MLB DEBUT: 2013 | POTENTIAL: #3 starter/setup reliever | **8D**

Thrws L Age 24
2009 (1-S) Baylor

90-95	FB	++++
83-85	SL	+++
	CU	++

Year	Lev	Team	W	L	Sv	IP	K	ERA	WHIP	BF/G	OBA	H%	S%	xERA	Ctl	Dom	Cmd	hr/9	BPV
2009	A	Great Lakes	3	1	0	30	38	2.09	1.06	16.7	206	29	86	2.58	3.0	11.4	3.8	0.9	135
2010	A+	Inland Empire	6	4	0	101	99	2.93	1.23	21.5	210	27	77	2.73	4.3	8.8	2.1	0.5	93
2010	AA	Chattanooga	1	4	0	23	22	7.04	2.00	18.5	302	37	65	6.52	7.0	8.6	1.2	1.2	37
2011	Rk	AZL Dodgers	1	0	0	2	3	0.00	1.00	7.6	151	27	100	0.94	4.5	13.5	3.0	0.0	169
2011	A+	Rancho Cucam	3	2	0	34	30	3.97	1.62	15.1	278	35	75	4.61	4.8	7.9	1.7	0.5	66

Tall, athletic hurler with a electric 90-95 mph fastball and a hard slider that is his strikeout pitch. Missed significant action with a recurring groin injury, but when he was on the mound, he shined. Locates his fastball well, but will need to clean up his mechanics and become more consistent. Control is the only thing holding him back right now.

Miller, Matt

SP | **Milwaukee** | EXP MLB DEBUT: 2014 | POTENTIAL: #4 starter | **7C**

Thrws R Age 23
2010 (5) Michigan

90-92	FB	+++
80-82	SL	+++
	CU	++

Year	Lev	Team	W	L	Sv	IP	K	ERA	WHIP	BF/G	OBA	H%	S%	xERA	Ctl	Dom	Cmd	hr/9	BPV
2008	NCAA	Michigan	0	1	0	11	6	4.91	1.55	5.3	262	31	65	3.73	4.9	4.9	1.0	0.0	53
2009	NCAA	Michigan	1	2	3	41	43	3.72	1.41	7.6	206	28	72	2.84	6.1	9.4	1.5	0.2	96
2010	NCAA	Michigan	3	3	0	64	51	5.06	1.73	17.1	315	38	70	5.50	3.9	7.2	1.8	0.6	56
2010	Rk	Helena	7	2	0	71	53	4.06	1.28	20.8	239	28	70	3.58	3.5	6.7	1.9	0.9	61
2011	A	Wisconsin	6	8	0	111	89	4.38	1.41	21.4	246	30	67	3.47	4.5	7.2	1.6	0.3	73

Tall, athletic hurler had a solid debut in the PIO. Strong armed pitcher with a 90-93 mph fastball that tops out at 94 but tends to be straight. Compliments the FB with a slurve and an average change-up. Miller struggled at UM but offers some nice projection.

Miller, Shelby

SP | **St. Louis** | EXP MLB DEBUT: 2013 | POTENTIAL: #1 starter | **9B**

Thrws R Age 21
2009 (1) HS (TX)

93-97	FB	++++
75-77	CB	++++
83-85	CU	+++

Year	Lev	Team	W	L	Sv	IP	K	ERA	WHIP	BF/G	OBA	H%	S%	xERA	Ctl	Dom	Cmd	hr/9	BPV
2009	A	Quad Cities	0	0	0	3	2	6.00	2.33	7.7	371	44	71	7.48	6.0	6.0	1.0	0.0	38
2010	A	Quad Cities	7	5	0	104	140	3.63	1.25	17.6	248	37	72	3.30	2.9	12.1	4.2	0.6	149
2011	A+	Palm Beach	2	3	0	53	81	2.89	1.13	23.3	211	36	74	2.27	3.4	13.8	4.1	0.3	170
2011	AA	Springfield	9	3	0	86	89	2.71	1.22	21.8	229	31	77	2.62	3.4	9.3	2.7	0.2	115

Dynamic 21-year-old continues to develop. Miller features a 92-95 mph fastball that tops out at 97 and has good life and sink. He also has a plus curveball and change-up. When all three offerings are working, he can dominate. He has smooth, repeatable mechanics which gives him the tools to succeed as he moves up. Miller could make his MLB debut in late 2012.

Milone, Tom

SP | **Oakland** | EXP MLB DEBUT: 2011 | POTENTIAL: #5 starter | **7B**

Thrws L Age 25
2008 (10) USC

84-88	FB	+++
73-75	CB	++
	CU	++

Year	Lev	Team	W	L	Sv	IP	K	ERA	WHIP	BF/G	OBA	H%	S%	xERA	Ctl	Dom	Cmd	hr/9	BPV
2008	A	Hagerstown	0	3	0	37	27	2.91	1.13	20.9	256	32	71	2.59	1.5	6.5	4.5	0.0	138
2009	A+	Potomac	12	5	0	151	106	2.92	1.19	22.4	253	30	77	3.20	2.1	6.3	2.9	0.5	88
2010	AA	Harrisburg	12	5	0	158	155	2.85	1.16	23.3	265	34	77	3.32	1.3	8.8	6.7	0.6	179
2011	AAA	Syracuse	12	6	0	148	155	3.22	1.03	23.8	247	33	69	2.71	1.0	9.4	9.7	0.5	249
2011	MLB	Washington	1	0	0	26	15	3.81	1.23	21.1	276	31	70	3.79	1.4	5.2	3.8	0.7	89

Milone continues to have success despite a below average fastball, but has a solid-average curveball and above average changeup. He has a knack for mixing pitches and keeping hitters off-guard by changing eye level and velocity. There are times when he lives in the meaty part of the zone too often. Has the poise and moxie to have a lasting career, but he has limited upside.

Mitchell, D.J. — SP — New York (A)

EXP MLB DEBUT: 2012 — POTENTIAL: #4 starter — **7C**

Thrws R Age 25
2008 (10) Clemson
87-92 FB +++
76-79 CB ++
80-82 CU +++

Year	Lev	Team	W	L	Sv	IP	K	ERA	WHIP	BF/G	OBA	H%	S%	xERA	Ctl	Dom	Cmd	hr/9	BPV
2009	A	Charleston (SC)	4	1	0	37	42	1.95	1.00	23.6	229	32	81	2.10	1.5	10.2	7.0	0.2	210
2009	A+	Tampa	8	6	0	103	83	2.88	1.27	22.2	242	31	75	2.84	3.3	7.2	2.2	0.1	93
2010	AA	Trenton	11	4	0	133	96	4.06	1.39	24.4	254	30	72	3.93	3.9	6.5	1.7	0.7	56
2010	AAA	Scranton/W-B	2	0	0	17	16	3.66	1.51	24.8	281	37	73	3.89	3.7	8.4	2.3	0.0	97
2011	AAA	Scranton/W-B	13	9	0	161	112	3.18	1.35	24.0	254	30	77	3.66	3.5	6.3	1.8	0.6	62

Lean and athletic starter who sequences pitches well and thrives despite lack of plus stuff. Generates heavy sink on FB with clean, smooth, and repeatable delivery. Commands pitches well which resulted in finishing 2nd in IL in wins. Won't punch many batters out and hasn't found consistent complement to FB. Could be candidate for long relief.

Molina, Nestor — SP — Chicago (A)

EXP MLB DEBUT: 2012 — POTENTIAL: #4 starter — **7B**

Thrws R Age 23
2006 FA (Venezuela)
87-94 FB +++
75-78 CB +++
82-84 SP +++
CU +++

Year	Lev	Team	W	L	Sv	IP	K	ERA	WHIP	BF/G	OBA	H%	S%	xERA	Ctl	Dom	Cmd	hr/9	BPV
2009	A-	Auburn	0	1	0	5	6	1.73	1.92	12.3	380	48	100	8.19	1.7	10.4	6.0	1.7	115
2010	A	Lansing	8	2	4	76	61	3.19	1.10	8.1	229	28	71	2.61	2.4	7.2	3.1	0.5	102
2010	A+	Dunedin	0	0	0	4	3	2.20	1.71	9.3	377	45	86	6.00	0.0	6.6		0.0	
2011	A+	Dunedin	10	3	0	108	115	2.58	1.07	20.0	251	33	79	2.97	1.2	9.6	8.2	0.7	215
2011	AA	New Hampshire	2	0	0	22	33	0.41	0.64	15.2	162	29	93	0.15	0.8	13.5	16.5	0.0	450

Quick-armed righty posted incredible numbers in breakout campaign. Upside not high despite performance as he lacks a plus pitch. Deep repertoire is effective and can throw any pitch in any count. CU is nice neutralizer and keeps hitters from sitting on FB. Cuts and sinks FB to both sides of plate and keeps ball on ground.

Montero, Rafael — SP — New York (N)

EXP MLB DEBUT: 2015 — POTENTIAL: #3 starter — **8E**

Thrws R Age 21
2011 NDFA D.R.
91-93 FB ++++
SL ++
CU ++

Year	Lev	Team	W	L	Sv	IP	K	ERA	WHIP	BF/G	OBA	H%	S%	xERA	Ctl	Dom	Cmd	hr/9	BPV
2011	Rk	Kingsport	2	1	0	17	9	4.24	1.35	17.7	262	28	71	4.24	3.2	4.8	1.5	1.1	31
2011	Rk	GCL Mets	1	2	1	31	32	1.45	1.10	17.3	243	34	85	2.30	1.7	9.3	5.3	0.0	174
2011	A-	Brooklyn	1	0	0	5	5	3.60	0.80	9.1	175	18	67	2.44	1.8	9.0	5.0	1.8	125

Short and wiry, Montero is a bit of a late bloomer. Signed by the Mets in 2011, he features a nice three-pitch mix that includes a 91-93 mph fastball that tops out at 95, a slider, and a change-up. The slider and change-up are both below average, but he is able to locate well. Nice potential, but only if his secondary pitches improve.

Montgomery, Mike — SP — Kansas City

EXP MLB DEBUT: 2012 — POTENTIAL: #2 starter — **9C**

Thrws L Age 22
2008 (1-S) HS (CA)
87-96 FB ++++
74-78 CB ++++
78-81 CU +++

Year	Lev	Team	W	L	Sv	IP	K	ERA	WHIP	BF/G	OBA	H%	S%	xERA	Ctl	Dom	Cmd	hr/9	BPV
2009	A+	Wilmington	4	1	0	52	46	2.25	0.96	21.8	206	27	74	1.51	2.1	8.0	3.8	0.0	142
2010	Rk	AZL Royals	0	1	0	8	7	1.10	0.85	10.0	206	27	86	1.25	1.1	7.7	7.0	0.0	207
2010	A+	Wilmington	2	0	0	24	33	1.12	0.74	21.6	170	28	83	0.52	1.5	12.3	8.3	0.0	268
2010	AA	NW Arkansas	5	4	0	59	48	3.50	1.39	19.1	251	30	76	3.73	4.0	7.3	1.8	0.6	69
2011	AAA	Omaha	5	11	0	150	129	5.33	1.50	23.2	270	33	65	4.56	4.1	7.7	1.9	0.9	60

Tall and durable pitcher who saw performance, but not natural stuff, regress in dismal season. Still throws with easy arm action and velocity, but needs to recapture FB command. Root cause was inconsistent slot and mechanics and offseason rest could help. FB exhibits nasty late life and knockout CB tallies Ks. HR rate increased despite groundball tendencies.

Moore, Brandon — SP — New York (N)

EXP MLB DEBUT: 2013 — POTENTIAL: Reliever — **6C**

Thrws R Age 26
2008 (14) Indiana Wesleyan
87-90 FB +++
77-79 CB +++
80-83 CU +++

Year	Lev	Team	W	L	Sv	IP	K	ERA	WHIP	BF/G	OBA	H%	S%	xERA	Ctl	Dom	Cmd	hr/9	BPV
2009	A-	Brooklyn	6	3	0	82	71	2.09	0.95	23.8	209	26	80	1.94	1.9	7.8	4.2	0.4	135
2010	A	Savannah	3	4	2	79	98	2.50	0.92	21.2	217	31	75	2.05	1.3	11.1	8.9	0.6	248
2010	A+	St. Lucie	2	4	0	66	61	3.82	1.44	23.4	270	34	74	4.06	3.5	8.3	2.3	0.5	84
2010	AA	Binghamton	0	1	0	3	6	26.13	3.87	20.7	478	59	38	24.58	11.6	17.4	1.5	11.6	-253
2011	AA	Binghamton	10	8	1	133	105	4.47	1.49	22.0	294	35	71	4.79	2.8	7.1	2.5	0.8	67

Strong, athletic right-hander features a solid 3-pitch mix including an 87-90 mph fastball, a 77-79 mph power curve, and a decent change-up. Moore throws strikes and attacks hitters, but doesn't really have a plus offering. He struggled in '11 and at best looks like a back-end innings eater, but more likely he's destined to move to a relief role.

Moore, Matt — SP — Tampa Bay

EXP MLB DEBUT: 2011 — POTENTIAL: #1 starter — **9A**

Thrws L Age 23
2007 (8) New Mexico JC
89-97 FB ++++
80-83 CB ++++
80-82 CU ++++

Year	Lev	Team	W	L	Sv	IP	K	ERA	WHIP	BF/G	OBA	H%	S%	xERA	Ctl	Dom	Cmd	hr/9	BPV
2009	A	Bowling Green	8	5	0	123	176	3.15	1.27	19.3	199	32	75	2.57	5.1	12.9	2.5	0.4	132
2010	A+	Charlotte	6	11	0	144	208	3.37	1.18	22.2	211	34	71	2.49	3.8	13.0	3.4	0.4	149
2011	AA	Montgomery	8	3	0	102	131	2.20	0.94	21.3	191	28	81	1.92	2.5	11.5	4.7	0.7	163
2011	AAA	Durham	4	0	0	52	79	1.38	0.98	22.0	183	31	90	1.72	3.1	13.6	4.4	0.5	177
2011	MLB	Tampa Bay	1	0	0	9	15	2.97	1.32	12.6	260	43	82	3.96	3.0	14.8	5.0	1.0	167

Strong-framed and durable pitcher who has already inked long-term deal after playoff success. Dominated hitters at all levels with plus-plus FB and wipeout CB. Smooth delivery produces easy velocity and locates FB with precision. No apparent weakness in arsenal as third pitch (CU) also grades as a plus. Power CB may be best breaking pitch in baseball.

Moreno, Diego — RP — Pittsburgh

EXP MLB DEBUT: 2014 — POTENTIAL: Reliever — **7C**

Thrws R Age 25
2006 NDFA Venz.
94-98 FB ++++
85-87 SL ++++
CU ++

Year	Lev	Team	W	L	Sv	IP	K	ERA	WHIP	BF/G	OBA	H%	S%	xERA	Ctl	Dom	Cmd	hr/9	BPV
2009	A	West Virginia	1	3	5	45	57	2.60	0.96	9.4	186	27	75	1.80	2.8	11.4	4.1	0.6	154
2010	A+	Bradenton	4	1	1	38	57	1.18	0.50	4.5	115	18	88		1.2	13.5	11.4	0.7	331
2010	AA	Altoona	0	0	2	7	12	7.50	1.81	4.8	330	52	58	6.49	3.8	15.0	4.0	1.3	126
2011	A+	Bradenton	2	4	5	33	31	3.25	1.23	4.0	217	28	74	2.85	4.1	8.4	2.1	0.5	89
2011	AA	Altoona	0	0	0	11	14	4.91	1.18	6.3	244	35	58	3.28	2.5	11.5	4.7	0.8	148

Short, powerful reliever features a blazing 94-98 mph fastball and a devasting mid-80s slider that is a true swing-and-miss offering. Was not as dominant in '11. Had a brief stint at Double-A, but struggled and was sent back to High-A. At 25 there isn't much upside left, but the fastball/slider combination gives him potential.

Morey, Robert — SP — Florida

EXP MLB DEBUT: 2013 — POTENTIAL: #5 starter — **7D**

Thrws R Age 23
2010 (5) Virginia
86-91 FB +++
71-73 SL +++
80-82 CU ++

Year	Lev	Team	W	L	Sv	IP	K	ERA	WHIP	BF/G	OBA	H%	S%	xERA	Ctl	Dom	Cmd	hr/9	BPV
2008	NCAA	Virginia	2	0	2	27	30	6.62	1.62	7.5	260	35	57	4.46	5.6	9.9	1.8	0.7	80
2009	NCAA	Virginia	3	0	2	67	84	3.35	1.19	15.0	215	31	73	2.80	3.8	11.3	3.0	0.7	122
2010	NCAA	Virginia	9	4	0	98	77	4.22	1.27	25.1	233	27	69	3.59	3.8	7.1	1.9	1.0	60
2010	A	Greensboro	1	3	0	44	41	3.67	1.29	15.1	266	32	76	4.26	2.4	8.4	3.4	1.2	87
2011	A	Greensboro	7	7	0	140	107	5.14	1.54	23.5	292	34	67	4.97	3.3	6.9	2.1	0.9	54

Polished collegiate hurler scuffled in his full-season debut. Doesn't have great size or overpowering stuff, but does know how to pitch. Fastball sits in the 86-91 mph range and he complements the heat with a decent slider and an average change-up. Doesn't have the size or stuff to dominate at higher levers, but could carve out a role at the back end of a rotation.

Morgan, Adam — SP — Philadelphia

EXP MLB DEBUT: 2015 — POTENTIAL: #4 starter — **7C**

Thrws L Age 22
2011 (3) Alabama Tuscaloosa
87-92 FB +++
80-83 SL +++
CU ++

Year	Lev	Team	W	L	Sv	IP	K	ERA	WHIP	BF/G	OBA	H%	S%	xERA	Ctl	Dom	Cmd	hr/9	BPV
2009	NCAA	Alabama	4	2	0	58	44	4.18	1.45	19.1	281	31	76	5.04	3.1	6.8	2.2	1.4	44
2010	NCAA	Alabama	7	5	0	90	72	6.19	1.61	22.2	308	35	64	6.05	3.2	7.2	2.3	1.6	36
2011	NCAA	Alabama	5	7	0	97	77	4.64	1.34	25.2	275	34	63	3.73	2.4	7.1	3.0	0.4	94
2011	A-	Williamsport	3	3	0	53	43	2.03	1.05	18.7	219	27	81	2.22	2.4	7.3	3.1	0.3	109

Short, left-handed hurler had a solid pro debut. He features a nice 87-92 mph fastball that can at times be very good. But he also overthrows, causing it to be very straight. Morgan adds in a good, but inconsistent, 80-83 mph slider, and a decent change-up. His debut went well, but he needs to become more consistent to have long-term success.

Morris, Bryan — SP — Pittsburgh

EXP MLB DEBUT: 2012 — POTENTIAL: #4 starter/reliever — **7C**

Thrws R Age 25
2006 (1-S) Motlow St CC
88-94 FB ++++
80-83 SL +++
74-78 CB ++++
79-82 CU ++

Year	Lev	Team	W	L	Sv	IP	K	ERA	WHIP	BF/G	OBA	H%	S%	xERA	Ctl	Dom	Cmd	hr/9	BPV
2008	A	Great Lakes	2	4	0	81	72	3.21	1.29	19.6	244	31	76	3.35	3.4	8.0	2.3	0.6	86
2009	A+	Lynchburg	4	9	0	72	32	5.61	1.68	21.6	299	33	64	4.85	4.2	4.0	0.9	0.2	31
2010	A+	Bradenton	3	0	0	44	40	0.61	1.00	21.1	229	30	93	1.88	1.4	8.1	5.7	0.0	178
2010	AA	Altoona	6	4	0	89	84	4.25	1.33	19.4	257	32	70	3.94	3.1	8.5	2.7	0.9	84
2011	AA	Altoona	3	4	3	78	64	3.35	1.35	9.3	247	31	74	3.22	3.8	7.4	1.9	0.2	84

Well-proportioned lefty has a lively 88-94 mph fastball. Also throws a hard slider that allows him to miss bats, a curve, and a change-up. Does not change speeds well, but has the smooth arm action to improve. Oblique injury in May limited him to 6 starts. Showed better command, but 2012 will determine whether he is a starter or reliever.

Moskos, Daniel — SP — Pittsburgh

EXP MLB DEBUT: 2011 — POTENTIAL: Reliever — **7B**

Thrws L Age 26
2007 (1) Clemson
92-94 FB ++++
83-85 SL +++
74-79 CB +++

Year	Lev	Team	W	L	Sv	IP	K	ERA	WHIP	BF/G	OBA	H%	S%	xERA	Ctl	Dom	Cmd	hr/9	BPV
2009	AA	Altoona	11	10	0	149	77	3.74	1.46	23.6	275	30	75	4.31	3.5	4.7	1.3	0.7	36
2010	AA	Altoona	3	1	21	41	43	1.53	1.02	4.3	183	26	83	1.39	3.5	9.4	2.7	0.0	131
2010	AAA	Indianapolis	0	5	1	17	18	10.53	2.69	5.0	350	43	60	9.44	10.5	9.5	0.9	1.6	13
2011	AAA	Indianapolis	1	1	3	42	29	3.43	1.21	5.6	252	30	71	3.16	2.4	6.2	2.6	0.4	84
2011	MLB	Pittsburgh	1	1	0	24	11	2.99	1.58	3.4	299	34	79	4.36	3.4	4.1	1.2	0.0	45

Moskos, the 4th overall pick in '07, finally reached the majors where had modest success. Fastball velocity returned to the 92-94 mph range and was backed by a nice 83-85 mph slider. Strong, stocky frame makes him durable. Still struggles with consistency and location, but he definitely made progress and should be able to secure a relief role in '12.

Moviel, Scott — SP — New York (N)

Thrws R Age 24
2007 (2-S) HS, (OH)

EXP MLB DEBUT: 2013 | POTENTIAL: #5 starter | 6C

Velo	Pitch	Grade
87-93	FB	+++
80-83	CB	++
79-82	CU	+

Year	Lev	Team	W	L	Sv	IP	K	ERA	WHIP	BF/G	OBA	H%	S%	xERA	Ctl	Dom	Cmd	hr/9	BPV
2008	A+	St. Lucie	1	0	0	5	2	0.00	0.60	17.1	124	14	100		1.8	3.6	2.0	0.0	94
2009	Rk	GCL Mets	0	0	0	9	10	1.00	1.11	17.7	283	39	90	2.88	0.0	10.0		0.0	
2009	A+	St. Lucie	4	5	0	64	46	3.93	1.33	20.4	252	31	68	3.17	3.4	6.5	1.9	0.1	79
2010	A+	St. Lucie	3	7	2	110	90	5.56	1.65	18.9	289	35	65	4.88	4.5	7.4	1.6	0.6	59
2011	A+	St. Lucie	5	10	0	125	66	5.11	1.69	21.7	334	38	67	5.39	2.4	4.7	1.9	0.2	51

Tall, lanky right-hander (6'11", 235 lbs.) continues to regress. He can pitch downhill effectively, which allows his 88-92 mph fastball to jump up on hitters. Notches strikeouts with curveball, but command within strike zone continues to be poor and limits his effectiveness. A move to relief seems likely in the near future and he will need to show some signs of progress in '12.

Munson, Kevin — RP — Arizona

Thrws R Age 23
2010 (4) James Madison

EXP MLB DEBUT: 2012 | POTENTIAL: Setup reliever/closer | 7D

Velo	Pitch	Grade
90-94	FB	++++
	SL	+++

Year	Lev	Team	W	L	Sv	IP	K	ERA	WHIP	BF/G	OBA	H%	S%	xERA	Ctl	Dom	Cmd	hr/9	BPV
2010	NCAA	James Madison	8	1	10	55	70	1.64	1.04	7.6	175	27	85	1.63	3.9	11.5	2.9	0.3	140
2010	A	South Bend	2	0	3	16	17	1.12	0.81	4.9	150	20	92	1.01	2.8	9.5	3.4	0.6	137
2010	A+	Visalia	0	0	0	0	0			3.6							0.0		
2011	A+	Visalia	4	3	0	53	76	4.06	1.60	5.6	227	35	75	3.96	6.9	12.9	1.9	0.7	105
2011	AA	Mobile	0	0	0	3	2	0.00	1.33	6.2	262	32	100	3.19	3.0	6.0	2.0	0.0	81

Strong, athletic reliever with a nice two-pitch fastball/slider mix. His fastball sits in the 90-94 range and can top out at 95 mph. His slider has nice swing-and-miss potential and has good late depth. Showed ample dominance but also very little command. His delivery is a little needs work and his command must improve for pro ball.

Murphy, Griffin — SP — Toronto

Thrws L Age 21
2010 (2) HS (CA)

EXP MLB DEBUT: 2015 | POTENTIAL: #3 starter | 8E

Velo	Pitch	Grade
87-92	FB	+++
73-76	CB	+++
	CU	+++

Year	Lev	Team	W	L	Sv	IP	K	ERA	WHIP	BF/G	OBA	H%	S%	xERA	Ctl	Dom	Cmd	hr/9	BPV
2011	Rk	GCL Blue Jays	2	2	0	41	39	4.39	1.56	16.3	293	35	76	5.42	3.5	8.6	2.4	1.3	59

Tall and durable pitcher with clean mechanics and potential to move quickly if things click. Has arm speed and action to produce potentially-plus CU while showing exquisite feel for cutting and sinking FB to both sides of plate. Crude breaking ball can be hit hard and could benefit by adding SL to mix. Can be slow to plate, but holds runners well.

Musgrove, Joe — SP — Toronto

Thrws R Age 19
2011 (1-S) HS (CA)

EXP MLB DEBUT: 2015 | POTENTIAL: #3 starter | 8D

Velo	Pitch	Grade
87-95	FB	+++
77-81	CB	+++
	CU	+++

Year	Lev	Team	W	L	Sv	IP	K	ERA	WHIP	BF/G	OBA	H%	S%	xERA	Ctl	Dom	Cmd	hr/9	BPV
2011	Rk	GCL Blue Jays	0	1	0	21	16	4.67	0.99	10.1	221	27	50	2.19	1.7	6.8	4.0	0.4	123
2011	Rk	Bluefield	1	0	0	3	2	0.00	1.00	11.5	191	24	100	1.46	3.0	6.0	2.0	0.0	95

Large-framed pitcher who needs to improve secondary pitches to realize potential. Throws heavy FB low in zone to induce groundballs and mixes in CB to get hitters to chase. CB can be hit or miss depending on day. Rarely walks hitters, but Dom was low as he works quickly and efficiently. Not much effort in delivery, but needs to repeat arm speed.

Mutz, Nick — SP — Los Angeles (A)

Thrws R Age 22
2011 (9) Dakota State

EXP MLB DEBUT: 2014 | POTENTIAL: #3 starter | 8E

Velo	Pitch	Grade
89-96	FB	++++
82-85	SL	+++
	CT	+++
	CU	++

Year	Lev	Team	W	L	Sv	IP	K	ERA	WHIP	BF/G	OBA	H%	S%	xERA	Ctl	Dom	Cmd	hr/9	BPV
2011	Rk	Orem	2	3	2	23	25	2.34	1.08	7.5	235	28	90	3.62	1.9	9.7	5.0	1.6	125

Durable and strong pitcher with intriguing background and will likely be SP despite relief role upon signing. Loose, quick arm generates hard heat and mixes in hard SL that can be plus poitch. Spots lively FB exceptionally well while CU in development stage. Has effort in delivery, but maintains velocity deep into games.

Neal, Zach — SP — Florida

Thrws R Age 23
2010 (17) Oklahoma

EXP MLB DEBUT: 2013 | POTENTIAL: #4 starter | 7D

Velo	Pitch	Grade
88-92	SL	+++
	CB	+++
	CU	++
		++

Year	Lev	Team	W	L	Sv	IP	K	ERA	WHIP	BF/G	OBA	H%	S%	xERA	Ctl	Dom	Cmd	hr/9	BPV
2008	NCAA	Sam Houston St	3	2	0	46	32	5.65	1.62	17.1	340	39	65	5.84	1.6	6.2	4.0	0.8	85
2010	NCAA	Oklahoma	8	3	0	105	95	4.45	1.29	24.0	274	34	65	3.80	2.1	8.1	4.0	0.6	114
2010	Rk	GCL Marlins	1	0	0	10	16	0.88	0.88	12.6	218	39	89	1.39	0.9	14.1	16.0	0.0	432
2010	A-	Jamestown	1	1	0	20	21	1.78	1.04	19.5	250	33	85	2.67	0.9	9.4	10.5	0.4	268
2011	A	Greensboro	7	6	0	119	84	4.16	1.39	22.8	270	31	72	4.28	3.1	6.4	2.0	0.9	55

Athletic hurler doesn't overpower hitters, but has enough stuff to keep them honest and creates some decent deception. Solid full-season debut and features an 88-92 mph fastball that has a bit of armside run. Complements the heater with a slider, a curve, and a below-average change-up. Not the biggest arm in the system, but does project as a solid innings-eater.

Nelson, Jimmy — SP — Milwaukee

Thrws R Age 23
2010 (2) Alabama

EXP MLB DEBUT: 2014 | POTENTIAL: #3 starter | 8D

Velo	Pitch	Grade
92-95	FB	++++
84-87	SL	+++
	CU	++
		++

Year	Lev	Team	W	L	Sv	IP	K	ERA	WHIP	BF/G	OBA	H%	S%	xERA	Ctl	Dom	Cmd	hr/9	BPV
2008	NCAA	Alabama	3	3	0	41	37	6.33	1.99	11.0	313	38	68	6.40	6.3	8.1	1.3	0.9	41
2009	NCAA	Alabama	2	3	2	37	39	4.60	1.42	7.2	239	32	67	3.54	4.8	9.4	2.0	0.5	90
2010	NCAA	Alabama	9	3	0	110	98	4.01	1.30	25.2	262	31	73	4.23	2.7	8.0	3.0	1.2	76
2010	Rk	Helena	2	0	3	26	33	3.78	1.64	9.7	289	41	78	4.94	4.5	11.3	2.5	0.7	98
2011	A	Wisconsin	8	9	0	146	120	4.38	1.45	24.0	262	32	69	3.97	4.0	7.4	1.8	0.6	69

Nelson is a big-bodied right-hander who has a 92-95 mph sinking fastball that tops out at 97 mph. Nelson also has a good 80-84 mph slider, but his change-up remains a work in progress. He gets better movement on his two-seam fastball. He struggled with command and did not dominate in the MWL. Look for a better season in the in the FSL in '12.

Nicolino, Justin — SP — Toronto

Thrws L Age 20
2010 (2) HS (FL)

EXP MLB DEBUT: 2014 | POTENTIAL: #2 starter | 9D

Velo	Pitch	Grade
87-93	FB	++++
76-80	CB	++
	CU	++++

Year	Lev	Team	W	L	Sv	IP	K	ERA	WHIP	BF/G	OBA	H%	S%	xERA	Ctl	Dom	Cmd	hr/9	BPV
2011	A-	Vancouver	5	1	0	52	64	1.04	0.75	15.5	160	25	85	0.43	1.9	11.1	5.8	0.0	212
2011	A	Lansing	1	1	0	8	9	3.29	1.59	12.0	322	44	77	4.69	2.2	9.9	4.5	0.0	144

Tall and lean pitcher with the stat line of top-notch prospect. Has makings of becoming #2 starter due to quality offerings and above average command. While Dom was high, may fall at upper levels without big FB to set up plus CU. Throws decent FB now, but could add velocity with added strength. Advanced CU is best pitch, but needs better CB.

Norris, Daniel — SP — Toronto

Thrws L Age 19
2011 (2) HS (TN)

EXP MLB DEBUT: 2015 | POTENTIAL: #2 starter | 9D

Velo	Pitch	Grade
88-94	FB	+++
75-78	CB	+++
	CU	+++

Year	Lev	Team	W	L	Sv	IP	K	ERA	WHIP	BF/G	OBA	H%	S%	xERA	Ctl	Dom	Cmd	hr/9	BPV
2011		Did not play																	

Young and athletic pitcher with top-of-the-line stuff but is inexperienced. Quick arm action and speedy delivery offer good velocity and movement while living in lower half of strike zone. Complements FB with excellent CB and advanced CU for age. Key to development will be refining of mechanics and adding strength to pitch deep into games.

Nuding, Zach — SP — New York (A)

Thrws R Age 22
2010 (30) Weatherford JC

EXP MLB DEBUT: 2014 | POTENTIAL: #4 starter | 7D

Velo	Pitch	Grade
88-96	FB	++++
82-85	SL	++
	CU	++

Year	Lev	Team	W	L	Sv	IP	K	ERA	WHIP	BF/G	OBA	H%	S%	xERA	Ctl	Dom	Cmd	hr/9	BPV
2010	Rk	GCL Yankees	0	1	0	2	2	4.50	2.50	10.6	415	52	80	8.75	4.5	9.0	2.0	0.0	68
2011	Rk	GCL Yankees	0	0	0	7	8	2.57	0.86	8.6	233	34	67	1.56	0.0	10.3		0.0	
2011	A	Charleston (SC)	7	6	0	98	82	4.50	1.34	20.4	239	28	68	3.82	4.0	7.5	1.9	1.0	61
2011	A+	Tampa	0	0	0	3	1	0.00	1.33	12.5	262	29	100	3.22	3.0	3.0	1.0	0.0	42

Big and nasty pitcher with intimidating size, but pitches to contact. Has ability to produce quick and hard FB, but takes a few ticks off to add downward movement. Uses height and has a powerful delivery, but inconsistent arm slot has led to flyball tendencies. Has trouble staying on top of SL and will need second pitch to stay in rotation.

Oberholtzer, Brett — SP — Houston

Thrws L Age 22
2008 (8) HS, (DE)

EXP MLB DEBUT: 2012 | POTENTIAL: #4 starter | 7B

Velo	Pitch	Grade
88-92	FB	+++
79-82	SL	+++
75-77	CB	+++
	CU	

Year	Lev	Team	W	L	Sv	IP	K	ERA	WHIP	BF/G	OBA	H%	S%	xERA	Ctl	Dom	Cmd	hr/9	BPV
2009	Rk	Danville	6	2	0	67	56	2.01	0.78	20.1	196	25	73	1.06	0.8	7.5	9.3	0.1	253
2010	A	Rome	0	2	0	23	19	1.96	1.17	23.0	253	31	85	3.02	2.0	7.4	3.8	0.4	117
2010	A+	Myrtle Beach	6	6	2	112	107	4.17	1.26	20.8	280	36	66	3.75	1.4	8.6	5.9	0.6	159
2011	AA	Mississippi	9	9	0	127	93	3.75	1.27	24.7	249	30	70	3.24	3.0	6.6	2.2	0.4	78
2011	AA	Corpus Christi	2	3	0	27	28	5.31	1.40	19.1	268	34	63	4.35	3.3	9.3	2.8	1.0	86

Strong, stocky left-hander. He attacks hitters by pounding the strike zone. His best pitch is an 88-92 mph fastball that has good life. Complements the fastball with a nice slider, a solid change, and a 12-6 curveball. While his raw stuff isn't great, he has some nice deception in his high three-quarters delivery and commands all three offerings well.

Odorizzi, Jake — SP — Kansas City

Thrws R Age 22 | 2008 (1-S) HS (IL) | EXP MLB DEBUT: 2012 | POTENTIAL: #3 starter | 8B

Velo	Pitch	Grade
90-96	FB	++++
78-81	SL	+++
73-76	CB	++++
80-84	CU	++

Year	Lev	Team	W	L	Sv	IP	K	ERA	WHIP	BF/G	OBA	H%	S%	xERA	Ctl	Dom	Cmd	hr/9	BPV
2008	Rk	AZL Brewers	1	2	0	20	19	3.56	1.34	7.6	240	30	76	3.72	4.0	8.5	2.1	0.9	75
2009	Rk	Helena	1	4	0	47	43	4.40	1.36	16.4	293	37	67	4.23	1.7	8.2	4.8	0.6	129
2010	A	Wisconsin	7	3	1	120	135	3.44	1.16	20.8	226	31	70	2.72	3.0	10.1	3.4	0.5	126
2011	A+	Wilmington	5	4	0	78	103	2.88	1.15	20.7	236	35	76	2.76	2.5	11.9	4.7	0.5	164
2011	AA	NW Arkansas	5	3	0	68	54	4.75	1.29	23.4	255	28	69	4.59	2.9	7.1	2.5	1.7	47

Athletic and lean pitcher dominated A+ before struggling in AA. Possesses excellent pitch mix, highlighted by plus FB and CB. Repeats delivery consistently which creates deception, but will need to upgrade CU to complement FB and two breaking balls. Leaves balls up often and will allow HR. Clean arm action has led to durability and stamina.

Oliver, Andrew — SP — Detroit

Thrws L Age 24 | 2009 (2) Oklahoma State | EXP MLB DEBUT: 2010 | POTENTIAL: #3 starter | 8B

Velo	Pitch	Grade
87-95	FB	+++
78-81	CB	++++
82-84	SL	+++
81-84	CU	+++

Year	Lev	Team	W	L	Sv	IP	K	ERA	WHIP	BF/G	OBA	H%	S%	xERA	Ctl	Dom	Cmd	hr/9	BPV
2010	AA	Erie	6	4	0	77	70	3.62	1.28	22.6	254	31	74	3.70	2.9	8.2	2.8	0.8	88
2010	AAA	Toledo	3	4	0	53	49	3.23	1.28	24.2	223	27	79	3.49	4.2	8.3	2.0	1.0	71
2010	MLB	Detroit	0	4	0	22	18	7.36	1.77	20.2	295	34	58	5.92	5.3	7.4	1.4	1.2	32
2011	AAA	Toledo	8	12	0	147	143	4.71	1.56	24.8	264	33	71	4.62	4.9	8.8	1.8	0.9	65
2011	MLB	Detroit	0	1	0	9	5	6.85	2.07	22.5	298	28	75	8.32	7.8	4.9	0.6	2.9	-50

Aggressive and durable starter who finished 3rd in IL in Ks despite struggles. When on, uses electric FB to set up hitters before wiping out with sharp-biting, hard CB. Also uses a SL, but tends to elevate it. Struggled with FB location and saw Ctl rise as a result. Holds velocity, but needs to find consistency to win rotation slot.

Oliveros, Lester — RP — Minnesota

Thrws R Age 24 | 2005 FA (Venezuela) | EXP MLB DEBUT: 2011 | POTENTIAL: Setup reliever | 7C

Velo	Pitch	Grade
90-96	FB	+++
80-84	SL	+++
77-80	CU	+++

Year	Lev	Team	W	L	Sv	IP	K	ERA	WHIP	BF/G	OBA	H%	S%	xERA	Ctl	Dom	Cmd	hr/9	BPV
2011	AA	Erie	2	0	0	17	28	0.53	0.88	6.3	187	36	93	1.02	2.1	14.8	7.0	0.0	254
2011	AAA	Toledo	1	3	5	28	26	6.43	1.93	6.0	319	36	72	7.63	5.5	8.4	1.5	2.3	6
2011	MLB	Detroit	0	0	0	8	4	5.63	1.50	3.8	262	30	58	3.62	4.5	4.5	1.0	0.0	51
2011	AAA	Rochester	0	0	0	3	4	3.00	0.67	5.2	191	18	100	3.38	0.0	12.0		3.0	
2011	MLB	Minnesota	0	0	0	13	9	4.12	1.53	5.7	260	32	70	3.65	4.8	6.2	1.3	0.0	67

Athletic and strong reliever who had interesting campaign that saw him pitch in majors, but end year in Double-A. Likes to pitch aggressively with hard FB and mix in nice set of secondary pitches. Effort in delivery has kept him as a RP for entire career and is not likely to change. Spotty control needs attention or middle relief will be best option.

Oramas, Juan — SP — San Diego

Thrws L Age 22 | 2006 NDFA, Mexico | EXP MLB DEBUT: 2013 | POTENTIAL: #4 starter | 7C

Velo	Pitch	Grade
89-92	FB	+++
	CB	++
	CU	++

Year	Lev	Team	W	L	Sv	IP	K	ERA	WHIP	BF/G	OBA	H%	S%	xERA	Ctl	Dom	Cmd	hr/9	BPV
2010	A	Fort Wayne	0	1	0	15	25	1.20	0.80	10.9	175	34	83	0.69	1.8	15.0	8.3	0.0	285
2010	A+	Lake Elsinore	7	3	0	84	90	3.00	1.07	13.6	213	27	78	2.86	2.8	9.6	3.5	1.1	111
2011	AA	San Antonio	10	5	0	104	102	3.11	1.22	22.1	252	32	78	3.55	2.4	8.8	3.6	0.9	108
2011	AAA	Tucson	0	1	0	3	4	16.88	2.50	17.0	437	44	40	17.16	2.8	11.3	4.0	8.4	-134

Short, strong-armed left-hander continues to excel. He doesn't overpower hitters, but is a strike-throwing machine. Fastball sits in the 88-92 range and tops out at 94. He also throws an average curve and an improved change-up. He comes into the zone early to get ahead of hitters. A strike-thrower working in PETCO has a chance.

Ortega, Jose — RP — Detroit

Thrws R Age 23 | 2006 FA (Venezuela) | EXP MLB DEBUT: 2012 | POTENTIAL: Setup reliever | 7B

Velo	Pitch	Grade
90-96	FB	+++
80-84	SL	+++
	CU	++

Year	Lev	Team	W	L	Sv	IP	K	ERA	WHIP	BF/G	OBA	H%	S%	xERA	Ctl	Dom	Cmd	hr/9	BPV
2009	A-	Oneonta	2	2	1	34	32	3.97	1.50	5.9	226	29	73	3.61	6.1	8.5	1.4	0.5	74
2010	A	West Michigan	0	3	1	25	22	4.64	1.79	6.4	283	35	73	4.94	6.1	7.9	1.3	0.4	62
2010	A+	Lakeland	2	1	0	19	20	0.95	1.11	7.5	207	29	90	1.88	3.3	9.5	2.9	0.0	130
2010	AA	Erie	1	0	0	23	19	3.10	1.25	6.3	252	30	78	3.55	2.7	7.4	2.7	0.8	83
2011	AAA	Toledo	1	3	0	50	44	6.30	1.76	6.9	302	36	65	6.01	4.9	7.9	1.6	1.3	39

Short and quick-armed reliever who uses short arm action and high three quarters slot to generate sneaky quick FB. Heater can be flat and straight and often uses it too much. Needs to trust hard SL which exhibits late movement at times. Projects to setup reliever where his max-effort delivery plays best. Doesn't change speeds much, but likely won't have to.

Osich, Josh — RP — San Francisco

Thrws L Age 23 | 2011 (6) Oregon | EXP MLB DEBUT: 2013 | POTENTIAL: reliever | 8C

Velo	Pitch	Grade
93-95	FB	++++
	SL	++
	CU	++

Year	Lev	Team	W	L	Sv	IP	K	ERA	WHIP	BF/G	OBA	H%	S%	xERA	Ctl	Dom	Cmd	hr/9	BPV
2011		Did not play																	

Strong and athletic, but also injury prone. He had Tommy John surgery in '10 but is healthy now. Has a good 92-95 mph fastball. His slider tends to be inconsistent, and his change-up is a work in progress but shows potential. Can spot fastball effectively and should move up quickly, though it will likely be in relief.

Ottavino, Adam — SP — St. Louis

Thrws R Age 26 | 2006 (1) Northeastern | EXP MLB DEBUT: 2010 | POTENTIAL: Setup reliever | 7C

Velo	Pitch	Grade
88-93	FB	+++
77-79	SL	+++
72-75	CB	++
78-81	CU	++

Year	Lev	Team	W	L	Sv	IP	K	ERA	WHIP	BF/G	OBA	H%	S%	xERA	Ctl	Dom	Cmd	hr/9	BPV
2008	AA	Springfield	3	7	0	115	96	5.24	1.61	21.2	291	34	70	5.45	4.1	7.5	1.8	1.3	43
2009	AAA	Memphis	7	12	0	144	119	4.75	1.55	23.3	258	31	70	4.36	5.1	7.4	1.5	0.8	56
2010	AAA	Memphis	5	3	0	47	43	4.00	1.17	20.9	244	30	68	3.40	2.3	8.2	3.6	1.0	102
2010	MLB	St. Louis	0	2	0	22	12	8.55	2.08	21.7	373	39	61	8.79	3.7	4.9	1.3	2.0	-23
2011	AAA	Memphis	7	8	0	141	120	4.85	1.60	23.9	279	34	71	4.91	4.5	7.7	1.7	0.9	54

Tall, sturdy former 1st rounder hasn't lived up to expectations. Still has a decent 90-93 mph fastball that can hit 95 and a nice sinking change-up and a decent slider, but substandard control and inconsistent mechanics continue to limit his effectiveness. Has not yet been tried in a relief role and could be the 2012 version of Lance Lynn.

Owens, Henry — SP — Boston

Thrws L Age 19 | 2011 (1-S) HS (CA) | EXP MLB DEBUT: 2015 | POTENTIAL: #3 starter | 8D

Velo	Pitch	Grade
86-93	FB	+++
72-75	CB	+++
78-83	SL	+++
	CU	++

Year	Lev	Team	W	L	Sv	IP	K	ERA	WHIP	BF/G	OBA	H%	S%	xERA	Ctl	Dom	Cmd	hr/9	BPV
2011		Did not play																	

Tall and lean pitcher who is very raw, yet has upside. Throws with quick arm that adds to pitch movement. Doesn't possess much projection despite slender frame, but has good CB and SL. Can cut and sink FB effectively and induces weak contact by solid pitch sequencing. Needs larger variance in velocity between FB and CU, but CU can be average.

Owens, Rudy — SP — Pittsburgh

Thrws L Age 24 | 2006 (28) HS, (AZ) | EXP MLB DEBUT: 2012 | POTENTIAL: #4 starter | 7B

Velo	Pitch	Grade
88-93	FB	+++
	CB	+++
	CU	+++

Year	Lev	Team	W	L	Sv	IP	K	ERA	WHIP	BF/G	OBA	H%	S%	xERA	Ctl	Dom	Cmd	hr/9	BPV
2008	A-	State College	3	6	0	58	45	4.97	1.31	16.0	278	34	59	3.64	2.0	7.0	3.5	0.3	105
2009	A	West Virginia	10	1	0	100	91	1.71	0.86	19.4	201	25	86	1.87	1.3	8.2	6.1	0.7	170
2009	A+	Lynchburg	1	1	0	23	22	3.90	1.34	16.0	308	38	75	4.96	0.8	8.6	11.0	1.2	241
2010	AA	Altoona	12	6	0	150	132	2.46	0.98	21.9	227	28	78	2.44	1.4	7.9	5.7	0.7	158
2011	AAA	Indianapolis	9	7	0	112	71	5.06	1.44	22.7	290	33	65	4.60	2.6	5.7	2.2	0.8	54

Polished, athletic lefty scuffled at Triple-A and ended the season on the DL with shoulder fatigue. When healthy he features an 88-93 mph fastball, an above-average curve, and a decent change-up. His calling card is plus control and the ability to throw strikes. Will need to prove that '11 was a fluke and should see time in Pittsburgh in '12.

Parker, Jarrod — SP — Oakland

Thrws R Age 23 | 2007 (1) HS, (IN) | EXP MLB DEBUT: 2012 | POTENTIAL: #1 starter | 9C

Velo	Pitch	Grade
90-95	FB	++++
79-82	SL	++++
73-76	CB	++
77-81	CU	+++

Year	Lev	Team	W	L	Sv	IP	K	ERA	WHIP	BF/G	OBA	H%	S%	xERA	Ctl	Dom	Cmd	hr/9	BPV
2008	A	South Bend	12	5	0	117	117	3.46	1.25	19.9	255	33	73	3.42	2.5	9.0	3.5	0.6	114
2009	A+	Visalia	1	0	0	19	21	0.95	0.84	17.4	183	27	88	0.93	1.9	9.9	5.3	0.0	188
2009	AA	Mobile	4	6	0	78	74	3.69	1.49	21.0	271	35	74	3.89	3.9	8.5	2.2	0.2	91
2011	AA	Mobile	11	8	0	130	112	3.80	1.28	20.5	234	29	70	3.12	3.8	7.7	2.0	0.5	83
2011	MLB	Arizona	0	0	0	5	1	0.00	0.96	19.7	214	23	100	1.68	1.7	1.7	1.0	0.0	44

Athletic hurler with quick arm action and easy velocity. Was healthy in '11 after TJS in '09. Started slowly, but development of 2-seam fastball gave him better movement and was 6-2 with a 2.84 ERA in the 2nd half. Works off his 90-95 mph fastball and can spot fastball to both sides of the plate. Curveball, slider, and 4-seamer round out his arsenal.

Paulino, Brenny — SP — Detroit

Thrws R Age 19 | 2009 FA (DR) | EXP MLB DEBUT: 2015 | POTENTIAL: #2 starter | 9D

Velo	Pitch	Grade
89-97	FB	++++
75-80	CB	++
	CU	++

Year	Lev	Team	W	L	Sv	IP	K	ERA	WHIP	BF/G	OBA	H%	S%	xERA	Ctl	Dom	Cmd	hr/9	BPV
2011	Rk	GCL Tigers	4	3	0	45	45	2.39	1.15	16.3	211	29	78	2.22	3.6	9.0	2.5	0.2	113
2011	A+	Lakeland	0	2	0	5	7	22.94	3.53	16.2	385	55	28	10.69	15.9	12.4	0.8	0.0	68

Tall and lean pitcher with loads of projection in quick arm. Was outstanding in Rookie ball before being shelled in limited High-A time. Loose arm action produces exemplary FB velocity while CB improved throughout year. Needs significant work on CU, especially with repeating arm speed, but is coachable. Could stand to be more efficient.

Paxton, James — SP — Seattle

Thrws L Age 23 · 2010 (4) Kentucky · EXP MLB DEBUT: 2012 · POTENTIAL: #2 starter · 9C

Velo	Pitch	Grade
89-96	FB	++++
79-83	CB	++++
	CU	+++

Year	Lev	Team	W	L	Sv	IP	K	ERA	WHIP	BF/G	OBA	H%	S%	xERA	Ctl	Dom	Cmd	hr/9	BPV
2007	NCAA	Kentucky	2	0	1	17	10	6.80	2.09	3.4	292	32	68	6.52	8.4	5.2	0.6	1.0	10
2008	NCAA	Kentucky	4	2	1	52	43	2.94	1.36	12.8	238	29	81	3.58	4.3	7.4	1.7	0.7	67
2009	NCAA	Kentucky	5	3	0	78	115	5.88	1.32	24.9	274	41	57	4.43	2.3	13.3	5.8	1.3	162
2011	A	Clinton	3	3	0	56	80	2.73	1.34	23.3	222	36	78	2.76	4.8	12.9	2.7	0.2	139
2011	AA	Jackson	3	0	0	39	51	1.85	1.05	21.6	203	31	85	2.10	3.0	11.8	3.9	0.5	154

Tall and strong hurler with impressive offerings. Began in Low-A before moving to Double-A and continued to dominante. Registers high Dom with lively, hard FB and potent CB while also keeping ball on ground. Future success hinges on improvement in CU, though delivery can be slow and control is inconsistent. Could be dynamic late-innings reliever.

Peacock, Brad — SP — Oakland

Thrws R Age 24 · 2006 (41) U. of Miami · EXP MLB DEBUT: 2012 · POTENTIAL: #3 starter · 8B

Velo	Pitch	Grade
91-95	FB	++++
76-78	CB	+++
83-85	CU	+++

Year	Lev	Team	W	L	Sv	IP	K	ERA	WHIP	BF/G	OBA	H%	S%	xERA	Ctl	Dom	Cmd	hr/9	BPV
2010	A+	Potomac	4	9	0	103	118	4.45	1.30	22.4	273	36	67	4.11	2.2	10.3	4.7	1.0	133
2010	AA	Harrisburg	2	2	0	38	30	4.71	1.44	23.2	235	26	70	4.19	5.2	7.1	1.4	1.2	44
2011	AA	Harrisburg	10	2	0	98	129	2.02	0.87	22.6	183	28	78	1.31	2.1	11.8	5.6	0.4	196
2011	AAA	Syracuse	5	1	0	48	48	3.19	1.25	21.7	210	26	78	3.16	4.5	9.0	2.0	0.9	81
2011	MLB	Washington	2	0	0	12	4	0.75	1.08	15.6	171	19	92	1.48	4.5	3.0	0.7	0.0	53

The 23-year-old Peacock just keeps getting better. He has a plus 91-94 mph fastball that now tops at 97 mph, along with a plus 12-6 curveball and a good change-up. He throws all three for strikes and keeps the ball in the park. He limited opposing hitters to an impressive .187 oppBA and had a WHIP of 0.99. Not flashy, but gets the job done.

Peavey, Greg — SP — New York (N)

Thrws R Age 23 · 2010 (6) Oregon State · EXP MLB DEBUT: 2013 · POTENTIAL: #4 starter · 7C

Velo	Pitch	Grade
88-93	FB	++++
84-85	SL	+++
	CU	++

Year	Lev	Team	W	L	Sv	IP	K	ERA	WHIP	BF/G	OBA	H%	S%	xERA	Ctl	Dom	Cmd	hr/9	BPV
2008	NCAA	Oregon State	2	3	1	49	35	4.96	1.47	14.0	270	29	70	5.01	3.9	6.4	1.7	1.5	31
2009	NCAA	Oregon State	4	3	0	62	42	5.79	1.56	21.0	285	33	62	4.77	3.9	6.1	1.6	0.7	45
2010	NCAA	Oregon State	6	3	0	99	72	3.64	1.27	27.0	258	31	70	3.23	2.6	6.5	2.5	0.3	87
2011	A	Savannah	6	2	0	78	69	3.12	1.10	21.9	254	32	71	2.81	1.3	8.0	6.3	0.3	173
2011	A+	St. Lucie	5	4	0	59	39	3.97	1.37	19.0	284	34	69	3.74	2.3	5.9	2.6	0.2	84

Compact, athletic right-hander had a solid pro debut. Has a nice 88-93 mph fastball, a sharp slider, and decent change-up. Peavy does have some effort to his delivery and has lost velocity since high school, and his slider can flatten out when he overthrows it. If he can sharpen his breaking ball and change-up, he has a chance to develop into a solid #4 starter.

Pelzer, Wynn — RP — Baltimore

Thrws R Age 26 · 2007 (9) South Carolina · EXP MLB DEBUT: 2012 · POTENTIAL: Closer · 8D

Velo	Pitch	Grade
89-97	FB	++++
81-84	SL	+++
80-82	CU	+

Year	Lev	Team	W	L	Sv	IP	K	ERA	WHIP	BF/G	OBA	H%	S%	xERA	Ctl	Dom	Cmd	hr/9	BPV
2009	A+	Lake Elsinore	11	8	0	150	147	3.95	1.28	22.8	240	32	68	3.09	3.5	8.8	2.5	0.4	101
2010	AA	San Antonio	6	9	0	94	83	4.21	1.68	19.2	278	34	77	5.07	5.4	7.9	1.5	0.9	52
2010	AA	Bowie	1	0	0	20	20	4.50	1.55	8.7	299	38	72	5.08	3.2	9.0	2.9	0.9	82
2011	AA	Bowie	5	7	1	76	65	4.14	1.59	11.6	262	32	75	4.49	5.3	7.7	1.4	0.7	58
2011	AAA	Norfolk	0	1	0	11	7	3.21	1.61	6.2	222	27	78	3.36	7.2	5.6	0.8	0.0	61

Aggressive and quick-armed pitcher has rotated between pen and rotation, though max-effort delivery projects best in short stints. Induces GB with heavy, lively FB and can punch out hitters with hard SL. Has trouble throwing strikes and lacks touch and feel for changing speeds. Likes to challenge hitters, but can overthrow and lose life on plus FB.

Pena, Ariel — SP — Los Angeles (A)

Thrws R Age 23 · 2007 FA (DR) · EXP MLB DEBUT: 2013 · POTENTIAL: #4 starter · 7C

Velo	Pitch	Grade
90-93	FB	+++
79-82	SL	+++
	CU	+++

Year	Lev	Team	W	L	Sv	IP	K	ERA	WHIP	BF/G	OBA	H%	S%	xERA	Ctl	Dom	Cmd	hr/9	BPV
2009	Rk	AZL Angels	5	4	0	49	47	3.85	1.24	14.2	249	32	68	3.11	2.7	8.6	3.1	0.4	112
2010	A	Cedar Rapids	7	5	0	103	88	3.76	1.49	24.6	243	30	75	3.87	5.2	7.7	1.5	0.6	65
2010	A+	Rancho Cucam	0	1	0	10	8	8.91	2.28	17.2	260	33	57	5.53	11.6	7.1	0.6	0.0	59
2011	A+	Inland Empire	10	6	0	151	180	4.46	1.55	24.5	265	37	71	4.30	4.8	10.7	2.2	0.6	95
2011	AAA	Salt Lake	0	0	0	4	3	2.25	2.75	22.3	383	46	91	8.74	9.0	6.8	0.8	0.0	35

Tall and durable pitcher who finished 2nd in CAL in Ks. Drastic increase in K rate by adding pitch movement and deception. No pitch stands out, but sequences three average pitches. FB and SL are best, while CU can be thrown with same arm speed. Control and command affected by choppy delivery and inconsistent release point.

Peralta, Wily — SP — Milwaukee

Thrws R Age 23 · 2005 NDFA D.R. · EXP MLB DEBUT: 2012 · POTENTIAL: #2 starter · 9D

Velo	Pitch	Grade
92-95	FB	++++
80-83	SL	+++
	CU	+++

Year	Lev	Team	W	L	Sv	IP	K	ERA	WHIP	BF/G	OBA	H%	S%	xERA	Ctl	Dom	Cmd	hr/9	BPV
2009	A	Wisconsin	4	4	1	103	118	3.49	1.33	15.9	238	33	73	3.22	4.0	10.3	2.6	0.4	110
2010	A+	Brevard County	6	3	0	105	75	3.86	1.35	23.1	256	30	71	3.56	3.4	6.4	1.9	0.4	69
2010	AA	Huntsville	2	3	0	42	29	3.63	1.59	23.2	266	30	81	4.89	5.1	6.2	1.2	1.1	32
2011	AA	Huntsville	9	7	0	119	117	3.47	1.29	23.3	240	31	74	3.40	3.6	8.8	2.4	0.7	91
2011	AAA	Nashville	2	0	0	31	40	2.03	1.03	23.9	194	31	78	1.51	3.2	11.6	3.6	0.0	162

Peralta is a solid, stocky righty who had a huge breakout. He has a plus 92-95 mph fastball that tops out at 97 with some nice late sink. He complements the fastball with a low-80s slider and an improved change-up. His raw stuff is plus, but he needs to improve control and command before he can dominate. Not a staff ace, but a solid #2 and soon.

Perez, Alexander — SP — Cleveland

Thrws R Age 22 · 2006 FA (DR) · EXP MLB DEBUT: 2014 · POTENTIAL: #3 starter · 8D

Velo	Pitch	Grade
89-93	FB	+++
77-79	CB	++++
78-81	CU	++

Year	Lev	Team	W	L	Sv	IP	K	ERA	WHIP	BF/G	OBA	H%	S%	xERA	Ctl	Dom	Cmd	hr/9	BPV
2008	Rk	GCL Indians	2	4	0	50	49	4.30	1.06	19.5	207	26	60	2.60	2.9	8.8	3.1	0.9	104
2009	A	Lake County	5	4	0	83	76	3.04	1.12	21.8	228	28	77	3.10	2.6	8.2	3.2	1.0	96
2009	A+	Kinston	1	2	0	31	31	2.89	1.32	16.1	267	35	78	3.47	2.6	9.0	3.4	0.3	119
2010	A+	Kinston	0	1	0	6	8	2.90	1.13	12.2	222	35	71	2.10	2.9	11.6	4.0	0.0	164

Thin and injury-prone pitcher who did not pitch in '11 after only 6 innings in '10. Development stalled due to Tomm John surgery, but has intriguing pitch mix when healthy. Explosive arm action produces FB movement while plus CB can wipe out hitters from both sides. Despite injury, has easy, clean arm action. Needs CU to stick as starter.

Perez, Carlos — SP — Atlanta

Thrws L Age 20 · 2010 NDFA D.R. · EXP MLB DEBUT: 2013 · POTENTIAL: #3 starter · 8D

Velo	Pitch	Grade
88-92	FB	+++
	CB	++
	CU	+++

Year	Lev	Team	W	L	Sv	IP	K	ERA	WHIP	BF/G	OBA	H%	S%	xERA	Ctl	Dom	Cmd	hr/9	BPV
2009	Rk	GCL Braves	1	2	0	30	23	5.36	1.59	13.3	291	35	65	4.80	3.9	6.9	1.8	0.6	57
2010	Rk	Danville	2	0	0	32	27	1.13	1.06	20.7	181	24	88	1.49	3.9	7.6	1.9	0.0	105
2010	A	Rome	0	1	0	7	4	3.86	1.57	15.4	288	31	80	5.38	3.9	5.1	1.3	1.3	18
2011	A	Rome	4	10	1	125	109	4.82	1.63	19.9	281	35	70	4.67	4.8	7.8	1.7	0.5	65

Live-armed hurler struggled in full-season. Has a 88-92 mph sinking fastball, but it could not find the strike zone. Mixes in an average curve and a potentially plus change-up. Curve and change need greater consistency before they can be true weapons. The Braves have time to move slowly, but Perez will need to show more in '12.

Perez, David — SP — Texas

Thrws R Age 19 · 2009 FA (DR) · EXP MLB DEBUT: 2015 · POTENTIAL: #1 starter · 9E

Velo	Pitch	Grade
90-97	FB	++++
82-84	CB	+++
	CU	+

Year	Lev	Team	W	L	Sv	IP	K	ERA	WHIP	BF/G	OBA	H%	S%	xERA	Ctl	Dom	Cmd	hr/9	BPV
2011	A-	Spokane	1	4	0	30	43	8.67	1.79	10.7	228	35	48	4.39	8.7	12.9	1.5	0.6	100

Tall and lanky pitcher who exhibited incredible upside in first year in U.S. Easy, loose arm generates plus FB and wicked CB can be out pitch. Uses height well to pitch on downward angle and keeps ball on ground. Repeats delivery well for size and youth, but had trouble limiting walks. May take a while to develop and change-up needs major work.

Perez, Martin — SP — Texas

Thrws L Age 21 · 2007 FA (Venezuela) · EXP MLB DEBUT: 2012 · POTENTIAL: #2 starter · 9C

Velo	Pitch	Grade
86-95	FB	++++
78-82	CB	+++
77-81	CU	+++

Year	Lev	Team	W	L	Sv	IP	K	ERA	WHIP	BF/G	OBA	H%	S%	xERA	Ctl	Dom	Cmd	hr/9	BPV
2009	A	Hickory	5	5	1	93	105	2.32	1.23	17.2	238	33	81	2.85	3.2	10.1	3.2	0.3	126
2009	AA	Frisco	1	3	0	21	14	5.57	1.62	18.6	329	37	66	5.72	2.1	6.0	2.8	0.9	58
2010	AA	Frisco	5	8	0	99	101	5.99	1.68	18.6	295	37	65	5.54	4.5	9.2	2.0	1.1	61
2011	AA	Frisco	4	2	0	88	83	3.17	1.32	21.4	244	31	77	3.45	3.7	8.5	2.3	0.6	87
2011	AAA	Round Rock	4	4	0	49	37	6.43	1.88	23.0	343	40	65	6.49	3.7	6.8	1.9	0.7	44

Short and strong pitcher who is on cusp of breakout in upper minors. Plagued by inconsistency but has pitches and dominance to be front-of-rotation starter. FB thrown with minimal effort and features solid movement. Mixes in CB and CU that project as plus pitches. Effective natural stuff, but can overthrow and suffer from command problems.

Petricka, Jacob — SP — Chicago (A)

Thrws R Age 24 · 2010 (2) Indiana State · EXP MLB DEBUT: 2013 · POTENTIAL: #3 starter · 8C

Velo	Pitch	Grade
90-96	FB	++++
80-83	CB	+++
	CU	++

Year	Lev	Team	W	L	Sv	IP	K	ERA	WHIP	BF/G	OBA	H%	S%	xERA	Ctl	Dom	Cmd	hr/9	BPV
2010	Rk	Bristol	2	4	0	34	38	2.89	0.94	16.1	206	29	68	1.68	1.8	10.0	5.4	0.3	180
2010	A	Kannapolis	0	1	0	9	10	3.91	2.28	5.2	334	45	81	6.64	7.8	9.8	1.3	0.0	73
2011	Rk	Bristol	0	0	0	4	5	0.00	1.00	7.6	262	39	100	2.29	0.0	11.3		0.0	
2011	A	Kannapolis	3	1	0	41	48	2.84	1.26	21.0	251	36	75	2.82	2.8	10.5	3.7	0.0	145
2011	A+	Winston-Salem	4	7	0	67	46	4.42	1.44	22.0	273	32	68	3.99	3.5	6.2	1.8	0.4	63

Tall and lean pitcher with more skills than numbers suggest. Effectively maintains velocity on plus FB and spins quality CB to keep hitters honest. CU has potential to be average third pitch. Keeps ball on ground by pitching downhill, but struggles to repeat delivery and arm slot. Doesn't walk many, though command isn't polished. Could be scary good RP.

Pettibone, John — SP — Philadelphia

EXP MLB DEBUT: 2015 | POTENTIAL: #3 starter | 8D

Thrws R Age 21
2008 (3) HS (CA)

Velo	Pitch	Grade
92-94	FB	+ + + +
80-83	SL	+ + +
	CU	+ +

Year	Lev	Team	W	L	Sv	IP	K	ERA	WHIP	BF/G	OBA	H%	S%	xERA	Ctl	Dom	Cmd	hr/9	BPV
2008	Rk	GCL Phillies	0	1	0	1	0	0.00	4.00	6.8	515	52	100	15.28	9.0	0.0	0.0	0.0	-48
2009	A-	Williamsport	2	4	0	35	36	5.38	1.51	16.9	272	37	60	3.74	4.1	9.2	2.3	0.0	103
2010	A	Lakewood	8	6	0	131	84	3.50	1.18	21.9	236	27	72	3.11	2.8	5.8	2.0	0.7	65
2011	A+	Clearwater	10	11	0	161	115	2.96	1.14	23.6	247	30	73	2.75	1.9	6.4	3.4	0.3	107

Pettibone is a tall, projectable right-hander who had a nice breakout. The velocity on his fastball jumped to 92-94 mph and now tops out at 96 mph. He mixes in an 80-83 mph slider and a decent change-up. Being a bit more aggressive on the mound could lead to more dominance. He still has a ways to go, but there is more here that it looked liked initially.

Phillips, Zachary — RP — Baltimore

EXP MLB DEBUT: 2011 | POTENTIAL: Situational reliever | 6A

Thrws L Age 25
2004 (23) Sacramento CC

Velo	Pitch	Grade
86-92	FB	+ + +
75-79	CB	+ + +
	CU	+ + +

Year	Lev	Team	W	L	Sv	IP	K	ERA	WHIP	BF/G	OBA	H%	S%	xERA	Ctl	Dom	Cmd	hr/9	BPV
2010	AA	Frisco	0	0	4	16	23	1.11	0.86	5.0	165	28	86	0.76	2.8	12.8	4.6	0.0	195
2010	AAA	Oklahoma City	3	2	1	50	40	3.23	1.58	6.7	261	33	78	3.95	5.2	7.2	1.4	0.2	69
2011	AAA	Round Rock	1	3	3	44	38	4.48	1.61	5.9	286	35	72	4.78	4.3	7.7	1.8	0.6	64
2011	AAA	Norfolk	1	1	1	13	7	2.73	1.44	4.0	244	28	79	3.22	4.8	4.8	1.0	0.0	56
2011	MLB	Baltimore	0	0	0	8	8	1.13	1.00	3.1	210	26	100	2.71	2.3	9.0	4.0	1.1	117

Athletic and strong reliever who reached BAL after trade from TEX. Has stuff and delivery to become situational RP. Sequences three pitches well and has been tough on LHH due to big CB. Control problems have curtailed efforts to pitch in key spots and will need to harness mechanical inconsistencies. Likes to bury heavy FB and counter with CB.

Pill, Tyler — SP — New York (N)

EXP MLB DEBUT: 2014 | POTENTIAL: #4 starter | 7D

Thrws R Age 22
2011 (4) Cal State Fullerton

Velo	Pitch	Grade
88-92	FB	+ + +
85-87	CT	+ +
	CB	+ +
	CU	+ +

Year	Lev	Team	W	L	Sv	IP	K	ERA	WHIP	BF/G	OBA	H%	S%	xERA	Ctl	Dom	Cmd	hr/9	BPV
2009	NCAA	Cal St Fullerton	11	3	0	102	74	4.06	1.08	23.4	252	29	64	3.24	1.1	6.5	5.7	0.9	137
2010	NCAA	Cal St Fullerton	4	4	0	61	58	3.38	1.09	24.0	238	30	70	2.80	1.9	8.5	4.5	0.6	135
2011	NCAA	Cal St Fullerton	6	1	0	90	99	2.10	1.01	21.6	221	30	80	2.17	1.9	9.9	5.2	0.4	168
2011	Rk	GCL Mets	0	0	0	2	1	4.50	1.50	4.3	347	39	67	4.95	0.0	4.5		0.0	
2011	A-	Brooklyn	1	0	0	7	9	3.86	1.00	3.8	168	27	57	1.15	3.9	11.6	3.0	0.0	154

Short, athletic lefty. His fastball sits in the 88-92 range but has some nice deception and good command. Complements the fastball with a change, curveball, and cutter, though none project to be plus pitches. He does throw strikes and could end up as a solid back-end starter.

Pimentel, Stolmy — SP — Boston

EXP MLB DEBUT: 2014 | POTENTIAL: #3 starter | 8D

Thrws R Age 22
2006 FA (DR)

Velo	Pitch	Grade
88-95	FB	+ + +
74-76	CB	+ +
78-82	CU	+ + + +

Year	Lev	Team	W	L	Sv	IP	K	ERA	WHIP	BF/G	OBA	H%	S%	xERA	Ctl	Dom	Cmd	hr/9	BPV
2008	A-	Lowell	5	2	0	63	61	3.14	1.08	18.9	223	27	75	2.95	2.4	8.7	3.6	1.0	108
2009	A	Greenville	10	7	0	117	103	3.84	1.40	20.6	290	35	75	4.60	2.2	7.9	3.6	0.9	91
2010	A+	Salem	9	11	0	128	102	4.07	1.26	20.1	249	30	69	3.55	2.9	7.2	2.4	0.8	76
2011	A+	Salem	6	4	0	51	35	4.57	1.29	19.1	257	28	69	4.33	2.8	6.2	2.2	1.4	44
2011	AA	Portland	0	9	0	50	30	9.16	1.96	16.0	347	38	52	7.43	4.1	5.4	1.3	1.4	2

Tall and projectable pitcher who got slayed in AA and performed only marginally better in A+. Owns one of top CU in org, but hasn't yet found consistency in CB. Can be guilty of throwing too many FB to heart of plate. Doesn't register many Ks despite nice velocity and change-of-pace offering. Lacks deception in quick delivery and may head to bullpen.

Pinder, Branden — RP — New York (A)

EXP MLB DEBUT: 2014 | POTENTIAL: Setup reliever | 7B

Thrws R Age 23
2011 (16) Long Beach St

Velo	Pitch	Grade
90-96	FB	+ + + +
79-82	SL	+ + +
	CU	+ +

Year	Lev	Team	W	L	Sv	IP	K	ERA	WHIP	BF/G	OBA	H%	S%	xERA	Ctl	Dom	Cmd	hr/9	BPV
2010	NCAA	Long Beach St	4	7	0	85	45	4.86	1.50	21.6	306	33	69	5.17	2.3	4.8	2.0	1.0	37
2011	NCAA	Long Beach St	3	5	4	63	58	5.29	1.25	14.3	265	35	53	3.00	2.1	8.3	3.9	0.0	133
2011	A-	Staten Island	2	2	14	31	38	1.16	0.68	4.5	155	23	85	0.47	1.5	11.0	7.6	0.3	241

Tall and physical reliever who was converted to bullpen upon signing. Low three-quarters slot deceives, but also has lively and quick FB that he can blow by hitters. Hard SL has been effective against RHH, but will need better CU or other change-of-pace pitch for LHH. Possesses excellent durability and could advance quickly.

Pomeranz, Drew — SP — Colorado

EXP MLB DEBUT: 2011 | POTENTIAL: #2 starter | 9C

Thrws L Age 23
2010 (1) Mississippi

Velo	Pitch	Grade
90-94	FB	+ + + +
77-81	CB	+ + +
83-86	SL	+ +
81-83	CU	+ +

Year	Lev	Team	W	L	Sv	IP	K	ERA	WHIP	BF/G	OBA	H%	S%	xERA	Ctl	Dom	Cmd	hr/9	BPV
2010	NCAA	Mississippi	9	2	0	100	139	2.25	1.20	25.2	201	31	84	2.60	4.4	12.5	2.8	0.6	130
2011	A+	Kinston	3	2	0	77	95	1.87	1.14	20.3	205	31	84	2.15	3.7	11.1	3.0	0.2	136
2011	AA	Akron	0	1	0	14	17	2.57	1.14	18.5	202	29	80	2.50	3.9	10.9	2.8	0.6	120
2011	AA	Tulsa	1	0	0	10	7	0.00	0.20	15.1	66	9	100		0.0	6.3		0.0	
2011	MLB	Colorado	2	1	0	18	13	5.47	1.33	18.8	271	33	54	3.29	2.5	6.5	2.6	0.0	94

Tall, projectable lefty has a lively 90-94 mph fastball that showed improved velocity. Also has a nice power curveball, slider, and a change-up that is a work in progress. Offerings are accentuated by deceptive delivery, though doesn't repeat consistently. Has the stamina and size to be a durable starter and should get a shot at cracking the starting rotation in '12.

Poreda, Aaron — SP — Pittsburgh

EXP MLB DEBUT: 2009 | POTENTIAL: Reliever | 7D

Thrws L Age 25
2007 (1) San Francisco

Velo	Pitch	Grade
88-96	FB	+ + +
77-81	SL	+ +
80-84	CU	+ +

Year	Lev	Team	W	L	Sv	IP	K	ERA	WHIP	BF/G	OBA	H%	S%	xERA	Ctl	Dom	Cmd	hr/9	BPV
2009	MLB	Chicago Wsox	1	0	0	11	12	2.45	1.55	4.8	225	32	82	3.20	6.5	9.8	1.5	0.0	100
2009	MLB	San Diego	0	0	0	2	0	4.29	2.86	3.0	144	14	83	5.69	21.4	0.0	0.0	0.0	26
2010	AA	San Antonio	0	1	0	25	25	2.52	1.76	6.0	203	27	86	3.83	9.4	9.0	1.0	0.4	78
2010	AAA	Portland	1	1	0	29	22	4.97	1.76	6.6	137	18	69	2.78	11.8	6.8	0.6	0.0	81
2011	AAA	Tucson	4	3	0	69	79	5.46	1.85	7.9	250	35	69	4.65	8.2	10.3	1.3	0.4	81

Athletic pitcher with plus arm strength that provides velocity and movement. Problems with command failed to improve and he walked almost as many as he struck out. Worked exclusively in relief, but fared no better. Works off fastball that has late sink. He also has a decent slider and some nice deception, but he struggles to repeat his low three-quarters delivery.

Portillo, Adys — SP — San Diego

EXP MLB DEBUT: 2013 | POTENTIAL: #3 starter | 7D

Thrws R Age 20
2008 NDFA Venz.

Velo	Pitch	Grade
87-92	FB	+ + + +
	CB	+ +
	CU	+ +

Year	Lev	Team	W	L	Sv	IP	K	ERA	WHIP	BF/G	OBA	H%	S%	xERA	Ctl	Dom	Cmd	hr/9	BPV
2009	Rk	AZL Padres	1	9	0	52	44	5.17	1.82	18.6	313	39	70	5.47	4.8	7.6	1.6	0.3	61
2010	A-	Eugene	2	6	0	62	62	4.79	1.53	19.3	239	32	67	3.63	5.8	9.0	1.6	0.3	85
2010	A	Fort Wayne	0	0	0	2	1	4.50	1.50	8.6	262	18	100	7.85	4.5	4.5	1.0	4.5	-84
2011	A	Fort Wayne	3	11	0	82	97	7.13	1.75	16.3	278	37	59	5.45	6.0	10.6	1.8	1.1	67

Tall, athletic hurler has good stuff, but well-below average control (41 BB in 64 IP). Features a nice low-90s fastball and could add velocity as he matures. Secondary offerings still very much in progress, though change-up has nice potential. Struggles with consistent mechanics and control. Lots of upside, but also lots of work to be done.

Pounders, Brooks — RP — Kansas City

EXP MLB DEBUT: 2014 | POTENTIAL: Reliever | 6C

Thrws R Age 21
2009 (2) HS (CA)

Velo	Pitch	Grade
88-92	FB	+ + +
	CB	+ +
	SL	+ +
	CU	+ +

Year	Lev	Team	W	L	Sv	IP	K	ERA	WHIP	BF/G	OBA	H%	S%	xERA	Ctl	Dom	Cmd	hr/9	BPV
2009	Rk	GCL Pirates	2	2	0	23	20	3.10	1.29	10.6	225	28	76	2.95	4.3	7.8	1.8	0.4	83
2010	A-	State College	3	3	1	42	29	4.49	1.31	10.9	252	28	68	3.99	3.2	6.2	1.9	1.1	50
2011	A	West Virginia	5	5	3	66	72	3.68	1.14	7.3	247	31	73	3.60	1.9	9.8	5.1	1.2	136

Tall, stocky righty is developing into a solid relief prospect. In high school his fastball was in the 90-94 range, but as a professional he's been in the 88-92 range. Also throws a curve, slider, and change-up, but none grade out even above-average. His size gives him potential, but he is still a ways away from contributing and will need to work hard to stay in shape.

Pryor, Stephen — RP — Seattle

EXP MLB DEBUT: 2013 | POTENTIAL: Setup reliever | 8D

Thrws R Age 22
2010 (5) Tennessee Tech

Velo	Pitch	Grade
91-97	FB	+ + + +
82-86	SL	+ + +
	CU	+

Year	Lev	Team	W	L	Sv	IP	K	ERA	WHIP	BF/G	OBA	H%	S%	xERA	Ctl	Dom	Cmd	hr/9	BPV
2010	NCAA	Tennessee Tech	4	4	4	41	75	5.71	1.39	7.2	232	42	60	3.87	4.8	16.5	3.4	1.1	146
2010	A-	Everett	0	0	4	18	26	0.50	0.77	5.9	121	22	93	0.08	3.5	12.9	3.7	0.0	186
2010	A	Clinton	0	2	1	17	29	3.71	1.35	5.9	262	47	70	3.14	3.2	15.4	4.8	0.0	196
2011	A+	High Desert	1	0	4	27	34	7.67	2.00	5.9	269	38	60	5.54	8.7	11.3	1.3	0.7	77
2011	AA	Jackson	2	1	6	22	27	1.22	0.72	4.6	126	20	81	0.01	2.8	10.9	3.9	0.0	177

Tall and slender reliever who misses bats consistently with plus FB and hard SL, but also misses strike zone. Throws with pure arm strength and ideal arm slot. Repeats delivery and can be tough to make hard contact against. Does not have a dependable third pitch and works from behind in count too often, limiting use of SL.

Purke, Matt — SP — Washington

EXP MLB DEBUT: 2014 | POTENTIAL: #2 starter | 8D

Thrws L Age 21
2011 (3) TCU

Velo	Pitch	Grade
91-94	FB	+ + + +
78-81	SL	+ +
76-78	CU	+ + +

Year	Lev	Team	W	L	Sv	IP	K	ERA	WHIP	BF/G	OBA	H%	S%	xERA	Ctl	Dom	Cmd	hr/9	BPV
2010	NCAA	Texas Christian	16	0	0	116	142	3.02	1.08	22.6	217	31	72	2.35	2.6	11.0	4.2	0.5	151
2011	NCAA	Texas Christian	5	1	0	52	61	1.72	1.07	18.5	197	28	85	1.98	3.4	10.5	3.1	0.3	133

The 21-year-old slipped in the draft due to shoulder bursitis and struggles with command. When healthy, he has an easy 91-94 mph fastball that tops out at 96. He also has a quality slider and a nice change-up. Purke slings from a low three-quarters slot and throws across this body, raising concerns about his long-term durabilty. A high risk, high reward hurler.

Putnam, Zach — RP — Cleveland

EXP MLB DEBUT: 2011 | POTENTIAL: Setup reliever | 7B

Thrws R Age 24
2008 (5) Michigan

Velo	Pitch	Grade
87-94	FB	+++
77-79	SL	+++
72-74	CB	++
78-80	CU	++

Year	Lev	Team	W	L	Sv	IP	K	ERA	WHIP	BF/G	OBA	H%	S%	xERA	Ctl	Dom	Cmd	hr/9	BPV
2009	AA	Akron	4	2	2	56	57	4.16	1.37	7.1	271	36	68	3.68	2.9	9.1	3.2	0.3	112
2010	AA	Akron	4	1	3	51	41	3.87	1.31	10.6	287	35	69	3.81	1.6	7.2	4.6	0.4	126
2010	AAA	Columbus	0	1	0	24	24	3.36	1.12	5.6	227	29	72	2.87	2.6	9.0	3.4	0.7	113
2011	AAA	Columbus	6	3	9	69	68	3.65	1.22	6.3	239	30	72	3.29	3.0	8.9	3.0	0.8	99
2011	MLB	Cleveland	1	1	0	7	9	6.34	1.41	3.8	333	45	56	5.60	0.0	11.4		1.3	

Athletic sinkerballer with deep arsenal for a reliever. Mostly works off two-seam FB and can succeed, but quality hitters may lay off it. Needs to upgrade secondary pitches, particularly SL. Keeps ball on the ground with sinker and splitter while CU is nice change-of-pace. Has posted nice Dom in minors, but likely more of a groundball reliever in majors.

Quackenbush, Kevin — RP — San Diego

EXP MLB DEBUT: 2013 | POTENTIAL: Reliever | 7B

Thrws R Age 23
2011 (8) South Florida

Velo	Pitch	Grade
90-93	FB	++++
	SL	++
	CU	++

Year	Lev	Team	W	L	Sv	IP	K	ERA	WHIP	BF/G	OBA	H%	S%	xERA	Ctl	Dom	Cmd	hr/9	BPV
2009	NCAA	South Florida	2	2	6	32	39	3.94	1.56	7.0	256	35	77	4.42	5.3	11.0	2.1	0.8	87
2010	NCAA	South Florida	2	5	4	33	49	4.61	1.48	5.7	243	38	70	3.98	5.2	13.3	2.6	0.8	116
2011	NCAA	South Florida	1	2	12	33	45	0.82	0.63	4.1	130	22	86		1.9	12.2	6.4	0.0	237
2011	A-	Eugene	1	0	9	20	33	0.45	0.94	4.5	186	35	95	1.16	2.7	14.7	5.5	0.0	222
2011	A	Fort Wayne	1	1	9	21	38	0.85	0.85	4.3	168	36	89	0.73	2.6	16.2	6.3	0.0	252

Tall, strong-armed reliever was absolutely dominant in '11. Uses 90-93 mph fastball that tops out at 95 mph with great effect. He hides the ball well and though he throws a slider and a change-up, neither is above-average. He throws strikes and competes very well and had a nice professional debut.

Quintana, Jose — SP — New York (A)

EXP MLB DEBUT: 2014 | POTENTIAL: #4 starter | 7D

Thrws L Age 23
2006 FA (Columbia)

Velo	Pitch	Grade
86-91	FB	+++
74-78	CB	+++
	CU	+++

Year	Lev	Team	W	L	Sv	IP	K	ERA	WHIP	BF/G	OBA	H%	S%	xERA	Ctl	Dom	Cmd	hr/9	BPV
2010	Rk	GCL Yankees	3	1	1	23	32	2.34	0.95	5.8	177	30	73	1.11	3.1	12.5	4.0	0.0	178
2010	A	Charleston (SC)	0	1	0	15	12	4.77	1.39	12.7	205	25	65	3.16	6.0	7.2	1.2	0.6	64
2011	A+	Tampa	10	2	1	102	88	2.91	1.12	13.4	230	29	74	2.62	2.5	7.8	3.1	0.4	108

Quick-armed pitcher who has gone back and forth between starting and relieving. Throws consistent and high-quality strikes while having touch of deception in delivery. Mixes pitches effectively and needs to have command as he lacks swing-and-miss offering. Dom has fallen as he has advanced, but has excellent pitchability and moxie.

Quirarte, Edwin — RP — San Francisco

EXP MLB DEBUT: 2013 | POTENTIAL: reliever | 7C

Thrws R Age 25
2008 (5) Cal State Northridge

Velo	Pitch	Grade
90-93	FB	+++
	SP	+++
	SL	++

Year	Lev	Team	W	L	Sv	IP	K	ERA	WHIP	BF/G	OBA	H%	S%	xERA	Ctl	Dom	Cmd	hr/9	BPV
2009	A	Augusta	6	4	8	36	18	4.48	1.66	5.4	324	36	72	5.42	2.7	4.5	1.6	0.5	36
2009	A+	San Jose	0	3	4	21	18	4.67	1.51	5.7	311	38	68	4.74	2.1	7.6	3.6	0.4	101
2010	A+	San Jose	2	9	6	62	38	3.77	1.26	6.2	243	27	72	3.56	3.2	5.5	1.7	0.9	50
2011	A+	San Jose	2	1	1	12	14	2.21	1.31	4.2	304	39	93	5.08	0.7	10.3	14.0	1.5	306
2011	AA	Richmond	1	2	0	46	38	5.47	1.76	6.0	319	39	68	5.65	3.9	7.4	1.9	0.6	58

Aggressive collegiate closer relies on a low-90s fastball, a splitter, and comps it with an above-average slider. Struggled to start the season at Double-A, but was much better when set back to the CAL. Generates lots of groundball outs (1.90 GB/FB ratio). Lacks a true plus pitch and will need to be more dominant as he moves up.

Raley, Brooks — SP — Chicago (N)

EXP MLB DEBUT: 2012 | POTENTIAL: #5 starter | 7D

Thrws L Age 23
2009 (7) Texas A&M

Velo	Pitch	Grade
88-91	FB	++
78-80	SL	+++
73-75	CB	+++
78-80	CU	+

Year	Lev	Team	W	L	Sv	IP	K	ERA	WHIP	BF/G	OBA	H%	S%	xERA	Ctl	Dom	Cmd	hr/9	BPV
2009	NCAA	Texas A&M	7	3	0	93	95	3.77	1.14	24.6	234	30	68	3.02	2.5	9.2	3.7	0.8	117
2009	Rk	AZL Cubs	0	1	0	4	3	4.39	0.98	5.2	147	10	67	2.98	4.4	6.6	1.5	2.2	31
2009	A-	Boise	0	0	0	6	2	1.48	0.66	10.6	149	12	100	1.55	1.5	3.0	2.0	1.5	41
2010	A+	Daytona	8	6	0	136	97	3.50	1.43	21.4	282	33	76	4.26	2.8	6.4	2.3	0.6	67
2011	AA	Tennessee	8	10	0	136	80	4.23	1.58	23.0	307	34	76	5.47	3.0	5.3	1.8	1.1	31

Strong, athletic lefty has decent stuff, but lacks a plus offering. Fastball is a nice 88-92 sinker. Also has a slurvy slider and a decent curveball. Change-up could develop into a fourth above-average offering. Made 25 starts at Double-A, but did nothing to stand out. Lack of dominance and inability to miss bats makes him a back end starter at best.

Ramirez, Erasmo — SP — Seattle

EXP MLB DEBUT: 2012 | POTENTIAL: #4 starter | 7B

Thrws R Age 22
2007 FA (Nicaragua)

Velo	Pitch	Grade
86-92	FB	+++
83-85	SL	+++
76-79	CB	+++
	CU	+++

Year	Lev	Team	W	L	Sv	IP	K	ERA	WHIP	BF/G	OBA	H%	S%	xERA	Ctl	Dom	Cmd	hr/9	BPV
2010	A	Clinton	10	4	1	151	117	2.98	1.08	22.7	250	29	75	3.10	1.3	7.0	5.6	0.8	141
2011	AA	Jackson	7	6	0	110	81	4.74	1.33	24.0	290	34	65	4.34	1.6	6.6	4.3	0.8	102
2011	AAA	Tacoma	3	2	0	42	35	5.13	1.52	26.1	300	36	67	5.01	2.8	7.5	2.7	0.9	71

Short and athletic sinkerballer who bypassed High-A and had moderate success despite being young for level. Efficiently sequences pitches and fools hitters with deceptive CU and arm speed. Effectively commands pitches to both sides with deep arsenal, but can be hittable. K rate likely to fall further as he progresses.

Ramirez, J.C. — SP — Philadelphia

EXP MLB DEBUT: 2013 | POTENTIAL: #4 starter/reliever | 7C

Thrws R Age 23
2005 NDFA, Nicaragua

Velo	Pitch	Grade
92-94	FB	++++
77-80	SL	+++
	CU	+

Year	Lev	Team	W	L	Sv	IP	K	ERA	WHIP	BF/G	OBA	H%	S%	xERA	Ctl	Dom	Cmd	hr/9	BPV
2008	A	Wisconsin	6	9	0	124	113	4.14	1.21	20.0	243	30	66	3.21	2.8	8.2	3.0	0.7	99
2009	A+	High Desert	8	10	0	142	111	5.13	1.45	21.7	276	32	66	4.74	3.4	7.0	2.1	1.1	52
2010	A+	Clearwater	4	3	0	64	55	4.07	1.25	23.7	258	33	65	3.17	2.4	7.7	3.2	0.3	109
2010	AA	Reading	3	4	0	77	60	5.48	1.46	25.4	290	33	65	5.11	2.8	7.0	2.5	1.3	53
2011	AA	Reading	11	13	0	144	89	4.50	1.38	23.3	262	29	69	4.19	3.4	5.6	1.6	0.9	42

Tall right-hander features a 92-94 mph sinking fastball, a slider, and a change-up. The slider and change-up still need some work and he struggled at times throwing strikes. Ramirez has power stuff, but needs to become more consistent and miss more bats. A move to relief seems possible, as it would allow his sinker/slider mix to play up.

Ramirez, Neil — SP — Texas

EXP MLB DEBUT: 2012 | POTENTIAL: #3 starter | 8C

Thrws R Age 23
2007 (1-S) HS (VA)

Velo	Pitch	Grade
90-94	FB	+++
80-83	CB	++++
79-81	CU	++

Year	Lev	Team	W	L	Sv	IP	K	ERA	WHIP	BF/G	OBA	H%	S%	xERA	Ctl	Dom	Cmd	hr/9	BPV
2009	A	Hickory	3	6	0	66	56	4.77	1.50	15.9	237	28	70	4.28	5.6	7.6	1.4	1.1	49
2010	A	Hickory	10	8	0	140	142	4.43	1.33	20.8	275	35	68	4.19	2.4	9.1	3.8	0.9	108
2011	A+	Myrtle Beach	0	0	0	4	9	0.00	0.48	13.8	78	26	100	0.00	2.1	19.3	9.0	0.0	344
2011	AA	Frisco	1	0	0	19	24	1.89	1.11	12.4	195	29	85	2.16	3.8	11.4	3.0	0.5	133
2011	AAA	Round Rock	4	3	0	74	86	3.64	1.32	17.1	232	32	74	3.40	4.3	10.4	2.5	0.7	101

Tall and projectable pitcher was standout in first year above Low-A. Thrived with cleaner, improved delivery and knockout CB. Posted high Dom and showed ability to dominate with three pitches. Ceiling isn't as high as stats suggest, but is solid best to succeed. Missed time with shoulder stiffness, but appears healthy for long-term.

Ramirez, Noe — SP — Boston

EXP MLB DEBUT: 2014 | POTENTIAL: #3 starter | 8C

Thrws R Age 22
2011 (4) Cal St Fullerton

Velo	Pitch	Grade
86-93	FB	+++
80-85	SL	++
81-84	CU	++++

Year	Lev	Team	W	L	Sv	IP	K	ERA	WHIP	BF/G	OBA	H%	S%	xERA	Ctl	Dom	Cmd	hr/9	BPV
2009	NCAA	Cal St Fullerton	9	2	0	110	100	3.35	1.03	21.2	225	27	71	2.77	2.0	8.2	4.2	0.9	120
2010	NCAA	Cal St Fullerton	12	1	0	106	119	2.54	1.05	25.6	235	32	79	2.79	1.6	10.1	6.3	0.8	177
2011	NCAA	Cal St Fullerton	8	3	0	82	91	1.75	0.85	23.2	183	27	77	0.96	2.0	10.0	5.1	0.0	184

Tall and slender starter may be big-time sleeper. Has impeccable feel and touch for changing speeds. Repeats arm speed and slot and can register Ks by deception. Breaking ball needs to be upgraded. Dictates at-bats by getting ahead with FB and inducing weak contact with CU. Has sound mechanics, but a few minor adjustments may lead to greater velocity.

Ranaudo, Anthony — SP — Boston

EXP MLB DEBUT: 2013 | POTENTIAL: #2 starter | 9D

Thrws R Age 22
2010 (1-S) LSU

Velo	Pitch	Grade
88-96	FB	++++
77-80	CB	+++
81-84	CU	+++

Year	Lev	Team	W	L	Sv	IP	K	ERA	WHIP	BF/G	OBA	H%	S%	xERA	Ctl	Dom	Cmd	hr/9	BPV
2008	NCAA	Louisiana St	1	0	0	12	13	0.00	0.92	5.6	129	16	110	1.25	4.5	9.8	2.2	0.8	111
2009	NCAA	Louisiana St	12	3	0	124	159	3.05	1.15	25.9	210	29	79	3.03	3.6	11.5	3.2	1.1	116
2010	NCAA	Louisiana St	5	3	0	51	54	7.38	1.70	15.4	294	36	58	6.02	4.7	9.5	2.0	1.6	48
2011	A	Greenville	4	1	0	46	50	3.33	1.11	18.1	212	28	72	2.68	3.1	9.8	3.1	0.8	113
2011	A+	Salem	5	5	0	81	67	4.33	1.36	21.2	259	31	68	3.83	3.3	7.4	2.2	0.7	75

Tall and projectable starter who succeeded despite inconsistent year. Height and arm slot are potent against hitters from both sides, particularly with plus FB and nice secondary pitches. Can nibble too much and leaves balls up in zone, but has the arsenal to be near top of rotation. Erratic CU while FB command needs to be fine-tuned.

Rasmussen, Rob — SP — Florida

EXP MLB DEBUT: 2012 | POTENTIAL: #3 starter | 7B

Thrws L Age 23
2010 (2) UCLA

Velo	Pitch	Grade
90-93	FB	+++
73-76	CB	+++
84-87	SL	+++
	CU	++

Year	Lev	Team	W	L	Sv	IP	K	ERA	WHIP	BF/G	OBA	H%	S%	xERA	Ctl	Dom	Cmd	hr/9	BPV
2008	NCAA	UCLA	0	2	0	17	8	5.76	2.09	9.4	340	37	71	6.81	5.8	4.2	0.7	0.5	12
2009	NCAA	UCLA	4	2	1	44	51	6.52	1.76	11.3	294	38	65	6.04	5.3	10.4	2.0	1.4	57
2010	NCAA	UCLA	11	3	0	109	128	2.72	1.13	22.7	222	30	80	2.88	2.9	10.6	3.7	0.8	126
2010	A	Greensboro	0	0	0	6	4	1.45	1.29	5.1	255	31	88	2.99	2.9	5.8	2.0	0.0	81
2011	A+	Jupiter	12	10	0	148	118	3.65	1.42	22.5	251	30	75	3.83	4.3	7.2	1.7	0.6	64

Smallish collegiate lefty starter has a nice 90-93 mph fastball, and complements it with a good 73-76 mph curve, 83-85 mph slider, and an improved change-up. Throws all of his offerings for strikes and know how to pitch. Held his own in the FSL but is not going to dominate, but he competes well.

Ray, Robbie — SP — Washington

EXP MLB DEBUT: 2014 | POTENTIAL: #5 starter | **7D**

Thrws L Age 20
2010 (12) HS (TN)

- 91-94 FB +++
- 72-74 CB +++
- CU +++

Year	Lev	Team	W	L	Sv	IP	K	ERA	WHIP	BF/G	OBA	H%	S%	xERA	Ctl	Dom	Cmd	hr/9	BPV
2011	A	Hagerstown	2	3	0	89	95	3.13	1.22	18.0	221	30	74	2.62	3.8	9.6	2.5	0.3	112

The 20-year-old lefty had an impressive full season debut in the SAL. In high school Ray had a 91-94 mph fastball, but it sat at 88-92 in '11. Mixes in an inconsistent curveball and an improved change-up. He does get some nice deception from his whip-like arm action and registered more Ks than IP. Not a ton of upside, but still has some potential.

Reckling, Trevor — SP — Los Angeles (A)

EXP MLB DEBUT: 2012 | POTENTIAL: #3 starter | **8D**

Thrws L Age 23
2007 (8) HS (NJ)

- 87-93 FB +++
- 78-82 SL ++++
- 77-80 CU ++++

Year	Lev	Team	W	L	Sv	IP	K	ERA	WHIP	BF/G	OBA	H%	S%	xERA	Ctl	Dom	Cmd	hr/9	BPV
2009	A+	Rancho Cucam	1	2	0	19	16	0.95	0.63	21.9	144	16	100	0.89	1.4	7.6	5.3	0.9	155
2009	AA	Arkansas	8	7	0	135	106	2.93	1.43	25.0	236	29	79	3.33	5.0	7.1	1.4	0.3	72
2010	AA	Arkansas	3	6	0	79	62	4.56	1.38	23.7	249	30	66	3.55	4.0	7.1	1.8	0.5	71
2010	AAA	Salt Lake	4	7	0	69	46	8.58	2.15	24.6	337	37	60	7.74	6.5	6.0	0.9	1.4	0
2011	AA	Arkansas	4	7	0	99	63	3.73	1.40	24.6	271	30	77	4.44	3.2	5.7	1.8	1.0	43

Long-time prospect has struggled in recent years as command hasn't improved. Pitches backwards with plus secondary pitches including deceptive CU and big-breaking CB. Dom has fallen dramatically as he's struggled to get ahead of hitters. Forced to use fringe-average FB when behind in count and can be hit hard. Still a glimmer of hope.

Redding, Jon Michael — SP — Los Angeles (N)

EXP MLB DEBUT: 2012 | POTENTIAL: #5 starter | **7C**

Thrws R Age 24
2008 (5) Florida CC

- 89-92 FB +++
- 75-77 CB ++
- CU ++

Year	Lev	Team	W	L	Sv	IP	K	ERA	WHIP	BF/G	OBA	H%	S%	xERA	Ctl	Dom	Cmd	hr/9	BPV
2008	Rk	Ogden	0	4	0	31	36	5.21	1.61	10.6	308	40	70	5.59	3.2	10.4	3.3	1.2	90
2009	A	Great Lakes	16	3	0	133	96	4.60	1.41	21.7	284	33	67	4.27	2.6	6.5	2.5	0.6	71
2010	A+	Inland Empire	4	10	0	144	86	5.56	1.60	23.6	304	34	64	5.05	3.3	5.4	1.6	0.6	42
2011	A+	Rancho Cucam	11	7	0	137	130	3.67	1.34	22.8	254	32	73	3.63	3.4	8.5	2.5	0.6	90

Undersized JuCo starter had some success in '11 in a repeat of the CAL. Isn't overpowering, as fastball sits in the 88-92 range, but he controls it well and keeps runners off base. Reeding also throws a good curveball and a below average change. While he lacks dominance, he goes after hitters and keeps the ball on the ground. Double-A will provide a real test.

Reed, Addison — RP — Chicago (A)

EXP MLB DEBUT: 2011 | POTENTIAL: Closer | **8A**

Thrws R Age 23
2010 (3) San Diego State

- 90-97 FB ++++
- 82-85 SL ++++
- CU +++

Year	Lev	Team	W	L	Sv	IP	K	ERA	WHIP	BF/G	OBA	H%	S%	xERA	Ctl	Dom	Cmd	hr/9	BPV
2011	A	Kannapolis	0	0	0	8	11	1.13	0.63	6.9	151	26	80	0.01	1.1	12.4	11.0	0.0	330
2011	A+	Winston-Salem	2	0	1	28	39	1.60	0.89	6.9	209	33	83	1.63	1.3	12.5	9.8	0.3	283
2011	AA	Birmingham	0	1	2	20	33	0.89	0.79	5.6	149	29	88	0.39	2.7	14.7	5.5	0.0	229
2011	AAA	Charlotte	0	0	2	21	28	1.28	0.52	6.4	119	16	89	0.23	1.3	11.9	9.3	0.9	273
2011	MLB	Chicago Wsox	0	0	0	7	12	3.80	1.55	5.2	333	53	80	5.91	1.3	15.2	12.0	1.3	294

A tall and strong reliever who pitched on five levels, including the majors. Posted dominating numbers with plus repertoire. Throws hard with fast arm action and has chance for more velocity. Locates heater with precision and consistently works ahead in count. Power SL breaks hard and CU is effective. Pitches up in the zone, but has velocity to do so.

Reed, Chris — SP — Los Angeles (N)

EXP MLB DEBUT: 2014 | POTENTIAL: #3 starter/power reliever | **8C**

Thrws L Age 22
2011 (1) Stanford

- 90-94 FB ++++
- 82-84 SL ++++
- 75-78 CU ++

Year	Lev	Team	W	L	Sv	IP	K	ERA	WHIP	BF/G	OBA	H%	S%	xERA	Ctl	Dom	Cmd	hr/9	BPV
2009	NCAA	Stanford	0	0	0	2	1	17.14	3.33	2.2	458	50	43	11.91	8.6	4.3	0.5	0.0	0
2010	NCAA	Stanford	2	0	0	20	14	6.24	1.88	5.0	288	34	65	5.35	6.7	6.2	0.9	0.4	41
2011	NCAA	Stanford	6	2	9	49	48	2.56	1.02	6.7	201	27	73	1.76	2.7	8.8	3.2	0.2	129
2011	A+	Rancho Cucam	0	1	0	7	9	7.71	1.86	10.9	313	43	58	6.42	5.1	11.6	2.3	1.3	70

Was the first college closer taken in the '11 draft. He has good size and athleticism. He features a 91-94 mph fastball with good movement, a plus 82-84 mph slider, and decent change-up. The Dodgers are attempting to convert him to a starting role. If Reed doesn't stick as a starter, he can easily move back to relief.

Reifer, Adam — RP — St. Louis

EXP MLB DEBUT: 2012 | POTENTIAL: Setup reliever | **8C**

Thrws R Age 26
2007 (11) UC Riverside

- 92-98 FB ++++
- 89-91 SL +++
- 84-87 CU +++

Year	Lev	Team	W	L	Sv	IP	K	ERA	WHIP	BF/G	OBA	H%	S%	xERA	Ctl	Dom	Cmd	hr/9	BPV
2008	A-	Batavia	2	1	22	30	41	2.99	1.10	3.7	175	27	74	2.02	4.5	12.3	2.7	0.6	133
2009	A+	Palm Beach	4	7	21	48	50	4.49	1.56	3.9	273	36	70	4.23	4.5	9.4	2.1	0.4	89
2010	AA	Springfield	3	1	17	54	52	3.00	1.26	4.3	258	34	76	3.24	2.5	8.7	3.5	0.3	118
2010	AAA	Memphis	1	0	0	1	0	0.00	1.00	3.8	0	0	100		9.0	0.0	0.0	0.0	55
2011	AAA	Memphis	0	1	0	6	1	1.48	1.31	5.0	289	27	100	4.95	1.5	1.5	1.0	1.5	-17

Tall, strong-armed reliever with heavy 95-97 mph fastball that tops out at 99. Teams the heavy fastball with a very good slider, giving him a solid one-two punch. His fastball tends to flatten out but he has enough velocity to get away with it. Major knee injury in April caused him to miss almost the entire season. Will need to prove he's healthy in '12.

Rice, Jason — RP — Atlanta

EXP MLB DEBUT: 2011 | POTENTIAL: Setup reliever | **7D**

Thrws R Age 26
2005 (11) Chaffey JC

- 90-98 FB ++++
- 76-80 CB +++
- CU +

Year	Lev	Team	W	L	Sv	IP	K	ERA	WHIP	BF/G	OBA	H%	S%	xERA	Ctl	Dom	Cmd	hr/9	BPV
2007	A+	Winston-Salem	3	3	0	31	43	5.77	1.86	6.3	200	30	69	4.48	10.4	12.4	1.2	0.9	89
2008	A	Kannapolis	8	8	1	115	109	4.45	1.46	20.5	283	36	68	4.14	3.1	8.5	2.7	0.4	95
2009	A+	Salem	1	3	0	70	94	2.44	1.13	6.7	161	26	78	1.64	5.3	12.1	2.3	0.3	136
2010	AA	Portland	3	2	13	60	71	2.85	1.25	5.1	210	28	81	3.11	4.5	10.7	2.4	0.9	100
2011	AAA	Pawtucket	4	5	4	85	89	3.70	1.40	8.2	243	32	74	3.66	4.4	9.4	2.1	0.6	88

Short and aggressive reliever who has been passed from org to org despite plus velocity and Dom ability. Mechanics are erratic, especially when he rushes delivery, but quick, live arm generates explosive FB movement. Can spin a good CB, but FB is most dependable offering. Likes to challenge hitters inside, but doesn't repeat delivery.

Richards, Garrett — SP — Los Angeles (A)

EXP MLB DEBUT: 2011 | POTENTIAL: #2 starter | **9C**

Thrws R Age 24
2009 (1-S) Oklahoma

- 90-97 FB ++++
- 77-80 CB ++++
- 84-87 SL +++
- 80-83 CU ++

Year	Lev	Team	W	L	Sv	IP	K	ERA	WHIP	BF/G	OBA	H%	S%	xERA	Ctl	Dom	Cmd	hr/9	BPV
2009	Rk	Orem	3	1	0	35	30	1.54	1.17	17.5	272	35	85	2.90	1.0	7.7	7.5	0.0	204
2010	A	Cedar Rapids	8	4	0	108	108	3.41	1.17	22.7	232	30	71	2.81	2.8	9.0	3.2	0.5	114
2010	A+	Rancho Cucam	4	1	0	34	41	3.95	1.37	20.5	283	38	74	4.52	2.4	10.8	4.6	1.1	127
2011	AA	Arkansas	12	2	0	143	103	3.15	1.14	25.7	234	27	74	2.91	2.5	6.5	2.6	0.6	82
2011	MLB	Los Angeles (A)	0	2	0	14	9	7.07	1.64	8.9	288	19	86	9.79	4.5	5.8	1.3	5.8	-115

Big and strong pitcher who finished 3rd in TL in ERA. Possesses excellent, natural stuff highlighted by plus FB and CB. Throws with quick, smooth arm action and adds sink at lower velocity. K rate dropped despite power arsenal, though should increase once mechanics become more consistent. Needs to improve potentially-average CU and SL.

Rienzo, Andre — SP — Chicago (A)

EXP MLB DEBUT: 2013 | POTENTIAL: #3 starter | **8D**

Thrws R Age 23
2006 FA (Brazil)

- 90-94 FB ++++
- 81-83 SL +++
- CU ++

Year	Lev	Team	W	L	Sv	IP	K	ERA	WHIP	BF/G	OBA	H%	S%	xERA	Ctl	Dom	Cmd	hr/9	BPV
2009	Rk	Bristol	2	6	0	54	49	4.16	1.26	17.0	265	33	67	3.64	2.2	8.2	3.8	0.7	110
2010	A	Kannapolis	8	4	0	101	125	3.65	1.26	20.6	250	36	70	3.20	2.9	11.1	3.9	0.4	140
2011	A+	Winston-Salem	6	5	0	116	118	3.41	1.50	20.0	248	33	76	3.68	5.1	9.2	1.8	0.3	89

Tall and thin pitcher who doesn't stand out for any one pitch or attribute, but succeeds by mixing pitches and commanding FB to both sides of plate. Secondary pitches need work, particularly CU, which he thows with a slower arm speed. Control not as sharp, but has improved his strikeout ability. Flyball pitcher who also struggles with LHH.

Riordan, Cory — SP — Colorado

EXP MLB DEBUT: 2014 | POTENTIAL: Long reliever | **6C**

Thrws R Age 26
2007 (6) Fordham

- 88-92 FB ++++
- SL +++
- CB ++
- CU ++

Year	Lev	Team	W	L	Sv	IP	K	ERA	WHIP	BF/G	OBA	H%	S%	xERA	Ctl	Dom	Cmd	hr/9	BPV
2008	A	Asheville	8	9	0	167	160	3.66	1.28	26.4	282	35	74	4.22	1.6	8.6	5.5	1.0	137
2009	A+	Modesto	12	7	0	169	134	3.94	1.38	25.4	279	34	72	4.08	2.6	7.1	2.8	0.6	83
2010	AA	Tulsa	8	5	0	161	135	4.02	1.28	24.5	270	32	72	4.19	2.1	7.5	3.6	1.1	87
2011	AA	Tulsa	1	12	0	142	100	5.38	1.39	22.1	300	33	64	5.12	1.6	6.3	4.0	1.3	77
2011	AAA	Colorado Spgs	0	0	0	7	4	3.86	1.00	26.7	262	31	57	2.35	0.0	5.1		0.0	

Tall, crafty righty got hammered at Double-A Tulsa. Doesn't blow hitters away, but has a nice 88-92 mph fastball and a solid 4-pitch mix. Has good control, but gave up 21 home runs and a .299 BAA. Not a ton of upside here, but knows how to pitch and could develop into a solid back of the roation guy.

Rivas, Amaury — SP — Milwaukee

EXP MLB DEBUT: 2012 | POTENTIAL: #4 starter | **7D**

Thrws R Age 26
2005 NDFA D.R.

- 90-93 FB +++
- SL ++
- CU ++

Year	Lev	Team	W	L	Sv	IP	K	ERA	WHIP	BF/G	OBA	H%	S%	xERA	Ctl	Dom	Cmd	hr/9	BPV
2008	A	West Virginia	8	3	0	90	70	3.50	1.28	19.4	246	28	77	3.86	3.2	7.0	2.2	1.1	61
2008	A+	Brevard County	1	2	0	30	20	4.20	1.53	18.7	293	34	73	4.70	3.3	6.0	1.8	0.6	53
2009	A+	Brevard County	13	7	0	133	123	2.98	1.14	20.3	225	28	77	2.90	2.9	8.3	2.9	0.7	98
2010	AA	Huntsville	11	6	0	141	114	3.38	1.31	23.3	246	30	74	3.32	3.5	7.3	2.1	0.4	80
2011	AAA	Nashville	7	12	0	150	108	4.73	1.54	23.4	263	30	70	4.52	4.9	6.5	1.3	0.8	44

Rivas isn't overpowering, but knows how to pitch. His fastball sits in the 90-93 range and tops out at 95. He gets good sinking action when he doesn't overthrow and complements it with a plus change-up and an average slider. Rivas struggled with control in '11 and will need to adjust as he needs to be sharp to be effective.

Rivero, Felipe — SP — Tampa Bay

EXP MLB DEBUT: 2015 | POTENTIAL: #4 starter | 8E / BPV

Thrws L Age 20
2008 FA (Venezuela)

86-93	FB	+++	
72-78	CB	++++	
	CU	++	

Year	Lev	Team	W	L	Sv	IP	K	ERA	WHIP	BF/G	OBA	H%	S%	xERA	Ctl	Dom	Cmd	hr/9	BPV
2011	Rk	Princeton	3	3	0	60	57	4.64	1.28	17.6	274	34	66	4.19	1.9	8.5	4.4	1.0	112

Short and athletic pitcher hasn't gotten past short-season ball yet, but has skill set to advance rapidly. Uses quick arm to produce outstanding pitch movement, particularly with FB. Already possesses plus CB that he throws for strikes and can also get hitters to chase. CU is quite crude and will need to be developed in order to last as starter.

Robertson, Tyler — RP — Minnesota

EXP MLB DEBUT: 2012 | POTENTIAL: Situational reliever | 6B / BPV

Thrws L Age 24
2006 (3) HS (CA)

87-94	FB	+++	
74-76	CB	+++	
70-74	CU	++	

Year	Lev	Team	W	L	Sv	IP	K	ERA	WHIP	BF/G	OBA	H%	S%	xERA	Ctl	Dom	Cmd	hr/9	BPV
2008	A+	Fort Myers	5	3	0	82	73	2.74	1.33	22.7	252	32	79	3.32	3.4	8.0	2.4	0.3	92
2009	A+	Fort Myers	8	8	0	143	103	3.33	1.33	22.8	256	31	75	3.50	3.2	6.5	2.0	0.4	72
2010	AA	New Britain	4	13	0	144	91	5.43	1.65	23.9	308	34	68	5.66	3.6	5.7	1.6	1.1	29
2010	AAA	Rochester	0	1	0	5	6	5.40	1.60	22.1	299	43	63	4.34	3.6	10.8	3.0	0.0	123
2011	AA	New Britain	10	3	16	89	88	3.63	1.30	6.7	257	33	73	3.58	2.9	8.9	3.0	0.6	102

Tall and aggressive sinkerballer who converted to closer in '11 and was dynamite. Pitches inside with average FB, but thrives on inducing groundballs. Stiff delivery forced move to pen and lacks projection. Tough on LHH and RHH with nice CB. Not much of a closer candidate in majors as he generally has been hittable and doesn't have consistent second pitch.

Robles, Mauricio — SP — Seattle

EXP MLB DEBUT: 2012 | POTENTIAL: #3 starter | 8D / BPV

Thrws L Age 23
2006 FA (Venezuela)

87-95	FB	+++	
81-85	CB	+++	
76-78	CU	+++	

Year	Lev	Team	W	L	Sv	IP	K	ERA	WHIP	BF/G	OBA	H%	S%	xERA	Ctl	Dom	Cmd	hr/9	BPV
2010	AA	W. Tennessee	6	6	0	114	120	4.11	1.34	21.6	241	31	71	3.64	4.0	9.5	2.4	0.8	89
2010	AAA	Tacoma	3	1	0	28	34	3.54	1.39	23.6	194	27	76	3.04	6.4	10.9	1.7	0.6	98
2011	A+	High Desert	0	2	0	12	9	12.64	2.48	16.0	358	40	46	8.98	8.2	6.7	0.8	1.5	-4
2011	AA	Jackson	0	1	0	8	6	4.39	1.83	19.1	232	26	75	5.07	8.8	6.6	0.8	1.1	31
2011	AAA	Tacoma	1	2	0	11	8	8.92	1.89	13.1	183	15	56	5.89	11.4	6.5	0.6	2.4	-4

Aggressive and strong-framed pitcher who missed time while recovering from TJ surgery. Has nice upside, but may be better served in pen where velocity and aggressiveness would play up. Walks have been problematic due to inconsistent secondary pitches Needs to trust stuff and work ahead in count more often.

Rodriguez, Armando — SP — New York (N)

EXP MLB DEBUT: 2013 | POTENTIAL: #4 starter | 7C / BPV

Thrws R Age 24
2007 NDFA Dominican Republic

88-92	FB	+++	
85-87	CT	+++	
78-81	SL	+++	
75-77	CU	++	

Year	Lev	Team	W	L	Sv	IP	K	ERA	WHIP	BF/G	OBA	H%	S%	xERA	Ctl	Dom	Cmd	hr/9	BPV
2009	Rk	Kingsport	3	1	0	45	36	2.99	1.31	20.7	234	29	77	3.11	4.0	7.2	1.8	0.4	77
2009	A	Savannah	2	1	0	16	24	2.22	0.86	19.9	99	19	71	0.09	5.0	13.3	2.7	0.0	171
2010	A	Savannah	8	9	0	146	152	3.08	1.11	21.2	220	30	71	2.33	2.8	9.4	3.3	0.3	127
2011	A+	St. Lucie	4	4	0	75	74	3.96	1.19	18.8	221	26	72	3.50	3.5	8.9	2.6	1.3	78

Tall, strong right-hander continues to make steady progress. He does not have an overpowering fastball--it sits in the 88-92 range--but locates it well and complements it with a cutter, a slider, and a change-up. He attacks hitters on both sides of the plate and is tough to hit. He has strong frame and competes well.

Rodriguez, Eduardo — SP — Baltimore

EXP MLB DEBUT: 2014 | POTENTIAL: #4 starter | 7B / BPV

Thrws L Age 19
2010 FA (Venezuela)

88-93	FB	+++	
75-80	CB	+++	
	CU	+++	

Year	Lev	Team	W	L	Sv	IP	K	ERA	WHIP	BF/G	OBA	H%	S%	xERA	Ctl	Dom	Cmd	hr/9	BPV
2011	Rk	GCL Orioles	1	1	1	44	46	1.83	1.02	15.4	183	26	80	1.38	3.5	9.4	2.7	0.0	131
2011	A-	Aberdeen	0	0	0	4	4	6.75	1.75	18.3	347	41	67	7.65	2.3	9.0	4.0	2.3	56

Tall and lean pitcher who performed admirably in short-season ball. Routinely fools hitters with uncanny ability to move ball around zone and mess with a hitter's timing. Sinking FB is sneaky quick and can drop CB in for strikes. May not have plus stuff, but repeats delivery and arm speed. Should develop better CU with more innings and could reach BAL at early age.

Rodriguez, Julio — SP — Philadelphia

EXP MLB DEBUT: 2014 | POTENTIAL: #3 starter | 8D / BPV

Thrws R Age 21
2008 (8) HS, (P.R.)

89-92	FB	+++	
75-77	CB	++++	
82-83	CU	++	

Year	Lev	Team	W	L	Sv	IP	K	ERA	WHIP	BF/G	OBA	H%	S%	xERA	Ctl	Dom	Cmd	hr/9	BPV
2008	Rk	GCL Phillies	0	1	0	10	8	12.48	2.38	7.5	387	42	48	10.39	5.3	7.1	1.3	2.7	-32
2009	Rk	GCL Phillies	1	2	0	49	56	3.11	1.02	17.2	206	27	75	2.66	2.6	10.2	4.0	1.1	126
2010	A-	Williamsport	2	2	0	34	36	2.65	1.18	19.4	207	28	79	2.55	4.0	9.5	2.4	0.5	105
2010	A	Lakewood	5	1	0	56	90	1.44	0.96	16.3	168	31	87	1.33	3.5	14.4	4.1	0.3	184
2011	A+	Clearwater	16	7	0	156	168	2.77	1.01	22.2	188	25	76	2.12	3.2	9.7	3.0	0.7	116

Tall, slender righty was one of the most dominant starters in the FSL. Does not blow people away and instead uses a sharp curveball and locates a 89-92 mph fastball. He gets plenty of swings-and-misses on his curve, but often it dives out of the zone and more mature hitters might lay off. He doesn't get a lot of attention, but there is a lot to like here.

Rodriguez, Santos — RP — Chicago (A)

EXP MLB DEBUT: 2013 | POTENTIAL: Setup reliever | 7C / BPV

Thrws L Age 24
2006 FA (DR)

89-97	FB	++++	
81-84	SL	++	
82-84	CU	+++	

Year	Lev	Team	W	L	Sv	IP	K	ERA	WHIP	BF/G	OBA	H%	S%	xERA	Ctl	Dom	Cmd	hr/9	BPV
2009	A	Kannapolis	0	0	0	4	8	0.00	1.00	5.1	210	48	100	1.56	2.3	18.0	8.0	0.0	289
2010	A+	Winston-Salem	2	0	0	40	59	3.59	1.47	5.4	193	33	73	2.59	7.2	13.2	1.8	0.0	135
2011	A+	Winston-Salem	2	3	2	62	49	3.77	1.66	6.9	286	34	78	4.89	4.8	7.1	1.5	0.6	54

Tall and lean reliever who repeated High-A, but saw Dom fall. Improved control, but became more hittable. Max-effort delivery should keep him in pen where plus FB and ability to retire LHH come in handy. Uses height to throw on downhill plane, though he doesn't spin a quality breaking ball. Exhibits good arm speed on CU which gives him second useful pitch.

Rodriguez, Wilking — SP — Tampa Bay

EXP MLB DEBUT: 2014 | POTENTIAL: #4 starter | 8E / BPV

Thrws R Age 22
2007 FA (Venezuela)

90-96	FB	++++	
75-80	CB	++	
	CU	++	

Year	Lev	Team	W	L	Sv	IP	K	ERA	WHIP	BF/G	OBA	H%	S%	xERA	Ctl	Dom	Cmd	hr/9	BPV
2009	Rk	Princeton	1	6	0	56	52	3.21	1.00	16.5	218	27	71	2.51	1.9	8.4	4.3	0.8	128
2010	A	Bowling Green	4	10	0	106	93	4.24	1.29	19.8	267	32	69	4.01	2.4	7.9	3.3	0.9	91
2011	A-	Hudson Valley	1	1	0	8	9	6.67	1.48	17.4	304	42	50	4.14	2.2	10.0	4.5	0.0	149
2011	A	Bowling Green	0	3	0	36	34	4.72	1.44	17.1	271	34	67	4.25	3.5	8.5	2.4	0.7	80

Projectable and live-armed pitcher who began season late due to shoulder issue. Problem may have stemmed from overthrowing, but has loose, quick arm that produces plus FB movement and velocity. Secondary offerings can be hittable, but is at best when sequencing pitches. Throws consistent strikes, though will need to add strength for durability and stamina.

Roemer, Wes — SP — Arizona

EXP MLB DEBUT: 2012 | POTENTIAL: #5 starter/reliever | 6C / BPV

Thrws R Age 25
2007 (1-S) Cal St Fullerton

85-92	FB	+++	
79-84	SL	+++	
79-82	CU	+++	

Year	Lev	Team	W	L	Sv	IP	K	ERA	WHIP	BF/G	OBA	H%	S%	xERA	Ctl	Dom	Cmd	hr/9	BPV
2009	AA	Mobile	9	9	0	134	98	4.29	1.30	25.2	259	30	69	3.88	2.9	6.6	2.3	0.9	64
2010	AA	Mobile	2	1	0	52	43	2.41	1.21	26.3	261	31	84	3.65	1.9	7.4	3.9	0.9	104
2010	AAA	Reno	2	6	0	71	57	7.08	1.81	23.6	310	34	65	7.10	4.9	7.2	1.5	2.1	3
2011	AA	Mobile	8	7	0	139	97	4.53	1.39	24.4	280	32	68	4.37	2.6	6.3	2.4	0.8	62
2011	AAA	Reno	0	1	0	24	18	3.73	1.29	24.7	277	30	81	5.02	1.9	6.7	3.6	1.9	60

Short/athletic pitcher who throws strikes and pitches aggressively. Lacks velocity to miss bats. Looked very pedestrian in stint at Double-A. Typically shows solid control with plenty of GB outs. Not a ton of upside, but he does throw plenty of strikes.

Rogers, Mark — SP — Milwaukee

EXP MLB DEBUT: 2010 | POTENTIAL: #1 starter | 8E / BPV

Thrws R Age 26
2004 (1) HS, (ME)

90-94	FB	++++	
83-86	SL	+++	
73-76	CB	+++	
80-83	CU	++	

Year	Lev	Team	W	L	Sv	IP	K	ERA	WHIP	BF/G	OBA	H%	S%	xERA	Ctl	Dom	Cmd	hr/9	BPV
2010	AAA	Nashville	0	0	0	4	3	2.20	1.46	17.6	206	26	83	2.79	6.6	6.6	1.0	0.0	74
2010	MLB	Milwaukee	0	0	0	10	11	1.80	0.50	8.3	66	10	60		2.7	9.9	3.7	0.0	178
2011	Rk	AZL Brewers	0	0	0	13	11	4.85	1.38	10.9	262	32	65	3.95	3.5	7.6	2.2	0.7	74
2011	A+	Brevard County	0	3	0	16	17	9.50	2.30	16.5	326	39	61	8.66	8.4	9.5	1.1	2.2	3
2011	AAA	Nashville	0	2	0	15	12	13.20	2.87	17.1	332	40	50	8.66	13.2	7.2	0.5	0.6	25

Athletic, power pitcher was hammered in '11, going 0-5 with a 9.35 ERA and was suspended for a second time for banned stimulants. When healthy, he has a plus mid-90s fastball, a power slider, a curve, and a change-up. He tends to miss spots and overthrow his fastball. When he is on, he can be very effective, but frequently the results are just too inconsistent.

Romero, Enny — SP — Tampa Bay

EXP MLB DEBUT: 2014 | POTENTIAL: #2 starter | 9D / BPV

Thrws L Age 21
2008 FA (DR)

90-94	FB	++++	
78-84	CB	++	
80-83	CU	+++	

Year	Lev	Team	W	L	Sv	IP	K	ERA	WHIP	BF/G	OBA	H%	S%	xERA	Ctl	Dom	Cmd	hr/9	BPV
2009	Rk	GCL Rays	2	4	0	39	33	4.83	1.51	15.4	256	32	67	3.97	4.8	7.6	1.6	0.5	69
2010	Rk	Princeton	4	1	0	69	72	1.95	0.94	20.0	207	29	79	1.71	1.8	9.4	5.1	0.3	170
2010	A-	Hudson Valley	1	0	0	5	4	1.80	1.20	20.1	66	9	83	0.71	9.0	7.2	0.8	0.0	102
2011	A	Bowling Green	5	5	0	114	140	4.26	1.51	19.0	244	34	72	4.01	5.4	11.1	2.1	0.7	94

Long, lean, and projectable lefty with lofty ceiling due to power repertoire. Throws hard and could add a few ticks by growing into slender frame. Doesn't repeat delivery, but should improve with more innings. FB thrown with quick arm and plenty of downward life. CU has above average potential, but CB needs significant work.

Rondon, Bruce

RP | Detroit | EXP MLB DEBUT: 2013 | POTENTIAL: Closer | 8C

Thrws R Age 21
2007 FA (Venezuela)

90-98	FB	++++
83-86	SL	++++
	CU	+

Year	Lev	Team	W	L	Sv	IP	K	ERA	WHIP	BF/G	OBA	H%	S%	xERA	Ctl	Dom	Cmd	hr/9	BPV
2009	Rk	GCL Tigers	0	1	0	11	15	4.86	1.80	17.1	277	42	70	4.52	6.5	12.2	1.9	0.0	112
2010	Rk	GCL Tigers	0	0	15	25	26	0.71	0.99	4.0	134	18	96	1.13	5.0	9.3	1.9	0.4	112
2010	A+	Lakeland	0	0	2	6	7	1.45	0.65	5.4	103	9	100	0.98	2.9	10.2	3.5	1.5	125
2011	A	West Michigan	2	2	19	40	61	2.03	1.40	4.1	163	30	84	2.08	7.7	13.7	1.8	0.0	142

Aggressive reliever who intimidates with his hard FB and willingness to challenge inside. Can tally Ks with hard FB and SL. Mechanics and arm action have led to constant control problems as he can overthrow and his FB flattens. Low arm angle and arm speed provide deception, but will need to improve efforts against LHH. If he improves his Ctl, watch out.

Rondon, Hector

SP | Cleveland | EXP MLB DEBUT: 2013 | POTENTIAL: #3 starter | 8C

Thrws R Age 24
2006 FA (Venezuela)

88-94	FB	++++
79-82	SL	+++
77-80	CB	++
79-82	CU	+++

Year	Lev	Team	W	L	Sv	IP	K	ERA	WHIP	BF/G	OBA	H%	S%	xERA	Ctl	Dom	Cmd	hr/9	BPV
2008	A+	Kinston	11	6	0	145	145	3.60	1.19	21.5	241	31	71	3.21	2.6	9.0	3.5	0.7	111
2009	AA	Akron	7	5	0	72	73	2.75	1.06	18.6	228	30	74	2.36	2.0	9.1	4.6	0.4	149
2009	AAA	Columbus	4	5	0	74	64	4.01	1.30	25.4	284	34	72	4.30	1.6	7.8	4.9	1.0	119
2010	AAA	Columbus	1	3	0	31	33	8.65	1.86	20.9	353	40	61	9.16	2.9	9.5	3.3	3.5	7
2011	A-	Mahoning Vall	0	0	0	3	2	3.00	1.00	5.7	262	32	67	2.35	0.0	6.0		0.0	

Advanced and projectable pitcher who missed most of '10 and '11 season after TJ surgery. When healthy, quick arm action adds life to pitches from mid three quarters slot. Commands FB, but often elevates SL and CU. Keeps walks to minimum and can use any pitch in any count. A second elbow surgery in November will likely lead to shortened '12 campaign.

Rosenbaum, Danny

SP | Washington | EXP MLB DEBUT: 2013 | POTENTIAL: #4 starter | 6C

Thrws L Age 24
2009 (22) Xavier

88-92	FB	+++
	SL	++
	CU	++++

Year	Lev	Team	W	L	Sv	IP	K	ERA	WHIP	BF/G	OBA	H%	S%	xERA	Ctl	Dom	Cmd	hr/9	BPV
2009	Rk	GCL Nationals	4	1	0	37	38	1.95	1.03	12.9	217	30	81	2.04	2.2	9.2	4.2	0.2	148
2010	A	Hagerstown	2	5	0	101	84	2.32	1.22	22.7	250	31	82	3.14	2.5	7.5	3.0	0.4	100
2010	A+	Potomac	3	2	0	43	31	2.09	1.12	21.2	224	27	83	2.53	2.7	6.5	2.4	0.4	87
2011	A+	Potomac	6	5	0	132	108	2.59	1.17	26.3	233	29	77	2.63	2.8	7.4	2.6	0.3	100
2011	AA	Harrisburg	3	1	0	39	27	2.30	0.97	24.7	197	24	74	1.45	2.5	6.2	2.5	0.0	104

Short right-hander put up some nice numbers in '11, going 9-6 with a 2.52 ERA. Rosenbaum throws a decent sinking 88-92 mph fastball, a slider, and a change-up. His breaking ball needs more consistency, but the change has the potential to be plus. Not much upside, but he throws strikes, limits HR, and gets hitters out.

Rosenthal, Trevor

SP | St. Louis | EXP MLB DEBUT: 2014 | POTENTIAL: #2 starter | 9D

Thrws R Age 22
2009 (21) Cowley County CC

90-94	FB	++++
80-83	CB	+++
75-78	CU	++

Year	Lev	Team	W	L	Sv	IP	K	ERA	WHIP	BF/G	OBA	H%	S%	xERA	Ctl	Dom	Cmd	hr/9	BPV
2009	Rk	GCL Cardinals	4	1	0	24	26	4.88	1.46	7.3	270	37	63	3.57	3.8	9.8	2.6	0.0	114
2010	Rk	Johnson City	3	0	1	32	30	2.25	0.94	12.0	203	27	76	1.68	2.0	8.4	4.3	0.3	147
2011	A	Quad Cities	7	7	0	120	133	4.12	1.25	22.2	247	34	66	3.22	2.9	10.0	3.4	0.5	121

Strong, athletic hurler whose stock in on the rise. Has a 90-94 mph fastball that tops out at 96 mph. Complements the fastball with a good change-up and a decent curveball. Gets good torque from his lower half to generate plus arm speed and easy velocity. Combines plus stuff with above-average command. Look for a breakout in 2012.

Rosin, Seth

RP | San Francisco | EXP MLB DEBUT: 2014 | POTENTIAL: reliever | 7B

Thrws R Age 23
2010 (4) Minnesota

91-93	FB	+++
	CB	++
	CU	++

Year	Lev	Team	W	L	Sv	IP	K	ERA	WHIP	BF/G	OBA	H%	S%	xERA	Ctl	Dom	Cmd	hr/9	BPV
2008	NCAA	Minnesota	1	1	2	47	32	4.39	1.38	14.2	289	34	66	3.86	2.1	6.1	2.9	0.2	89
2009	NCAA	Minnesota	7	1	0	77	65	4.21	1.27	21.0	274	33	67	3.85	1.9	7.6	4.1	0.7	110
2010	NCAA	Minnesota	9	4	0	103	95	4.72	1.09	25.2	256	31	59	3.53	1.0	8.3	7.9	1.1	186
2010	A-	Salem-Keizer	1	1	0	11	9	4.91	0.91	6.8	225	29	40	1.62	0.8	7.4	9.0	0.0	243
2011	A	Augusta	2	3	2	89	93	3.34	1.25	9.3	244	33	72	2.98	3.0	9.4	3.1	0.3	119

Tall, strong-bodied hurler worked both as a starter and in relief. Features a 91-93 mph fastball, decent slider, and average change-up. Throws strikes with regularity, but fastball lacks movement and is likely better suited in a relief role. Does command the strike zone effectively and has three usable offerings. Worked effectively in relief in the AFL.

Ross, Joe

SP | San Diego | EXP MLB DEBUT: 2015 | POTENTIAL: #3 starter | 8D

Thrws R Age 19
2011 (1) HS, (CA)

91-94	FB	+++
78-82	CB	+++
	CU	+++

Year	Lev	Team	W	L	Sv	IP	K	ERA	WHIP	BF/G	OBA	H%	S%	xERA	Ctl	Dom	Cmd	hr/9	BPV
2011	Rk	AZL Padres	0	0	0	1	0	0.00	2.00	4.8	415	41	100	7.58	0.0	0.0		0.0	

Ross is the younger brother of A's prospect Tyson Ross. He features a nice 91-94 mph fastball, a plus power 11-5 curveball, and an inconsistent change-up. Struggles with command at times and needs to be more consistent with his mechanics, but is athletic and should get stronger as he matures. Profiles as a solid #3 starter.

Ross, Robbie

SP | Texas | EXP MLB DEBUT: 2013 | POTENTIAL: #3 starter | 8B

Thrws L Age 23
2008 (2) HS (KY)

87-94	FB	+++
81-85	SL	+++
79-83	CU	+++

Year	Lev	Team	W	L	Sv	IP	K	ERA	WHIP	BF/G	OBA	H%	S%	xERA	Ctl	Dom	Cmd	hr/9	BPV
2009	A-	Spokane	4	4	0	74	76	2.67	1.15	19.6	246	32	79	3.04	2.1	9.2	4.5	0.6	137
2010	A	Hickory	8	7	0	94	62	2.59	1.16	23.4	251	30	77	2.79	1.9	5.9	3.1	0.2	100
2010	A+	Bakersfield	4	4	0	52	49	5.37	1.62	21.0	314	39	66	5.29	2.9	8.5	2.9	0.7	83
2011	A+	Myrtle Beach	9	4	0	123	98	2.27	1.06	22.7	227	29	77	2.09	2.0	7.2	3.5	0.1	124
2011	AA	Frisco	1	1	0	38	36	2.61	1.00	24.2	235	28	82	3.08	1.2	8.5	7.2	1.2	175

Short and athletic hurler who led CAR in ERA and oppBA en route to pitcher of year. Upside limited by size and delivery, but induces weak contact with deception. Keeps ball down and rarely allows HR. Changes speeds effectively with lively FB and both his hard SL and CU are legitimately solid-average. One of top control pitchers in system.

Rowland, Robby

SP | Arizona | EXP MLB DEBUT: 2014 | POTENTIAL: #4 starter | 8E

Thrws R Age 20
2010 (3) HS, (CA)

88-92	FB	+++
70-73	CB	++
80-82	SL	++

Year	Lev	Team	W	L	Sv	IP	K	ERA	WHIP	BF/G	OBA	H%	S%	xERA	Ctl	Dom	Cmd	hr/9	BPV
2010	Rk	Missoula	4	6	0	54	40	5.67	1.54	16.8	289	33	64	5.18	3.5	6.7	1.9	1.2	42
2011	Rk	Missoula	2	7	0	68	52	8.07	1.65	21.7	331	36	53	6.89	2.3	6.9	3.1	2.0	35

Lanky, projectable RHP got torched in full-season debut. At 6'6" 205, he has good size, is athletic, and features a good 88-92 mpb fastball. Complements the FB with a slow 12-6 curveball and a potentially good slider. Will likely need to decide between the curve and the slider. Look for better results in '12.

Royse, Thomas

SP | Chicago (A) | EXP MLB DEBUT: 2014 | POTENTIAL: #4 starter | 7D

Thrws R Age 23
2010 (3) Louisville

87-92	FB	+++
77-79	SL	+++
80-82	CU	++

Year	Lev	Team	W	L	Sv	IP	K	ERA	WHIP	BF/G	OBA	H%	S%	xERA	Ctl	Dom	Cmd	hr/9	BPV
2008	NCAA	Louisville	4	0	1	50	51	4.84	1.39	8.1	294	36	69	5.12	2.0	9.1	4.6	1.4	105
2009	NCAA	Louisville	3	2	2	41	48	3.50	1.09	13.4	232	33	67	2.56	2.2	10.5	4.8	0.4	159
2010	NCAA	Louisville	9	1	0	104	99	2.85	1.21	26.2	254	32	80	3.56	2.2	8.6	3.8	0.9	110
2010	Rk	Great Falls	1	1	0	34	28	3.43	1.00	13.0	226	28	66	2.34	1.6	7.4	4.7	0.5	136

Tall pitcher who missed season after TJ surgery. Relies on location and pitch movement more than stuff. Commands average, sinking FB to both sides of plate and uses tight SL as go-to secondary offering. Rarely walks hitters and provides deception with athletic delivery. Lack of formidable arm strength may lead him to relief work.

Ruffin, Chance

RP | Seattle | EXP MLB DEBUT: 2011 | POTENTIAL: Closer | 8B

Thrws R Age 23
2010 (1-S) Texas

88-93	FB	+++
78-82	SL	++++
76-80	CB	++
	CU	++

Year	Lev	Team	W	L	Sv	IP	K	ERA	WHIP	BF/G	OBA	H%	S%	xERA	Ctl	Dom	Cmd	hr/9	BPV
2010	NCAA	Texas	6	1	14	64	97	1.12	0.95	6.5	188	31	93	1.75	2.7	13.6	5.1	0.6	189
2011	AA	Erie	3	3	10	34	43	2.12	1.15	4.4	193	28	84	2.30	4.2	11.4	2.7	0.5	125
2011	AAA	Toledo	0	0	9	14	17	1.90	1.41	4.6	259	36	89	3.88	3.8	10.8	2.8	0.6	108
2011	MLB	Detroit	0	0	0	3	3	5.63	1.56	7.0	357	33	100	10.52	0.0	8.4		5.6	
2011	MLB	Seattle	1	0	0	14	15	3.86	1.57	4.7	248	31	80	4.77	5.8	9.6	1.7	1.3	60

Short and aggressive reliever who can dominate in short stints. Reached majors on basis of his potent FB/SL combination. Commands FB to get ahead of hitters and punches them out with plus SL. Slows arm speed on CU and may abandon as a result. Control comes and goes and will need to clean up before given prominent role in bullpen.

Russell, Max

SP | Los Angeles (A) | EXP MLB DEBUT: 2013 | POTENTIAL: #4 starter | 7C

Thrws L Age 23
2010 (4) Florida Southern

88-92	FB	+++
75-79	CB	+++
78-82	SL	++
	CU	+++

Year	Lev	Team	W	L	Sv	IP	K	ERA	WHIP	BF/G	OBA	H%	S%	xERA	Ctl	Dom	Cmd	hr/9	BPV
2010	Rk	Orem	4	0	0	31	31	3.46	0.96	16.9	235	29	69	2.95	0.9	8.9	10.3	1.2	244
2010	A	Cedar Rapids	2	3	0	42	30	5.34	1.50	22.7	317	34	72	6.41	1.7	6.4	3.8	2.1	45
2011	A	Cedar Rapids	5	10	0	114	85	3.79	1.28	23.4	239	27	74	3.78	3.6	6.7	1.9	1.1	54
2011	A+	Inland Empire	1	2	0	41	34	4.17	1.22	23.7	266	32	67	3.77	1.8	7.5	4.3	0.9	109

Deceptive and aggressive pitcher who allows lots of HR despite high groundball rate. Mixes four pitches well, but pitches off average FB. Slow CB may be best pitch while CT shows flashes. Has good idea on how to set up hitters and shows moxie on mound. Not overpowering by any means, but can give hitters different looks.

Ryan, Kyle — SP — Detroit

Thrws L Age 20 | 2010 (12) HS (FL) | EXP MLB DEBUT: 2015 | POTENTIAL: #4 starter | 7C

86-93	FB	+++
77-79	CB	+++
	CU	++

Year	Lev	Team	W	L	Sv	IP	K	ERA	WHIP	BF/G	OBA	H%	S%	xERA	Ctl	Dom	Cmd	hr/9	BPV
2010	Rk	GCL Tigers	2	4	0	54	46	4.17	1.31	18.6	276	35	67	3.63	2.2	7.7	3.5	0.3	110
2011	A	West Michigan	6	10	0	137	99	3.15	1.28	23.4	273	33	74	3.38	2.0	6.5	3.3	0.2	103

Tall and lean pitcher with nice projection. Doesn't throw hard, but uses low three-quarters slot to keep hitters off-guard. Keeps ball low and induces fair share of grounders. Lacks an out pitch, but can get hitters to chase slow CB. Not much separation between FB and CU. Throws strikes and pitches to contact.

Salcedo, Adrian — SP — Minnesota

Thrws R Age 21 | 2007 FA (DR) | EXP MLB DEBUT: 2014 | POTENTIAL: #3 starter | 8C

89-93	FB	+++
77-79	CB	++
80-83	SL	+++
	CU	+++

Year	Lev	Team	W	L	Sv	IP	K	ERA	WHIP	BF/G	OBA	H%	S%	xERA	Ctl	Dom	Cmd	hr/9	BPV
2009	Rk	GCL Twins	3	2	0	61	58	1.47	1.03	21.4	258	34	85	2.48	0.4	8.5	19.3	0.1	456
2010	Rk	Elizabethton	4	3	1	66	65	3.27	0.98	15.7	228	30	66	2.22	1.4	8.9	6.5	0.4	187
2010	A+	Fort Myers	1	3	0	27	16	6.31	1.85	21.1	355	39	66	6.88	2.7	5.3	2.0	1.0	28
2011	A	Beloit	6	6	0	135	92	2.93	1.17	18.6	256	31	74	2.95	1.8	6.1	3.4	0.3	104

Tall and thin pitcher who fits MIN mold by commanding strike zone and possessing nice CU. Quick arm action produces pitch movement and clean delivery offers projection. Uses two breaking balls and SL currently better than CB. Doesn't miss bats that stuff would suggest, but upside remains.

Sampson, Keyvius — SP — San Diego

Thrws R Age 21 | 2009 (4) HS, (FL) | EXP MLB DEBUT: 2014 | POTENTIAL: #3 starter | 8C

90-93	FB	++++
73-75	CB	+++
	CU	++

Year	Lev	Team	W	L	Sv	IP	K	ERA	WHIP	BF/G	OBA	H%	S%	xERA	Ctl	Dom	Cmd	hr/9	BPV
2009	Rk	AZL Padres	0	0	0	3	3	3.00	0.33	4.7	106	15	0		0.0	9.0		0.0	
2009	A-	Eugene	0	0	0	5	5	3.60	1.20	10.1	175	25	67	1.76	5.4	9.0	1.7	0.0	109
2010	A-	Eugene	3	3	0	43	58	3.56	1.21	17.3	224	33	73	3.10	3.6	12.1	3.4	0.8	130
2011	A	Fort Wayne	12	3	0	118	143	2.90	1.10	19.3	196	28	75	2.29	3.7	10.9	2.9	0.6	124

Short, athletic righty uses a 90-94 mph fastball with good late movement to dominate. Fastball showed more velocity in '11. Also throws an average curveball and a plus change-up. Showed solid mechanics and decent command. Will vary arm slot and needs to mix in his off-speed pitches more frequently and effectively, but the upside is very good.

Sanchez, Aaron — SP — Toronto

Thrws R Age 19 | 2010 (1-S) HS (CA) | EXP MLB DEBUT: 2015 | POTENTIAL: #3 starter | 8D

88-95	FB	++++
77-81	CB	+++
	CU	++

Year	Lev	Team	W	L	Sv	IP	K	ERA	WHIP	BF/G	OBA	H%	S%	xERA	Ctl	Dom	Cmd	hr/9	BPV
2010	Rk	GCL Blue Jays	0	2	0	19	28	1.42	1.63	10.6	262	41	93	4.31	5.7	13.3	2.3	0.5	117
2010	A-	Auburn	0	1	0	6	9	4.50	1.50	13.0	191	34	67	2.65	7.5	13.5	1.8	0.0	136
2011	Rk	Bluefield	3	2	1	42	43	5.55	1.49	16.5	274	35	63	4.53	3.8	9.2	2.4	0.9	80
2011	A-	Vancouver	0	1	0	11	13	4.82	1.43	15.9	202	30	63	2.62	6.4	10.4	1.6	0.0	111

Tall and very projectable pitcher who uses mid three-quarters arm slot and height well to throw downhill. Velocity has increased, but moving parts in delivery create command issues at times. Release point has been inconsistent, but can snap off excellent CB that shows glimpses of becoming second plus pitch. CU remains below average.

Sanchez, Angel — SP — Los Angeles (N)

Thrws R Age 22 | 2010 NDFA D.R. | EXP MLB DEBUT: 2014 | POTENTIAL: #2 starter | 8D

90-94	FB	+++
	CB	+++
	CU	++++

Year	Lev	Team	W	L	Sv	IP	K	ERA	WHIP	BF/G	OBA	H%	S%	xERA	Ctl	Dom	Cmd	hr/9	BPV
2011	A	Great Lakes	8	4	0	99	84	2.82	1.12	19.5	205	26	75	2.34	3.5	7.6	2.2	0.5	91

Tall, slender, athletic hurler had an impressive showing in the MWL. Fastball sits in the 90-94 mph range and tops out at 95. Complements it with a plus change-up and a decent curveball. At 6'3" 175 lbs., he has room for growth and additional velocity. Still some work to do, but a very impressive debut.

Sanchez, Eduardo — RP — St. Louis

Thrws R Age 23 | 2005 NDFA Venz. | EXP MLB DEBUT: 2011 | POTENTIAL: Future closer | 8A

95-97	FB	++++
	SL	++++

Year	Lev	Team	W	L	Sv	IP	K	ERA	WHIP	BF/G	OBA	H%	S%	xERA	Ctl	Dom	Cmd	hr/9	BPV
2010	AA	Springfield	1	1	11	26	27	3.12	1.15	4.3	231	30	75	2.94	2.8	9.3	3.4	0.7	115
2010	AAA	Memphis	0	0	3	27	31	1.67	1.15	4.1	200	27	90	2.52	4.0	10.3	2.6	0.7	111
2011	AA	Springfield	0	1	0	4	3	4.39	1.22	5.5	206	26	60	2.18	4.4	6.6	1.5	0.0	85
2011	AAA	Memphis	1	0	0	3	3	0.00	0.00	4.2	0	0			0.0	9.0		0.0	
2011	MLB	St. Louis	3	1	5	30	35	1.80	1.00	4.4	142	21	83	1.17	4.8	10.5	2.2	0.3	127

Short, wiry reliever generates plus velocity. His fastball sits at 95-97 mph and tops out at 99. He also throws a nice slider that plays up because of the fastball velocity. Despite his size he is able to keep the ball down and overpower hitters. He dominated at every level in '11, likely has a secure spot in the Cardinals pen and has the potential to close.

Santiago, Hector — SP — Chicago (A)

Thrws L Age 24 | 2006 (30) Okaloosa-Walton JC | EXP MLB DEBUT: 2011 | POTENTIAL: #4 starter | 7D

88-93	FB	+++
77-80	CB	+++
	CU	+++

Year	Lev	Team	W	L	Sv	IP	K	ERA	WHIP	BF/G	OBA	H%	S%	xERA	Ctl	Dom	Cmd	hr/9	BPV
2009	A+	Winston-Salem	4	4	1	58	66	3.88	1.36	6.4	248	33	73	3.76	3.9	10.2	2.6	0.8	99
2010	A+	Winston-Salem	4	5	2	60	61	4.19	1.36	6.8	271	35	69	3.91	2.8	9.1	3.2	0.6	105
2011	A+	Winston-Salem	2	3	0	44	43	3.68	1.18	22.0	234	28	76	3.76	2.9	8.8	3.1	1.4	82
2011	AA	Birmingham	7	5	0	83	74	3.57	1.32	23.0	233	29	73	3.16	4.2	8.0	1.9	0.4	83
2011	MLB	Chicago Wsox	0	0	0	5	2	0.00	0.39	8.2	65	7	100	0.00	1.8	3.5	2.0	0.0	105

Short and strong pitcher who converted to starter. Has stamina and arm strength to maintain velocity and generally pitches off FB early in count. Pitches inside effectively and can pepper outer half of plate with CU with screwball action. Very tough on LHH and could be solid lefty specialist at worst. May not have dependable CB, but FB/CU combo is stellar.

Satterwhite, Cody — RP — Detroit

Thrws R Age 25 | 2008 (2) Mississippi | EXP MLB DEBUT: 2013 | POTENTIAL: Closer | 8D

90-96	FB	+++
81-85	SL	+++
80-82	CU	+++

Year	Lev	Team	W	L	Sv	IP	K	ERA	WHIP	BF/G	OBA	H%	S%	xERA	Ctl	Dom	Cmd	hr/9	BPV
2008	NCAA	Mississippi	3	5	0	72	55	5.36	1.65	20.2	285	31	72	5.82	4.7	6.9	1.4	1.6	21
2008	Rk	GCL Tigers	0	0	1	2	2	0.00	2.38	3.6	403	50	100	8.20	4.3	8.6	2.0	0.0	68
2008	A+	Lakeland	0	0	2	18	22	4.48	1.55	4.6	239	36	68	3.37	6.0	10.9	1.8	0.0	111
2009	AA	Erie	4	6	12	49	52	3.48	1.49	6.2	249	32	79	4.23	4.9	9.5	1.9	0.9	75
2011	Rk	GCL Tigers	0	0	1	10	10	3.60	1.50	5.4	316	42	73	4.37	1.8	9.0	5.0	0.0	151

Tall and projectable reliever with demeanor and arsenal to close games, but cannot stay healthy. Limited time in past two years due to shoulder surgery, though DET has hope that velocity will return. Not much movement to FB, but has velocity to pitch up. Combines FB with hard SL that serves as K pitch. Max-effort delivery doesn't help health.

Scahill, Rob — SP — Colorado

Thrws R Age 24 | 2009 (8) Bradley | EXP MLB DEBUT: 2012 | POTENTIAL: Power reliever | 7D

90-95	FB	+++
83-86	SL	+++
	CU	++

Year	Lev	Team	W	L	Sv	IP	K	ERA	WHIP	BF/G	OBA	H%	S%	xERA	Ctl	Dom	Cmd	hr/9	BPV
2008	NCAA	Bradley	4	6	0	83	79	5.52	1.43	25.3	250	31	61	3.95	4.4	8.5	1.9	0.8	74
2009	NCAA	Bradley	3	3	0	60	59	4.05	1.42	25.4	245	33	69	3.29	4.5	8.9	2.0	0.2	96
2009	A-	Tri-City	1	4	0	63	58	3.14	1.24	17.0	246	32	74	2.98	2.9	8.3	2.9	0.3	108
2010	A+	Modesto	10	7	0	156	140	4.73	1.49	24.9	282	35	67	4.33	3.4	8.1	2.4	0.5	81
2011	AA	Tulsa	12	11	0	160	104	3.93	1.40	25.0	266	30	73	4.05	3.4	5.8	1.7	0.7	53

Strong-armed righty has a nice 90-94 mph fastball with good sinking action. Compliments the fastball with nice slider. Scahill survived the CAL by keeping the ball down in the zone and generating groundball outs. He also has a power slider and a curveball. None are above-average and there isn't much margin for error.

Scarpetta, Cody — SP — Milwaukee

Thrws R Age 23 | 2007 (11) HS, (IL) | EXP MLB DEBUT: 2014 | POTENTIAL: #3 starter | 8D

90-94	FB	++++
75-78	CB	+++
	CU	++

Year	Lev	Team	W	L	Sv	IP	K	ERA	WHIP	BF/G	OBA	H%	S%	xERA	Ctl	Dom	Cmd	hr/9	BPV
2008	Rk	AZL Brewers	1	0	0	15	27	0.59	1.05	9.8	157	34	94	1.12	4.7	16.0	3.4	0.0	190
2009	A	Wisconsin	4	11	0	105	116	3.43	1.31	16.7	219	30	74	2.94	4.7	9.9	2.1	0.4	102
2009	AA	Huntsville	0	0	0	5	1	5.40	1.20	20.1	262	23	60	4.58	1.8	1.8	1.0	1.8	-20
2010	A+	Brevard County	7	12	0	128	142	3.87	1.46	20.3	250	35	72	3.57	4.7	10.0	2.1	0.3	101
2011	AA	Huntsville	8	5	0	117	98	3.85	1.38	21.3	233	28	73	3.47	4.7	7.5	1.6	0.6	69

Big, stocky pitcher has plus raw stuff, but struggled with command. He has a nice 90-94 mph sinking FB and also throws a good, hard 12-6 CB and a CU that flashes as plus. Command issues will catch up with him eventually, but so far he has been effectively wild and has yet to post an ERA over 4.00 as a professional.

Scheppers, Tanner — RP — Texas

Thrws R Age 25 | 2009 (1) Fresno State | EXP MLB DEBUT: 2012 | POTENTIAL: Closer | 9D

90-98	FB	++++
82-84	CB	++
86-89	SL	+++
81-85	CU	++

Year	Lev	Team	W	L	Sv	IP	K	ERA	WHIP	BF/G	OBA	H%	S%	xERA	Ctl	Dom	Cmd	hr/9	BPV
2008	NCAA	Fresno State	8	2	1	70	109	2.95	1.25	23.8	214	36	77	2.77	4.4	14.0	3.2	0.5	148
2010	AA	Frisco	0	0	2	11	19	0.82	0.27	5.7	88	14	100		0.0	15.5		0.8	
2010	AAA	Oklahoma City	1	3	4	69	71	5.48	1.62	10.2	296	38	65	5.00	3.9	9.3	2.4	0.7	81
2011	AA	Frisco	2	1	0	23	24	3.13	1.17	5.4	217	29	73	2.54	3.5	9.4	2.7	0.4	112
2011	AAA	Round Rock	2	0	2	20	20	4.46	1.73	8.4	288	38	71	4.53	5.3	8.9	1.7	0.0	86

Tall and aggressive reliever missed time early with back injury and returned with customary delivery and command issues. Possesses one of top FB in minors. 4-seam FB exhibits nasty late life and hard slider registers strikeouts. Often overthrows which leads to mechanical problems. Starting role may be out of question due to lack of offspeed offering.

Schmidt, Nick — SP — Colorado

EXP MLB DEBUT: 2012 | POTENTIAL: #4 starter | **6C**

Thrws L Age 26
2007 (1) Arkansas

Velo	Pitch	Grade
87-91	FB	++
77-80	CB	+++
79-81	CU	+++

Year	Lev	Team	W	L	Sv	IP	K	ERA	WHIP	BF/G	OBA	H%	S%	xERA	Ctl	Dom	Cmd	hr/9	BPV
2009	A	Fort Wayne	4	0	0	51	59	2.81	1.19	15.8	208	31	74	2.10	4.0	10.4	2.6	0.0	129
2009	A+	Lake Elsinore	2	8	0	48	27	7.88	1.98	20.9	334	36	60	7.16	5.1	5.1	1.0	1.3	0
2010	A+	Lake Elsinore	6	9	0	97	87	4.36	1.41	17.1	256	33	68	3.62	4.0	8.1	2.0	0.4	84
2011	Rk	AZL Padres	1	1	0	8	9	4.50	1.38	16.8	262	37	64	3.25	3.4	10.1	3.0	0.0	126
2011	A+	Lake Elsinore	3	5	0	63	58	3.85	1.35	21.9	258	31	74	4.09	3.3	8.3	2.5	1.0	76

Projectable pitcher who relies on command, movement, and ability to change speeds. Needs to prove he can stay healthy as he logged only 14 starts in '11. Repeats delivery well, has a plus change-up and keeps ball low with sinking fastball. Will need to be more efficient with pitches. Struggled in the AFL so the odds are long.

Shafer, Aaron — SP — Atlanta

EXP MLB DEBUT: 2012 | POTENTIAL: #5 starter | **6C**

Thrws R Age 25
2008 (2) Wichita St

Velo	Pitch	Grade
88-92	FB	+++
72-75	CB	++
79-81	CU	++++

Year	Lev	Team	W	L	Sv	IP	K	ERA	WHIP	BF/G	OBA	H%	S%	xERA	Ctl	Dom	Cmd	hr/9	BPV
2009	A	Peoria	11	8	0	116	81	4.50	1.32	19.2	271	30	68	4.30	2.4	6.3	2.6	1.1	61
2010	A+	Daytona	2	1	5	46	47	0.97	0.84	7.1	182	25	89	1.12	1.9	9.2	4.7	0.2	166
2010	AA	Tennessee	2	2	2	34	30	5.03	1.29	5.6	262	32	61	3.81	2.6	7.9	3.0	0.8	89
2011	A+	Lynchburg	3	3	0	65	40	3.05	1.31	24.4	250	29	77	3.35	3.3	5.5	1.7	0.4	61
2011	AA	Mississippi	3	2	0	44	37	4.69	1.50	27.2	295	36	67	4.44	2.9	7.6	2.6	0.4	85

Tall, athletic pitcher with smooth arm action and a repeatable three-quarters delivery. Fastball has late life but velocity is fringe at best. He changes speeds effectively and uses all quadrants of the strike zone. Curveball needs better rotation. At 25, looks like a 5th starter at best.

Shipers, Jordan — SP — Seattle

EXP MLB DEBUT: 2014 | POTENTIAL: #4 starter | **7C**

Thrws L Age 21
2010 (16) HS (MO)

Velo	Pitch	Grade
88-92	FB	+++
80-82	SL	++
78-81	CU	+++

Year	Lev	Team	W	L	Sv	IP	K	ERA	WHIP	BF/G	OBA	H%	S%	xERA	Ctl	Dom	Cmd	hr/9	BPV
2011	A-	Everett	1	5	0	49	47	4.76	1.54	21.5	265	33	69	4.42	4.8	8.6	1.8	0.7	70

Short and lean pitcher with advanced feel for pitching, but hasn't yet translated to success. Pitches backwards at times and uses CU early in count to set up average FB. Generally commands pitches, but control can waver when attempting to overthrow. Pitches with effort and will need to smooth out arm action.

Shoemaker, Matt — SP — Los Angeles (A)

EXP MLB DEBUT: 2012 | POTENTIAL: #4 starter | **7B**

Thrws R Age 25
2008 FA (Eastern Michigan)

Velo	Pitch	Grade
87-92	FB	+++
78-80	CB	+++
	CU	+++

Year	Lev	Team	W	L	Sv	IP	K	ERA	WHIP	BF/G	OBA	H%	S%	xERA	Ctl	Dom	Cmd	hr/9	BPV
2009	A+	Rancho Cucam	1	0	0	17	13	3.16	0.88	21.1	225	25	69	2.54	0.5	6.8	13.0	1.1	292
2010	A+	Rancho Cucam	7	8	0	122	119	4.94	1.45	26.1	286	35	67	4.77	2.9	8.8	3.1	1.0	84
2010	AAA	Salt Lake	2	1	0	15	9	5.96	1.85	23.5	320	37	64	5.37	4.8	5.4	1.1	0.0	47
2011	AA	Arkansas	12	5	0	156	129	2.48	1.07	26.4	231	27	83	3.02	2.0	7.4	3.7	1.0	101
2011	AAA	Salt Lake	0	2	0	21	12	8.14	1.90	24.8	321	35	57	6.73	5.1	5.1	1.0	1.3	4

Tall and strong pitcher who was TL pitcher of year after finishing 1st in ERA and Ks. Got bombed in Triple-A, but exhibits above average feel for pitching. Lacks a plus pitch but throws quality strikes and commands FB to both sides of plate. Lacks big break in CB, but is effective against RHH.

Shreve, Colby — SP — Philadelphia

EXP MLB DEBUT: 2013 | POTENTIAL: Reliever | **7C**

Thrws R Age 24
2008 (6) S Nevada CC

Velo	Pitch	Grade
89-95	FB	++++
80-83	SL	++
79-82	CU	+++

Year	Lev	Team	W	L	Sv	IP	K	ERA	WHIP	BF/G	OBA	H%	S%	xERA	Ctl	Dom	Cmd	hr/9	BPV
2010	A	Lakewood	7	5	0	109	76	3.96	1.15	18.8	236	27	68	3.22	2.5	6.3	2.5	0.9	71
2011	A	Lakewood	5	5	2	72	65	2.75	1.36	9.1	259	33	81	3.67	3.4	8.1	2.4	0.5	87
2011	A+	Clearwater	1	1	0	12	14	3.69	1.56	7.6	317	39	88	6.61	2.2	10.3	4.7	2.2	85

Tall, slender (6'5" 200 lbs.) right-handed reliever put up solid numbers at Low and High-A in '11. Has a lively 90-95 mph fastball and a nice slider. Shows and ability to mix speeds well, but needs to spin ball better and repeat his arm slot. Struggled against more advanced hitters in the AFL and will need to prove he can get Double-A hitters out.

Simmons, Crawford — SP — Kansas City

EXP MLB DEBUT: 2014 | POTENTIAL: #3 starter | **8E**

Thrws L Age 21
2009 (14) HS (GA)

Velo	Pitch	Grade
86-91	FB	+++
77-79	CB	++
78-81	CU	++++

Year	Lev	Team	W	L	Sv	IP	K	ERA	WHIP	BF/G	OBA	H%	S%	xERA	Ctl	Dom	Cmd	hr/9	BPV
2010	Rk	Burlington	6	2	0	78	70	2.77	1.04	21.5	220	27	77	2.64	2.2	8.1	3.7	0.8	113
2011	Rk	AZL Royals	0	0	0	1	1	9.00	2.00	4.8	415	52	50	7.49	0.0	9.0		0.0	
2011	A	Kane County	0	3	0	10	12	7.13	1.88	15.8	313	44	58	5.28	5.3	10.7	2.0	0.0	98

Athletic and efficient pitcher who nursed elbow injury and didn't see much game action. Has pitchability of a veteran but needs time to develop breaking ball and increase velocity. FB is merely average, though could throw harder with minor adjustments in delivery. CU is best present offering and can throw strikes with any pitch.

Simon, Kyle — SP — Baltimore

EXP MLB DEBUT: 2014 | POTENTIAL: #4 starter | **7C**

Thrws R Age 21
2011 (4) Arizona

Velo	Pitch	Grade
86-93	FB	+++
83-87	CT	+++
81-83	SL	++
	CU	+++

Year	Lev	Team	W	L	Sv	IP	K	ERA	WHIP	BF/G	OBA	H%	S%	xERA	Ctl	Dom	Cmd	hr/9	BPV
2009	NCAA	Arizona	3	5	0	74	42	6.06	1.78	18.0	336	38	64	5.80	3.2	5.1	1.6	0.4	41
2010	NCAA	Arizona	8	6	0	109	62	4.29	1.55	25.1	300	34	73	4.91	3.0	5.1	1.7	0.7	41
2011	NCAA	Arizona	11	3	0	129	86	2.72	0.97	25.7	239	29	70	2.09	0.8	6.0	7.8	0.1	203
2011	A-	Aberdeen	1	0	1	8	2	0.00	0.75	4.8	117	13	100	0.09	3.4	2.3	0.7	0.0	59
2011	A	Delmarva	0	2	0	8	7	4.39	0.98	3.9	206	24	57	2.59	2.2	7.7	3.5	1.1	100

Tall and durable pitcher who began pro career as RP, but will likely return to starting. Works off sinker and can use number of secondary pitches to keep hitters guessing. Can cut and sink FB to both sides of plate. Throws with easy arm action and offers hint of deception with high arm slot. Not likely to post high Dom, but will be groundballer.

Simpson, Hayden — SP — Chicago (N)

EXP MLB DEBUT: 2013 | POTENTIAL: #3 starter | **8D**

Thrws R Age 23
2010 (1) S. Arkansas

Velo	Pitch	Grade
90-93	FB	++++
82-84	SL	+++
	CB	+++
	CU	++

Year	Lev	Team	W	L	Sv	IP	K	ERA	WHIP	BF/G	OBA	H%	S%	xERA	Ctl	Dom	Cmd	hr/9	BPV
2011	Rk	AZL Cubs	0	4	0	17	11	8.37	2.15	7.8	349	40	58	7.10	5.8	5.8	1.0	0.5	25
2011	A	Peoria	1	6	0	61	46	5.74	1.69	17.2	306	35	68	5.96	4.0	6.8	1.7	1.3	30

Smallish righty has shown nothing to justify high pick. Features a 90-93 mph fastball that tops out at 96 and complements with a good slider and a curveball. Struggled in the pitcher-friendly MWL. Still some potential, but so far we have seen little of it.

Sisco, Jake — SP — Cleveland

EXP MLB DEBUT: 2014 | POTENTIAL: #2 starter | **9D**

Thrws R Age 20
2011 (3) Merced JC

Velo	Pitch	Grade
90-95	FB	+++
77-81	CB	+++
80-84	SL	++++
	CU	++

Year	Lev	Team	W	L	Sv	IP	K	ERA	WHIP	BF/G	OBA	H%	S%	xERA	Ctl	Dom	Cmd	hr/9	BPV
2011	Rk	AZL Indians	2	4	0	34	31	5.28	1.67	12.8	294	38	65	4.47	4.5	8.2	1.8	0.0	84

Lean and projectable hurler with deep arsenal of average to above-average offerings. SL is best pitch and can get hitters to chase out of zone. FB exhibits good velocity and movement. Arm action and frame suggest more velocity forthcoming. Inconsistent CU can be good pitch, but can slow arm speed and hitters get good looks.

Skaggs, Tyler — SP — Arizona

EXP MLB DEBUT: 2012 | POTENTIAL: #2 starter | **8B**

Thrws L Age 20
2009 (1-S) HS, (CA)

Velo	Pitch	Grade
87-92	FB	++++
70-73	CB	+++
	SL	++
	CU	++

Year	Lev	Team	W	L	Sv	IP	K	ERA	WHIP	BF/G	OBA	H%	S%	xERA	Ctl	Dom	Cmd	hr/9	BPV
2009	Rk	AZL Angels	0	0	0	6	7	0.00	0.83	7.3	191	29	100	1.00	1.5	10.5	7.0	0.0	227
2010	A	Cedar Rapids	8	4	0	82	82	3.62	1.21	17.4	252	33	71	3.32	2.3	9.0	3.9	0.7	121
2010	A	South Bend	1	1	0	16	20	1.69	1.06	15.5	224	32	88	2.48	2.3	11.3	5.0	0.6	166
2011	A+	Visalia	5	5	0	100	125	3.23	1.15	23.4	223	32	72	2.66	3.1	11.2	3.7	0.5	139
2011	AA	Mobile	4	1	0	57	73	2.52	1.05	22.1	218	32	79	2.44	2.4	11.5	4.9	0.6	164

Tall, lanky lefty with easy velocity and smooth mechanics. FB sits at 88-92 mph with good deception; he locates it well and isn't afraid to pitch inside. CBI is plus and enabled him to dominate. Can rush delivery at times and SL and CU are only average, but fastball and curveball give him two above-average offerings.

Slaats, Josh — SP — Colorado

EXP MLB DEBUT: 2013 | POTENTIAL: #4 starter | **7C**

Thrws R Age 23
2010 (5) Hawaii

Velo	Pitch	Grade
88-93	FB	+++
	SL	+++
	CU	+++

Year	Lev	Team	W	L	Sv	IP	K	ERA	WHIP	BF/G	OBA	H%	S%	xERA	Ctl	Dom	Cmd	hr/9	BPV
2008	NCAA	Hawaii	0	5	1	39	24	7.14	2.07	14.7	312	36	63	6.22	7.1	5.5	0.8	0.5	28
2009	NCAA	Hawaii	2	2	4	27	30	8.33	1.70	6.8	276	37	48	4.90	5.7	10.0	1.8	0.7	77
2010	NCAA	Hawaii	5	4	0	74	75	3.77	1.42	18.5	257	35	71	3.41	4.0	9.1	2.3	0.1	103
2010	A-	Tri-City	1	3	0	32	42	1.96	0.93	15.1	181	27	82	1.65	2.8	11.8	4.2	0.6	161
2011	A	Asheville	7	3	0	125	103	4.18	1.49	24.5	277	33	74	4.59	3.7	7.4	2.0	0.9	61

Big and strong, he has a nice low-90s fastball, slider, and change-up. The slider and change-up need refinement, but has the stuff to emerge as a solid mid-rotation starter. His curve can be plus at times, but is still inconsistent. Will need to show better command as he moves up, but he has some nice potential.

Slama, Anthony — RP — Minnesota

EXP MLB DEBUT: 2010 | POTENTIAL: Setup reliever | 7D

Thrws R Age 28
2006 (39) San Diego

Velo	Pitch	Grade
87-93	FB	+++
72-76	SL	+++
80-84	CU	+

Year	Lev	Team	W	L	Sv	IP	K	ERA	WHIP	BF/G	OBA	H%	S%	xERA	Ctl	Dom	Cmd	hr/9	BPV
2009	AAA	Rochester	0	2	4	15	19	3.55	1.25	5.6	204	32	68	2.19	4.7	11.3	2.4	0.0	132
2010	AAA	Rochester	2	2	17	65	74	2.21	1.12	4.8	183	25	84	2.28	4.4	10.2	2.3	0.7	108
2010	MLB	Minnesota	0	1	0	4	5	8.57	2.62	4.6	336	42	70	9.53	10.7	10.7	1.0	2.1	9
2011	AAA	Rochester	3	2	1	37	42	2.92	1.16	5.5	206	27	79	2.91	3.9	10.2	2.6	1.0	101
2011	MLB	Minnesota	0	0	0	2	3	0.00	0.95	4.0	0	0	100		8.6	12.9	1.5	0.0	164

Strong-framed and aggressive reliever who missed 2H with elbow ailment. Stats are better than true skills. Doesn't have plus pitch and has erratic FB command. Struggles with release point and has been flyball pitcher. Offers deceptive delivery, pitch movement, and hard SL that have been very effective against RHH.

Smith, Eric — SP — Arizona

EXP MLB DEBUT: 2012 | POTENTIAL: #4 starter | 7D

Thrws R Age 23
2009 (2) Rhode Island

Velo	Pitch	Grade
88-92	FB	+++
84-87	SL	+++
80-82	CU	+++

Year	Lev	Team	W	L	Sv	IP	K	ERA	WHIP	BF/G	OBA	H%	S%	xERA	Ctl	Dom	Cmd	hr/9	BPV
2009	Rk	Missoula	0	3	0	25	21	4.29	1.51	12.1	236	30	70	3.61	5.7	7.5	1.3	0.4	70
2009	A	South Bend	0	0	0	16	10	2.80	1.37	22.5	261	28	85	4.31	3.4	5.6	1.7	1.1	38
2010	A	South Bend	5	5	0	86	65	3.55	1.36	22.5	259	31	73	3.59	3.3	6.8	2.0	0.4	74
2010	A+	Visalia	4	4	0	50	36	5.02	1.71	22.8	283	33	71	5.12	5.4	6.5	1.2	0.7	41
2011	A+	Visalia	5	13	0	150	103	6.36	1.89	25.3	320	37	65	6.08	5.1	6.2	1.2	0.7	34

Athletic starter got torched in full season in the CAL. Does have a nice 90-93 fastball, a good slider and solid change-up. He will remain a starter for now, though he did relieve in the past. Sub-par command continues to be his nemesis (85 BB/103 K). Nothing else is going to get better until he shows improvement.

Smith, Will — SP — Kansas City

EXP MLB DEBUT: 2013 | POTENTIAL: #3 starter | 8D

Thrws L Age 22
2007 (8) Gulf Coast CC

Velo	Pitch	Grade
87-93	FB	+++
74-80	CB	+++
78-82	CU	++

Year	Lev	Team	W	L	Sv	IP	K	ERA	WHIP	BF/G	OBA	H%	S%	xERA	Ctl	Dom	Cmd	hr/9	BPV
2010	A+	Rancho Cucam	2	2	0	37	31	4.61	1.32	25.6	256	30	67	3.97	3.2	7.5	2.4	1.0	70
2010	AA	Arkansas	1	2	0	18	8	7.42	2.31	23.3	391	41	69	9.21	4.5	4.0	0.9	1.5	-25
2010	AAA	Salt Lake	2	4	0	53	40	5.60	1.60	26.1	303	35	66	5.42	3.4	6.8	2.0	1.0	47
2010	A+	Wilmington	4	1	0	54	51	2.82	0.96	25.6	239	29	76	2.85	0.7	8.5	12.8	1.0	296
2011	AA	NW Arkansas	13	9	0	161	108	3.85	1.34	24.8	273	31	72	4.05	2.5	6.0	2.4	0.7	65

Tall and physical lefty who relies on groundballs and ability to retire LHH. Gets ahead of hitters consistently with reliable FB that he locates to both sides of plate and drops in quality CB for strikes. Hasn't yet developed pitch to tackle RHH. Not a high Dom pitcher, but has stamina to pitch deep into games.

Smoker, Josh — RP — Washington

EXP MLB DEBUT: 2013 | POTENTIAL: reliever | 6C

Thrws L Age 23
2007 (1-S) HS (GA)

Velo	Pitch	Grade
85-89	FB	+++
78-81	SL	++
72-76	CB	+++
81-83	SP	+++

Year	Lev	Team	W	L	Sv	IP	K	ERA	WHIP	BF/G	OBA	H%	S%	xERA	Ctl	Dom	Cmd	hr/9	BPV
2008	Rk	GCL Nationals	2	1	0	26	16	1.38	1.26	17.8	214	26	88	2.40	4.5	5.5	1.2	0.0	71
2008	A	Hagerstown	0	4	0	18	21	11.50	2.22	18.2	379	47	49	9.65	4.5	10.5	2.3	2.5	16
2009	Rk	GCL Nationals	4	2	0	42	31	3.41	1.33	17.5	279	33	74	3.80	2.1	6.6	3.1	0.4	91
2010	A	Hagerstown	3	10	3	91	92	6.52	1.78	14.0	292	36	65	6.10	5.5	9.1	1.6	1.5	41
2011	A+	Potomac	5	2	2	50	56	2.33	1.37	4.6	184	25	86	2.96	6.6	10.0	1.5	0.7	89

Former 1st round pick pitched exclusively in relief in '11 with positive results. His fastball velocity now sits in the 88-92 mph range and he also throws a slider, curveball, change-up, and splitter. That mix of pitches doesn't help as much in relief, but he made steady progress and still has some potential.

Smyly, Drew — SP — Detroit

EXP MLB DEBUT: 2012 | POTENTIAL: #3 starter | 8C

Thrws L Age 23
2010 (2) Arkansas

Velo	Pitch	Grade
87-93	FB	+++
80-83	SL	+++
75-79	CB	+++
	CU	+++

Year	Lev	Team	W	L	Sv	IP	K	ERA	WHIP	BF/G	OBA	H%	S%	xERA	Ctl	Dom	Cmd	hr/9	BPV
2009	NCAA	Arkansas	3	1	0	58	60	4.66	1.41	15.3	258	33	68	4.18	3.9	9.3	2.4	0.9	82
2010	NCAA	Arkansas	9	1	0	103	114	2.80	1.17	22.9	226	30	81	3.19	3.1	10.0	3.2	1.0	107
2011	A+	Lakeland	7	3	0	80	77	2.58	1.15	22.7	239	32	76	2.50	2.4	8.7	3.7	0.1	133
2011	AA	Erie	4	3	0	45	53	1.19	1.04	21.8	201	29	89	1.81	3.0	10.6	3.5	0.2	146

DET minor league pitcher of year after breakout performance. Exhibits polish with deep arsenal and prefers to pitch to contact. Can register Ks with CB and CU, though Dom may decline at higher levels as neither are plus pitches. FB velocity is fine and shows excellent movement. Doesn't allow many HR and works quickly.

Snell, Blake — SP — Tampa Bay

EXP MLB DEBUT: 2015 | POTENTIAL: #3 starter | 8E

Thrws L Age 19
2011 (1-S) HS (WA)

Velo	Pitch	Grade
87-92	FB	+++
78-80	CB	+++
	CU	+++

Year	Lev	Team	W	L	Sv	IP	K	ERA	WHIP	BF/G	OBA	H%	S%	xERA	Ctl	Dom	Cmd	hr/9	BPV
2011	Rk	GCL Rays	1	2	0	26	26	3.10	1.57	10.4	290	39	78	4.15	3.8	9.0	2.4	0.0	101

Tall and lean starter who uses height to create downward angle to plate. Velocity is merely average, but has some projection left. Lives in bottom half of strike zone with sinker and adds average CB and CU to mix. Similar to other youngsters, needs innings to generate consistent secondary offerings. Has chance to be special, but needs time.

Snodgress, Scott — SP — Chicago (A)

EXP MLB DEBUT: 2013 | POTENTIAL: #4 starter | 7B

Thrws L Age 22
2011 (5) Stanford

Velo	Pitch	Grade
90-94	FB	+++
80-82	CB	+++
	CU	++

Year	Lev	Team	W	L	Sv	IP	K	ERA	WHIP	BF/G	OBA	H%	S%	xERA	Ctl	Dom	Cmd	hr/9	BPV
2009	NCAA	Stanford	1	3	1	32	17	5.89	1.65	8.4	312	34	64	5.52	3.4	4.8	1.4	0.8	26
2010	NCAA	Stanford	1	2	1	37	38	5.59	1.68	7.6	240	32	65	4.19	7.1	9.2	1.3	0.5	75
2011	NCAA	Stanford	2	2	2	31	38	4.65	1.77	5.7	236	34	72	4.18	8.1	11.0	1.4	0.3	94
2011	Rk	Great Falls	3	3	0	59	68	3.35	1.32	15.3	268	36	77	3.91	2.6	10.4	4.0	0.8	125

Athletic and tall pitcher with projectable frame, though arm action not conducive to more velocity. Works off sneaky quick FB and mixes in average CB for good measure, though doesn't command FB well. Will need better CU to stay in rotation and offers mediocre upside despite success in first pro season.

Snow, Forrest — RP — Seattle

EXP MLB DEBUT: 2012 | POTENTIAL: Setup reliever | 7B

Thrws R Age 23
2010 (36) Washington

Velo	Pitch	Grade
87-95	FB	++++
80-83	CB	++
74-77	CU	+++

Year	Lev	Team	W	L	Sv	IP	K	ERA	WHIP	BF/G	OBA	H%	S%	xERA	Ctl	Dom	Cmd	hr/9	BPV
2010	A-	Everett	0	0	3	25	26	0.00	0.68	8.8	102	15	100	0.00	3.2	9.3	2.9	0.0	151
2010	A	Clinton	0	1	6	20	26	1.35	0.80	4.8	138	21	87	0.75	3.2	11.7	3.7	0.5	162
2011	A	Clinton	2	7	0	74	71	3.64	1.09	22.3	229	30	66	2.57	2.3	8.6	3.7	0.5	125
2011	A+	High Desert	2	3	0	33	20	8.16	1.87	25.9	344	36	58	7.62	3.5	5.4	1.5	1.9	-6
2011	AAA	Tacoma	1	2	0	35	36	5.38	1.25	15.9	256	32	58	3.83	2.6	9.2	3.6	1.0	104

Long and lean hurler who was fully healthy and improved velocity and pitch movement, particularly with plus FB. Changes speeds effectively and hard sinker is tough to lift. CB hasn't yet developed, but has potential to be decent third pitch. Bullpen may be best role where FB/CU combo could be dynamite in short stints.

Soliman, Manuel — SP — Minnesota

EXP MLB DEBUT: 2014 | POTENTIAL: #3 starter | 8E

Thrws R Age 22
2007 FA (DR)

Velo	Pitch	Grade
88-94	FB	+++
80-82	SL	+++
79-82	CU	++

Year	Lev	Team	W	L	Sv	IP	K	ERA	WHIP	BF/G	OBA	H%	S%	xERA	Ctl	Dom	Cmd	hr/9	BPV
2010	Rk	Elizabethton	5	2	0	64	74	3.50	1.06	20.8	206	28	68	2.40	2.9	10.4	3.5	0.7	129
2011	A	Beloit	7	11	0	136	120	3.97	1.31	20.1	250	30	73	4.01	3.3	7.9	2.4	1.1	69

Tall and strong pitcher has excellent control despite relative inexperience (former 3Bman). Throws consistent strikes with clean arm action and loose, repeatable delivery. Projection remains and could add more velocity in time. Has been durable and has deep arsenal, though no above average pitch at present. SL can get Ks, but CU is iffy.

Solis, Sammy — SP — Washington

EXP MLB DEBUT: 2013 | POTENTIAL: #3 starter | 8C

Thrws L Age 23
2010 (1-S) San Diego

Velo	Pitch	Grade
92-94	FB	++++
80-82	CU	++++
78-80	CB	++

Year	Lev	Team	W	L	Sv	IP	K	ERA	WHIP	BF/G	OBA	H%	S%	xERA	Ctl	Dom	Cmd	hr/9	BPV
2009	NCAA	San Diego	1	1	0	12	16	4.50	1.08	23.4	278	42	54	2.72	0.0	12.0		0.0	
2010	NCAA	San Diego	9	2	0	92	92	3.42	1.21	24.7	240	32	72	3.01	2.8	9.0	3.2	0.5	113
2010	A	Hagerstown	0	0	0	4	3	0.00	0.50	6.6	151	19	100	0.00	0.0	6.8		0.0	
2011	A	Hagerstown	2	1	0	40	40	4.04	1.27	23.4	256	33	69	3.56	2.7	9.0	3.3	0.7	107
2011	A+	Potomac	6	2	0	56	53	2.73	1.28	23.0	278	35	82	4.02	1.8	8.5	4.8	0.8	127

He improved as much as any player in the organization. Solis uses his strong frame to generate a 92-94 mph, topping out at 96. He mixes in a plus curve and an improved change-up. Missed action with a groin injury, but looked impressive in the AFL. Has the potential to be a solid mid-rotation lefty.

Soptic, Jeff — SP — Chicago (A)

EXP MLB DEBUT: 2015 | POTENTIAL: #2 starter/Closer | 8D

Thrws R Age 21
2011 (3) Johnson Cty CC

Velo	Pitch	Grade
91-98	FB	++++
84-88	SL	+++
	CU	+

Year	Lev	Team	W	L	Sv	IP	K	ERA	WHIP	BF/G	OBA	H%	S%	xERA	Ctl	Dom	Cmd	hr/9	BPV
2011	Rk	Bristol	0	1	1	2	2	0.00	1.82	3.4	244	32	100	4.14	8.2	8.2	1.0	0.0	76

Strong-armed and tall pitcher with incredible velocity. Raw pitch mix highlighted by straight FB and SL that can be knockout pitch. Mechanics need to be overhauled and inconsistent release point has brought command issues. Needs change-of-pace pitch to stick as SP, but future is bright with proper coaching and development.

Soto, Giovanni — SP — Cleveland

Thrws L Age 21
2009 (21) HS (PR)

Velo	Pitch	Grade
85-89	FB	+++
77-80	SL	+++
75-78	CB	++
	CU	++

EXP MLB DEBUT: 2013 · POTENTIAL: #5 starter · 7D

Year	Lev	Team	W	L	Sv	IP	K	ERA	WHIP	BF/G	OBA	H%	S%	xERA	Ctl	Dom	Cmd	hr/9	BPV
2009	Rk	GCL Tigers	4	0	1	45	37	1.19	1.17	13.9	206	27	89	2.05	4.0	7.4	1.9	0.0	97
2010	A	West Michigan	6	6	0	82	76	2.63	1.22	20.7	244	32	78	2.84	2.7	8.3	3.0	0.2	113
2010	A	Lake County	3	2	0	31	31	3.77	1.06	20.1	201	23	71	3.07	3.2	9.0	2.8	1.5	84
2011	Rk	AZL Indians	0	0	0	5	7	1.80	1.00	6.4	221	36	80	1.75	1.8	12.6	7.0	0.0	233
2011	A+	Kinston	4	4	0	64	64	3.23	1.20	17.2	237	30	75	3.16	3.0	9.0	3.0	0.7	105

Tall and slender, he relies on pitching down in strike zone with sinker. Few pitches come out straight due to quick arm action. Below average velocity, but is effective moving around plate. Maintains stuff throughout game and can eat innings with loose mechanics. Lacks a dominant secondary pitch, but has posted high Dom due to trickery.

Spoone, Chorye — RP — Boston

Thrws R Age 26
2005 (8) Catonsville CC

Velo	Pitch	Grade
88-94	FB	+++
79-81	CB	+++
82-85	CU	++

EXP MLB DEBUT: 2012 · POTENTIAL: Middle reliever · 7D

Year	Lev	Team	W	L	Sv	IP	K	ERA	WHIP	BF/G	OBA	H%	S%	xERA	Ctl	Dom	Cmd	hr/9	BPV
2009	A-	Aberdeen	0	0	0	3	3	0.00	1.33	12.5	106	15	100	1.39	9.0	9.0	1.0	0.0	109
2009	A+	Frederick	0	2	0	14	12	9.57	2.20	17.7	299	34	57	7.69	8.9	7.7	0.9	1.9	2
2010	AA	Bowie	7	6	0	132	88	4.02	1.60	24.3	262	30	76	4.62	5.4	6.0	1.1	0.8	37
2011	AA	Bowie	5	5	1	87	64	4.13	1.42	16.1	252	30	71	3.76	4.2	6.6	1.6	0.5	61
2011	AAA	Norfolk	2	1	0	34	16	5.54	1.96	20.4	299	33	70	5.58	6.9	4.2	0.6	0.3	26

Durable and strong pitcher who once was one of BAL's top prospects. Pitched as both SP and RP. Groundball specialist with stellar velocity, but misses strike zone often and fails to capitalize on sinker/CB combination. Doesn't strike out many, but could work well in short stints by throwing even harder.

Spruill, Zeke — SP — Atlanta

Thrws R Age 22
2008 (2) HS, (GA)

Velo	Pitch	Grade
90-94	FB	+++
76-83	SL	+++
79-82	CU	++

EXP MLB DEBUT: 2012 · POTENTIAL: #3 starter · 7C

Year	Lev	Team	W	L	Sv	IP	K	ERA	WHIP	BF/G	OBA	H%	S%	xERA	Ctl	Dom	Cmd	hr/9	BPV
2009	A	Rome	8	6	1	116	95	3.03	1.24	23.6	268	32	78	3.69	1.9	7.4	4.0	0.7	108
2010	Rk	GCL Braves	0	0	0	3	1	3.00	1.67	6.7	321	35	80	4.94	3.0	3.0	1.0	0.0	30
2010	A+	Myrtle Beach	3	5	0	65	41	5.54	1.48	20.0	312	36	61	4.81	1.8	5.7	3.2	0.6	76
2011	A+	Lynchburg	7	9	0	129	92	3.20	1.01	24.8	229	27	69	2.40	1.6	6.4	4.0	0.5	117
2011	AA	Mississippi	3	2	0	45	16	3.20	1.38	27.0	262	27	78	3.89	3.4	3.2	0.9	0.6	24

He pounded strike zone with a sinking fastball en-route to a breakout season. Fastball sits in the 90-94 range, but generates more groundballs than strikeouts. Is complemented with a decent change-up and an inconsistent slider. Spruill held his own once promoted to Double-A and now profiles as a solid #3 or #4 starter.

Stephenson, Robert — SP — Cincinnati

Thrws R Age 20
2011 (1) HS, (CA)

Velo	Pitch	Grade
93-96	FB	++++
78-80		+++

EXP MLB DEBUT: 2015 · POTENTIAL: #2 starter · 9D

Year	Lev	Team	W	L	Sv	IP	K	ERA	WHIP	BF/G	OBA	H%	S%	xERA	Ctl	Dom	Cmd	hr/9	BPV
2011		Did not play																	

Electric-armed hurler uses a max effort delivery to throw FB in the 93-96 range. He complements the heater with a CB and an rarely used CU. Needs to learn how to pitch and not just throw. There is some effort to his delivery that could be ironed out to give his CU better deception. Lots of potential, but a work in progress.

Sterling, Felix — SP — Cleveland

Thrws R Age 19
2009 FA (DR)

Velo	Pitch	Grade
89-94	FB	++++
83-86	SL	+++
	CU	++

EXP MLB DEBUT: 2015 · POTENTIAL: #2 starter · 9D

Year	Lev	Team	W	L	Sv	IP	K	ERA	WHIP	BF/G	OBA	H%	S%	xERA	Ctl	Dom	Cmd	hr/9	BPV
2010	Rk	AZL Indians	2	3	0	51	57	3.17	1.17	17.0	217	30	72	2.50	3.5	10.0	2.9	0.4	121
2011	Rk	AZL Indians	2	3	0	26	31	4.14	1.30	17.9	261	35	71	4.02	2.8	10.7	3.9	1.0	117
2011	A	Lake County	2	3	0	41	35	4.16	1.36	19.1	211	25	71	3.41	5.5	7.7	1.4	0.9	62

Large and strong pitcher succeeded in first year in U.S. with impressive pitchability and moxie. Doesn't have great projection, but offers pure arm strength and effective FB. Hard SL serves as wipeout pitch and shows potential for solid-average CU. Command and control need to be ironed out to reach ceiling.

Stewart, Ethan — SP — Philadelphia

Thrws L Age 21
2010 (47) New Mexico JC

Velo	Pitch	Grade
88-92	FB	+++
	CB	++
	CU	++

EXP MLB DEBUT: 2015 · POTENTIAL: #5 starter · 7D

Year	Lev	Team	W	L	Sv	IP	K	ERA	WHIP	BF/G	OBA	H%	S%	xERA	Ctl	Dom	Cmd	hr/9	BPV
2011	Rk	GCL Phillies	4	4	0	54	54	3.65	1.44	21.0	272	34	77	4.34	3.5	9.0	2.6	0.8	84
2011	A-	Williamsport	1	0	0	9	6	2.00	1.67	20.2	262	29	93	4.97	6.0	6.0	1.0	1.0	30

Tall, projectable lefty from Canada had an impressive pro debut. He has a nice 90-93 mph FB, with a CB and CU that show potential. His front-side mechanics are not very good and could lead to struggles with control, but he uses his lower half well and has good size.

Stoffel, Jason — RP — Houston

Thrws R Age 23
2009 (4) Arizona

Velo	Pitch	Grade
92-96	FB	++++
	CB	++
	CU	+++

EXP MLB DEBUT: 2012 · POTENTIAL: reliever · 8C

Year	Lev	Team	W	L	Sv	IP	K	ERA	WHIP	BF/G	OBA	H%	S%	xERA	Ctl	Dom	Cmd	hr/9	BPV
2009	Rk	AZL Giants	0	0	2	9	6	1.96	0.87	3.8	236	29	75	1.67	0.0	5.9		0.0	
2009	A-	Salem-Keizer	1	0	2	10	13	0.00	0.69	4.4	174	28	100	0.44	0.9	11.6	13.0	0.0	363
2010	A+	San Jose	2	4	25	50	66	4.84	1.57	4.2	280	40	69	4.66	4.3	11.8	2.8	0.7	106
2011	AA	Richmond	1	2	13	31	31	4.04	1.60	4.3	279	37	73	4.34	4.6	8.9	1.9	0.3	85
2011	AA	Corpus Christi	1	3	4	16	19	5.63	1.69	4.0	285	36	71	5.95	5.1	10.7	2.1	1.7	56

Strong-armed reliever has a nice 90-94 fastball, along with power curve and a good changeup. At 6'2", 220 he isn't particularly athletic, but projects as a solid setup man. Struggled a bit in '11, but did strike out more than a batter an inning. If control and conditioning can improve, he should be able to get major league hitters out.

Stowell, Bryce — RP — Cleveland

Thrws R Age 25
2008 (22) UC Irvine

Velo	Pitch	Grade
89-96	FB	++++
82-84	SL	+++
	CU	+

EXP MLB DEBUT: 2012 · POTENTIAL: Setup reliever/Closer · 7A

Year	Lev	Team	W	L	Sv	IP	K	ERA	WHIP	BF/G	OBA	H%	S%	xERA	Ctl	Dom	Cmd	hr/9	BPV
2010	AA	Akron	1	0	7	22	33	0.00	1.18	6.3	194	34	100	1.86	4.5	13.4	3.0	0.0	160
2010	AAA	Columbus	1	1	0	19	28	5.63	1.46	4.8	169	26	62	3.18	8.0	13.1	1.6	0.9	106
2011	A-	Mahoning Vall	0	0	1	2	3	0.00	1.00	7.6	151	27	100	0.94	4.5	13.5	3.0	0.0	169
2011	A	Lake County	0	1	0	17	26	2.63	1.05	6.6	142	26	72	0.99	5.3	13.7	2.6	0.0	163
2011	AA	Akron	1	0	0	19	28	1.88	1.15	5.8	182	30	86	2.11	4.7	13.2	2.8	0.5	142

Athletic and strong reliever has progressed slowly despite age and power stuff. Throws with max effort, but quick FB exhibits tailing action. Mixes in power SL for good measure to register Ks. Has closer-type stuff, but needs to harness arm strength to throw more consistent strikes. An inconsistent release point may be the culprit for lack of command.

Straily, Dan — SP — Oakland

Thrws R Age 23
2009 (24) Marshall

Velo	Pitch	Grade
89-93	FB	+++
80-83	CB	++++
	CU	++

EXP MLB DEBUT: 2013 · POTENTIAL: #4 starter · 7C

Year	Lev	Team	W	L	Sv	IP	K	ERA	WHIP	BF/G	OBA	H%	S%	xERA	Ctl	Dom	Cmd	hr/9	BPV
2008	NCAA	Marshall	5	4	0	82	57	4.28	1.38	21.5	259	30	69	3.88	3.5	6.3	1.8	0.7	58
2009	NCAA	Marshall	4	3	0	71	58	4.30	1.60	24.2	285	35	72	4.53	4.3	7.3	1.7	0.4	66
2009	A-	Vancouver	5	3	0	59	66	4.12	1.42	15.6	284	38	72	4.40	2.7	10.1	3.7	0.8	113
2010	A	Kane County	10	7	0	148	149	4.32	1.34	22.0	248	32	69	3.75	3.7	9.1	2.4	0.8	87
2011	A+	Stockton	11	9	0	160	154	3.88	1.25	23.3	262	33	69	3.47	2.2	8.7	3.9	0.6	119

Big and durable hurler who has consistently pitched well. Throws any pitch in any count, including plus CB and solid-average FB with nice movement. Natural stuff is quite good and induces groundballs by keeping ball down. Can cut and sink ball and intent to pitch to contact as opposed to dominance. Not much upside, but has value.

Sturdevant, Tyler — RP — Cleveland

Thrws L Age 26
2009 (27) New Mexico St

Velo	Pitch	Grade
87-93	FB	+++
78-79	CB	++
	CT	+++

EXP MLB DEBUT: 2012 · POTENTIAL: Middle reliever · 7D

Year	Lev	Team	W	L	Sv	IP	K	ERA	WHIP	BF/G	OBA	H%	S%	xERA	Ctl	Dom	Cmd	hr/9	BPV
2010	A	Lake County	3	0	2	35	56	0.77	0.71	7.8	146	27	92	0.40	2.0	14.3	7.0	0.3	251
2010	A+	Kinston	3	2	0	29	35	3.72	1.34	8.1	255	35	75	3.95	3.4	10.9	3.2	0.9	108
2011	A+	Kinston	4	2	1	41	44	1.98	0.95	7.4	211	28	83	2.16	1.8	9.7	5.5	0.7	166
2011	AA	Akron	3	1	2	30	34	3.30	1.30	6.5	262	36	76	3.62	2.7	10.2	3.8	0.6	125
2011	AAA	Columbus	0	0	1	3	4	5.63	2.50	8.5	399	54	75	8.40	5.6	11.3	2.0	0.0	85

Durable reliever who relies on throwing strikes and tallying Ks. No one pitch stands out from another, but succeeds with cutting and sinking FB to both sides of plate. More or less a one-pitch reliever as CB lacks bite and doesn't change speeds. Upside limited, but can be useful situational reliever.

Suarez, Larry — SP — Chicago (N)

Thrws R Age 22
2006 NDFA Venz.

Velo	Pitch	Grade
89-95	FB	++++
80-83	SL	+++
80-82	CU	+

EXP MLB DEBUT: 2014 · POTENTIAL: Power reliever · 7D

Year	Lev	Team	W	L	Sv	IP	K	ERA	WHIP	BF/G	OBA	H%	S%	xERA	Ctl	Dom	Cmd	hr/9	BPV
2010	A-	Boise	0	0	0	18	20	5.44	1.70	11.8	300	38	71	6.03	4.5	9.9	2.2	1.5	56
2010	A	Peoria	1	3	1	47	51	4.98	1.55	7.6	278	36	69	4.83	4.2	9.8	2.3	1.0	78
2011	A	Peoria	0	0	1	16	23	0.00	1.13	6.3	224	35	106	2.62	2.8	12.9	4.6	0.6	168
2011	A+	Daytona	1	1	0	12	12	3.00	1.33	6.2	278	31	92	5.49	2.3	9.0	4.0	2.3	70
2011	AA	Tennessee	0	2	0	16	11	7.31	1.75	12.2	328	37	58	6.29	3.4	6.2	1.8	1.1	31

Tall/strong-bodied pitcher was moved to relief with solid results. Has a nice mid-90s fastball and the quick arm action to snap-off a nasty slider. Improved control in '11 gives him a change to help at the next level. Pitched at three different levels in 2011 and generated more groundball outs.

Sulbaran, J.C. — SP — Cincinnati

EXP MLB DEBUT: 2014 | POTENTIAL: #3 starter | **8D**

Thrws R | Age 22
2008 (30) HS, (FL)

- 88-92 FB ++++
- CB +++
- CU ++

Year	Lev	Team	W	L	Sv	IP	K	ERA	WHIP	BF/G	OBA	H%	S%	xERA	Ctl	Dom	Cmd	hr/9	BPV
2009	A	Dayton	5	5	0	92	100	5.27	1.57	19.3	266	32	72	5.55	5.0	9.8	2.0	1.9	46
2010	A	Dayton	4	6	0	79	83	5.01	1.61	21.9	259	34	69	4.44	5.6	9.4	1.7	0.7	75
2011	A+	Bakersfield	9	6	0	137	155	4.60	1.39	22.2	266	36	67	3.95	3.3	10.2	3.1	0.7	108

Strong righty with some nice projection if his breaking ball develops. Solid 88-92 mph fastball with late movement. Also has a good but inconsistent curveball and a potentially plus change-up. Inconsistent front-side mechanics cause him to fly open early and lead to subpar control. Held his own in the CAL and is a potential sleeper in 2012.

Summers, Matt — RP — Minnesota

EXP MLB DEBUT: 2014 | POTENTIAL: Setup reliever | **7B**

Thrws R | Age 22
2011 (4) UC-Irvine

- 87-95 FB ++++
- 79-83 CB +++
- CU +

Year	Lev	Team	W	L	Sv	IP	K	ERA	WHIP	BF/G	OBA	H%	S%	xERA	Ctl	Dom	Cmd	hr/9	BPV
2009	NCAA	Cal-Irvine	0	0	0	7	6	7.71	2.14	5.8	336	42	60	6.35	6.4	7.7	1.2	0.0	59
2010	NCAA	Cal-Irvine	2	2	0	30	32	8.64	1.92	6.8	320	40	55	6.89	5.4	9.5	1.8	1.5	41
2011	NCAA	Cal-Irvine	10	2	0	103	90	1.74	0.91	25.7	180	24	80	1.18	2.6	7.8	3.0	0.1	126
2011	Rk	Elizabethton	1	1	6	20	36	0.89	0.79	3.6	162	34	88	0.51	2.2	16.0	7.2	0.0	270

Athletic and durable reliever who relies more on deception and trickery than natural stuff. Uses short arm action in full-effort delivery. Has good velocity in plus FB and mixes in CB for good measure. LHH did not get a hit against him in '11. Likely to remain in bullpen where groundball tendencies enhance his overall package as setup reliever.

Surkamp, Eric — SP — San Francisco

EXP MLB DEBUT: 2011 | POTENTIAL: #5 starter | **7B**

Thrws L | Age 24
2008 (6) NC State

- 87-90 FB +++
- 75-78 CB +++
- CU ++

Year	Lev	Team	W	L	Sv	IP	K	ERA	WHIP	BF/G	OBA	H%	S%	xERA	Ctl	Dom	Cmd	hr/9	BPV
2009	A	Augusta	11	5	0	131	169	3.30	1.28	23.4	259	38	74	3.35	2.7	11.6	4.3	0.4	152
2010	A+	San Jose	4	2	0	101	108	3.12	1.00	22.7	217	29	69	2.14	2.0	9.6	4.9	0.4	159
2011	A+	San Jose	1	0	0	6	5	0.00	0.83	21.9	191	25	100	1.03	1.5	7.5	5.0	0.0	167
2011	AA	Richmond	10	4	0	142	165	2.03	1.08	24.1	215	31	82	2.21	2.8	10.5	3.8	0.3	144
2011	MLB	San Francisco	2	2	0	26	13	5.84	1.87	20.5	302	34	67	5.46	5.8	4.5	0.8	0.3	27

Tall lefty keeps hitters off balance with an 87-90 mph sinking fastball. Complements it with a plus sweeping curveball and an improved change-up was key to 2011 breakout. Has some nice deception with a low three-quarters delivery. Willing to pitch to both sides of the plate and effectively changes eye level. Not much margin for error, but knows how to pitch.

Swagerty, Jordan — RP — St. Louis

EXP MLB DEBUT: 2012 | POTENTIAL: reliever | **8B**

Thrws R | Age 22
2010 (2) Arizona State

- 88-95 FB ++++
- 83-85 CU ++++
- CB ++

Year	Lev	Team	W	L	Sv	IP	K	ERA	WHIP	BF/G	OBA	H%	S%	xERA	Ctl	Dom	Cmd	hr/9	BPV
2009	NCAA	Arizona State	4	1	4	58	51	4.50	1.41	9.8	294	36	69	4.56	2.2	7.9	3.6	0.8	97
2010	NCAA	Arizona State	2	0	14	37	48	2.19	1.19	4.4	246	35	88	3.46	2.4	11.7	4.8	1.0	148
2011	A	Quad Cities	3	1	0	30	30	1.50	0.67	20.9	175	23	83	0.98	0.6	9.0	15.0	0.6	371
2011	A+	Palm Beach	2	2	5	54	52	1.83	1.07	9.6	216	29	82	2.06	2.7	8.7	3.3	0.2	127
2011	AA	Springfield	0	0	3	9	7	2.97	1.43	4.3	238	27	83	4.02	4.9	6.9	1.4	1.0	49

Short, athletic righty has a quick and deceptive delivery. He features an 90-94 mph sinking fastball that gets in on hitters quickly. His best pitch a plus 83-85 mph slurve that has big, late-breaking action. He also has a nice change-up. Swagerty pitches aggressively and his solid three-pitch mix gives him a chance to start.

Syndergaard, Noah — SP — Toronto

EXP MLB DEBUT: 2014 | POTENTIAL: #2 starter | **9D**

Thrws R | Age 19
2010 (1-S) HS (TX)

- 90-97 FB ++++
- 78-80 CB ++
- CU ++

Year	Lev	Team	W	L	Sv	IP	K	ERA	WHIP	BF/G	OBA	H%	S%	xERA	Ctl	Dom	Cmd	hr/9	BPV
2010	Rk	GCL Blue Jays	0	1	0	13	6	2.75	1.15	10.4	229	26	73	2.30	2.7	4.1	1.5	0.0	65
2011	Rk	Bluefield	4	0	0	32	37	1.41	1.06	17.7	203	29	88	1.98	3.1	10.4	3.4	0.3	139
2011	A-	Vancouver	1	2	0	18	22	2.00	1.11	17.7	228	34	80	2.13	2.5	11.0	4.4	0.0	168
2011	A	Lansing	0	0	0	9	9	3.00	1.11	17.7	240	33	70	2.30	2.0	9.0	4.5	0.0	156

Tall and powerful pitcher who succeeded despite only one dependable offering. Thrives with plus FB that he locates with precision to both sides of plate. Has velocity to pitch up, but also can cut and sink it to bottom half of zone. Doesn't trust secondary offerings, though both CB and CU can be good. Slows arm speed on CU at present.

Tago, Peter — SP — Colorado

EXP MLB DEBUT: 2015 | POTENTIAL: #3 starter | **8D**

Thrws R | Age 19
2010 (2) HS, (CA)

- 91-94 FB ++++
- 73-75 CB ++
- CU ++

Year	Lev	Team	W	L	Sv	IP	K	ERA	WHIP	BF/G	OBA	H%	S%	xERA	Ctl	Dom	Cmd	hr/9	BPV
2011	A	Asheville	3	5	0	90	58	7.09	1.78	21.8	257	28	59	5.18	7.2	5.8	0.8	1.0	25

Lean, athletic righty has surprising velocity and movement. Is still very raw, but he has a ton and upside. Has a loose delivery and clean arm action that projects to deliver consistent mid-90s heat. Needs to tighten the rotation on his curveball, but it shows good potential. Also has a nice change-up. Pitch mix gives him a chance at the next level.

Taillon, Jameson — SP — Pittsburgh

EXP MLB DEBUT: 2014 | POTENTIAL: #1 starter | **9C**

Thrws R | Age 20
2010 (1) HS, (TX)

- 94-97 FB ++++
- 80-83 CB ++++
- 84-86 SL +++
- CU ++

Year	Lev	Team	W	L	Sv	IP	K	ERA	WHIP	BF/G	OBA	H%	S%	xERA	Ctl	Dom	Cmd	hr/9	BPV
2011	A	West Virginia	2	3	0	92	97	4.00	1.20	16.1	255	33	69	3.56	2.1	9.5	4.4	0.9	127

Tall, athletic hurler features a 94-97 mph FB that tops out at 99. Complements it with a plus SL and two-plane power curveball. Improved CU gives him potential for a fourth plus offering. At 6'6" he has the frame to dominate and be durable. Should have the tools to move quickly once they take the leash off.

Tanner, Clayton — SP — Cincinnati

EXP MLB DEBUT: 2012 | POTENTIAL: #4 starter | **7C**

Thrws L | Age 25
2006 (3) HS, (CA)

- 85-90 FB +++
- 77-81 SL ++++
- CU ++

Year	Lev	Team	W	L	Sv	IP	K	ERA	WHIP	BF/G	OBA	H%	S%	xERA	Ctl	Dom	Cmd	hr/9	BPV
2008	A+	San Jose	10	8	0	117	84	3.69	1.39	20.5	273	33	71	3.56	3.0	6.5	2.2	0.1	82
2009	A+	San Jose	12	6	0	139	121	3.17	1.25	21.8	252	30	80	3.92	2.7	7.8	2.9	1.2	77
2010	AA	Richmond	9	9	0	149	79	3.68	1.44	23.5	263	29	75	4.04	3.9	4.8	1.2	0.6	39
2011	AA	Richmond	6	10	0	119	90	4.30	1.30	22.3	263	30	69	4.03	2.6	6.8	2.6	1.0	68
2011	AAA	Louisville	0	0	0	3	4	0.00	1.00	11.5	106	18	100	0.52	6.0	12.0	2.0	0.0	148

Athletic pitcher with plus slider and fastball location, which compensates for below average velocity and sub-standard control. Isn't overpowering, but knows how to locate and keep hitters off balance. Not a lot of upside, but could see a few seasons as a back end starter.

Tapia, Domingo — SP — New York (N)

EXP MLB DEBUT: 2015 | POTENTIAL: #3 starter | **8E**

Thrws R | Age 20
2009 NDFA D.R.

- 96-98 FB ++++
- CB +
- CU +

Year	Lev	Team	W	L	Sv	IP	K	ERA	WHIP	BF/G	OBA	H%	S%	xERA	Ctl	Dom	Cmd	hr/9	BPV
2010	Rk	GCL Mets	4	3	0	47	29	3.45	1.26	19.2	270	32	69	3.11	1.9	5.6	2.9	0.0	95
2011	Rk	Kingsport	5	5	0	50	30	3.78	1.32	18.8	262	30	71	3.67	2.9	5.4	1.9	0.5	58
2011	A-	Brooklyn	1	0	0	6	6	0.00	0.83	21.9	228	31	100	1.45	0.0	9.0		0.0	

Tall, wiry right-hander might have the best fastball in the Mets system. It sits in the 96-98 mph range and tops out at 100. Also throws a two seam fastball, curveball, and a change-up. At 6'4" 185 lbs. he is very projectable but also very raw. If the secondary pitches improve, he could have a huge breakout.

Tazawa, Junichi — SP — Boston

EXP MLB DEBUT: 2009 | POTENTIAL: #4 starter | **7B**

Thrws R | Age 26
2008 FA (Japan)

- 88-94 FB +++
- 77-81 SL +++
- 75-78 CB +++
- 79-82 CU +++

Year	Lev	Team	W	L	Sv	IP	K	ERA	WHIP	BF/G	OBA	H%	S%	xERA	Ctl	Dom	Cmd	hr/9	BPV
2009	MLB	Boston	2	3	0	25	13	7.53	2.07	20.5	378	40	65	8.30	3.2	4.7	1.4	1.4	-5
2011	A+	Salem	0	1	0	19	13	6.13	1.36	13.3	271	28	59	5.15	2.8	6.1	2.2	1.9	27
2011	AA	Portland	3	2	0	23	27	4.70	1.17	11.5	236	31	63	3.49	2.7	10.6	3.9	1.2	117
2011	AAA	Pawtucket	1	1	0	14	19	2.55	1.21	7.1	260	39	81	3.38	1.9	12.1	6.3	0.6	190
2011	MLB	Boston	0	0	0	3	4	6.00	1.33	4.2	262	31	67	5.95	3.0	12.0	4.0	3.0	69

Short and athletic pitcher with MLB experience, but can't stay healthy. Has deep arsenal of pitches in magic bag and still has potential to be reliable starter. Mixes pitches with precision and unusual delivery allows deception by hiding ball. FB tends to be flat at higher velocities and may not have ideal putaway pitch to tally Ks. CU can be plus at times.

Teheran, Julio — SP — Atlanta

EXP MLB DEBUT: 2011 | POTENTIAL: #1 starter | **9B**

Thrws R | Age 21
2007 NDFA D.R.

- 92-96 FB ++++
- 75-79 CB ++++
- 79-82 CU ++++
- 80-83 SL ++

Year	Lev	Team	W	L	Sv	IP	K	ERA	WHIP	BF/G	OBA	H%	S%	xERA	Ctl	Dom	Cmd	hr/9	BPV
2010	A	Rome	2	2	0	39	45	1.15	0.84	20.5	173	25	88	1.03	2.3	10.4	4.5	0.2	170
2010	A+	Myrtle Beach	4	4	0	63	76	3.00	1.09	24.7	239	33	76	3.04	1.9	10.8	5.8	0.9	169
2010	AA	Mississippi	3	2	0	40	38	3.38	1.15	22.7	205	27	70	2.39	3.8	8.6	2.2	0.5	99
2011	AAA	Gwinnett	15	3	0	144	122	2.56	1.19	23.1	232	29	78	2.70	3.0	7.6	2.5	0.3	98
2011	MLB	Atlanta	1	1	0	19	10	5.16	1.51	16.6	279	28	72	5.66	3.8	4.7	1.3	1.9	-3

Strong-armed, athletic hurler saw gains across the board. Features a 93-96 mph fastball with good movement. Maintains velocity deep into outings and can drop curveball in for strikes. Change-up remains plus and gives him the potential to dominate. Was 15-3 with a 2.55 at Triple-A. Should compete for the 4th or 5th slot in Atlanta in 2012.

Tepesch, Nick — SP — Texas

Thrws R Age 23
2010 (14) Missouri

Velo	Pitch	Grade
87-94	FB	+++
78-80	CB	++
	CT	+++
	CU	

EXP MLB DEBUT: 2014 | POTENTIAL: #4 starter | 8E

Year	Lev	Team	W	L	Sv	IP	K	ERA	WHIP	BF/G	OBA	H%	S%	xERA	Ctl	Dom	Cmd	hr/9	BPV
2008	NCAA	Missouri	1	3	4	29	17	4.93	1.54	5.8	286				3.7	5.2	1.4		
2009	NCAA	Missouri	6	5	1	84	84	6.31	1.63	20.8	315				3.0	9.0	3.0		
2010	NCAA	Missouri	6	6	0	98	75	4.22	1.37	27.5	281	33	71	4.32	2.5	6.9	2.8	0.8	74
2011	A	Hickory	7	5	0	138	118	4.04	1.30	19.6	274	33	71	4.12	2.2	7.7	3.6	0.9	94

Tall and strong pitcher who has flown under radar despite commandable FB and excellent control. A tad old for level, but has goods to succeed. Doesn't have much deception and can be slow to plate, though has added cutter to repertoire. Clean arm action enhances FB movement, but will need to upgrade breaking ball.

Thompson, Aaron — SP — Minnesota

Thrws L Age 25
2005 (1-S) HS, (NM)

Velo	Pitch	Grade
86-91	FB	+++
77-83	SL	+++
71-75	CB	++
80-83	CU	++

EXP MLB DEBUT: 2011 | POTENTIAL: #5 starter | 6C

Year	Lev	Team	W	L	Sv	IP	K	ERA	WHIP	BF/G	OBA	H%	S%	xERA	Ctl	Dom	Cmd	hr/9	BPV
2010	AA	Harrisburg	4	13	0	136	95	5.81	1.59	23.1	299	34	64	5.37	3.5	6.3	1.8	1.1	39
2010	AAA	Syracuse	1	0	0	5	4	1.80	1.60	22.1	262	33	88	3.85	5.4	7.2	1.3	0.0	74
2011	AA	Altoona	4	7	0	83	51	5.19	1.44	12.7	299	34	63	4.61	2.2	5.5	2.6	0.6	62
2011	AAA	Indianapolis	1	0	0	19	10	2.84	1.68	17.1	300	35	81	4.64	4.3	4.7	1.1	0.0	47
2011	MLB	Pittsburgh	0	0	0	7	1	7.50	2.64	9.8	390	36	76	11.01	7.5	1.3	0.2	2.5	-87

Former 1st round pick has not lived up to expectations. He remains athletic and has four pitches that he can sometimes throw for strikes. There is still a chance he can make it. He repeats high three-quarters delivery, but lacks a quality change-up and at best projects as a back of the rotation guy.

Thompson, Jake — SP — Tampa Bay

Thrws R Age 22
2010 (2) Long Beach State

Velo	Pitch	Grade
88-94	FB	+++
83-88	SL	+++
	CU	+++

EXP MLB DEBUT: 2014 | POTENTIAL: #4 starter | 7B

Year	Lev	Team	W	L	Sv	IP	K	ERA	WHIP	BF/G	OBA	H%	S%	xERA	Ctl	Dom	Cmd	hr/9	BPV
2008	NCAA	Long Beach St	2	5	0	67	42	4.96	1.65	23.1	322	37	69	5.28	2.8	5.6	2.0	0.4	54
2009	NCAA	Long Beach St	4	7	0	85	42	5.61	1.36	25.4	301	32	59	4.74	1.4	4.4	3.2	1.0	61
2010	NCAA	Long Beach St	5	4	0	90	73	5.19	1.39	27.1	286	35	60	3.93	2.3	7.3	3.2	0.3	99
2010	A-	Hudson Valley	2	1	0	40	33	1.35	0.85	14.7	199	26	82	1.16	1.4	7.4	5.5	0.0	175
2010	A+	Charlotte	2	0	0	11	6	0.00	0.36	17.5	61	7	100	0.00	1.6	4.9	3.0	0.0	135

Aggressive and durable starter with miniscule Dom, but quality pitches in arsenal. Toys with hitters by changing speeds and moving pitches around strike zone. Can be guilty of too many strikes, but mixes in SL and solid-average CU that can become plus. Can tally Ks, but works quickly and pitches to contact early in count.

Thomson, Matt — SP — Oakland

Thrws R Age 24
2010 (12) San Diego

Velo	Pitch	Grade
89-93	FB	++++
80-83	SL	+++
79-83	CB	++
	CU	++

EXP MLB DEBUT: 2013 | POTENTIAL: #4 starter | 7D

Year	Lev	Team	W	L	Sv	IP	K	ERA	WHIP	BF/G	OBA	H%	S%	xERA	Ctl	Dom	Cmd	hr/9	BPV
2009	NCAA	San Diego	5	5	2	81	88	5.99	1.37	21.2	264	35	54	3.79	3.2	9.8	3.0	0.6	108
2010	NCAA	San Diego	1	3	7	42	56	3.41	1.37	6.6	274	41	75	3.81	2.8	11.9	4.3	0.4	149
2010	A-	Vancouver	3	2	0	46	61	2.15	0.93	14.4	212	34	74	1.49	1.6	11.9	7.6	0.0	244
2010	A+	Stockton	1	0	0	5	10	0.00	0.80	18.1	124	33	100	0.13	3.6	18.0	5.0	0.0	243
2011	A	Burlington	0	0	0	4	5	6.75	2.50	10.6	383	53	70	8.06	6.8	11.3	1.7	0.0	81

Tall and strong pitcher who missed most of season with shoulder injury. Versatile, he has] solid velocity and quick FB exhibits downward movement. Pitches effectively inside to RHH and rarely beats hiimself. Needs to upgrade SL and show more confidence in CU. May be best in pen if secondary pitches continue to lag.

Thornburg, Tyler — SP — Milwaukee

Thrws R Age 23
2010 (3) Charleston Southern

Velo	Pitch	Grade
91-94	FB	++++
75-78	CB	+++
	CU	++

EXP MLB DEBUT: 2013 | POTENTIAL: #3 starter | 8B

Year	Lev	Team	W	L	Sv	IP	K	ERA	WHIP	BF/G	OBA	H%	S%	xERA	Ctl	Dom	Cmd	hr/9	BPV
2009	NCAA	Charleston S.	4	4	1	31	35	3.76	1.58	8.5	222	31	75	3.51	6.9	10.1	1.5	0.3	93
2010	NCAA	Charleston S.	5	4	0	78	88	4.15	1.23	26.4	220	30	65	2.77	3.9	10.1	2.6	0.5	112
2010	Rk	Helena	1	0	1	23	38	1.95	1.13	10.1	187	32	88	2.37	4.3	14.8	3.5	0.8	156
2011	A	Wisconsin	7	0	0	68	76	1.58	1.09	22.2	203	28	87	2.14	3.3	10.0	3.0	0.4	127
2011	A+	Brevard County	3	6	0	68	84	3.57	1.15	22.5	190	27	70	2.39	4.4	11.1	2.5	0.7	117

Short but athletic, he had an impressive breakout. His fastball consistently sits in the low 90s and tops at 95. He has an extremely high three-quarters delivery that gives him deception. He complements the heat with a power curveball and nice change-up. Does have a maximum effort delivery, but there is potential.

Tillman, Daniel — RP — Los Angeles (A)

Thrws R Age 23
2010 (2) Florida Southern

Velo	Pitch	Grade
90-96	FB	++++
82-85	SL	+++

EXP MLB DEBUT: 2013 | POTENTIAL: Closer | 8D

Year	Lev	Team	W	L	Sv	IP	K	ERA	WHIP	BF/G	OBA	H%	S%	xERA	Ctl	Dom	Cmd	hr/9	BPV
2010	Rk	Orem	2	2	10	32	50	1.96	1.03	5.6	203	36	79	1.58	2.8	14.0	5.0	0.0	204
2011	A	Cedar Rapids	5	3	12	66	70	2.04	1.29	7.5	221	31	83	2.63	4.4	9.5	2.2	0.1	110
2011	A+	Inland Empire	1	0	2	8	8	4.50	1.13	4.5	237	29	63	3.36	2.3	9.0	4.0	1.1	112

Quick-armed reliever works with aggressive, late-innings mentality and can dominate in short stints. Arm strength and loose action provide enough velocity and mixes in a nasty SL that serves as K pitch. Will likely stay in bullpen as he lacks touch and feel for changing speeds and will need to hone control and command.

Tolleson, Shawn — RP — Los Angeles (N)

Thrws R Age 24
2010 (30) Baylor

Velo	Pitch	Grade
90-93	FB	++++
	CT	+++
	SL	+++
	CU	++

EXP MLB DEBUT: 2012 | POTENTIAL: reliever | 8B

Year	Lev	Team	W	L	Sv	IP	K	ERA	WHIP	BF/G	OBA	H%	S%	xERA	Ctl	Dom	Cmd	hr/9	BPV
2010	NCAA	Baylor	2	7	1	76	84	5.20	1.71	21.6	320	42	70	5.84	3.4	9.9	2.9	0.9	83
2010	Rk	Ogden	1	1	17	28	39	0.64	0.78	3.9	176	28	95	0.97	1.6	12.4	7.8	0.3	249
2011	A	Great Lakes	1	0	10	15	33	0.00	0.80	3.9	159	46	100	0.46	2.4	19.8	8.3	0.0	315
2011	A+	Rancho Cucam	2	0	3	9	17	0.98	0.54	6.2	72	10	100		2.9	16.6	5.7	1.0	230
2011	AA	Chattanooga	4	2	12	44	55	1.63	1.20	4.7	252	37	88	3.06	2.2	11.2	5.0	0.4	165

30th round pick in '10 looks like a steal. Attacks hitters with a 90-93 mph fastball, a cutter and a decent slider. Dodgers converted him to relief and he was fantastic. Tolleson locates all three offerings well and simply over-matched hitters - 18 BB/105 K in 69 IP. Could reach the majors as soon as 2012.

Torres, Alex — SP — Tampa Bay

Thrws L Age 24
2005 FA (Venezuela)

Velo	Pitch	Grade
87-94	FB	+++
78-82	CB	+++
76-78	CU	++++

EXP MLB DEBUT: 2011 | POTENTIAL: #3 starter | 8B

Year	Lev	Team	W	L	Sv	IP	K	ERA	WHIP	BF/G	OBA	H%	S%	xERA	Ctl	Dom	Cmd	hr/9	BPV
2009	AA	Arkansas	3	1	0	26	25	2.77	1.54	22.7	239	32	80	3.37	5.9	8.7	1.5	0.0	90
2009	AA	Montgomery	0	2	0	8	7	3.29	1.46	17.6	232	27	82	4.14	5.5	7.7	1.4	1.1	51
2010	AA	Montgomery	11	6	0	142	150	3.48	1.45	22.5	253	34	77	3.86	4.4	9.5	2.1	0.6	89
2011	AAA	Durham	9	7	0	146	156	3.08	1.49	23.3	245	33	80	3.72	5.1	9.6	1.9	0.4	90
2011	MLB	Tampa Bay	1	1	0	8	9	3.38	1.88	9.4	262	37	80	4.51	7.9	10.1	1.3	0.0	90

Short and solid pitcher who reached TAM after leading IL in Ks. Throws with outstanding arm speed, particularly with plus CU that creates deception and plus movement. CB can also be good, giving him two solid secondary offerings. Movement on FB can be too much for own good and needs to become more efficient to pitch deeper into games.

Turnbull, Kylin — SP — Washington

Thrws L Age 22
2011 (4) Santa Barbara JC,CA

Velo	Pitch	Grade
88-92	FB	++
80-84	SL	++
	CU	+

EXP MLB DEBUT: 2015 | POTENTIAL: #5 Starter/reliever | 6C

Year	Lev	Team	W	L	Sv	IP	K	ERA	WHIP	BF/G	OBA	H%	S%	xERA	Ctl	Dom	Cmd	hr/9	BPV
2011		Did not play																	

At 6'5' 205 he has a lean, projectable frame. His fastball currently sits in the low-90s and tops out at 94. Turnbull also throws an inconsistent slider and lacks a quality third offering. He sometimes struggles with control and his velocity tends to flucuate, suggesting concerns about stamina and durability.

Turner, Jacob — SP — Detroit

Thrws R Age 21
2009 (1) HS (MO)

Velo	Pitch	Grade
89-95	FB	++++
78-83	CB	++++
78-81	CU	+++

EXP MLB DEBUT: 2011 | POTENTIAL: #1 starter | 9B

Year	Lev	Team	W	L	Sv	IP	K	ERA	WHIP	BF/G	OBA	H%	S%	xERA	Ctl	Dom	Cmd	hr/9	BPV
2010	A	West Michigan	2	3	0	54	51	3.67	1.15	19.5	258	33	69	3.27	1.5	8.5	5.7	0.7	153
2010	A+	Lakeland	4	2	0	61	51	2.95	1.10	18.4	235	29	73	2.64	2.1	7.5	3.6	0.4	116
2011	AA	Erie	3	5	0	113	90	3.50	1.18	26.7	242	29	72	3.21	2.5	7.2	2.8	0.7	87
2011	AAA	Toledo	1	0	0	17	20	3.16	1.05	22.1	237	33	71	2.60	1.6	10.5	6.7	0.5	195
2011	MLB	Detroit	0	1	0	12	8	8.85	1.72	18.5	331	35	50	7.29	3.0	5.9	2.0	2.2	0

Tall and strong pitcher with pitch mix, tenacity, and smooth mechanics to front a rotation. Very polished for age and sequences pitches with precision. Hasn't been dominant, but focused on improving consistency on secondary offerings. Throws heavy FB with late life and spots to both sides of plate. Still offers projection and repeats arm speed.

Tuttle, Dan — SP — Cincinnati

Thrws R Age 21
2009 (5) HS, (NC)

Velo	Pitch	Grade
89-94	FB	+++
79-82	SL	+++
	CU	++

EXP MLB DEBUT: 2013 | POTENTIAL: reliever | 7C

Year	Lev	Team	W	L	Sv	IP	K	ERA	WHIP	BF/G	OBA	H%	S%	xERA	Ctl	Dom	Cmd	hr/9	BPV
2009	Rk	GCL Reds	1	2	0	32	30	1.68	1.31	14.7	261	34	88	3.35	2.8	8.4	3.0	0.3	108
2010	Rk	Billings	5	3	0	58	52	4.34	1.50	19.3	261	32	73	4.45	4.5	8.1	1.8	0.9	61
2011	Rk	AZL Reds	3	1	0	23	35	3.91	1.22	18.6	227	39	64	2.35	3.5	13.7	3.9	0.0	174
2011	A	Dayton	4	3	0	57	50	4.89	1.38	21.8	265	34	62	3.63	3.3	7.9	2.4	0.3	90

Athletic RHP with some nice upside potential, pitched exclusively in relief in '11. Features a low-90s fastball that tops out at 94, a hard-breaking slider, and a potential changeup. Whip like delivery generates good movement, but occasionally leads to struggles with control. Generates plenty of groundball outs, but profiles as nothing more than a middle reliever.

Urbina, Juan — SP — New York (N)

EXP MLB DEBUT: 2014 | POTENTIAL: #2 starter | **8D**

Thrws L Age 19
2009 NDFA Venz.

Velo	Pitch	Grade
88-91	FB	++++
75-77	CB	++
80-83	CU	++
	SL	

Year	Lev	Team	W	L	Sv	IP	K	ERA	WHIP	BF/G	OBA	H%	S%	xERA	Ctl	Dom	Cmd	hr/9	BPV
2010	Rk	GCL Mets	5	3	0	48	38	5.05	1.41	18.5	285	33	65	4.58	2.6	7.1	2.7	0.9	70
2011	Rk	Kingsport	4	6	0	56	49	5.95	1.57	20.5	301	35	65	5.69	3.2	7.9	2.5	1.4	50

Lanky and projectable lefty features an 87-91 mph fastball that tops out at 93. His best pitch is a solid change-up that he uses effectively. He also has a curve and a slider, but both are below average. His mechanics are relatively clean and repeatable, though he does throw across his body. Still very raw and needs polish, but he has a live arm.

Velasquez, Vincent — SP — Houston

EXP MLB DEBUT: 2015 | POTENTIAL: #2 starter | **8E**

Thrws R Age 20
2010 (2) HS, (CA)

Velo	Pitch	Grade
90-93	FB	++++
74-77	CB	+++
80-83	CU	+++

Year	Lev	Team	W	L	Sv	IP	K	ERA	WHIP	BF/G	OBA	H%	S%	xERA	Ctl	Dom	Cmd	hr/9	BPV
2010	Rk	Greeneville	2	2	0	29	25	3.09	1.00	13.9	226	26	76	3.02	1.5	7.7	5.0	1.2	124

The loose and projectable prepster has an ideal pitcher's frame. Injured his elbow and had TJS at the end of '10 and missed all of '11. Prior to the injury he flashed three potentially plus offerings in a sinking fastball, a solid curveball, and a plus change-up. Will need to show he can come back, but he still has good potential.

Ventura, Yordano — SP — Kansas City

EXP MLB DEBUT: 2014 | POTENTIAL: #2 starter | **9E**

Thrws R Age 21
2008 FA (DR)

Velo	Pitch	Grade
92-98	FB	++++
79-83	CB	++
	CU	+++

Year	Lev	Team	W	L	Sv	IP	K	ERA	WHIP	BF/G	OBA	H%	S%	xERA	Ctl	Dom	Cmd	hr/9	BPV
2010	Rk	AZL Royals	4	2	0	52	58	3.28	1.26	15.2	250	34	75	3.29	2.9	10.0	3.4	0.5	121
2011	A	Kane County	4	6	0	84	88	4.28	1.26	18.1	257	33	67	3.71	2.6	9.4	3.7	0.9	111

Short-statured pitcher with high upside predicated on filthy FB and CU. Generates velocity, but delivery can be borderline violent which may eventually lead to bullpen role. Overthrows instead of focusing on changing speeds and mixing in breaking ball. Needs to develop CB in order to have lasting career as starter.

Villanueva, Elih — SP — Florida

EXP MLB DEBUT: 2011 | POTENTIAL: #5 starter | **7D**

Thrws R Age 25
2008 (27) Florida State

Velo	Pitch	Grade
86-89	FB	+++
77-80	CB	+++
73-74	CU	++

Year	Lev	Team	W	L	Sv	IP	K	ERA	WHIP	BF/G	OBA	H%	S%	xERA	Ctl	Dom	Cmd	hr/9	BPV
2009	A+	Jupiter	9	12	0	158	110	3.47	1.12	23.9	263	31	69	3.20	1.0	6.3	6.1	0.6	151
2009	AA	Jacksonville	0	1	0	10	5	4.50	1.50	21.6	299	34	67	4.15	2.7	4.5	1.7	0.0	57
2010	AA	Jacksonville	14	4	0	179	115	2.26	0.96	24.1	213	24	81	2.32	1.7	5.8	3.4	0.8	95
2011	AAA	New Orleans	7	11	0	165	105	5.35	1.56	25.8	300	33	68	5.55	3.2	5.7	1.8	1.3	28
2011	MLB	Florida	0	1	0	3	2	24.00	3.33	18.5	371	38	22	12.82	15.0	6.0	0.4	3.0	-65

Strong, wide-bodied righty came back to earth after a stellar campaign in '10. Below average velocity on fastball limits upside, but he mixes pitches while throwing strikes. Profiles as a solid back of the rotation guy, but does have the potential for a bit more. 2012 will be an important season for him.

Villareal, Brayan — SP — Detroit

EXP MLB DEBUT: 2011 | POTENTIAL: #4 starter | **7C**

Thrws R Age 25
2005 FA (Venezuela)

Velo	Pitch	Grade
88-95	FB	+++
81-84	SL	+++
	CU	+++

Year	Lev	Team	W	L	Sv	IP	K	ERA	WHIP	BF/G	OBA	H%	S%	xERA	Ctl	Dom	Cmd	hr/9	BPV
2009	A	West Michigan	5	5	2	103	118	2.88	1.15	15.8	226	32	75	2.63	3.0	10.3	3.5	0.4	131
2010	A+	Lakeland	7	4	0	85	90	3.49	1.13	21.0	233	30	72	3.04	2.4	9.5	3.9	0.8	122
2010	AA	Erie	0	4	0	43	46	3.75	1.23	21.9	233	29	74	3.67	3.3	9.6	2.9	1.3	89
2011	AAA	Toledo	3	5	0	66	40	5.05	1.42	16.5	259	29	65	4.15	4.0	5.5	1.4	0.8	40
2011	MLB	Detroit	1	1	0	16	14	6.75	1.94	4.8	318	37	68	7.10	5.6	7.9	1.4	1.7	18

Short and athletic pitcher didn't fare well in brief stint with DET, but has goods to be a contributor. Dom decreasing at higher levels and can be victimized by pitching backwards. Uses SL early in count to set up average FB. Can sneak FB by hitters, but doesn't change speeds effectively. Arm slot varies, though appears to do so purposely to keep hitters off-guard.

Vizcaino, Arodys — SP — Atlanta

EXP MLB DEBUT: 2011 | POTENTIAL: #3 starter/Setup Reliever | **9C**

Thrws R Age 21
20007 NDFA D.R.

Velo	Pitch	Grade
89-96	FB	++++
80-83	CB	++++
83-85	CU	++

Year	Lev	Team	W	L	Sv	IP	K	ERA	WHIP	BF/G	OBA	H%	S%	xERA	Ctl	Dom	Cmd	hr/9	BPV
2010	A+	Myrtle Beach	0	0	0	13	11	4.77	1.44	18.7	301	36	67	4.64	2.0	7.5	3.7	0.7	96
2011	A+	Lynchburg	2	2	0	40	37	2.47	1.02	17.1	215	27	79	2.41	2.2	8.3	3.7	0.7	119
2011	AA	Mississippi	2	3	0	49	55	3.84	1.26	18.2	241	33	69	3.20	3.3	10.1	3.1	0.5	115
2011	AAA	Gwinnett	1	0	0	7	8	1.29	1.00	4.5	262	34	100	3.51	0.0	10.3		1.3	
2011	MLB	Atlanta	1	1	0	17	17	4.74	1.46	4.3	249	32	67	3.80	4.7	8.9	1.9	0.5	83

Strong-armed, athletic pitcher with quick arm action. Features a dominant 92-95 mph FB and a plus CB. Can be too aggressive and inefficient by overthrowing. Fared well after being to relief because of organizational depth. Needs to show improved command, but could quickly emerge as a dominant setup man or a mid-rotation starter.

Volz, Kendal — RP — Kansas City

EXP MLB DEBUT: 2012 | POTENTIAL: Setup reliever | **7C**

Thrws R Age 24
2009 (9) Baylor

Velo	Pitch	Grade
87-92	FB	+++
80-84	SL	+++
80-83	CU	+++

Year	Lev	Team	W	L	Sv	IP	K	ERA	WHIP	BF/G	OBA	H%	S%	xERA	Ctl	Dom	Cmd	hr/9	BPV
2009	NCAA	Baylor	3	7	2	86	78	4.50	1.50	24.8	273	33	72	4.72	4.0	8.2	2.1	1.0	61
2010	A	Greenville	6	5	0	116	94	3.72	1.21	18.0	279	33	71	3.85	1.1	7.3	6.7	0.8	161
2011	A+	Salem	2	3	2	51	56	3.35	1.06	6.4	226	29	73	2.97	2.1	9.9	4.7	1.1	135
2011	A+	Wilmington	1	0	1	11	7	1.64	1.09	7.2	262	31	83	2.58	0.8	5.7	7.0	0.0	184
2011	AA	NW Arkansas	0	0	1	6	7	7.26	1.45	8.8	222	28	50	4.29	5.8	10.2	1.8	1.5	65

Large and strong pitcher who converted from SP to RP in '11. FB exhibits nasty movement and hitters have difficulty putting into air. Over-reliance on FB, but has decent secondary offerings. Neither SL or CU offer much in the way of strikeouts and he can be hittable by throwing too many strikes. Not much upside, but safe bet to succeed.

Von Rosenberg, Zack — SP — Pittsburgh

EXP MLB DEBUT: 2012 | POTENTIAL: #2 starter | **8D**

Thrws R Age 21
2009 (6) HS, (LA)

Velo	Pitch	Grade
90-92	FB	+++
74-76	CB	+++
	CU	+++

Year	Lev	Team	W	L	Sv	IP	K	ERA	WHIP	BF/G	OBA	H%	S%	xERA	Ctl	Dom	Cmd	hr/9	BPV
2009	Rk	GCL Pirates	0	0	0	1	1	0.00	0.00	2.8	0	0			0.0	9.0		0.0	
2010	A-	State College	1	6	0	59	39	3.20	1.24	18.4	265	31	75	3.56	2.0	5.9	3.0	0.6	82
2011	A	West Virginia	5	9	0	125	114	5.75	1.33	19.2	288	34	59	4.81	1.7	8.2	5.0	1.4	110

Tall, projectable righty took a step back in '11. Fastball has good velocity and now sits at 90-92 mph but tends to be flat, but he shows good command of it. Good changeup and the makings of a nice slurvy curveball. He finished the year on a high note (3.91 ERA in August with 6 BB/28 K) and is still only 20, but will need to show more in '12.

Wagner, Neil — RP — Oakland

EXP MLB DEBUT: 2011 | POTENTIAL: Setup reliever | **7E**

Thrws R Age 28
2005 (21) North Dakota St

Velo	Pitch	Grade
90-96	FB	++++
	SL	++
	SP	++

Year	Lev	Team	W	L	Sv	IP	K	ERA	WHIP	BF/G	OBA	H%	S%	xERA	Ctl	Dom	Cmd	hr/9	BPV
2010	AA	Akron	1	1	4	14	15	6.38	1.70	4.9	299	41	58	4.62	4.5	9.6	2.1	0.0	98
2010	AA	Midland	6	2	1	48	45	3.73	1.70	6.6	288	37	77	4.64	5.0	8.4	1.7	0.2	77
2011	AA	Midland	1	3	4	37	53	3.40	1.19	5.3	229	38	68	2.31	3.2	12.9	4.1	0.0	172
2011	AAA	Sacramento	2	1	2	29	34	3.10	1.28	5.4	248	34	77	3.40	3.1	10.6	3.4	0.6	121
2011	MLB	Oakland	0	0	0	5	4	7.20	1.80	3.9	299	33	63	6.57	5.4	7.2	1.3	1.8	12

Big and powerful-armed RP who appeared in majors for first time. Keeps ball down with explosive FB thrown from high three-quarters slot. High groundball rate gives him chance to evolve into setup reliever. Lacks consistent secondary stuff and only SL shows potential. Lacks touch for changing speeds and LHH have been troublesome.

Walker, Taijuan — SP — Seattle

EXP MLB DEBUT: 2013 | POTENTIAL: #1 starter | **9C**

Thrws R Age 19
2010 (1-S) HS (CA)

Velo	Pitch	Grade
89-98	FB	+++++
82-86	SL	+++
75-79	CB	+++
80-82	CU	++

Year	Lev	Team	W	L	Sv	IP	K	ERA	WHIP	BF/G	OBA	H%	S%	xERA	Ctl	Dom	Cmd	hr/9	BPV
2010	Rk	AZL Mariners	1	1	0	7	9	1.29	0.71	6.2	92	16	80		3.9	11.6	3.0	0.0	169
2011	A	Clinton	6	5	0	96	113	2.90	1.12	21.1	203	29	74	2.21	3.6	10.6	2.9	0.4	127

Lean and athletic pitcher who dominated level thanks to plus-plus FB and improved location. Throws with minimal effort and adds hint of movement to induce weak contact and plentiful groundballs. CB and SL give him two nice breaking pitches, while CU shows glimpses of being fourth average offering. Significant upside.

Warren, Adam — SP — New York (A)

EXP MLB DEBUT: 2012 | POTENTIAL: #4 starter | **7A**

Thrws R Age 24
2009 (4) North Carolina

Velo	Pitch	Grade
87-95	FB	++++
80-82	SL	++
76-80	CB	++
77-80	CU	+++

Year	Lev	Team	W	L	Sv	IP	K	ERA	WHIP	BF/G	OBA	H%	S%	xERA	Ctl	Dom	Cmd	hr/9	BPV
2009	NCAA	North Carolina	10	2	0	98	103	3.31	1.24	23.4	231	31	74	2.95	3.6	9.5	2.6	0.5	107
2009	A-	Staten Island	4	2	0	56	50	1.44	1.05	18.1	236	31	86	2.26	1.6	8.0	5.0	0.2	156
2010	A+	Tampa	7	5	0	81	67	2.22	1.10	21.2	240	30	79	2.49	1.9	7.4	3.9	0.2	128
2010	AA	Trenton	4	2	0	54	59	3.16	1.20	21.8	243	33	73	2.88	2.7	9.8	3.7	0.3	133
2011	AAA	Scranton/W-B	6	8	0	152	111	3.61	1.30	23.2	253	29	74	3.70	3.1	6.6	2.1	0.8	65

Durable and athletic pitcher with compact delivery, smarts, and polish. Has been consistent performer and uses four-pitch arsenal to keep hitters guessing. FB is best pitch and exhibits plenty of late movement. Has been victim of long ball and flyball tendencies may not work in NYY. Loses command at times, but generally throws strikes.

Watts, Dakota — RP — Minnesota

EXP MLB DEBUT: 2013 | POTENTIAL: Closer | 8E

Thrws R Age 24
2009 (16) Cal St Stanislaus

91-98	FB	++++
81-85	SL	+++

Year	Lev	Team	W	L	Sv	IP	K	ERA	WHIP	BF/G	OBA	H%	S%	xERA	Ctl	Dom	Cmd	hr/9	BPV
2010	A	Beloit	2	1	2	46	55	2.34	1.32	6.4	192	28	83	2.60	5.8	10.7	1.8	0.4	108
2010	A+	Fort Myers	4	2	6	31	29	3.19	1.23	7.4	229	29	75	3.01	3.5	8.4	2.4	0.6	93
2010	AA	New Britain	0	0	0	3	5	14.06	1.88	7.5	307	50	17	5.13	5.6	14.1	2.5	0.0	130
2011	A+	Fort Myers	2	2	8	31	25	4.63	1.48	5.3	267	33	67	3.89	4.1	7.2	1.8	0.3	74
2011	AA	New Britain	1	2	2	34	28	7.92	1.79	6.8	304	36	53	5.68	5.0	7.4	1.5	0.8	46

Tall and strong reliever who has shown improvement despite stats. Has among top FB in minors with velocity and vicious late movement. Rarely allows HR and generally records Ks or groundball outs. Though control and command have improved, he still struggles with walks. Unusual, max-effort delivery effective in short stints.

Weathers, Casey — RP — Chicago (N)

EXP MLB DEBUT: 2012 | POTENTIAL: Setup reliever/closer | 7C

Thrws R Age 27
2007 (1) Vanderbilt

90-98	FB	++++
82-87	SL	++++
82-85	CU	+

Year	Lev	Team	W	L	Sv	IP	K	ERA	WHIP	BF/G	OBA	H%	S%	xERA	Ctl	Dom	Cmd	hr/9	BPV
2007	A+	Modesto	0	0	0	1	2	0.00	2.00	4.8	0	0	100	2.09	18.0	18.0	1.0	0.0	184
2008	AA	Tulsa	2	1	2	44	54	3.06	1.41	4.2	215	32	77	2.90	5.7	11.0	1.9	0.2	113
2010	A-	Tri-City	0	0	0	11	21	0.00	0.63	3.9	60	16	100	-0.89	4.0	16.9	4.2	0.0	233
2010	A+	Modesto	0	1	4	18	25	6.92	1.92	4.3	260	38	64	5.51	8.4	12.4	1.5	1.0	78
2011	AA	Tulsa	2	2	0	45	48	5.38	1.77	4.7	201	27	69	4.04	9.6	9.6	1.0	0.6	75

Short, powerful reliever has yet to regain his form following TJ surgery. His velocity is back in the mid-90s, but he can't seem to find the strike zone. Features a lively plus mid-90s fastball and a swing-and-miss slider. Change-up is ineffective and will need to improve. Will need to show some signs of life in 2012.

Webster, Allen — SP — Los Angeles (N)

EXP MLB DEBUT: 2013 | POTENTIAL: #2 starter | 9D

Thrws R Age 22
2008 (18) HS. (NC)

90-95	FB	++++
82-85	SL	+++
77-80	CB	+++
82-84	CU	+++

Year	Lev	Team	W	L	Sv	IP	K	ERA	WHIP	BF/G	OBA	H%	S%	xERA	Ctl	Dom	Cmd	hr/9	BPV
2009	Rk	Ogden	2	0	0	21	21	3.00	1.29	21.6	280	37	77	3.69	1.7	9.0	5.3	0.4	150
2009	Rk	AZL Dodgers	2	1	0	47	56	2.10	1.04	15.2	208	31	78	1.71	2.7	10.7	4.0	0.0	161
2010	A	Great Lakes	12	9	0	131	114	2.88	1.31	20.8	244	31	78	3.26	3.6	7.8	2.2	0.4	86
2011	A+	Rancho Cucam	5	2	0	54	62	2.33	1.24	24.4	232	33	82	2.83	3.5	10.3	3.0	0.3	123
2011	AA	Chattanooga	6	3	0	91	73	5.04	1.51	21.9	282	34	66	4.55	3.6	7.2	2.0	0.7	64

Smallish (6'2", 165 lbs.) RHP had impressive full-season debut, going 11-5 with a 4.03 ERA. Pitches off a 90-95 mph sinking FB. CU is next best though CB and SL show potential and throws all four offerings for strikes. Durability is a concern and he tired down the stretch. Struggled when promoted to Double-A, but has plus potential.

Weiland, Kyle — SP — Houston

EXP MLB DEBUT: 2011 | POTENTIAL: #3 starter | 8B

Thrws R Age 25
2008 (3) Notre Dame

88-95	FB	++++
78-81	CB	+++
80-85	CU	+++

Year	Lev	Team	W	L	Sv	IP	K	ERA	WHIP	BF/G	OBA	H%	S%	xERA	Ctl	Dom	Cmd	hr/9	BPV
2008	A-	Lowell	3	3	0	60	68	1.50	0.77	14.3	175	26	80	0.79	1.5	10.2	6.8	0.2	219
2009	A+	Salem	7	9	0	132	112	3.47	1.33	21.1	242	31	73	3.15	3.9	7.6	2.0	0.3	85
2010	AA	Portland	5	9	0	128	120	4.43	1.26	20.9	237	29	66	3.49	3.4	8.4	2.4	0.9	82
2011	AAA	Pawtucket	8	10	0	128	126	3.58	1.27	21.8	230	29	73	3.25	3.9	8.9	2.3	0.7	89
2011	MLB	Boston	0	3	0	24	13	7.81	1.69	15.6	298	30	56	6.38	4.5	4.8	1.1	1.9	-9

Lean but strong pitcher who improved command. Generally focuses on inducing groundballs, but has velocity and secondary pitches to register Ks. Two-seamer exhibits life down in zone while big CB can be dropped for strikes. CU has moments of effectiveness and he gives hitters different looks with CT. Needs to maintain velocity late in games.

Wells, Ben — SP — Chicago (N)

EXP MLB DEBUT: 2014 | POTENTIAL: #3 starter | 7D

Thrws R Age 19
2010 (7) HS, (AK)

90-93	FB	+++
	CB	++
	CU	++

Year	Lev	Team	W	L	Sv	IP	K	ERA	WHIP	BF/G	OBA	H%	S%	xERA	Ctl	Dom	Cmd	hr/9	BPV
2011	A-	Boise	4	4	0	77	53	4.67	1.32	20.0	276	32	63	3.80	2.2	6.2	2.8	0.5	81

Strong, advanced 18-year-old has a solid pro debut. Uses a heavy 90-93 mph sinking fastball that tops out at 95. Secondary offerings are not advanced. Curveball and change-up both need work, but he has a good approach and clean, repeatable mechanics and nice long-term potential. Look for a breakout in 2012.

West, Matt — RP — Texas

EXP MLB DEBUT: 2014 | POTENTIAL: Setup reliever | 7C

Thrws R Age 23
2007 (2) HS (TX)

89-96	FB	+++
81-84	CB	+++
	CU	++

Year	Lev	Team	W	L	Sv	IP	K	ERA	WHIP	BF/G	OBA	H%	S%	xERA	Ctl	Dom	Cmd	hr/9	BPV
2011	A-	Spokane	1	2	9	26	35	3.12	0.92	4.2	239	34	71	2.76	0.3	12.1	35.0	1.0	784
2011	A+	Myrtle Beach	0	0	0	1	0	0.00	1.00	3.8	262	26	100	2.41	0.0	0.0		0.0	0

Powerful reliever who converted from 3B to RP to take advantage of arm strength. Dominated with surprising command and explosiveness. FB can be flat, but has velocity and tenacity to pitch up in zone and get hitters to chase. Commands hard CB and is ideal complement to quick FB. CU in development stage, but will likely stay as RP.

Wheeler, Zack — SP — New York (N)

EXP MLB DEBUT: 2014 | POTENTIAL: #1 starter | 9D

Thrws R Age 22
2009 (1) HS, (GA)

91-95	FB	++++
78-82	SL	+++
83-85	CU	++

Year	Lev	Team	W	L	Sv	IP	K	ERA	WHIP	BF/G	OBA	H%	S%	xERA	Ctl	Dom	Cmd	hr/9	BPV
2010	A	Augusta	3	3	0	58	70	4.02	1.46	11.9	223	33	69	2.95	5.9	10.8	1.8	0.0	114
2011	A+	San Jose	7	5	0	88	98	3.99	1.38	23.1	230	31	72	3.50	4.8	10.0	2.1	0.7	92
2011	A+	St. Lucie	2	2	0	27	31	2.00	1.15	17.9	255	37	81	2.58	1.7	10.3	6.2	0.0	196

Tall, lanky right-hander has a plus 91-95 mph FB with late life. He also features a power CB and an average CU, though both need work. Wheeler has repeatable mechanics and generates easy velocity. Command has been a problem in the past, but was improved in '11. If that trend continues, he could be very fun to watch.

Wieland, Joe — SP — San Diego

EXP MLB DEBUT: 2012 | POTENTIAL: #3 starter | 8B

Thrws R Age 22
2008 (4) HS, (NV)

88-93	CB	+++
80-83	CU	+++
79-82		+++

Year	Lev	Team	W	L	Sv	IP	K	ERA	WHIP	BF/G	OBA	H%	S%	xERA	Ctl	Dom	Cmd	hr/9	BPV
2010	A	Hickory	7	4	0	89	71	3.34	1.11	23.3	251	31	69	2.85	1.5	7.2	4.7	0.4	135
2010	A+	Bakersfield	4	3	0	59	62	5.19	1.31	22.1	287	37	61	4.30	1.5	9.5	6.2	0.9	157
2011	A+	Myrtle Beach	6	3	0	85	96	2.11	0.96	23.0	245	33	83	2.68	0.4	10.1	24.0	0.7	549
2011	AA	Frisco	4	0	0	44	36	1.23	1.05	24.3	220	27	91	2.29	2.3	7.4	3.3	0.4	112
2011	AA	San Antonio	3	1	0	26	18	2.77	1.12	20.5	239	29	72	2.33	2.1	6.2	3.0	0.0	108

A strike-throwing machine who dominates without an overpowering fastball. Heater sits in the 88-92 range, but does have some good late action. Complements the fastball with a good curveball and a nice change-up. Throws strikes, has plus command, and is fearless. Walked only 21 and should get a crack at the Padres rotation in 2012.

Wilk, Adam — SP — Detroit

EXP MLB DEBUT: 2011 | POTENTIAL: #5 starter | 6A

Thrws L Age 24
2009 (11) Long Beach State

86-92	FB	+++
78-81	CB	+++
80-82	CU	+++

Year	Lev	Team	W	L	Sv	IP	K	ERA	WHIP	BF/G	OBA	H%	S%	xERA	Ctl	Dom	Cmd	hr/9	BPV
2009	A	West Michigan	2	1	0	36	33	1.50	0.89	19.1	228	29	87	2.06	0.5	8.2	16.5	0.5	390
2010	A+	Lakeland	9	5	0	143	100	3.02	1.10	23.4	256	30	73	3.00	1.2	6.3	5.3	0.5	137
2010	AA	Erie	2	0	0	23	14	1.16	0.65	26.8	133	15	86	0.31	1.9	5.4	2.8	0.4	108
2011	AAA	Toledo	8	6	0	102	76	3.26	1.16	22.6	267	30	79	4.07	1.2	6.7	5.4	1.3	116
2011	MLB	Detroit	0	0	0	13	10	5.50	1.30	10.8	275	29	64	5.21	2.1	6.9	3.3	2.1	49

Tall and lean pitcher with ability to hit spots and locate FB to all parts of strike zone. Command and control-oriented nature limits upside, but is very efficient and holds velocity and quick arm action deep into games. Adds and subtracts, cuts and sinks, and can be crafty. Won't overpower or register strikeouts, but may be ideal option for swingman role.

Williams, Corey — RP — Minnesota

EXP MLB DEBUT: 2014 | POTENTIAL: Setup reliever | 8D

Thrws L Age 21
2011 (3) Vanderbilt

86-94	FB	+++
78-83	SL	++
	CU	+++

Year	Lev	Team	W	L	Sv	IP	K	ERA	WHIP	BF/G	OBA	H%	S%	xERA	Ctl	Dom	Cmd	hr/9	BPV
2010	NCAA	Vanderbilt	1	0	1	17	17	2.65	1.18	5.7	226	31	75	2.29	3.2	9.0	2.8	0.0	123
2011	NCAA	Vanderbilt	2	0	2	38	37	4.49	1.15	5.2	218	28	60	2.59	3.3	8.7	2.6	0.5	105
2011	Rk	Elizabethton	1	1	1	11	11	4.02	1.52	6.9	275	37	71	3.81	4.0	8.8	2.2	0.0	99

Athletic and strong pitcher who has upside as power reliever. Has quick arm action to produce heavy FB, but more intent on pitching to contact than strikeouts. Repeats mechanics and release point and CU is next best offering after FB. Breaking ball has moments, but hasn't trusted it in crucial spots.

Wilson, Alex — SP — Boston

EXP MLB DEBUT: 2012 | POTENTIAL: #3 starter | 8C

Thrws R Age 25
2009 (2) Texas A&M

88-95	FB	+++
81-85	SL	++++
80-85	CU	++

Year	Lev	Team	W	L	Sv	IP	K	ERA	WHIP	BF/G	OBA	H%	S%	xERA	Ctl	Dom	Cmd	hr/9	BPV
2009	A-	Lowell	0	1	0	36	33	0.50	0.47	9.1	90	13	88	-0.93	1.8	8.3	4.7	0.0	186
2010	A+	Salem	2	1	0	55	50	3.42	1.05	19.4	216	27	69	2.48	2.4	8.2	3.3	0.7	111
2010	AA	Portland	4	5	0	78	56	6.68	1.65	21.8	301	33	62	6.18	3.9	6.5	1.6	1.7	16
2011	AA	Portland	9	4	0	112	99	3.05	1.25	21.7	246	30	77	3.35	3.0	8.0	2.7	0.6	90
2011	AAA	Pawtucket	1	0	0	21	24	3.43	1.24	21.3	243	33	75	3.46	3.0	10.3	3.4	0.9	114

Short and strong starter with clean, loose mechanics and potent high three-quarters slot. Has the arm strength to throw hard while also mixing in plus, tight SL that is legitimate swing-and-miss pitch. Has been HR prone from time to time, but has sufficient control and command. Could be dynamite late-innings reliever if CU fails to come around.

Wimmers, Alex — SP — Minnesota

EXP MLB DEBUT: 2013 | POTENTIAL: #3 starter | **8B**

Thrws R Age 23
2010 (1) Ohio State

Velo	Pitch	Grade
87-93	FB	+++
80-83	CB	+++
79-82	CU	++++

Year	Lev	Team	W	L	Sv	IP	K	ERA	WHIP	BF/G	OBA	H%	S%	xERA	Ctl	Dom	Cmd	hr/9	BPV
2009	NCAA	Ohio State	9	2	0	104	136	3.28	1.30	26.8	214	31	77	3.15	4.8	11.7	2.5	0.8	111
2010	NCAA	Ohio State	9	0	0	73	86	1.60	1.11	28.7	220	33	84	2.03	2.8	10.6	3.7	0.0	153
2010	A+	Fort Myers	2	0	0	15	23	0.59	0.72	13.5	123	23	91		3.0	13.6	4.6	0.0	209
2011	Rk	GCL Twins	0	0	0	1	1	0.00	1.00	3.8	0	0	100	0.00	9.0	9.0	1.0	0.0	130
2011	A+	Fort Myers	2	3	1	40	39	4.25	1.24	13.6	198	24	69	3.18	4.9	8.7	1.8	1.1	71

Tall and athletic pitcher who possesses solid pitch mix, but will need better FB command and consistency in delivery. Best pitch is CU which has chance to be plus, particularly with quick arm. Has enough velocity on FB and bite on CB to have upside.

Winkler, Danny — SP — Colorado

EXP MLB DEBUT: 2014 | POTENTIAL: #4 starter/reliever | **7C**

Thrws R Age 22
2011 (20) Central Florida

Velo	Pitch	Grade
91-93	FB	+++
81-83	SL	+++
	CU	++

Year	Lev	Team	W	L	Sv	IP	K	ERA	WHIP	BF/G	OBA	H%	S%	xERA	Ctl	Dom	Cmd	hr/9	BPV
2011	Rk	Casper	4	3	0	57	65	3.94	1.45	20.3	284	38	75	4.66	3.0	10.2	3.4	0.9	103

Short righty had a solid professional debut. Attacks hitters with a 91-93 mph fastball and a plus slider. Currently lacks size, physicality, and stamina need to remain a starter. Will need to get stronger or be moved to a relief role where he could flourish due to fastball/slider combination.

Withrow, Chris — SP — Los Angeles (N)

EXP MLB DEBUT: 2013 | POTENTIAL: #2 starter | **9D**

Thrws R Age 23
2007 (1) HS, (TX)

Velo	Pitch	Grade
89-94	FB	++++
74-78	CB	+++
79-81	CU	+++

Year	Lev	Team	W	L	Sv	IP	K	ERA	WHIP	BF/G	OBA	H%	S%	xERA	Ctl	Dom	Cmd	hr/9	BPV
2008	A+	Inland Empire	0	0	0	4	1	4.50	2.00	4.8	151	16	75	3.58	13.5	2.3	0.2	0.0	42
2009	A+	Inland Empire	6	6	0	86	105	4.70	1.45	19.4	248	36	66	3.54	4.7	11.0	2.3	0.3	111
2009	AA	Chattanooga	2	2	0	27	26	3.99	1.33	18.7	239	30	71	3.47	4.0	8.6	2.2	0.7	85
2010	AA	Chattanooga	4	9	0	129	120	5.99	1.66	21.5	286	35	64	5.19	4.8	8.4	1.7	0.9	57
2011	AA	Chattanooga	6	6	0	128	130	4.21	1.45	21.9	235	31	71	3.62	5.3	9.1	1.7	0.6	82

Athletic pitcher with plus velocity and ability to dominate. Fastball sits in the 90-95 mph range and tops out at 98 with excellent late movement. Curve is a plus offering with nice downward action, but tends to be inconsistent. His change-up is still needs work. Good potential but is still raw and needs to improve command.

Wojciechowski, Asher — SP — Toronto

EXP MLB DEBUT: 2013 | POTENTIAL: #4 starter | **7C**

Thrws R Age 23
2010 (1-S) The Citadel

Velo	Pitch	Grade
88-96	FB	+++
81-84	SL	+++
	CU	+

Year	Lev	Team	W	L	Sv	IP	K	ERA	WHIP	BF/G	OBA	H%	S%	xERA	Ctl	Dom	Cmd	hr/9	BPV
2008	NCAA	The Citadel	5	1	0	76	78	4.50	1.45	23.2	246	32	69	3.79	4.7	9.2	2.0	0.6	84
2009	NCAA	The Citadel	3	3	0	69	75	4.42	1.37	24.2	238	33	66	3.30	4.4	9.8	2.2	0.4	101
2010	NCAA	The Citadel	12	3	0	125	155	3.59	1.14	29.2	239	34	70	3.03	2.3	11.1	4.8	0.7	154
2010	A-	Auburn	0	0	0	12	11	0.75	0.83	14.6	151	21	90	0.58	3.0	8.3	2.8	0.0	132
2011	A+	Dunedin	11	9	0	130	96	4.70	1.44	22.2	298	34	69	4.94	2.1	6.6	3.1	1.0	69

Large-framed starter who provides ample durability and stamina. Produces big FB with exceptional arm strength and quick arm action. Tinkering with mechanics has caused stat line to suffer, but has tools to succeed. Good, hard SL is second best pitch, but will need to improve CU (or add change-of-pace pitch) to more effectively battle LHH.

Wood, Austin — RP — Detroit

EXP MLB DEBUT: 2012 | POTENTIAL: Middle reliever | **7D**

Thrws L Age 25
2009 (5) Texas

Velo	Pitch	Grade
86-93	FB	+++
74-78	CB	+++
	CU	+++

Year	Lev	Team	W	L	Sv	IP	K	ERA	WHIP	BF/G	OBA	H%	S%	xERA	Ctl	Dom	Cmd	hr/9	BPV
2009	Rk	GCL Tigers	1	0	0	1	1	9.00	2.00	4.8	415	52	50	7.49	0.0	9.0		0.0	
2009	A+	Lakeland	0	0	0	5	4	0.00	0.80	6.0	221	28	100	1.30	0.0	7.2		0.0	
2010	A+	Lakeland	0	0	0	1	3	0.00	0.00	1.6	0	0			0.0	24.5		0.0	
2011	AA	Erie	5	5	6	62	61	3.18	1.37	5.2	245	31	79	3.70	4.1	8.8	2.2	0.7	83
2011	Rk	Orem	0	0	0	1	1	24.55	3.64	3.6	563	59	33	23.66	0.0	8.2		8.2	

Injury-riddled pitcher who returned after missing most of '10. Quick arm action adds nice movement to average FB and he can locate it well down in the zone. Doesn't have a wipeout offering, but has good secondary pitches to keep hitters guessing. Can take a few ticks off FB and is able to repeat arm speed on CU. Not much upside, but is tough against LHH.

Workman, Brandon — SP — Boston

EXP MLB DEBUT: 2014 | POTENTIAL: #4 starter | **7B**

Thrws R Age 23
2010 (2) Texas

Velo	Pitch	Grade
88-94	FB	+++
86-89	CT	+++
77-80	CB	++++
	CU	++

Year	Lev	Team	W	L	Sv	IP	K	ERA	WHIP	BF/G	OBA	H%	S%	xERA	Ctl	Dom	Cmd	hr/9	BPV
2008	NCAA	Texas	5	2	1	53	49	5.08	1.47	10.8	279	34	67	4.70	3.4	8.3	2.5	1.0	70
2009	NCAA	Texas	3	5	0	75	82	3.48	1.15	14.9	215	28	72	2.86	3.4	9.8	2.9	0.8	107
2010	NCAA	Texas	12	2	0	104	101	3.37	1.16	24.4	250	32	72	3.13	2.0	8.7	4.4	0.6	131
2011	A	Greenville	6	7	0	131	115	3.71	1.23	20.4	257	32	71	3.49	2.3	7.9	3.5	0.7	104

Tall and durable pitcher who succeeded in first pro season by commanding deep pitch mix at will. Best pitch is hard CB that he can get hitters to chase or drop in for strikes early in count. Throws from three-quarters slot and whips quality FB into strike zone. CU remains below average, but should improve with better arm speed.

Wright, Mike — SP — Baltimore

EXP MLB DEBUT: 2014 | POTENTIAL: #3 starter | **8D**

Thrws R Age 22
2011 (3) East Carolina

Velo	Pitch	Grade
87-92	FB	+++
82-85	SL	+++
	CU	+++

Year	Lev	Team	W	L	Sv	IP	K	ERA	WHIP	BF/G	OBA	H%	S%	xERA	Ctl	Dom	Cmd	hr/9	BPV
2010	NCAA	East Carolina	2	2	0	35	31	6.94	1.54	6.9	332	39	56	6.21	1.3	8.0	6.2	1.5	120
2011	NCAA	East Carolina	6	4	0	100	75	2.79	1.11	24.6	223	28	73	2.28	2.7	6.8	2.5	0.2	98
2011	Rk	GCL Orioles	0	0	0	1	1	0.00	0.00	2.8	0	0			0.0	9.0		0.0	
2011	A-	Aberdeen	2	1	0	31	29	3.77	1.13	17.5	249	31	69	3.29	1.7	8.4	4.8	0.9	131
2011	A	Delmarva	1	1	0	13	12	10.91	1.89	15.6	361	42	41	8.07	2.7	8.2	3.0	2.0	34

Tall and slender pitcher who thrives with sinker/slider combination. Spots sinker down in strike zone and keeps walks to a minimum. Hitters have trouble elevating pitches and quick arm adds hint of deception. Inconsistent CU and lack of Dom potential may lead to bullpen role, but will be given shot to develop change-of-pace pitch as starter.

Yambati, Robinson — SP — Kansas City

EXP MLB DEBUT: 2015 | POTENTIAL: #2 starter | **9E**

Thrws R Age 21
2008 FA (DR)

Velo	Pitch	Grade
87-96	FB	+++
80-82	SL	+++
	CU	+++

Year	Lev	Team	W	L	Sv	IP	K	ERA	WHIP	BF/G	OBA	H%	S%	xERA	Ctl	Dom	Cmd	hr/9	BPV
2009	Rk	AZL Royals	2	3	1	27	18	8.97	2.03	11.0	349	39	54	7.24	4.6	6.0	1.3	1.0	18
2010	Rk	AZL Royals	8	2	0	66	64	2.72	1.16	18.8	259	35	74	2.69	1.6	8.7	5.3	0.0	168
2011	Rk	Burlington	0	5	0	17	9	19.36	3.20	12.9	476	49	37	14.98	5.8	4.7	0.8	3.1	-89

Tall and thin pitcher with dynamic upside, but little production so far. Beffudles onlookers with inconsistent velocity--FB is mid-90s in one outing and barely touches 90 in the next. Long arms and quick action provides pitch movement, but has trouble repeating delivery. Plenty of projection, but needs time to iron out mechanical issues.

Yan, Johan — RP — Texas

EXP MLB DEBUT: 2012 | POTENTIAL: Situational reliever | **6A**

Thrws R Age 23
2005 FA (DR)

Velo	Pitch	Grade
86-92	FB	+++
80-82	SL	++
	CU	++

Year	Lev	Team	W	L	Sv	IP	K	ERA	WHIP	BF/G	OBA	H%	S%	xERA	Ctl	Dom	Cmd	hr/9	BPV
2009	Rk	AZL Rangers	3	2	1	25	21	9.36	1.92	7.9	305	38	47	5.62	6.1	7.6	1.2	0.4	54
2010	A-	Spokane	0	1	0	3	2	2.90	1.94	7.4	364	43	83	6.33	2.9	5.8	2.0	0.0	59
2010	A	Hickory	0	2	2	40	36	2.70	1.00	6.9	199	25	74	1.95	2.7	8.1	3.0	0.5	113
2011	A+	Myrtle Beach	5	3	10	41	48	1.53	1.12	6.2	222	31	89	2.49	2.8	10.5	3.7	0.4	138
2011	AA	Frisco	0	0	2	26	18	0.34	1.03	5.3	196	24	96	1.59	3.1	6.2	2.0	0.0	95

Tall and lean reliever who signed as INF, but converted to RP in '09. Low arm slot has been effective against RHH and hitters from both sides have difficulty squaring up balls. Has enough velocity due to sidearm angle and has ideal groundball rate for situational pitching. Not much upside, but unique delivery has value.

Younginer, Madison — SP — Boston

EXP MLB DEBUT: 2015 | POTENTIAL: #3 starter | **8E**

Thrws R Age 21
2009 (7) HS (SC)

Velo	Pitch	Grade
89-95	FB	+++
73-77	CB	+++
80-82	CU	+++

Year	Lev	Team	W	L	Sv	IP	K	ERA	WHIP	BF/G	OBA	H%	S%	xERA	Ctl	Dom	Cmd	hr/9	BPV
2010	A-	Lowell	3	7	0	62	40	4.79	1.40	18.7	243	29	64	3.38	4.5	5.8	1.3	0.3	60
2011	A-	Lowell	1	6	0	61	48	5.30	1.55	19.1	271	33	65	4.41	4.6	7.1	1.5	0.6	58

Tall, lanky, and projectable hurler who repeated short-season ball, but didn't dazzle. Has tendency to pitch backwards and using CU to set up FB with late life. CB can be plus pitch at times, but shows inconsistent break. Could increase velocity with smoother mechanics, but pitches up too frequently.

Zych, Tony — RP — Chicago (N)

EXP MLB DEBUT: 2013 | POTENTIAL: Possible closer | **7C**

Thrws R Age 21
2011 (4) Louisville

Velo	Pitch	Grade
94-97	FB	++++
83-85	SL	+++

Year	Lev	Team	W	L	Sv	IP	K	ERA	WHIP	BF/G	OBA	H%	S%	xERA	Ctl	Dom	Cmd	hr/9	BPV
2009	NCAA	Louisville	6	2	2	44	31	3.27	1.09	8.2	234	24	80	3.73	2.0	6.3	3.1	1.6	62
2010	NCAA	Louisville	5	2	0	59	50	5.17	1.39	11.3	274	34	62	4.04	2.9	7.6	2.6	0.6	83
2011	NCAA	Louisville	0	2	13	30	30	3.00	1.43	4.6	255	34	79	3.60	4.2	9.0	2.1	0.3	94
2011	Rk	AZL Cubs	0	0	0	2	3	4.50	1.50	4.3	262	43	67	3.53	4.5	13.5	3.0	0.0	147
2011	A-	Boise	0	0	0	2	2	0.00	0.50	3.3	0	0	100		4.5	9.0	2.0	0.0	151

Tall, athletic reliever has a plus 94-97 mph FB and a plus SL. Throws from a low three-quarters slot adding some nice deception and good movement. As a result, command can sometimes be an issue. Pitched effectively in the 2010 Cape Cod league and could move up quickly as he has plenty of closer experience in college.

MAJOR LEAGUE EQUIVALENTS

In his 1985 *Baseball Abstract*, Bill James introduced the concept of major league equivalencies. His assertion was that, with the proper adjustments, a minor leaguer's statistics could be converted to an equivalent major league level performance with a great deal of accuracy.

Because of wide variations in the level of play among different minor leagues, it is difficult to get a true reading on a player's potential. For instance, a .300 batting average achieved in the high-offense Pacific Coast League is not nearly as much of an accomplishment as a similar level in the Eastern League. MLEs normalize these types of variances, for all statistical categories.

The actual MLEs are not projections. They represent how a player's previous performance might look at the major league level. However, the MLE stat line can be used in forecasting future performance in just the same way as a major league stat line would.

The model we use contains a few variations to James' version and updates all of the minor league and ballpark factors. In addition, we designed a module to convert pitching statistics, which is something James did not originally do.

Do MLEs really work?

Used correctly, MLEs are excellent indicators of potential. But just like we cannot take traditional major league statistics at face value, the same goes for MLEs. The underlying measures of base skill — batting eye ratios, pitching command ratios, etc. — are far more accurate in evaluating future talent than raw home runs, batting averages or ERAs.

The charts we present here also provide the unique perspective of looking at up to five years' worth of data. Ironically, the longer the history, the less likely the player is a legitimate prospect — he should have made it to the majors before compiling a long history in AA and/or AAA ball. Of course, the shorter trends are more difficult to read despite them often belonging to players with higher ceilings. But even here we can find small indications of players improving their skills, or struggling, as they rise through more difficult levels of competition. Since players — especially those with any talent — are promoted rapidly through major league systems, a two or three-year scan is often all we get to spot any trends.

Here are some things to look for as you scan these charts:

Target players who...

- spent a full year in AA and then a full year in AAA
- had consistent playing time from one year to the next
- improved their base skills as they were promoted

Raise the warning flag for players who...

- were stuck at a level for multiple seasons, or regressed
- displayed marked changes in playing time from one year to the next
- showed large drops in BPIs from one year to the next

Players are listed on the charts if they spent at least part of 2007-2011 in Triple-A or Double-A and had at least 100 AB or 30 IP within those two levels. Each is listed with the organization with which they finished the season.

Only statistics accumulated in Triple-A and Double-A ball are included (players who split a season are indicated as a/a); Single-A stats are excluded.

Each player's actual AB and IP totals are used as the base for the conversion. However, it is more useful to compare performances using common levels, so rely on the ratios and sabermetric gauges. Complete explanations of these formulas appear in the Glossary.

BATTER	B	Yr	Age	Pos	Lev	Tm	AB	R	H	D	T	HR	RBI	BB	K	SB	CS	BA	OB	Slg	OPS	bb%	Ct%	Eye	PX	SX	RC/G	BPV
Adams,David	R	10	23	4	aa	NYY	152	25	40	13	2	3	26	16	27	4	2	264	333	432	765	9%	83%	0.59	116	132	5.17	48
Adams,Ryan	R	10	23	4	aa	BAL	530	65	143	38	0	14	54	36	96	2	3	270	317	420	736	6%	82%	0.38	104	42	4.75	40
		11	24	4	aaa	BAL	377	36	94	24	2	9	29	23	114	4	2	249	293	395	688	6%	70%	0.20	98	77	4.04	28
Almonte,Zoilo	B	11	22	8	aa	NYY	175	18	40	10	1	3	18	11	49	3	1	229	274	349	623	6%	72%	0.22	82	90	3.30	15
Alonso,Yonder	L	09	22	3	aa	CIN	105	10	29	10	0	2	12	12	13	1	0	276	350	429	779	10%	88%	0.92	114	36	5.72	57
		10	23	3	a/a	CIN	507	54	130	32	1	14	54	44	77	10	4	257	317	406	722	8%	85%	0.58	100	71	4.61	38
		11	24	8	aaa	CIN	358	34	91	20	3	10	42	35	70	4	6	254	321	411	731	9%	80%	0.50	100	72	4.51	36
Amarista,Alexi	L	10	21	4	a/a	LAA	256	29	72	7	2	1	22	10	14	6	4	280	307	335	643	4%	95%	0.73	38	97	3.63	23
		11	22	4	aaa	LAA	363	33	87	20	3	3	34	14	63	10	9	240	268	336	604	4%	83%	0.22	69	103	2.86	13
Anderson,Bryan	L	07	21	2	aa	STL	389	44	107	14	1	5	45	28	59	0	1	275	325	356	681	7%	85%	0.48	54	39	4.24	24
		08	22	2	aa	STL	315	31	86	16	1	3	33	28	45	2	0	273	332	359	692	8%	86%	0.63	63	57	4.50	30
		09	23	2	aa	STL	163	17	35	6	2	3	9	8	32	1	0	215	251	331	583	5%	80%	0.25	72	103	2.84	6
		10	24	2	aaa	STL	270	27	60	10	0	8	30	19	40	0	0	221	272	345	616	6%	85%	0.47	77	25	3.23	15
		11	25	2	aaa	STL	335	27	75	15	0	5	26	25	89	1	1	224	278	313	591	7%	73%	0.28	63	32	3.01	6
Anderson,Lars	L	08	21	3	aa	BOS	133	22	40	14	0	4	24	23	34	1	0	304	407	501	908	15%	75%	0.69	141	46	8.21	73
		09	22	3	aa	BOS	447	42	102	26	0	7	43	54	92	2	0	228	311	334	645	11%	79%	0.58	76	42	3.78	19
		10	23	3	a/a	BOS	471	47	120	40	2	11	53	38	96	2	3	254	310	416	726	8%	80%	0.40	115	52	4.53	40
		11	24	3	aaa	BOS	491	53	120	33	2	11	63	65	131	4	0	244	333	387	720	12%	73%	0.50	98	71	4.78	32
Avery,Xavier	L	10	21	8	aa	BAL	107	8	24	5	0	3	14	5	25	8	0	221	257	356	613	5%	76%	0.20	87	91	3.44	14
		11	22	8	aa	BAL	557	63	137	29	2	4	23	42	163	32	15	246	299	327	626	7%	71%	0.26	60	111	3.36	12
Barfield,Jeremy	R	11	23	8	aa	OAK	495	39	104	20	2	7	51	29	103	1	1	210	254	301	555	6%	79%	0.28	61	50	2.57	1
Bell,Josh	B	10	24	5	aaa	BAL	316	34	79	22	0	12	40	18	63	2	5	251	291	431	722	5%	80%	0.28	118	40	4.13	38
		11	25	5	aaa	BAL	395	47	87	10	1	16	43	29	133	3	0	220	274	372	646	7%	66%	0.22	87	72	3.54	14
Beltre,Engel	L	10	21	8	aa	TEX	181	12	45	4	4	1	12	8	19	7	2	250	283	336	619	4%	89%	0.42	49	150	3.36	12
		11	22	8	aa	TEX	437	49	92	14	6	1	21	21	109	12	6	211	247	277	524	5%	75%	0.19	44	150	2.25	-8
Benson,Joe	R	10	23	8	aa	MIN	373	50	81	17	5	17	38	29	90	11	11	217	274	426	700	7%	76%	0.32	123	139	3.57	29
		11	24	8	aa	MIN	400	50	98	26	3	10	49	42	118	9	10	245	317	400	717	10%	71%	0.36	103	98	4.22	31
Blackmon,Charles	L	10	24	8	aa	COL	337	41	91	21	3	10	42	24	33	14	8	271	319	436	755	7%	90%	0.72	107	113	4.81	49
Cardenas,Adrian	L	09	22	4	aa	OAK	508	59	130	35	2	3	59	40	51	6	8	256	311	352	663	7%	90%	0.78	74	69	3.77	32
		10	23	4	a/a	OAK	404	50	105	20	1	3	40	38	38	5	10	260	324	337	660	9%	91%	1.00	57	60	3.69	30
		11	24	8	aaa	OAK	491	48	124	23	3	3	35	32	67	9	7	253	298	330	628	6%	86%	0.48	56	84	3.40	17
Carpenter,Matt	L	10	25	5	aa	STL	396	57	105	22	2	8	39	48	70	9	2	264	344	388	732	11%	82%	0.69	84	96	5.03	36
		11	26	5	aaa	STL	434	42	102	23	2	8	48	58	82	3	5	235	325	353	678	12%	81%	0.71	80	52	4.04	25
Carroll,Sawyer	L	09	23	8	aa	SD	82	14	22	4	2	1	11	15	14	1	1	263	375	394	769	15%	83%	1.03	82	147	5.55	42
		10	24	8	aa	SD	458	41	91	17	2	5	46	48	118	1	8	199	275	277	552	9%	74%	0.41	53	44	2.47	-3
		11	25	8	aa	SD	460	48	94	18	4	11	50	45	122	8	2	204	275	333	608	9%	73%	0.37	79	109	3.17	8
Carter,Chris	R	10	24	3	aaa	OAK	465	64	96	24	1	20	65	51	97	1	1	207	285	388	673	10%	79%	0.53	112	54	3.79	26
		11	25	3	aaa	OAK	296	37	63	14	1	11	48	28	102	3	1	213	281	378	659	9%	66%	0.27	102	77	3.66	19
Castillo,Angel	R	11	22	8	a/a	LAA	365	36	65	11	1	4	18	18	118	13	5	178	217	247	463	5%	68%	0.15	46	112	1.73	-19
Castillo,Welington	R	08	21	2	aa	CHC	203	19	54	10	0	3	19	11	40	0	0	264	302	358	660	5%	80%	0.28	67	23	3.89	21
		09	22	2	aa	CHC	319	23	69	15	0	10	32	12	62	1	0	216	245	357	602	4%	81%	0.19	90	30	2.94	13
		10	23	2	aaa	CHC	239	25	52	15	1	10	41	14	42	0	3	217	260	410	670	5%	82%	0.33	122	46	3.38	29
		11	24	2	aaa	CHC	227	24	52	7	0	10	22	12	66	0	0	229	268	392	660	5%	71%	0.18	96	23	3.59	19
Castillo,Wilkin	B	07	23	2	aa	ARI	410	41	113	28	3	6	38	15	53	15	16	277	302	402	704	3%	87%	0.28	89	97	3.82	35
		08	24	25	a/a	CIN	428	32	91	16	1	5	36	19	49	4	4	213	247	289	536	4%	89%	0.39	53	55	2.33	1
		09	25	2	aaa	CIN	122	9	24	5	1	2	6	1	18	3	1	193	199	293	492	1%	85%	0.05	65	43	1.83	-8
		10	26	2	aaa	CIN	317	33	67	14	2	7	26	9	45	8	4	212	234	337	571	3%	86%	0.21	80	109	2.54	8
		11	27	2	aaa	ATL	279	15	60	10	1	4	28	6	58	4	4	215	232	301	533	2%	79%	0.10	57	59	2.18	-3
Cavazos-Galvez,Brian	R	11	24	3	aa	LA	411	43	93	22	3	10	44	8	75	9	13	226	241	367	608	2%	82%	0.11	91	104	2.55	15
Chambers,Adron	L	10	24	8	a/a	STL	321	46	76	8	4	4	25	29	51	11	6	238	302	324	626	8%	84%	0.58	51	134	3.40	12
		11	25	8	aaa	STL	426	51	95	15	3	6	30	37	105	15	15	223	285	315	600	8%	75%	0.35	59	108	2.82	6
Chavez,Johermyn	R	11	22	8	aa	SEA	439	38	83	14	3	10	40	40	141	5	10	189	257	303	560	8%	68%	0.28	70	76	2.40	-3
Chiang,Chih-Hsien	L	10	23	8	aa	BOS	438	40	106	37	1	8	48	23	46	1	0	242	280	386	666	5%	89%	0.50	105	47	3.77	34
		11	24	8	aa	SEA	451	63	118	38	3	13	69	25	107	6	5	262	300	446	746	5%	76%	0.23	125	99	4.61	43
Chirinos,Robinson	R	07	23	6	aa	CHC	127	9	25	4	2	2	13	11	27	1	1	199	261	306	566	8%	79%	0.40	64	97	2.65	1
		08	24	5	aa	CHC	103	9	21	7	2	0	6	8	15	0	0	205	260	308	568	7%	86%	0.53	74	96	2.73	9
		09	25	2	aa	CHC	35	3	8	3	0	0	4	6	3	0	1	215	324	295	619	14%	91%	1.77	71	34	3.19	36
		10	26	2	a/a	CHC	319	42	86	24	0	13	50	30	35	1	6	268	332	464	796	9%	89%	0.87	129	33	5.28	60
		11	27	2	aaa	TAM	282	17	58	10	1	4	17	21	86	1	1	206	261	291	552	7%	70%	0.24	56	43	2.57	-3
Colon,Christian	R	11	22	6	aa	KC	491	51	111	13	2	5	45	33	54	12	8	226	275	291	566	6%	89%	0.61	43	88	2.69	5
Cooper,David	L	09	23	3	aa	TOR	473	60	119	32	0	10	63	57	93	0	0	252	332	383	715	11%	80%	0.61	93	28	4.68	34
		10	24	3	aa	TOR	498	44	109	27	1	16	58	39	60	0	0	218	275	372	647	7%	88%	0.65	99	24	3.53	27
		11	25	3	aaa	TOR	467	47	134	41	1	6	59	42	54	1	4	287	346	418	763	8%	88%	0.78	99	33	5.28	52
Cowgill,Collin	R	10	24	8	aa	ARI	502	73	133	34	4	13	68	47	64	20	10	266	329	428	757	9%	87%	0.74	107	118	4.99	48
		11	25	8	aaa	ARI	395	53	110	20	6	7	39	28	76	17	4	278	326	413	739	7%	81%	0.37	86	155	5.01	36
Cox,Zack	L	11	22	5	aa	STL	352	35	83	15	0	6	31	19	78	0	1	236	275	330	604	5%	78%	0.24	64	31	3.11	10
Cozart,Zack	R	11	26	6	aaa	CIN	323	41	82	21	1	5	23	17	62	6	2	254	291	372	663	5%	81%	0.27	84	91	3.82	25
Culberson,Charlie	R	11	22	4	aa	SF	553	59	133	33	2	8	48	19	138	12	4	241	266	351	617	3%	75%	0.14	78	100	3.19	15
Danks,Jordan	L	09	23	8	aa	CHW	284	43	63	11	1	6	17	32	65	6	3	221	300	328	628	10%	77%	0.50	69	94	3.46	12
		10	24	8	aaa	CHW	445	47	92	23	2	7	32	32	127	12	7	207	260	313	573	7%	71%	0.25	73	99	2.67	4
		11	25	8	aaa	CHW	463	51	102	21	4	13	51	48	184	14	5	220	294	367	661	9%	60%	0.26	91	124	3.75	16
Darnell,James	R	10	24	5	aa	SD	373	39	83	18	1	8	43	39	60	2	0	223	297	339	636	10%	84%	0.65	77	57	3.60	19
		11	25	5	a/a	SD	422	54	99	21	1	13	52	47	99	1	1	235	311	382	693	10%	77%	0.47	94	50	4.23	26
Decker,Jaff	L	11	21	8	aa	SD	496	67	95	23	1	13	69	82	168	11	6	192	306	321	627	14%	66%	0.49	83	82	3.45	8
Dominguez,Chris	R	11	25	5	aa	SF	295	28	63	20	2	5	36	7	88	1	6	214	232	346	578	2%	70%	0.08	92	80	2.37	11
Dominguez,Matt	R	09	20	5	aa	FLA	97	9	18	7	0	2	8	13	21	0	0	181	280	319	598	12%	78%	0.63	99	22	3.09	13
		10	21	5	aa	FLA	504	52	117	32	1	11	69	49	84	0	2	232	301	367	668	9%	83%	0.59	93	30	3.86	27
		11	22	5	a/a	FLA	340	34	73	16	1	8	40	21	62	0	1	215	260	338	599	6%	82%	0.34	81	43	2.95	12

BATTER	B	Yr	Age	Pos	Lev	Tm	AB	R	H	D	T	HR	RBI	BB	K	SB	CS	BA	OB	Slg	OPS	bb%	Ct%	Eye	PX	SX	RC/G	BPV
Donaldson,Josh	R	10	25	2	aaa	OAK	294	35	55	11	1	12	45	31	56	2	1	186	263	346	609	9%	81%	0.55	95	65	3.06	12
		11	26	2	aaa	OAK	444	51	88	22	0	10	46	33	123	8	5	198	254	315	569	7%	72%	0.27	79	76	2.62	4
Dozier,Brian	R	11	24	6	aa	MIN	311	43	84	20	6	4	24	21	51	8	8	270	316	412	728	6%	84%	0.41	94	150	4.36	37
Dykstra,Allan	L	11	24	3	aa	NYM	390	40	85	18	1	13	55	50	153	1	1	218	307	369	676	11%	61%	0.33	95	44	4.00	18
Eaton,Adam	L	11	23	8	aa	ARI	212	22	57	7	4	3	20	21	38	7	7	269	335	382	717	9%	82%	0.55	68	133	4.32	29
Erickson,Gorman	B	11	23	2	aa	LA	142	13	32	7	0	5	19	8	25	1	0	225	267	380	647	5%	82%	0.32	98	40	3.50	22
Escobar,Eduardo	B	10	22	6	aa	CHW	202	19	48	7	2	3	19	8	30	3	0	240	269	340	609	4%	85%	0.27	63	101	3.24	11
		11	23	6	aaa	CHW	489	46	118	21	3	4	41	24	117	11	9	241	277	321	598	5%	76%	0.21	56	93	2.94	8
Exposito,Luis	R	09	23	2	aa	BOS	92	12	30	6	0	2	10	3	22	1	2	326	347	457	804	3%	76%	0.14	91	53	5.63	49
		10	24	2	aa	BOS	473	47	113	41	1	8	68	39	67	1	2	238	297	379	676	8%	86%	0.58	104	41	3.92	34
		11	25	2	aaa	BOS	330	27	74	18	0	6	29	21	86	0	2	224	271	333	604	6%	74%	0.24	76	22	3.02	11
Fairley,Wendell	L	11	23	8	aa	SF	98	9	24	3	2	0	6	7	29	2	2	245	295	316	612	7%	70%	0.24	45	148	3.14	5
Farris,Eric	R	10	25	4	aaa	MIL	230	21	53	8	1	2	12	7	22	11	2	230	251	296	548	3%	90%	0.31	46	109	2.61	2
		11	26	4	aaa	MIL	538	47	116	21	3	4	37	22	86	14	8	216	246	288	535	4%	84%	0.26	51	99	2.31	-2
Federowicz,Tim	R	11	24	2	a/a	LA	422	40	94	21	0	9	44	28	100	1	0	223	271	336	608	6%	76%	0.28	77	39	3.16	12
Flowers,Tyler	R	09	24	2	a/a	CHW	353	59	97	25	1	15	49	60	99	3	0	275	380	478	857	14%	72%	0.60	131	70	7.02	58
		10	25	2	aaa	CHW	346	33	65	18	1	13	40	43	101	2	1	189	279	363	642	11%	71%	0.43	109	49	3.45	17
		11	26	2	aaa	CHW	222	28	51	7	0	14	25	33	100	2	0	230	329	450	780	13%	55%	0.33	126	41	5.38	35
Frazier,Todd	R	09	24	8	a/a	CIN	514	57	137	41	1	16	64	41	69	8	9	267	321	442	764	7%	87%	0.59	120	59	4.89	50
		10	25	8	aaa	CIN	480	55	108	29	3	14	51	36	108	11	5	226	279	388	667	7%	77%	0.33	105	101	3.68	25
		11	26	5	aaa	CIN	315	34	69	15	1	12	33	25	97	12	5	219	276	387	664	7%	69%	0.26	104	95	3.58	21
Galvis,Freddy	B	09	20	6	aa	PHI	61	5	12	0	0	1	4	2	6	0	1	189	216	241	457	3%	91%	0.37	27	47	1.54	-19
		10	21	6	aa	PHI	501	45	106	14	2	4	37	23	66	11	5	212	246	273	519	4%	87%	0.34	42	93	2.24	-5
		11	22	6	a/a	PHI	543	63	136	25	4	7	35	25	93	19	14	250	283	350	633	4%	83%	0.27	67	113	3.24	17
Gillaspie,Conor	L	10	23	5	aa	SF	491	50	132	24	7	7	58	31	59	0	4	269	313	387	701	6%	88%	0.53	76	72	4.26	32
		11	24	5	aaa	SF	428	40	103	18	4	7	39	42	92	6	11	241	309	350	659	9%	79%	0.46	71	80	3.55	19
Gillespie,Cole	R	08	24	8	aa	MIL	462	55	109	33	2	11	60	59	88	12	1	237	323	384	707	11%	81%	0.67	102	98	4.61	34
		09	25	8	a/a	ARI	374	43	86	16	8	9	38	41	66	9	6	229	306	387	693	10%	82%	0.63	95	147	4.06	28
		10	26	8	aaa	ARI	264	32	61	12	5	5	29	27	34	5	6	230	301	362	663	9%	87%	0.79	82	124	3.56	27
		11	27	8	aaa	ARI	484	52	108	15	11	6	41	41	112	12	6	223	284	337	621	8%	77%	0.37	67	170	3.27	9
Gillies,Tyson	L	10	22	8	aa	PHI	105	11	21	2	1	2	5	4	18	2	2	202	232	298	530	4%	83%	0.23	55	111	2.12	-5
Gindl,Caleb	L	10	22	8	aa	MIL	463	49	111	30	1	7	48	46	65	8	6	240	308	354	663	9%	86%	0.71	83	67	3.81	28
		11	23	8	aaa	MIL	472	59	122	19	3	11	42	46	111	4	6	258	324	381	706	9%	76%	0.41	77	73	4.35	26
Gomez,Hector	R	11	23	6	aa	COL	425	32	89	21	5	11	35	13	98	11	4	209	233	360	593	3%	77%	0.13	94	124	2.72	11
Grandal,Yasmani	B	11	23	2	a/a	CIN	168	16	45	15	0	3	20	13	46	0	1	268	320	411	731	7%	73%	0.28	107	26	4.69	39
Green,Grant	R	11	24	6	aa	OAK	530	53	124	27	1	6	43	27	140	4	9	234	271	323	594	5%	74%	0.19	64	55	2.82	8
Green,Taylor	L	09	23	5	aa	MIL	306	28	71	14	0	4	35	29	32	0	1	232	299	317	616	9%	90%	0.91	61	24	3.34	21
		10	24	5	aa	MIL	393	40	88	25	1	11	64	37	57	0	2	224	292	377	668	9%	85%	0.65	102	33	3.76	30
		11	25	5	a/a	MIL	431	54	120	31	1	17	65	41	93	1	0	278	341	473	814	9%	78%	0.44	127	46	6.02	54
Guyer,Brandon	R	09	24	8	aa	CHC	189	18	32	12	1	1	12	8	30	6	6	171	204	259	463	4%	84%	0.26	68	115	1.48	-10
		10	25	8	aa	CHC	369	56	109	35	4	10	42	20	41	22	4	297	333	489	822	5%	89%	0.50	132	150	6.17	63
		11	26	8	aaa	TAM	388	60	102	24	4	10	47	27	94	12	7	263	311	423	734	7%	76%	0.29	104	134	4.54	36
Gyorko,Jedd	R	11	23	5	aa	SD	236	30	55	9	0	5	29	20	61	1	0	233	293	335	628	8%	74%	0.33	67	51	3.50	12
Hagerty,Jason	B	11	24	2	aa	SD	130	11	23	5	1	1	13	11	49	0	1	177	241	254	495	8%	62%	0.22	53	76	1.98	-15
Hamilton,Mark	L	07	23	3	aa	STL	248	25	52	13	0	5	32	19	45	1	1	211	268	321	589	7%	82%	0.43	75	43	2.92	10
		08	24	3	aa	STL	245	20	49	10	0	6	22	26	53	0	0	200	276	310	586	10%	78%	0.49	71	16	2.97	6
		09	25	3	aa	STL	293	36	74	18	0	9	35	30	65	0	1	253	323	411	734	9%	78%	0.46	104	28	4.76	36
		10	26	3	aaa	STL	258	36	60	16	0	11	40	23	54	0	0	232	295	421	715	8%	79%	0.42	120	34	4.34	35
		11	27	3	aaa	STL	252	31	68	20	0	1	26	29	55	0	0	270	345	361	706	10%	78%	0.53	76	29	4.71	32
Harper,Bryce	L	11	19	8	aa	WAS	129	12	32	7	1	3	10	13	26	6	2	248	317	388	704	9%	80%	0.50	91	100	4.41	30
Harrilchak,Cory	L	11	24	8	aa	ATL	429	32	95	22	4	5	41	31	84	7	8	221	274	326	600	7%	80%	0.37	72	86	2.90	11
Havens,Reese	L	10	24	4	aa	NYM	68	9	20	2	1	4	9	4	11	0	3	288	327	519	846	5%	83%	0.35	128	97	5.16	56
		11	25	4	aa	NYM	211	26	49	12	1	4	18	19	71	1	0	232	296	355	651	8%	66%	0.27	84	73	3.74	17
Hazelbaker,Jeremy	L	11	24	8	aa	BOS	354	42	81	18	2	8	29	30	117	25	9	229	289	359	648	8%	67%	0.26	85	130	3.55	16
Henry,Justin	L	10	25	4	a/a	DET	356	35	80	17	2	1	22	40	54	13	11	224	304	290	594	10%	85%	0.74	51	89	2.95	11
		11	26	8	a/a	DET	395	43	104	22	5	0	35	48	62	17	11	263	343	344	687	11%	84%	0.77	60	121	4.23	28
Hernandez,Gorkys	R	09	22	8	aa	PIT	556	65	144	24	3	2	41	31	103	17	18	259	298	324	622	5%	81%	0.30	49	96	3.12	12
		10	23	8	aa	PIT	368	36	86	10	2	2	21	25	77	14	3	234	284	288	572	6%	79%	0.33	37	108	2.96	-0
		11	24	8	aaa	PIT	424	37	104	22	7	1	31	26	98	16	10	245	289	337	626	6%	77%	0.27	64	144	3.26	14
Hill,Steven	R	09	25	2	aa	STL	464	47	109	22	1	13	48	27	84	1	2	236	278	374	652	5%	82%	0.32	89	42	3.55	22
		10	26	2	a/a	STL	395	44	86	23	1	15	65	29	79	1	0	217	270	393	663	7%	80%	0.37	112	51	3.64	26
		11	27	3	a/a	STL	148	16	32	4	0	8	20	8	49	1	0	216	256	405	662	5%	67%	0.16	108	42	3.53	20
Hudson,Kyle	L	11	24	8	a/a	BAL	337	39	90	9	1	0	17	34	87	27	11	267	334	300	634	9%	74%	0.39	26	107	3.73	8
Iglesias,Jose	R	10	21	6	aa	BOS	221	23	60	11	2	0	10	6	34	4	2	270	290	340	630	3%	85%	0.18	54	103	3.46	16
		11	22	6	aaa	BOS	357	30	80	10	0	1	27	18	60	10	4	224	261	261	522	5%	83%	0.30	29	75	2.34	-7
Jackson,Brett	L	10	22	8	aa	CHC	228	35	56	12	3	5	21	23	47	14	5	246	315	390	705	9%	79%	0.49	92	157	4.34	30
		11	23	8	a/a	CHC	431	57	100	20	3	14	39	49	154	14	8	232	310	390	700	10%	64%	0.32	98	113	4.15	24
Jackson,Ryan	R	11	23	6	aa	STL	533	41	117	27	2	6	46	28	104	1	0	220	258	311	570	5%	80%	0.27	66	51	2.75	6
Jimenez,Luis	R	11	23	5	aa	LAA	490	52	126	35	1	15	79	22	79	13	7	257	289	424	714	4%	84%	0.28	112	82	4.17	38
Jones,Mycal	R	11	24	8	aa	ATL	373	46	78	21	1	5	26	41	105	12	7	209	287	311	598	10%	72%	0.39	73	94	3.04	8
Joseph,Corban	L	10	22	4	aa	NYY	111	9	20	5	2	0	11	13	27	1	0	182	269	264	532	11%	76%	0.49	56	121	2.51	-6
		11	23	4	aa	NYY	499	59	121	33	5	5	46	48	116	3	3	242	309	359	668	9%	77%	0.41	83	92	3.92	23
Kieschnick,Roger	L	10	24	8	aa	SF	223	19	52	8	3	3	20	15	49	2	3	233	280	334	614	6%	78%	0.30	63	95	3.12	10
		11	25	8	aa	SF	459	58	105	20	5	13	53	28	134	11	8	229	273	379	652	6%	71%	0.21	92	130	3.38	18
Komatsu,Erik	L	11	24	8	aa	WAS	448	48	109	22	1	6	38	50	73	17	10	243	319	337	656	10%	84%	0.68	66	82	3.78	22
Kozma,Peter	R	09	21	6	aa	STL	407	40	77	13	2	4	29	33	65	3	2	189	250	261	511	8%	84%	0.51	48	76	2.19	-7
		10	22	6	aa	STL	503	53	105	24	1	9	56	43	84	10	2	209	271	314	585	8%	83%	0.51	72	86	2.97	9
		11	23	6	aaa	STL	398	34	70	14	1	2	33	26	101	1	2	176	226	231	458	6%	75%	0.26	41	55	1.70	-19

BATTER	B	Yr	Age	Pos	Lev	Tm	AB	R	H	D	T	HR	RBI	BB	K	SB	CS	BA	OB	Slg	OPS	bb%	Ct%	Eye	PX	SX	RC/G	BPV
Krauss,Marc	L	11	24	8	aa	ARI	433	48	91	23	6	11	45	44	136	1	3	210	283	367	650	9%	69%	0.32	99	101	3.50	17
Kuhn,Tyler	L	10	24	8	aa	CHW	384	42	93	14	3	5	40	30	68	5	6	243	297	333	629	7%	82%	0.44	59	84	3.36	14
		11	25	5	a/a	CHW	505	56	144	28	8	1	47	37	94	12	8	285	334	378	712	7%	81%	0.39	66	129	4.56	30
Laird,Brandon	R	10	23	5	a/a	NYY	531	72	133	24	1	24	85	36	96	2	2	251	299	432	731	6%	82%	0.38	109	54	4.52	36
		11	24	5	aaa	NYY	462	43	109	24	0	16	58	15	93	0	0	236	260	392	652	3%	80%	0.16	100	22	3.47	23
Lake,Junior	R	11	21	6	aa	CHC	242	31	54	9	1	5	13	10	64	14	2	223	254	331	585	4%	74%	0.16	69	135	2.97	6
Lambo,Andrew	L	09	21	8	aa	LA	492	61	115	35	1	10	53	34	84	3	3	234	284	372	656	7%	83%	0.41	97	64	3.61	26
		10	22	8	aa	PIT	272	31	67	11	1	5	29	19	55	1	1	246	296	349	645	7%	80%	0.35	68	59	3.63	17
		11	23	8	a/a	PIT	437	43	90	25	0	8	46	33	113	4	3	206	262	318	580	7%	74%	0.29	79	55	2.78	7
Lavarnway,Ryan	R	10	23	0	aa	BOS	158	19	40	10	0	6	28	19	31	0	0	254	333	428	761	11%	81%	0.61	113	20	5.22	43
		11	24	2	a/a	BOS	435	57	112	24	0	23	71	43	119	1	1	257	324	471	796	9%	73%	0.36	131	34	5.49	47
Lee,Hak-Ju	L	11	21	6	aa	TAM	100	12	17	1	3	1	5	8	24	4	2	170	231	270	501	7%	76%	0.33	51	223	1.99	-16
Liddi,Alex	R	10	22	5	aa	SEA	502	61	122	32	5	11	72	40	119	4	9	243	299	392	691	7%	76%	0.34	99	90	3.88	29
		11	23	5	aaa	SEA	559	75	111	25	2	17	64	38	204	3	1	199	250	342	591	6%	64%	0.19	90	89	2.85	7
Lin,Che-Hsuan	R	10	22	8	aa	BOS	458	65	115	18	3	1	25	53	45	19	15	251	329	310	639	10%	90%	1.18	44	106	3.53	25
		11	23	8	a/a	BOS	466	55	103	17	2	1	28	45	70	22	8	221	290	273	562	9%	85%	0.64	39	111	2.83	3
Loewen,Adam	L	10	26	8	aa	TOR	459	49	90	26	2	9	49	46	124	12	6	196	270	321	590	9%	73%	0.37	84	94	2.89	8
		11	27	8	aaa	TOR	520	47	116	34	3	10	48	35	178	6	9	223	272	358	630	6%	66%	0.20	93	77	3.13	17
Lombardozzi,Steve	B	11	23	4	a/a	WAS	556	70	154	23	7	6	42	31	85	24	9	277	315	376	691	5%	85%	0.36	64	140	4.27	26
Lough,David	L	09	24	8	aa	KC	236	32	70	13	1	7	25	10	23	10	5	295	323	444	767	4%	90%	0.42	96	101	5.07	46
		10	25	8	aaa	KC	460	48	111	14	8	8	43	30	55	11	6	242	288	357	645	6%	88%	0.54	68	131	3.53	20
		11	26	8	aaa	KC	456	60	122	22	9	6	45	24	55	10	9	268	304	395	699	5%	88%	0.44	81	147	4.06	31
Mahoney,Joseph	L	10	24	3	aa	BAL	191	24	56	11	1	8	24	13	31	7	1	292	337	482	819	6%	84%	0.42	118	95	6.16	55
		11	25	3	aa	BAL	315	36	83	21	4	10	56	20	92	6	2	263	307	451	758	6%	71%	0.22	119	126	4.94	41
Marrero,Chris	R	09	21	3	aa	WAS	75	8	19	6	0	1	10	7	16	0	1	256	320	377	697	9%	79%	0.45	92	36	4.16	32
		10	22	3	aa	WAS	524	65	142	27	0	15	73	38	88	1	3	271	320	408	729	7%	83%	0.43	90	34	4.68	36
		11	23	3	aaa	WAS	483	48	129	27	0	11	56	46	106	2	2	267	331	391	722	9%	78%	0.43	85	33	4.73	33
Marte,Starling	R	11	23	8	aa	PIT	536	74	160	35	6	9	41	17	106	19	13	299	320	437	757	3%	80%	0.16	94	133	4.83	41
Martinez,Francisco	R	11	21	5	aa	SEA	477	68	124	19	5	8	57	19	118	8	11	260	288	371	659	4%	75%	0.16	70	119	3.47	19
Martinez,Jose	R	07	22	6	aa	STL	250	30	66	11	0	8	38	12	19	0	0	264	298	404	702	5%	92%	0.63	88	30	4.30	37
		08	23	46	aa	STL	483	39	106	17	1	6	53	16	34	1	5	219	244	296	541	3%	93%	0.47	52	39	2.31	4
		11	24	8	aa	CHW	200	16	53	12	1	1	13	13	29	4	2	265	310	350	660	6%	86%	0.45	65	73	3.88	24
Martin,Leonys	L	11	23	8	a/a	TEX	287	36	74	14	3	3	29	18	35	13	11	258	302	359	661	6%	88%	0.51	69	124	3.46	25
Mastroianni,Darin	R	09	24	8	aa	TOR	247	36	62	10	2	1	23	36	47	36	8	253	349	319	668	13%	81%	0.78	47	150	4.55	19
		10	25	8	aa	TOR	525	72	130	22	5	3	33	56	83	33	11	247	320	322	642	10%	84%	0.68	53	136	3.79	18
		11	26	8	a/a	TOR	488	60	103	21	7	2	24	41	97	22	12	211	272	295	567	8%	80%	0.42	57	155	2.66	2
Mercer,Jordy	R	10	24	5	aa	PIT	485	53	119	28	1	2	52	24	57	6	1	245	281	319	600	5%	88%	0.42	59	81	3.18	14
		11	25	6	a/a	PIT	491	60	105	26	1	14	52	27	86	7	7	214	255	356	611	5%	82%	0.31	93	80	2.91	16
Mesoraco,Devin	R	10	22	2	a/a	CIN	239	37	61	13	2	14	35	19	41	1	1	255	310	502	812	7%	83%	0.46	146	84	5.47	55
		11	23	2	aaa	CIN	436	45	110	31	2	12	54	40	95	1	1	252	315	415	730	8%	78%	0.42	110	51	4.68	38
Mills,Beau	L	09	23	3	aa	CLE	516	53	128	31	1	12	74	29	90	1	2	249	289	382	671	5%	83%	0.33	91	42	3.84	27
		10	24	3	aa	CLE	427	41	87	22	1	7	55	33	59	2	1	205	261	308	569	7%	86%	0.55	72	57	2.73	9
		11	25	3	a/a	CLE	349	39	85	20	1	13	52	25	69	0	0	244	294	418	712	7%	80%	0.36	111	36	4.33	34
Mitchell,Jermaine	L	10	26	8	a/a	OAK	132	12	23	3	2	0	9	14	34	2	7	171	251	221	472	10%	74%	0.41	32	117	1.53	-22
		11	27	8	a/a	OAK	536	75	136	22	10	9	51	60	142	18	23	254	329	382	711	10%	74%	0.42	79	153	4.02	26
Montero,Jesus	R	09	20	2	aa	NYY	167	19	55	11	0	9	34	14	19	0	0	327	378	560	937	8%	89%	0.72	143	10	8.31	82
		10	21	2	aaa	NYY	453	60	125	30	2	22	68	44	78	0	0	275	340	493	833	9%	83%	0.57	136	41	6.20	59
		11	22	2	aaa	NYY	420	46	115	17	1	18	58	32	104	0	0	274	325	448	773	7%	75%	0.31	104	28	5.34	40
Moore,Jeremy	L	11	24	8	aaa	LAA	426	49	100	19	10	10	43	13	133	14	12	235	257	397	654	3%	69%	0.10	97	199	3.12	20
Moore,Tyler	R	11	24	3	aa	WAS	519	56	123	32	3	24	72	24	154	2	0	237	271	449	720	4%	70%	0.16	131	74	4.19	36
Navarro,Yamaico	R	09	22	6	aa	BOS	135	13	24	7	1	2	9	12	23	4	1	180	247	292	539	8%	83%	0.53	76	106	2.45	2
		10	23	6	a/a	BOS	382	44	99	25	2	8	48	36	45	14	7	259	323	398	721	9%	88%	0.80	95	95	4.54	42
		11	24	6	aaa	KC	220	25	49	10	2	4	15	16	47	4	7	223	275	341	616	7%	79%	0.34	76	100	2.86	13
Neal,Thomas	R	10	23	8	aa	SF	525	60	144	38	1	10	60	39	84	10	5	274	325	407	732	7%	84%	0.47	95	73	4.78	40
		11	24	8	aaa	CLE	256	31	63	12	2	1	20	11	65	6	7	246	277	320	597	4%	75%	0.17	54	110	2.81	8
Nieuwenhuis,Kirk	L	10	23	8	a/a	NYM	514	66	119	36	2	14	56	28	104	10	9	231	271	389	660	5%	80%	0.27	107	93	3.41	27
		11	24	8	aaa	NYM	188	26	48	15	2	4	11	25	68	4	2	255	343	420	763	12%	64%	0.37	113	119	5.24	39
Noriega,Gabriel	B	11	21	6	aa	SEA	93	7	20	4	0	0	6	2	22	1	0	215	232	258	490	2%	76%	0.09	38	54	2.03	-11
Norris,Derek	R	11	22	2	aa	WAS	334	62	63	16	1	16	38	63	124	11	4	189	317	386	704	16%	63%	0.51	119	108	4.31	22
Nunez,Gustavo	B	11	23	6	aa	DET	121	10	23	3	0	2	6	4	29	3	3	190	216	264	480	3%	76%	0.14	48	71	1.68	-14
Ortiz,Ryan	R	11	24	2	aa	OAK	152	13	29	3	0	1	10	14	47	1	0	191	259	230	489	8%	69%	0.30	28	45	2.10	-19
Pacheco,Jordan	R	10	25	2	aa	COL	78	9	24	5	0	1	14	5	5	1	1	308	348	406	754	6%	93%	0.92	74	47	5.21	51
		11	26	2	aaa	COL	363	29	76	16	2	2	25	15	54	1	2	209	241	281	522	4%	85%	0.28	52	60	2.21	-3
Parker,Stephen	L	11	24	5	a/a	OAK	529	52	122	24	1	6	52	48	133	1	1	231	295	314	608	8%	75%	0.36	59	44	3.28	9
Parmelee,Chris	L	10	23	3	aa	MIN	411	40	99	22	1	5	34	33	55	2	2	241	297	336	633	7%	87%	0.60	68	50	3.51	20
		11	24	3	aa	MIN	530	55	131	28	4	8	60	51	102	0	1	247	313	360	674	9%	81%	0.50	77	55	4.06	24
Pastornicky,Tyler	R	10	21	6	aa	ATL	134	19	31	4	1	2	12	14	18	9	2	231	305	323	628	10%	86%	0.78	58	129	3.66	16
		11	22	6	a/a	ATL	459	53	129	13	4	6	36	26	51	22	12	281	320	366	686	5%	89%	0.51	53	115	4.09	26
Pedroza,Jaime	B	10	24	4	aa	LA	411	38	94	17	2	5	27	43	83	8	10	229	302	315	618	10%	80%	0.52	59	70	3.18	11
		11	25	4	aa	LA	268	20	53	13	2	4	17	26	91	6	7	198	269	306	575	9%	66%	0.29	73	89	2.58	2
Peguero,Francisco	R	11	23	8	aa	SF	285	29	81	11	6	4	31	4	49	7	1	284	294	407	701	1%	83%	0.08	75	159	4.36	27
Perez,Nelson	L	11	24	8	aa	CHC	237	20	50	15	1	6	23	14	98	1	2	211	255	359	614	6%	59%	0.14	99	60	2.97	14
Phelps,Cord	B	10	24	4	a/a	CLE	442	51	118	25	4	6	42	31	56	3	7	266	315	379	694	7%	87%	0.56	77	75	4.10	32
		11	25	4	aaa	CLE	378	39	94	22	3	10	48	40	102	2	7	249	321	402	723	10%	73%	0.39	99	65	4.35	32
Pill,Brett	R	09	25	3	aa	SF	527	58	138	35	1	14	90	30	66	5	3	262	302	412	714	5%	87%	0.46	101	61	4.40	38
		10	26	3	aaa	SF	520	43	116	29	0	10	57	20	51	5	2	223	252	336	588	4%	90%	0.40	79	55	2.85	15
		11	27	3	aaa	SF	536	49	126	28	2	15	64	15	67	4	8	235	256	379	635	3%	88%	0.22	93	57	3.08	21

BATTER	B	Yr	Age	Pos	Lev	Tm	AB	R	H	D	T	HR	RBI	BB	K	SB	CS	BA	OB	Slg	OPS	bb%	Ct%	Eye	PX	SX	RC/G	BPV
Recker,Anthony	R	07	24	2	aa	OAK	201	12	35	10	0	3	16	13	54	0	1	175	226	269	495	6%	73%	0.25	68	23	1.95	-9
		08	25	2	aa	OAK	430	41	96	24	3	8	46	31	109	1	2	223	275	345	621	7%	75%	0.29	83	64	3.23	14
		09	26	2	aa	OAK	329	28	68	12	1	9	37	24	78	1	0	207	261	333	593	7%	76%	0.31	78	45	2.96	7
		10	27	2	a/a	OAK	288	30	60	14	1	7	31	20	61	1	1	209	260	341	601	6%	79%	0.32	86	56	2.98	12
		11	28	2	aaa	OAK	345	38	72	18	1	9	30	35	105	4	6	209	282	345	627	9%	70%	0.33	89	65	3.16	13
Rizzo,Anthony	L	10	21	3	aa	BOS	414	49	102	32	0	14	60	33	71	5	1	246	303	427	729	7%	83%	0.47	122	64	4.60	42
		11	22	3	aaa	SD	356	40	89	25	1	14	63	29	110	4	7	250	306	444	750	8%	69%	0.26	126	58	4.50	40
Robinson,Clint	L	11	26	3	aaa	KC	503	59	133	30	0	14	68	39	102	1	1	264	317	408	725	7%	80%	0.38	96	36	4.68	35
Robinson,Trayvon	B	09	22	8	aa	LA	57	7	13	1	1	2	9	9	16	3	2	228	333	386	719	14%	72%	0.56	85	147	4.35	22
		10	23	8	aa	LA	434	60	109	20	3	7	43	52	101	28	19	251	331	357	688	11%	77%	0.51	70	120	3.97	23
		11	24	8	aaa	SEA	377	43	83	7	3	15	43	30	156	5	7	220	278	374	652	4%	82%	0.25	19	69	1.84	-15
Rojas,Miguel	R	11	22	6	aa	CIN	239	18	52	5	0	0	16	11	44	8	8	218	252	238	490	4%	82%	0.25	19	96	2.32	-5
Romine,Andrew	B	10	25	6	aa	LAA	383	42	94	13	2	2	26	37	54	16	11	246	313	306	619	9%	86%	0.69	43	96	3.32	14
		11	26	6	aa	LAA	381	41	81	7	1	2	22	27	105	14	7	213	265	252	517	7%	72%	0.26	27	99	2.27	-13
Romine,Austin	R	10	22	2	aa	NYY	455	51	110	26	0	9	58	32	76	2	0	242	292	360	652	7%	83%	0.42	52	52	3.74	23
		11	23	2	a/a	NYY	351	36	89	11	0	6	40	27	69	2	2	254	307	336	643	7%	80%	0.39	54	41	3.67	15
Rosario,Wilin	R	10	22	2	aa	COL	270	34	74	13	1	17	42	17	43	1	0	273	317	520	837	6%	84%	0.40	145	51	5.98	59
		11	23	2	aa	COL	405	37	92	14	3	17	34	13	93	1	2	227	251	402	654	3%	77%	0.14	102	62	3.33	21
Russell,Kyle	L	10	24	8	aa	LA	273	26	55	19	1	7	20	20	93	2	2	200	255	352	607	7%	66%	0.22	103	66	2.95	14
		11	25	8	a/a	LA	432	42	83	24	2	12	45	31	188	4	1	192	246	340	586	5%	56%	0.16	96	88	2.79	7
Sanchez,Hector	B	11	22	2	aaa	SF	153	10	33	8	0	1	17	8	24	2	0	216	255	288	542	5%	84%	0.33	56	26	2.41	2
Sappelt,Dave	R	11	24	8	aaa	CIN	297	30	80	14	2	6	22	23	46	3	5	269	322	391	712	7%	85%	0.50	79	66	4.35	32
Schafer,Logan	L	11	25	8	a/a	MIL	359	45	93	18	4	4	30	25	53	11	9	259	307	365	672	7%	85%	0.47	71	119	3.77	25
Short,Brandon	R	11	23	8	aa	CHW	526	62	124	26	4	12	49	32	142	17	10	236	280	369	648	6%	73%	0.23	86	118	3.42	18
Sierra,Moises	R	11	23	8	aa	TOR	495	67	123	17	3	15	55	32	106	13	16	248	294	386	680	6%	79%	0.30	83	99	3.57	23
Silverio,Alfredo	R	11	24	8	aa	LA	533	65	133	35	9	11	61	21	109	8	14	250	278	411	689	4%	80%	0.19	105	134	3.56	30
Skipworth,Kyle	L	11	21	2	aa	FLA	396	26	71	11	1	8	36	27	165	0	4	179	232	273	504	6%	58%	0.16	58	30	1.98	-13
Snyder,Brandon	R	09	23	3	a/a	BAL	463	57	130	35	2	13	84	47	100	3	2	281	347	449	796	9%	78%	0.47	114	63	5.79	50
		10	24	3	aaa	BAL	339	28	78	20	1	8	34	22	81	3	1	231	277	364	641	6%	76%	0.27	90	59	3.50	19
		11	25	3	aaa	BAL	448	42	101	18	1	12	54	24	103	1	2	225	265	350	615	5%	77%	0.23	79	43	3.12	12
Sogard,Eric	L	09	23	4	aa	SD	458	63	112	20	2	4	40	46	42	8	7	244	313	321	634	9%	91%	1.10	55	84	3.53	26
		10	24	4	aaa	OAK	514	56	122	22	4	3	44	52	49	10	12	237	307	312	619	9%	90%	1.06	53	84	3.24	22
		11	25	6	aaa	OAK	315	37	74	13	1	3	25	26	41	9	4	235	293	311	604	8%	87%	0.63	54	91	3.21	13
Solarte,Yangervis	B	10	23	5	aa	MIN	127	11	30	8	0	2	15	2	14	1	1	239	251	347	598	2%	89%	0.14	79	49	2.87	15
		11	24	4	aa	MIN	459	46	129	33	2	4	35	18	42	4	5	281	308	388	696	4%	91%	0.43	81	64	4.19	36
Soto,Neftali	R	11	22	3	a/a	CIN	396	51	97	16	2	25	58	19	110	0	1	245	280	485	764	5%	72%	0.17	138	53	4.64	42
Strieby,Ryan	R	09	24	3	aa	DET	294	52	79	15	1	15	47	45	68	2	0	268	365	483	848	13%	77%	0.67	130	69	6.70	56
		10	25	8	aaa	DET	290	23	61	13	0	8	38	25	72	1	1	211	274	344	618	8%	75%	0.35	85	27	3.21	12
		11	26	3	aaa	DET	487	51	104	24	0	15	59	45	195	4	2	214	280	355	635	8%	60%	0.23	91	52	3.42	13
Taylor,Michael	R	09	24	8	a/a	PHI	428	61	124	25	3	19	70	39	61	18	6	291	350	495	845	8%	86%	0.64	126	110	6.43	62
		10	25	8	aaa	OAK	464	54	99	20	4	4	53	35	67	11	7	213	268	298	566	7%	86%	0.52	59	111	2.66	6
		11	26	8	aaa	OAK	349	33	72	12	0	10	42	30	98	9	6	206	269	327	596	8%	72%	0.31	75	64	2.89	6
Tejeda,Oscar	R	11	22	4	aa	BOS	457	37	103	25	1	3	30	21	108	10	4	225	259	304	564	4%	78%	0.19	84	147	2.91	13
Tekotte,Blake	L	10	23	8	aa	SD	268	37	57	7	5	8	31	23	59	5	10	212	273	362	635	8%	78%	0.38	92	105	3.74	20
		11	24	8	aa	SD	414	55	92	21	1	12	48	51	133	26	14	222	308	365	672	11%	68%	0.38	92	105	3.74	20
Triunfel,Carlos	R	10	21	6	aa	SEA	470	41	108	10	1	5	34	10	43	2	10	230	247	289	536	2%	91%	0.24	38	46	2.16	-3
		11	22	6	a/a	SEA	506	37	120	24	2	4	32	20	102	4	8	237	266	316	582	4%	80%	0.20	58	54	2.72	7
Trout,Mike	R	11	20	8	aa	LAA	353	72	108	17	9	10	34	38	80	29	11	306	373	490	863	10%	77%	0.48	109	223	6.81	56
Valaika,Chris	R	10	25	4	aaa	CIN	424	38	110	24	1	4	40	15	63	2	4	259	285	348	633	3%	85%	0.24	67	47	3.38	19
		11	26	4	aaa	CIN	417	28	89	15	0	5	26	15	79	1	0	213	241	285	526	3%	81%	0.19	50	34	2.31	-4
Valdespin,Jordany	L	10	23	4	aa	NYM	112	6	22	7	0	0	6	1	17	3	3	196	204	259	462	1%	85%	0.06	55	70	1.50	-11
		11	24	6	a/a	NYM	511	51	125	26	3	12	45	19	109	27	21	245	272	378	649	4%	79%	0.17	87	112	3.08	21
Villar,Jonathan	B	11	20	6	aa	HOU	324	38	66	14	2	8	19	21	109	10	6	204	252	333	586	6%	66%	0.19	94	93	2.96	6
Vogt,Stephen	L	11	27	2	a/a	TAM	510	47	121	27	6	12	74	24	100	3	2	237	272	384	656	4%	80%	0.24	94	93	3.56	23
Waring,Brandon	R	10	25	5	aa	BAL	472	54	101	27	1	19	55	44	144	0	1	214	281	397	677	9%	70%	0.31	115	36	3.80	25
		11	26	5	aa	BAL	406	49	80	18	2	19	48	26	141	0	0	197	245	392	637	6%	65%	0.18	116	59	3.18	17
Weglarz,Nick	L	09	22	8	aa	CLE	339	64	73	16	1	14	60	73	71	2	3	215	353	393	747	18%	79%	1.02	109	64	5.02	37
		10	23	8	a/a	CLE	312	40	78	24	1	10	37	40	55	2	2	250	335	429	765	11%	82%	0.73	121	56	5.18	48
		11	24	8	aa	CLE	134	20	21	7	0	2	10	30	48	0	1	157	311	254	565	18%	64%	0.63	69	42	2.85	-7
Welty,Ronnie	R	11	23	8	aa	BAL	390	40	82	18	2	12	38	42	134	9	3	210	287	359	646	10%	66%	0.31	109	93	3.57	15
Wheeler,Ryan	L	10	22	5	aa	ARI	67	7	16	3	0	3	9	4	13	0	0	239	282	418	700	6%	81%	0.31	109	20	4.09	31
		11	23	5	aa	ARI	480	50	124	28	2	12	64	32	112	2	3	258	305	400	705	6%	77%	0.29	94	55	4.27	31

PITCHER	Th	Yr	Age	Lev	Org	W	L	G	Sv	IP	H	ER	HR	BB	K	ERA	WHIP	BF/G	OBA	bb/9	K/9	Cmd	HR/9	H%	S%	BPV
Abreu,Juan	R	10	25	aa	ATL	4	2	39	11	44	51	19	2	24	39	3.85	1.71	5.2	284	5.0	7.9	1.6	0.5	36%	77%	65
		11	26	aaa	HOU	5	2	48	4	58	48	16	5	34	62	2.45	1.42	5.2	222	5.3	9.7	1.8	0.8	30%	86%	83
Adams,Austin	R	11	25	aa	CLE	11	10	26	0	136	176	71	6	67	106	4.72	1.79	24.6	307	4.5	7.0	1.6	0.4	38%	73%	57
Alderson,Tim	R	09	21	aa	PIT	9	2	20	0	111	123	53	9	24	56	4.32	1.32	23.6	275	1.9	4.5	2.3	0.7	31%	68%	55
		10	22	aa	PIT	7	6	18	0	89	125	64	10	25	49	6.46	1.68	22.8	324	2.5	4.9	2.0	1.0	36%	61%	31
		11	23	aa	PIT	0	4	42	0	74	80	40	6	26	46	4.88	1.43	7.7	269	3.2	5.5	1.7	0.7	31%	66%	49
Archer,Chris	R	10	22	aa	CHC	8	2	13	0	70	53	16	2	38	58	2.06	1.30	22.7	206	4.9	7.5	1.5	0.3	27%	84%	83
		11	23	a/a	TAM	9	7	27	0	147	160	73	11	83	112	4.43	1.65	25.0	272	5.1	6.9	1.4	0.6	33%	73%	51
Aumont,Phillippe	R	10	22	aa	PHI	1	6	11	0	49	60	45	4	37	32	8.23	1.97	21.9	295	6.8	5.9	0.9	0.7	34%	56%	27
		11	23	a/a	PHI	2	5	43	7	54	49	19	2	24	67	3.11	1.37	5.4	239	4.1	11.2	2.8	0.4	36%	77%	121
Axelrod,Dylan	R	10	25	aa	CHW	0	1	2	0	10	10	4	0	3	6	4.00	1.33	21.3	255	3.0	5.7	1.9	0.0	31%	67%	78
		11	26	a/a	CHW	9	3	26	0	151	160	62	4	42	108	3.71	1.34	24.7	267	2.5	6.5	2.6	0.3	33%	71%	87
Barnes,Scott	L	09	22	aa	CLE	2	2	6	0	31	42	27	8	15	26	7.79	1.83	24.7	316	4.3	7.5	1.7	2.3	35%	61%	4
		10	23	aa	CLE	6	11	26	0	138	142	92	14	59	110	5.98	1.46	23.2	261	3.8	7.1	1.9	0.9	31%	59%	57
		11	24	a/a	CLE	8	4	18	0	99	97	44	12	37	89	4.04	1.36	23.5	252	3.4	8.1	2.4	1.1	31%	73%	72
Bauer,Trevor	R	11	20	aa	ARI	1	1	4	0	17	21	15	2	7	23	8.07	1.70	19.3	303	3.9	12.2	3.1	1.1	44%	51%	101
Bellamy,Kyle	R	10	23	aa	CHW	2	2	20	0	25	36	23	1	23	17	8.21	2.34	6.6	329	8.2	6.1	0.7	0.4	39%	62%	31
Berger,Eric	L	09	23	aa	CLE	3	1	6	0	33	39	13	1	18	29	3.63	1.71	25.6	288	4.8	7.9	1.7	0.3	37%	78%	71
		10	24	a/a	CLE	5	6	23	0	112	122	69	10	72	78	5.55	1.73	22.6	271	5.8	6.2	1.1	0.8	32%	68%	36
		11	25	a/a	CLE	2	1	42	0	71	82	38	6	38	71	4.83	1.68	7.8	282	4.7	8.9	1.9	0.7	37%	72%	69
Betances,Dellin	R	10	23	aa	NYY	0	0	3	0	14	11	7	4	3	18	4.47	0.99	18.4	211	1.9	11.5	6.0	2.6	24%	70%	131
		11	24	a/a	NYY	4	9	25	0	126	120	66	12	74	119	4.69	1.54	22.5	246	5.3	8.5	1.6	0.9	31%	70%	65
Brackman,Andrew	R	10	25	aa	NYY	5	7	15	0	80	91	33	4	31	60	3.66	1.51	23.7	279	3.4	6.7	2.0	0.5	34%	76%	67
		11	26	aaa	NYY	3	6	33	1	96	106	91	15	87	58	8.55	2.01	14.3	274	8.1	5.5	0.7	1.4	30%	57%	5
Brasier,Ryan	R	10	23	aa	LAA	7	12	28	0	142	147	96	31	67	78	6.08	1.51	22.5	262	4.2	4.9	1.2	2.0	27%	65%	-2
		11	24	a/a	LAA	2	2	50	19	52	49	18	3	21	43	3.16	1.33	4.5	241	3.7	7.3	2.0	0.5	30%	77%	78
Brewer,Charles	R	11	23	aa	ARI	5	1	11	0	52	53	17	2	18	40	2.90	1.37	20.4	259	3.1	6.8	2.2	0.4	32%	79%	80
Bromberg,David	R	10	23	a/a	MIN	6	9	26	0	151	164	68	12	46	94	4.05	1.39	25.0	271	2.7	5.6	2.0	0.7	31%	72%	56
		11	24	aa	MIN	1	3	8	0	37	55	27	2	15	18	6.48	1.88	22.2	336	3.6	4.5	1.2	0.6	38%	64%	23
Bush,Matt	R	11	25	aa	TAM	5	3	36	5	50	54	29	5	24	64	5.25	1.54	6.2	267	4.2	11.4	2.7	0.9	38%	66%	101
Carignan,Andrew	R	11	25	a/a	OAK	0	0	24	3	28	23	8	2	9	28	2.66	1.15	4.8	219	3.0	9.0	3.0	0.6	29%	79%	110
Carpenter,Chris	R	11	26	a/a	CHC	3	4	32	2	43	48	31	5	27	27	6.64	1.77	6.2	279	5.7	5.6	1.0	1.1	31%	63%	19
Carpenter,David	R	11	24	aa	LAA	1	0	19	5	19	14	0	0	5	13	0.00	1.03	3.9	207	2.4	6.3	2.6	0.0	26%	100%	107
Carreno,Joel	R	11	24	aa	TOR	7	9	24	0	135	118	63	14	71	130	4.22	1.40	24.3	231	4.7	8.7	1.8	0.9	29%	72%	71
Carter,Anthony	R	10	24	aa	CHW	1	4	46	22	57	58	33	8	24	49	5.14	1.44	5.4	258	3.8	7.8	2.0	1.3	31%	67%	53
		11	25	a/a	CHW	1	2	47	8	62	82	54	9	36	52	7.88	1.92	6.3	313	5.3	7.6	1.4	1.2	38%	59%	30
Castillo,Richard	R	11	22	aa	STL	1	1	24	0	44	59	18	3	18	36	3.70	1.75	8.6	314	3.7	7.3	2.0	0.6	39%	79%	60
Castro,Simon	R	10	22	a/a	SD	7	7	26	0	140	128	52	7	41	101	3.34	1.21	22.2	238	2.6	6.5	2.5	0.5	29%	72%	84
		11	23	a/a	SD	7	8	22	0	115	127	61	10	30	84	4.74	1.37	22.4	274	2.4	6.5	2.8	0.7	33%	65%	75
Clemens,Paul	R	11	23	a/a	HOU	8	7	26	0	144	138	63	12	57	108	3.92	1.36	23.7	248	3.6	6.7	1.9	0.7	30%	72%	64
Cleto,Maikel	R	11	22	a/a	STL	7	5	20	0	106	97	45	6	49	87	3.86	1.38	22.7	239	4.2	7.4	1.8	0.5	30%	72%	73
Cloyd,Tyler	R	10	23	aa	PHI	1	1	2	0	9	5	4	3	1	5	4.12	0.69	16.2	164	1.0	4.9	4.7	3.1	9%	67%	57
		11	24	aa	PHI	6	3	18	0	107	114	38	7	15	81	3.18	1.21	24.5	269	1.2	6.9	5.5	0.6	33%	75%	139
Cohoon,Mark	L	10	23	aa	NYM	5	4	13	0	71	78	33	5	14	46	4.18	1.31	23.1	274	1.8	5.8	3.2	0.7	32%	68%	82
		11	24	a/a	NYM	5	14	27	0	146	197	93	17	54	80	5.72	1.72	25.1	316	3.3	4.9	1.5	1.0	35%	68%	21
Colome,Alexander	R	11	22	aa	TAM	3	4	9	0	52	43	25	5	26	27	4.25	1.33	24.5	221	4.5	4.7	1.1	0.8	24%	69%	38
Cook,Ryan	R	10	23	a/a	ARI	1	1	4	0	23	22	14	2	11	15	5.43	1.42	25.2	245	4.3	5.8	1.4	0.8	28%	61%	46
		11	24	a/a	ARI	1	5	48	19	61	43	15	2	20	50	2.20	1.04	5.0	196	2.9	7.4	2.5	0.3	25%	79%	105
Cortes,Dan	R	11	24	aaa	SEA	1	2	32	3	39	42	19	2	25	40	4.33	1.73	5.7	270	5.8	9.2	1.6	0.5	36%	75%	74
Cosart,Jarred	R	11	21	aa	HOU	1	2	7	0	36	34	19	4	12	20	4.60	1.24	21.6	241	2.9	4.8	1.7	0.9	27%	64%	44
Crosby,Casey	L	11	23	aa	DET	9	7	25	0	132	138	70	12	74	99	4.78	1.61	23.9	264	5.1	6.8	1.3	0.8	32%	71%	47
Darnell,Logan	L	11	22	aa	MIN	1	1	5	0	31	40	19	2	4	17	5.71	1.43	26.7	308	1.1	4.9	4.3	0.7	35%	59%	93
Delgado,Randall	R	10	21	aa	ATL	3	5	8	0	43	38	26	2	19	40	5.36	1.32	22.9	232	4.0	8.3	2.1	0.4	31%	57%	91
		11	22	a/a	ATL	7	7	25	0	139	147	67	15	55	120	4.34	1.46	24.3	266	3.6	7.8	2.2	1.0	33%	72%	65
Dolis,Rafael	R	10	23	aa	CHC	5	4	12	0	55	72	28	3	26	39	4.57	1.78	21.6	309	4.2	6.4	1.5	0.5	37%	74%	48
		11	24	aa	CHC	8	5	51	17	73	69	30	2	34	40	3.69	1.42	6.2	244	4.3	5.0	1.2	0.3	29%	73%	52
Doubront,Felix	L	09	22	aa	BOS	8	6	26	0	121	140	58	8	52	87	4.31	1.59	21.0	284	3.9	6.5	1.7	0.6	34%	73%	54
		10	23	a/a	BOS	8	3	17	0	80	85	30	1	32	62	3.38	1.46	20.6	267	3.6	7.0	1.9	0.1	34%	75%	81
		11	24	a/a	BOS	3	5	19	0	75	81	42	11	27	57	4.97	1.43	17.2	269	3.2	6.8	2.1	1.3	31%	68%	49
Eovaldi,Nathan	R	11	21	aa	LA	6	5	20	0	103	77	29	3	39	88	2.53	1.13	20.8	204	3.4	7.7	2.3	0.2	27%	77%	101
Eppley,Cody	R	10	25	a/a	TEX	3	2	37	10	51	52	20	3	23	49	3.45	1.45	6.0	257	4.0	8.5	2.1	0.5	34%	77%	83
		11	26	aaa	TEX	4	2	43	10	55	57	26	3	34	43	4.22	1.65	5.9	262	5.5	7.0	1.3	0.5	32%	74%	55
Familia,Jeurys	R	11	22	aa	NYM	4	4	17	0	88	88	35	9	32	84	3.57	1.37	22.1	256	3.3	8.6	2.6	0.9	33%	77%	83
Fiers,Michael	R	10	25	aa	MIL	1	1	10	1	31	32	16	3	10	30	4.49	1.35	13.3	261	2.9	8.6	3.0	1.0	33%	69%	88
		11	26	a/a	MIL	13	3	34	5	126	95	29	12	37	109	2.08	1.05	14.7	205	2.7	7.8	2.9	0.8	25%	86%	97
Fleming,Marquis	R	11	25	a/a	TAM	5	4	43	4	83	69	36	5	43	87	3.93	1.36	8.2	223	4.7	9.5	2.0	0.5	31%	71%	93
Friedrich,Christian	L	10	23	aa	COL	3	6	18	0	87	121	64	12	35	64	6.60	1.79	22.8	322	3.6	6.6	1.8	1.3	37%	64%	30
		11	24	aa	COL	6	10	25	0	133	180	87	24	42	80	5.89	1.66	24.4	316	2.8	5.4	1.9	1.6	34%	68%	16
Gardner,Joe	R	11	23	aa	COL	10	11	25	0	134	157	74	8	53	65	4.98	1.57	24.0	287	3.5	4.4	1.2	0.6	32%	67%	33
Gast,John	L	11	22	aa	STL	4	4	13	0	79	77	31	7	28	46	3.52	1.33	25.9	250	3.2	5.2	1.6	0.7	28%	75%	48
Gibson,Kyle	R	10	23	a/a	MIN	7	5	19	0	108	111	44	5	26	72	3.66	1.27	23.8	260	2.2	6.0	2.8	0.4	31%	70%	85
		11	24	aaa	MIN	3	8	18	0	95	125	59	10	28	72	5.61	1.60	24.0	309	2.7	6.8	2.6	0.9	37%	65%	61
Godfrey,Graham	R	09	25	aa	OAK	11	8	28	0	159	174	67	8	49	85	3.77	1.40	24.6	273	2.8	4.8	1.7	0.4	31%	73%	52
		10	26	a/a	OAK	4	8	29	0	125	151	83	9	62	81	6.00	1.71	19.9	293	4.5	5.8	1.3	0.6	34%	64%	40
		11	27	a/a	OAK	14	3	20	0	111	108	35	6	31	75	2.79	1.25	23.2	250	2.5	6.0	2.4	0.4	30%	78%	79
Gray,Sonny	R	11	22	aa	OAK	1	0	5	0	20	15	1	0	5	16	0.44	1.04	15.8	209	2.4	7.1	2.9	0.0	28%	95%	117
Griffin,A.J.	R	11	23	a/a	OAK	2	4	7	0	38	47	25	6	12	24	5.87	1.55	24.3	298	2.8	5.7	2.0	1.4	33%	64%	30
Griffith,Nevin	R	11	22	aa	CHW	5	9	25	0	108	117	93	11	105	76	7.72	2.05	21.6	270	8.8	6.3	0.7	0.9	32%	61%	27

PITCHER	Th	Yr	Age	Lev	Org	W	L	G	Sv	IP	H	ER	HR	BB	K	ERA	WHIP	BF/G	OBA	bb/9	K/9	Cmd	HR/9	H%	S%	BPV
Guerra,Deolis	R	09	20	aa	MIN	6	3	12	0	62	68	42	4	17	42	6.06	1.36	22.2	271	2.5	6.1	2.5	0.6	32%	53%	72
		10	21	a/a	MIN	2	13	24	0	127	167	92	17	41	75	6.54	1.63	24.1	310	2.9	5.3	1.8	1.2	35%	61%	27
		11	22	aa	MIN	8	7	37	1	95	107	60	8	27	79	5.72	1.41	11.1	279	2.5	7.5	2.9	0.8	34%	59%	82
Gutierrez,Carlos	R	09	23	aa	MIN	1	3	22	0	52	73	45	6	26	25	7.84	1.90	11.4	325	4.5	4.4	1.0	1.1	36%	69%	5
		10	24	a/a	MIN	5	8	34	2	126	157	70	7	52	71	5.01	1.65	16.9	299	3.7	5.1	1.4	0.5	34%	69%	39
		11	25	aaa	MIN	2	3	43	0	62	70	38	2	33	44	5.50	1.65	6.6	278	4.8	6.4	1.3	0.3	34%	64%	58
Hagadone,Nick	L	10	25	aa	CLE	2	2	19	1	48	51	28	5	35	37	5.33	1.78	11.9	265	6.5	6.9	1.1	1.0	32%	71%	36
		11	26	aa	CLE	4	4	46	4	71	66	26	5	23	63	3.33	1.25	6.4	240	2.9	7.9	2.7	0.6	31%	74%	93
Harvey,Matt	R	11	22	aa	NYM	5	3	12	0	60	61	31	3	21	56	4.64	1.38	21.4	259	3.2	8.4	2.6	0.5	34%	65%	93
Heath,Deunte	R	08	23	aa	ATL	4	5	13	0	66	88	48	5	33	39	6.60	1.82	24.1	312	4.5	5.3	1.2	0.7	36%	63%	28
		09	24	a/a	ATL	2	6	32	1	98	128	73	7	54	76	6.71	1.85	14.6	308	4.9	6.9	1.4	0.7	37%	62%	45
		10	25	aa	CHW	2	4	39	2	57	63	28	6	37	68	4.37	1.75	6.8	275	5.8	10.6	1.8	0.9	38%	76%	76
		11	26	aaa	CHW	4	7	30	1	103	124	70	17	74	96	6.15	1.93	16.6	293	6.5	8.4	1.3	1.5	36%	71%	28
Heckathorn,Kyle	R	11	23	aa	MIL	0	4	7	0	36	50	33	8	17	21	8.08	1.85	24.7	321	4.2	5.2	1.2	1.9	34%	58%	-8
Hembree,Heath	R	11	22	aa	SF	1	1	28	17	29	23	11	1	13	29	3.52	1.26	4.3	217	4.1	9.1	2.2	0.3	30%	71%	103
Hendriks,Liam	R	11	22	a/a	MIN	12	6	25	0	139	147	56	4	21	92	3.59	1.20	23.0	266	1.3	5.9	4.5	0.3	32%	68%	124
Herrera,Kelvin	R	11	21	KC	KC	5	0	37	13	53	36	11	4	12	49	1.93	0.90	5.5	188	2.0	8.2	4.1	0.7	24%	83%	132
Hoover,J.J.	R	10	23	aa	ATL	3	1	4	0	20	18	9	1	15	30	4.13	1.63	23.0	229	6.9	13.4	1.9	0.5	38%	74%	117
		11	24	a/a	ATL	3	6	43	2	106	88	36	5	41	99	3.10	1.22	10.2	223	3.5	8.4	2.4	0.4	29%	75%	99
Hutchison,Drew	R	11	21	aa	TOR	3	0	3	0	15	11	2	0	9	19	1.41	0.88	19.0	204	1.2	11.3	9.5	0.0	32%	82%	282
Hyatt,Austin	R	10	24	aa	PHI	1	0	4	0	22	24	14	4	9	20	5.60	1.53	24.5	274	3.9	8.2	2.1	1.7	32%	68%	42
		11	25	aa	PHI	12	6	28	0	154	157	77	22	49	137	4.50	1.34	23.5	259	2.9	8.0	2.8	1.3	31%	70%	72
Jeffress,Jeremy	R	10	23	aa	MIL	1	1	11	3	14	9	2	0	2	14	1.32	0.80	4.8	184	1.3	8.7	6.6	0.0	26%	82%	209
		11	24	a/a	KC	3	6	25	2	56	65	37	6	38	35	5.98	1.85	10.6	286	6.1	5.7	0.9	1.0	33%	68%	21
Jenkins,Chad	R	11	24	aa	TOR	5	7	16	0	100	110	57	9	28	63	5.11	1.37	26.9	272	2.5	5.7	2.2	0.8	31%	63%	56
Jones,Beau	L	09	23	aa	TEX	3	4	36	2	54	69	34	2	32	48	5.66	1.87	7.2	304	5.3	7.9	1.5	0.3	39%	68%	63
		10	24	aa	TEX	3	0	34	3	52	45	23	0	33	51	3.99	1.49	6.8	229	5.6	8.8	1.6	0.0	32%	70%	95
		11	25	a/a	TEX	0	1	43	1	68	72	28	9	29	47	3.74	1.48	7.0	265	3.9	6.2	1.6	1.2	30%	79%	37
Judy,Josh	R	09	24	aa	CLE	4	3	36	11	49	43	24	2	20	55	4.35	1.28	5.7	232	3.6	10.1	2.8	0.4	33%	64%	117
		10	25	aa	CLE	3	0	40	2	49	61	18	5	14	49	3.22	1.54	5.5	298	2.7	9.1	3.4	0.9	39%	82%	93
		11	26	aaa	CLE	6	2	50	23	52	50	21	5	26	49	3.57	1.46	4.6	249	4.4	8.4	1.9	0.8	32%	78%	71
Kelly,Casey	R	10	21	aa	BOS	3	5	21	0	95	124	60	10	31	72	5.68	1.63	20.6	309	3.0	6.9	2.3	0.9	37%	65%	56
		11	22	aa	SD	11	6	27	0	142	153	58	6	43	95	3.70	1.38	22.6	269	2.7	6.0	2.2	0.4	32%	72%	73
Kimball,Cole	R	10	25	aa	WAS	5	1	38	12	54	43	20	6	34	57	3.33	1.44	6.2	216	5.7	9.5	1.6	0.9	28%	80%	75
Kluber,Corey	R	09	23	aa	SD	2	4	9	0	45	48	24	4	34	29	4.74	1.83	23.8	269	6.8	5.8	0.9	0.8	31%	75%	29
		10	24	a/a	CLE	9	9	29	0	160	190	70	7	56	143	3.94	1.53	24.6	289	3.1	8.0	2.6	0.4	37%	74%	87
		11	25	aaa	CLE	7	11	27	0	151	175	107	18	72	116	6.36	1.64	25.4	285	4.3	6.9	1.6	1.1	34%	61%	41
Kontos,George	R	08	23	aa	NYY	6	11	27	0	151	169	89	20	63	123	5.28	1.53	24.9	277	3.7	7.3	2.0	1.2	33%	67%	50
		09	24	aa	NYY	4	5	13	0	71	79	36	8	33	52	4.57	1.58	24.6	277	4.2	6.6	1.6	1.0	32%	73%	41
		10	25	a/a	NYY	0	3	19	0	34	42	19	4	13	26	4.99	1.60	8.1	297	3.3	6.8	2.0	1.1	35%	71%	46
		11	26	aaa	NYY	4	4	40	2	89	93	37	18	30	72	3.73	1.38	9.6	263	3.0	7.2	2.4	1.8	29%	82%	41
Lamb,John	L	10	20	aa	KC	2	1	7	0	33	38	21	2	11	24	5.71	1.50	20.8	283	3.1	6.6	2.1	0.5	34%	60%	67
		11	21	aa	KC	1	2	8	0	35	35	12	3	12	18	3.20	1.33	18.6	254	3.0	4.7	1.6	0.7	29%	77%	46
Leesman,Charles	L	10	24	aa	CHW	5	2	11	0	63	57	25	1	22	44	3.52	1.24	23.9	235	3.1	6.2	2.0	0.1	29%	69%	83
		11	25	aa	CHW	10	7	27	0	152	183	90	6	95	96	5.34	1.83	26.7	292	5.6	5.7	1.0	0.3	35%	69%	42
Lee,Chen	R	10	24	aa	CLE	5	4	44	0	72	67	30	6	22	71	3.73	1.23	6.8	241	2.7	8.8	3.3	0.8	31%	71%	105
		11	25	aa	CLE	6	1	44	1	71	62	23	3	24	80	2.87	1.21	6.7	230	3.0	10.1	3.3	0.4	33%	76%	129
Lehman,Patrick	R	11	25	aa	WAS	1	2	29	6	34	27	18	2	4	27	4.70	0.90	4.5	211	1.1	7.2	6.5	0.6	26%	45%	175
Lindsay,Shane	R	10	26	a/a	CLE	1	2	33	1	40	40	29	1	51	46	6.62	2.26	6.3	255	11.3	10.2	0.9	0.2	37%	68%	77
		11	27	a/a	CHW	3	3	50	4	70	41	23	3	70	74	3.00	1.58	6.3	165	9.0	9.4	1.0	0.4	23%	81%	89
Locke,Jeff	L	10	23	aa	PIT	3	2	10	0	57	64	26	5	11	47	4.09	1.31	24.2	277	1.7	7.4	4.3	0.8	34%	70%	110
		11	24	a/a	PIT	8	10	28	0	153	165	75	10	54	109	4.39	1.43	23.8	269	3.2	6.4	2.0	0.6	32%	69%	64
Lo,Chia-Jen	R	09	24	aa	HOU	2	0	30	2	39	33	11	1	20	33	2.62	1.35	5.5	225	4.5	7.6	1.7	0.2	29%	80%	84
		10	25	aa	HOU	0	1	7	0	15	11	4	0	11	10	2.53	1.40	9.3	194	6.3	6.3	1.0	0.0	25%	80%	75
Lueke,Josh	R	11	27	aaa	SEA	2	4	30	11	42	36	12	1	11	28	2.51	1.10	5.7	223	2.4	6.0	2.5	0.2	28%	76%	95
Lynn,Lance	R	11	24	aaa	STL	7	3	12	0	75	85	33	2	24	53	3.99	1.46	27.4	280	2.9	6.3	2.2	0.2	34%	71%	76
Magnuson,Trystan	R	10	25	aa	TOR	3	0	46	5	73	82	24	1	11	50	3.01	1.28	6.7	278	1.4	6.1	4.5	0.1	34%	75%	125
		11	26	aaa	OAK	4	2	30	5	45	38	16	4	18	37	3.11	1.23	6.3	221	3.6	7.3	2.0	0.7	27%	77%	76
Maine,Scott	L	09	25	a/a	ARI	4	5	48	7	62	79	24	2	22	52	3.44	1.63	5.9	305	3.1	7.6	2.4	0.3	39%	78%	81
		10	26	a/a	CHC	4	2	45	10	57	52	23	5	25	51	3.65	1.35	5.4	236	4.0	8.1	2.0	0.8	30%	75%	74
		11	27	aaa	CHC	4	3	38	12	51	42	22	3	24	57	3.84	1.29	5.7	219	4.2	9.9	2.3	0.5	31%	70%	104
Main,Michael	R	10	22	aa	SF	0	3	5	0	13	25	28	3	14	6	19.09	2.95	15.5	393	9.5	4.1	0.4	2.0	41%	31%	-52
Manzanillo,Santo	R	11	23	aa	MIL	0	1	20	7	20	14	6	2	12	17	2.49	1.30	4.3	196	5.3	7.4	1.4	1.0	23%	86%	61
Marinez,Jhan	R	10	22	aa	FLA	1	0	15	6	16	10	5	1	7	18	2.78	1.05	4.3	175	3.9	10.0	2.6	0.6	25%	75%	117
		11	23	aa	FLA	3	8	56	2	58	51	25	7	43	67	3.89	1.62	4.7	233	6.6	10.4	1.6	1.0	32%	79%	73
Marte,Luis	R	09	23	aa	DET	5	8	19	0	105	125	59	21	28	70	5.03	1.45	24.2	289	2.4	6.0	2.5	1.8	31%	71%	33
		10	24	a/a	DET	2	2	39	7	49	53	33	6	27	44	6.06	1.62	5.7	269	4.9	8.0	1.6	1.1	33%	63%	49
		11	25	a/a	DET	4	0	25	3	56	38	15	3	22	55	2.42	1.08	9.0	190	3.6	8.8	2.5	0.6	25%	80%	105
Martinez,Carlos	R	09	26	aa	WAS	7	6	28	2	79	107	52	8	29	33	5.93	1.71	13.1	316	3.3	3.8	1.2	0.9	34%	65%	12
		11	27	a/a	WAS	3	4	33	2	66	103	59	9	19	27	7.72	1.86	9.5	349	2.7	3.8	1.4	1.3	37%	58%	-1
Martin,Ethan	R	11	22	aa	LA	5	3	21	2	40	32	18	3	25	38	3.92	1.40	8.3	213	5.5	8.5	1.5	0.6	28%	72%	78
Martin,Rafael	R	10	26	aa	WAS	5	4	47	0	67	75	40	7	30	44	5.40	1.56	6.4	276	4.0	5.8	1.5	0.9	32%	66%	38
		11	27	aa	WAS	4	1	32	13	36	33	9	1	10	34	2.34	1.19	4.6	239	2.5	8.5	3.4	0.3	32%	80%	121
Mathieson,Scott	R	10	26	aaa	PHI	3	6	54	26	64	60	27	10	26	69	3.76	1.33	5.1	242	3.6	9.7	2.7	1.4	31%	78%	77
		11	27	aaa	PHI	2	2	30	5	82	91	41	11	55	64	4.47	1.78	12.9	274	6.1	7.0	1.2	1.3	32%	78%	29
McAllister,Zach	R	11	24	aaa	CLE	12	9	25	0	155	174	64	10	31	106	3.72	1.33	26.3	278	1.8	6.2	3.4	0.6	33%	72%	90
McGuire,Deck	R	11	22	aa	TOR	2	1	4	0	21	23	12	4	7	20	5.17	1.43	22.5	273	3.1	8.5	2.8	2.0	32%	71%	52
McPherson,Kyle	R	11	24	aa	PIT	8	5	16	0	89	87	36	7	21	65	3.65	1.21	23.1	251	2.1	6.5	3.1	0.7	30%	71%	86

PITCHER	Th	Yr	Age	Lev	Org	W	L	G	Sv	IP	H	ER	HR	BB	K	ERA	WHIP	BF/G	OBA	bb/9	K/9	Cmd	HR/9	H%	S%	BPV
Miley,Wade	L	10	24	aa	ARI	5	2	13	0	72	74	23	6	30	52	2.83	1.44	24.2	260	3.7	6.5	1.8	0.8	31%	83%	56
		11	25	a/a	ARI	8	3	22	0	130	137	63	9	41	81	4.37	1.37	25.3	266	2.8	5.6	2.0	0.7	31%	68%	58
Miller,Aaron	L	10	23	aa	LA	1	4	6	0	23	30	19	3	18	17	7.26	2.06	19.1	308	6.9	6.8	1.0	1.2	36%	65%	19
Miller,Shelby	R	11	21	aa	STL	9	3	16	0	87	69	22	1	28	77	2.30	1.12	21.9	214	2.9	8.0	2.7	0.1	29%	78%	113
Milone,Tom	L	10	24	aa	WAS	12	5	27	0	158	195	66	11	24	129	3.76	1.38	25.2	297	1.4	7.3	5.4	0.6	37%	74%	135
		11	25	aaa	WAS	12	6	24	0	148	160	64	10	16	126	3.91	1.19	25.4	270	1.0	7.6	7.9	0.6	34%	67%	194
Molina,Nestor	R	11	22	aa	TOR	2	0	5	0	22	14	1	0	2	29	0.49	0.71	16.0	175	0.8	12.0	14.7	0.0	29%	92%	400
Moore,Brandon	R	10	25	aa	NYM	0	1	1	0	3	8	9	4	4	5	27.50	4.07	21.7	482	12.2	13.8	1.1	12.2	51%	38%	-302
		11	26	aa	NYM	10	8	26	1	133	172	70	11	41	86	4.72	1.60	23.1	307	2.8	5.8	2.1	0.7	36%	71%	50
Moore,Matt	L	11	22	a/a	TAM	12	3	27	0	155	108	35	10	44	185	2.03	0.98	22.4	193	2.5	10.7	4.3	0.6	28%	83%	152
Moreno,Diego	R	10	24	aa	PIT	0	0	7	2	7	12	7	1	3	10	9.21	2.05	5.1	355	3.9	11.9	3.0	1.3	49%	54%	79
Morris,Bryan	R	10	24	aa	PIT	6	4	19	0	89	100	49	9	30	68	5.00	1.46	20.5	278	3.0	6.9	2.3	0.9	33%	67%	60
		11	25	aa	PIT	3	4	35	3	78	84	35	2	33	50	4.05	1.50	9.8	269	3.8	5.8	1.5	0.2	33%	71%	61
Moskos,Daniel	L	09	23	aa	PIT	11	10	27	0	149	184	74	11	57	62	4.48	1.61	25.0	297	3.4	3.7	1.1	0.7	32%	73%	21
		10	24	a/a	PIT	3	6	56	22	58	59	31	3	34	49	4.78	1.59	4.7	257	5.3	7.7	1.5	0.5	33%	69%	66
		11	25	aaa	PIT	1	1	30	3	42	47	19	2	11	22	4.08	1.38	6.0	276	2.4	4.8	2.0	0.4	32%	70%	58
Oberholtzer,Brett	L	11	22	aa	HOU	11	12	27	0	155	152	68	8	46	107	3.95	1.28	24.1	251	2.7	6.2	2.3	0.5	30%	69%	75
Odorizzi,Jake	R	11	21	aa	KC	5	3	12	0	69	69	37	11	20	45	4.90	1.30	24.2	257	2.6	5.9	2.3	1.4	28%	66%	43
Oliveros,Lester	R	10	22	aa	DET	1	2	24	14	25	22	16	3	20	31	5.74	1.67	4.8	231	7.2	11.1	1.6	1.1	32%	67%	76
		11	23	a/a	MIN	3	3	34	5	48	55	24	7	21	47	4.50	1.58	6.3	281	3.9	8.8	2.2	1.2	35%	75%	62
Oliver,Andrew	L	11	24	aaa	DET	8	12	26	0	147	179	99	18	82	115	6.06	1.77	26.5	294	5.0	7.0	1.4	1.1	35%	67%	35
Oramas,Juan	L	11	21	a/a	SD	10	6	20	0	108	99	34	9	25	97	2.85	1.15	22.0	238	2.1	8.1	3.9	0.7	30%	78%	116
Ortega,Jose	R	10	22	aa	DET	1	0	15	0	23	25	9	2	7	16	3.49	1.38	6.6	270	2.7	6.2	2.3	0.8	32%	77%	63
		11	23	aaa	DET	1	3	33	0	50	72	44	8	27	36	7.93	1.98	7.4	330	4.9	6.5	1.3	1.5	38%	60%	13
Ottavino,Adam	R	08	23	aa	STL	3	7	24	0	115	143	72	14	48	82	5.63	1.66	22.0	298	3.8	6.4	1.7	1.1	35%	67%	37
		09	24	aaa	STL	7	12	27	0	144	156	86	11	77	103	5.38	1.62	24.2	271	4.8	6.4	1.3	0.7	32%	66%	47
		10	25	aaa	STL	5	3	9	0	47	44	21	4	11	37	4.00	1.17	21.4	242	2.1	7.1	3.4	0.8	29%	67%	97
		11	26	aaa	STL	7	8	26	0	141	174	82	13	71	94	5.26	1.74	25.3	297	4.6	6.0	1.3	0.8	35%	70%	35
Owens,Rudy	L	10	23	aa	PIT	12	6	26	0	150	138	47	11	22	111	2.82	1.07	23.0	240	1.3	6.7	5.0	0.7	29%	76%	133
		11	24	aaa	PIT	9	7	21	0	112	148	73	10	31	56	5.88	1.59	24.1	310	2.5	4.5	1.8	0.8	35%	62%	33
Parker,Jarrod	R	09	21	aa	ARI	4	6	16	0	78	92	41	3	32	68	4.72	1.60	22.1	288	3.7	7.9	2.1	0.3	37%	69%	79
		11	23	aa	ARI	11	8	26	0	131	124	62	7	52	93	4.25	1.35	21.5	246	3.6	6.4	1.8	0.5	30%	68%	66
Paxton,James	L	11	23	aa	SEA	3	0	7	0	39	31	9	2	13	45	2.05	1.12	22.5	214	3.0	10.4	3.5	0.4	31%	83%	135
Peacock,Brad	R	11	23	a/a	WAS	15	3	25	0	147	113	47	10	46	147	2.88	1.09	23.5	208	2.8	9.0	3.2	0.6	28%	75%	116
Pelzer,Wynn	R	10	24	aa	BAL	7	9	32	0	114	152	68	15	63	82	5.40	1.88	17.1	313	5.0	6.4	1.3	1.2	36%	73%	23
		11	25	a/a	BAL	5	8	37	1	88	105	51	8	56	57	5.28	1.84	11.3	290	5.8	5.9	1.0	0.8	34%	72%	29
Peralta,Wily	R	10	21	aa	MIL	2	3	8	0	42	47	19	5	24	26	4.06	1.69	24.2	277	5.1	5.6	1.1	1.1	31%	79%	24
		11	22	a/a	MIL	11	7	26	0	151	134	55	9	56	141	3.26	1.26	24.2	233	3.3	8.4	2.5	0.5	31%	75%	96
Perez,Martin	L	10	19	aa	TEX	5	8	24	0	99	125	76	14	46	96	6.93	1.72	19.2	301	4.2	8.7	2.1	1.2	38%	60%	53
		11	20	a/a	TEX	8	6	27	0	137	158	68	10	52	105	4.49	1.53	22.6	283	3.4	6.9	2.0	0.7	34%	71%	62
Phillips,Zachary	L	09	23	aa	TEX	0	0	20	2	33	32	7	1	20	24	1.96	1.55	7.4	248	5.3	6.6	1.2	0.3	31%	88%	62
		10	24	a/a	TEX	3	2	45	5	67	69	25	1	35	52	3.32	1.55	6.7	261	4.7	7.0	1.5	0.1	33%	77%	72
Pimentel,Stolmy	R	11	21	aa	BOS	0	9	15	0	50	80	55	7	22	26	9.81	2.03	16.6	354	3.9	4.6	1.2	1.3	39%	50%	-3
Pomeranz,Drew	L	11	23	aa	COL	1	1	5	0	24	14	5	1	6	19	1.73	0.80	17.9	162	2.2	7.2	3.3	0.4	20%	81%	122
Poreda,Aaron	L	08	22	aa	CHW	3	4	15	0	87	98	39	7	23	64	4.03	1.39	25.0	278	2.4	6.6	2.8	0.7	33%	72%	76
		09	23	a/a	SD	5	7	20	0	107	88	49	3	73	93	4.12	1.50	23.7	220	6.1	7.8	1.3	0.3	29%	71%	77
		10	24	a/a	SD	1	2	39	0	54	32	23	1	62	42	3.83	1.74	6.5	169	10.3	7.0	0.7	0.2	22%	76%	72
		11	25	aaa	SD	4	3	41	0	70	62	33	2	56	67	4.28	1.69	7.8	233	7.2	8.7	1.2	0.2	32%	73%	79
Pryor,Stephen	R	11	22	aa	SEA	2	1	17	6	23	10	3	0	7	24	1.30	0.73	4.9	128	2.7	9.6	3.6	0.0	20%	80%	162
Putnam,Zach	R	09	22	aa	CLE	4	2	33	2	56	71	35	2	19	52	5.60	1.60	7.7	302	3.0	8.3	2.7	0.3	39%	63%	92
		10	23	a/a	CLE	4	2	37	3	75	85	34	4	16	58	4.07	1.34	8.7	279	1.9	6.9	3.6	0.5	34%	69%	103
		11	24	aaa	CLE	6	3	44	9	69	68	31	6	23	56	4.10	1.33	6.7	254	3.0	7.4	2.4	0.7	31%	70%	78
Quirarte,Edwin	R	11	25	aa	SF	1	2	35	0	46	75	37	4	21	31	7.21	2.08	6.6	357	4.2	5.9	1.4	0.7	42%	64%	29
Raley,Brooks	L	11	23	aa	CHC	8	10	26	0	136	191	73	18	44	67	4.84	1.72	24.4	324	2.9	4.4	1.5	1.2	35%	74%	13
Ramirez,Erasmo	R	11	21	a/a	SEA	10	8	26	0	153	177	76	11	28	105	4.47	1.34	25.0	284	1.7	6.2	3.7	0.6	34%	67%	94
Ramirez,J.C.	R	10	22	aa	PHI	3	4	13	0	77	96	51	12	23	51	5.95	1.54	26.5	299	2.7	5.9	2.2	1.4	34%	64%	36
		11	23	aa	PHI	11	13	26	0	144	160	81	16	53	75	5.04	1.48	24.4	276	3.3	4.7	1.4	1.0	30%	67%	28
Ramirez,Neil	R	11	22	a/a	TEX	5	3	24	0	93	82	36	7	41	93	3.50	1.31	16.5	230	3.9	9.0	2.3	0.7	30%	75%	89
Reckling,Trevor	L	09	20	aa	LAA	8	7	23	0	135	133	55	4	72	93	3.68	1.52	26.1	253	4.8	6.2	1.3	0.3	31%	75%	61
		10	21	a/a	LAA	7	13	28	0	148	177	109	14	74	96	6.59	1.70	24.4	290	4.5	5.8	1.3	0.9	34%	60%	33
		11	22	aa	LAA	4	7	17	0	99	118	49	12	33	54	4.47	1.53	25.9	290	3.0	4.9	1.6	1.1	32%	73%	28
Reed,Addison	R	11	23	a/a	CHW	0	1	24	4	42	21	6	3	10	53	1.39	0.75	6.4	149	2.2	11.4	5.3	0.6	22%	87%	187
Reifer,Adam	R	10	24	a/a	STL	4	1	52	17	55	58	19	2	14	43	3.04	1.31	4.5	264	2.4	7.0	3.0	0.3	33%	76%	96
Rice,Jason	R	10	24	aa	BOS	3	2	48	13	60	53	22	6	29	58	3.32	1.37	5.4	231	4.4	8.7	2.0	0.9	29%	79%	74
		11	25	aaa	BOS	4	5	44	4	85	96	48	7	46	71	5.02	1.67	8.9	279	4.8	7.5	1.5	0.7	34%	70%	54
Richards,Garrett	R	11	23	aa	LAA	12	2	22	0	143	143	61	11	39	86	3.85	1.27	27.2	255	2.5	5.4	2.2	0.7	29%	71%	62
Riordan,Cory	R	10	24	aa	COL	8	5	27	0	161	206	96	26	39	108	5.35	1.52	26.5	305	2.2	6.0	2.8	1.5	34%	68%	45
		11	25	a/a	COL	1	12	28	0	149	193	89	22	23	79	5.36	1.44	23.3	307	1.4	4.8	3.5	1.3	33%	65%	56
Rivas,Amaury	R	10	25	aa	MIL	11	6	25	0	141	149	62	7	58	98	3.96	1.47	24.8	266	3.7	6.2	1.7	0.5	32%	73%	61
		11	26	aaa	MIL	7	12	28	0	151	167	83	14	81	89	4.95	1.65	24.6	276	4.8	5.3	1.1	0.8	31%	71%	30
Robertson,Tyler	L	10	23	a/a	MIN	4	14	28	0	149	202	97	16	56	81	5.85	1.73	24.8	317	3.4	4.9	1.4	1.0	35%	67%	22
		11	24	aa	MIN	10	3	55	16	90	95	38	5	29	70	3.85	1.38	7.0	267	2.9	7.0	2.4	0.5	33%	72%	80
Robles,Mauricio	L	10	22	a/a	SEA	9	7	27	0	142	123	63	10	67	144	3.98	1.33	22.4	229	4.2	9.1	2.2	0.7	30%	71%	89
		11	23	a/a	SEA	1	3	6	0	20	14	14	3	20	13	6.31	1.69	15.4	194	8.9	5.7	0.6	1.4	20%	64%	21
Rogers,Mark	R	10	25	a/a	MIL	6	8	25	0	116	100	53	3	74	100	4.08	1.50	20.5	228	5.8	7.8	1.3	0.2	30%	71%	77
		11	26	aaa	MIL	0	2	5	0	15	23	23	1	22	10	13.54	2.95	17.6	342	12.9	6.1	0.5	0.6	40%	50%	15
Rondon,Hector	R	09	22	a/a	CLE	11	10	27	0	146	158	66	11	29	130	4.05	1.28	22.7	270	1.8	8.0	4.6	0.7	34%	69%	124
		10	23	aaa	CLE	1	3	7	0	31	50	30	10	10	30	8.79	1.89	21.5	352	2.7	8.8	3.2	3.0	40%	59%	14

PITCHER	Th	Yr	Age	Lev	Org	W	L	G	Sv	IP	H	ER	HR	BB	K	ERA	WHIP	BF/G	OBA	bb/9	K/9	Cmd	HR/9	H%	S%	BPV
Ruffin,Chance	R	11	23	a/a	DET	3	3	44	19	49	43	13	3	22	49	2.46	1.32	4.7	231	4.0	9.1	2.3	0.6	31%	84%	93
Sanchez,Eduardo	R	09	21	aa	STL	2	0	41	10	50	32	15	4	17	50	2.74	0.99	4.8	182	3.1	9.1	2.9	0.7	24%	75%	114
		10	22	a/a	STL	1	1	50	14	53	41	13	3	17	53	2.26	1.10	4.3	209	2.9	8.9	3.1	0.5	28%	81%	116
Santiago,Hector	L	11	24	aa	CHW	7	5	15	0	83	87	44	6	45	63	4.73	1.57	25.0	263	4.8	6.8	1.4	0.6	32%	70%	55
Satterwhite,Cody	R	09	23	aa	DET	4	6	34	12	49	53	23	6	26	44	4.22	1.61	6.5	270	4.8	8.1	1.7	1.1	33%	77%	52
Scahill,Rob	R	11	24	aa	COL	12	11	27	0	161	189	83	14	59	81	4.63	1.54	26.5	287	3.3	4.5	1.4	0.8	32%	71%	30
Scarpetta,Cody	R	11	23	aa	MIL	8	5	23	0	117	111	56	9	61	86	4.33	1.47	22.4	246	4.7	6.6	1.4	0.7	30%	71%	55
Scheppers,Tanner	R	10	24	a/a	TEX	1	3	36	6	80	97	52	7	30	78	5.85	1.59	10.0	293	3.4	8.8	2.6	0.8	38%	63%	80
		11	25	a/a	TEX	4	1	28	2	44	46	20	1	21	36	4.13	1.53	6.9	265	4.3	7.4	1.7	0.2	34%	71%	76
Shafer,Aaron	R	10	24	aa	CHC	2	2	25	2	34	39	23	3	10	25	6.00	1.46	6.0	283	2.7	6.7	2.4	0.8	34%	58%	65
		11	25	aa	ATL	3	2	7	0	44	59	26	2	14	31	5.27	1.65	29.0	314	2.9	6.2	2.2	0.4	38%	66%	63
Skaggs,Tyler	L	11	20	aa	ARI	4	1	10	0	58	48	17	4	14	64	2.67	1.06	23.0	220	2.1	9.9	4.7	0.6	31%	77%	150
Slama,Anthony	R	09	26	a/a	MIN	4	4	62	29	81	68	31	5	42	87	3.39	1.36	5.6	224	4.7	9.7	2.1	0.6	31%	76%	94
		10	27	aaa	MIN	2	4	54	17	65	45	18	5	32	60	2.42	1.19	5.0	193	4.4	8.3	1.9	0.7	25%	83%	84
		11	28	aaa	MIN	3	2	27	1	37	33	15	4	18	31	3.63	1.37	5.9	234	4.3	7.6	1.8	0.9	29%	76%	64
Smyly,Drew	L	11	22	aa	DET	4	3	8	0	46	34	7	1	14	44	1.35	1.06	22.7	205	2.8	8.8	3.1	0.2	28%	88%	126
Snow,Forrest	R	11	22	aaa	SEA	1	2	9	0	35	32	17	3	8	32	4.38	1.14	15.9	236	2.1	8.2	3.9	0.7	30%	62%	117
Spoone,Chorye	R	08	23	aa	BAL	3	3	9	0	41	47	27	5	27	27	5.87	1.81	21.6	283	5.9	5.9	1.0	1.1	32%	69%	21
		10	25	aa	BAL	7	6	24	0	132	167	79	17	84	67	5.38	1.90	26.5	302	5.8	4.5	0.8	1.1	33%	73%	4
		11	26	a/a	BAL	7	6	31	1	122	156	82	8	71	62	6.06	1.86	18.8	304	5.3	4.6	0.9	0.6	34%	66%	22
Stoffel,Jason	R	11	23	aa	HOU	2	5	50	17	48	55	24	4	23	43	4.56	1.63	4.3	282	4.3	8.1	1.9	0.7	36%	72%	66
Stowell,Bryce	R	10	24	aa	CLE	2	1	31	7	42	29	13	2	28	52	2.87	1.35	5.8	191	6.0	11.2	1.9	0.4	29%	79%	111
		11	25	aa	CLE	1	0	13	0	19	14	5	1	11	23	2.33	1.30	6.3	203	5.0	10.6	2.1	0.5	30%	83%	108
Sturdevant,Tyler	R	11	26	a/a	CLE	3	1	21	3	34	43	16	2	12	30	4.24	1.63	7.3	305	3.1	8.1	2.6	0.5	39%	74%	80
Suarez,Larry	R	11	22	aa	CHC	0	2	6	0	16	24	15	2	6	9	8.21	1.87	12.8	341	3.3	5.3	1.6	1.2	38%	55%	16
Surkamp,Eric	L	11	24	aa	SF	10	4	23	0	142	133	42	6	46	135	2.63	1.26	25.8	242	2.9	8.6	2.9	0.4	32%	79%	109
Tanner,Clayton	L	10	23	aa	SF	9	9	27	0	149	178	80	11	65	66	4.83	1.63	25.1	290	3.9	4.0	1.0	0.7	32%	70%	22
		11	24	a/a	CIN	6	10	23	0	123	133	61	14	36	79	4.49	1.38	22.9	271	2.7	5.8	2.2	1.0	31%	70%	51
Tazawa,Junichi	R	09	23	a/a	BOS	9	7	20	0	109	107	44	9	28	81	3.63	1.24	22.7	251	2.3	6.7	2.9	0.7	30%	72%	83
		11	25	a/a	BOS	4	3	16	0	37	41	20	4	10	37	4.82	1.37	10.0	272	2.5	8.8	3.5	1.0	35%	67%	95
Teheran,Julio	R	10	20	aa	ATL	3	2	7	0	40	29	15	2	15	37	3.48	1.11	23.0	199	3.5	8.4	2.4	0.4	27%	68%	104
		11	21	aaa	ATL	15	3	25	0	145	136	48	5	47	111	2.98	1.27	24.2	244	2.9	6.9	2.4	0.3	31%	76%	87
Thompson,Aaron	L	08	22	aa	FLA	2	5	16	0	81	124	59	9	42	49	6.54	2.04	25.2	343	4.7	5.4	1.2	1.0	39%	68%	13
		09	23	aa	WAS	5	12	26	0	146	184	86	12	55	88	5.29	1.63	25.6	301	3.4	5.4	1.6	0.7	35%	67%	39
		10	24	a/a	WAS	5	13	27	0	141	197	113	18	56	85	7.20	1.79	24.6	323	3.6	5.4	1.5	1.1	36%	60%	20
		11	24	a/a	PIT	5	7	33	0	103	142	64	6	29	48	5.62	1.66	14.3	322	2.5	4.2	1.7	0.5	36%	65%	35
Tolleson,Shawn	R	11	23	aa	LA	4	2	38	12	44	44	8	2	10	47	1.62	1.21	4.8	254	1.9	9.6	5.0	0.4	35%	88%	155
Turner,Jacob	R	11	20	a/a	DET	4	5	20	0	131	128	58	11	33	95	3.95	1.23	27.2	251	2.2	6.5	2.9	0.7	30%	69%	83
Villanueva,Elih	R	10	24	aa	FLA	14	4	28	0	179	166	58	18	38	99	2.91	1.14	26.0	241	1.9	5.0	2.6	0.9	27%	79%	64
		11	25	a/a	FLA	7	11	28	0	165	218	103	22	60	91	5.61	1.69	27.2	312	3.3	5.0	1.5	1.2	34%	68%	18
Vizcaino,Arodys	R	11	21	a/a	ATL	3	3	17	0	57	56	25	4	17	56	3.90	1.29	14.0	252	2.8	8.9	3.2	0.6	33%	70%	107
Wagner,Neil	R	09	26	aa	CLE	1	3	46	2	61	64	30	4	38	57	4.43	1.68	6.1	266	5.6	8.4	1.5	0.7	34%	74%	64
		10	27	aa	OAK	7	3	46	5	63	90	38	1	37	45	5.42	2.01	6.7	328	5.3	6.5	1.2	0.2	40%	71%	49
		11	28	a/a	OAK	3	4	50	6	66	66	26	2	23	68	3.52	1.34	5.6	254	3.1	9.3	3.0	0.2	35%	72%	116
Warren,Adam	R	10	23	aa	NYY	4	2	10	0	54	56	23	2	16	52	3.77	1.33	23.0	261	2.7	8.7	3.2	0.3	35%	71%	112
		11	24	aaa	NYY	6	8	27	0	152	180	83	19	59	91	4.92	1.56	25.3	288	3.5	5.4	1.6	1.1	32%	71%	29
Watts,Dakota	R	10	23	aa	MIN	0	0	2	0	3	4	5	0	2	4	14.06	1.88	7.7	300	5.6	11.3	2.0	0.0	17%	17%	105
		11	24	aa	MIN	1	2	23	2	34	46	32	2	19	22	8.38	1.89	7.2	314	5.0	5.8	1.2	0.6	37%	53%	33
Webster,Allen	R	11	21	aa	LA	6	3	18	0	91	103	49	6	30	65	4.88	1.46	22.2	279	3.0	6.4	2.1	0.6	34%	66%	65
Weiland,Kyle	R	10	24	aa	BOS	5	9	25	0	128	129	75	14	48	98	5.25	1.39	22.1	257	3.4	6.9	2.0	1.0	31%	63%	58
		11	25	aaa	BOS	8	10	24	0	128	135	69	12	60	100	4.87	1.52	23.7	265	4.2	7.0	1.7	0.8	32%	69%	54
Wilk,Adam	L	10	23	aa	DET	2	0	3	0	23	11	3	1	5	12	1.16	0.69	27.9	140	1.9	4.7	2.4	0.4	16%	87%	94
		11	24	aaa	DET	8	6	18	0	103	126	48	18	14	61	4.17	1.37	24.5	296	1.3	5.4	4.3	1.6	32%	76%	71
Wilson,Alex	R	10	24	aa	BOS	4	5	16	0	78	108	67	15	33	47	7.72	1.81	23.1	322	3.8	5.4	1.4	1.8	35%	59%	-1
		11	25	a/a	BOS	10	4	25	0	133	146	58	11	46	98	3.89	1.45	23.2	273	3.1	6.6	2.1	0.7	33%	74%	63
Withrow,Chris	R	10	21	aa	LA	4	9	27	0	129	153	88	12	66	98	6.13	1.70	22.1	289	4.6	6.8	1.5	0.8	35%	63%	44
		11	22	aa	LA	6	6	25	0	129	114	59	7	64	115	4.10	1.38	22.1	233	4.5	8.0	1.8	0.5	30%	70%	80
Wood,Austin	L	11	25	aa	DET	5	5	50	6	63	67	27	6	28	48	3.84	1.52	5.6	269	4.0	6.9	1.7	0.8	32%	76%	55
Yan,Johan	R	11	23	aa	TEX	0	0	19	2	27	20	1	0	9	15	0.40	1.11	5.7	208	3.1	5.0	1.6	0.0	25%	96%	78

This section of the book may be the smallest as far as word count is concerned, but may be the most important, as this is where players' skills and potential are tied together and ranked against their peers. The rankings that follow are divided into long-term potential in the major leagues and shorter-term fantasy value.

TOP 100: Lists the top 100 minor league prospects in terms of long-range potential in the major leagues. First an overall MLBA Top 100, then both authors provide their own lists.

ORGANIZATIONAL: Lists the top 15 minor league prospects within each organization in terms of long-range potential in the major leagues.

POSITIONAL: Lists the top 15 prospects, by position, in terms of long-range potential in the major leagues.

TOP POWER: Lists the top 25 prospects that have the potential to hit for power in the major leagues, combining raw power, plate discipline, and at the ability to make their power game-usable.

TOP BA: Lists the top 25 prospects that have the potential to hit for high batting average in the major leagues, combining contact ability, plate discipline, hitting mechanics and strength.

TOP SPEED: Lists the top 25 prospects that have the potential to steal bases in the major leagues, combining raw speed and base-running instincts.

TOP FASTBALL: Lists the top 25 pitchers that have the best fastball, combining velocity and pitch movement.

TOP BREAKING BALL: Lists the top 25 pitchers that have the best breaking ball, combining pitch movement, strikeout potential, and consistency.

2012 TOP FANTASY PROSPECTS: Lists the top 100 minor league prospects that will have the most value to their respective fantasy teams in 2012.

TOP 100 ARCHIVE: Takes a look back at the top 100 lists from the past eight years.

The rankings in this book are the creation of the minor league department at BaseballHQ.com. While several baseball personnel contributed player information to the book, no opinions were solicited or received in comparing players.

TOP 100 PROSPECTS OF 2012

1	Bryce Harper	OF	WAS
2	Matt Moore	LHP	TAM
3	Mike Trout	OF	LAA
4	Julio Teheran	RHP	ATL
5	Jesus Montero	C	NYY
6	Jurickson Profar	SS	TEX
7	Manny Machado	SS	BAL
8	Gerrit Cole	RHP	PIT
9	Devin Mesoraco	C	CIN
10	Wil Myers	OF	KC
11	Miguel Sano	3B	MIN
12	Jacob Turner	RHP	DET
13	Anthony Rendon	3B	WAS
14	Trevor Bauer	RHP	ARI
15	Nolan Arenado	3B	COL
16	Jameson Taillon	RHP	PIT
17	Shelby Miller	RHP	STL
18	Dylan Bundy	RHP	BAL
19	Brett Jackson	OF	CHC
20	Drew Pomeranz	LHP	COL
21	Martin Perez	LHP	TEX
22	Yonder Alonso	1B	SD
23	Taijuan Walker	RHP	SEA
24	Danny Hultzen	LHP	SEA
25	Gary Brown	OF	SF
26	Anthony Rizzo	1B	CHC
27	Bubba Starling	OF	KC
28	Travis d'Arnaud	C	TOR
29	Mike Montgomery	LHP	KC
30	Jake Odorizzi	RHP	KC
31	Hak-Ju Lee	SS	TAM
32	Jonathan Singleton	1B	HOU
33	Garrett Richards	RHP	LAA
34	Manny Banuelos	LHP	NYY
35	James Paxton	LHP	SEA
36	Jarrod Parker	RHP	OAK
37	Carlos Martinez	RHP	STL
38	Jake Marisnick	OF	TOR
39	Yasmani Grandal	C	SD
40	Trevor May	RHP	PHI
41	Gary Sanchez	C	NYY
42	Mike Olt	3B	TEX
43	Wilin Rosario	C	COL
44	John Lamb	LHP	KC
45	Francisco Lindor	SS	CLE
46	Dellin Betances	RHP	NYY
47	Michael Choice	OF	OAK
48	Arodys Vizcaino	RHP	ATL
49	Trayvon Robinson	OF	SEA
50	Matt Harvey	RHP	NYM

51	Will Middlebrooks	3B	BOS
52	Jedd Gyorko	3B	SD
53	Randall Delgado	RHP	ATL
54	Zack Wheeler	RHP	NYM
55	Zach Lee	RHP	LA
56	Tyler Skaggs	LHP	ARI
57	Nick Castellanos	3B	DET
58	Robbie Erlin	LHP	SD
59	Christian Yelich	OF	MIA
60	Anthony Gose	OF	TOR
61	Addison Reed	RHP	CHW
62	Javier Baez	SS	CHC
63	Starling Marte	OF	PIT
64	Kaleb Cowart	3B	LAA
65	George Springer	OF	HOU
66	Jarred Cosart	RHP	HOU
67	Jean Segura	2B	LAA
68	Kolten Wong	2B	STL
69	Nick Franklin	SS	SEA
70	Alex Torres	RHP	TAM
71	Rymer Liriano	OF	SD
72	Josh Bell	OF	PIT
73	Leonys Martin	OF	TEX
74	Joe Wieland	RHP	SD
75	Joe Benson	OF	MIN
76	Wily Peralta	RHP	MIL
77	Tim Wheeler	OF	COL
78	Oscar Taveras	OF	STL
79	Xander Bogaerts	SS	BOS
80	Archie Bradley	RHP	ARI
81	Kyle Gibson	RHP	MIN
82	Allen Webster	RHP	LA
83	C.J. Cron	1B	LAA
84	Grant Green	OF	OAK
85	Brad Peacock	RHP	OAK
86	Chris Dwyer	LHP	KC
87	Billy Hamilton	SS	CIN
88	A.J. Cole	RHP	OAK
89	Aaron Hicks	OF	MIN
90	Noah Syndergaard	RHP	TOR
91	Tyrell Jenkins	RHP	STL
92	Anthony Ranaudo	RHP	BOS
93	Jed Bradley	LHP	MIL
94	Nathan Eovaldi	RHP	LA
95	Andrelton Simmons	SS	ATL
96	Taylor Guerrieri	RHP	TAM
97	Cheslor Cuthbert	3B	KC
98	Edward Salcedo	3B	ATL
99	Domingo Santana	OF	HOU
100	Jesse Biddle	LHP	PHI

ROB GORDON'S TOP 100

#	Player	Pos	Team	#	Player	Pos	Team
1	Bryce Harper	OF	WAS	51	Jedd Gyorko	3B	SD
2	Matt Moore	LHP	TAM	52	Zach Lee	RHP	LA
3	Mike Trout	OF	LAA	53	Dellin Betances	RHP	NYY
4	Shelby Miller	RHP	STL	54	Anthony Gose	OF	TOR
5	Julio Teheran	RHP	ATL	55	Jake Marisnick	OF	TOR
6	Jurickson Profar	SS	TEX	56	Zack Wheeler	RHP	NYM
7	Jesus Montero	C	NYY	57	Michael Choice	OF	OAK
8	Devin Mesoraco	C	CIN	58	John Lamb	LHP	KC
9	Manny Machado	SS	BAL	59	Wily Peralta	RHP	MIL
10	Trevor Bauer	RHP	ARI	60	Jean Segura	2B	LAA
11	Jameson Taillon	RHP	PIT	61	Alex Colome	RHP	TAM
12	Anthony Rendon	3B	WAS	62	Xander Bogaerts	SS	BOS
13	Wil Myers	OF	KC	63	Archie Bradley	RHP	ARI
14	Gerrit Cole	RHP	PIT	64	Brad Peacock	RHP	OAK
15	Travis d'Arnaud	C	TOR	65	Oscar Taveras	OF	STL
16	Miguel Sano	3B	MIN	66	Trayvon Robinson	OF	SEA
17	Martin Perez	LHP	TEX	67	Billy Hamilton	SS	CIN
18	Drew Pomeranz	LHP	COL	68	A.J. Cole	RHP	OAK
19	Jacob Turner	RHP	DET	69	Alex Torres	RHP	TAM
20	Yonder Alonso	1B	SD	70	Kaleb Cowart	3B	LAA
21	Anthony Rizzo	1B	CHC	71	Addison Reed	RHP	CHW
22	Nolan Arenado	3B	COL	72	Francisco Lindor	SS	CLE
23	Robbie Erlin	LHP	SD	73	Nick Franklin	SS	SEA
24	Gary Brown	OF	SF	74	Tyrell Jenkins	RHP	STL
25	Wilin Rosario	C	COL	75	Jed Bradley	LHP	MIL
26	Brett Jackson	OF	CHC	76	Nathan Eovaldi	RHP	LA
27	Jonathan Singleton	1B	HOU	77	Allen Webster	RHP	LA
28	Hak-Ju Lee	SS	TAM	78	Will Middlebrooks	3B	BOS
29	Carlos Martinez	RHP	STL	79	Cheslor Cuthbert	3B	KC
30	Dylan Bundy	RHP	BAL	80	Christian Yelich	OF	MIA
31	Danny Hultzen	LHP	SEA	81	Kolten Wong	2B	STL
32	Taijuan Walker	RHP	SEA	82	Starling Marte	OF	PIT
33	Trevor May	RHP	PHI	83	Aaron Hicks	OF	MIN
34	Jake Odorizzi	RHP	KC	84	George Springer	OF	HOU
35	Tyler Skaggs	LHP	ARI	85	Grant Green	OF	OAK
36	Yasmani Grandal	C	SD	86	Drew Hutchison	RHP	TOR
37	Jarrod Parker	RHP	OAK	87	Tyler Thornburg	RHP	MIL
38	Matt Harvey	RHP	NYM	88	James Darnell	3B	SD
39	James Paxton	LHP	SEA	89	Josh Bell	OF	PIT
40	Garrett Richards	RHP	LAA	90	Taylor Jungmann	RHP	MIL
41	Arodys Vizcaino	RHP	ATL	91	C.J. Cron	1B	LAA
42	Mike Olt	3B	TEX	92	Joe Benson	OF	MIN
43	Bubba Starling	OF	KC	93	Chad James	LHP	MIA
44	Mike Montgomery	LHP	KC	94	Alex Meyer	RHP	WAS
45	Gary Sanchez	C	NYY	95	Anthony Ranaudo	RHP	BOS
46	Randall Delgado	RHP	ATL	96	Ryan Lavarnway	C	BOS
47	Leonys Martin	OF	TEX	97	Chad Bettis	RHP	COL
48	Nick Castellanos	3B	DET	98	Rymer Liriano	OF	SD
49	Manny Banuelos	LHP	NYY	99	Marcell Ozuna	OF	MIA
50	Joe Wieland	RHP	SD	100	Tim Wheeler	OF	COL

JEREMY DELONEY'S TOP 100

#	Player	Pos	Team	#	Player	Pos	Team
1	Bryce Harper	OF	WAS	51	Mike Olt	3B	TEX
2	Matt Moore	LHP	TAM	52	Yasmani Grandal	C	SD
3	Mike Trout	OF	LAA	53	Josh Bell	OF	PIT
4	Jesus Montero	C	NYY	54	Carlos Martinez	RHP	STL
5	Julio Teheran	RHP	ATL	55	Trevor May	RHP	PHI
6	Jurickson Profar	SS	TEX	56	Zack Wheeler	RHP	NYM
7	Manny Machado	SS	BAL	57	Kolten Wong	2B	STL
8	Dylan Bundy	RHP	BAL	58	Jedd Gyorko	3B	SD
9	Gerrit Cole	RHP	PIT	59	Addison Reed	RHP	CHW
10	Jacob Turner	RHP	DET	60	Tim Wheeler	OF	COL
11	Miguel Sano	3B	MIN	61	Arodys Vizcaino	RHP	ATL
12	Brett Jackson	OF	CHC	62	Kaleb Cowart	3B	LAA
13	Wil Myers	OF	KC	63	Kyle Gibson	RHP	MIN
14	Nolan Arenado	3B	COL	64	Chris Dwyer	LHP	KC
15	Devin Mesoraco	C	CIN	65	Randall Delgado	RHP	ATL
16	Taijuan Walker	RHP	SEA	66	Zach Lee	RHP	LA
17	Anthony Rendon	3B	WAS	67	Nick Franklin	SS	SEA
18	Danny Hultzen	LHP	SEA	68	Joe Benson	OF	MIN
19	Bubba Starling	OF	KC	69	Wilin Rosario	C	COL
20	Mike Montgomery	LHP	KC	70	Matt Harvey	RHP	NYM
21	Drew Pomeranz	LHP	COL	71	Noah Syndergaard	RHP	TOR
22	Trevor Bauer	RHP	ARI	72	Nick Castellanos	3B	DET
23	Martin Perez	LHP	TEX	73	Alex Torres	RHP	TAM
24	Francisco Lindor	SS	CLE	74	C.J. Cron	1B	LAA
25	Jameson Taillon	RHP	PIT	75	Anthony Gose	OF	TOR
26	Gary Brown	OF	SF	76	Andrelton Simmons	SS	ATL
27	Yonder Alonso	1B	SD	77	Jean Segura	2B	LAA
28	Manny Banuelos	LHP	NYY	78	Taylor Guerrieri	RHP	TAM
29	Jake Marisnick	OF	TOR	79	Edward Salcedo	3B	ATL
30	Javier Baez	SS	CHC	80	Grant Green	OF	OAK
31	Will Middlebrooks	3B	BOS	81	Anthony Ranaudo	RHP	BOS
32	Jake Odorizzi	RHP	KC	82	Domingo Santana	OF	HOU
33	Shelby Miller	RHP	STL	83	Jesse Biddle	LHP	PHI
34	Anthony Rizzo	1B	CHC	84	Tyler Skaggs	LHP	ARI
35	Jarred Cosart	RHP	HOU	85	Jonathan Schoop	SS	BAL
36	Garrett Richards	RHP	LAA	86	Aaron Hicks	OF	MIN
37	John Lamb	LHP	KC	87	Allen Webster	RHP	LA
38	James Paxton	LHP	SEA	88	Brandon Nimmo	OF	NYM
39	Hak-Ju Lee	SS	TAM	89	Joe Panik	SS	SF
40	Jonathan Singleton	1B	HOU	90	Deck McGuire	RHP	TOR
41	Trayvon Robinson	OF	SEA	91	Josh Vitters	3B	CHC
42	Michael Choice	OF	OAK	92	Jeurys Familia	RHP	NYM
43	Dellin Betances	RHP	NYY	93	Andy Oliver	LHP	DET
44	Rymer Liriano	OF	SD	94	Bryce Brentz	OF	BOS
45	Christian Yelich	OF	MIA	95	Oscar Taveras	OF	STL
46	Jarrod Parker	RHP	OAK	96	Sebastian Valle	C	PHI
47	Gary Sanchez	C	NYY	97	Sonny Gray	RHP	OAK
48	Travis d'Arnaud	C	TOR	98	Tyler Pastronicky	SS	ATL
49	George Springer	OF	HOU	99	Xander Bogaerts	SS	BOS
50	Starling Marte	OF	PIT	100	Kyle Parker	OF	COL

TOP PROSPECTS BY ORGANIZATION

AL EAST

BALTIMORE ORIOLES
1. Manny Machado, SS
2. Dylan Bundy, RHP
3. Jonathan Schoop, SS
4. Parker Bridwell, RHP
5. Nick Delmonico, 3B
6. Bobby Bundy, RHP
7. Dan Klein, RHP
8. Roderick Bernadina, OF
9. Xavier Avery, OF
10. Mike Wright, RHP
11. Jason Esposito, 3B
12. L.J. Hoes, 2B
13. Eduardo Rodriguez, LHP
14. Joseph Mahoney, 1B
15. Wynn Pelzer, RHP

BOSTON RED SOX
1. Will Middlebrooks, 3B
2. Anthony Ranaudo, RHP
3. Bryce Brentz, OF
4. Xander Bogaerts, SS
5. Jose Iglesias, SS
6. Matt Barnes, RHP
7. Garin Cecchini, 3B
8. Brandon Jacobs, OF
9. Sean Coyle, 2B
10. Lars Anderson, 1B
11. Alex Wilson, RHP
12. Noe Ramirez, RHP
13. Williams Jerez, OF
14. Ryan Lavarnway, C
15. Felix Doubront, LHP

NEW YORK YANKEES
1. Jesus Montero, C
2. Manny Banuelos, LHP
3. Dellin Betances, RHP
4. Gary Sanchez, C
5. Ravel Santana, OF
6. Mason Williams, OF
7. Dante Bichette, 3B
8. Angelo Gumbs, 2B
9. Cito Culver, SS
10. Adam Warren, RHP
11. Ramon Flores, OF
12. Austin Romine, C
13. Claudio Custodio, SS
14. Brett Marshall, RHP
15. Slade Heathcott, OF

TAMPA BAY RAYS
1. Matt Moore, LHP
2. Hak-Ju Lee, SS
3. Alex Torres, LHP
4. Taylor Guerrieri, RHP
5. Enny Romero, LHP
6. Mikie Mahtook, OF
7. Alexander Colome, RHP
8. Drew Vettleson, OF
9. Chris Archer, RHP
10. Brandon Guyer, OF
11. Josh Sale, OF
12. Nick Barnese, RHP
13. Parker Markel, RHP
14. Granden Goetzman, OF
15. Tyler Goeddel, 3B

TORONTO BLUE JAYS
1. Jake Marisnick, OF
2. Travis d'Arnaud, C
3. Noah Syndergaard, RHP
4. Anthony Gose, OF
5. Deck McGuire, RHP
6. Daniel Norris, LHP
7. Justin Nicolino, LHP
8. Drew Hutchison, RHP
9. Adonys Cardona, RHP
10. David Cooper, 1B
11. Aaron Sanchez, RHP
12. Joe Musgrove, RHP
13. Adeiny Hechavarria, SS
14. Chris Hawkins, OF
15. A.J. Jimenez, C

AL CENTRAL

CHICAGO WHITE SOX
1. Addison Reed, RHP
2. Jacob Petricka, RHP
3. Eduardo Escobar, SS
4. Trayce Thompson, OF
5. Jhan Marinez, RHP
6. Gregori Infante, RHP
7. Erik Johnson, RHP
8. Simon Castro, RHP
9. Brandon Short, OF
10. Keenyn Walker, OF
11. Jeff Soptic, RHP
12. Nestor Molina, RHP
13. Tyler Flowers, C
14. Kevan Smith, C
15. Jared Mitchell, OF

CLEVELAND INDIANS
1. Francisco Lindor, SS
2. Dillon Howard, RHP
3. Felix Sterling, RHP
4. Nick Hagadone, LHP
5. Luigi Rodriguez, OF
6. Chen Lee, RHP
7. Jake Sisco, RHP
8. Tony Wolters, SS
9. Jason Knapp, RHP
10. Jorge Martinez, SS
11. LeVon Washington, OF
12. Nick Weglarz, OF
13. Elvis Araujo, LHP
14. Chun Chen, C
15. Kelvin De La Cruz, LHP

DETROIT TIGERS
1. Jacob Turner, RHP
2. Nick Castellanos, 3B
3. Andy Oliver, LHP
4. Casey Crosby, LHP
5. Drew Smyly, LHP
6. Brenny Paulino, RHP
7. Avisail Garcia, OF
8. Bruce Rondon, RHP
9. Aaron Westlake, 1B
10. Danry Vasquez, OF
11. Ryan Strieby, 1B
12. Jose Ortega, RHP
13. Daniel Fields, OF
14. Matt Hoffman, LHP
15. James McCann, C

KANSAS CITY ROYALS
1. Wil Myers, OF
2. Bubba Starling, OF
3. Mike Montgomery, LHP
4. Jake Odorizzi, RHP
5. John Lamb, LHP
6. Chris Dwyer, LHP
7. Cheslor Cuthbert, 3B
8. Christian Colon, 2B/SS
9. Kelvin Herrera, RHP
10. Yordano Ventura, RHP
11. Jorge Bonifacio, OF
12. Brett Eibner, OF
13. Jason Adam, RHP
14. Elier Hernandez, OF
15. Noel Arguelles, LHP

MINNESOTA TWINS
1. Miguel Sano, 3B
2. Kyle Gibson, RHP
3. Joe Benson, OF
4. Aaron Hicks, OF
5. Eddie Rosario, 2B
6. Alex Wimmers, RHP
7. Oswaldo Arcia, OF
8. Levi Michael, SS
9. Adrian Salcedo, RHP
10. Brian Dozier, 2B
11. Chris Parmelee, 1B/RF
12. Madison Boer, RHP
13. Liam Hendriks, RHP
14. Carlos Gutierrez, RHP
15. Max Kepler, OF

AL WEST

LOS ANGELES ANGELS
1. Mike Trout, OF
2. Garrett Richards, RHP
3. Kaleb Cowart, 3B
4. C.J. Cron, 1B
5. Jean Segura, 2B/SS
6. Taylor Lindsey, 2B
7. Fabio Martinez, RHP
8. Chevez Clarke, OF
9. John Hellweg, RHP
10. Randal Grichuk, OF
11. Nick Maronde, LHP
12. Cam Bedrosian, RHP
13. Daniel Tillman, RHP
14. Luis Jimenez, 3B
15. Trevor Reckling, LHP

OAKLAND ATHLETICS
1. Michael Choice, OF
2. Jarrod Parker, RHP
3. Grant Green, OF
4. Sonny Gray, RHP
5. Brad Peacock, RHP
6. Derek Norris, C
7. Michael Taylor, OF
8. A.J. Cole, RHP
9. Vicmal de la Cruz, OF
10. Yordy Cabrera, SS
11. Renato Nunez, 3B
12. Chris Carter, 1B
13. Ian Krol, LHP
14. Stephen Parker, 3B
15. Aaron Shipman, OF

SEATTLE MARINERS
1. Taijuan Walker, RHP
2. Danny Hultzen, LHP
3. James Paxton, LHP
4. Trayvon Robinson, OF
5. Nick Franklin, SS
6. Vicente Campos, RHP
7. Guillermo Pimentel, OF
8. Phillips Castillo, OF
9. Alex Liddi, 3B
10. Chance Ruffin, RHP
11. Martin Peguero, SS
12. Francisco Martinez, 3B
13. Vince Catricala, 3B
14. Jabari Blash, OF
15. Mauricio Robles, LHP

TEXAS RANGERS
1. Jurickson Profar, SS
2. Martin Perez, LHP
3. Mike Olt, 3B
4. Robbie Ross, LHP
5. Tanner Scheppers, RHP
6. David Perez, RHP
7. Jorge Alfaro, C
8. Barret Loux, RHP
9. Luis Sardinas, SS
10. Leonys Martin, OF
11. Cody Buckel, RHP
12. Roman Mendez, RHP
13. Kevin Matthews, LHP
14. Zach Cone, OF
15. Neil Ramirez, RHP

TOP PROSPECTS BY ORGANIZATION

NL EAST

ATLANTA BRAVES
1. Julio Teheran, RHP
2. Randall Delgado, RHP
3. Arodys Vizcaino, RHP
4. Andrelton Simmons, SS
5. Christian Bethancourt, C
6. Brandon Drury, 3B
7. Sean Gilmartin, LHP
8. Tyler Pastornicky, SS
9. J.R. Graham, RHP
10. J.J. Hoover, RHP
11. Joe Terdoslavich, 1B
12. Edward Salcedo, SS
13. Zeke Spruill, RHP
14. Tommy LaStella, 2B
15. Matt Lipka, SS

MIAMI MARLINS
1. Christian Yelich, 1B
2. Chad James, LHLP
3. Jose Fernandez, RHP
4. Marcell Ozuna, OF
5. J.T. Realmuto, C
6. Matt Dominguez, 3B
7. Rob Rasmussen, LHP
8. Isaac Galloway, 0F
9. Noah Perio, 2B
10. Elih Villanueva, RHP
11. Adam Conley, LHP
12. Tom Koehler, RHP
13. Kyle Jensen, OF
14. Mason Hope, RHP
15. Jesus Solorzano, OF

NEW YORK METS
1. Matt Harvey, RHP
2. Zack Wheeler, RHP
3. Jeurys Familia, RHP
4. Michael Fulmer, RHP
5. Brandon Nimmo, OF
6. Cesar Puello, OF
7. Wilmer Flores, SS
8. Jordany Valdespin, SS
9. Matt Den Dekker, OF
10. Kirk Nieuwenhuis, OF
11. Reese Havens, SS
12. Aderlin Rodriguez, 3B
13. Jefry Marte, 3B
14. Cory Vaughn, OF
15. Danny Muno, 2B

PHILADELPHIA PHILLIES
1. Trevor May, RHP
2. Jesse Biddle, LHP
3. Phillippe Aumont, RHP
4. Sebastian Valle, C
5. Brody Colvin, RHP
6. John Pettibone, RHP
7. Freddy Galvis, SS
8. Tyler Cloyd, RHP
9. Maikel Franco, 3B
10. Jiwan James, OF
11. Cameron Rupp, C
12. Larry Greene, OF
13. Tyson Gillies, OF
14. Justin De Fratus, RHP
15. Julio Rodriguez, RHP

WASHINGTON NATIONALS
1. Bryce Harper, OF
2. Anthony Rendon, 3B
3. Alex Meyer. RHP
4. Brian Goodwin, OF
5. Matt Purke, LHP
6. Sammy Solis, LHP
7. Chris Marrero, 1B
8. Destin Hood, RHP
9. Robbie Ray, LHP
10. Tyler Moore, RHP
11. Steve Lombardozzi, 2B
12. Jeff Kobernus, 2B
13. Matt Skole, 3B
14. Eury Perez, OF
15. Cole Kimball, RHP

NL CENTRAL

CHICAGO CUBS
1. Anthony Rizzo, 1B
2. Brett Jackson, OF
3. Javier Baez, SS
4. Matt Szczur, OF
5. Dillon Maples, RHP
6. Trey McNutt, RHP
7. Josh Vitters, 3B
8. Junior Lake, SS
9. Marco Hernandez, 2B
10. Gioskar Amaya, 3B
11. Rafael Dolis, RHP
12. Ronald Torreyes, 2B
13. Dave Sappelt, OF
14. Jeimer Candelario, 3B
15. Welington Castillo, C

CINCINNATI REDS
1. Devin Mesoraco, C
2. Billy Hamilton, SS
3. Daniel Corcino, RHP
4. Robert Stephenson, RHP
5. Zack Cozart, SS
6. Didi Gregorius, SS
7. Neftali Soto, 1B
8. Todd Frazier, 3B/OF
9. Tony Cingrani, LHP
10. Yorman Rodriguez, OF
11. Ryan LaMarre, OF
12. Chris Valaika, 2B
13. Donnie Joseph, LHP
14. Ryan Wright, 2B
15. Amir Garrett, LHP

HOUSTON ASTROS
1. Jonathan Singleton, 1B
2. George Springer, OF
3. Jarred Cosart, RHP
4. Kyle Weiland, RHP
5. Domingo Santana, OF
6. Jonathan Villar, SS
7. Paul Clemens, RHP
8. Brett Oberholtzer, LHP
9. Delino DeShields, 2B
10. Mike Foltynewicz, RHP
11. Mike Kvasnicka, 3B
12. Telvin Nash, OF
13. Adrian Houser, RHP
14. Ariel Ovando, OF
15. Jay Austin, OF

MILWAUKEE BREWERS
1. Wily Peralta, RHP
2. Taylor Jungmann, RHP
3. Jed Bradley, LHP
4. Tyler Thornburg, RHP
5. Jimmy Nelson, RHP
6. Taylor Green, 3B
7. Logan Schafer, OF
8. Cody Scarpetta, RHP
9. Scooter Gennett, 2B
10. Kentrail Davis. OF
11. Caleb Gindl, OF
12. Jorge Lopez, RHP
13. Michael Fiers, RHP
14. Orlando Arcia, SS
15. Nick Bucci, RHP

PITTSBURGH PIRATES
1. Jameson Taillon, RHP
2. Gerrit Cole, RHP
3. Starling Marte, OF
4. Josh Bell, OF
5. Kyle McPherson, RHP
6. Luis Heredia, RHP
7. Robbie Grossman, OF
8. Stetson Allie, RHP
9. Jeff Locke, LHP
10. Alex Dickerson, OF
11. Colton Cain, RHP
12. Tony Sanchez, C
13. Nick Kingham, RHP
14. Matt Curry, 1B
15. Bryan Morris, RHP

ST. LOUIS CARDINALS
1. Shelby Miller, RHP
2. Carlos Martinez, RHP
3. Oscar Taveras, OF
4. Tyrell Jenkins, RHP
5. Kolten Wong, 2B
6. Zack Cox, 3B
7. Eduardo Sanchez, RHP
8. Lance Lynn, RHP
9. Matt Adams, 1B
10. Jordan Swagerty, RHP
11. Trevor Rosenthal, RHP
12. Ryan Jackson, SS
13. Tommy Pham, OF
14. Matt Carpenter, 3B
15. Seth Blair, RHP

NL WEST

ARIZONA DIAMONDBACKS
1, Trevor Bauer, RHP
2. Tyler Skaggs, LHP
3. Archie Bradley, RHP
4. A.J. Pollock, OF
5. Pat Corbin, LHP
6. Matt Davidson, 3B
7. Adam Eaton, OF
8. Chris Owings, SS
9. Ryan Wheeler, 3B
10. Andrew Chafin, LHP
11. David Holmberg, LHP
12. Bobby Borchering, 3B
13. Marc Krauss, OF
14. Charles Brewer, RHP
15. Wade Miley, LHP

COLORADO ROCKIES
1. Nolan Arenado, 3B
2. Drew Pomeranz, LHP
3. Wilin Rosario, C
4. Chad Bettis, RHP
5. Tim Wheeler, OF
6. Kyle Parker, OF
7. Charles Blackmon OF
8. Edwar Cabrera, LHP
9. Tyler Matzek, LHP
10. Josh Rutledge, SS
11. Trevor Story, SS
12. Tyler Anderson, LHP
13. Rosell Herrera, SS
14. Joe Gardner, RHP
15. Rafael Ortega, OF

LOS ANGELES DODGERS
1. Zach Lee, RHP
2. Allen Webster, RHP
3. Nathan Eovaldi, RHP
4. Chris Withrow, RHP
5. Joc Pederson, OF
6. Shawn Tolleson, RHP
7. Aaron Miller, LHP
8. Angel Sanchez, RHP
9. Garrett Gould, RHP
10. Alfredo Silverio, OF
11. Ethan Martin, RHP
12. Chris Reed, LHP
13. Ralston Cash, RHP
14. Tim Federowicz, C
15. Scott Van Slyke, 1B

SAN DIEGO PADRES
1. Robbie Erlin, LHP
2. Yonder Alonso, 1B
3. Jedd Gyorko, 3B
4. Yasmani Grandal, C
5. Keyvius Sampson, RHP
6. Rymer Liriano, OF
7. Casey Kelly, RHP
8. James Darnell, OF
9. Joe Wieland, RHP
10. Brad Boxberger, RHP
11. Cory Spangenberg, 2B
12. Reymond Fuentes, OF
13. Austin Hedges, C
14. Jaff Decker, OF
15. Yoan Alcantara, RHP

SAN FRANCISCO GIANTS
1. Gary Brown, OF
2. Francisco Peguero, OF
3. Joe Panik, 2B
4. Andrew Susac, C
5. Heath Hembree, RHP
6. Ehire Adrianza, SS
7. Eric Surkamp, LHP
8. Kyle Crick, RHP
9. Tommy Joseph, C
10. Charlie Culberson, 2B
11. Hector Sanchez, C
12. Jesus Galindo, OF
13. Clayton Blackburn, RHP
14. Jarrett Parker, OF
15. Joan Gregorio, RHP

TOP PROSPECTS BY POSITION

CATCHER
1. Jesus Montero, NYY
2. Devin Mesoraco, CIN
3. Travis d'Arnaud, TOR
4. Wilin Rosario, COL
5. Yasmani Grandal, SD
6. Gary Sanchez, NYY
7. Christian Bethancourt, ATL
8. Ryan Lavarnway, BOS
9. Andrew Susac, SF
10. Carlos Perez, TOR
11. Derek Norris, OAK
12. Sebastian Valle, PHI
13. Tony Sanchez, PIT
14. Tyler Flowers, CHW
15. Tommy Joseph, SF

FIRST BASE
1. Yonder Alonso, SD
2. Anthony Rizzo, CHC
3. Jonathan Singleton, HOU
4. C.J. Cron, LAA
5. Lars Anderson, BOS
6. Chris Carter, OAK
7. David Cooper, TOR
8. Chris Parmelee, MIN
9. Matt Adams, STL
10. Matt Davidson, ARI
11. Tyler Moore, WAS
12. Chris Marrero, WAS
13. Aaron Westlake, DET
14. Dan Vogelbach, CHC
15. Matt Curry, PIT

SECOND BASE
1. Jean Segura, LAA
2. Kolten Wong, STL
3. Cory Spangenberg, SD
4. Taylor Lindsey, LAA
5. Eddie Rosario, MIN
6. Joe Panik, SF
7. Jonathan Schoop, BAL
8. Ryan Adams, BAL
9. Ivan DeJesus, LA
10. Sean Coyle, BOS
11. Tommy LaStella, ATL
12. Scooter Gennett, MIL
13. Steve Lombardozzi, WAS
14. Claudio Custodio, NYY
15. Ronald Torreyes, CHC

THIRD BASE
1. Miguel Sano, MIN
2. Nolan Arenado, COL
3. Anthony Rendon, WAS
4. Will Middlebrooks, BOS
5. Michael Olt, TEX
6. Jedd Gyorko, SD
7. Kaleb Cowart, LAA
8. Nick Castellanos, DET
9. Edward Salcedo, ATL
10. Josh Vitters, CHC
11. Cheslor Cuthbert, KC
12. Matt Dominguez, MIA
13. Todd Frazier, CIN
14. Garin Cecchini, BOS
15. Zack Cox, STL

SHORTSTOP
1. Jurickson Profar, TEX
2. Manny Machado, BAL
3. Hak-Ju Lee, TAM
4. Xander Bogaerts, BOS
5. Billy Hamilton, CIN
6. Francisco Lindor, CLE
7. Nick Franklin, SEA
8. Javier Baez, CHC
9. Christian Colon, KC
10. Jose Iglesias, BOS
11. Wilmer Flores, NYM
12. Zack Cozart, CIN
13. Trevor Story, COL
14. Andrelton Simmons, ATL
15. Tyler Pastornicky, ATL

OUTFIELD
1. Bryce Harper, WAS
2. Mike Trout, LAA
3. Brett Jackson, CHC
4. Wil Myers, KC
5. Bubba Starling, KC
6. Gary Brown, SF
7. Jake Marisnick, TOR
8. Trayvon Robinson, SEA
9. Michael Choice, OAK
10. Rymer Liriano, SD
11. Christian Yelich, MIA
12. George Springer, HOU
13. Starling Marte, PIT
14. Josh Bell, PIT
15. Tim Wheeler, COL
16. Joe Benson, MIN
17. Anthony Gose, TOR
18. Grant Green, OAK
19. Domingo Santana, HOU
20. Aaron Hicks, MIN
21. Brandon Nimmo, NYM
22. Bryce Brentz, BOS
23. Oscar Taveras, STL
24. Kyle Parker, COL
25. Ravel Santana, NYY
26. Francisco Peguero, SF
27. Oswaldo Arcia, MIN
28. Cesar Puello, NYM
29. Guillermo Pimentel, SEA
30. Mikie Mahtook, TAM
31. Mason Williams, NYY
32. Jiwan James, PHI
33. Drew Vettleson, TAM
34. Brandon Guyer, TAM
35. Brandon Jacobs, BOS
36. Robbie Grossman, PIT
37. Marcell Ozuna, MIA
38. Jorge Bonifacio, KC
39. Leonys Martin, TEX
40. Alfredo Silverio, LA
41. Matt Szczur, CHC
42. A.J. Pollock, ARI
43. Luigi Rodriguez, CLE
44. Avisail Garcia, DET
45. Trayce Thompson, CHW

STARTING PITCHER
1. Matt Moore, LHP, TAM
2. Shelby Miller, RHP, STL
3. Julio Teheran, RHP, ATL
4. Trevor Bauer, RHP, ARI
5. Jameson Taillon, RHP, PIT
6. Gerrit Cole, RHP, PIT
7. Martin Perez, LHP, TEX
8. Drew Pomeranz, LHP, COL
9. Robbie Erlin, LHP, SD
10. Jacob Turner, RHP, DET
11. Carlos Martinez, RHP, STL
12. Dylan Bundy, RHP, BAL
13. Danny Hultzen, LHP, SEA
14. Taijuan Walker, RHP, SEA
15. Trevor May, RHP, PHI

16. Jake Odorizzi, RHP, KC
17. Tyler Skaggs, LHP, ARI
18. Jarrod Parker, RHP, OAK
19. Matt Harvey, RHP, NYM
20. James Paxton, LHP, SEA
21. Garrett Richards, RHP, LAA
22. Arodys Vizcaino, RHP, ATL
23. Mike Montgomery, LHP, KC
24. Randall Delgado, RHP, ATL
25. Manny Banuelos, LHP, NYY
26. Joe Wieland, RHP, SD
27. Zach Lee, RHP, LA
28. Dellin Betances, RHP, NYY
29. Zack Wheeler, RHP, NYM
30. John Lamb, LHP, KC

31. Wily Peralta, RHP, MIL
32. Alexander Colome, RHP, TAM
33. Archie Bradley, RHP, ARI
34. A.J. Cole, RHP, OAK
35. Brad Peacock, RHP, OAK
36. Alex Torres, LHP, TAM
37. Tyrell Jenkins, RHP, STL
38. Jed Bradley, LHP, MIL
39. Nathan Eovaldi, RHP, LA
40. Allen Webster, RHP, LA
41. Drew Hutchison, RHP, TOR
42. Tyler Thornburg, RHP, MIL
43. Taylor Jungmann, RHP, MIL
44. Chad James, LHP, MIA
45. Alex Meyer, RHP, WAS

46. Anthony Ranaudo, RHP, BOS
47. Chad Bettis, RHP, COL
48. Kyle Gibson, RHP, MIN
49. Andrew Oliver, LHP, DET
50. Sonny Gray, RHP, OAK
51. Matt Barnes, RHP, BOS
52. Deck McGuire, RHP, TOR
53. Jeurys Familia, RHP, NYM
54. Jason Knapp, RHP, CLE
55. Chris Dwyer, LHP, KC
56. Jarred Cosart, RHP, HOU
57. Casey Crosby, LHP, DET
58. Fabio Martinez, RHP, LAA
59. Chris Withrow, RHP, LA
60. Vicente Campos, RHP, SEA

61. Jose Fernandez, RHP, MIA
62. Daniel Corcino, RHP, CIN
63. Michael Fulmer, RHP, NYM
64. Taylor Guerrieri, RHP, TAM
65. Brenny Paulino, RHP, DET
66. Kyle Weiland, RHP, HOU
67. Daniel Norris, LHP, TOR
68. Jake Sisco, RHP, CLE
69. Noah Syndergaard, RHP, TOR
70. Robert Stephenson, RHP, CIN
71. Trevor Rosenthal, RHP, STL
72. Adonys Cardona, RHP, TOR
73. Rob Rasmussen, LHP, MIA
74. Justin Nicolino, LHP, TOR
75. Dillon Howard, RHP, CLE

RELIEF PITCHER
1. Addison Reed, RHP, CHW
2. Eduardo Sanchez, RHP, STL
3. Tanner Scheppers, RHP, TEX
4. Nick Hagadone, LHP, CLE
5. Phillippe Aumont, RHP, PHI
6. Brad Boxberger, RHP, SD
7. Chance Ruffin, RHP, SEA
8. Kelvin Herrera, RHP, KC
9. Shawn Tolleson, RHP, LA
10. Heath Hembree, RHP, SF
11. Juan Abreu, RHP, HOU
12. Jhan Marinez, RHP, CHW
13. Carlos Gutierrez, RHP, MIN
14. Chen Lee, RHP, CLE
15. Santo Manzanillo, RHP, MIL

TOP PROSPECTS BY SKILLS

2012 TOP FANTASY PROSPECTS

TOP POWER
Jesus Montero, C, NYY
Bryce Harper, OF, WAS
Devin Mesoraco, C, CIN
Michael Choice, OF, OAK
Matt Adams, 1B, STL
Miguel Sano, 3B, MIN
Yonder Alonso, 1B, SD
Nolan Arenado, 3B, COL
Gary Sanchez, C, NYY
Anthony Rizzo, 1B, CHC
Manny Machado, SS, BAL
Mike Olt, 3B, TEX
Tim Wheeler, OF, COL
Anthony Rendon, 3B, WAS
Alex Liddi, 3B, SEA
Jedd Gyorko, 3B, SD
Will Middlebrooks, 3B, BOS
Chris Carter, 1B, OAK
Brett Eibner, OF, KC
Ryan Lavarnway, C, BOS
Angelo Songco, OF, LA
Christian Yelich, OF, MIA
Bobby Borchering, 1B, ARI
Xander Bogaerts, SS, BOS
Wilin Rosario, C, COL

TOP BA
Christian Yelich, OF, MIA
Mike Trout, OF, LAA
Nolan Arenado, 3B, COL
Wil Myers, OF, KC
Gary Brown, OF, SF
Jesus Montero, C, NYY
Yonder Alonso, 1B, SD
Kolton Wong, 2B, STL
Brett Jackson, OF, CHC
Manny Machado, SS, BAL
Jedd Gyorko, 3B, SD
Jurickson Profar, SS, TEX
Oscar Taveras, OF, STL
Bryce Harper, OF, WAS
Jake Marisnick, OF, TOR
Francisco Lindor, SS, CLE
Hak-Ju Lee, SS, TAM
David Cooper, 1B, TOR
Miguel Sano, 3B, MIN
James Darnell, OF, SD
Brandon Guyer, OF, TAM
Anthony Rizzo, 1B, CHC
Cory Spangenberg, 2B, SD
Jonathan Singleton, 1B, PHI
Matt Adams, 1B, STL

TOP SPEED
Billy Hamilton, SS, CIN
Gary Brown, OF, SF
Rymer Liriano, OF, SD
Anthony Gose, OF, TOR
Reymond Fuentes, OF, SD
Mike Trout, OF, LAA
Xavier Avery, OF, BAL
Starling Marte, OF, PIT
Jeff Kobernus, 2B, WAS
Jake Marisnick, OF, TOR
Eury Perez, OF, WAS
Jace Peterson, SS, SD
Bubba Starling, OF, KC
Ryan LaMarre, OF, CIN
Hak-Ju Lee, SS, TAM
Kentrail Davis, OF, MIL
Jurickson Profar, SS, TEX
Rafael Ortega, OF, COL
Mason Williams, OF, NYY
Keenyn Walker, OF, CHW
Jared Mitchell, OF, CHW
Jean Segura, 2B, LAA
Andrelton Simmons, SS, ATL
Jiwan James, OF, PHI
Brett Jackson, OF, CHC

TOP FASTBALL
Jameson Taillon, RHP, PIT
Dylan Bundy, RHP, BAL
Julio Teheran, RHP, ATL
Gerrit Cole, RHP, PIT
Taijuan Walker, RHP, SEA
Shelby Miller, RHP, STL
Trevor Bauer, RHP, ARI
Jacob Turner, RHP, DET
Garrett Richards, RHP, LAA
Carlos Martinez, RHP, STL
Martin Perez, LHP, TEX
James Paxton, LHP, SEA
Trevor May, RHP, PHI
Jarred Cosart, RHP, HOU
Arodys Vizcaino, RHP, ATL
Mike Montgomery, LHP, KC
Wily Peralta, RHP, MIL
Dellin Betances, RHP, NYY
Jason Knapp, RHP, CLE
Nick Hagadone, LHP, CLE
Zack Wheeler, RHP, NYM
Archie Bradley, RHP, ARI
Noah Syndergaard, RHP, TOR
Jeurys Familia, RHP, NYM
Addison Reed, RHP, CHW

TOP BREAKING BALL
Matt Moore, LHP, TAM
Jacob Turner, RHP, DET
Jameson Taillon, RHP, PIT
Dylan Bundy, RHP, BAL
Trevor Bauer, RHP, ARI
Shelby Miller, RHP, STL
Gerrit Cole, RHP, PIT
Garrett Richards, RHP, LAA
Drew Pomeranz, LHP, COL
James Paxton, LHP, SEA
Chris Archer, RHP, TAM
Mike Montgomery, LHP, KC
Tyler Skaggs, LHP, ARI

Sonny Gray, RHP, OAK
Robbie Erlin, LHP, SD
Carlos Martinez, RHP, STL
Casey Kelly, RHP, SD
Jarrod Parker, RHP, OAK
Alex Wilson, RHP, BOS
Andrew Oliver, LHP, DET
Arodys Vizcaino, RHP, ATL
Zack Wheeler, RHP, NYM
Jordan Swaggerty, RHP, STL
Sammy Solis, LHP, WAS
Casey Crosby, LHP, DET
Robbie Erlin, LHP, SD

1. Mike Trout (OF, LAA)
2. Matt Moore (LHP, TAM)
3. Jesus Montero (C, NYY)
4. Randall Delgado (RHP, ATL)
5. Julio Teheran (RHP, ATL)
6. Trevor Bauer (RHP, ARI)
7. Drew Pomeranz (LHP, COL)
8. Bryce Harper (OF, WAS)
9. Devin Mesoraco (C, CIN)
10. Wilin Rosario (C, COL)

11. Brett Jackson (OF, CHC)
12. Manny Banuelos (LHP, NYY)
13. Dellin Betances (RHP, NYY)
14. Addison Reed (RHP, CWS)
15. Arodys Vizcaino (RHP, ATL)
16. James Darnell (3B/OF, SD)
17. Jacob Turner (RHP, DET)
18. Jarrod Parker (RHP, OAK)
19. Alex Liddi (3B, SEA)
20. Liam Hendriks (RHP, MIN)

21. Brad Peacock (RHP, OAK)
22. Joe Benson (OF, MIN)
23. Lars Anderson (1B, BOS)
24. Mike Montgomery (LHP, KC)
25. Martin Perez (LHP, TEX)
26. Jake Odorizzi (RHP, KC)
27. Matt Harvey (RHP, NYM)
28. Tom Milone (LHP, OAK)
29. Matt Dominguez (3B, MIA)
30. Matt Adams (1B, STL)

31. Leonys Martin (OF, TEX)
32. Shelby Miller (RHP, STL)
33. Taylor Green (3B, MIL)
34. Austin Romine (C, NYY)
35. Zack Cox (3B, STL)
36. Alex Torres (LHP, TAM)
37. Alex White (RHP, COL)
38. Junichi Tazawa (RHP, BOS)
39. Garrett Richards (RHP, LAA)
40. Starling Marte (OF, PIT)

41. Will Middlebrooks (3B, BOS)
42. Eric Surkamp (RHP, SF)
43. Nathan Eovaldi (RHP, LA)
44. Charlie Blackmon (OF, COL)
45. Robbie Erlin (LHP, SD)
46. Hak-Ju Lee (SS, TAM)
47. Casey Kelly (RHP, SD)
48. Tyler Skaggs (LHP, ARI)
49. Neil Ramirez (RHP, TEX)
50. Wily Peralta (RHP, MIL)

51. Travis D'Arnaud (C, TOR)
52. Jedd Gyorko (3B, SD)
53. Joe Wieland (RHP, SD)
54. David Cooper (1B, TOR)
55. Jose Iglesias (SS, BOS)
56. Brandon Guyer (OF, TAM)
57. James Paxton (LHP, SEA)
58. Andy Oliver (LHP, DET)
59. Jarred Cosart (RHP, HOU)
60. Grant Green (OF, OAK)

61. Tanner Scheppers (RHP, TEX)
62. Ryan Lavarnway (C, BOS)
63. Tim Beckham (SS, TAM)
64. Josh Vitters (3B, CHC)
65. Derek Norris (C, OAK)
66. Chris Archer (RHP, TAM)
67. Brad Boxberger (RHP, SD)
68. Pat Corbin (LHP, ARI)
69. A.J. Pollock (OF, ARI)
70. Nick Franklin (SS, SEA)

71. Anthony Gose (OF, TOR)
72. Wil Myers (OF, KC)
73. Allen Webster (RHP, LA)
74. Tim Wheeler (OF, COL)
75. Alex Colome (RHP, TAM)
76. Sonny Gray (RHP, OAK)
77. Drew Hutchison (RHP, TOR)
78. Phillippe Aumont (RHP, PHI)
79. Anthony Rendon (3B, WAS)
80. Tony Sanchez (C, PIT)

81. Collin Cowgill (OF, ARI)
82. Deck McGuire (RHP, TOR)
83. Thomas Neal (OF, CLE)
84. Adeiny Hechavarria (SS, TOR)
85. Drew Smyly (LHP, DET)
86. Jeurys Familia (RHP, NYM)
87. Adam Eaton (OF, ARI)
88. Christian Colon (SS, KC)
89. Reese Havens (2B, NYM)
90. Kirk Nieuwenhuis (OF, NYM)

91. Simon Castro (RHP, CWS)
92. J.J. Hoover (RHP, ATL)
93. Scott Van Slyke (1B, LA)
94. Casey Crosby (LHP, DET)
95. Ryan Wheeler (3B, ARI)
96. Nick Hagadone (LHP, CLE)
97. Steve Lombardozzi (2B, WAS)
98. David Phelps (RHP, NYY)
99. Chris Marrero (1B, WAS)
100. Brian Dozier (SS, MIN)

TOP 100 PROSPECTS ARCHIVE

2011

1. Bryce Harper (OF, WAS)
2. Domonic Brown (OF, PHI)
3. Jesus Montero (C, NYY)
4. Mike Trout (OF, LAA)
5. Jeremy Hellickson (RHP, TAM)
6. Aroldis Chapman (LHP, CIN)
7. Eric Hosmer (1B, KC)
8. Dustin Ackley (2B, SEA)
9. Desmond Jennings (OF, TAM)
10. Julio Teheran (RHP, ATL)

11. Mike Moustakas (3B, KC)
12. Brandon Belt (1B, SF)
13. Freddie Freeman (1B, ATL)
14. Michael Pineda (RHP, SEA)
15. Matt Moore (LHP, TAM)
16. Mike Montgomery (LHP, KC)
17. Brett Jackson (OF, CHC)
18. Nick Franklin (SS, SEA)
19. Jameson Taillon (RHP, PIT)
20. Jacob Turner (RHP, DET)

21. Shelby Miller (RHP, STL)
22. Martin Perez (LHP, TEX)
23. Wil Myers (C, KC)
24. Kyle Gibson (RHP, MIN)
25. Lonnie Chisenhall (3B, CLE)
26. Tyler Matzek (LHP, COL)
27. Brett Lawrie (2B, TOR)
28. Yonder Alonso (1B, CIN)
29. Jarrod Parker (RHP, ARI)
30. Jonathan Singleton (1B, PHI)

31. Tanner Scheppers (RHP, TEX)
32. Kyle Drabek (RHP, TOR)
33. Jason Knapp (RHP, CLE)
34. Manny Banuelos (LHP, NYY)
35. Alex White (RHP, CLE)
36. Jason Kipnis (2B, CLE)
37. Wilin Rosario (C, COL)
38. Manny Machado (SS, BAL)
39. Chris Sale (LHP, CHW)
40. Devin Mesoraco (C, CIN)

41. Tyler Chatwood (RHP, LAA)
42. John Lamb (LHP, KC)
43. Danny Duffy (LHP, KC)
44. Trevor May (RHP, PHI)
45. Mike Minor (LHP, ATL)
46. Jarred Cosart (RHP, PHI)
47. Tony Sanchez (C, PIT)
48. Brody Colvin (RHP, PHI)
49. Zach Britton (LHP, BAL)
50. Dee Gordon (SS, LA)

51. Miguel Sano (3B, MIN)
52. Grant Green (SS, OAK)
53. Danny Espinosa (SS, WAS)
54. Simon Castro (RHP, SD)
55. Derek Norris (C, WAS)
56. Chris Archer (RHP, CHC)
57. Jurickson Profar (SS, TEX)
58. Zack Cox (3B, STL)
59. Billy Hamilton (2B, CIN)
60. Gary Sanchez (C, NYY)

61. Zach Lee (RHP, LA)
62. Drew Pomeranz (LHP, CLE)
63. Randall Delgado (RHP, ATL)
64. Michael Choice (OF, OAK)
65. Nick Weglarz (OF, CLE)
66. Nolan Arenado (3B, COL)
67. Chris Carter (1B/OF, OAK)
68. Arodys Vizcaino (RHP, ATL)
69. Trey McNutt (RHP, CHC)
70. Dellin Betances (RHP, NYY)

71. Aaron Hicks (OF, MIN)
72. Aaron Crow (RHP, KC)
73. Jake McGee (LHP, TAM)
74. Lars Anderson (1B, BOS)
75. Fabio Martinez (RHP, LAA)
76. Ben Revere (OF, MIN)
77. Jordan Lyles (RHP, HOU)
78. Casey Kelly (RHP, SD)
79. Trayvon Robinson (OF, LA)
80. Craig Kimbrel (RHP, ATL)

81. Jose Iglesias (SS, BOS)
82. Garrett Richards (RHP, LAA)
83. Allen Webster (RHP, LA)
84. Chris Dwyer (LHP, KC)
85. Alex Colome (RHP, TAM)
86. Zack Wheeler (RHP, SF)
87. Andy Oliver (LHP, DET)
88. Andrew Brackman (RHP, NYY)
89. Wilmer Flores (SS, NYM)
90. Christian Friedrich (LHP, COL)

91. Anthony Ranaudo (RHP, BOS)
92. Aaron Miller (LHP, LA)
93. Matt Harvey (RHP, NYM)
94. Mark Rogers (RHP, MIL)
95. Jean Segura (2B, LAA)
96. Hank Conger (C, LAA)
97. J.P. Arencibia (C, TOR)
98. Matt Dominguez (3B, FLA)
99. Jerry Sands (1B, LA)
100. Nick Castellanos (3B, DET)

2010

1. Stephen Strasburg (RHP, WAS)
2. Jason Heyward (OF, ATL)
3. Jesus Montero (C, NYY)
4. Buster Posey (C, SF)
5. Justin Smoak (1B, TEX)
6. Pedro Alvarez (3B, PIT)
7. Carlos Santana (C, CLE)
8. Desmond Jennings (OF, TAM)
9. Brian Matusz (LHP, BAL)
10. Neftali Feliz (RHP, TEX)

11. Brett Wallace (3B, TOR)
12. Mike Stanton (OF. FLA)
13. M. Bumgarner (LHP, SF)
14. J. Hellickson (RHP, TAM)
15. Dustin Ackley (1B/OF, SEA)
16. Aroldis Chapman (LHP, CIN)
17. Yonder Alonso (1B, CIN)
18. Alcides Escobar (SS, MIL)
19. Brett Lawrie (2B, MIL)
20. Starlin Castro (SS, CHC)

21. Logan Morrison (1B, FLA)
22. Mike Montgomery (LHP, KC)
23. Domonic Brown (OF, PHI)
24. Josh Vitters (3B, CHC)
25. R. Westmoreland (OF, BOS)
26. Todd Frazier (3B/OF, CIN)
27. Eric Hosmer (1B, KC)
28. Freddie Freeman (1B, ATL)
29. Derek Norris (C, WAS)
30. Martin Perez (LHP, TEX)

31. Wade Davis (RHP, TAM)
32. Trevor Reckling (LHP, LAA)
33. Jordan Walden (RHP, LAA)
34. Mat Gamel (3B, MIL)
35. Tyler Flowers (C, CHW)
36. T. Scheppers (RHP, TEX)
37. Casey Crosby (LHP, DET)
38. Austin Jackson (OF, DET)
39. Devaris Gordon (SS, LA)
40. Kyle Drabek (RHP, TOR)

41. Ben Revere (OF, MIN)
42. Michael Taylor (OF, OAK)
43. Jacob Turner (RHP, DET)
44. Tim Beckham (SS, TAM)
45. Carlos Triunfel (SS, SEA)
46. Aaron Crow (RHP, KC)
47. Matt Moore (LHP, TAM)
48. Jarrod Parker (RHP, ARI)
49. F. Martinez (OF, NYM)
50. C. Friedrich (LHP, COL)

51. Jenrry Mejia (RHP, NYM)
52. Tyler Matzek (LHP, COL)
53. Brett Jackson (OF, CHC)
54. Aaron Hicks (OF, MIN)
55. Jhoulys Chacin (RHP, COL)
56. Josh Bell (3B, BAL)
57. Brandon Allen (1B, ARI)
58. Chris Carter (1B, OAK)
59. Jason Knapp (RHP, CLE)
60. Danny Duffy (LHP, KC)

61. Tim Alderson (RHP, PIT)
62. Matt Dominguez (3B, FLA)
63. Mike Moustakas (3B, KC)
64. Jake Arrieta (RHP, BAL)
65. Carlos Carrasco (RHP, CLE)
66. Wilmer Flores (SS, NYM)
67. Drew Storen (RHP, WAS)
68. Lonnie Chisenhall (3B, CLE)
69. Aaron Poreda (LHP, SD)
70. A. Cashner (RHP, CHC)

71. Tony Sanchez (C, PIT)
72. Julio Teheran (RHP, ATL)
73. Jose Tabata (OF, PIT)
74. Jason Castro (C, HOU)
75. Casey Kelly (RHP, BOS)
76. Alex White (RHP, CLE)
77. Jay Jackson (RHP, CHC)
78. Dan Hudson (RHP, CHW)
79. Brandon Erbe (RHP, BAL)
80. Zack Wheeler (RHP, SF)

81. Shelby Miller (RHP, STL)
82. Jordan Lyles (RHP, HOU)
83. Simon Castro (RHP, SD)
84. Aaron Miller (LHP, LA)
85. Michael Ynoa (RHP, OAK)
86. Ethan Martin (RHP, LA)
87. Scott Elbert (LHP, LA)
88. Nick Weglarz (OF, CLE)
89. Donavan Tate (OF, SD)
90. Jordan Danks (OF, CHW)

91. Hector Rondon (RHP, CLE)
92. Chris Heisey (OF, CIN)
93. Kyle Gibson (RHP, MIN)
94. Mike Leake (RHP, CIN)
95. Mike Trout (OF, LAA)
96. Jake McGee (LHP, TAM)
97. Chad James (LHP, FLA)
98. C. Bethancourt (C, NYY)
99. Miguel Sano (SS, MIN)
100. Noel Arguelles (LHP, KC)

TOP 100 PROSPECTS ARCHIVE

2009

1. Matt Wieters (C, BAL)
2. David Price (LHP, TAM)
3. Rick Porcello (RHP, DET)
4. Colby Rasmus (OF, STL)
5. Madison Bumgarner (LHP, SF)
6. Neftali Feliz (RHP, TEX)
7. Jason Heyward (OF, ATL)
8. Andrew McCutchen (OF, PIT)
9. Pedro Alvarez (3B, PIT)
10. Cameron Maybin (OF, FLA)

11. Trevor Cahill (RHP, OAK)
12. Mike Moustakas (3B/SS, KC)
13. Jordan Zimmermann (RHP, WAS)
14. Travis Snider (OF, TOR)
15. Tim Beckham (SS, TAM)
16. Eric Hosmer (1B, KC)
17. Tommy Hanson (RHP, ATL)
18. Dexter Fowler (OF, COL)
19. Brett Anderson (LHP, OAK)
20. Carlos Triunfel (SS/2B, SEA)

21. Buster Posey (C, SF)
22. Chris Tillman (RHP, BAL)
23. Brian Matusz (LHP, BAL)
24. Justin Smoak (1B, TEX)
25. Jarrod Parker (RHP, ARI)
26. Derek Holland (LHP, TEX)
27. Lars Anderson (1B, BOS)
28. Michael Inoa (RHP, OAK)
29. Mike Stanton (OF, FLA)
30. Taylor Teagarden (C, TEX)

31. Gordon Beckham (SS, CHW)
32. Brett Wallace (3B, STL)
33. Matt LaPorta (OF, CLE)
34. Jordan Schafer (OF, ATL)
35. Carlos Santana (C, CLE)
36. Aaron Hicks (OF, MIN)
37. Adam Miller (RHP, CLE)
38. Elvis Andrus (SS, TEX)
39. Alcides Escobar (SS, MIL)
40. Wade Davis (RHP, TAM)

41. Austin Jackson (OF, NYY)
42. Jesus Montero (C, NYY)
43. Tim Alderson (RHP, SF)
44. Jhoulys Chacin (RHP, COL)
45. Phillippe Aumont (RHP, SEA)
46. James McDonald (RHP, LA)
47. Reid Brignac (SS, TAM)
48. Desmond Jennings (OF, TAM)
49. Fernando Martinez (OF, NYM)
50. JP Arencibia (C, TOR)

51. Wilmer Flores (SS, NYM)
52. Brett Cecil (LHP, TOR)
53. Aaron Poreda (LHP, CHW)
54. Jeremy Jeffress (RHP, MIL)
55. Michael Main (RHP, TEX)
56. Josh Vitters (3B, CHC)
57. Mat Gamel (3B, MIL)
58. Yonder Alonso (1B, CIN)
59. Gio Gonzalez (LHP, OAK)
60. Michael Bowden (RHP, BOS)

61. Angel Villalona (1B, SF)
62. Carlos Carrasco (RHP, PHI)
63. Jake Arrieta (RHP, BAL)
64. Jordan Walden (RHP, LAA)
65. Freddie Freeman (1B, ATL)
66. Logan Morrison (1B, FLA)
67. Shooter Hunt (RHP, MIN)
68. Junichi Tazawa (RHP, BOS)
69. Nick Adenhart (RHP, LAA)
70. Jose Tabata (OF, PIT)

71. Adrian Cardenas (SS/2B, OAK)
72. Chris Carter (3B/OF, OAK)
73. Ben Revere (OF, MIN)
74. Josh Reddick (OF, BOS)
75. Jeremy Hellickson (RHP, TAM)
76. Justin Jackson (SS, TOR)
77. Wilson Ramos (C, MIN)
78. Jason Castro (C, HOU)
79. Julio Borbon (OF, TEX)
80. Tyler Flowers (C, CHW)

81. Gorkys Hernandez (OF, ATL)
82. Neftali Soto (3B, CIN)
83. Henry Rodriguez (RHP, OAK)
84. Dan Duffy (LHP, KC)
85. Daniel Cortes (RHP, KC)
86. Dayan Viciedo (3B, CHW)
87. Matt Dominguez (3B, FLA)
88. Jordan Danks (OF, CHW)
89. Chris Coghlan (2B, FLA)
90. Brian Bogusevic (OF, HOU)

91. Ryan Tucker (RHP, FLA)
92. Jonathon Niese (LHP, NYM)
93. Martin Perez (LHP, TEX)
94. James Simmons (RHP, OAK)
95. Nick Weglarz (OF/1B, CLE)
96. Daniel Bard (RHP, BOS)
97. Yamaico Navarro (SS, BOS)
98. Jose Ceda (RHP, FLA)
99. Jeff Samardzija (RHP, CHC)
100. Jason Donald (SS, PHI)

2008

1. Jay Bruce (OF, CIN)
2. Evan Longoria (3B, TAM)
3. Clay Buchholz (RHP, BOS)
4. Clayton Kershaw (LHP, LAD)
5. Joba Chamberlain (RHP, NYY)
6. Colby Rasmus (OF, STL)
7. Cameron Maybin (OF, FLA)
8. Homer Bailey (RHP, CIN)
9. David Price (LHP, TAM)
10. Andrew McCutchen (OF, PIT)

11. Brandon Wood (3B/SS, LAA)
12. Matt Wieters (C, BAL)
13. Jacoby Ellsbury (OF, BOS)
14. Travis Snider (OF, TOR)
15. Reid Brignac (SS, TAM)
16. Jacob McGee (LHP, TAM)
17. Wade Davis (RHP, TAM)
18. Adam Miller (RHP, CLE)
19. Rick Porcello (RHP, DET)
20. Franklin Morales (LHP, COL)

21. Carlos Triunfel (SS, SEA)
22. Andy LaRoche (3B/OF, LAD)
23. Jordan Schafer (OF, ATL)
24. Kosuke Fukodome (OF, CHC)
25. Jose Tabata (OF, NYY)
26. Carlos Gonzalez (OF, OAK)
27. Joey Votto (1B/OF, CIN)
28. Daric Barton (1B, OAK)
29. Angel Villalona (3B, SF)
30. Eric Hurley (RHP, TEX)

31. Nick Adenhart (RHP, LAA)
32. Fernando Martinez (OF, NYM)
33. Ross Detwiler (LHP, WAS)
34. Johnny Cueto (RHP, CIN)
35. Chris Marrero (OF, WAS)
36. Jason Heyward (OF, ATL)
37. Mike Moustakas (SS, KC)
38. Elvis Andrus (SS, TEX)
39. Taylor Teagarden (C, TEX)
40. Ian Kennedy (RHP, NYY)

41. Kasey Kiker (LHP, TEX)
42. Scott Elbert (LHP, LAD)
43. Justin Masterson (RHP, BOS)
44. Max Scherzer (RHP, ARI)
45. Brandon Jones (OF, ATL)
46. Josh Vitters (3B, CHC)
47. Jarrod Parker (RHP, ARI)
48. Matt Antonelli (2B, SD)
49. Gio Gonzalez (LHP, CHW)
50. Ian Stewart (3B, COL)

51. Chase Headley (3B, SD)
52. Anthony Swarzak (RHP, MIN)
53. Jair Jurrjens (RHP, DET)
54. Billy Rowell (3B, BAL)
55. Jeff Clement (C, SEA)
56. Tyler Colvin (OF, CHC)
57. Neil Walker (3B, PIT)
58. Geovany Soto (C/1B, CHC)
59. Steven Pearce (1B/OF, PIT)
60. Fautino de los Santos (RHP, CHW)

61. Manny Parra (LHP, MIL)
62. Matt LaPorta (OF, MIL)
63. Austin Jackson (OF, NYY)
64. Carlos Carrasco (RHP, PHI)
65. Jed Lowrie (SS/2B, BOS)
66. Deolis Guerra (RHP, NYM)
67. Jonathon Meloan (RHP, LAD)
68. Chin-Lung Hu (SS, LAD)
69. Blake Beaven (RHP, TEX)
70. Michael Main (RHP, TEX)

71. Gorkys Hernandez (OF, ATL)
72. Jeff Niemann (RHP, TAM)
73. Desmond Jennings (OF, TAM)
74. Radhames Liz (RHP, BAL)
75. Chuck Lofgren (LHP, CLE)
76. Luke Hochevar (RHP, KC)
77. Brent Lillibridge (SS, ATL)
78. Jaime Garcia (LHP, STL)
79. Bryan Anderson (C, STL)
80. Troy Patton (LHP, BAL)

81. Nolan Reimold (OF, BAL)
82. Matt Latos (RHP, SD)
83. Tommy Hanson (RHP, ATL)
84. Aaron Poreda (LHP, CHW)
85. Cole Rohrbough (LHP, ATL)
86. Lars Anderson (1B, BOS)
87. Chris Volstad (RHP, FLA)
88. Henry Sosa (RHP, SF)
89. Madison Bumgarner (LHP, SF)
90. Michael Bowden (RHP, BOS)

91. Hank Conger (C, LAA)
92. JR Towles (C, HOU)
93. Greg Reynolds (RHP, COL)
94. Adrian Cardenas (2B/SS, PHI)
95. Chris Nelson (SS, COL)
96. Ryan Kalish (OF, BOS)
97. Dexter Fowler (OF, COL)
98. James McDonald (RHP, LAD)
99. Beau Mills (3B/1B, CLE)
100. Michael Burgess (OF, WAS

TOP 100 PROSPECTS ARCHIVE

2007

1. Delmon Young (OF, TAM)
2. Alex Gordon (3B, KC)
3. Daisuke Matsuzaka (RHP, BOS)
4. Justin Upton (OF, ARI)
5. Homer Bailey (RHP, CIN)
6. Philip Hughes (RHP, NYY)
7. Brandon Wood (SS, LAA)
8. Jay Bruce (OF, CIN)
9. Billy Butler (OF, KC)
10. Cameron Maybin (OF, DET)

11. Andrew McCutchen (OF, PIT)
12. Troy Tulowitzki (SS, COL)
13. Evan Longoria (3B, TAM)
14. Jose Tabata (OF, NYY)
15. Reid Brignac (SS, TAM)
16. Chris Young (OF, ARI)
17. Adam Miller (RHP, CLE)
18. Mike Pelfrey (RHP, NYM)
19. Carlos Gonzalez (OF, ARI)
20. Tim Lincecum (RHP, SF)

21. Andy LaRoche (3B, LAD)
22. Fernando Martinez (OF, NYM)
23. Yovani Gallardo (RHP, MIL)
24. Colby Rasmus (OF, STL)
25. Ryan Braun (3B, MIL)
26. Scott Elbert (LHP, LAD)
27. Nick Adenhart (RHP, LAA)
28. Andrew Miller (LHP, DET)
29. Billy Rowell (3B, BAL)
30. John Danks (LHP, CHW)

31. Luke Hochevar (RHP, KC)
32. Erick Aybar (SS, LAA)
33. Jacoby Ellsbury (OF, BOS)
34. Eric Hurley (RHP, TEX)
35. Ian Stewart (3B, COL)
36. Clay Buchholz (RHP, BOS)
37. Elvis Andrus (SS, ATL)
38. Jason Hirsh (RHP, COL)
39. Hunter Pence (OF, HOU)
40. Franklin Morales (LHP, COL)

41. Adam Lind (OF, TOR)
42. Travis Snider (OF, TOR)
43. Jeff Niemann (RHP, TAM)
44. Clayton Kershaw (LHP, LAD)
45. James Loney (1B, LAD)
46. Chris Iannetta (C, COL)
47. Elijah Dukes (OF, TAM)
48. Chuck Lofgren (LHP, CLE)
49. Joey Votto (1B, CIN)
50. Jacob McGee (LHP, TAM)

51. Adam Jones (OF, SEA)
52. Brad Lincoln (RHP, PIT)
53. Brian Barton (OF, CLE)
54. Will Inman (RHP, MIL)
55. Wade Davis (RHP, TAM)
56. Donald Veal (LHP, CHC)
57. Michael Bowden (RHP, BOS)
58. Ryan Sweeney (OF, CHW)
59. Josh Fields (3B, CHW)
60. Jarrod Saltalamacchia (C, ATL)

61. Felix Pie (OF, CHC)
62. Brandon Erbe (RHP, BAL)
63. Giovanny Gonzalez (LHP, CHW)
64. Trevor Crowe (OF, CLE)
65. Travis Buck (OF, OAK)
66. Daric Barton (1B, OAK)
67. Kevin Kouzmanoff (3B, SD)
68. Jeff Clement (C, SEA)
69. Neil Walker (C, PIT)
70. Troy Patton (LHP, HOU)

71. Brandon Morrow (RHP, SEA)
72. Dustin Pedroia (2B, BOS)
73. Blake DeWitt (2B, LAD)
74. Carlos Carrasco (RHP, PHI)
75. Jonathon Meloan (RHP, LAD)
76. Hank Conger (C, LAA)
77. Sean Rodriguez (SS, LAA)
78. Humberto Sanchez (RHP, NYY)
79. Phil Humber (RHP, NYM)
80. Edinson Volquez (RHP, TEX)

81. Dustin Nippert (RHP, ARI)
82. Anthony Swarzak (RHP, MIN)
83. Chris Parmalee (OF/1B, MIN)
84. Ubaldo Jimenez (RHP, COL)
85. Dexter Fowler (OF, COL)
86. Drew Stubbs (OF, CIN)
87. Miguel Montero (C, ARI)
88. Carlos Gomez (OF, NYM)
89. Kevin Slowey (RHP, MIN)
90. Nolan Reimold (OF, BAL)

91. Daniel Bard (RHP, BOS)
92. Chris Nelson (SS, COL)
93. Cedric Hunter (OF, SD)
94. Angel Villanoa (3B, SF)
95. Jamie Garcia (LHP, STL)
96. Travis Wood (LHP, CIN)
97. Cesar Carillo (RHP, SD)
98. Pedro Beato (RHP, BAL)
99. Joba Chamberlain (RHP, NYY)
100. Kei Igawa (LHP, NYY)

2006

1. Delmon Young (OF, TAM)
2. Justin Upton (OF/SS, ARI)
3. Brandon Wood (SS, LAA)
4. Ian Stewart (3B, COL)
5. Prince Fielder (1B, MIL)
6. Jeremy Hermida (OF, FLA)
7. Chad Billingsley (RHP, LAD)
8. Stephen Drew (SS, ARI)
9. Andy Marte (3B, BOS)
10. Francisco Liriano (LHP, MIN)

11. Alex Gordon (3B, KC)
12. Jarrod Saltalamacchia (C, ATL)
13. Carlos Quentin (OF, ARI)
14. Lastings Milledge (OF, NYM)
15. Conor Jackson (1B, ARI)
16. Joel Guzman (SS, LAD)
17. Nick Markakis (OF, BAL)
18. Adam Miller (RHP, CLE)
19. Matt Cain (RHP, SF)
20. Erick Aybar (SS, LAA)

21. Billy Butler (OF, KC)
22. Justin Verlander (RHP, DET)
23. Howie Kendrick (2B, LAA)
24. Andy LaRoche (3B, LAD)
25. Troy Tulowitski (SS, COL)
26. Jered Weaver (RHP, LAA)
27. Ryan Zimmerman (3B, WAS)
28. Chris Young (OF, ARI)
29. Elvis Andrus (SS, ATL)
30. Daric Barton (1B, OAK)

31. Scott Olson (LHP, FLA)
32. Jon Lester (LHP, BOS)
33. Cole Hamels (LHP, PHI)
34. Anthony Reyes (RHP, STL)
35. Mike Pelfrey (RHP, NYM)
36. Andrew McCutchen (OF, PIT)
37. Ryan Braun (3B, MIL)
38. Chris Nelson (SS, COL)
39. Kendry Morales (1B/OF, LAA)
40. Anibal Sanchez (RHP, FLA)

41. Hanley Ramirez (SS, FLA)
42. John Danks (LHP, TEX)
43. Edison Volquez (RHP, TEX)
44. Russell Martin (C, LAD)
45. Dustin Nippert (RHP, ARI)
46. Jon Papelbon (RHP, BOS)
47. Carlos Gonzales (OF, ARI)
48. Felix Pie (OF, CHC)
49. Yusmeiro Petit (RHP, FLA)
50. Dustin Pedroia (2B, BOS)

51. Joel Zumaya (RHP, DET)
52. Gio Gonzalez (LHP, PHI)
53. Hayden Penn (RHP, BAL)
54. Nolan Reimold (OF, BAL)
55. Homer Bailey (RHP, CIN)
56. Mark Pawelek (LHP, CHC)
57. Neil Walker (C, PIT)
58. Philip Hughes (RHP, NYY)
59. Jonathon Broxton (RHP, LAD)
60. Dustin McGowan (RHP, TOR)

61. Cameron Maybin (OF, DET)
62. Scott Elbert (LHP, LAD)
63. Andrew Lerew (RHP, ATL)
64. Yuniel Escobar (SS, ATL)
65. Jose Tabata (OF, NYY)
66. Craig Hansen (RHP, BOS)
67. Javier Herrera (OF, OAK)
68. James Loney (1B, LAD)
69. Matt Kemp (OF, LAD)
70. Jairo Garcia (RHP, OAK)

71. Ryan Sweeney (OF, CHW)
72. Thomas Diamond (RHP, TEX)
73. Cesar Carillo (RHP, SD)
74. Adam Loewen (LHP, BAL)
75. Chuck Tiffany (LHP, LAD)
76. Brian Anderson (OF, CHW)
77. Jeremy Sowers (LHP, CLE)
78. Matt Moses (3B, MIN)
79. Angel Guzman (RHP, CHC)
80. Jeff Clement (C, SEA)

81. Kenji Jojima (C, SEA)
82. Fernando Nieve (RHP, HOU)
83. Corey Hart (OF/3B, MIL)
84. Eric Duncan (3B, NYY)
85. Justin Huber (1B, KC)
86. Jeff Niemann (RHP, TAM)
87. Cliff Pennington (SS, OAK)
88. Jeff Mathis (C, LAA)
89. Troy Patton (LHP, HOU)
90. Jay Bruce (OF, CIN)

91. Colby Rasmus (OF, STL)
92. Jeff Bianchi (SS, KC)
93. Joaquin Arias (SS, TEX)
94. Eddy Martinez-Esteve (OF, SF)
95. Jason Kubel (OF, MIN)
96. Adam Jones (OF, SEA)
97. Ian Kinsler (2B, TEX)
98. Eric Hurley (RHP, TEX)
99. Anthony Swarzak (RHP, MIN)
100. Josh Barfield (2B, SD)

TOP 100 PROSPECTS ARCHIVE

2005

1. Delmon Young (OF, TAM)
2. Casey Kotchman (1B, LAA)
3. Felix Hernandez (RHP, SEA)
4. Ian Stewart (3B, COL)
5. Andy Marte (3B, ATL)
6. Rickie Weeks (2B, MIL)
7. Adam Miller (RHP, CLE)
8. Prince Fielder (1B, MIL)
9. Scott Kazmir (LHP, TAM)
10. Dallas McPherson (3B, LAA)

11. Jeff Francis (LHP, COL)
12. Jeff Francouer (OF, ATL)
13. Chris Nelson (SS, COL)
14. Hanley Ramirez (SS, BOS)
15. Matt Cain (RHP, SF)
16. Edwin Jackson (RHP, LA)
17. Joel Guzman (SS, LA)
18. JJ Hardy (SS, MIL)
19. Carlos Quentin (OF, ARI)
20. Lastings Milledge (OF, NYM)

21. Jeremy Hermida (OF, FLA)
22. Daric Barton (C/1B, OAK)
23. James Loney (1B, LA)
24. Chad Billingsley (RHP, LA)
25. John Danks (LHP, TEX)
26. Josh Barfield (2B, SD)
27. Ervin Santana (RHP, LAA)
28. Ryan Sweeney (OF, CHW)
29. Kendry Morales (1B/OF, LAA)
30. Erick Aybar (SS, LAA)

31. Conor Jackson (OF, ARI)
32. Yuresimo Petit (RHP, NYM)
33. Anthony Reyes (RHP, STL)
34. Joe Blanton (RHP, OAK)
35. Michael Aubrey (1B, CLE)
36. Nick Swisher (OF, OAK)
37. Jason Kubel (OF, MIN)
38. Michael Hinckley (LHP, WAS)
39. Gavin Floyd (RHP, PHI)
40. Jose Capellan (RHP, MIL)

41. Dan Meyer (LHP, OAK)
42. Eric Duncan (3B, NYY)
43. Cole Hamels (LHP, PHI)
44. Jeremy Reed (OF, SEA)
45. Jesse Crain (RHP, MIN)
46. Franklin Gutierrez (OF, CLE)
47. Shin Soo Choo (OF, SEA)
48. Guillermo Quiroz (C, TOR)
49. Jeff Mathis (C, LAA)
50. Jeff Niemann (RHP, TAM)

51. JD Durbin (RHP, MIN)
52. Dustin McGowan (RHP, TOR)
53. Scott Olsen (LHP, FLA)
54. Francisco Rosario (RHP, TOR)
55. Aaron Hill (SS, TOR)
56. Jason Bartlett (SS, MIN)
57. Brian Anderson (OF, CHW)
58. Sergio Santos (SS, ARI)
59. Jered Weaver (RHP, LAA)
60. Justin Verlander (RHP, DET)

61. Russ Adams (SS, TOR)
62. Brandon League (RHP, TOR)
63. Brandon McCarthy (RHP, CHW)
64. Juan Dominguez (RHP, TEX)
65. Huston Street (RHP, OAK)
66. Jairo Garcia (RHP, OAK)
67. John Maine (RHP, BAL)
68. Javier Herrera (OF, OAK)
69. Chuck Tiffany (LHP, LA)
70. Angel Guzman (RHP, CHC)

71. Felix Pie (OF, CHC)
72. Josh Fields (3B, CHW)
73. Fernando Nieve (RHP, HOU)
74. Chris Burke (2B, HOU)
75. Ian Kinsler (SS, TEX)
76. Brian Dopirak (1B, CHC)
77. John VanBenscoten (RHP, PIT)
78. Zach Duke (LHP, PIT)
79. Greg Miller (LHP, LA)
80. Ryan Howard (1B, PHI)

81. Dan Johnson (1B, OAK)
82. Andy LaRoche (3B, LA)
83. Merkin Valdez (RHP, SF)
84. Homer Bailey (RHP, CIN)
85. Nick Marakis (OF, BAL)
86. Ubaldo Jimenez (RHP, COL)
87. Phil Humber (RHP, NYM)
88. Edwin Encarnacion (3B, CIN)
89. Kyle Davies (RHP, ATL)
90. Vince Sinisi (OF, TEX)

91. Thomas Diamond (RHP, TEX)
92. Stephen Drew (SS, ARI)
93. Denny Bautista (RHP, KC)
94. Matt Moses (3B, MIN)
95. Chris Snyder (C, ARI)
96. Billy Butler (3B, KC)
97. Brian McCann (C, ATL)
98. Mark Teahen (3B, KC)
99. Corey Hart (OF, MIL)
100. Matt Bush (SS, SD)

2004

1. Joe Mauer (C, MIN)
2. BJ Upton (SS, TAM)
3. Zach Greinke (RHP, KC)
4. Andy Marte (3B, ATL)
5. Casey Kotchman (1B, LAA)
6. Edwin Jackson (RHP, LA)
7. Justin Morneau (1B, MIN)
8. Scott Kazmir (LHP, NYM)
9. Cole Hamels (LHP, PHI)
10. Alexis Rios (OF, TOR)

11. JJ Hardy (SS, MIL)
12. Rickie Weeks (2B, MIL)
13. Delmon Young (OF, TAM)
14. Prince Fielder (1B, MIL)
15. Bobby Crosby (SS, OAK)
16. Greg Miller (LHP, LA)
17. David Wright (3B, NYM)
18. Dustin McGowan (RHP, TOR)
19. Jeremy Reed (OF, CHW)
20. Khalil Greene (SS, SD)

21. Josh Barfield (2B, SD)
22. Gavin Floyd (RHP, PHI)
23. Chin-hui Tsao (RHP, COL)
24. Jeff Mathis (C, LAA)
25. Grady Sizemore (OF, CLE)
26. Ervin Santana (RHP, LAA)
27. Joe Blanton (RHP, OAK)
28. Hanley Ramirez (SS, BOS)
29. Jeff Francouer (OF, ATL)
30. Scott Hairston (2B, ARI)

31. Jeremy Hermida (OF, FLA)
32. Angel Guzman (RHP, CHC)
33. John VanBenschoten (RHP, PIT)
34. Gabe Gross (OF, TOR)
35. Guillermo Quiroz (C, TOR)
36. Dallas McPherson (3B, LAA)
37. Merkin Valdez (RHP, SF)
38. Clint Nageotte (RHP, SEA)
39. Adam Wainwright (RHP, STL)
40. Joel Hanrahan (RHP, LA)

41. James Loney (1B, LA)
42. Franklin Gutierrez (OF, CLE)
43. Juan Dominguez (RHP, TEX)
44. Ian Stewart (3B, COL)
45. Adrian Gonzalez (1B, TEX)
46. Andy Sisco (LHP, CHC)
47. Chris Snelling (OF, SEA)
48. Ryan Harvey (OF, CHC)
49. Justin Jones (LHP, CHC)
50. Sergio Santos (SS, ARI)

51. Sean Burnett (LHP, PIT)
52. Kris Honel (RHP, CHW)
53. Francisco Cruceta (RHP, CLE)
54. Bobby Jenks (RHP, LAA)
55. Adam Loewen (LHP, BAL)
56. Brandon Claussen(LHP, CIN)
57. Ryan Wagner (RHP, CIN)
58. Dioner Navarro (C, NYY)
59. Neal Cotts (LHP, CHW)
60. Jeff Allison (RHP, FLA)

61. Brian Bullington (RHP, PIT)
62. Jason Bay (OF, PIT)
63. Taylor Buchholz (RHP, HOU)
64. Felix Pie (OF, CHC)
65. John Maine (RHP, BAL)
66. Blake Hawksworth (RHP, STL)
67. Clint Everts (RHP, MON)
68. Matt Moses (3B/SS, MIN)
69. Conor Jackson (OF, ARI)
70. Jeff Francis (LHP, COL)

71. Brad Nelson (OF/1B, MIL)
72. Jose Lopez (SS/2B, SEA)
73. Michael Aubrey (1B, CLE)
74. Macay McBride (LHP, ATL)
75. Manny Parra (RHP, MIL)
76. Boof Bonser (RHP, MIN)
77. JD Durbin (RHP, MIN)
78. Aaron Hill (SS, TOR)
79. John Danks (LHP, TEX)
80. Ryan Sweeney (OF, CHW)

81. Chris Lubanski (OF, KC)
82. Jesse Crain (RHP, MIN)
83. Jason Stokes (1B, FLA)
84. Matt Cain (RHP, SF)
85. Rett Johnson (RHP, SEA)
86. Russ Adams (SS, TOR)
87. Scott Olsen (LHP, FLA)
88. David Bush (RHP, TOR)
89. Mike Jones (RHP, MIL)
90. Corey Hart (3B/1B, MIL)

91. Dan Meyer (LHP, ATL)
92. Kyle Sleeth (RHP, DET)
93. Travis Blackley (LHP, SEA)
94. Ramon Nivar (OF, TEX)
95. Shin-Soo Choo (OF, SEA)
96. Jason Bartlett (SS, MIN)
97. Adam LaRoche (1B, ATL)
98. Denny Bautista (RHP, BAL)
99. Jason Arnold (RHP, TOR)
100. Kazuhito Tadano (RHP, CLE)

AVG: Batting Average (see also BA)

BA: Batting Average (see also AVG)

Base Performance Indicator (BPI): A statistical formula that measures an isolated aspect of a player's situation-independent raw skill or a gauge that helps capture the effects of random chance has on a skill. Although there are many such formulas, there are only a few that we are referring to when the term is used in this book. For pitchers, our BPI's are control (bb%), dominance (k/9), command (k/bb), opposition on base average (OOB), ground/line/fly ratios (G/L/F), and expected ERA (xERA). Random chance is measured witih the hit rate (H%) and strand rate (S%).

*Base Performance Value (BPV): A single value that describes a pitcher's overall raw skill level. This is more useful than any traditional statistical gauge to track performance trends and project future statistical output. The BPV formula combines and weights several BPIs:

(Dominance Rate x 6) + (Command ratio x 21) – Opposition HR Rate x 30) – ((Opp. Batting Average - .275) x 200)

The formula combines the individual raw skills of power, command, the ability to keep batters from reaching base, and the ability to prevent long hits, all characteristics that are unaffected by most external team factors. In tandem with a pitcher's strand rate, it provides a complete picture of the elements that contribute to a pitcher's ERA, and therefore serves as an accurate tool to project likely changes in ERA. BENCHMARKS: We generally consider a BPV of 50 to be the minimum level required for long-term success. The elite of bullpen aces will have BPV's in the excess of 100 and it is rare for these stoppers to enjoy long-term success with consistent levels under 75.

Batters Faced per Game *(Craig Wright)*

((IP x 2.82) + H + BB) / G

A measure of pitcher usage and one of the leading indicators for potential pitcher burnout.

Batting Average (BA, or AVG)

(H/AB)

Ratio of hits to at-bats, though it is a poor evaluative measure of hitting performance. It neglects the offensive value of the base on balls and assumes that all hits are created equal.

Batting Eye (Eye)

(Walks / Strikeouts)

A measure of a player's strike zone judgment, the raw ability to distinguish between balls and strikes. BENCHMARKS: The best hitters have eye ratios over 1.00 (indicating more walks than strikeouts) and are the most likely to be among a league's .300 hitters. At the other end of the scale are ratios

less than 0.50, which represent batters who likely also have lower BAs.

bb%: Walk rate (hitters)

bb/9: Opposition Walks per 9 IP

BF/Gm: Batters Faced Per Game

BPI: Base Performance Indicator

*BPV: Base Performance Value

Cmd: Command ratio

Command Ratio (Cmd)

(Strikeouts / Walks)

This is a measure of a pitcher's raw ability to get the ball over the plate. There is no more fundamental a skill than this, and so it is accurately used as a leading indicator to project future rises and falls in other gauges, such as ERA. Command is one of the best gauges to use to evaluate minor league performance. It is a prime component of a pitcher's base performance value. BENCHMARKS: Baseball's upper echelon of command pitchers will have ratios in excess of 3.0. Pitchers with ratios under 1.0 — indicating that they walk more batters than they strike out — have virtually no potential for long term success. If you make no other changes in your approach to drafting a pitching staff, limiting your focus to only pitchers with a command ratio of 2.0 or better will substantially improve your odds of success.

Contact Rate (ct%)

((AB - K) / AB)

Measures a batter's ability to get wood on the ball and hit it into the field of play. BENCHMARK: Those batters with the best contact skill will have levels of 90% or better. The hackers of society will have levels of 75% or less.

Control Rate (bb/9), or Opposition Walks per Game

BB Allowed x 9 / IP

Measures how many walks a pitcher allows per game equivalent. BENCHMARK: The best pitchers will have bb/9 levels of 3.0 or less.

ct%: Contact rate

Ctl: Control Rate

Dom: Dominance Rate

Dominance Rate (k/9), or Opposition Strikeouts per Game

(K Allowed x 9 / IP)

Measures how many strikeouts a pitcher allows per game equivalent. BENCHMARK: The best pitchers will have k/9 levels of 6.0 or higher.

*Expected Earned Run Average *(Gill and Reeve)*

(.575 x H [per 9 IP]) + (.94 x HR [per 9 IP]) + (.28 x BB [per 9 IP]) - (.01 x K [per 9 IP]) - Normalizing Factor

"xERA represents the expected ERA of the pitcher based on a normal distribution of his statistics. It is not influenced by situation-dependent factors." xERA erases the inequity between starters' and relievers' ERA's, eliminating the effect that a pitcher's success or failure has on another pitcher's ERA.

Similar to other gauges, the accuracy of this formula changes with the level of competition from one season to the next. The normalizing factor allows us to better approximate a pitcher's actual ERA. This value is usually somewhere around 2.77 and varies by league and year. BENCHMARKS: In general, xERA's should approximate a pitcher's ERA fairly closely. However, those pitchers who have large variances between the two gauges are candidates for further analysis.

Extra-Base Hit Rate (X/H)

(2B + 3B + HR) / Hits

X/H is a measure of power and can be used along with a player's slugging percentage and isolated power to gauge a player's ability to drive the ball. BENCHMARKS: Players with above average power will post X/H of greater than 38% and players with moderate power will post X/H of 30% or greater. Weak hitters with below average power will have a X/H level of less than 20%.

Eye: Batting Eye

h%: Hit rate (batters)

H%: Hits Allowed per Balls in Play (pitchers)

Hit Rate (h% or H%)

(H—HR) / (AB – HR - K)

The percent of balls hit into the field of play that fall for hits.

hr/9: Opposition Home Runs per 9 IP

ISO: Isolated Power

Isolated Power (ISO)

(Slugging Percentage - Batting Average)

Isolated Power is a measurement of power skill. Subtracting a player's BA from his SLG, we are essentially pulling out all the singles and single bases from the formula. What remains are the extra-base hits. ISO is not an absolute measurement as it assumes that two doubles is worth one home run, which certainly is not the case, but is another statistic that is a good measurement of raw power. BENCHMARKS: The game's top sluggers will tend to have ISO levels over .200. Weak hitters will be under .100.

k/9: Dominance rate (opposition strikeouts per 9 IP)

Major League Equivalency (Bill James)

A formula that converts a player's minor or foreign league statistics into a comparable performance in the major leagues. These are not projections, but conversions of current performance. Contains adjustments for the level of play in individual leagues and teams. Works best with Triple-A stats, not quite as well with Double-A stats, and hardly at all with the lower levels. Foreign conversions are still a work in process. James' original formula only addressed batting. Our research has devised conversion formulas for pitchers, however, their best use comes when looking at BPI's, not traditional stats.

MLE: Major League Equivalency

OBP: On Base Percentage (batters)

OBA: Opposition Batting Average (pitchers)

On Base Percentage (OBP)

(H + BB) / (AB + BB)

Addressing one of the two deficiencies in BA, OBP gives value to those events that get batters on base, but are not hits. By adding walks (and often, hit batsmen) into the basic batting average formula, we have a better gauge of a batter's ability to reach base safely. An OBP of .350 can be read as "this batter gets on base 35% of the time."

Why this is a more important gauge than batting average? When a run is scored, there is no distinction made as to how that runner reached base. So, two thirds of the time — about how often a batter comes to the plate with the bases empty — a walk really is as good as a hit. BENCHMARKS: We all know what a .300 hitter is, but what represents "good" for OBP? That comparable level would likely be .400, with .275 representing the level of futility.

On Base Plus Slugging Percentage (OPS): A simple sum of the two gauges, it is considered as one of the better evaluators of overall performance. OPS combines the two basic elements of offensive production — the ability to get on base (OBP) and the ability to advance baserunners (SLG). BENCHMARKS: The game's top batters will have OPS levels over .900. The worst batters will have levels under .600.

Opposition Batting Average (OBA)

(Hits Allowed / ((IP x 2.82) + Hits Allowed))

A close approximation of the batting average achieved by opposing batters against a particular pitcher. BENCHMARKS: The converse of the benchmark for batters, the best pitchers will have levels under .250; the worst pitchers levels over .300.

Opposition Home Runs per Game (hr/9)

(HR Allowed x 9 / IP)

Measures how many home runs a pitcher allows per game equivalent. BENCHMARK: The best pitchers will have hr/9 levels of under 1.0.

Opposition On Base Average (OOB)

(Hits Allowed + BB) / ((IP x 2.82) + H + BB)

A close approximation of the on base average achieved by opposing batters against a particular pitcher. BENCHMARK: The best pitchers will have levels under .300; the worst pitchers levels over .375.

Opposition Strikeouts per Game: See Dominance Rate.

Opposition Walks per Game: See Control Rate.

OPS: On Base Plus Slugging Percentage

RC: Runs Created

RC/G: Runs Created Per Game

Runs Created *(Bill James)*

(H + BB - CS) x (Total bases + (.55 x SB)) / (AB + BB)

A formula that converts all offensive events into a total of runs scored. As calculated for individual teams, the result approximates a club's actual run total with great accuracy.

Runs Created Per Game *(Bill James)*

Runs Created / ((AB - H + CS) / 25.5)

RC expressed on a per-game basis might be considered the hypothetical ERA compiled against a particular batter. BENCHMARKS: Few players surpass the level of a 10.00 RC/G in any given season, but any level over 7.50 can still be considered very good. At the bottom are levels below 3.00.

S%: Strand Rate

Save: There are six events that need to occur in order for a pitcher to post a single save...

1. The starting pitcher and middle relievers must pitch well.
2. The offense must score enough runs.
3. It must be a reasonably close game.
4. The manager must choose to put the pitcher in for a save opportunity.
5. The pitcher must pitch well and hold the lead.
6. The manager must let him finish the game.

Of these six events, only one is within the control of the relief pitcher. As such, projecting saves for a reliever has little to do with skill and a lot to do with opportunity. However, pitchers with excellent skills sets may create opportunity for themselves.

Situation Independent: Describing a statistical gauge that measures performance apart from the context of team, ballpark, or other outside variables. Strikeouts and Walks, inasmuch as they are unaffected by the performance of a batter's surrounding team, are considered situation independent stats.

Conversely, RBIs are situation dependent because individual performance varies greatly by the performance of other batters on the team (you can't drive in runs if there is nobody on base). Similarly, pitching wins are as much a measure of the success of a pitcher as they are a measure of the success of the offense and defense performing behind that pitcher, and are therefore a poor measure of pitching performance alone.

Situation independent gauges are important for us to be able to separate a player's contribution to his team and isolate his performance so that we may judge it on its own merits.

Slg: Slugging Percentage

Slugging Percentage (Slg)

(Singles + (2 x Doubles) + (3 x Triples) + (4 x HR)) / AB

A measure of the total number of bases accumulated per at bat. It is a misnomer; it is not a true measure of a batter's slugging ability because it includes singles. SLG also assumes that each type of hit has proportionately increasing value (i.e. a double is twice as valuable as a single, etc.) which is not true. BENCHMARKS: The top batters will have levels over .500. The bottom batters will have levels under .300.

Strand Rate (S%)

(H + BB - ER) / (H + BB - HR)

Measures the percentage of allowed runners a pitcher strands, which incorporates both individual pitcher skill and bullpen effectiveness. BENCHMARKS: The most adept at stranding runners will have S% levels over 75%. Once a pitcher's S% starts dropping down below 65%, he's going to have problems with his ERA. Those pitchers with strand rates over 80% will have artificially low ERAs, which will be prone to relapse.

Strikeouts per Game: See Opposition Strikeouts per game.

Walks + Hits per Innings Pitched (WHIP): The number of baserunners a pitcher allows per inning. BENCHMARKS: Usually, a WHIP of under 1.20 is considered top level and over 1.50 is indicative of poor performance. Levels under 1.00 — allowing fewer runners than IP — represent extraordinary performance and are rarely maintained over time.

Walk rate (bb%)

(BB / (AB + BB))

A measure of a batter's eye and plate patience. BENCHMARKS: The best batters will have levels of over 10%. Those with the least plate patience will have levels of 5% or less.

Walks per Game: See Opposition Walks per Game.

WHIP: Walks + Hits per Innings Pitched

Wins: There are five events that need to occur in order for a pitcher to post a single win...

1. He must pitch well, allowing few runs.
2. The offense must score enough runs.
3. The defense must successfully field all batted balls.
4. The bullpen must hold the lead.
5. The manager must leave the pitcher in for 5 innings, and not remove him if the team is still behind.

X/H: Extra-base Hit Rate

*xERA: Expected ERA

* Asterisked formulas have updated versions in the Baseball Forecaster. *However, those updates include statistics like Ground Ball Rate, Fly Ball Rate or Line Drive Rate, for which we do not have reliable data for minor leaguers. So we use the previous version of those formulas, as listed here, for the players in this book.*

TEAM AFFILIATIONS

TEAM	ORG	LEAGUE	LEV
Aberdeen	BAL	New York-Penn League	SS
Akron	CLE	Eastern League	AA
Albuquerque	LAD	Pacific Coast League	AAA
Altoona	PIT	Eastern League	AA
Arkansas	LAA	Texas League	AA
Asheville	COL	South Atlantic League	A-
Auburn	WAS	New York-Penn League	SS
Augusta	SF	South Atlantic League	A-
AZL Angels	LAA	Arizona League	Rk
AZL Athletics	OAK	Arizona League	Rk
AZL Brewers	MIL	Arizona League	Rk
AZL Cubs	CHC	Arizona League	Rk
AZL Diamondbacks	ARI	Arizona League	Rk
AZL Dodgers	LAD	Arizona League	Rk
AZL Giants	SF	Arizona League	Rk
AZL Indians	CLE	Arizona League	Rk
AZL Mariners	SEA	Arizona League	Rk
AZL Padres	SD	Arizona League	Rk
AZL Rangers	TEX	Arizona League	Rk
AZL Reds	CIN	Arizona League	Rk
AZL Royals	KC	Arizona League	Rk
Bakersfield	CIN	California League	A+
Batavia	STL	New York-Penn League	SS
Beloit	MIN	Midwest League	A-
Billings	CIN	Pioneer League	Rk
Binghamton	NYM	Eastern League	AA
Birmingham	CHW	Southern League	AA
Bluefield	TOR	Appalachian League	Rk
Boise	CHC	Northwest League	SS
Bowie	BAL	Eastern League	AA
Bowling Green	TAM	Midwest League	A-
Bradenton	PIT	Florida State League	A+
Brevard County	MIL	Florida State League	A+
Bristol	CHW	Appalachian League	Rk
Brooklyn	NYM	New York-Penn League	SS
Buffalo	NYM	International League	AAA
Burlington	KC	Appalachian League	Rk
Burlington	OAK	Midwest League	A-
Carolina	CLE	Carolina League	A+
Cedar Rapids	LAA	Midwest League	A-
Charleston	NYY	South Atlantic League	A-
Charlotte	TAM	Florida State League	A+
Charlotte	CHW	International League	AAA
Chattanooga	LAD	Southern League	AA
Clearwater	PHI	Florida State League	A+
Clinton	SEA	Midwest League	A-
Colorado Springs	COL	Pacific Coast League	AAA
Columbus	CLE	International League	AAA

TEAM	ORG	LEAGUE	LEV
Connecticut	DET	New York-Penn League	SS
Corpus Christi	HOU	Texas League	AA
Danville	ATL	Appalachian League	Rk
Dayton	CIN	Midwest League	A-
Daytona	CHC	Florida State League	A+
Delmarva	BAL	South Atlantic League	A-
Dunedin	TOR	Florida State League	A+
Durham	TAM	International League	AAA
Elizabethton	MIN	Appalachian League	Rk
Erie	DET	Eastern League	AA
Eugene	SD	Northwest League	SS
Everett	SEA	Northwest League	SS
Fort Myers	MIN	Florida State League	A+
Fort Wayne	SD	Midwest League	A-
Frederick	BAL	Carolina League	A+
Fresno	SF	Pacific Coast League	AAA
Frisco	TEX	Texas League	AA
GCL Astros	HOU	Gulf Coast League	Rk
GCL Blue Jays	TOR	Gulf Coast League	Rk
GCL Braves	ATL	Gulf Coast League	Rk
GCL Cardinals	STL	Gulf Coast League	Rk
GCL Marlins	FLA	Gulf Coast League	Rk
GCL Mets	NYM	Gulf Coast League	Rk
GCL Nationals	WAS	Gulf Coast League	Rk
GCL Orioles	BAL	Gulf Coast League	Rk
GCL Phillies	PHI	Gulf Coast League	Rk
GCL Pirates	PIT	Gulf Coast League	Rk
GCL Rays	TAM	Gulf Coast League	Rk
GCL Red Sox	BOS	Gulf Coast League	Rk
GCL Tigers	DET	Gulf Coast League	Rk
GCL Twins	MIN	Gulf Coast League	Rk
GCL Yankees	NYY	Gulf Coast League	Rk
Grand Junction	COL	Pioneer League	Rk
Great Falls	CHW	Pioneer League	Rk
Great Lakes	LAD	Midwest League	A-
Greeneville	HOU	Appalachian League	Rk
Greensboro	FLA	South Atlantic League	A-
Greenville	BOS	South Atlantic League	A-
Gwinnett	ATL	International League	AAA
Hagerstown	WAS	South Atlantic League	A-
Harrisburg	WAS	Eastern League	AA
Helena	MIL	Pioneer League	Rk
Hickory	TEX	South Atlantic League	A-
High Desert	SEA	California League	A+
Hudson Valley	TAM	New York-Penn League	SS
Huntsville	MIL	Southern League	AA
Idaho Falls	KC	Pioneer League	Rk
Indianapolis	PIT	International League	AAA

TEAM	ORG	LEAGUE	LEV
Inland Empire	LAA	California League	A+
Iowa	CHC	Pacific Coast League	AAA
Jackson	SEA	Southern League	AA
Jacksonville	FLA	Southern League	AA
Jamestown	FLA	New York-Penn League	SS
Johnson City	STL	Appalachian League	Rk
Jupiter	FLA	Florida State League	A+
Kane County	KC	Midwest League	A-
Kannapolis	CHW	South Atlantic League	A-
Kingsport	NYM	Appalachian League	Rk
Lake County	CLE	Midwest League	A-
Lake Elsinore	SD	California League	A+
Lakeland	DET	Florida State League	A+
Lakewood	PHi	South Atlantic League	A-
Lancaster	HOU	California League	A+
Lansing	TOR	Midwest League	A-
Las Vegas	TOR	Pacific Coast League	AAA
Lehigh Valley	PHI	International League	AAA
Lexington	HOU	South Atlantic League	A-
Louisville	CIN	International League	AAA
Lowell	BOS	New York-Penn League	SS
Lynchburg	ATL	Carolina League	A+
Mahoning Valley	CLE	New York-Penn League	SS
Memphis	STL	Pacific Coast League	AAA
Midland	OAK	Texas League	AA
Mississippi	ATL	Southern League	AA
Missoula	ARI	Pioneer League	Rk
Mobile	ARI	Southern League	AA
Modesto	COL	California League	A+
Montgomery	TAM	Southern League	AA
Myrtle Beach	TEX	Carolina League	A+
Nashville	MIL	Pacific Coast League	AAA
New Britain	MIN	Eastern League	AA
New Hampshire	TOR	Eastern League	AA
New Orleans	FLA	Pacific Coast League	AAA
Norfolk	BAL	International League	AAA
Northwest Arkansas	KC	Texas League	AA
Ogden	LAD	Pioneer League	Rk
Oklahoma City	HOU	Pacific Coast League	AAA
Omaha	KC	Pacific Coast League	AAA
Orem	LAA	Pioneer League	Rk
Palm Beach	STL	Florida State League	A+
Pawtucket	BOS	International League	AAA
Pensacola	CIN	Southern League	AA
Peoria	CHC	Midwest League	A-
Portland	BOS	Eastern League	AA
Potomac	WAS	Carolina League	A+
Princeton	TAM	Appalachian League	Rk

TEAM	ORG	LEAGUE	LEV
Pulaski	SEA	Appalachian League	Rk
Quad Cities	STL	Midwest League	A-
Rancho Cucamonga	LAD	California League	A+
Reading	PHI	Eastern League	AA
Reno	ARI	Pacific Coast League	AAA
Richmond	SF	Eastern League	AA
Rochester	MIN	International League	AAA
Rome	ATL	South Atlantic League	A-
Round Rock	TEX	Pacific Coast League	AAA
Sacramento	OAK	Pacific Coast League	AAA
Salem	BOS	Carolina League	A+
Salem-Keizer	SF	Northwest League	SS
Salt Lake	LAA	Pacific Coast League	AAA
San Antonio	SD	Texas League	AA
San Jose	SF	California League	A+
Savannah	NYM	South Atlantic League	A-
Scranton/			
Wilkes-Barre	NYY	International League	AAA
South Bend	ARI	Midwest League	A-
Spokane	TEX	Northwest League	SS
Springfield	STL	Texas League	AA
St. Lucie	NYM	Florida State League	A+
State College	PIT	New York-Penn League	SS
Staten Island	NYY	New York-Penn League	SS
Stockton	OAK	California League	A+
Syracuse	WAS	International League	AAA
Tacoma	SEA	Pacific Coast League	AAA
Tampa	NYY	Florida State League	A+
Tennessee	CHC	Southern League	AA
Toledo	DET	International League	AAA
Trenton	NYY	Eastern League	AA
Tri-City	HOU	New York-Penn League	SS
Tri-City	COL	Northwest League	SS
Tucson	SD	Pacific Coast League	AAA
Tulsa	COL	Texas League	AA
Vancouver	TOR	Northwest League	SS
Vermont	OAK	New York-Penn League	SS
Visalia	ARI	California League	A+
West Michigan	DET	Midwest League	A-
West Virginia	PIT	South Atlantic League	A-
Williamsport	PHI	New York-Penn League	SS
Wilmington	KC	Carolina League	A+
Winston-Salem	CHW	Carolina League	A+
Wisconsin	MIL	Midwest League	A-
Yakima	ARI	Northwest League	SS

10 REASONS
why <u>winners</u> rely on
BASEBALL HQ PRODUCTS
for fantasy baseball information

1 **NO OTHER RESOURCE** provides you with more vital intelligence to help you win. Compare the depth of our offerings in these pages with any other information product or service.

2 **NO OTHER RESOURCE** provides more exclusive information, like cutting-edge component skills analyses, revolutionary strategies like the LIMA Plan, and innovative gaming formats like Rotisserie 500. *You won't find these anywhere else on the internet, guaranteed.*

3 **NO OTHER RESOURCE** has as long and consistent a track record of success in top national competitions... Our writers and readers have achieved 27 first place finishes, plus another 22 second and third place finishes since 1997. *No other resource comes remotely close.*

4 **NO OTHER RESOURCE** has as consistent a track record in projecting impact performances. In 2011, our readers had surprises like Alex Avila, Peter Bourjos, J.J. Hardy, Matt Kemp, Cameron Maybin, Mike Morse, Matt Wieters, Ben Zobrist, Johnny Cueto, Kyle Farnsworth, Zack Greinke, Aaron Harang, Fernando Salas and James Shields on their teams, *and dozens more.*

5 **NO OTHER RESOURCE** is supported by more than 50 top writers and analysts — all paid professionals and proven winners, not weekend hobbyists or corporate staffers.

6 **NO OTHER RESOURCE** has a wider scope, providing valuable information not only for Rotisserie, but for alternative formats like simulations, salary cap contests, online games, points, head-to-head, dynasty leagues and others.

7 **NO OTHER RESOURCE** is as highly regarded by its peers in the industry. Baseball HQ is the *only* three-time winner of the Fantasy Sports Trade Association's "Best Fantasy Baseball Online Content" award and Ron Shandler was a key subject in Sam Walker's *Fantasyland.*

8 **NO OTHER RESOURCE** is as highly regarded *outside* of the fantasy industry. Many Major League general managers are regular customers. We were advisors to the St. Louis Cardinals in 2004 and our former Minor League Director is now a scout for the organization.

9 **NO OTHER RESOURCE** has been creating fantasy baseball winners for as long as we have. Our 26 years of stability *guarantees your investment.*

10 Year after year, more than 90% of our customers report that Baseball HQ products and services have helped them improve their performance in their fantasy leagues. <u>That's the bottom line</u>.

TO ORDER
MAIL check or money order to:
Big Lead Sports/FSV, 1500 Broadway, Suite 810, New York, NY 10036
PHONE 1-800-422-7820
FAX: 540-772-1969
ONLINE secure order form: *http://orders.baseballhq.com/*

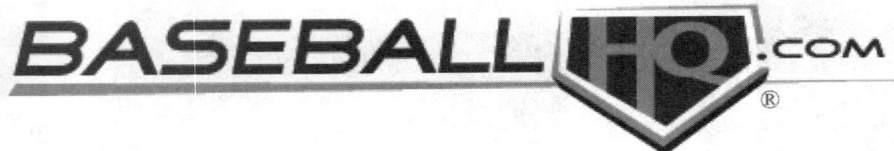

First Pitch
Forums & Conferences

Get a head start on the 2012 season with a unique opportunity to go one-on-one with some of the top writers and analysts in the fantasy baseball industry. First Pitch Forums bring the experts to some of the top cities in the USA for lively and informative symposium sessions.

These 3+ hour sessions combine player analysis with fantasy drafting, interactive activities and fun! You've never experienced anything so informational and entertaining! We've selected the top issues, topics, players and strategies that could make or break your fantasy season.

Our "Quest for Fire" program in 2011 was a rousing success, identifying many of last year's surprise players, such as Erik Bedard, Bartolo Colon, Lucas Duda, Kyle Farnsworth, Aaron Harang, Derek Holland, Eric Hosmer, Cory Luebke, Cameron Maybin, Mike Morse, Bud Norris, Fernando Salas, Jarrod Saltalamacchia, James Shields and Matt Wieters.

So we are going to be on the lookout for Black Swans again, in 2012, based on...

- ◘ Playing time opportunity
- ◘ Injury prognoses
- ◘ Bullpen volatility
- ◘ Minor league scouting
- ◘ Statistical analysis
- ◘ Breakout profile modeling
- ◘ and much more!

Ron Shandler and *Baseball Injury Report's* Rick Wilton chair the sessions, bringing a dynamic energy to every event. They are joined by guest experts from BaseballHQ.com and some of the leading sports media sources, like ESPN.com, MLB.com, USA Today Sports Weekly, Baseball America, Rotowire.com, Mastersball.com, KFFL.com and Sirius/XM Radio.

Program description, forum sites and directions at
http://www.baseballhq.com/ seminars/

What you get for your registration

- ◘ 3+ hours of baseball talk with some of the baseball industry's top writers and analysts
- ◘ The chance to have *your* questions answered, 1-on-1 with the experts
- ◘ The opportunity to network with fellow fantasy leaguers from your area
- ◘ Freebies and discounts from leading industry vendors

2012 SITES

February 18	**LOS ANGELES**
February 19	**SAN FRANCISCO**
February 25	**CHICAGO**
February 26	**DETROIT**
March 2	**WASHINGTON DC**
March 3	**NEW YORK**
March 4	**BOSTON**

REGISTRATION: $39 per person in advance
$49 per person at the door

(Note: Schedule is preliminary and subject to change.)

Don't forget - November 2-4 in Phoenix!